1998
CHILDREN'S
WRITER'S &
ILLUSTRATOR'S
MARKET

Managing Editor, Annuals Department: Cindy Laufenberg
Supervising Editor: Mark Garvey
Production Editors: Anne Bowling, Mary Cox, Tara Horton

International Standard Serial Number 0897-9790
International Standard Book Number 0-89879-819-1

Cover illustration: Brenda Grannan
Portraits: Ann Barrow

Attention Booksellers: This is an annual directory of F&W Publications.
Return deadline for this edition is April 30, 1999.

1998
CHILDREN'S WRITER'S & ILLUSTRATOR'S MARKET

850 PLACES TO SELL YOUR WORK

EDITED BY
ALICE P. BUENING

WRITER'S DIGEST BOOKS
CINCINNATI, OHIO

Contents

Reprinted with permission of Dutton.

Page 15

The Markets

The Resources

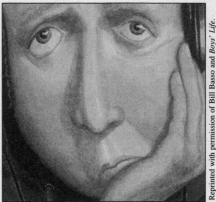

Page 196

Reprinted with permission of Bill Basso and *Boys' Life*.

From the Editor

Several years ago I was getting ready for work with my radio tuned to "Morning Edition," as always, and I heard the most wonderful story. A reporter told of a shipload of 29,000 plastic tub toys that had washed overboard and were cruising the world's oceans. Scientists had been watching them to study currents, tides and winds, and hundreds of them had washed up on beaches in the Gulf of Alaska.

I burst out laughing. What a great image—thousands and thousands of bright little ducks, turtles, frogs and beavers bobbing along the surf. I asked everyone I ran into if they happened to catch that story, and told them about it if they hadn't.

A few years later, I was at a children's literature conference in Indiana where illustrator/author **David Wisniewski** was giving a presentation. He was a terrific speaker—interesting, funny, candid, great artwork. Wisniewski talked about the books he was working on. One of them was *Ducky*. He was illustrating the story, written by Eve Bunting, about a duck who had washed overboard with thousands of other tub toys, spent time worriedly floating, and finally washed up on an Alaskan beach to be found by an excited young boy.

Wow! I wondered if Eve Bunting and I had been listening to the radio at the same time. I wondered how many other people had heard that same report. Was Bunting the only one who thought, *That would make a terrific children's book*?

Bunting knows what all good writers and illustrators do: You don't have to look far for a great idea. Ideas are all around us. Life is the ultimate idea generator. You just have to pay attention.

Judy Blume feels such observation is part of a writer's nature. "Writers are observers," she says. "That's what we do, that's what we are—we're sponges." It was a big thrill for me to hear more of Blume's thoughts on the writing life, her audience and her books. See Judy Blume: Telling the Best Story She Can Tell on page 57 to hear the rest of our conversation.

I was also excited when I heard through a mutual friend that **Richard Peck** was interested in writing an article for me. As the author of almost two dozen novels for young adults over several decades, Peck shares his unique view of YA fiction in That Was Then, This Is Now: A Look at YA Past & Present on page 51.

For a look at the creative world from the perspective of other authors and illustrators, read the Insider Reports in this edition. You'll find an interview with the above-mentioned Wisniewski (who happened to win the Caldecott Medal in 1997) on page 88. Hear from **Robert Sabuda**, best known for his amazing pop-up books, but also an accomplished picture book illustrator, on page 72. Author **Brian Cleary** writes about the importance of humor in children's books on page 122. And **Elaine Marie Alphin** shares her wealth of experience writing for the book and magazine markets on page 220.

Also look at publishing through the eyes of editors like **Louise May** of educational publisher Mondo Books (page 136), **Laura Minchew** of religious publisher Tommy Nelson

© 1997 David Wisniewski for Clarion Books

(page 144), **Susan Kent Cakars**, formerly of concept book publisher Magination Press (page 128), and **Mary Lou Carney**, editor of *Guideposts for Kids* (page 214).

Of course, observation is not just important to the creative aspect of your career in children's publishing. You must also pay attention to what's going on in the business side of the industry. There are a number of business-related articles in this edition such as Before Your First Sale (page 6), Ten Tips & Twenty Questions for Your Next Book Deal (page 31), and For Illustrators: Straight Talk on Your Business Plan (page 36). And in an effort to give you the most complete publisher information available, we've added mission statements to many of the book publishers and magazines listed here, added more contact names for each publisher, and worked hard gathering information for a list of "must-have" publishers and publications.

Your research of potential publishers shouldn't stop with *Children's Writer's & Illustrator's Market*. Always send for guidelines and catalogs and sample copies of magazines. Go to conferences and local meetings. Get to know other writers and illustrators in your area. And hang out at the children's section of your local bookstore—it's packed with pages and pages of other people's ideas, and may spark a few of your own. (While you're there, check out a copy of *Ducky.*)

And if you have any ideas about how I can make this book more helpful to you—or any questions, comments, thoughts or observations to share—I'd love to hear them. I get some of my best ideas from you.

Alice P. Buening
cwim@fwpubs.com

How to Use This Book to Sell Your Work

As a writer, illustrator or photographer first picking up *Children's Writer's & Illustrator's Market*, you may not know quite how to start using the book. Your impulse may be to flip through the book and quickly make a mailing list, then submit to everyone in hopes that someone will take interest in your work. Well, there's more to it. Finding the right market takes time and research. The more you know about a company that interests you, the better chance you have of getting work accepted.

We've made your job a little easier by putting a wealth of information at your fingertips. Besides providing listings, this directory includes a number of tools to help you determine which markets are the best ones for your work. By using these tools, as well as researching on your own, you raise your odds of being published.

USING THE INDEXES

This book lists hundreds of potential buyers of freelance material. To learn which companies want the type of material you're interested in submitting, start with the indexes.

The Age-level Index

Age groups are broken down into these categories in the Age-level Index:
- **Picture books** or **picture-oriented material** are written and illustrated for preschoolers to 8-year-olds.
- **Young readers** are for 5- to 8-year-olds.
- **Middle readers** are for 9- to 11-year-olds.
- **Young adults** are for ages 12 and up.

These age breakdowns may vary slightly from publisher to publisher, but using them as guidelines will help you target appropriate markets. For example, if you've written an article about the latest teen fashions, check the Magazines Age-level Index under the Young Adult subheading. Using this list, you'll quickly find the listings for young adult magazines.

The Subject Index

But let's narrow the search further. Take your list of young adult magazines, turn to the Subject Index, and find the Fashion subheading. Then highlight the names that appear on both lists (Young Adult and Fashion). Now you have a smaller list of all the magazines that would be interested in your teen fashion article. Read through those listings and decide which ones sound best for your work.

Illustrators and photographers can use the Subject Index as well. If you specialize in painting animals, for instance, consider sending samples to book and magazine publishers listed under Animals and, perhaps, Nature/Environment. Illustrators can simply send general examples of their style (in the form of tearsheets or postcards) to art directors to keep on file. The indexes may be more helpful to artists sending manuscripts/illustration packages. Always read the listings for the potential markets to see the type of work art directors prefer and what type of samples they'll keep on file.

The Photography Index

You'll find lists of book and magazine publishers, as well as greeting card, puzzle and game manufacturers, that buy photos from freelancers in the Photography Index. Copy the lists and read the listings for specific needs. Send for photo guidelines if they're offered.

USING THE LISTINGS

Many listings begin with one or more symbols. Here's what each stands for:

(‡) indicates a listing is new to this edition.

(□) indicates a listing is a book packager or producer.

(★) indicates a company publishes educational material.

(❦) indicates a listing is Canadian.

(*) indicates a contest, organization or workshop is open to students.

In the Book Publishers section, you'll find contact names after **Manuscript Acquisitions** and **Art Acquisitions**. Contact names in Magazines follow boldface titles such as **Fiction Editor**, **Articles Editor** or **Art Director**. Following contact information in many of these listings, we've added mission statements. Read these to get a general idea of the aim of certain publishers and magazines to help you decide whether to explore them further.

The subheadings under each listing contain more specific information about what a company needs. In Book Publishers and Magazines, for example, you'll find such things as age levels and subjects needed under the Fiction and Nonfiction subheads. Here's an example from a listing in the Book Publishers section:

Fiction: Picture books: adventure, animal, contemporary, fantasy, humor. Young readers: animal, contemporary, humor, sports, suspense/mystery. Middle readers: adventure, humor, sports. Young adults: humor, problem novels.

Also check the listings for information on how to submit your work and response time. In Book Publishers and Magazines, writers will find this information under the How to Contact/ Writers subhead:

How to Contact/Writers: Query with outline/synopsis and 2 sample chapters. Reports on queries in 6 weeks.

For information on submission procedures and formats, turn to Before Your First Sale on page 6.

Also look for information regarding payment and rights purchased. Some markets pay on acceptance, others on publication. Some pay a flat rate for manuscripts and artwork, others pay advances and royalties. Knowing how a market operates will keep you from being shocked when you discover your paycheck won't arrive until your manuscript is published—a year after it was accepted. This information is found under Terms in Book Publishers, Magazines and Play Publishers. Here's an example from the Magazines section:

Terms: Pays on acceptance. Buys first North American serial rights or reprint rights. Pays $50-100 for stories/articles. Pays illustrators $75-125 for b&w or color inside; $150-200 for color cover.

Under Tips you'll find special advice straight from an editor or art director about what their company wants or doesn't want, or other helpful advice:

Tips: "We are looking for picture books centered on a strong, fully-developed protaganist who grows or changes during the course of the story."

Additional information about specific markets in the form of comments from the editor of this book is set off by bullets (●) within listings:

- This publisher accepts only queries and manuscripts submitted by agents.

Many listings indicate whether submission guidelines are available. If a publisher you're interested in offers guidelines, send for them and read them. The same is true with catalogs. Sending for catalogs and seeing and reading about the books a publisher produces gives you a better idea whether your work would fit in. (You may even want to look at a few of the books in the catalog at a library or bookstore.) Note that a number of publishers offer guidelines and catalogs on their websites.

Especially for artists and photographers

Along with information for writers, listings provide information for photographers and illustrators. Illustrators will find numerous markets that maintain files of samples for possible future assignments. If you're both a writer and illustrator, look for markets that accept manuscript/illustration packages. You'll find sample illustrations from various publishers sprinkled throughout the listings. These illustrations serve as examples of the kind of art these particular companies buy. Read the captions for additional information about the artwork and the market.

If you're a photographer, after consulting the Photography Index, read the information under the Photography subhead within listings to see what format buyers prefer. For example, some want 35mm color transparencies, others want b&w prints. Note the type of photos a buyer wants to purchase and the procedures for submitting. It's not uncommon for a market to want a résumé and promotional literature, as well as tearsheets from previous work. Listings also note whether model releases and/or captions are required.

Especially for young writers

If you're a parent, teacher or student, you may be interested in Young Writer's & Illustrator's Markets. The listings in this section encourage submissions from young writers and artists. Some may require a written statement from a teacher or parent, noting the work is original. Also watch for age limits.

Young people should also check Contests & Awards for contests that accept work by young writers and artists. Some of the contests listed are especially for students; others accept both student and adult work. These are marked with a an asterisk (*). Some listings in Clubs & Organizations and Conferences & Workshops may also be of interest to students. Organizations and conferences which are open to or are especially for students are also marked with an asterisk.

COMMON ABBREVIATIONS

Throughout the listings, the following abbreviations are used:
- **ms** or **mss** stands for manuscript or manuscripts.
- **SASE** refers to a self-addressed, stamped envelope.
- **SAE** refers to a self-addressed envelope.
- **IRC** stands for International Reply Coupon. These are required with SAEs sent to markets in countries other than your own.

Before Your First Sale

If you're just beginning to pursue your career as a children's book writer or illustrator, it's important to learn the proper procedures, formats and protocol for the publishing industry. This article outlines the basics you need to know before you head to the post office with your submissions.

FINDING THE BEST MARKETS FOR YOUR WORK

Researching publishers well is a basic element of submitting your work successfully. Editors and art directors hate to receive inappropriate submissions—handling them wastes a lot of their time, not to mention your time and money, and they are the main reason some publishers have chosen not to accept material over the transom. By randomly sending out material without knowing a company's needs, you're sure to meet with rejection.

If you're interested in submitting to a particular magazine, write to request a sample copy, or see if it's available in your local library or bookstore. For a book publisher, obtain a book catalog and check a library or bookstore for titles produced by that publisher. Many publishers and magazines now have websites that include catalogs or sample articles (websites are given within the listings). Studying such materials carefully will better acquaint you with a publisher's or magazine's writing, illustration and photography styles and formats.

Most of the book publishers and magazines listed in this book (as well as some multimedia, greeting card and paper product producers) offer some sort of writer's, artist's or photographer's guidelines for a self-addressed, stamped envelope (SASE). Guidelines are also often found on publishers' websites. It's important to read and study guidelines before submitting work. You'll get a better understanding of what a particular publisher wants. You may even decide, after reading the submission guidelines, that your work isn't right for a company you considered.

SUBMITTING YOUR WORK

Throughout the listings you'll read requests for particular elements to include when contacting markets. Here are explanations of some of these important submission components.

Queries, cover letters and proposals

A query letter is a no-more-than-one-page, well-written piece meant to arouse an editor's interest in your work. Many query letters start with leads similar to those of actual manuscripts. In the rest of the letter, briefly outline the work you're proposing and include facts, anecdotes, interviews or other pertinent information that give the editor a feel for the manuscript's premise— entice her to want to know more. End your letter with a straightforward request to write (or submit) the work, and include information on its approximate length, date it could be completed, and whether accompanying photos or artwork are available.

Arthur Levine, editor-in-chief of Scholastic imprint Arthur Levine Books, recommends writers send queries that present their books as a publisher's catalog would present them. Read through a good catalog and examine how the publisher gives enticing summaries of their books in a spare amount of words. It's also important that query letters give editors a taste of your writing style. For examples of an effective query letter and cover letter, see pages 8 and 9. For good advice and more samples of queries, cover letters and other correspondence, consult *How to Write Attention-Grabbing Query & Cover Letters*, by John Wood (Writer's Digest Books).

- **Query letters for nonfiction.** Queries are usually required when submitting nonfiction material to a publisher. The goal of a nonfiction query is to convince the editor your idea is perfect for her readership and that you're qualified to do the job. Note any previous writing experience and include published samples to prove your credentials, especially samples related to the subject matter you're querying about.

• **Query letters for fiction.** More and more, queries are being requested for fiction manuscripts. For a fiction query, explain the story's plot, main characters, conflict and resolution. Just as in nonfiction queries, make the editor eager to see more.

• **Cover letters for writers.** Some editors prefer to review complete manuscripts, especially for fiction. In such cases, the cover letter (which should be no longer than one page) serves as your introduction, establishes your credentials as a writer, and gives the editor an overview of the manuscript. If the editor asked for a manuscript because of a query, note this in your cover letter.

• **Cover letters for illustrators and photographers.** For an illustrator or photographer the cover letter serves as an introduction to the art director and establishes credentials as a professional when submitting samples. Explain what services you can provide as well as what type of follow-up contact you plan to make, if any.

• **Résumés.** Often writers, illustrators and photographers are asked to submit résumés with cover letters and samples. They can be created in a variety of formats, from a single page listing information, to color brochures featuring your work. Keep your résumé brief, and focus on your achievements, including your clients and the work you've done for them, as well as your educational background and any awards you've received. Do not use the same résumé you'd use for typical job applications.

• **Book proposals.** Throughout the listings in the Book Publishers section, publishers refer to submitting a synopsis, outline and sample chapters. Depending on an editor's preference, some or all of these components, along with a cover letter, make up a book proposal.

A *synopsis* summarizes the book, covering the basic plot (including the ending). It should be easy to read and flow well.

An *outline* covers your book chapter by chapter and provides highlights of each. If you're developing an outline for fiction, include major characters, plots and subplots, and book length.

Sample chapters give a more comprehensive idea of your writing skill. Some editors may request the first two or three chapters to see how your material is set up. Find out what the editor wants before writing or revising sample chapters.

Manuscript formats

When submitting a complete manuscript, follow some basic guidelines. In the upper-left corner of your title page, type your legal name (not pseudonym), address and phone number. In the upper-right corner, type the approximate word length. All material in the upper corners should be typed single-spaced. Then type the title (centered) almost halfway down that page, the word "by" two spaces under that, and your name or pseudonym two spaces under "by."

The first page should also include the title (centered) one-third of the way down. Two spaces under that type "by" and your name or pseudonym. To begin the body of your manuscript, drop down two double spaces and indent five spaces for each new paragraph. There should be one-inch margins around all sides of a full typewritten page. (Manuscripts with wide margins are more readable and easier to edit.)

Set your computer or typewriter on double-space for the manuscript body. From page two to the end of the manuscript, include your last name followed by a comma and the title (or key words of the title) in the upper-left corner. The page number should go in the top right corner. Drop down two double spaces to begin the body of each page. If you're submitting a novel, type each chapter title one third of the way down the page. For more information on manuscript formats, read *Writer's Digest Guide to Manuscript Formats*, by Dian Buchman and Seli Groves, or *Manuscript Submissions*, by Scott Edelstein (both Writer's Digest Books).

May 1, 1997

Sara Murray-Plumer
123 Your Street
Indianapolis IN 46207
Work Phone: 317-555-5493
Home: 317-555-9823

Danny Lee
Fiction Editor
Jack And Jill
Children's Better Health Institute
1100 Waterway Blve.
Indianapolis, IN 46206

Dear Mr. Lee:

The enclosed manuscript, "In A Minute," offers a brief glimpse of cultures around the world in a one-minute journey around the globe. This article mixes fiction and nonfiction to give children ages seven to ten an idea of how different children share one minute in time.

"In A Minute" will appeal to your target audience, since *Jack And Jill* readers are beginning to tell time and broaden their focus beyond their backyard. This story touches on the notion of time zones, multiple cultures and how people around the world can be unique and, yet, so similar.

I am currently evaluating additional options for this manuscript with other publishers. If you are interested in "In A Minute," but would like some changes, please let me know. I will be happy to work with you on revisions. I have included a self-addressed postcard. I would appreciate your mailing this card to indicate you have successfully received my manuscript.

I hope you'll share my enthusiasm for "In A Minute."

Sincerely,

Sara Murray-Plumer

Sara Murray-Plumer

Enc.

This cover letter was so effective that Sara Murray-Plumer got interest from two magazines for her story "In A Minute." *Jack And Jill* and *Spider* both wanted to publish her story, but she eventually chose *Spider*. Note that Plumer starts with a short but fact-filled description of her article and follows by pointing out why it's right for *Jack And Jill*. Telling that she's submitted the piece to other publishers and letting the editor know she's open to working with him on revisions shows her professionalism.

April 28, 1997

Sara Murray-Plumer
123 Your Street
Indianapolis IN 46207
Work phone: 317-555-5493
Home phone: 317-555-9823

Jonathan Lanman
Vice President & Associate Publisher
Atheneum Books
1230 Avenue of the Americas
New York, NY 10020

Dear Mr. Lanman:

Enclosed is the outline for *Caught by the Net*, a 4,700-word mystery written for middle graders. This story combines the compelling readability of a mystery with the emerging fascination of the Internet.

This mystery follows young Maddie as she tries to find her missing tutor and gets caught up in an intriguing puzzle. She uses a computer and accesses the Internet to unravel a string of clues, while avoiding the illusive "M," who is framing her tutor.

Caught by the Net is marketable for a number of reasons. First, it incorporates a growing topic for both young and old—the Internet. Secondly, as you know, many kids will read a mystery before they'll read anything else. And, finally, the story has a subtle taste of classic literature.

I have worked as a public relations professional for more than six years. I am involved in SCBWI, including sitting on Indiana's SCBWI steering committee. One of my stories was published in *Spider* earlier this year, and I write a nonfiction piece for each issue of *U*S* Kids*.

If you are interested in *Caught by the Net*, please let me know and I will send you the entire manuscript. Use the enclosed form and SASE to note your level of interest. I am currently evaluating additional options for this manuscript with other publishers.

I hope you'll share my enthusiasm for *Caught by the Net*.

Sincerely,

Sara Murray-Plumer

Sara Murray-Plumer

Enc.

This letter written by Sara Murray-Plumer was submitted with an outline for a book idea. Again, she opens with a enticing summary of the story, then explains what's marketable about it. A little on her work background and writing credits, as well as her involvement in SCBWI show the editor her level of professionalism. Exercising editorial etiquette, she also lets the editor know she's submitted the work elsewhere.

Picture book formats

The majority of editors prefer to see complete manuscripts for picture books. When typing the text of a picture book, don't include page breaks. And unless you are an illustrator, don't worry about supplying art. Editors will find their own illustrators for picture books. Most of the time, a writer and an illustrator who work on the same book never meet. The editor acts as a go-between in case either the writer or illustrator has any problems. *How to Write and Sell Children's Picture Books*, by Jean E. Karl (Writer's Digest Books), offers advice on preparing text and marketing your work.

If you're an illustrator who has written your own book, create a dummy or storyboard containing both art and text. Then submit it along with your complete manuscript and sample pieces of final art (color photocopies or slides—never originals). Publishers interested in picture books specify in their listings what should be submitted. For a step-by-step guide on creating a good dummy, refer to *How to Write and Illustrate Children's Books and Get Them Published*, edited by Treld Pelkey Bicknell and Felicity Trotman (North Light Books), or Frieda Gates's book, *How to Write, Illustrate, and Design Children's Books* (Lloyd-Simone Publishing Company).

Writers may also want to learn the art of dummy making to help them through their writing process with things like pacing, rhythm and length. For a great explanation and helpful hints, see *You Can Write Children's Books*, by Tracey Dils (Writer's Digest Books).

Mailing submissions

Your main concern when packaging material is to be sure it arrives undamaged. If your manuscript is less than six pages, simply fold it in thirds and send it in a #10 (business-size) envelope. For a SASE, either fold another #10 envelope in thirds or insert a #9 (reply) envelope which fits in a #10 neatly without folding.

Another option is folding your manuscript in half in a 6×9 envelope, with a #9 or #10 SASE enclosed. For larger manuscripts use a 9×12 envelope both for mailing the submission and as a SASE (which can be folded in half). Book manuscripts require sturdy packaging for mailing. Include a self-addressed mailing label and return postage.

If asked to send artwork and photographs, remember they require a bit more care in packaging to guarantee they arrive in good condition. Sandwich illustrations and photos between heavy cardboard that is slightly larger than the work. The cardboard can be secured by rubber bands or with tape. If you tape the cardboard together, check that the artwork doesn't stick to the tape. Be sure your name and address appear on the back of each piece of art or each photo in case the material becomes separated. For the packaging use either a manila envelope, foam-padded envelope, brown paper or a mailer lined with plastic air bubbles. Bind non-joined edges with reinforced mailing tape and affix a typed mailing label or clearly write your address.

Mailing material first class ensures quick delivery. Also, first-class mail is forwarded for one year if the addressee has moved and can be returned if undeliverable. If you're concerned about your original material safely reaching its destination, consider other mailing options, such as UPS or certified mail. If material needs to reach your editor or art director quickly, use overnight delivery services.

Remember, companies outside your own country can't use your country's postage when returning a manuscript to you. When mailing a submission to another country, include a self-addressed envelope and International Reply Coupons or IRCs. (You'll see this term in many Canadian listings.) Your postmaster can tell you, based on a package's weight, the correct number of IRCs to include to ensure its return.

If it's not necessary for an editor to return your work (such as with photocopies) don't include return postage. You may want to track the status of your submission by enclosing a postage-paid reply postcard with options for the editor to check, such as "Yes, I am interested," "I'll keep the material on file," or "No, the material is not appropriate for my needs at this time."

Some writers, illustrators and photographers simply include a deadline date. If you don't hear from the editor or art director by the specified date, your manuscript, artwork or photos are automatically withdrawn from consideration. Because many publishing houses and companies are overstocked with material, a minimum deadline should be at least three months.

Unless requested, it's never a good idea to use a company's fax number or e-mail address to send manuscript submissions. This can disrupt a company's internal business.

Keeping submission records

It's important to keep track of the material you submit. When recording each submission, include the date it was sent, the business and contact name, and any enclosures (such as samples of writing, artwork or photography). You can create a record-keeping system of your own or

---

The Seven Deadly Sins of Submission

1. Sending your manuscript or query on paper in screaming colors. Ditto the envelope.

Also forgo smiley faces, cutsie stickers, photos of your family and homemade bookmarks. None of these show how clever you are. What they will do is mark you as an amateur.

2. Including illustrations if you aren't really, truly and absolutely a bona fide artist— or at least a darn good amateur.

First of all, you don't have to be an artist to sell a book for children. Nine times out of ten, publishers find their own illustrators. Secondly, it isn't your artistic ability you're trying to sell—it's your writing ability. If an editor likes your work, you'll have plenty of time later to discuss the kind of art you think would work best with it. But when you're at the submission stage, a poorly drawn sketch can cast a pall over the whole enchilada. An editor blazing through a fat stack of unsolicited submissions may well assume that where there's poor art, there's poor story. Ouch.

3. Telling the editor in your cover letter that your kids absolutely love the story. (Or if you're a teacher, that the kids in your classroom do.)

They're your kids! Of course they do! They probably love a lot of things you do. And for that matter, they may love your story because it genuinely *is* fabulous. But few editors will be swayed by the affectionate people within your own orbit.

4. Explaining in your cover letter that until now, the only thing you've ever written is a grocery list or the monthly updates in your church bulletin.

This is a case where less is more, so if you've got relevant writing experience, by all means say so. But if you don't—don't. As much as editors admire enthusiasm, most will assume that if you're submitting through the slush, the odds are high that you're new to writing for kids. It doesn't bother them. Don't let if bother you.

5. Stuffing your envelope with a bunch of submissions.

The rule is one at a time, so don't throw everything you've got at the wall to see what sticks. Send your best work, and only your best work. Trying to make an editor figure out what you couldn't is almost certain to boomerang. In fact, the editor might just send the whole package back unread.

6. Comparing your work to that of famous authors.

There's nothing wrong with trying to mimic an author's style. Actually, it's almost a time-honored strategy for learning the craft. But resist announcing that your work is like Dr. Seuss' or Judy Blume's or . . . whoever's. It's yours, and it's on that basis that an editor will judge it.

7. Not including a SASE.

Kiss of death. If you want an answer, pony up. It's that simple.

—*Laura Belgrave, freelance editor and creator of* The Slush Pile *(www.theslushpile.com).*

look for record-keeping software in your area computer store. The 1998 *Writer's Market: the Electronic Edition* CD-ROM features a submission tracker that can be copied to your hard drive.

Keep copies of articles or manuscripts you send together with related correspondence to make follow-up easier. When you sell rights to a manuscript, artwork or photos, you can "close" your file on a particular submission by noting the date the material was accepted, what rights were purchased, the publication date and payment.

Often writers, illustrators and photographers fail to follow up on overdue responses. If you don't hear from a publisher within their stated response time, wait another month or so and follow up with a note asking about the status of your submission. Include the title or description, date sent, and a SASE for response. Ask the contact person when she anticipates making a decision. You may refresh the memory of a buyer who temporarily forgot about your submission. At the very least you'll receive a definite "no," and free yourself to send the material to another publisher.

Simultaneous submissions

If you opt for simultaneous (also called "multiple") submissions—sending the same material to several editors at the same time—be sure to inform each editor your work is being considered elsewhere. Many editors are reluctant to receive simultaneous submissions but understand that for hopeful freelancers, waiting several months for a response can be frustrating. In some cases, an editor may actually be more inclined to read your manuscript sooner if she knows it's being considered by another publisher. The Society of Children's Book Writers and Illustrators cautions writers against simultaneous submissions. The official recommendation of SCBWI is to submit to one publisher at a time, but wait only three months (note you'll do so in your cover letter). If no response is received, then send a note withdrawing your manuscript from consideration. SCBWI considers simultaneous submissions acceptable only if you have a manuscript dealing with a timely issue.

It's especially important to keep track of simultaneous submissions, so if you get an offer on a manuscript sent to more than one publisher, you can instruct other publishers to withdraw your work from consideration.

AGENTS AND REPS

Most children's writers, illustrators and photographers, especially those just beginning, are confused about whether to enlist the services of an agent or representative. Some are confident with their own negotiation skills and believe acquiring an agent or rep is not in their best interest. Others feel uncomfortable in the business arena or are not willing to sacrifice valuable creative time for marketing.

About half of children's publishers accept unagented work, so it's possible to break into children's publishing without an agent. Some agents avoid working with children's books because traditionally low advances and trickling royalty payments over long periods make children's books less lucrative. And it's practically impossible to find an agent interested in marketing articles and short stories—there simply isn't enough financial incentive.

Having an agent, though, may speed up the process of getting your work reviewed, especially by publishers who don't accept unagented submissions. If an agent has a good reputation and submits your manuscript to an editor, that manuscript may actually bypass the first-read stage (done by editorial assistants and junior editors) and end up on the editor's desk sooner.

A reputable agent should be familiar with the needs of the current market and evaluate your work accordingly. She should also determine the quality of your work and whether it is saleable. When your manuscript sells, she should negotiate a favorable contract and clear up any questions you have about payments. Representation does not guarantee sale of your work. It just means an agent or rep sees potential in your writing, art or photos.

Literary agents typically charge a 15 percent commission from the sale of writing; art and photo representatives usually charge a 25 to 30 percent commission. These fees are taken from advances and royalty earnings. Higher percentages are charged for sale of foreign rights.

Just as when approaching a publisher, the manuscript, artwork or photos, and query or cover letter you submit to a potential agent must be attractive and professional looking.

For a detailed directory of literary agents, refer to *Guide to Literary Agents*; for listings of art reps, consult *Artist's & Graphic Designer's Market*; and for photo reps, see *Photographer's Market* (all Writer's Digest Books).

Ten Commandments for Freelance Children's Illustrators

I. Do put your name and address on every single sample and slide.

Keep art directors informed if you change address or phone number.

II. Do research where you're going to send your samples.

Know the art director's name, if possible. Be familiar with the artists that particular publisher is already working with and decide if you're compatible.

III. Do edit mercilessly!

Send only your best work. Omit any pices that are obviously student assignments. Include an adequate number of pieces, but don't overdo.

IV. Do send both color and black and white samples. Show your range.

If you work comfortably in a number of styles or media, show one or two samples of each.

V. Do include samples showing children (and other people), animals and something to show how you would handle narrative illustration, perhaps an illustration to accompany a familiar story.

I've had artists who sent some pieces that re-illustrated several stories that had appeared in *Cricket*. While not necessary, it's an easy way to show an art director you are familiar with his publication and it's a good excercise in designing an illustration in conjunction with type.

VI. Do send a personal letter, not photocopies or generic greetings.

Don't be overly cute, flip or self-congratulatory. Do give a strong sense of your own unique personality, vision, style and taste.

VII. Don't send anything larger than 8½ × 11 if at all possible. Don't send originals or anything irreplaceable if lost.

VIII. Do enclose a SASE if you expect a reply or the return of artwork.

If you are asking for samples to be returned, give at least one or two pieces that may be kept on file. This is especially true if you send slides or tranparencies. Most photocopiers can't reproduce them. Art directors need something to show editors and to remind themselves of who you are.

IX. Do follow up with a card, note or additional sample. Don't call.

Keep a file or log of what samples you've sent to whom, and when. The same sample over and over again, while it perhaps reinforces who you are, doesn't generate any excitement, nor does it let art directors know you are continuing to do new and vital work.

X. Do know your craft and offer reproducible results; become familiar with the printing process.

Ensure that art done on assignment is of the same or higher quality and in the same style as the work in your portfolio. Talk with a local printer or color separator. Find out what happens when art is shot in halftone, or what colors or media do and do not reproduce well in standard four-color separation.

—Ron McCutchan, art director, The Cricket Magazine Group

First Books

BY ANNE BOWLING

Getting your first break in the world of writing and illustrating for children is a tricky path to navigate. There are no definite directions, and no straight lines from point A to point B—it seems every writer and illustrator who has had the pleasure of first publication has gotten there a different way.

Here four newcomers to children's publishing share their stories, and each is distinctly different. Some were able to work fulltime on their projects, others stole late evening and weekend hours to complete their books. Some networked with professional organizations and writer's groups, others chose to go it alone. Some found having an agent was the best route to take, others had their plain brown envelopes picked right out of the slush pile.

These writers' and illustrators' stories do share a few common lessons: believe in your work and have the will to persist. And while you should use planning and care in the steps you take toward submission, most important is your love of the creative process.

NAN PARSON ROSSITER
Rugby & Rosie (Dutton Children's Books)

Nan Parson Rossiter, a fulltime mother and freelance artist who focused most of her work in advertising, hadn't really planned to write a children's book. But she had been moved by a friend's story of raising a seeing-eye dog pup during its first year, and the result of that conversation was *Rugby & Rosie*, published by Dutton Children's Books in 1997.

© Bruce Rossiter

"I don't remember ever actually thinking I wanted to be a children's book author," Rossiter says. "I was just thinking, 'What would make a good story?' The idea for *Rugby & Rosie* came all at once—names and everything. I told my husband and then my parents. And then I wrote it down—and I cried."

Rossiter's tale is the story of Rosie, a golden retriever puppy who comes to live with a young boy, his family and their chocolate Labrador Rugby. Rosie will stay only until she is old enough to begin her training as a guide dog for the blind. In what *Publishers Weekly* called a "heart-tugging debut," Rossiter explores the boy's emotions of love, loss and hope during his year with the visiting Rosie.

While Rossiter finished her manuscript in "just a few days," creating the submission package took a bit longer. "I worked on the illustrations on and off until I had seven finished, which was some time later," Rossiter says. Using color photocopies, she created dummies that she submitted one or two at a time to prospective publishers.

"I received about a dozen form letters rejecting my story, and I was about to abandon the whole idea," she says. "But I happened to be working on a freelance job for the art director with Penguin. I asked if he would give my story to someone—anyone! He did, and Dutton called about a month later."

The timing of the acceptance was perfect for Rossiter, who was growing increasingly frustrated with her work in freelance illustration. She had worked in the field for eight years, and

Rugby & Rosie

Nan Parson Rossiter

Writer/illustrator Nan Parson Rossiter used a warm, autumnal palette to create the paintings for *Rugby & Rosie* (Dutton Children's Books), which *Publishers Weekly* called "perfect for lovers of dog stories that mix in just a touch of rue." Rossiter's first book is the bittersweet story of Rosie, a golden retriever pup being prepared for life as a seeing-eye dog, and her impact on the family that adopts her for one year. Rossiter spent "just a few days" on her manuscript, she says, but the illustration and publication processes took longer—six years from start to finish. The project enabled Rossiter to move away from her freelance illustration work, and she is working on a second picture book for Dutton.

with two agents she kept busy, but "I wasn't enjoying the work anymore," she says. "Most of the time it seemed I only painted a finished version of someone else's sketch. On a November morning I called my agent and told him I was through with freelancing, and to please return my portfolio to me. That was the very afternoon Dutton called and said they wanted to publish *Rugby & Rosie*."

Three years passed between the time Rossiter conceived her idea and Dutton responded, and another three years would pass before the book was published. But after that November phone call, the pace of the project picked up considerably.

Until the following spring, Rossiter worked with an editor on the manuscript, the pacing and the sketches for the book. She began the final illustrations in May of 1995, with a deadline to complete 21 paintings by September 1. "That was a tight deadline under normal circumstances, and I had two busy toddlers filling my days," she recalls.

Painting in her studio, which occupies a corner of her living room (surrounded by "the construction and demolition team" of sons Cole and Noah), Rossiter worked "every spare minute and every evening into the night," she says. "Weekends my husband Bruce kept our sons busy outside or took them on day trips. It was difficult, because I missed doing things with them, but wonderful because my dream had come true. I definitely could not have done it without Bruce's support."

Rossiter's summer of painting culminated in a series of illustrations that *Publishers Weekly* described as "drenched in autumnal hues and elegiac golden light, bespeaking a deep and unrequited nostalgia—perfect for lovers of dog stories that mix in just a touch of rue."

While painting in oils was new for her, the book's palette of warm colors was a natural fit. "I have always felt the late afternoons of autumn to be the most melancholy of times. They are bittersweet, but I love them more than any other. The story of *Rugby & Rosie* is also bittersweet, so I thought the palette seemed fitting."

Rossiter is now working on a second picture book for Dutton, tentatively titled *South*, which is the story of two Canada geese, one of which is injured. Her advice to other writers is to follow the formula that worked for her. "I had an idea I really believed was special," she says. "I thought it had lessons and levels beyond the average children's book, and I just went with it. I prayed for guidance in working in a style that was unfamiliar to me—actually, I prayed about every aspect of this experience, from finding the right publisher (or any publisher!) to staying positive and persevering. It couldn't have worked out better."

HELEN KIM
The Long Season of Rain (Henry Holt & Co., Inc.)

Seattle-based author Helen Kim had no idea a National Book Award nomination lay in her future when she sat down to write the first lines of *The Long Season of Rain*. Kim completed the first sentence—and eventually the first 50 pages—of her novel as a project for a continuing education course in creative writing.

"This started out as an assignment," says Kim, who now teaches creative writing and literature at a Seattle community college. "I thought I was writing a short story, but it didn't want to stop."

The result of Kim's five-year writing project, a young adult novel published in 1996 by Henry Holt & Co., was the coming-of-age story told through Junehee Lee, an 11-year-old girl living in Seoul, Korea. In a household dominated by women, a young boy orphaned during a rainy-season mudslide comes to stay, and

A lover of writing from her childhood in Korea, author Helen Kim struggled to master English before penning her first novel *The Long Season of Rain* (Henry Holt & Co., Inc.). It's a challenge, Kim says, to "understand the language in a poetic way, to be able to hear the rhythm and know the nuances." The coming-of-age story of 11-year-old Junehee Lee was quickly accepted by an editor at Edge Books, an imprint of Henry Holt dedicated to publishing multicultural literary fiction for young adults. Kim's novel received a National Book Award nomination and starred reviews from *Publisher's Weekly* and *School Library Journal*.

Reprinted with permission of Henry Holt & Co., Inc.

sets off an emotional chain reaction that leaves a permanent imprint on the family's members.

Distinguished as a Best Book by both *Publishers Weekly* and *School Library Journal*, *The Long Season of Rain* was called "a devastatingly clear-eyed view of societal restrictions and their effects on the young narrator's life" by *The Horn Book Magazine*. The novel's distinction as a National Book Award finalist is even more impressive considering Kim did not begin writing in English until she was in her teens.

Kim first experienced "a connection to writing" in third grade in Seoul when she wrote a short composition about her family that won first prize in her school, she says. Three years later, her family immigrated to New Jersey, and while she continued to write poems and short stories in Korean, her education in English had begun.

"I think I wanted to write even then," Kim says, "but there was this long transitional period between ages 12 and 30 when I was writing in Korean, and then Kunglish, and then I started to write in English. All along I wanted to write, but I never felt comfortable with English enough to really start writing."

After completing her masters degree in 1990, she began applying herself to fiction writing in English, and "the writing was horrible," she says. "It's one thing to have a command of the language to have a conversation, and another to understand the language in a poetic way, to be able to hear the rhythm and know the nuances."

But Kim persisted in completing the first 50 pages of her novel, and shipped it off with a grant application to the New Jersey State Council on the Arts. She proposed to write a novel in the tradition of Salinger and Steinbeck, centered on a universal theme, using simple and direct language that anyone ages 12 and up could read.

"It was a long, long shot," Kim says of the application, "because they select 50 out of over 1,000 people. I was shocked and really happy when they gave me the grant. I woke up one morning and there was something in the mail from the assemblymen of my county, and I thought, 'Is this an election year?' I was about to dump it when something about the way it was typed made me stop. So I opened it and it said, 'You have received a $12,000 grant for your novel,' and I thought, 'Oh my God, $12,000!' I couldn't stop saying that for the whole day.''

Kim spent the next five years writing and revising her novel. During that time, "I didn't think at all about whether it would be published or not published," she says. "Those thoughts never occurred to me. I just wrote. And I think it's because I held it off for so many years, that when I started to write the novel was coming off full force, and I was already in it, and not really thinking about the future but just about being in the process."

Kim spent a year in a creative writing program at New York University, where she connected with colleagues who would become long-term, trusted critics. Attending other writers' conferences gave her added support from colleagues and the attention of an agent who would later place her novel with Henry Holt.

Her workshop and conference experiences "were extremely positive," Kim says. "But it's essential that you find the right group to look at your work. When you're starting out, and you don't really know if your work is good, and you have someone who doesn't know your writing well critique it in a negative way, that can do some damage. You need to be very sensitive to who can critique your work and help you nurture the book."

The fact that *The Long Season of Rain* was published as a young adult novel was a surprise to Kim. The book was originally presented to publishers as adult fiction, and received two offers as such. But a proposal came in to publish the novel as young adult from an editor at Henry Holt's Edge Books, an imprint that specializes in multicultural literary fiction for young adults. The manuscript had come to Holt at a serendipitous time, as that publisher was broadening its definition of young adult fiction to supply young readers with material more akin to literature.

"I think Edge Books is trying to spearhead a movement for sophisticated young adult readers who are often lost in the shuffle," Kim says. "Now is an excellent time for serious writers to write young adult fiction."

But Kim cautions, "Young adults are not unsophisticated in their reading, so when you sit down to write, you are not writing for children. They understand the complexity of emotion. Even though my novel is told by an 11-year-old girl, what was happening in her house was very complex in terms of emotion. And the readers are able to understand that perfectly."

To other new authors, Kim advises, "Get an agent, because it is almost impossible to do it without an agent. It takes so much longer, it takes so much more effort, most publishers don't read your work unless it is through an agent, or somehow their editor has gotten ahold of you through connections," she says.

Agents not only increase a writer's chances of publication, but can direct writers to specific editors for their work, says Kim. "Ask your agent what kind of editor that person is beforehand," she advises. "My editor and I sat down and went through page by page, and I know not all editors do that. Remember, the agent is working for you—you ask all the questions you need to ask, like, 'Will this editor do some line editing with me?' Your agent has that information."

Already Kim is at work on her second novel. As yet untitled, this sequel to *The Long Season of Rain* follows Junehee Lee's exploration of her family's life after they immigrate to the U.S., as Junehee moves through her teens and into her early twenties. Pyungsoo, the orphan boy and catalyst for conflict in the first novel, figures prominently in the second, Kim promises, as he comes to America with the family and wreaks havoc. Kim declines to promise a publication date: after five years writing the first novel, "God knows how long this will take me," she says.

Lastly, Kim recommends, "Tell the truth, and desire solitude, because you will be in solitude a lot, and love the process. Because what happens after you finish writing really has very little to do with you."

BARBARA MAITLAND
The Bear Who Didn't Like Honey (ABC, All Books for Children)

Children's book author Barbara Maitland says poetry is a major influence on her prose, and it's easy to hear in the sing-song rhythms of her first picture book *The Bear Who Didn't Like Honey*.

"I read a lot of poetry," she says, "And that influences the way I write—each word must be considered carefully, both because of the length restrictions of picture books, and because the words will probably be read aloud."

Published by ABC, All Books for Children in the U.K., and Orchard Books in the U.S., *The Bear Who Didn't Like Honey* (for ages 3-6) is the story of Little Bear, taunted as "Scaredy Bear" by his brother and sisters for his timidity. He explains away his fears creatively: the water—it's too cold; the dark—he's not sleepy; and honeybees—he just doesn't like honey. But when he finds a smaller cub trapped in a tree, he finds the bravery to rescue him, and discovers his own inner courage.

That her stories achieve poetic precision is no surprise—the Little Bear manuscript went through about 40 revisions, which Maitland says is typical. Her writing steps begin with outlining the basic plot and characters by hand. Maitland then enters the story into her computer, editing as she goes. She prints out the second version, revises that, retypes, and repeats the process "until every word that's left is there for a reason," she says.

"The discipline imposed by the length is probably the biggest challenge of writing picture books and easy readers," Maitland says. "I overcome this by not worrying about the length at all in the early drafts, but just getting down the story I want to tell. Then I focus on telling the same story in the appropriate amount of words, as part of the tightening and polishing process."

An English major and long-time lover of children's books, Maitland came to writing for children through a creative writing class. "In one exercise we were asked to recall an early memory, and describe an event from that perspective. The exercise opened up a flood of memories which I continued to write down long after I'd finished the class."

Her first two efforts at writing for children, which now stay in her "useful writing exercise/ potential material for something else" file, had lessons to teach, she says.

"On reflection, they were not stories at all. I didn't draw on the memories as raw material to develop into something else, but pretty much presented them as the end product. I knew from my research that editors receive many such manuscripts, whose only merit is their warm and fuzzy glow for the person whose experience is involved, but I was too close to see that applied to what I had written. Now I always allow a cooling-off time, essential if I'm to approach what I've written, see its flaws, and rewrite effectively."

The inspiration for Little Bear's story came during a hiking trip in the Adirondacks. Maitland came across a mother bear and her cubs "and I couldn't get the image of those bear cubs reaching up for berries out of my mind," she says. "They looked so vulnerable. I kept wondering what it must be like to be a little bear, learning for the first time how to get along in the woods."

For submission of the Little Bear manuscript, Maitland had done her homework. Using *Children's Writer's & Illustrator's Market*, she identified publishers who accepted unsolicited simultaneous submissions and published a high percentage of first-time writers.

Of the three publishers she targeted, ABC, All Books for Children in London notified her that her manuscript had been accepted. "I spent the next week six feet above the ground," Maitland says, "telling relatives, friends and complete strangers in checkout lines that I'd just had my first book accepted."

The book was co-editioned by ABC, which meant Maitland has had her book published in

The Bear Who Didn't Like Honey was the breakthrough picture book for author Barbara Maitland, who persisted in writing although two earlier manuscripts were given up for lost. "I felt in my bones as I was writing [this book] that it was good," Maitland says, and editors at ABC, All Books for Children in London agreed. (The book was published in the U.S. by Orchard Books.) Her first two manuscripts taught her to allow a "cooling-off" period in her writing, Maitland says, which is the best way to "approach what I've written, see its flaws, and rewrite." Maitland has two more books on deck: *Moo in the Morning* (Farrar, Strauss & Giroux), scheduled for Spring 1998 publication, and *The Bookstore Ghost* (Puffin), scheduled for Fall.

Danish, Dutch, French and German, as well as in English for the U.S. and U.K. "My contract with ABC specified I would receive one copy of each of the co-editions—undoubtedly the best parcel I've ever received!" When she visits classrooms in local schools with her book, Maitland says, the children are intrigued by seeing Little Bear's name as *Lille Bjorn*, *Kleine Beer* and *Petit Ours*. Maitland now dedicates more than 20 hours each week (outside a fulltime job) to her writing, working "in the evenings and on weekends. I need at least three hours to get settled in and produce. I think about what I'm writing, or make notes about it, every day. I always carry a notebook. On days when I just don't get the chance to sit down at my desk, I'll read an SCBWI newsletter, or a book about writing, or research markets for current projects. This works for me because I feel like I'm keeping my hand in, doing necessary, writing-related things."

Since publication of *The Bear Who Didn't Like Honey*, Maitland has had two other books accepted: *Moo in the Morning*, a picture book scheduled for Spring of 1998 published by ABC in the U.K. and Farrar, Strauss & Giroux in the U.S., and *The Bookstore Ghost*, an easy reader, scheduled for Fall of 1998 from Puffin Books.

To other writers working toward their first publication, Maitland advises: "Write, and write, and keep improving your writing. When you reach the point where you truly believe in a manuscript, submit, submit, and keep submitting." While there are manuscripts Maitland no longer submits because they weren't ready, she says, "I have one manuscript that has been out 19 times. I can stand the rejection because I believe in it and think it deserves a chance. When it comes back, I print out a fresh copy and send it back out there. ·

"My experience showed me that you don't need contacts within the publishing world in order to get published. I knew no one, and my plain, brown envelope was pulled out of the slush pile. I hope anyone who has a rejected manuscript stuffed away somewhere will take it out, take a good, clear-eyed look at it, and if they still like what they see—resubmit!"

DWIGHT BEEN
Waking Upside Down (Atheneum Books for Young Readers)

A misunderstanding led San Francisco graphic designer Dwight Been to try his hand at illustrating children's books. About five years ago, Been overheard—or thought he overheard—another freelance designer say he was working on a children's book.

"The idea stuck in my head and grew until I was really interested," Been says. "I took a course in children's book illustration, and got together a portofolio. When I ran into that same freelancer a couple of years later, it turned out he never was working on a children's book. I must have totally misunderstood what he was saying all those years back, but it got me into children's book illustrating!"

Published in 1996 by Atheneum Books for Young Readers, an imprint of Simon & Schuster, *Waking Upside Down* (written by Philip Heckman) was Been's first full book illustration project.

The story features Morton, a little boy who resents being displaced from his own room by his twin sisters, who need the bigger bedroom. After settling into sleep surrounded by the girls' bunny wallpaper ("nobody could sleep in such a stupid room, he thought"), Morton awakes in an upside-down house. The story charts Morton's adventure as he moves from room to room, dancing with the ceiling fan, climbing the fireplace bricks and eventually settling down to sleep among the stars his sisters had painted on the ceiling.

The project required that Been "spend a lot of time staring at the ceiling," he says, to convincingly capture the angles and perspectives in scenes such as Morton filling a glass of water from the faucet, swinging from a hall light fixture and hiding from his dad, who got up in the middle of the night for orange juice.

"I did a number of sketches, and took a lot of photos, and turned them upside down," Been says. "The faucet was a tricky one. I had a friend pose with an empty glass, took some photos and added the faucet later. Another tricky thing to figure out was the gravity in the house. Everything had the normal gravitational pull except Morton, and his clothes were pulled to the ceiling. I couldn't get on the ceiling and sketch it out—I just had to imagine it, which I think led to the eventual crazy perspectives in the book."

The project appealed to Been immediately when he was contacted by Macmillan (purchased by Simon & Schuster while the book was being produced), although he confesses, "I wouldn't have turned down any manuscript from Macmillan." Using watercolor washes and Prismacolor for detail and depth, Been created a soft, shadowy world for Morton not unlike the work of contemporaries Maurice Sendak and Chris Van Allsburg, whose work Been says he admires.

But his primary artistic influences are fine artists from the past, Been says. "When I was starting to develop my style, I remembered how much I liked Thomas Hart Benton, the American painter and muralist from the '30s and '40s. The movement in his compositions was so lyrical, they would have made great children's books. I also love to look at the sketches and graphic

The bizarre perspectives of an inverted house were a challenge for illustrator Dwight Been, whose first full-book illustration project was *Waking Upside Down*. As the title implies, main character Morton awakes to find his house not quite the way he left it, and spends an entertaining evening exploring his topsy-turvy environment. A San Francisco-based graphic designer, Been attracted the attention of Simon & Schuster by sending out samples of his work in a "mass mailing blitz to any and every children's publisher across the country I could find." Although he had experience creating cover and inside art for other books, his first full-book illustration project was "trial by fire," Been says.

work of artists like Toulouse-Lautrec and Honore Daumier from the 1800s, and imagine them drawing a kids' book.

"I think if you look to current children's illustrators for influence, you'll end up imitating them if not just ripping them off," Been says. "Find out who influenced the illustrators you admire. Go outside of your immediate genre for influences and you'll never end up with a knock-off, imitative style."

While *Waking Upside Down* was Been's first full-book illustration, he broke into the field doing cover and inside art illustrations for Price Stern Sloan's Very Scary Stories series. Then a new member of the Society of Children's Book Writers and Illustrators, Been took his portfolio and sample kits to an SCBWI illustrators' weekend in Los Angeles. "The reviews went well, and several months later I got a call from the publisher. I had no monsters or scary drawings in my portfolio, but they liked my style and asked if I could do scary drawings. Of course, I said, 'Sure.' " Been signed a contract for a color cover and 11 inside black and white illustrations for *Even More Scary Stories for Sleepovers*. Having completed that project, Been said, "I thought, 'Hey this isn't so hard. I'll sit back and wait for more of those calls to come rolling in.' Which, of course, didn't happen." Been broke the inertia by sending out some 50 sample kits and a "mass mailing blitz to any and every children's publisher across the country I could find in the *Literary Market Place*."

That mailing effort brought him to *Waking Upside Down*, and the learning curve involved in a first book project. "It was total trial by fire," Been says. "No matter how hard you work on your portfolio, there is no way of knowing what lies in store for your first full-length color book.

"There are things you need to discover about yourself," Been says, "such as how tight to render the dummy and how much spontaneity to leave for the final art; which elements of your style stay constant over 15 boards and which ones have a tendency to change. Over the course of 15 illustrations plus front and back cover plus end papers you find out what your strengths are and what elements you need to develop further. I remember being in the middle of doing the final boards and feeling totally overwhelmed. You don't see how you'll ever be able to complete this humongous project, but somehow you do, and you say, 'Gosh, that wasn't so bad!' "

Since publication, Been has visited schools and done a number of bookstore signings, and plans to increase his trips to libraries for readings. "It's a blast to do," he says, "because the kids will always get you with a question you've never considered. It's great stimulation for new ideas!"

Been says he's looking forward to future book illustration projects, in particular a project with his sister (a published author), which he says would be his "dream job." To other illustrators waiting for their first break, Been advises: "Try to develop a style you really like. You're going to get some harsh critiques and rejections out there, so make sure you like your style before asking others to love it," he says. "Also, enjoy doing it!"

The Business of Writing & Illustrating

A career in children's publishing involves more than just writing skills or artistic talent. Successful authors and illustrators must be able to hold their own in negotiations, keep records, understand contract language, grasp copyright law, pay taxes and take care of a number of other business concerns. Although agents and reps, accountants and lawyers, and writers organizations offer help in sorting out such business issues, it's wise to have a basic understanding of them going in. This article offers just that—basic information. For a more in-depth look at the subjects covered here, check your library or bookstore for books and magazines to help you, some of which are mentioned. We also tell you how to get information on issues like taxes and copyright from the federal government.

CONTRACTS & NEGOTIATION

Before you see your work in print or begin working with an editor or art director on a project, there is negotiation. And whether negotiating a book contract, a magazine article assignment, or an illustration or photo assignment there are a few things to keep in mind. First, if you find any clauses vague or confusing in a contract, get legal advice. The time and money invested in counseling up front could protect you from problems later. If you have an agent or rep, she will review any contract.

A contract is an agreement between two or more parties that specifies the fees to be paid, services rendered, deadlines, rights purchased and, for artists and photographers, whether original work is returned. Most companies have standard contracts for writers, illustrators and photographers. The specifics (such as royalty rates, advances, delivery dates, etc.) are typed in after negotiations.

Though it's okay to conduct negotiations over the phone, get a written contract once both parties have agreed on terms. Never depend on oral stipulations; written contracts protect both parties from misunderstandings. Watch for clauses that may not be in your best interest, such as "work-for-hire." When you do work-for-hire, you give up all rights to your creations.

Some reputable children's magazines, such as *Highlights for Children*, buy all rights, and many writers and illustrators believe it's worth the concession in order to break into the field. However, once you become more established in the field, it's in your best interest to keep rights to your work.

When negotiating a book deal, find out whether your contract contains an option clause. This clause requires the author to give the publisher a first look at her next work before offering it to other publishers. Though it's editorial etiquette to give the publisher the first chance at publishing your next work, be wary of statements in the contract that could trap you. Don't allow the publisher to consider the next project for more than 30 days and be specific about what type of work should actually be considered "next work." (For example, if the book under contract is a young adult novel, specify that the publisher will receive an exclusive look at only your next young adult novel.) See Ten Tips & Twenty Questions for Your Next Book Deal on page 31 for some great suggestions on making the most of negotiations. For more tips on contracts, SCBWI members can send a SASE for their publication "Answers to Some Questions About Contracts."

Book publishers' payment methods

Book publishers pay authors and artists in royalties, a percentage of either the wholesale or retail price of each book sold. From large publishing houses, the author usually receives an advance issued against future royalties before the book is published. Half of the advance amount is issued upon signing the book contract; the other half is issued when the book is finished. For illustrations, one third of the advance should be collected upon signing the contract; one third upon delivery of sketches; and one third upon delivery of finished art.

After your book has sold enough copies to earn back your advance, you'll start to get royalty checks. Some publishers hold a reserve against returns, which means a percentage of royalties is held back in case books are returned from bookstores. If you have a reserve clause in your contract, find out the exact percentage of total sales that will be withheld and the time period the publisher will hold this money. You should be reimbursed this amount after a reasonable time period, such as a year. Royalty percentages vary with each publisher, but there are standard ranges.

Book publishers' rates

According to the latest figures from the Society of Children's Book Writers and Illustrators, picture book writers can expect advances of $3,500-5,000; picture book illustrators' advances range from $7,000-10,000; text and illustration packages can score $8,000-10,000. Royalties for picture books are generally about five percent (split between the author and illustrator) but can go as high as ten percent. Those who both write and illustrate a book, of course, receive the full royalty.

Advances for chapter books and middle-grade novels vary slightly from picture books. Hardcover titles can fetch authors advances of $4,000-6,000 and ten percent royalties; paperbacks bring in slightly lower advances of $3,000-5,000 and royalties of six to eight percent. Fees for young adult novels are generally the same, but additional length may increase fees and royalties.

As you might expect, advance and royalty figures vary from house to house and are affected by the time of year, the state of the economy and other factors. Some smaller houses may not even pay royalties, just flat fees. First-time writers and illustrators generally start on the low end of the scale, while established and high-profile writers are paid more.

Pay rates for magazines

For writers, fee structures for magazines are based on a per-word rate or range for a specific article length. Artists and photographers have a few more variables to contend with before contracting their services.

Payment for illustrations and photos can be set by such factors as whether the piece(s) will be black and white or four-color, how many are to be purchased, where the work appears (cover or inside), circulation and the artist's or photographer's prior experience.

Remaindering

When a book goes out of print, a publisher will sell any existing copies to a wholesaler who, in turn, sells the copies to stores at a discount. When the books are "remaindered" to a wholesaler, they are usually sold at a price just above the cost of printing. When negotiating a contract with a publisher you may want to discuss the possibility of purchasing the remaindered copies before they are sold to a wholesaler, then you can market the copies you purchased and still make a profit.

KNOW YOUR RIGHTS

A copyright is a form of protection provided to creators of original works, published or unpublished. In general, copyright protection ensures the writer, illustrator or photographer the power to decide how her work is used and allows her to receive payment for each use.

Essentially, copyright also encourages the creation of new works by guaranteeing the creator power to sell rights to the work in the marketplace. The copyright holder can print, reprint or copy her work; sell or distribute copies of her work; or prepare derivative works such as plays, collages or recordings. The Copyright Law is designed to protect work (created on or after January 1, 1978) for her lifetime plus 50 years.

If you collaborate with someone else on a written or artistic project, the copyright will last for the lifetime of the last survivor plus 50 years. The creators' heirs may hold a copyright for an additional 50 years. After that, the work becomes public domain. Works created anonymously or under a pseudonym are protected for 100 years, or 75 years after publication. Under work-for-hire agreements, you relinquish your copyright to your "employer."

Copyright notice and registration

Some feel a copyright notice should be included on all work, registered or not. Others feel it is not necessary and a copyright notice will only confuse publishers about whether the material is registered (acquiring rights to previously registered material is a more complicated process).

Although it's not necessary to include a copyright notice on unregistered work, if you don't feel your work is safe without the notice, it is your right to include one. Including a copyright notice—© (year of work, your name)—should help safeguard against plagiarism.

Registration is a legal formality intended to make copyright public record, and can help you win more money in a court case. By registering work within three months of publication or before an infringement occurs, you are eligible to collect statutory damages and attorney's fees. If you register later than three months after publication, you will qualify only for actual damages and profits.

Ideas and concepts are not copyrightable, only expressions of those ideas and concepts. A character type or basic plot outline, for example, is not subject to a copyright infringement lawsuit. Also, titles, names, short phrases or slogans, and lists of contents are not subject to copyright protection, though titles and names may be protected through the Trademark Office.

You can register a group of articles, illustrations or photos if it meets these criteria:
- the group is assembled in order, such as in a notebook;
- the works bear a single title, such as "Works by (your name)";
- it is the work of one writer, artist or photographer;
- the material is the subject of a single claim to copyright.

It's a publisher's responsibility to register your book for copyright. If you've previously registered the same material, you must inform your editor and supply the previous copyright information, otherwise, the publisher can't register the book in its published form.

For more information about the proper way to register works, contact the Copyright Office, Library of Congress, Washington DC 20359. The forms available are TX for writing (books, articles, etc.); VA for pictures (photographs, illustrations); and PA for plays and music. (To order copyright forms by phone, call (202)707-9100.) For information about how to use the copyright forms, request a copy of Circular I on Copyright Basics. All of the forms and circulars are free. Send the completed registration form along with the stated fee and a copy of the work to the Copyright Office.

For specific answers to questions about copyright (but not legal advice), call the Copyright Public Information Office at (202)707-3000 weekdays between 8:30 a.m. and 5 p.m. EST. Forms can also be downloaded from the Library of Congress website: http://lcweb.loc.gov/copyright. The site also includes tips on filling out forms, general copyright information and links to other sites related to copyright issues. For members of SCBWI, information about copyrights and the law is available. Send a SASE to the Society of Children's Book Writers and Illustrators, 22736 Vanowen St., Suite 106, West Hills CA 91307. Request "Copyright Facts for Writers."

The rights publishers buy

The copyright law specifies that a writer, illustrator or photographer generally sells one-time rights to her work unless she and the buyer agree otherwise in writing. Many publications will want more exclusive rights to your work than just one-time usage; some will even require you to sell all rights. Be sure you are monetarily compensated for the additional rights you relinquish. If you must give up all rights to a work, carefully consider the price you're being offered to determine whether you'll be compensated for the loss of other potential sales.

Writers who only give up limited rights to their work can then sell reprint rights to other publications, foreign rights to international publications, or even movie rights, should the opportunity arise. Artists and photographers can sell their work to other markets such as paper product companies who may use an image on a calendar, greeting card or mug. Illustrators and photographers may even sell original work after it has been published. And there are now galleries throughout the U.S. that display the work of children's illustrators.

Rights acquired through the sale of a book manuscript are explained in each publisher's contract. Take time to read relevant clauses to be sure you understand what rights each contract is specifying before signing. Be sure your contract contains a clause allowing all rights to revert back to you in the event the publisher goes out of business. (You may even want to have the contract reviewed by an agent or an attorney specializing in publishing law.)

The following are the rights you'll most often sell to publishers, periodicals and producers in the marketplace:

First rights. The buyer purchases the rights to use the work for the first time in any medium. All other rights remain with the creator. When material is excerpted from a soon-to-be-published book for use in a newspaper or periodical, first serial rights are also purchased.

One-time rights. The buyer has no guarantee that she is the first to use a piece. One-time permission to run written work, illustrations or photos is acquired, then the rights revert back to the creator.

First North American serial rights. This is similar to first rights, except that companies who distribute both in the U.S. and Canada will stipulate these rights to ensure that another North American company won't come out with simultaneous usage of the same work.

Second serial (reprint) rights. In this case newspapers and magazines are granted the right to reproduce a work that has already appeared in another publication. These rights are also purchased by a newspaper or magazine editor who wants to publish part of a book after the book has been published. The proceeds from reprint rights for a book are often split 50-50 between the author and his publishing company.

Simultaneous rights. More than one publication buys one-time rights to the same work at the same time. Use of such rights occurs among magazines with circulations that don't overlap, such as many religious publications.

All rights. Just as it sounds, the writer, illustrator or photographer relinquishes all rights to a piece—she no longer has any say in who acquires rights to use it. All rights are purchased by publishers who pay premium usage fees, have an exclusive format, or have other book or magazine interests from which the purchased work can generate more mileage. If a company insists on acquiring all rights to your work, see if you can negotiate for the rights to revert back to you after a reasonable period of time. If they agree to such a proposal, get it in writing.

Note: Writers, illustrators and photographers should he wary of "work-for-hire" arrangements. If you sign an agreement stipulating that your work will be done as work-for-hire, you will not control the copyrights of the completed work—the company who hired you will be the copyright owner.

Foreign serial rights. Be sure before you market to foreign publications that you have sold only North American—not worldwide—serial rights to previous markets. If so, you are free to market to publications that may be interested in material that's appeared in a North American-based periodical.

Syndication rights. This is a division of serial rights. For example, if a syndicate prints portions of a book in installments in its newspapers, it would be syndicating second serial rights. The syndicate would receive a commission and leave the remainder to be split between the author and publisher.

Subsidiary rights. These include serial rights, dramatic rights, book club rights or translation rights. The contract should specify what percentage of profits from sales of these rights go to the author and publisher.

Dramatic, television and motion picture rights. During a specified time the interested party tries to sell a story to a producer or director. Many times options are renewed because the selling process can be lengthy.

Display rights or electronic publishing rights. They're also known as "Data, Storage and Retrieval." Usually listed under subsidiary rights, the marketing of electronic rights in this era of rapidly expanding capabilities and markets for electronic material can be tricky. Display rights can cover text or images to be used in a CD-ROM or online, or may cover use of material in formats not even fully developed yet. If a display rights clause is listed in your contract, try to negotiate its elimination. Otherwise, be sure to pin down which electronic rights are being purchased. Demand the clause be restricted to things designed to be read-only. By doing this, you maintain your rights to use your work for things such as games and interactive software.

RUNNING YOUR BUSINESS

An important part of being a freelance writer, illustrator or photographer is running your freelance business. It's imperative to maintain accurate business records to determine if you're making a profit as a freelancer. Keeping correct, organized records will also make your life easier as you approach tax time.

When setting up your system, begin by keeping a bank account and ledger for your business finances apart from your personal finances. Also, if writing, illustration or photography is secondary to another freelance career, keep separate business records for each.

You will likely accumulate some business expenses before showing any profit when you start out as a freelancer. To substantiate your income and expenses to the IRS, keep all invoices, cash receipts, sales slips, bank statements, canceled checks and receipts related to travel expenses and entertaining clients. For entertainment expenditures, record the date, place and purpose of the business meeting as well as gas mileage. Keep records for all purchases, big and small— don't take the small purchases for granted; they can add up to a substantial amount. File all receipts in chronological order. Maintaining a separate file for each month simplifies retrieving records at the end of the year.

Record keeping

When setting up a single-entry bookkeeping system, record income and expenses separately. Use some of the subheads that appear on Schedule C (the form used for recording income from a business) of the 1040 tax form so you can easily transfer information onto the tax form when filing your return. In your ledger include a description of each transaction—the date, source of income (or debts from business purchases), description of what was purchased or sold, the amount of the transaction and whether payment was by cash, check or credit card.

Don't wait until January 1 to start keeping records. The moment you first make a business-related purchase or sell an article, book manuscript, illustration or photo, begin tracking your profits and losses. If you keep records from January 1 to December 31, you're using a calendar-year accounting period. Any other accounting period is called a fiscal year.

There are two types of accounting methods you can choose from—the cash method and the accrual method. The cash method is used more often: You record income when it is received and expenses when they're disbursed.

Using the accrual method, you report income at the time you earn it rather than when it's actually received. Similarly, expenses are recorded at the time they're incurred rather than when you actually pay them. If you choose this method, keep separate records for "accounts receivable" and "accounts payable."

Satifsying the IRS

To successfully—and legally—work as a freelancer, you must know what income you should report and what deductions you can claim. But before you can do that, you must prove to the IRS you're in business to make a profit, that your writing, illustration or photography is not merely a hobby.

The Tax Reform Act of 1986 says you should show a profit for three years out of a five-year period to attain professional status. The IRS considers these factors as proof of your professionalism:

- accurate financial records;
- a business bank account separate from your personal account;
- proven time devoted to your profession;
- whether it's your main or secondary source of income;
- your history of profits and losses;
- the amount of training you have invested in your field;
- your expertise.

If your business is unincorporated, you'll fill out tax information on Schedule C of Form 1040. If you're unsure of what deductions you can take, request the IRS publication containing this information. Under the Tax Reform Act, only 30 percent of business meals, entertainment and related tips, and parking charges are deductible. Other deductible expenses allowed on Schedule C include: car expenses for business-related trips; professional courses and seminars; depreciation of office equipment, such as a computer; dues and publications; and miscellaneous expenses, such as postage used for business needs.

If you're working out of a home office, a portion of your mortgage interest (or rent), related utilities, property taxes, repair costs and depreciation may he deducted as business expenses— under special circumstances. To learn more about the possibility of home office deductions, consult IRS Publication 587, Business Use of Your Home.

The method of paying taxes on income not subject to withholding is called "estimated tax" for individuals. If you expect to owe more than $500 at year's end and if the total amount of income tax that will be withheld during the year will be less than 90% of the tax shown on the current year's return, you'll generally make estimated tax payments. Estimated tax payments are made in four equal installments due on April 15, June 15, September 15 and January 15 (assuming you're a calendar-year taxpayer). For more information, request Publication 533, Self-Employment Tax.

The Internal Revenue Service's website (http://www.irs.ustreas.gov/) offers tips and instant access to IRS forms and publications.

Social Security tax

Depending on your net income as a freelancer, you may be liable for a Social Security tax. This is a tax designed for those who don't have Social Security withheld from their paychecks. You're liable if your net income is $400 or more per year. Net income is the difference between your income and allowable business deductions. Request Schedule SE, Computation of Social Security Self-Employment Tax, if you qualify.

If completing your income tax return proves to be too complex, consider hiring an accountant (the fee is a deductible business expense) or contact the IRS for assistance (look in the White Pages under U.S. Government - Internal Revenue Service). In addition to numerous publications to instruct you in various facets of preparing a tax return, the IRS also has walk-in centers in some cities.

Insurance

As a self-employed professional be aware of what health and business insurance coverage is available to you. Unless you're a Canadian who is covered by national health insurance or a fulltime freelancer covered by your spouse's policy, health insurance will no doubt be one of your biggest expenses. Under the terms of a 1985 government act (COBRA), if you leave a job with health benefits, you're entitled to continue that coverage for up to 18 months—you pay 100 percent of the premium and sometimes a small administration fee. Eventually, you must search for your own health plan. You may also need disability and life insurance. Disability insurance is offered through many private insurance companies and state governments. This insurance pays a monthly fee that covers living and business expenses during periods of long-term recuperation from a health problem. The amount of money paid is based on the recipient's annual earnings.

Before contacting any insurance representative, talk to other writers, illustrators or photographers to learn which insurance companies they recommend. If you belong to a writers' or artists' organization, ask the organization if it offers insurance coverage for professionals. (SCBWI has a plan available. Look through the Clubs & Organizations section for other groups that may offer coverage.) Group coverage may be more affordable and provide more comprehensive coverage than an individual policy.

Ten Tips and Twenty Questions for Your Next Book Deal

BY STEPHEN E. GILLEN

If you've been published, then you've seen it before—a *whereas* and a *therefore* followed by eight or more pages of pre-printed, pedantic prose offered up by the editor as his/her "standard publishing contract." Other than a few tiny spaces for your name, the title of your work, and the manuscript delivery date, the bulk of it looks as though it were long ago locked down in Century Schoolbook type.

But the truth is that there's more to review than the spelling of your name, choice of title, and projected completion date, and more to negotiate than you might realize. Here are ten tips to help you understand what is (or ought to be) worthy of negotiation and twenty questions to help you gather the information that will best enable you (or your attorney or agent) to make it very uncomfortable indeed for the editor/publisher to resist your well-reasoned requests.

THE BOOK DEAL—10 TIPS

The first tip is far and away the most important and least appreciated. Read it slowly . . . let it sink in . . . and believe it before you go on.

1. You have more leverage than you think. Editors are under ever-increasing pressure to sign new titles, meet publication dates and deliver sales results. For many of them, these factors have a direct bearing on their year-end compensation (a circumstance that can work to an author's significant bargaining advantage as year end approaches). While there are many aspiring first-time authors out there, only a relative handful will be published. If you have attracted interest or a contract offer, you have already made the cut—a reasonable list of tactfully stated concerns and requested amendments will only reinforce the impression that you are a competent and thorough professional. Moreover, the editor will have invested a significant amount of time in reviewing your proposal, perhaps getting outside reviews, preparing a proforma profit and loss analysis, and drafting a publication plan and recommendation for his/her superiors—if you are not signed all of this effort will have been for naught.

2. Only sell them what they intend to use. Beware of "work-for-hire" provisions, grants of "all right, title and interest," and broadly stated grants of electronic rights. If your publisher intends to publish a hardcover edition for distribution in North America, then the grant of rights should convey North American hardcover rights only. Alternate editions can be addressed by amendment to your book contract if and when the publisher expresses an interest in publishing them.

3. Don't leave the back door standing open. It's one thing to be signed to a publishing contract, but unfortunately (and perhaps unfairly) quite another to actually be published. Editors come and go and markets change. An open-ended manuscript acceptability standard can leave you holding an unpublished manuscript. Most form contracts will require you to deliver a completed

---

STEPHEN E. GILLEN *is Of Counsel with the firm of Frost & Jacobs LLP in Cincinnati, Ohio. His practice is concentrated in publishing, licensing, copyrights, trademarks and related matters. The firm maintains a website at http://www.frojac.com where additional articles and links to other sites of interest to writers can be found.*

manuscript that is acceptable to the publisher in form and content. This arguably allows the publisher to reject your completed work for any reason (provided it is not acting in bad faith). You should strive for an acceptability clause requiring only that the finished manuscript conform in coverage and quality to the sample chapters provided with your prospectus or, alternatively, a clause requiring the manuscript be professionally competent and fit for publication. You should also ask for language that obliges the publisher to provide you with detailed editorial comments and at least one opportunity to revise.

4. Don't promise what you can't deliver. Publishers usually require their authors to make certain representations and warranties about the work submitted—that it isn't libelous, that it doesn't infringe third party copyrights, and so on. Be careful that these representations apply only to work as supplied by you and not to the work of other contributors or editors. Also, we all know that every editor likes to put his mark on a work by changing the title. Be sure you do not warrant that the title does not infringe trademark or other rights (unless, of course, it is indeed your title).

Most contracts will also require you to indemnify the publisher for any damage or cost incurred as a result of your breach of the foregoing warranties. It is reasonable for you to ask that such indemnification be limited to defects as determined by a court of competent jurisdiction and also to ask that your obligation to indemnify the publisher be capped at the total royalties and other payments you actually receive from the publisher's exploitation of your work.

5. Don't let the editor put words in your mouth. Contracts typically give the publisher the right to select an editor to edit the work. However, you can win the battle for editorial control (or at least negotiate a peace with honor) by asking that the editor's authority be limited to copyediting and changes reasonably necessary to conform the manuscript to house style and further that substantive changes not be made without your approval.

6. The copyright is yours . . . to have and to hold. U.S. Copyright law vests the copyright in the human creator at the moment the work is fixed in a tangible medium of expression—put pen to paper and the copyright is yours. Ask that the publisher register it in your name. The publisher's legitimate interests are adequately protected by an appropriate assignment of rights and you are protected by holding all of the residual and derivative rights (not to mention having the psychic income that comes from being the record holder of a copyright—as writers, we have to take our income where we find it).

7. Don't take yourself out of the market. Watch out for the "no compete" provisions. Publishers often ask that you not publish or assist in publishing any other work that might compete. These restrictions are usually very broadly drafted and open-ended in scope. As such, they may be unenforceable as an unreasonable restraint of trade. Better, however, to try to narrow them before you sign.

8. A word about royalties. Royalties are the proverbial two birds in the bush. It's far better to negotiate for non-refundable advances. In any event, know whether your royalties will be based on list price, invoice price or net receipts. If they are based on the latter, ask the publisher for its discount schedule and for some historical averages so you can compare apples to apples in the event you are the happy holder of two or more contract offers.

9. Don't become an indentured servant. Some publishers still routinely include options clauses in their publishing contracts. This gives the publisher dibs on your next manuscript. Tell them that if they do a great job with the current one, you will certainly be back with the next.

10. Don't become trade bait. Publishers are merging, consolidating and selling lists. The best thing you have going for you is the support and confidence of the editor who felt strongly enough about your manuscript to try to sign you—now, his interests parallel yours and his reputation is on the line. You lose this advantage if your book is sold to another house, so it is in your best interests to try to negotiate for the right to approve any assignment of your book contract. A great reluctance on the part of the publisher to agree should send you a signal about its own feelings of security.

Odds are, you will not prevail on all of these issues. But odds are equally as good that you will not lose on all of them either.

In any event, you will not get that for which you do not ask. So ask away. At the end of the day you will have a better deal and a more informed relationship with your publisher. But do not ask yet—doing a little preparation first will put you in a better position to negotiate later.

BEHIND THE DEAL—20 QUESTIONS (OR HOW TO WIN THE GAME BEFORE YOUR EDITOR KNOWS IT HAS STARTED)

Now that you have some idea of what is or might be negotiable in a book publishing contract, it's time to do some serious sleuthing. Negotiations are ultimately influenced by which side knows the most about the other side's positions. The editor starts this contest with an advantage gained from experience in the market, experience doing other similar deals (undoubtedly many more than you have done), and the benefits of your perspective as reflected in your proposal. The way you get on an even footing with your editor/publisher is by knowing what to ask, and just as importantly, when to ask it.

What follows is a list of 20 questions (more or less) that you can employ to learn more about your publisher's plans for, and expectations of, your work—information that will help you evaluate your leverage and your editor's weaknesses. Ask them in the context of negotiating a book contract and the editor will evade them, hedge or refuse to answer. Ask them after the editor has indicated an interest in your work but before you engage in active contract-focused negotiations—in the context of learning more about your editor/publisher, more about their list and their business, more about the market and your potential competition—and you may catch the editor still in his selling mode. Ask them yourself and in person or over the phone. Negotiations may be formal and may be best handled by your attorney or agent in order to preserve your relationship with your editor. But information gathering will be most effective if you do it in person. A question perceived as innocuous when asked by you will be viewed with suspicion if posed by your agent or attorney. It may take some prodding, probing, wheedling and cajoling, but the information you gather will prove valuable so take copious notes.

Ask about the editor's background

1. How long have you been with Publisher X? Editors move from house to house and it will be helpful to know how long your editor has been in his current position.
2. Where were you before? The experience he gained at other houses will tell you something about his knowledge of the market and the business.
3. Did you come up through the sales side or through editorial? The editor with a sales background will have a significantly different negotiating focus from the editor with an editorial background.
4. Tell me about your current list. How many titles are there? What disciplines (if an educational work)? What curricular level (if an educational work)? What are your lead titles? What sort of market share do you have? Are any of them market leaders? The answers to these questions will tell you something about your editor's place in the pecking order and about how much attention your project is likely to get.

Next, find out how important your project is to his bonus (no editor will knowingly tell you, but the answers to these questions may provide a few clues):
5. How many new books do you sign in a typical year? The answer to this question will tell you something about the editor's annual signing goals.
6. How many have you signed so far this year? The answer to this question will give you some idea of where the editor is in relation to his goals. If the editor is close to his annual average, it could well be that signing you will make the difference between earning or not earning a bonus. You will probably never know for certain how important your project is, but you may at least get a clue.

Find out where your book fits in

7. How would you envision positioning my book vis-à-vis the competition? This will tell you what your editor sees as your work's competitive advantages—information that will prove useful should you decide to approach other publishers with your project.

8. Who are your principal competitors in this market? If you have not already submitted to these competitors, you should seriously consider doing so immediately. The best leverage you can have in negotiating a book contract is to know that there is another interested publisher in the wings.

9. Do you have any titles (published or signed) similar to mine? For obvious reasons, you want to know if the editor will have divided loyalties. Moreover, when it comes time to talk about the scope of your non-compete clause, it is very helpful to be able to point out specifically that the publisher is not similarly constrained.

10. If the proposal or partial manuscript has been reviewed, check the reviews to see who is identified as a competitor. Again, you want to know about the other publishers who might also be interested in your work.

Get the numbers (the answers to these questions will help you secure a reasonable advance against royalties):

11. How big a market are we talking about? This will give you a sense of how the publisher views your book and whether you both see it the same way.

12. What sort of market penetration does Publisher X generally expect with a new book? In combination with the answer to question #11, this will give you a way of corroborating the editor's sales projections.

13. How many units would an average book sell in the market for which my book is targeted? First year? Lifetime? How many do you think the market leader sells? The answers to these questions, once you know the cover price, will let you estimate revenues and royalties so you can make a credible, objectively supportable request for advances.

14. How many units does a book like mine have to sell to break even? The answer to this question will tell you at what volume the publisher covers its costs.

15. How many units would it have to sell before you would consider it a roaring success? The answer to this question will tell you at what point the publisher has made its customary margin. The break-even volume and the volume necessary to a target margin are natural break points for a sliding royalty scale. Consider accepting the rate first offered up to break even, but ask for a higher rate up to the target margin, and ask for the moon beyond that.

16. How would you see it priced? As noted, this information helps you project revenues and royalties, but it also will tell you something about the titles your editor views as competitive— because they will necessarily fall in the same price range.

17. Do you think it would travel well? If the editor says no, then it will be very hard for him to push for exclusive, perpetual foreign and translation rights.

18. Tell me about Publisher X's foreign sales ability? Sub-rights licensing (translations and adaptations)? New media capability? Again, rights the editor is not positioned to aggressively exploit should not be part of the package.

Get the promotion plan:

19. What would you envision doing to promote a book like mine? Promotional brochure (How many pages? Full color? How big a mailing?) How many review copies/comps? Presentation at sales conference? Author appearance? Newspaper/journal ads? Anything else? Most publishing contracts say very little about what the publisher will do to market and promote your work. If you get a sales pitch from the editor, make an effort to reduce it to writing and reference it in the publishing contract.

Check the back door

20. Roughly what percent of the titles you sign actually make it into print? The answer to this question will tell you how important it is to introduce an objective acceptability standard into the manuscript delivery clause.

21. Is there anything else I should know about you or about how you see my book fitting into your list? If your editor is still talking, you should still be taking notes.

You will not get answers to all of these questions. And you will not get answers to any of them without a fair amount of prodding. But the time and effort you spend will tell you volumes about your editor and will pay many dividends when the time comes to negotiate that contract. Knock 'em dead!

For Illustrators: Straight Talk On Your Business Plan

BY DAVID A. NILES

Remember how you used to dream of your idyllic life-to-come as a children's book illustrator? Working at home in your own familiar place . . . clad in shorts and tee . . . maybe even in your PJs . . . seated by your studio window overlooking the brook that babbles its way past your meadow, while you create lovely images that every editor and his mother will love you for? Remember? In such moments of reverie, did it ever occur to you that there would be another, more daunting side to your dream? Possibly not.

At that early time, the B-word, *business*, probably hadn't stolen its way into your illustration vocabulary. Certainly you were possessed of genuine artistic purpose. You had worked hard in order to refine your art and design skills, had achieved academically, shown your work in a number of places, had pleased a number of small clients, and had been encouraged by some flattering comments. But when you put it all together, did it make a whole? Did you ever think of your artist role as being only part of who you were? Possibly it hadn't occurred to you that if you're going to be successful as a children's book illustrator, you must prepare yourself for a business career too!

College art courses often seem to ignore such practical issues as how to set up your freelance business, price your work, market and promote your talents, and other business skills that can add up to survival. Art is a competitive field, and without those practical skills, other less talented but more enlightened people may have an advantage over you in the marketplace.

Success in the business of art begins with establishing a business plan. And by calling it a plan, I'm not talking about the kind of casual internal conversation you may carry on with yourself while driving to the local art supply store. I'm talking about a process that will require you to sit down with pen and paper and really consider how you intend to plan your art business and make it creatively, as well as financially, profitable.

For starters, let's say you've just left an illustration staff job and are going into business fulltime, with children's book illustration as your goal. At this point it may help to look at the advantages you had as a staff artist that you may be leaving behind. Think about how many things were organized and provided by your employer. Your work was carefully planned with great consideration for quality, your hours and work schedules were fixed, your workload was generally constant, your workplace was furnished with the necessary equipment and resources, you had a steady income that included a paid vacation, all the bookkeeping was done by your employer, and you probably were furnished with disability insurance, a medical plan and possibly a profit-sharing plan as well. Now, let's look at the other side of the ledger and see how that compares with being in business for yourself as a freelancer.

As a self-employed illustrator, you can adjust your own work schedule because your work hours are flexible, but this doesn't guarantee you'll have income-producing work every time

DAVID A. NILES *writes on issues of professional illustrative practice for art journals and the World Wide Web. A past vice president of the Boston Chapter of the Graphic Artists Guild as well as a freelance illustrator, his career has also included the Rhode Island School of Design, where he served as associate professor of illustration for 18 years. He lives in Massachusetts.*

you step into your studio. Your timetable will be determined by the nature and the number of projects you undertake, though as your own boss you'll have the power to adjust the schedule based on your own creative needs. Your workplace can be located wherever you choose to live, and under such a plan, you can enjoy a level of freedom that was never possible when you worked on staff. As an employee, your planning was done for you; once you work for yourself, the plan *starts with you*! And you have sole responsibility for molding it, orchestrating it, and sustaining it throughout your career. Challenging? You bet!

The following questions and answers are to assist you in establishing a basic plan for doing business as an illustrator in the children's book field—one that should get you started on the road to a stronger and more profitable career. I suppose we could give it a lofty title such as "An Analysis of Planning For a Freelance Illustration Business" or "A Policy For Running My Own Freelance Business," but why not simply call it . . . "The Plan."

THE PLAN

To start formulating your plan, spend some time thinking about how you should respond to the following questions. Consider each item on the basis of your own goals and aspirations as a professional. It might help to write down your answers to make them available for later review.

1. What do you do?

Here, simply describe the nature of your work—what kind of illustration you do, or what you ultimately aspire to do.

2. What do you call your business?

The simplest form of titling is your name and what you do: Jane Reed, Illustrator. Though some prefer to use a cute or snappy title such as "Spotlight Studio" or "Studio One," this tends to imply that you have a staff and take on projects beyond children's books. Your place in the industry will be more secure if you use your name and your art specialty. Your creditors, the IRS, your agent, and your clients, among others, will come to know you more readily by your professional name than by any obscure title you may dream up for your studio.

3. What kind of product or service do you provide?

State this straightforwardly. You illustrate books for children. If you wish to clarify this even more, you can add that you illustrate textbooks or educational materials for CD-ROM, you do animation for multimedia, or perhaps you write and illustrate picture books.

4. What are your business hours?

As you begin your freelance career, you might think you'll work anytime you feel like working. This is a common view of freelancing. However, it's wise to devise a work schedule that is as regular as it would be if you worked for someone else. And if you aren't working on a project for a client, you should be taking care of various studio and professional chores that are required of a business.

These chores include billing, filing, promotional planning, keeping your portfolio up-to-date, working on your marketing plan, writing the stories you plan to illustrate, phoning prospective clients, mailing promotional packages, writing proposals, contacting editors, etc.—business surely, and a process characterized by *bus*yness. If this means being in your studio at 8 o'clock in the morning and remaining there well into the evening, so be it. There will be days when a deadline will require many consecutive hours of highly-focused work. Your business hours should be set at a realistic level, not unlike a normal 9 to 5 work day.

5. Who are your present clients?

Whether you have many clients or only a few, list them. Whether they fit your specific role as book illustrator or not, list everybody you are working for. You may be surprised at what this list tells you. Moreover, this list will grow along with your business as you add clients and customers who are willing to use your talents.

6. Who are your potential clients?

Here's where you can put your dreams down on paper. If you'd like to work for certain clients who are household names or for certain editors who have very unique and special reputations in the book trade, write down their names.

7. What steps do you take to market and promote your talent?

You can remain in your studio, creating wonderful original work for your portfolio, but if you don't get that work out into the world, you might as well forget freelancing and work for someone else. Marketing means analyzing the potential markets that exist, and devising strategies by which those markets can be exposed to your creative work. Gaining the attention of those people and publishers you wish to work for will require careful planning, and it isn't something you do only when things get slow.

Marketing and promoting your work and your talent is a constant process that must take a high priority if you are to achieve your career goals. This will require much of your time and some expense. Many illustrators are now using the World Wide Web to promote their work. In addition, many use a comprehensive mail-marketing program to place samples of their latest work in the hands of the clients on their wish lists. Research all possible resources for information about the publishing community so you can identify potential clients' needs and requirements.

In addition to *Children's Writer's & Illustrator's Market*, here are a few resources to check out, including websites:

- The Children's Book Council: http://www.cbcbooks.org/memlst.txt
- Society of Children's Book Writers and Illustrators: http://www.scbwi.org
- The Graphic Artists Guild: http://www.gag.org
- Inkspot: Children's Illustrator Directory and Resource: http://www.inkspot.com/author/illustrators.html
- *Literary Marketplace* (LMP): This is the yellow pages of the publishing industry. A complete source available in most libraries.
- *Graphic Artists Guild Handbook of Pricing & Ethical Guidelines*: This comprehensive book is in its ninth edition, covering pricing and professional trade practices throughout the visual communications industry. An absolute must.

Contact the Children's Book Council or SCBWI for ideas and direction. Attend conferences and talk with agents and editors about your work. Look around for other illustrators with greater experience to get their opinions and ideas. If you belong to a Graphic Artists Guild chapter, helpful information will be available through their meetings and publications.

8. How do you price your work?

Publishers' budgets reflect anticipated unit sales. Book publishing's typical advance and royalty system means that when the publisher has commissioned you for a project, they are assuming financial risk. For that reason, iIllustrators usually have little say over how much they might be offered to illustrate a picture book. The anticipated sales curve for the particular book determines the income you will realize for your efforts. If you're hired to do jackets or illustrations for young adult books, you will generally be paid a flat fee.

Whether you're working under a flat fee or a royalty contract, you should figure in both cases that you are working under an hourly pay system you structure and apply to everything you do. In effect, you place a monetary value on the time you spend working by the hour. Each hour you spend in the studio must be paid for, either by your client, or you, even if you are involved in personal work that your business requires.

Understanding the economics of your situation is crucial if you're to remain profitable. You need to have an accurate idea of how much it costs annually to run your business—a total of your rent, supplies, travel, research, promotional printing, computer expense and any other costs. For a strong resource on these important matters, consult the *Graphic Artists Guild Handbook of Pricing & Ethical Guidelines* (mentioned above), available in most bookstores.

The Children's Book Council and SCBWI also provide guidance on these crucial financial matters. And workshops dealing with pricing and billing are held on a regular basis both locally and nationally by the Graphic Artists Guild.

9. Are you prepared to negotiate terms on a contract?

Negotiation need not be scary. Just remember that a contract—any contract—has no function until it is signed and agreed to. You should fully understand any and all terms on a contract before you sign. If there's a question on any aspect of a contract, speak out and request that it be explained—it may be a point that can be negotiated.

Be aware that an aggressive spirit will most surely guarantee you won't prevail. It might even cause you to lose you the assignment. Good negotiation will never happen under adversarial conditions. A publisher will know the minute you walk in the door that you intend to win, and they simply won't let that happen. Should you fail to reach an agreement, it's best to accept it and leave in good faith. Remember that you may come back to negotiate another day.

Note that book publishers often use work-for-hire contracts for illustration. When you are hired to work for them, you may be expected to sign such a contract, thus relinquishing all future rights to the work. It's possible that certain details of work-for-hire contracts can be negotiated such as return of original work or reuse of your work in another medium. Again, if there's a question, request that it be explained.

For helpful advice on contracts and negotiation, SCBWI members can send a SASE for their publication called "Answers to Some Questions About Contracts."

10. How do you bill clients?

An important part of running your freelance business is creating a billing system. Part of your billing policy should include the practice of sending invoices stating the fee and terms that have been agreed upon by you and your client. Your billing policy should be discussed and put down on paper, before any misunderstandings have had a chance to develop. That way, if clients are slow in paying, you'll have a system in place that will encourage them to pay what they owe. If you experience inordinate difficulties in collecting from a client, don't be afraid to go all the way, even if it means using a collection agency. If they're that difficult to deal with, you probably wouldn't wish to work for them again.

11. What type of record-keeping system do you use?

Keeping good records for your freelance art business is a difficult and ongoing task. You might consider hiring a financial consultant, accountant or even an intern to keep things organized; in the long term it will pay for itself. Many people get into trouble by not separating personal and business expenses, which often occurs when they use the same credit cards for both. Start off playing it smart. Get separate credit cards for your personal and business expenses. But don't stop there—get separate bank accounts, account books, file drawers, everything. As the old proverb goes, "a place for everything, and everything in its place."

12. How do you handle the freelance cash-flow roller coaster?

People accustomed to receiving a weekly pay check sometimes have difficulties adjusting to the sporadic cash flow situation that is a fact of life when you freelance. Three weeks of checks flowing in, then three months of no payments at all. Scary? You bet. But the best way to deal with this is not to overspend a windfall. You may get paid for a large project with what seems like all the money in the world. Treat that money as though it's got to sustain you for months by budgeting it with care. If you set up a payment schedule from your own account, it can often take you through a lean period during which you have little or no cash flow.

Will Rogers once wrote: "Even if you're on the right track, you'll get run over if you just sit there." With a good plan in hand, you'll be better positioned to move toward your goals. You will not just be "sitting there." Living a full life as a creator of images for children is dependent on many factors, but the most crucial of all is the manner in which you run your creative business. If you are as creative in the management of your business as you are in the creation of your captivating images for children, success will soon be your willing partner.

Promoting Your Work Through School Appearances

BY ALICE P. BUENING

Writers and illustrators just embarking on their careers may not know what's in store for them in the way of promoting their books. Some work under the misconception that they will finish a book and their publishers will market it—while they remain in their offices or studios working on their next projects. I've heard an author say this attitude is akin to "giving birth to a baby and thinking, 'Okay, I'm done with it.' "

Of course publishers market the books on their lists. But let's say a publisher releases 75 new titles a year. That publisher also has several hundred titles on their backlist. All these books will

Jacket illustration © 1993 Daniel Pinkwater. Reprinted with permission of Simon & Schuster.

Any author or illustrator who's had a tough day at a school should pick up a copy of Daniel Pinkwater's *Author's Day* (Atheneum), a funny look at an author appearance gone wrong. In the book writer Bramwell Wink-Porter is off to Melvinville Elementary School, where there hangs a banner proclaiming "Welcome Mr. Bramwell Wink-Porter, author of *Fuzzy Bunny*." Wink-Porter's book, however, is *The Bunny Brothers*; someone else wrote *The Fuzzy Bunny*. From there the fictitious author endures pancakes with green crayons in them, a fainting teacher, a bite by a rabbit, being tied to a chair by rambunctious sixth-graders, and a sandwich of bologna and shredded carrots with extra mayonnaise, "The favorite lunch of Fuzzy Bunny in your wonderful book."

appear in their catalog. Some of the titles will have special marketing campaigns through the company's publicity department. But we're talking a lot of books. The average publisher simply does not have the resources or staff to go all out in promoting hundreds of individual titles each year. That leaves much of the promotional burden on the shoulders of authors or illustrators, if they so choose. Telling people about your books, in fact, could be considered part of the role of an author or illustrator. And one important way to promote your work is by appearing at schools.

For many authors and illustrators, school visits are an enjoyable, rewarding way to sell books, stay in touch with their audience, and earn extra income. Once they develop a polished presentation, speakers may receive anywhere from $250-1,500 or more per day plus expenses, and school appearances also often include book signings. Authors and illustrators report that they also gain energy, inspiration and feedback by meeting the audience and fans of their books.

In order for these appearances to go smoothly many details must be taken care of including setting up the visit, planning the presentations, having the right equipment on hand at the school, and coordinating book sales. Publishers may serve as go-betweens for schools and authors and illustrators. Larger publishers may have special appearance coordinators on staff, so if doing school visits interests you, let your publisher know, and talk to the appropriate person on their staff. Other publishers provide no assistance in setting up school gigs, so authors and illustrators must send promotional material to schools on their own. Some local groups, such as teachers organizations or public library consortiums, compile directories of local authors who visit schools, supplying basic information about fees, types of programs offered, grade levels preferred and book titles. Network with authors and illustrators in your area to find out if such a resource exists and how you can be included.

Not surprisingly, a number of authors and illustrators have turned to the World Wide Web as a promotional tool. A site called *Invite An Author to Your School* (http://www.snowcrest.net/kidpower/authors.html) offers writers and illustrators free listings, including contact information and book titles, with links to their personal websites.

If you've never done a school appearance, the thought of it may scare you a bit. It's a good idea to contact authors or illustrators in your area, and ask if you can tag along on one of their appearances. Offer to do a few free visits at schools in your area, or at the schools your own children attend.

When giving presentations to kids, work from your strengths and interact with your audience. If you're funny, use that. If you're an illustrator, demonstrate how you draw a character or show slides of your illustration process. Bring in a book dummy and explain how a book is made. Answer kids' questions. Have the class help you write a story or a poem or make a picture—whatever will keep their attention. (An author in my area whose books feature cowboy characters dresses up like a cowgirl and performs with a lasso. She's on the road two weeks a month during the school year.)

What follows are answers to some questions posed to three people with much experience in the area of school appearances. They offer advice and suggestions helpful for both those new to school appearances and those who've been at it for a while.

DAVID GREENBERG
Author—Portland, Oregon

Last year, David Greenberg set out to create a nationwide sourcebook called *Authors and Illustrators Who Visit Schools* (similar to sourcebooks of illustrators' work that are sent to art directors). Greenberg planned to offer interested parties (for a price) a full page in a catalog and website for one year, mailing the print version to 65,000 public school librarians.

Unfortunately, the plan didn't work out—he didn't get enough interest to launch the catalog in 1997—so he developed Plan B: He banded together with four other authors to share the cost of mailing to 30,000 K-8 schools in the U.S., including information about each of them (see page 43 for a sample page) and referring recipients to their website and cyber-catalog (http://www.teleport.com/~authilus). The website, *Authors and Illustrators Who Visit Schools*, features a page for each author with detailed descriptions of presentations, listings of book titles, full-color photos and book jackets, and contact information. Greenberg is hopeful that if their beginning effort is successful, they'll be able to entice more authors and illustrators to jump on board.

Greenberg's titles include *Slugs* and *Bugs* (both published by Little, Brown & Co.), *The Great School Lunch Rebellion* and *Your Dog Might Be a Werewolf, Your Toes Could All Explode* (both published by Bantam). He's been visiting schools for more than 20 years, and makes about 100 appearances a school year.

How do you benefit from your school appearances? How do you think students benefit?

I love presenting to kids. It energizes me. It inspires me. It keeps me close to the language, the humor and thought processes. I think students benefit because they are inspired in that the sheer humanness of the presenter makes book writing seem more possible for them. It's like the difference between reading a play to yourself and seeing it performed.

Why do you think it's important for authors and illustrators to visit schools?

It seems to me that too many of us have only a theoretical understanding of children, referenced only from our own childhoods. If we're going to write for children, we should be milling about among them. Working in schools gives us this opportunity.

It is important for schools, teachers and students because it makes books relevant, in the same manner that cows make milk relevant. When you meet an author, a book is no longer a product to be purchased or taken from a library shelf. It becomes the animate manifestation of a living person.

How did you come up with the idea of the catalog and the website?

Whenever I visit schools, the most common question I get from librarians, principals or PTA liaisons upon leaving is, "Who do you know of that might present for us next year?" Schools clearly have no central source for finding authors. And, oddly, publishers are often passive or unresponsive in helping out, even though it would be in their best interests to do so.

It occurred to me that if I could find writers who were genuinely interested in presenting at schools, who were experienced at presenting, who were professionals, and if I could put them all in a catalog, it would be of benefit to the authors and great benefit to the schools. In addition, by banding together and sharing costs of printing and postage, we could radically lower the cost of sending out our mailing.

Describe what you do at a school visit.

I give schools a menu of options from which to choose. The main thing I do is present at assemblies. These presentations are based upon my writing which happens to be children's poetry. I dynamically, expressively read my poems, and talk to kids about the qualities that activate the writing. I do writing workshops in which I present unique writing lessons I've developed. I do teacher inservices, in which I give teachers many unique, practical writing lessons to use with kids. I do family presentations for which kids come back in the evening with their families and they, as a team, write together.

Do you often get mail from children after you speak at their school? How do you handle this?

It's the nature of visiting schools that authors are very likely to receive letters (often many letters—monsoons of letters) from children, sometimes from teachers. I think it's vital that an

DAVID GREENBERG, Author

TITLES:
- SLUGS (Little, Brown & Co.)
- BUGS (Little, Brown & Co.)
- THE GREAT SCHOOL LUNCH REBELLION (Bantam)
- YOUR DOG MIGHT BE A WEREWOLF, YOUR TOES COULD ALL EXPLODE (Bantam)

AWARDS: THE GREAT SCHOOL LUNCH REBELLION was the 1990 recipient of the Children's Choice award.

PROGRAMS AVAILABLE:

GRADES: K-12.

LENGTH: Depending upon grade and type of presentation, from thirty to sixty minutes.

AUDIENCE SIZE: As a very rough guideline, around two hundred maximum per assembly, one hundred maximum per writing workshop. Inservices and Family Evening sessions can accommodate any number.

ASSEMBLIES: Greenberg dynamically and expressively reads, or, better yet, performs his rollicking poems for kids. His poems are filled with alliteration, acrobatic meter patterns, snazzy rhymes. Students regularly are so captivated by the joy of Greenberg's performances that they leave his assembly quoting their favorite lines. Greenberg also weaves into his presentation explanations of the various elements that activate his poetry. He discusses the craft of writing and the fierce perseverance necessary to succeed. He emphasizes the key importance of the writing process.

WRITING WORKSHOPS: These are intensive, personalized writing sessions that exude a spirit of love for language. Based upon unique, highly motivational lessons, students write impressively thoughtful work.

FAMILY EVENING PRESENTATIONS: Loads of fun, the purpose of these sessions is to bring kids and parents together in an important educational activity. Greenberg starts the evening session by reading several of his poems. Next, he demonstrates a writing activity at the overhead, and family groups collaboratively try their hand at the same sort of writing (which always has some sort of family theme). Kids clamber to take completed work home as a memento.

TEACHER INSERVICES: These are refreshingly fun in tone, yet absolutely practical in content. They provide teachers with numerous, unique and compelling writing lessons that they can implement in their classes immediately.

A WORD FROM DAVID GREENBERG: *"It is my goal that when kids leave my assemblies they say to themselves 'I want to be a writer when I grow up!.' In my assemblies I do far more than read my poems and talk about what goes into them. I make a major point of talking about the many many rejections I've received for my writing, and how in the face of this I've stuck in there. Likewise, I feel that there are many kids who face adversity, not only in their curriculum, but in their daily lives, and I hope to serve as an example and inspiration for them to keep kicking, keep trying. Such tenacity, I think, underlies success as a writer, and, probably, at any endeavor."*

FEES: $795 for the first two presentations of a day. Each presentation thereafter on that same day is $110 each. Afternoon Inservices and evening Family Presentations are $200 each. *There is no additional fee for expenses*. The only exception to this is if David Greenberg is asked to travel to an area that cannot be integrated into one of his tours. In this case, a fee will have to be negotiated and expenses charged in addition.

DAVID GREENBERG CONTACT INFORMATION:

4131 NE Wistaria Dr., Portland, OR 97212
Phone Number: 503/287-2167
Fax Number: 503/287-8137
E-Mail: seminar@juno.com

This page is an example of the promotional material sent out to K-8 schools throughout the country by author David Greenberg. His website *Authors and Illustrators Who Visit Schools* (http://www.teleport.com/~authilus) features similar information, but complete with color covers and expanded summaries of his books. Greenberg makes about 100 school appearances each year.

author respond to every letter. If an entire class writes, an author should thoughtfully respond to the class. If individual kids write, an author should respond thoughtfully to each.

I know this letter writing may seem burdensome, especially when you receive piles of letters, and they all seem so similar. Though these letters may seem inconsequential to the recipient, they often are of utmost importance to the sender—they are waiting in suspense to hear back from the author. And if they never do, they are disappointed and disillusioned. Teachers have more than once ruefully spoken to me of all those authors who never write back.

If they do get letters back, they are overjoyed. The event is memorable and positive. They share the letter with their families and friends and cherish it. I've also heard from teachers what a marvelous, positive difference it made for a particular child that I wrote back to him or her.

What's your advice for authors and illustrators who have never presented to children?

One—Be professional. Too many authors dress slovenly, show up late, don't return phone calls, are unprepared. In short too many authors are not outstanding role models for our profession or adulthood. We have a very serious responsibility to positively influence kids, and we must never take this lightly.

Two—Speak many places for free in order to familiarize yourself with your audience and to gain experience at speaking. A school should not be expected to pay a large sum of money to someone who, although he's a great author, is an incompetent presenter. It's vital that you know the difference in learning and listening styles between lower elementary, upper elementary, junior high and senior high.

Three—Speak at no charge to as many local or national teachers' and librarians' associations as you can. Volunteer to speak to local teacher college classes. In this way, you will start to form a reputation as a worthy speaker, and you will begin to receive invitations to speak.

What problems have school appearances posed for you?

If you're outstanding as a presenter and develop a reputation that brings you a great deal of work, you must try to form some sort of balance between school presenting and your own writing and your family life. It is very easy, given the travel demands of speaking, to let it entirely take over you life.

Do you have any other advice to share?

I cannot stress enough how strongly I feel about professionalism. When authors visit schools, they take on the temporary status of celebrity—children (and teachers) hang on their every word, every behavioral nuance. The story of their visit will be repeated to countless parents, friends, siblings, passed down through the years. This is no time to push an anti-authority or counterculture agenda. This is not time to act the prima donna. We are the responsible adults who are helping to steward these children—many of whom live in very difficult circumstances—to adulthood. We can be nothing less than positive role models in every aspect of our visit. Anything less than this is a discredit to our profession and harmful to children. On the other hand, in the measure that we take our roles seriously (and joyously) we can make great positive differences in children's lives.

HEIDI PETACH
Illustrator/Author—Cincinnati, Ohio

Armed with a bevy of promotional material whipped up in Adobe Illustrator and Microsoft Word, illustrator/author Heidi Petach feels organization and careful preparation are paramount when gearing up for school appearances. She's created a school visit info sheet (pictured on page 47) to keep details straight for herself, a sheet of quotes about her collected from previous school and conference appearances, a page of book reviews, a bibliography and bio, and even a classroom discovery guide relating to her book *Goldilocks and the Three Hares*.

Among Petach's many other titles are *Pig Out!*, by Portia Aborio (Putnam & Grosset); *The Little Ballerina*, by Katherine Ross (Random House); and *The Monster That Glowed in the Dark*, by Annie Ingle (also Random House). She's been visiting schools since 1989, and makes about two dozen appearances every school year.

What were your experiences when you first began visiting schools? What did you learn early on?

When I first started, my fee was lower and I found myself staying up nights and weekends in the studio making up for lost time and money. I now charge more, have the experience to know what works best, both for me and for the schools, and feel more in control of the situation. People at schools are very cooperative if you let them know exactly what you need and exactly what you in turn will provide for them. I was apprehensive at first about raising my fees, but by that point, word-of-mouth recommendations began setting things in motion on their own, and I have no trouble getting bookings.

How much is your publisher involved in setting up your school gigs? Does this vary with different publishers you've worked with?

Yes, it varies quite a lot. And it also depends on how many books you've done with them. Generally, publishers don't market you very aggressively until you've had at least three successful books with them. The larger publishers have entire departments for educational marketing. They go to the large conventions such as the ALA (American Library Association), they have author/illustrator packets they send out to interested schools that feature each of their authors and illustrators who are willing to do school visits, their requirements and fees.

Out of all the publishers I've worked with, the one who worked best with me is Putnam & Grosset. They sent me a questionnaire to fill out for their school visits packets, made a bio sheet for me, had 8×10 glossies of me on hand to give out, and asked my permission to use all pertinent material for a website they were making for school visit info.

This doesn't mean I don't keep aggressively pursuing school visits on my own or come up with ideas to help promote my books to schools. I put together a "Classroom Discovery Guide" with fun and creative ideas, as well as age-appropriate activities and worksheets that use my *Goldilocks and the Three Hares* in the elementary school. I tested it out thoroughly in local schools, got great suggestions from both the children and their teachers, and Putnam printed it and sends it free to any school that requests it.

I thought it would be fun to have a video of *Goldilocks and the Three Hares* à la "Reading Rainbow" and got corporate funding to have it professionally made. It's been shown in local classrooms via WCET's [her local PBS station] educational cable hookup. And Putnam & Grosset distributes it free to schools who request it. All the schools have to do is provide a SASE. Your publisher can be a great help. But it certainly doesn't hurt to provide materials for them to make their job easier. Everyone benefits.

How do you benefit from the visits?

I love doing school visits. It keeps me in tune with how kids are—what they like, what they dislike. The younger ones in particular are refreshingly honest. It's a perk for me, particularly in midwinter when I feel as isolated as a hermit in my studio.

I'll never forget the school I visited that had a big banner welcoming me at the entrance. Then, as I stepped inside, the entrance hallway was lined with life-sized paper people. The first grade classes wondered what I might look like and created wonderful paper collages, complete with button jewelry, hats and purses, along with descriptions. After my presentation, the third graders sent me acrostics based on my name, and I was amazed at how well they had listened. Tiny details just mentioned in passing popped up.

Why do you think it's important for authors and illustrators to do school visits?

To keep that spark alive—that close connection between you, your work, and the children who will be enjoying it. The interaction is so important—it's exhilarating, humbling, and makes all the hard, lonely work in the studio or at the computer worthwhile. And for the kids, it opens a mysterious door and lets them feel like they're part of a larger process. It opens up their vision to experience what it's like to be someone else. It's a sharing of the creative process in both directions.

What do you do during a typical school visit?

I enjoy doing school assemblies. I split the assemblies up by age, going into slightly less detail and time for the younger children. My presentation is fast paced and funny. I show them slides of what my studio looks like, how I work, how my family, friends and pets get into my books, give them a tour of my publisher's offices, and tell the stories behind the stories.

I also bring along visuals to show them—actual sketches, dummies, finished art, color proofs—and explain the printing process in simple terms. Then I field questions for five or ten minutes. I love the spontaneous interactions—I never know what I'll be asked! Sometimes the questions are thoughtful, such as where I got my training and how old I was when I first tried writing and illustrating my first book. Sometimes they just ask, "How old are you? How much money do you make?"

I also autograph books. This is usually done in the school library, and I specify that each book have a slip of paper in it with the child's name spelled correctly. I prefer that kids order the books from the local bookstore or the publisher. Some people make extra money buying the books themselves, but for me, that is too much hassle, and it's nice to help support a bookstore. After all, they help me.

What's your advice for other authors and illustrators who've never presented to school children?

Do your homework. Find out what authors and illustrators will be presenting in your local schools and ask if you can observe in the background. That's how I started. If you have children, volunteer to do a presentation at their school for free. This will build your confidence, and you'll quickly discover exactly what you need to put in your school information sheets regarding requirements—what you expect the school to provide, where, when and what your fee will be. Also spell out what you'll provide—be specific. Some schools need contracts and this sheet usually suffices.

Make out a checklist of things to bring so you don't leave anything behind. I always bring a back-up remote control for a Kodak carousel slide projector, for instance, in case the school's doesn't work. This has been immensely helpful. Also, having a flashlight (to shed light on your notes during slide presentations) and asking for a glass of water are good ideas. One thing I've learned to head off problems in advance of slide shows is to be sure the room can be darkened considerably so the slides will show up well, and that the screen is large enough. Also be sure to specify if a mike or power cords will be needed.

I fill out a form I've made up for myself when I get the initial inquiry (it's usually by phone) so I don't forget to get the contact person's name, school name, phone number, etc. Always follow up promptly with your promotional material—cover letter, school visit info sheet, bio, bibliography, quotes from other school visits, etc. And never forget to send a thank you note to the school afterwards. These can be creative and tie in with the theme of your latest book.

Heidi Petach School Visit

School _____

Address _____

_____

Contact Person _____

Phone _____ Date Contacted _____

Date of Visit _____

Times of Assemblies _____

_____

_____

Target Time for Prior Set-up _____ Fee _____ (Due on day of visit)

Book Sale? _____ Handled by: _____

Heidi Petach will provide prior to visit:
❑ Bios
❑ School Visit Info Sheet
❑ School Visit Quotes
❑ *Goldilocks and the Three Hares* Reviews
❑ Bibliography
❑ Sample copy of *Goldilocks and the Three Hares Classroom Discovery Guide* (Teachers' and students' pages using the book in a cross-curriculum program)
❑ *Goldilocks and the Three Hares* video order form (free from publisher + postage and padded mailer)
❑ Autographed OWLphabet print for school (school has permission to photocopy it to give to students on day of visit).

Heidi Petach will bring on day of visit:
❑ Slides ❑ CD player ❑ Visuals (sketches, dummies, art, mechanicals, progs, proof sheets, etc.)

School will provide prior to visit: ❑ Directions on how to get there

School will provide by target set-up time:
❑ Very large screen in room that can be darkened considerably
❑ Kodak Carousel projector placed at a distance for the slides to fill the screen
❑ Microphone, chair, and water placed by projector, as well as power for CD
❑ Table at front for visuals

8943 Renetta Court ❖ Cincinnati, OH 45251 ❖ 513/522-1780

This school visit sheet created by Heidi Petach helps the illustrator/author keep track of pertinent information about an appearance. Petach fills in the information as soon as someone from a school contacts her. The boxes help her keep track of what she's sent them, and once a booking is made, she sends a copy of the form to the school to serve as a contract. "It spells out very clearly what I'll need," she says. "I've never had a problem with equipment not being there." Petach has created a number of attractive promotional pieces to send to schools in her area, and has also created classroom activities related to her books.

BRUCE BALAN
Author—Los Altos, California

A trip to *Bruce Balan's Office* (http://cyber.kdz.com/balan) offers visitors information on how to invite him to your school (among many other things). He answers questions like "What do you do?" and "Where have you spoken before?" Even "What if I want to invite a different author?" Balan also details what he does during an appearance (complete with digital photos of previous school appearances) and shows full-color covers with descriptions of all of his titles, including a link to his super cool site for his Cyber.kdz series (published by Avon Books).

In addition to Cyber.kdz, Balan has written a number of picture books including *The Moose in the Dress*, illustrated by Denise Teasedale (Random House) and *Pie in the Sky*, illustrated by Clare Skilbeck. His story book *BUOY—Home At Sea* will be released in June 1998 by Bantam. Balan has been visiting schools since the late '80s and does at least one a month during the school year.

How effective has the website been for you as far as booking school visits?

Bruce Balan's Office has been effective for providing information to people who already know me. I have not received jobs from people who found me via the website.

What, then, are the advantages to having your own website?

My website is a great place to let current readers know about other books I've written. It's easy to offer teachers curriculum materials, and an easy place to tell people to look to get more info on school visits. The Web offers good general promotion by keeping my name out there.

Do you think it will become a more important promotional tool for authors in the next few years?

Definitely, because access to author information is so easy via the Web. If I were a Net-savvy teacher looking for an author to invite, I could start by searching the Web for my favorite authors to find out if they have pages and if they do school visits. I don't think you *have* to be on the Web, but as all authors and illustrators know, promoting ourselves in this competitive market is tough. The Web gives you a lot of exposure compared to the time, effort and money involved. Though that investment is not unsubstantial, it's nothing when compared to print advertising, mass mailings or radio and TV ads.

How do you get school gigs?

Word of mouth is the best way—teacher/librarian to teacher/librarian. Also, referrals from other writers and booksellers. Santa Clara County has an event where authors can each have five minutes to present to district teachers and librarians. This has been very effective.

Why do you think it's important for you to do school visits?

I go back to one of my first school visits (in 1988 or '89). I was very nervous and expressed this to the librarian. "How could I compete with all the media kids are exposed to? How could I entertain them?" She said, "It's not important that you compete. It's important that you are a real person. Because if they see that you are a real person, it opens the possibility that they, too, could be writers." I've always remembered that, and that's the basis of my presentation: We are all writers.

When a child sees that being something "special" like a writer is something they can do, then they know they can be anything special. That's exciting.

It's also important to me because I love it! It's really fun. It's not for everyone, though. It is exhausting. It's a lot of work and you can't just get up in front of the kids and bore them to

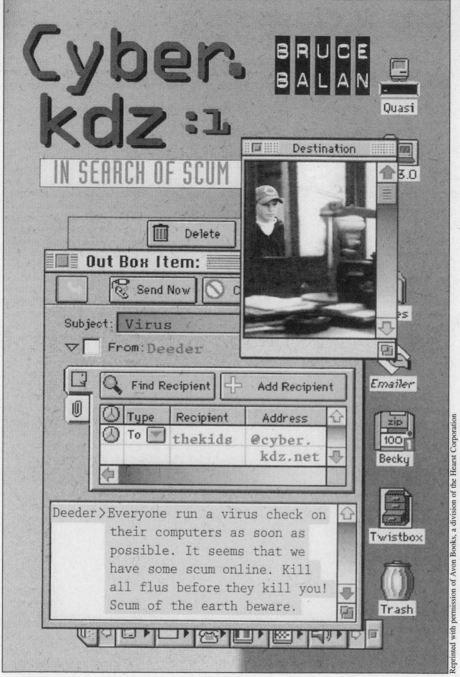

Author Bruce Balan utilizes the Web to promote his cool series Cyber.kdz to readers. His site http:// cyber.kds.com features previews of his soon-to-be-released titles (*Cyber.kdz: 6* release date is May 1998), digital photos of Cyber.kdz events, a calendar of events, a cyber-talk slang test, a mailing list to join, and a link to his site *Bruce Balan's Office*, which gives information on how to invite this tech-savvy author to a school. In addition to his series for Avon, Balan has written a number of picture books—you can find out all about them by visiting http://cyber.kdz/balan/books.html.

death. You have to talk *with* them, not *at* them. There are too many authors who don't understand that.

Why would you recommend other writers do school appearances?

It gets you away from your desk and into the real world. It puts you in touch with your audience. It allows you to see the effect your writing has on your readers. (This can be good or bad, but it's usually good.)

How involved is your publisher in setting things up for you?

Not at all. I do it myself.

What do you do during the actual visit?

I read some of my books. I talk about the process of writing and being published. Sometimes I talk about the Internet (if the group is of Cyber.kdz age). Sometimes I do a writing exercise. I answer a lot of questions. That's the best part. In fact, I try to let the questions drive my presentations.

How many books do you usually sell during a visit?

It varies widely, anywhere from 5 to 100. This is controlled by how well the school publicizes the event and the book sale, like whether they sent out notices and order forms before the presentation.

What's your advice for authors who've never presented to a school audience?

I love author visits. They are a blast and can be a good source of income. You have to balance that out with the time away from writing. But authors and illustrators need to remember they are visiting *students*. That's where the focus should be. Don't just get up in from of them and blah, blah, blah. Put some life into your presentation.

Also, you will always have some presentations that go poorly. It's just part of the business. Preparation is key. You should have an information sheet for the school and work with them to make the event a success. It's terrible to do a presentation and have the teacher in the back of the room stapling and grading assignments. If the teachers are excited and prepared for your visit, then the kids will be too.

That Was Then, This Is Now: A Look at YA Past & Present

BY RICHARD PECK

A generation ago, two novels came out of nowhere to recognize an overlooked readership and to transform the publishing industry. They were Judy Blume's *Are You There God? It's Me, Margaret* and S.E. Hinton's *The Outsiders*. No two titles could have anticipated the scope of what was about to be called "Young Adult." Significantly, though, Judy Blume's novel was about puberty, and S.E. Hinton's depicted adolescence.

Are You There God? It's Me, Margaret was arguably the first successful attempt in human history to give honest aid and comfort to girls embarking upon the physical and emotional ordeal of puberty. As proof of its durability, Judy Blume still takes heat from book-burning mothers. Her crime appears to be that she is making contact with their daughters just as they are losing it.

The 1967 appearance of *The Outsiders* created another sensation when its author was revealed to be a high-school girl. Evidently she'd avoided the sort of teacher who says, "Write what you know. Spill your own experience on the page." Wisely and professionally, she wrote not from experience but from observation. She seemed to know instinctively that nobody wants to read your diary except your mother. S.E. Hinton was a girl, but her novel was about boys. Like most writers, she was a solitary, watching at the edge of the action, but she wrote about people interacting in groups. She saw her school divided between the haves and the have-nots, between the overpraised and the overlooked ("Socs" and "Greasers" in her book).

Sensibly, she chose to celebrate the underclass, signaling her intent in the title, a very good place to signal intent. She had the extraordinary maturity to know that young readers identify most compassionately with the very people they wouldn't sit next to in class (see *Huckleberry Finn*.) Many a novel to come in this new field was to champion the underdog.

Though *The Outsiders* was florid melodrama, Hinton touched a deeper chord with her readers in creating a gang as a caring surrogate family. This pointed ahead to what young adult novels would be, stories of family life and the search for family. Since hers was about a family freed of parents, the world of young readers beat a path to her door. Publishers were suddenly in search of novels about the private life of the pubescent and adolescent.

It was a revolutionary literature for a revolutionary time. A novel is always about private life, and young people of 15 and 13 and 11 suddenly had more private life than their own parents. The authority of home and school imploded, leaving the young with options and decisions that earlier generations had never heard of, or read about. The parental divorce rate, the drug culture, the sexual revolution, the racially integrating school, the suburbanizing and malling of America: all these seemingly new issues demanded an airing, and the questions novels can ask.

Critics quickly saw every YA offering as a single-problem novel. After all, John Donovan's 1969 *I'll Get There. It Better Be Worth the Trip* dealt directly with homosexuality, a topic so hot that it's rarely mentioned in home or classroom 30 years later.

The critics wanted to know how any 200-page novel for young, inexperienced readers could

RICHARD PECK *has written 22 young adult novels, including* Secrets of the Shopping Mall. *His* Are You in the House Alone? *is an Edgar Allan Poe Award winner. His newest novel is* Strays Like Us *(Dial, 1998).*

do more than trivialize such a challenging topic. But even the earliest titles went well beyond docudramas of trendy topics, finding a range they maintain to this day. Suddenly there was science fiction/fantasy by Anne McCaffrey, Robin McKinley and William Sleator. Well ahead of the multicultural movement, novels by Nicholasa Mohr, Mildred Taylor and Virginia Hamilton explored ethnic identity and diversity. There was historical fiction and comedy and satire and mystery and suspense.

Young adult books mirrored the full range of adult fiction, though with a better-crafted economy and without the fashionable despair and pornography that masks weak writing. Deeply felt novels appeared, such as Paul Zindel's *The Pigman*, a quiet story about a boy and a girl and an old man that asked some questions about personal responsibility that parents ought to have asked. Bette Greene's *Summer of My German Soldier* found adult readers and a filming with its portrait of a Jewish girl on the Arkansas homefront during World War II. Judy Blume topped herself with *Forever*, a book clearly demonstrating that adolescent sexual activity is anything but a single problem.

In Robert Cormier's landmark *The Chocolate War*, young adult books found the gut issue in their readers' lives. Cormier depicted the peergroup leader the young set up over themselves when adult authority fails them. He recast *Lord of the Flies*, by William Golding, in an American school, making it far harder to deny. The book found readers where they were, and are—tied down by peergroup leaders in a world increasingly remote from adults. It was to be perhaps the most imitated of all young adult novels.

YA IN THE NINETIES

But to invoke one of S.E. Hinton's later titles, *That Was Then, This Is Now*. Where are young adult books and their readers now at the end of the 1990s?

In the publishing world the Golden Age is always behind us and the sky is forever falling. In the early 1970s when some of us were writing our first books, we were told we'd missed the boat. The federal money of President Johnson's Great Society had just stopped raining on schools and libraries, and the end was considered nigh. Now in the 1990s the question arises, will the series—romance and horror—inundate real books as publishing gives way to packaging?

Will R.L. Stine be the death of us all? And this concern about the young: does reading Goosebumps and Christopher Pike lead the impressionable on to reading anything at all but Stephen King? This echoes the earlier concern that Sweet Valley High readers were heading for an adult diet limited to Harlequin Romances and Danielle Steel. The question remains unresolved in the '90s. But in fact from Horatio Alger on to the dawn of YA, books for young readers were chiefly presented as series. Today series sales continue to allow publishers to acquire the "real" novel and even to produce it in hardback. Series, moreover, require a lot of authorship, and so provide publishing experience for new writers through such packagers as Daniel Weiss Associates and the several series from Bantam Doubleday Dell. The economic might of the series—feeding the young taste for the ritual of repetition—is a perennial fact of our working lives, and it works for us and against us.

Mention of series titles overstocking the shelves suggests the continuing advance of the megabookstore chains. They've made deep inroads upon the committed independent bookseller, and when they open at the shopping mall, they've found young readers where they live. The mall is better attended than the library and now, just possibly, the school.

In his excellent study, *From Romance to Realism: Fifty Years of Growth and Change in Young Adult Literature*, Michael Cart says, " . . . It is now the buyers for the chains—not librarians, not educators, and not psychologists—who dictate how we define 'young adults.' For them YAs are now 11- to 13- or 14-year olds."

This sharp focus on the younger reader forges the link between the books of middle grade and middle school, but creates chaotic changes in trim size, cover art and bookstore shelving. YA titles are often shelved indiscriminately, some titles randomly placed in the "Children's"

Throughout his career, Richard Peck has written in almost every genre and tackled many of the tough problems teens face. In the '90s Peck's titles turned high-tech with *Lost in Cyberspace* (1995, Dial Books for Young Readers), one of almost two dozen books he's written for young people since 1972. This books marries humor and science fictions in what *Kirkus Reviews* calls a "a fast-paced, fun-filled adventure that's virtually guaranteed," as readers follow sixth-grader Josh and his high-tech pal Aaron through experiments with "cellular reorganization."

Jacket painting © 1995 Broeck Steadman. Reprinted with permission of Dial Books for Young Readers.

section that no self-respecting seventh-grader would go near, others in "Young Adult" by personnel who don't even read as much as the suggested age-level on the covers. In a chain store's "Young Readers" section you're liable to find anything, including old classroom staples like Thornton Wilder's *The Bridge of San Luis Rey.*

But fears that the chains will carry only the series, the uncontroversial, and multiple copies of bestsellers seem so far unfounded. A chain store often has a better stock of quality YA titles than the independent bookseller's far shorter shelves.

Books for older adolescent readers, true coming-of-age novels such as Chris Crutcher's *Running Loose,* are in considerable eclipse now. Publishers aren't encouraging these manuscripts, though David Gale at Simon & Schuster is stoutly behind Rob Thomas's *Rats Saw God, Slave Day* and his forthcoming titles that aim at high school. But now in the nineties YA increasingly explores puberty more often than senior year.

This shift to the younger reader isn't entirely the book chains' doing. The middle-school librarian continues to promote leisure reading and YA books while high-school librarians often put more emphasis on reference. Publishers have never won the high-school teacher to the possibilities of YA, despite the potential for bringing fiction and young readers closer together. Classroom discussions pairing *The Chocolate War* and *Lord of the Flies* would be illuminating. Many a YA adult novel reinterprets an adult novel already in the curriculum. But the 1990s high school is polarized between the college-prep program and its full menu of "classics," and the remedial program in search of "materials" rather than readings.

No author dare write a novel expecting it to be adopted for the classroom of any grade. But middle-school teachers, alert to readings for this enigmatic age group, are increasingly receptive

In *The Great Interactive Dream Machine* (Dial, 1996), Richard Peck's sequel to *Lost in Cyberspace*, readers rejoin friends Josh and Aaron as they turn a computer into a wish-granting machine. In Peck's latest novel, *Strays Like Us* (Dial, May 1998) he writes for the same age level, telling the story of "an adolescent girl adapting to a new life and a new town after her mother abandons her to the care of her great aunt."

to YA titles, making Gary Paulsen's *Hatchet* (1987) and Lois Lowry's *The Giver* (1993) instant curriculum inclusions.

The new writer looking for publication might better explore the mysteries of middle school and puberty than the high-school scene. At least the emphasis is now on readers who are at just the age when we've traditionally lost most people to reading, even in far better times than these.

WHO ARE YA READERS?

But nothing is simple for this secret segment of the population. We're trying to make contact with people whose own parents haven't seen them for days. They make a nonsense of our age groupings because they read two years up. Upper grade school wants to read about middle school. Middle school wants to read about high school. And high-school freshmen want to read about anybody with a driver's license and the car to go with it. They look for protagonists 24 months older when life begins, in just the pattern they look for leadership in their own lives. They don't want to read about now. Nothing is happening now. *Are You There God? It's Me, Margaret* that Judy Blume wrote to reach readers at the point of puberty was soon to be carried around by fourth-graders, to prove their worldly sophistication.

YA readers are overwhelmingly suburban and even today mainly in public schools. They are the offspring of the first readers of YA fiction back in the S.E. Hinton era, those old revolutionaries of the bygone '60s and '70s, who as a generation have not aged well. Some of the best novels of recent lists provide real companionship to children coping with the continuing decline of family and the dislocations and aridity of suburban life that distance young people from extended family.

Titles from the past—*The Outsiders*, *Secrets of the Shopping Mall*—that are in fact fantasies about being free of family now give way to any number of books that enact the search for the

RECOMMENDED READS

The axiom that nobody but a reader ever became a writer is twice true for the still-mysterious young adult field. Here follows a list of recent titles that begin to suggest the range and the quality of the field now in the '90s:

Nothing But the Truth: A Documentary Novel, **by Avi (Orchard, 1991).** A confrontation between a ninth-grade boy and his teacher spirals into a very public controversy.

Uncle Vampire, **by Cynthia D. Grant (Atheneum, 1993).** This exploration of one of the last taboos, incest, was followed by two more novels on the same subject: Cynthia Voigt's *When She Hollers* (Scholastic, 1994), and Jacqueline Woodson's *I Hadn't Meant to Tell You This* (Delacorte, 1994).

Kokopelli's Flute, **by Will Hobbs (Atheneum, 1995).** Trying to safeguard the relics in ancient cliff ruins, a boy slips under the mystical power of a flute that turns him into a woodrat. See also this author's *Bearstone* and *Beardance.*

Under the Blood-Red Sun, **by Graham Salisbury (Delacorte, 1994).** A 13-year-old Japanese-American boy sees his Hawaiian family altered by the attack on Pearl Harbor, by the author of *Blue Skin of the Sea* (Delacorte, 1992.)

Dangerous Skies, **by Suzanne Fisher Staples (Farrar, 1996).** A black girl in the rural South is accused of a murder in a novel being compared to *To Kill a Mockingbird.*

Heart of a Jaguar, **by Marc Talbert (Simon & Schuster, 1995).** A boy struggling toward manhood in a drought-plagued Mayan village learns the true meaning of sacrifice.

Belle Prater's Boy, **by Ruth White (Farrar, 1996).** This Newbery Honor Book moves from fantasy to reality as a boy and a girl come to terms with parents who have left them.

Like Sisters on the Homefront, **by Rita Williams-Garcia (Lodestar/Dutton, 1995).** A 14-year-old and her baby are sent from inner city to rural Southern relatives in this portrayal of a search for roots and values.

---

absent parent. Sharon Creech's 1995 Newbery Medal winner, *Walk Two Moons*, is a girl's quest for her missing mother. Her 1997 *Chasing Redbird* is another girl's search for the spirit of her departed aunt. Young adult continues to center on the family and the American teenagers' great dream of creating a surrogate family of their friends.

Thus it's the best of times and the worst of times for books, their writers and young readers. The literacy rate continues to decline, but the young seem to have an unparalleled disposable income. High-school graduates who can read their diplomas are increasingly being called "gifted," but more and more schools conduct visiting author programs that stimulate sales and provide insight for future books. Both the librarian and the publisher are more selective now that the free-wheeling '80s are well behind us. But organizations within the National Council of Teachers of English, the American Library Association, and the International Reading Association have now been formed to provide programming and promotion for YA books, though their efforts are chiefly supported by middle-school teachers and librarians.

And the shift to the younger reader makes more titles eligible for the prestigious Newbery Medal, a great incentive to both hardback and paperback sales. Many larger bookstores feature Newbery Medal and Newbery Honor Books in prominent, separate displays. Some of the best contemporary fiction is appearing in the YA field now, often written by authors drawn from the adult list. But it's a field that needs a new name. Its current readers are less liable to be YAs than PLs—the pubescent literate.

Is there a sure-fire formula for writing a novel in this fluid field for these bewildering young readers? No, we're not talking formula fiction here. And the very basis of the novel form is that there are no sure things. But in an increasingly competitive field, publishers are still looking for the novel that touches these bases:

1. It is the story of a step—perhaps a single step that one young character takes nearer maturity and always independently because a novel for the young celebrates the individual, not the group.
2. It tells a family story, or the story of a search for family.
3. It may well be set in the past, but the author is wise to leave her own earlier self, his own coming-of-age, out of it.
4. It is a conversation overheard because a novel is only as strong as the voices that tell it, and our readers are lonely people looking for friends.
5. And it must end at a new beginning, with the sense of a lot of life left to be lived.

Even avid readers at this age read chiefly for escape. Of course, a novel must entertain first before it can do anything else. But the chief challenge in writing for this wonderful, needy readership is to include within the format of entertainment a message or two about growing up anyway, even today when maturing itself has become an elective. After all, these young readers are the adult book buyers and the library board members of the century lying dead ahead.

Judy Blume: Telling the Best Story She Can Tell

BY ALICE P. BUENING

When I first got my job as editor of *Children's Writer's & Illustrator's Market*, I excitedly told my husband I'd get to interview authors and illustrators. "Wow, maybe you could interview Judy Blume," he said, knowing she was my favorite author as a child. "Oh gosh no. She's way too famous. I doubt she'd talk to me," I said. "Besides I'd be so nervous, I probably couldn't think of anything to ask her."

Well that was five books ago. And it turns out that Judy Blume wasn't too famous to talk to me. I asked her about doing an interview as she signed my copy of *Are You There God? It's Me, Margaret* during an autograph party at a conference. "I do interviews," she said. "Here's where you can reach me." She jotted down the address of her agent. Then I ran up to my hotel room and called my husband, my mom, my sister and a few of my girlfriends to tell them I talked to Judy Blume and somehow managed not to wet my pants.

And when I finally did interveiw her, I found plenty of things to talk about. The questions were a little different than the ones I

Photo: Peter Simon

might have asked when I was a ten-year-old and an avid reader of her books, like *Starring Sally J. Freedman as Herself*; *Deenie*; *Forever*; *Then Again, Maybe I Won't*; and *Blubber*. Now I wanted to know about the book she's working on (untitled at presstime, and due out in spring 1998), her relationship with her audience, how she's dealt with censorship and tackling difficult issues, and how she manages to bring even an adult reader so in touch with the feelings and fears of childhood.

I just finished your book *Letters to Judy*. It was really hard to get through. By that I mean it's so difficult to hear the distress, hurt and loneliness of some of the children who've written to you. What effect have all the letters from kids had on you as a writer?

As a writer I think it can be very dangerous to allow yourself to think about [the problems of your audience] when you're writing. And in fact, during the years I was working on that book I couldn't write anything. It becomes too overwhelming. On the one hand it's a huge responsibility, but then when you sit down to write again, you've got to put it out of your mind.

When the book was first published, I heard from a couple of children's fiction writers who told me they were using it as an idea manual. That made me really, really uncomfortable, because I've never used it that way, and I don't like the idea of somebody else using it that way. I try to separate what kids write to me from what I'm writing myself.

Did you ever think that would be part of your responsibility as a writer—to answer all these kids' letters and be a sounding board for their problems?

Of course not. In my wildest imagination, I imagined being published. That's the first fantasy. I can run through the fantasies. The first is, "Please someday, let something be published." The next fantasy—and you get greedier with your fantasies—is, "Oh God, this is being published, I hope somebody will read it." And the fantasies grow from there.

But I never could've imagined anything quite like this. And it's been very hard to separate from it. I think I've finally managed to do it. At one point, I was so involved in one child's life, I had to consult a professional to help me help this child. My fantasy then ran to, "I could save her if only she were with me."

My professional training had nothing to do with social work or psychology, or being a counselor to people in need, so I never learned to step back the way professionals are trained to. It became very hard for me.

Was there an urge to reach out to all of the kids who wrote to you with their problems?

Yes. The urge was stronger than that—the urge was to save them. And I had to learn what I could do, how I could be responsible and helpful and supportive. I learned how to be supportive without thinking I had to save each one of them, because I can't. Nobody can.

The letters really escalated after *Letters to Judy* was published and they began to take over my life and I couldn't write. Thankfully, it's quieted down some. I think that for some of the topics kids wrote about, they didn't have any other outlet. In the last few years with so much talk about abuse and incest, I think they probably don't feel as alone as they once did.

In some schools now, they're taught what to do, how to contact agencies that can help them. I think right after *Letters to Judy* there was this tremendous outpouring. It was like, "Oh here's where we can go with our problems—we can go to Judy, and she'll help us." In England they have a name for it. It's called an Agony Aunt. But I did not want to become an Agony Aunt.

In the last few decades have the letters you've gotten from kids changed? Have their problems changed?

Their problems always have to do with the most important parts of their lives, which are family and friends and school. And about the universals of love and loss and fitting in and being accepted and disappointment.

Censorship has been an issue with you. Is there really a pamphlet on "How to Rid Your Schools and Libraries of Judy Blume Books?"

There was, yes. I don't know if it's still around. Actually, in some places the censors have done their jobs well, and you can't find some of my books easily. *Deenie* they have been very successful with. A lot of people ask me where they can find my new book *Deenie*. They know I've written a book called *Deenie*, and they assume it's new because they can't find it.

Have you gotten more flack about *Deenie*, which included masturbation or *Forever*, which included teen sex and birth control?

Deenie. Masturbation is the single greatest taboo in children's literature. And the censors are quiet, very quiet. The book is quietly removed, and I think it's shocking, and it does kids such

In her decades of writing for young people, Judy Blume has read thousands of letters from her readers. In the mid '80s, she decided to compile a collection of them. The result was *Letters to Judy: What Your Kids Wish They Could Tell You.* All royalties from the book go directly to the Kids Fund, an educational and charitable foundation which Blume helped set up, that offers grants to non-profit organizations for the development of programs addressing the needs and concerns of young people.

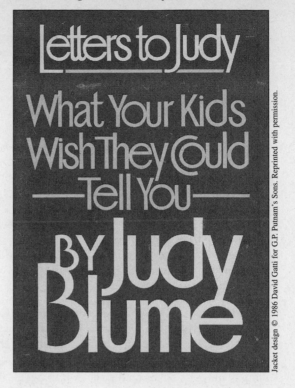

a disservice. It's so sad. It leaves them right back in the '50s when nobody would talk about it or acknowledge it.

Why do you think some adults are so scared to have their kids read about these kinds of things?

We're not talking about all parents, but we're talking about a group of vocal ones. I was once on a radio show with some parents who said to me, "We teach our children that masturbation is a sin and will be punished by God. You teach them that it's okay." You can't argue with that. They have every right to teach their children that it's a sin, but they don't have every right to say that no child should be allowed to read a book.

Deenie for me is so important because it reflects the way in which I grew up. My parents never talked to me about [masturbation], but they never told me there was anything wrong with it. It was such a secret, that you thought you were the only one who did it, so you thought maybe there was something wrong with you. To find it in a book would've been such a relief.

And there are different kinds of fears. One is the religious right who have been very vocal in the whole issue of banning books, and choosing not just what's right for their kids, but what's right for all kids. That's one kind of fear, and that fear is contagious.

And there's a lot of fear when it comes to dealing with your children. I think some parents just don't know how to talk to their kids about anything, and certainly not about their own sexuality. So they have the idea, "If my kid doesn't read about it, it's not ever going to happen, or they're never going to come to me and ask me about it, and that's what I'm going for—let them learn it the way I learned it." Meaning on the playground, from their school friends who don't know at all what they're talking about. It's an avoidance fear.

Some of the mothers in your books—Deenie's mother and Tony's (in *Then Again, Maybe I Won't*) and even Sally's to some extent—can be pretty insensitive to the feelings of their children. Where did that come from?

Probably because I had a warm nurturing father and a cool mother who couldn't talk to us about anything. Parents aren't perfect. In my new book, there's a very remote, difficult mother, so this young woman finds a mother substitute.

Is that a book for adults?

Actually, the hope is that it will reach a teenage audience as well as the twenty-somethings and thirty-somethings who grew up reading my books. It follows two girls who were 12 in 1977 up to 1995 when they're 30. It will probably be published adult, but we hope it will be acceptable to older teenagers.

I got a copy of *Forever* from the library. The jacket copy said it was a book for adults.

That was a total surprise to me. We're talking a really long time ago—1975—and it was a shocker. I was very very upset about it, because I didn't intend it to be for adults. That was a children's publisher covering their asses, really. They didn't know what to do with it, either. They'd never had a book like that.

I read *Forever* when I was in the sixth grade. I went to a Catholic school, and a teacher found out a lot of the girls were reading it, and it caused quite a stir. I realized after I re-read it as an adult why they were so upset.

You probably didn't get all that's in *Forever* when you were in the sixth grade. That's the great thing about kids—they read right over things. If they're curious enough, and realize they don't understand something, they'll come to you and ask questions. But, sometimes they'll read right over something and not even ask about it. They don't even notice that they don't get it. Kids are really very good at censoring themselves. Sometimes they'll read something and they'll write to me, "It made me feel funny. I'm not ready for this, so I put it down." I think you can really trust them in what they read and how.

Is it easier for writers to include sexual situations in YA books now than when you wrote *Forever*? Have publishers eased up? Have the censors?

There's still a lot of fear. There are some publishers who have decided to make a conscious effort to do realistic books for YAs. There are others who just won't have anything to do with it. It depends on the publishing company. But, generally, sexual language is looking for trouble.

What's your advice for writers who are tackling that kind of material?

For me the best thing is not to even know there's a problem, and to write from this place deep inside, where you're not thinking about anything but telling the best story you can tell. And if it becomes an issue, deal with it afterwards. One of the great fears, with this climate of censorship we have today, is that writers will censor themselves and the losers will be the kids.

Writers are hungry. They want to be published. If they think they can't be published by writing about something, then maybe they won't write about it. The '70s was a very writer- and kid-friendly time, because there was less fear in the marketplace and more concern about publishing the best books and getting them to the kids, books that kids could really relate to.

All publishing has changed drastically in the last couple of years. The whole marketplace—everything has changed. That's a topic I'm probably not even qualified to talk about, but it's become much more like the movie business—it's driven by the bottom line. It's all economics, the way things are marketed now.

So if you just look at children's publishing—has it changed? Yes. Is there more fear now in publishing? I don't know. There was, but maybe now people are sick of pandering to the censors.

Jacket painting © 1990 Floyd Cooper for Bradbury Press. Reprinted with permission.

Are You There God? It's Me, Margaret is the first in more than 20 books for young readers by Judy Blume. Since its publication in 1970, Blume has won more than 90 awards. Among them are "Children's Choice" awards in 30 states and internationally. In 1996 she received the American Library Association's Margaret A. Edwards award for lifetime achievement. This new and charming *Margaret* cover was painted by Floyd Cooper for a 1990 edition of the classic.

When published in 1975, Bradbury Press billed *Forever* as Judy Blume's first book for adults, a surprise to the author. Blume's often controversial story of first love and sexual awakening received this new jacket for its 20th anniversary in print, but Blume says her first generation of readers is often nostalgic about the original covers of the book they love.

Jacket by Janet Halverson for Bradbury Press. Reprinted with permission.

I think a lot of people are going back to saying, "Give us the best books."

As an adult, how are you so in touch with what it was like to be an 11-year-old? I've just re-read a lot of your books, and re-lived so many feelings, things that I'd forgotten about. How do you have that recall?

I don't think it is explainable. And I'm not sure I have it as much as I once did. When I started to write, I was young, and I was very in tune with kids. I was twenty-something and I had two kids, so I had adult responsibilities—but I don't think I was really much of an adult. I think I was still that kid, with adult responsibilities.

Also, I wasn't awfully happy in my twenties, so it was easier to identify with kids. Not my own kids who were very small, but with the child I was. And now, my own kids are in their thirties and I've got a five-year-old grandson. I find myself identifying a lot with him and understanding what's going on—you can really read it right there on his face.

I like kids. I like their honesty. I like the fact that everything is new in their lives, every experience. Some of them are going through hard times. My grandson is five and he's already experienced loss through divorce, although he sees both his parents all the time. It still was a great loss in his life when he was three and very hard for him. I see that. I feel for him more than anyone else. Kids just have so few choices—they're stuck with the decisions their parents make.

Is it true you got the idea for *Blubber* from things your daughter told you had happened at her school?

That was a long time ago. Her fourth- or fifth-grade class. They had a teacher who just had no idea of what was going on—no idea of classroom dynamics, or the way the kids were treating one another. I just read in the Sunday *New York Times*, about a third-grade teacher in a New York public school. He's trying to help his kids learn how to treat one another with respect, decency and understanding, and he thought it was really working. One day there was a substitute in his class, and the kids didn't know that he was actually in school, and he observed them. He was disappointed. All that work, all that discussion, and look how they were behaving toward one another! But you have to keep at it. You have to bring it out in the open in the classroom. If you're a teacher, you have to keep talking about it, you have to make kids aware.

Kids really can be mean. I was chubby when I was a kid, and I heard about it a lot.

I was just the opposite. I was painfully thin. And I heard about it constantly. I can remember still the absolute humiliation of being weighed in school and not weighing 50 I was really small. I always had to walk first on line because we walked by size. And I prayed when I got on that scale that it would be 50 and it wasn't. Now, I've got this little grandson who is tiny. I can tell you, it's going to be a long time until he weighs 50.

As your kids got older and you had them to observe, did that help your writing?

I worried a lot when they became older teenagers that it would be all over, that I'd lose it, because I think living with kids every day really does help. Although there are plenty of brilliant writers, like Maurice Sendak, who never had kids and are able to do it.

And it didn't go away, in fact, when my kids grew up. Maybe you lose some of those rich details, but if you observe kids outside, watch them on the playground, see them in school situations, you can get those details back. I think once you're so in touch with kids, you just don't lose it—it doesn't matter how old you get.

Writers are observers. I can't imagine a writer saying, "Now I know everything, so I'm not going to bother to observe anymore." That's what we do, that's what we are—we're sponges. I explain it to kids, that when I'm not writing, I'm a regular person, but as soon as I start a new book, I have these antennae that come out of my head and pick up everything that's around— the way people talk, what they say to one another. You can't write good fiction unless you're a natural observer.

And you can't just decide, "I'm going to write children's books." It just doesn't work that way. I don't think you make that decision. It's made someplace else. You write what comes naturally. Every now and then some wonderful adult novelist will decide, "This looks like so much fun. I'm going to do a picture book." I'm not saying that somebody can't write really well for all age groups. But when a person who's never done it spontaneously makes that decision—"I'm going to do it"—it just doesn't work.

Do writers you meet ask you for advice? What do you tell them?

You just have to do it. Nobody can tell you how to do it, you just do it. The only advice is supportive advice, which is don't give up easily if this is something you really want to do. And we all have to learn to deal with rejection and criticism. I have a daughter who writes, a very grown up daughter, and it's hard for her to face rejection. She writes wonderful things but she doesn't always send them in. But there's no way out of it. It doesn't matter how many books you publish, you still face rejection and criticism all the time. It's just a fact of life as a writer. And it's hard and it's painful, and I don't think it necessarily gets easier. You have to learn to accept it and deal with it.

If you would've begun writing in, say, 1995 instead of the late '60s, do you think it would have been more difficult for you to get your work published?

I don't know . . . I don't know. I think a fresh voice and good writing is always welcome— somebody is going to find you and nurture you. I don't know that everyone will be nurtured as a writer as well as I was because they all won't have Dick Jackson [her first editor]. And that

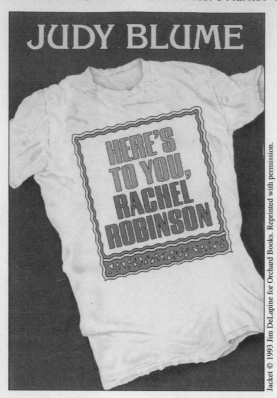

JUDY BLUME

HERE'S TO YOU, RACHEL ROBINSON

Jacket © 1993 Jim DeLapine for Orchard Books. Reprinted with permission.

In Judy Blume's 1993 novel *Here's to You, Rachel Robinson* (Orchard), a continuation of her best-selling *Just as Long as We're Together*, Rachel's life is turned upside down when her older brother, who's expelled from boarding school, returns home. Like all of Blume's books, the story faces real-life issues like relationships with siblings and parents, showing the stress and emotions of the main character. Her books have tackled such topics as divorce, kids' cruelty to kids, religion, masturbation, menstruation, moving and being the new kid in school.

was a very lucky break for me. But there's always room for that fresh voice and that new way of seeing things.

And certainly the hardest thing about writing when you've written twenty-some books is to be fresh and spontaneous. You know more about writing. You've got a lot more experience. But to be fresh and find a new voice is hard. My new book has been the hardest book I've ever written. It's probably been through about 20 drafts. That's not good for spontaneity. I wrote it first person present, first person past, third person present, third person past, first and third mixed, and it just became a nightmare.

It's not a warm and cozy book. It's pretty tough, and the friendship is not your basic wonderful friendship. It's a difficult book. But it's the story I needed to tell at the time, so there it is. I got myself into a real tough spot by again doing something that didn't neatly fit into any category. If you tell the story you want to tell, and the story doesn't fit in a category, even if you're Judy Blume, you're going to have a lot of trouble.

That's generally a problem with YA, isn't it?

Yes. Nobody knows what it is anymore. "YA" is ridiculous. YAs are read by ten-year-olds. The book I'm working on is not meant for a ten-year-old, so how do you publish something YA and say I want 16-36s to read this book? That's why my new book has been back and forth and back and forth—nobody's known what to do with it.

I think the publisher has probably come up with a wise plan, but it's a new plan, and it's a scary plan for them and the marketers—to publish something adult and try to reach a specific audience, especially in today's marketplace. And I won't do this again, I tell you that! My adult books have been hard for me, because I haven't known as I've been writing that they were. And

I don't think that's bad. I think as you write you should just tell a story and not wonder, "Who is this for?" Even though eventually, you have to ask.

I've seen the TV show based on your Fudge books, and I read on your website (http://www. judyblume.com) that there's a stage play based on your characters.

It's based on *Tales of a Fourth-Grade Nothing*. I love it. I've seen two productions. One I saw opening night at the Seattle Children's Theater. That was the very first production. I was scared to death that I would run out, and I loved it! I thought it was charming and true to the book. I was surprised how well the book translated and could be adapted for the stage.

I saw it again when it opened at the Kennedy Center. They did a production of it last fall. I took my grandson, and we had a wonderful time. In that production, Fudge was played by a 300-pound man. I thought, "Oh my God, what is this going to be like?" But it worked. It was very funny and believable. That Kennedy Center production is on the road. [See Blume's website for scheduled dates.]

Any parting words of advice for writers?

Don't let anyone discourage you. I had a lot of people who would have been very happy to discourage me. And I don't think you necessarily have to show your family and friends what you're writing, because they love you and they'll tell you it's wonderful.

One thing that helped me was taking a writing class. Of course, it depends on how lucky you are with who is leading the class. I hesitate to say teaching, because I think people can lead you and be supportive and encourage you and give positive criticisms, but they can't really teach you to write.

What was important to me in my writing course, and maybe this is what's important to people who have writing groups, is that you're together with a group of people who are interested in doing the same thing you're interested in doing and it can be inspiring. You need inspiration to go home and just get to it. I knew I was going to this class once a week. I knew I wanted to have material. Whatever gets you to do the writing and not postpone it—that's positive.

KEY TO SYMBOLS & ABBREVIATIONS

‡ Indicates a listing new in this edition.

❦ Indicates a Canadian listing.

★ Indicates a publisher produces educational material.

☐ Indicates a book packager/producer.

* Indicates a contest, organization or conference is open to students.

● Indicates a comment from the editor of *Children's Writer's & Illustrator's Market*.

ms or **mss** Stands for manuscript or manuscripts.

SASE Refers to a self-addressed stamped envelope.

SAE Refers to a self-addressed envelope.

IRC Stands for International Reply Coupon. These are required with SAEs sent to markets in countries other than your own.

b&w Stands for black and white.

IMPORTANT LISTING INFORMATION

• Listings are based on questionnaires, phone calls and updated copy. They are not advertisements nor are markets reported here necessarily endorsed by the editor of this book.

• Information in the listings comes directly from the companies and is as accurate as possible, but situations may change and needs may fluctuate between the publication of this directory and the time you use it.

• *Children's Writer's & Illustrator's Market* reserves the right to exclude any listing that does not meet its requirements.

COMPLAINT PROCEDURE

If you feel you have not been treated fairly by a listing in *Children's Writer's & Illustrator's Market*, we advise you to take the following steps:

• First try to contact the listing. Sometimes one phone call or a letter can quickly clear up the matter.

• Document all your correspondence with the listing. When you write to us with a complaint, provide the details of your submission, the date of your first contact with the listing and the nature of your subsequent correspondence.

• We will enter your letter into our files and attempt to contact the listing.

• The number and severity of complaints will be considered in our decision whether or not to delete the listing from the next edition.

Book Publishers

The children's book publishing industry is always in flux. In the last few years, the production of hardcover picture books, which had experienced a huge expansion (read: overpublishing), has leveled off. The industry has continued to consolidate, with 1997 bringing the merger of Penguin and Putnam. Publishers are streamlining, shortening their lists, and being more selective about the titles they choose.

The word "streamlining" should not make writers and illustrators worry too much, however. Publishers are still looking for quality material and good ideas, first-time authors are still being published, and many editors still accept unsolicited manuscripts or, at the very least, queries. A good book still has about the same chance of being published as in the past.

And although mergers often mean the demise of imprints, new publishing ventures are still sprouting up. A refreshing crop of new imprints and publishers emerged in the last few years, with missions to publish quality literature. Imprints like Arthur Levine Books (Scholastic) and DK Ink (DK Publishing) and new independent publishers like Front Street Books and Turtle Books could be signaling the state of things to come in children's publishing.

ARE PAPERBACKS DECLINING?

Children's paperbacks series (the equivalent to the bestseller in adult publishing) are still strong in sales, and established series continue to add titles to their lists. But the last few years have brought bad news for R.L. Stine and Scholastic—the "decline" of Goosebumps. The series reached its height in sales in early fall of 1996, reportedly moving upwards of one and a half million copies per title per month for new releases. Millions of copies were returned to the publisher, and by November 1996 sales had dropped precipitously, which was quite scary for Scholastic.

Why the big drop? It could be that Scholastic overpublished Goosebumps titles, or that the licensed merchandise associated with the books overpowered them. Or maybe it was because Goosebumps doesn't offer readers continuing characters to go back to again and again. It's probably a combination of factors. But even with a drop in sales of Goosebumps titles, series paperbacks are still firmly entrenched in the children's bestseller list—and the Paperback Group is still Scholastic's biggest area. Scholastic's newest paperback series, Animorphs, reached 8th on the *USA Today* bestseller list, proving that sci-fi featuring a compelling story and real kids can sell to middle-grade readers.

Many paperback series are produced by book packagers for large publishers like Scholastic and Bantam. Writing for packagers often involves a work-for-hire arrangement, and usually the books in a series are written by several authors under a single pseudonym. For writers interested in this route, packagers can provide regular income and good experience. There are a number of packagers among our listings, all marked with an open box (□).

Nonfiction books are still enjoying popularity, accounting for half of all children's books published. Both institutional (intended for libraries and schools) and retail nonfiction publishers are looking for books with strong graphic appeal, as more and more nonfiction picture books are being published. Nonfiction may be an area that will soon begin to surface in mass market paperbacks as well.

The awareness of the need for multicultural offerings is still alive in the children's book market. Books dealing with the African-American, Native American, Hispanic, and Asian-American experiences are being published in increasing numbers. Publishers like Lee & Low are specializing in this area of the market.

FINDING THE RIGHT PUBLISHER

So what can we expect from children's publishers in the next few years? As *Publishers Weekly* put it, "variety, quality and stimulating material that will provide fun for young readers and children's book admirers of all ages." As always, the key to marketing children's writing, illustration and photography is to match your interests with that of the publisher. To help you locate publishers seeking your type of work, we've included several indexes at the back of this book.

The Subject Index lists book and magazine publishers according to their fiction and nonfiction needs or interests. The Age-Level Index indicates which age groups publishers cater to. And we've compiled a Photography Index, indicating which markets buy photography for children's publications.

Use the indexes to hone your list of markets. For instance, if you specialize in contemporary fiction for young adults and you're trying to place a book manuscript, go first to the Subject Index. Locate the fiction categories under Book Publishers, find Contemporary, and copy the list. Now go to the Age-Level Index and find all the publishers on the Contemporary list that

---

POP-UP BOOKS

According to illustrator and paper engineer Robert Sabuda, pop-up (a.k.a. moveable) books have been "considered the stepchildren of children's publishing," thought of more as toys than literature, and priced below the cost of regular picture books. That makes Sabuda admittedly cranky, but his work is helping to change the opinion of pop-up books among consumers and publishers alike.

Moveable books, which have been produced in various forms since as far back as the 16th century, are more expensive to print than other books, because each one must be hand assembled. Many are made in a town in Popayan, Columbia, where pop-up books are a main industry. "It costs about $2 to put together a picture book—the binding, the printing and everything," says Sabuda. "And it's cheaper if you print more, because the film's already made." With pop-up books, the price does not go down because the books always have to be put together by hand. "Every single one has to be built," he says.

The retail price of pop-up books are slowly being pushed up largely because of Sabuda's books. His titles like *The Twelve Days of Christmas*, *The Christmas Alphabet*, and his latest moveable creation, *Cookie Count, A Tasty Pop-up*, have broken the $20 mark. "People don't care how expensive it is—if a book's really good, they're going to buy it."

Sabuda estimates that there are about 150 pop-up books published each year. Those interested in seeing some of the latest of these unique works of paper art can find them in an annual fall exhibit now in its tenth year at The University of Arizona.

Serious admirers of pop-up books can become members of the Moveable Book Society, an international organization of about 300 book artists and paper engineers, collectors, books dealers, and book lovers with one thing in common—"that quirk of really liking moveable books." MBS publishes a newsletter (for which Sabuda writes "scathing reviews" of pop-up books.). The organization also holds conferences in various locations worldwide. For more information about the Moveable Books Society, contact Ann Montanaro, P.O. Box 11654, New Brunswick NJ 08906.

When Sabuda began work on his first pop-up book, he learned about the process by taking apart other books, figuring out how they worked, and much trial and error. Starting last fall, Sabuda began sharing his expertise, teaching a class in paper engineering at the Pratt Institute in New York City. "It's not taught anywhere else that I'm aware of," he says. To learn more about the work of Robert Sabuda—and see work from one of his pop-up books—turn to the Insider Report on page 72.

are included under the Young Adults heading and highlight them. Read the listings for the highlighted publishers and see if your work matches their needs.

Photographers can also use the indexes to narrow their list of possible publishers. If you're interested in selling nature photos to kids' magazine, for example, first copy the Magazine list in the Photography Index. Next check the Subject Index under the Nature/Environment. Highlight those markets on the Magazine list and the Nature/Environment list. Again, read the highlighted listings to determine which magazines are most appropriate for your work.

Some writers who are really determined to get their work into print but who receive rejections from royalty publishers may look to subsidy and co-op publishers as an option. These publishers ask writers to pay all or part of the costs of producing a book. We strongly advise writers and illustrators to work only with publishers who pay them. For this reason, we've adopted a policy not to include any subsidy or co-op publishers in *Children's Writer's & Illustrator's Market*.

If you're interested in publishing your book just to share it with friends and relatives, self-publishing is a viable option, but it involves a lot of time and energy. You oversee all of the book production details. A local printer may be able to help you, or you may want to arrange some type of desktop computer publishing.

Whatever path you choose, keep in mind that the market is still flooded with submissions, so it's important for you to hone your craft and submit the best work possible. Competition from thousands of other writers and illustrators makes it more important than ever to research a publisher before submitting—read their guidelines, look at their catalog, check out a few of their titles, visit their website.

For insights and advice on getting published, from a variety of perspectives, be sure to read the Insider Reports in this section. We've talked to several editors—Susan Kent Cakars, former editor at Magination Press, about writing concept books (page 128); Louise May, senior editor at Mondo on what makes a good picture book for the educational market (page 136); and Tommy Nelson Editor Laura Minchew on religious children's publishing (page 144). Also hear from two illustrator/authors with very different styles, 1997 Caldecott Winner David Wisniewski (page 88), and artist/paper engineer Robert Sabuda (page 72 and sidebar); photographer Walter Wick, famous for his I Spy series (page 166); and Children's Choice Award winner Brian Cleary on the importance of humor in children's literature (page 122).

Information on publishers listed in the previous edition but not this edition of *Children's Writer's & Illustrator's Market* may be found in the General Index.

‡ABBEVILLE KIDS, Imprint of Abbeville Publishing Group, 488 Madison Ave., New York NY 10022. (212)888-1969. Fax: (212)644-5085. **Acquisitions:** Susan Costello, editorial director/editor-in-chief. Publishes hardcover and trade paperback originals. 75% of books from unagented writers. Abbeville Kids publishes children's fiction and nonfiction with an emphasis on illustrations and picture books.
  • Abbeville Kids rarely publishes unsolicited material.
Fiction: Recently published *Felix Explores Planet Earth*, by Annette Langen and Constanza Droop; and The *Silly Shapes* series, by Sophie Fatus.
Nonfiction: Picture books: art/architecture. Recently published *Heroes: Great Men Through the Ages*, written and illustrated by Rebecca Hazell.
How to Contact/Writers: Fiction: Query with complete ms and SASE. Nonfiction: Query with outline, TOC, CV, cover letter describing scope of project and SASE. Reports on queries in 3 months.
Illustration: Reviews ms/illustration packages. Submit photocopies.
Photography: Reviews ms/photo packages. Submit photocopies.
Terms: Pays royalty. Advance varies. Publishes book 18 months after acceptance of ms. Will consider simultaneous submissions. Book catalog and ms guidelines free; call customer service.

ABC, ALL BOOKS FOR CHILDREN, The All Children's Co., Ltd., 33 Museum St., London WC1A 1LD United Kingdom. (171)436-6300. Fax: (171)240-6923. Imprints: softbABCks (paperback); factbABCks (nonfiction). Book publisher. **Manuscript Acquisitions:** Carol Mackenzie. Publishes 40 picture books/year. 50% of books by first-time authors.

● See First Books for an interview with ABC author Barbara Maitland on her book *The Bear Who Didn't Like Honey.*

Fiction: Picture books: adventure, animal, concept, contemporary, multicultural, nature/environment. Average word length: picture books—under 1,000. Published *Angelina Ice Skates*, by Katharine Holabird, illustrated by Helen Craig; *Three Bags Full*, by Ragnhild Scamell, illustrated by Sally Hobson; and *My Map Book*, by Sara Fanelli.

Nonfiction: Picture books, young readers, middle readers: concept, history nature/environment.

How to Contact/Writers: Picture books: Submit complete manuscript. Nonfiction: Query. Reports on queries in 1 month; ms in 2-3 months. Publishes a book 12-18 months after acceptance. Will consider simultaneous submissions. Manuscripts returned only if envelope and postage are provided.

Illustration: Works with 15 illustrators/year. Uses color artwork only. Reviews ms/illustration packages from artists. Submit ms with 2 color photocopies. Illustrations only: Reports in 1 month. Samples returned with SASE (IRC); samples filed.

Terms: "Payment decided on individual basis." Sends galleys to authors; color proofs to illustrators. Original artwork returned at job's completion. Book catalog available for SAE (IRC).

ABINGDON PRESS, The United Methodist Publishing House, 201 Eighth Ave. S., Nashville TN 37203. (615)749-6384. Fax: (615)749-6512. Estab. 1789. **Acquisitions:** Peg Augustine, children's book editor. "Abingdon Press, America's oldest theological publisher, provides an ecumenical publishing program dedicated to serving the Christian community—clergy, scholars, church leaders, musicians and general readers—with quality resources in the areas of Bible study, the practice of ministry, theology, devotion, spirituality, inspiration, prayer, music and worship, reference, Christian education and church supplies."

Nonfiction: Picture books: religion. Does not want to see animal stories.

How to Contact/Writers: Query; submit outline/synopsis and 1 sample chapter. Reports on queries in 4-6 weeks; mss in 3 months.

Illustration: Uses color artwork only. Reviews ms/illustration packages from artists. Query with photocopies only. Samples returned with SASE; samples not filed.

Photography: Buys stock images. Wants scenics, landscape, still life and multiracial photos. Model/property release required. Uses color prints. Submit stock photo list.

‡★**ABSEY & CO.**, 5706 Root Rd., Suite #5, Spring TX 77389. E-mail: abseyandco@aol.com. **Acquisitions:** Karen Foster, editorial director. Publishes 5-10 titles/year. 50% of books from first-time authors; 50% from unagented writers. "We are looking primarily for education books, especially those with teaching strategies based upon research."

Fiction: "Since we are a small, new press, we are looking for good manuscripts with a firm intended audience. As yet, we haven't explored this market. We feel more comfortable starting with nonfiction—educational. A mistake we often see in submissions is writers underwrite or overwrite—a lack of balance."

Nonfiction: Recently published *Amazing Jones*, by Deanna Cera; and *Ancient Egyptian Jewelry*, by Carol Andrews.

How to Contact/Writers: Fiction: Query with SASE. Nonfiction: Query with outline and 1-2 sample chapters. Will consider simultaneous submissions. Reports on queries in 3 months.

Illustration: Reviews/ms illustration packages. Send photocopies, transparencies, etc.

Photography: Reviews ms/photo packages. Send photocopies, transparencies, etc.

Terms: Pays 8-15% royalty on wholesale price. Publishes book 1 year after acceptance of ms. Manuscript guidelines for #10 SASE.

‡**ACROPOLIS BOOKS**, 747 Sheridan Blvd., #1-A, Lakewood CO 80214. (303)231-9923. Fax: (303)235-0492. E-mail: acropolisbooks@worldnet.att.net. Website: http://www.acropolisbooks.com. Imprints: I Level, Awakening, Flashlight. Book publisher. **Acquisitions:** Constance J. Wilson, editor in chief. Publishes 2 picture books/year; 2 young readers/year; and 2 middle readers/year. 50% of books by first-time authors.

Fiction: Picture books, young readers: animal, folktales, poetry, religion. Middle readers, young adults/teens: folktales, poetry, religion. "No fantasy—please understand our focus. We are just bringing up our children's imprint—the books scheduled all have a gentle theme of wisdom and help a child understand his/her true identity."

Nonfiction: Picture books, young readers, middle readers: animal, religion, self help. Young adults/teens: religion, self help. Recently published *Closer Walk with God*, written by Jim Rosemergy (young adult); *Living Joyfully with Children*, written by Lin Sweet (adult); and *Oxford Books of English Mystical Verse* (adult).

How to Contact/Writers: Fiction: Submit complete manuscript. Reports on queries in 1 month; mss in 2 months. Publishes a book 18-24 months after acceptance. Will consider simultaneous submissions.

---

‡ **LISTINGS NEW TO THIS EDITION** are marked with a double dagger.

Illustration: Works with 3 illustrators/year. Reviews ms/illustration packages from artists. Illustrations only: Query first. Reports back in 2 months. Samples returned with SASE; samples filed for 6 months.

Photography: Buys stock and assigns work. Model/property releases required. Uses color prints. Submit cover letter, résumé, published samples, promo piece.

Terms: Pays authors royalty of 7-12.5% based on wholesale price. Offers advances (varies) based on wholesale price. Pays illustrators by the project or royalty (varies) based on wholesale price. Pays photographers by the project (varies). Sends galleys to authors; dummies to illustrators. Book catalog available for $3; ms guidelines for SASE.

Tips: "Understand our publishing focus on consciousness (wisdom through spiritual understanding) in expression today. We are interested in eternal, timeless truth, not specific religious/religions."

ADVOCACY PRESS, P.O. Box 236, Santa Barbara CA 93102. (805)962-2728. Fax: (805)963-3580. Division of The Girls Incorporated of Greater Santa Barbara. Book publisher. **Acquisitions:** Bill Sheehan. Publishes 2-4 children's books/year.

Fiction: Picture books, young readers, middle readers: adventure, animal, concepts in self-esteem, contemporary, fantasy, folktales, gender equity, multicultural, nature/environment, poetry. "Illustrated children's stories incorporate self-esteem, gender equity, self-awareness concepts." Published *Nature's Wonderful World in Rhyme* (birth-age 12, collection of poems); *Shadow and the Ready Time* (32-page picture book). "Most publications are 32-48 page picture stories for readers 4-11 years. Most feature adventures of animals in interesting/educational locales."

Nonfiction: Middle readers, young adults: careers, multicultural, self-help, social issues, textbooks.

How to Contact/Writers: "Because of the required focus of our publications, most have been written in-house." Reports on queries/mss in 1-2 months. Include SASE.

Illustration: "Require intimate integration of art with story. Therefore, almost always use local illustrators." Average about 30 illustrations per story. Reviews ms/illustration packages from artists. Submit ms with dummy. Contact: William Sheehan. Reports in 1-2 months. Samples returned with SASE.

Terms: Authors paid by royalty or outright purchase. Pays illustrators by project or royalty. Book catalog and ms guidelines for SASE.

Tips: "We are not presently looking for new titles."

AFRICA WORLD PRESS, P.O. Box 1892, Trenton NJ 08607. (609)844-9583. Fax: (609)844-0198. Book publisher. **Acquisitions:** Kassahun Checole, editor. Publishes 5 picture books/year; 15 young reader and young adult titles/year; 8 middle readers/year. Books concentrate on African-American life.

Fiction: Picture books, young readers: adventure, concept, contemporary, folktales, history, multicultural. Middle readers, young adults: adventure, contemporary, folktales, history, multicultural.

Nonfiction: Picture books, young readers, middle readers, young adults: concept, history, multicultural. Does not want to see self-help, gender or health books.

How to Contact/Writers: Query; submit outline/synopsis and 2 sample chapters. Reports on queries in 30-45 days; mss in 3 months. Will consider previously published work.

Illustration: Works with 10-20 illustrators/year. Reviews ms/illustration packages from artists. Query. Illustrations only: Query with samples. Reports in 3 months.

Terms: Pays authors royalty based on retail price. Pays illustrators by the project or royalty based on retail price. Book catalog available for SAE; ms and art guidelines available for SASE.

AFRICAN AMERICAN IMAGES, 1909 W. 95th St., Chicago IL 60643. (773)445-0322. Fax: (773)445-9844. Book publisher. **Acquisitions:** Jawanza Kunjufu, editor. Publishes 2 picture books/year; 1 young reader title/year; 1 middle reader title/year. 90% of books by first-time authors.

Fiction: Picture books, young readers, middle readers: multicultural. "We publish books from an Africentric frame of reference that promote self-esteem, collective values, liberation and skill development." Does not want to see poetry, essays, novels, autobiographies, biographies, religious materials or mss exclusively addressing the continent of Africa.

Nonfiction: Picture books, young readers, middle readers: multicultural.

How to Contact/Writers: Fiction/Nonfiction: Query or submit complete ms. Reports on queries in 2 weeks; mss in 6 weeks. Publishes a book 9 months after acceptance. Will consider simultaneous submissions. Include SASE for return of ms.

Illustration: Works with 4 children's illustrators/year. Illustrations only: Submit tearsheets. Reports on art samples in 2 weeks. Samples returned with SASE; samples filed.

Terms: Pays 10% royalty based on wholesale price. Illustrators paid by the project ($500-$1,000 range). Original artwork returned at job's completion. Book catalog, ms guidelines free on request.

ALADDIN PAPERBACKS, 1230 Avenue of the Americas, 4th Floor, New York NY 10020. Paperback imprint of Simon & Schuster Children's Publishing Children's Division. Vice President/Editorial Director: Ellen Krieger. **Manuscript Acquisitions:** Julia Richardson, editor. **Art Acquisitions:** Chani Yammer, art director. Publishes 130 titles/year.

- Aladdin publishes primarily reprints of successful hardcovers from other Simon & Schuster imprints.

Inventive illustration creates surprises for readers

Robert Sabuda

Robert Sabuda is more than an illustrator—you could say he's an inventor. Each book project he takes on offers a unique challenge and he often creates a new medium, a perfect method to enhance the story. He's worked in paper mosaic, linoleum cut prints, glass, and cut paper, and has engineered a number of intricate pop-up books.

Sabuda's interest in picture book illustration happened by accident. As a senior at Pratt Institute (where he's now on staff), he took an internship at Dial Books for Young Readers, where he learned the process of illustrating and making children's books.

"Doing that internship was very influential for me," says Sabuda. "When I went back to Pratt it was the first semester of my senior year, and I decided I wanted to be a children's book illustrator. I put together a portfolio of children's work and when I got out of college, I started illustrating picture books."

In 1994, Sabuda began work on *The Christmas Alphabet* (Orchard), his first pop-up book, an art form for which he's become well-known. (For more information on pop-up books, see the sidebar on page 68.) "I very much wanted to do a Christmas book, but everybody said, 'Don't do that—everyone does a Christmas book. If you're going to do one, you better do something really special, or no one is going to be interested.' " Sabuda's creative wheels began turning and he decided to do a Christmas pop-up book. This sent him into inventor mode.

"I purchased a bunch of pop-up books and took them all apart and figured out how they worked, what made things lift and fold. It was all trial and error, completely self-taught." Now Sabuda spends more time on pop-up books than traditional picture books.

"My pop-up books have really put me up into a high visibility. Not that I haven't done well with the picture books, but the pop-up books have been kind of amazing for me. I think people like to open a book and see a surprise inside—and a pop-up book is definitely a surprise."

Readers may find the illustrations in Sabuda's traditional picture books surprising as well. The illustrations for *St. Valentine* (Atheneum), which he also wrote, were created in paper mosaic, each piece about a quarter inch by a quarter inch. He painted all the paper first, then cut it into squares and used tweezers to pick up each piece and glue it onto a large sheet of gray paper. "I really like to challenge myself," says Sabuda. "I really want to feel I'm making a book in a traditional way, and I hope that subconsciously that's interpreted by the reader."

For his exquisite picture book *Arthur and the Sword* (Atheneum), Sabuda wanted a

INSIDER REPORT, *Sabuda*

medieval feel to the artwork. "I thought stained glass would be a great idea, so I made a piece of stained glass for a sample—I used actual glass and lead and put it all together. Of course, it looked fabulous in the real world, but the thing about a book is you have to able to reproduce it. So I took a piece of glass, and since I could control the color, I actually dyed the glass itself, and put lead onto the glass, and we took slides of that," enabling him to manipulate what the light would look like through the glass. "It was painstaking, but we got the results we wanted, so that made it worthwhile."

The images in Sabuda's *Tutankhamen's Gift* (Atheneum), were cut from solid sheets of black paper ("they look like sheets of black lace") overlaying painted hand-made Papyrus, for "a very heavy, Egyptian type of art." And for one of his latest books, *The Paper Dragon*, by Marguerite W. Davol, each illustration was cut from painted tissue paper created by Sabuda, adhered to handmade Japanese paper.

This detail from an illustration in *The Paper Dragon*, by Marguerite W. Davol, illustrates the care Robert Sabuda takes in matching just the right style of art for each book he creates. *Dragon* illustrations are made from cut tissue paper, which Sabuda painted, and adhered to handmade Japanese Sugikawashi paper.

INSIDER REPORT, *continued*

© 1996 Robert Sabuda. Reprinted with permission of Simon & Schuster.

Robert Sabuda's pop-up books are bringing the artform to a new level, evident in this spread from *The Twelve Days of Christmas*. Note the five gold rings adorning the reindeer's antlers and the six geese circling the slice of pie. For more on pop-up books, see the sidebar on page 68.

"I'm not comfortable doing the same exact thing over and over again; I always like to do something new," Sabuda says. Opportunities to use new techniques and media are not necessarily what draws him to a story, though. "The story or the subject matter really has to interest me. Like the Christmas books (*The Christmas Alphabet* and *The Twelve Days of Christmas*)—I could never put those kind of pop-up books together if I didn't love Christmas. It's always the idea of the story that has to interest me first, and from there I'll go to the artwork."

Sabuda remains very hands-on throughout the book production process "because I demand that. I'm not big on sitting back and hoping a book project comes out good when it's finished. If I ever get backed into a corner, I always say, 'My name's on the cover.' The book has to be top notch because it's a reflection of me as a book maker and an artist. I'm not hard to work with, but I know exactly what I want."

Sabuda recommends that those interested in working in the field of children's books be sure that's what they really want, and then do their best to learn about the market. "Gear your work to the market," he says. "Keep drawing—spend all your time drawing. And of course, read books. That's one of the things that most people who want to be children's book authors or illustrators miss—they think they know what's going on in the world of children's books, but very rarely do. People don't realize that there's research involved whenever you want to enter any kind of field. A lot of people skip the research, then they come up with something stale."

—*Alice P. Buening*

They publish very little original material and are unable to consider unsolicited manuscripts; accepting query letters only. Send SASE for writer's and artist's guidelines.

ALYSON PUBLICATIONS, INC., P.O. 4371, Los Angeles CA 90078. (213)871-1225. Fax: (213)467-6805. Book publisher. **Acquisitions:** Julie K. Trevelyan. Publishes 4 (projected) picture books/year and 3 (projected) young adult titles/year. "Alyson Wonderland is the line of children's books. We are looking for diverse depictions of family life for children of gay and lesbian parents."
Fiction: All levels: adventure, animal, contemporary, fantasy, history, humor, multicultural, nature/environment, science fiction. Young readers and middle readers: suspense, mystery. Teens: anthology.
Nonfiction: Teens: concept, social issues. "We like books that incorporate all racial, religious and body types, as well as dealing with children with gay and lesbian parents—which all our books must deal with. Our YA books should deal with issues faced by kids growing up gay or lesbian." Published *Heather Has Two Mommies*, by Lesléa Newman; and *Daddy's Wedding*, by Michael Willhoite.
How to Contact/Writers: Submit outline/synopsis and sample chapters (young adults); submit complete manuscript (picture books/young readers). Reports on queries/mss within 3 months. Include SASE.
Illustration: Works with 4 illustrators/year. Reviews mss/illustration packages from artists. Illustrations only: Submit "representative art that can be *kept on file*. Good quality photocopies are OK." Reports only if interested. Samples returned with SASE; samples kept on file.
Terms: Pays authors royalty of 8-12% based on retail price. "We *do* offer advances." Pays illustrators by the project (range: $25-500). Pays photographers per photo (range: $50-300). Book catalog and/or ms guidelines free for SASE.
Tips: "We only publish kids' books aimed at the children of gay or lesbian parents."

AMERICAN BIBLE SOCIETY, 1865 Broadway, New York NY 10023. Fax: (212)408-1435. Book publisher. Estab. 1816. **Manuscript Acquisitions:** Barbara Bernstengel. **Art Acquisitions:** Christina Murphy, product designer. Publishes 2 picture books/year; 1 young reader/year; and 1 young adult/year. Publishes books with spiritual/religious themes based on the Bible. Do not call. Submit all sample submissions, résumés, etc. for review via mail.
Nonfiction: All levels: activity books, multicultural, religion, self-help, nature/environment, reference, social issues and special needs. Multicultural needs include intercity lifestyle; African-American, Hispanic/Latino, Native American, Asian; mixed groups (such as choirs, classrooms, church events). "Unsolicited manuscripts will be returned unread! We prefer published writing samples with résumés so we can contact copywriters when an appropriate project comes up." Recently published *Teach Me, Jesus* children's activity booklet (ages 7-10, full color cover and 16 b&w interior illustrations and activities).
How to Contact/Writers: All mss developed inhouse. Query with résumé and writing samples. Contact: Barbara Bernstengel. Unsolicited mss rejected. No credit lines given.
Illustration: Works with 1 illustrator/year. "Would be more interested in artwork for children and teens which is influenced by the visual 'vocabulary' of videos." Reviews ms/illustration packages from artists. Contact: Christina Murphy. Illustrations only: Query with samples; arrange a personal interview to show portfolio; send "résumés, tearsheets and promotional literature to keep; slides will be returned promptly." Reports on queries within 1 month. Samples returned; samples sometimes filed. Book catalog free on written request.
Photography: Contact: Christina Murphy. Buys stock and assigns work. Looking for "nature, scenic, multicultural, intergenerational people shots; particularly interested in seeing photographs from the country of Israel, i.e., natural settings such as the Dead Sea as well as the Christian Easter Procession." Model/property releases required. Uses any size b&w prints; 35mm, 2¼×2¼ and 4×5 transparencies. Photographers should query with samples first before trying to arrange for a personal interview to show portfolio; provide résumé, promotional literature or tearsheets.
Terms: Photographers paid by the project (range: $800-5,000); per photo (range $100-400). Credit line given on most projects. Most photos purchased for all rights basis. Factors used to determine payment for ms/illustration package include "nature and scope of project; complexity of illustration and continuity of work; number of illustrations." Pays illustrators $200-30,000; based on fair market value. Sends 2 complimentary copies of published work to illustrators. ABS owns all publication rights to illustrations and mss.
Tips: Illustrators and photographers: "Submit in a form that we can keep on file if we like such as tearsheets, postcards, photocopies, etc."

□**ARROYO PROJECTS STUDIO**, 1413 Second St., Santa Fe NM 87505. Independent book producer/packager. Creative Director: Sally Blakemore. Publishes novelty books only (pop-up, concept, etc.)
   ● Arroyo is not accepting submissions due to a current glut of material. Please query for guidelines after June 1998.

ATHENEUM BOOKS FOR YOUNG READERS, 1230 Avenue of the Americas, New York NY 10020. (212)698-7200. Website: http://www.simonsays.com. Imprint of Simon & Schuster Children's Publishing Division. Book publisher. Vice President/Associate Publisher and Editorial Director: Jonathan Lanman. Estab. 1960.
Manuscript Acquisitions: Anne Schwartz, editorial director of Anne Schwartz Books; Jean Karl, editor of Jean Karl Books. Marcia Marshall, executive editor; Ana Cerro, editor. **Art Acquisitions:** Ann Boyco. Publishes 15-

20 picture books/year; 4-5 young readers/year; 20-25 middle readers/year; and 10-15 young adults/year. 10% of books by first-time authors; 50% of books from agented writers. "Atheneum publishes original hardcover trade books for children from pre-school age through young adult. The style and subject matter of the books we publish is almost unlimited. We do not, however, publish textbooks, coloring or activity books, greeting cards, magazines or pamphlets or religious publications. Anne Schwartz Books is a new and highly selective line of books recently added to the Atheneum imprint. The lists of Charles Scribner's Sons Books for Young Readers have been folded into the Atheneum program."

● See First Books for an interview with Atheneum illustrator Dwight Been on his book *Waking Upside Down*, by Philip Heckman. Atheneum's title *The View From Saturday*, by E.L. Konigsburg, received the 1997 Newbery Medal.

Fiction: Picture books and middle readers: animal, contemporary, fantasy. Young readers and young adults: contemporary, fantasy.

Nonfiction: All levels: animal, biography, history, nature/environment, science.

How to Contact/Writers: Fiction/Nonfiction: Query only for all projects. Reports on queries in 6-8 weeks. Publishes a book 18-24 months after acceptance. Will consider simultaneous submissions from previously unpublished authors; "we request that the author let us know it is a simultaneous submission."

Illustration: Works with 40-50 illustrators/year. Editorial reviews ms/illustration packages from artists. Query first. Illustrations only: Submit résumé, tearsheets. Samples returned with SASE; samples filed. Reports on art samples only if interested.

Terms: Pays authors in royalties of 8-10% based on retail price. Pays illustrators royalty of 5-6¼% or by the project. Pays photographers by the project. Sends galleys to authors; proofs to illustrators. Original artwork returned at job's completion. Ms guidelines for #10 SAE and 1 first-class stamp.

★A/V CONCEPTS CORP., 30 Montauk Blvd., Oakdale NY 11769. (516)567-7227. Fax: (516)567-8745. Educational book publisher. **Manuscript Acquisitions:** Laura Solimene, editor. **Art Acquisitions:** Phil Solimene, president. Publishes 6 young readers/year; 6 middle readers/year; 6 young adult titles/year. 20% of books by first-time authors. Primary theme of books and multimedia is classic literature 1 math, science, language arts, self esteem.

Fiction: Middle readers: hi-lo. Young adults: hi-lo, multicultural, special needs. "We hire writers to adapt classic literature."

Nonfiction: All levels: activity books. Young adults: hi-lo, multicultural, science, self help, textbooks. Average word length: middle readers—300-400; young adults—500-950.

How to Contact/Writers: Fiction: Submit outline/synopsis and 1 sample chapter. Reports on queries in 1 month.

Illustration: Works with 4-6 illustrators/year. Reviews ms/illustration packages from artists. Submit ms with 3-4 photocopies of final art. Illustrations only: Query with samples. Reports in 1 month. Samples returned with SASE; samples filed.

Photography: Submit samples.

Terms: Work purchased outright from authors (range $50-1,000). Pays illustrators by the project (range: $50-1,000). Pays photographers per photo (range: $25-250). Ms and art guidelines available for 9×12 SASE.

AVON BOOKS/BOOKS FOR YOUNG READERS (Avon Flare, Avon Camelot and Avon hardcover), 1350 Avenue of the Americas, New York NY 10019. (212)261-6817. A division of The Hearst Corporation. Book publisher. Elise Howard, executive editor. **Acquisitions:** Ruth Katcher, senior editor, Stephanie Siegel, assistant editor and Abigail McAden, editorial assistant. Publishes 12 hardcovers, 25-30 middle readers/year, 20-25 young adults/year. 10% of books by first-time authors; 60% of books from agented writers.

Fiction: Middle readers: comedy, contemporary, problem novels, sports, spy/mystery/adventure. Young adults: contemporary, problem novels, romance. Average length: middle readers—100-150 pages; young adults—150-250 pages. Avon does not publish preschool picture books.

Nonfiction: Middle readers: hobbies, music/dance, sports. Young adults: "growing up." Average length: middle readers—100-150 pages; young adults—150-250 pages.

How to Contact/Writers: "Please send for guidelines before submitting." Fiction/nonfiction: Submit outline/synopsis and 3 sample chapters. Reports on mss in 1-2 months. Publishes a book 18-24 months after acceptance. Will consider simultaneous submissions.

Illustration: Very rarely will review ms/illustration packages. Illustrations only: "Send samples we can keep. Need line art."

Terms: Pays authors in royalties of 6% based on retail price. Average advance payment is "very open." Book catalog available for 9×12 SAE and 4 first-class stamps; ms guidelines for #10 SASE.

★ **PUBLISHERS PRODUCING** educational material are marked with a star.

Tips: "We have three young readers imprints: Avon Camelot, books for the middle grades; Avon Flare, young adults; and Avon hardcover. Our list includes both individual titles and series, with the emphasis in our paperback originals on high quality recreational reading—a fresh and original writing style; identifiable, three-dimensional characters; a strong, well-paced story that pulls readers in and keeps them interested." Writers: "Make sure you really know what a company's list looks like before you submit work. Is your work in line with what they usually do? Is your work appropriate for the age group that this company publishes for? Keep aware of what's in your bookstore (but not what's in there for too long!)" Illustrators: "Submit work to art directors and people who are in charge of illustration at publishers. This is usually not handled entirely by the editorial department."

□★**B&B PUBLISHING, INC.**, 820 Wisconsin St., P.O. Box 96, Wallworth WI 53184. (414)275-9474. Fax: (414)275-9530. Book publisher, independent book producer/packager. **Acquisitions:** Katy O'Shea, managing director. Publishes 4 young adult titles/year. All titles are nonfiction, educational, usually curriculum related. "Especially interested in geography-based material."
Nonfiction: Middle readers, young adults: biography, careers, concept, geography, history, multicultural, nature/environment, reference, science, social issues. Multicultural needs include smaller ethnic groups, sociological perspective, true stories; no folktales. "Please no personal war experiences, most such material is unsuitable for younger readers." Average word length: middle readers—15,000; young adults—20,000. Recently published *Awesome Almanac*™ *Ohio*, by Margie Benson and *Awesome Almanac Texas*™, by Suzanne Martin.
How to Contact/Writers: Nonfiction: Query. Submit outline/synopsis and 1 sample chapter. Reports in 3 months. Usually publishes a book 1 year after acceptance. Will consider simultaneous and previously published submissions. "Send SASE or submission will not be acknowledged."
Illustration: Works with 3-4 illustrators/year. Reviews ms/illustration packages from artists. Query. Submit sample chapter with illustration. Reports back in 3 months. Illustrations only: Query with samples, resume, promo sheet and tearsheets. Reports only if interested on non-manuscript sample submissions. Samples returned with SASE; samples filed. Original artwork returned at job's completion.
Photography: Buys photos from freelancers. Contact: photo editor. Buys stock and assigns work. Photos used vary by project—wonders of the world, nature/environment, etc. Uses color or b&w prints and 35mm, 2¼×2¼, 4×4 or 8×10 transparencies. Submit cover letter, resume, published samples, stock photo list and promo piece.
Terms: Usually uses work-for-hire contracts for authors. Offers advances (up to $2,000). Pays illustrators by the project. Pays photographers by the project or per photo. Sends galleys to authors; dummies to illustrators. Ms guidelines available for SASE.

BANTAM DOUBLEDAY DELL, Books for Young Readers, 1540 Broadway, New York NY 10036. (212)354-6500. Book publisher Vice President/Publisher: Craig Virden. Deputy Publisher/Editor-in-Chief: Beverly Horowitz. **Acquisitions:** Michelle Poploff, editorial director, paperbacks; Françoise Bui, executive editor, series; Wendy Lamb, executive editor, hardcovers. Publishes 16 picture books/year; new line of first choice chapter yearling; 60 middle reader books/year; 60 young adult titles/year. 10% of books by first-time authors; 70% of books from agented writers. "Bantam Doubleday Dell Books for Young Readers publishes award-winning books by distinguished authors and the most promising new writers."
Fiction: Picture books: adventure, animal, contemporary, easy-to-read, fantasy, humor. Young readers: animal, contemporary, humor, easy-to-read, fantasy, sports, suspense/mystery. Middle readers: adventure, animal, contemporary, humor, easy-to-read, fantasy, sports, suspense/mystery. Young adults: adventure, contemporary issues, humor, coming-of-age, suspense/mystery. Published *Brian's Winter*, by Gary Paulsen; *Expecting The Unexpected*, by Mavis Jukes; and *Shadowmaker*, by Joan Lowery Nixon.
Nonfiction: "Bantam Doubleday Dell Books for Young Readers publishes a very limited number of nonfiction titles."
How to Contact/Writers: Submit through agent or query. "All unsolicited manuscripts returned unopened with the following exceptions: Unsolicited manuscripts are accepted for the Delacorte Press Prize for a First Young Adult Novel contest (see Contests & Awards section) and the Marguerite de Angeli Prize for a First Middle Grade Novel contest (see Contests & Awards section)." Reports on queries in 6-8 weeks; mss in 3 months.
Illustration: Number of illustrations used per fiction title varies considerably. Reviews ms/illustration packages from artists. Query first. Do not send originals. "If you submit a dummy, please submit the text separately." Reports on ms/art samples only if interested. Cannot return samples; samples filed. Illustrations only: Submit tearsheets, résumé, samples that do not need to be returned. Original artwork returned at job's completion.
Terms: Pays authors advance and royalty. Pays illustrators advance and royalty or flat fee.

★**BARRONS EDUCATIONAL SERIES**, 250 Wireless Blvd., Hauppauge NY 11788. (516)434-3311. Fax: (516)434-3723. Book publisher. Estab. 1945. **Acquisitions:** Grace Freedson. Publishes 20 picture books/year; 20 young readers/year; 20 middle reader titles/year; 10 young adult titles/year. 25% of books by first-time authors; 25% of books from agented writers. "Barrons tends to publish series of books, both for adults and children."
Fiction: Picture books: animal, concept, multicultural, nature/environment. Young readers: Adventure, multicultural, nature/environment, suspense/mystery. Middle readers: adventure, horror, multicultural, nature/environment, problem novels, suspense/mystery. Young adults: horror, problem novels. Recently published *Red Lace &*

Yellow Lace, by Mike Casey, adapted by Judith Herbst, illustrated by Jenny Stanley; and *What in the World is a Homophone?*, by Leslie Presson, illustrated by Jo-Ellen Bosson.

Nonfiction: Picture books: concept, reference. Young readers: how-to, reference, self help, social issues. Middle readers: hi-lo, how-to, reference, self help, social issues. Young adults: how-to, self help, social issues.

How to Contact/Writers: Fiction: Query. Nonfiction: Submit outline/synopsis and sample chapters. "Submissions must be accompanied by SASE for response." Reports on queries in 1 month; mss in 6-8 months. Publishes a book 1 year after acceptance. Will consider simultaneous submissions.

Illustration: Works with 10 illustrators/year. Reviews ms/illustration packages from artists. Query first; 3 chapters of ms with 1 piece of final art, remainder roughs. Illustrations only: Submit tearsheets or slides plus résumé. Reports in 3-8 weeks.

Terms: Pays authors in royalties of 10-16% based on wholesale price or buys ms outright for $2,000 minimum. Pays illustrators by the project based on retail price. Sends galleys to authors; dummies to illustrators. Book catalog, ms/artist's guidelines for 9×12 SAE.

Tips: Writers: "We are predominately on the lookout for preschool storybooks and concept books. No YA fiction/romance or novels." Illustrators: "We are happy to receive a sample illustration to keep on file for future consideration. Periodic notes reminding us of your work are acceptable." Children's book themes "are becoming much more contemporary and relevant to a child's day-to-day activities."

❦BEACH HOLME PUBLISHERS, 2040 W. 12th Ave., Suite 226, Vancouver, British Columbia V6J 2G2 Canada. (604)733-4868. E-mail: bhp@beachholme.bc.ca. Website: http://www.beachholme.bc.ca. Book publisher. **Manuscript Acquisitions:** Joy Gugeler, managing editor. **Art Acquisitions:** Joy Gugeler and Teresa Bubela. Publishes 4 young adult titles/year and 4 adult literary titles/year. 20% of books by first-time authors. "We publish primarily regional historical fiction. We publish novels for children aged 8-12. We are particularly interested in works that have a historical basis and are set in the Pacific Northwest, or northern Canada. Include ideas for teachers guides or resources and appropriate topics for a classroom situation if applicable."

● Beach Holme *only* accepts work from Canadian writers.

Fiction: Young adults: contemporary, folktales, history, multicultural, nature/environment, poetry. Multicultural needs include themes reflecting cultural heritage of the Pacific Northwest, i.e., first nations, Asian, East Indian, etc. Does not want to see generic adventure or mystery with no sense of place. Average word length: middle readers—15-20,000; young adults/teens—30,000-40,000. Recently published *Shabash!*, by Ann Walsh (ages 8-12, young adult fiction); *White Jade Tiger*, by Julie Lawson (ages 10+, young adult fiction); and *Finders Keepers*, by Andrea Spalding (ages 8-12, young adult fiction).

How to Contact/Writers: Fiction: Submit outline/synopsis and 3 sample chapters. Reports on queries in 4-8 weeks; mss in 2 months. Publishes a book 6 months-1 year after acceptance. Will consider simultaneous submissions (if specified).

Illustration: Works with 3 illustrators/year. Reports on submissions in 4 weeks in interested. Samples returned with SASE; samples filed.

Terms: Pays authors 10-12% royalty based on retail price. Offers advances (average amount: $500). Pays illustrators by the project (range: $500-1,000). Pays photographers by the project (range: $100-300). Sends galleys to authors. Book catalog available for 9×12 SAE and 3 first-class Canadian stamps; ms guidelines available with SASE.

Tips: "Research what we have previously published to familiarize yourself with what we are looking for. Please, be informed."

‡BEECH TREE BOOKS, 1350 Avenue of the Americas, New York NY 10019. (212)261-6500. Editor-in-Chief/Vice President: Paulette Clark Kaufman. A division of William Morrow & Co. Paperback book publisher. Publishes 40 titles/year.

Fiction: Middle readers, young adult: activity books, adventure, contemporary, family, history.

Nonfiction: Middle readers, young adult: biography.

How to Contact/Writers: Query.

★BEHRMAN HOUSE INC., 235 Watchung Ave., West Orange NJ 07052. (973)669-0447. Fax: (973)669-9769. Book publisher. Estab. 1921. Managing Editor: Adam Bengal. **Acquisitions:** Adam Siegel, project editor. Publishes 3 young reader titles/year; 3 middle reader titles/year; and 3 young adult titles/year. 12% of books by first-time authors; 2% of books from agented writers. "Behrman House publishes quality books of Jewish content—history, Bible, philosophy, holidays, ethics—for children and adults."

Fiction: All levels: Judaism.

Nonfiction: All levels: Judaism, Jewish educational textbooks. Average word length: young reader—1,200; middle reader—2,000; young adult—4,000. Published *My Jewish Year*, by Adam Fisher (ages 8-9); *Partners* *with God*, by Gila Gevirtz (ages 8-9); and *It's a Mitzvah!*, by Bradley Artson (adult).

How to Contact/Writers: Fiction/Nonfiction: Submit outline/synopsis and sample chapters. Reports on queries in 1 month; mss in 2 months. Publishes a book 2½ years after acceptance. Will consider simultaneous submissions.

Illustration: Works with 6 children's illustrators/year. Reviews ms/illustration packages from artists. "Query first." Illustrations only: Query with samples; send unsolicited art samples by mail. Reports on queries in 1 month; mss in 2 months.

Photography: Purchases photos from freelancers. Buys stock and assigns work. Uses photos of families involved in Jewish activities. Uses color and b&w prints. Photographers should query with samples. Send unsolicited photos by mail. Submit portfolio for review.

Terms: Pays authors in royalties of 3-10% based on retail price or buys ms outright for $1,000-5,000. Offers advance. Pays illustrators by the project (range: $500-5,000). Sends galleys to authors; dummies to illustrators. Book catalog free on request.

Tips: Looking for "religious school texts" with Judaic themes or general trade Judaica.

‡**THE BENEFACTORY**, One Post Rd., Fairfield CT 06430. (203)255-7744. Fax: (203)255-6200. Book publisher. Estab. 1990. **Acquisitions:** Cindy Germain, production manager. Publishes 6-8 picture books/year; 6-8 young readers/year. 50% of books by first-time authors. "The Benefactory has a license with The Humane Society of the United States. Each title is based on a true story about a real animal, and accompanied by a read-along audiocassette and plush animal. A percentage of revenues benefits the HSUS."

Nonfiction: Picture books: arts/crafts, nature/environment; young readers: animal, nature/environment. Average word length: picture books—1,200; young readers—1,500. Recently published *Chessie, the Travelin' Man*, written by Randy Houk, illustrated by Paula Bartlett (ages 5-10, picture book); *Condor Magic*, written by Lyn Littlefield Hoopes, illustrated by Peter C. Stone (ages 5-10, picture book); and *Caesar: On Deaf Ears*, written by Loren Spiotta Di Mare, illustrated by Kara Lee (ages 5-10, picture book).

How to Contact/Writers: Reports on queries in 3 weeks; ms in 6 months. Publishes a book 1 year after acceptance. Will consider simultaneous submissions.

Illustration: Works with 6-8 illustrators/year. Uses color artwork only. Reviews ms/illustration packages from artists. Query or send ms with dummy. Illustrations only: Send résumé, promo sheet and tearsheets to be kept on file. Reports in 6 months. Samples returned with SASE; samples filed.

Terms: Pays authors royalty of 3-5% based on wholesale price. Offers advances (average amount: $5,000). Pays illustrators royalty of 3-5% based on wholesale price. Sends galleys to authors; dummies to illustrators. Originals returned to artist at job's completion. Book catalog available for 8½×11 SASE; ms and art guidelines available for SASE.

BESS PRESS, 3565 Harding Ave., Honolulu HI 96816. (808)734-7159. Fax: (808)732-3627. E-mail: editor@bes spress.com. Website: http://www.besspress.com. **Manuscript Acquisitions:** Revé Shapard. **Art Acquisitions:** Carol Colbath. Publishes 1-2 picture books/year; 1-2 young readers/year; 0-1 middle readers/year. 60% of books by first-time authors. "Bess Press specializes in trade and educational titles about Hawaiian life and culture. We also publish introductory Asian language materials and educational titles about the Pacific islands."

Fiction: Picture books, young readers, middle readers: adventure, animal, anthology, concept, folktales, hi-lo, history, humor, multicultural, nature/environment, sports. Multicultural material must be specific to Hawaii. Published *Sumorella*, by Sandi Takayama, illustrated by Esther Szegedy (ages 3-8); and *Angel and Tutu*, by Helen M. Swanson (middle reader).

Nonfiction: Picture books: concept. Young readers: activity books. Picture books, middle readers, young readers: animal, hi-lo, history, multicultural, nature/environment, sports, textbooks. Published *State of Hawaii Coloring Book*, by Wren (ages 3-8, coloring book); and *Hawaiian Wildlife Coloring and Activity Book*, by Tammy Yee (ages 5-8, activity book).

How to Contact/Writers: Fiction/Nonfiction: Submit complete ms. Reports on queries in 2 weeks; on mss in 3-4 weeks. Publishes a book 6-12 months after acceptance. Will consider simultaneous submissions and previously published work.

Illustration: Works with 3 illustrators/year. Reviews ms/illustration packages from artists. Submit ms with dummy. Illustrations only: Query with samples. Reports only if interested. Samples returned with SASE; samples filed.

Terms: Pays authors royalty of 2½-10% based on wholesale price or work purchased outright. Pays illustrators by the project, royalty of 2½-5% based on wholesale price. Sends galleys to authors; dummies to illustrators. Original artwork returned at job's completion. Book catalog available for SASE.

Tips: Looks for "books with commercial or educational appeal in our primary markets—Hawaii, the Western

---

A SELF-ADDRESSED, STAMPED ENVELOPE (SASE) should always be included with submissions within your own country. When sending material to other countries, include a self-addressed envelope (SAE) and International Reply Coupons (IRCs).

United States and libraries. Primarily interested in books about Hawaiian life and culture."

BETHANY HOUSE PUBLISHERS, 11300 Hampshire Ave. S., Minneapolis MN 55438-2455. (612)829-2500. Book publisher. **Manuscript Acquisitions:** Rochelle Glöege, Natasha Sperling. **Art Acquisitions:** Cathy Engstrom. Publishes 2 young readers/year; 18 middle-grade readers/year; and 16 young adults/year. Bethany House Publishers is a non-profit publisher seeking to publish imaginative, excellent books that reflect an evangelical worldview without being preachy.
Fiction: Series for early readers, middle readers, young adults: historical and contemporary adventure, history, humor, multicultural, suspense/mystery, religion, sports, romance and current issues. Young adult: romance. Does not want to see poetry or science fiction. Average word length: early readers—6,000; young readers—20,000; young adults—40,000. Published *Too Many Secrets*, by Patricia H. Rushford (young adult/teens, mystery series); *The Ghost of KRZY*, by Bill Myers (middle-graders, mystery/humor series); and *The Mystery of the Dancing Angels*, by Elspeth Campbell Murphy (young readers, mystery series).
Nonfiction: Young readers, middle readers, young adults: religion/devotional, self-help, social issues. Published *Can I Be a Christian Without Being Weird?*, by Kevin Johnson (early teens, devotional book); and *Hot Topics, Tough Questions*, by Bill Myers (young adult/teen, Biblically based advice).
How to Contact/Writers: Fiction/Nonfiction: Query. Reports on queries in 2 months; mss in 4 months. Publishes a book 12-18 months after acceptance. Will consider simultaneous submissions.
Illustration: Works with 8 illustrators/year. Reviews illustration samples from artists. Illustrations only: Query with samples. Reports in 2 months. Samples returned with SASE.
Terms: Pays authors royalty based on net sales. Pays illustrators by the project. Pays photographers by the project. Sends galleys to authors. Book catalog available for 11 × 14 SAE and 5 first-class stamps.
Tips: "Research the market, know what is already out there. Study our catalog before submitting material. We look for an evangelical message woven delicately into a strong plot and topics that seek to broaden the reader's experience and perspective."

‡BEYOND WORDS PUBLISHING, INC., 20827 N.W. Cornell Rd., Hillsboro OR 97124. (503)531-8700. Fax: (503)531-8773. E-mail: beyondword@aol.com. Book publisher. Director, Children's Division: Michelle Roehm. Publishes 6-10 picture books/year. 40% of books by first-time authors. "Our company mision statement is 'Inspire to Integrity,' so it's crucial that your story inspires children in some way."
Fiction: Picture books: adventure, animal, contemporary, fantasy, folktales, history, multicultural, nature/environment. "We are looking for Native American, African-American, Asian-American, etc. authors/illustrators; stories that will appeal to girls and women." Average length: picture books—32 pages. Recently published *Frog Girl*, written and illustrated by Paul Owen Lewis (ages 5-10, Native American myth).
Nonfiction: Picture books, young readers: biography, geography, health, history, multicultural, nature/environment, reference, science, self-help. *The Book of Goddesses*, by Kris Waldherr (all ages, multicultural historic reference); and *Girls Know Best* (compilation of 38 girls' writing—ages 7-15).
How to Contact/Writers: Fiction: Submit complete ms. Nonfiction: Submit outline/synopsis. Reports on queries/mss in 6 months. Will consider simultaneous submissions and previously published work.
Illustration: Works with 4-6 illustrators/year. Reviews ms/illustration packages from artists. Submit ms with 2-3 pieces of final art. "No originals please!" Illustrations only: Send résumé, promo sheet, "samples—no originals!" Reports in 6 months only if interested. Samples returned with SASE; samples filed.
Photography: Works on assignment only.
Terms: Sends galleys to authors; dummies to illustrators. Book catalog for SAE; ms and artist's guidelines for SASE.
Tips: "Please research the books we have previously published. This will give you a good idea if your proposal fits with our company."

□★BLACKBIRCH PRESS, INC./BLACKBIRCH GRAPHICS, INC., 260 Amity Rd., Woodbridge CT 06525. Fax: (203)389-1596. Book publisher, independent book producer/packager. Senior Editor: Deborah Kops. **Manuscript Acquisitions:** Bruce Glassman. **Art Acquisitions:** Sonja Kalter. Publishes 20 middle readers, and 70 young adult titles/year. 15% of books by first-time authors.
Nonfiction: Picture books: animal, concept, geography, history, nature/environment, science. Young readers: animal, biography, geography, multicultural, nature/environment, special needs. Middle readers and young adults: geography, nature/environment, reference, special needs. Does not want to see dogs, spiritual, medical themes. Average word length: young adult readers—8,000-10,000; middle readers—5,000-7,000. Recently published *Mount Rushmore*, *Marine Biologist* (ages 8-10); and *Lennon & McCartney* (ages 11-15).
How to Contact/Writers: Nonfiction: Query. Materials will not be returned. Publishes a book 1 year after acceptance. Will consider simultaneous submissions.
Illustration: Works with 10 illustrators/year. Uses color artwork only. Reviews ms/illustration packages from artists. Submit query. Illustrations only: Query with samples; send résumé, promo sheet. Samples not returned; samples filed.
Photography: Buys photos from freelancers. Buys stock and assigns work. Uses animal, human culture, geography. Captions required. Uses 35mm, 2¼ × 2¼, 4 × 5 transparencies. Submit cover letter, published samples and promo piece.

Terms: Pays authors royalty or work purchased outright from author. Offers advances. Pays illustrators by the project or royalty. Pays photographers by the project, per photo or royalty. Original artwork returned at job's completion. Book catalog available for 8 × 10 SAE and 3 first-class stamps. Ms guidelines available for SASE.

‡**BLUE SKY MARKETING**, P.O. Box 21583, St. Paul MN 55121. (612)456-5602. Book publisher. President: Vic Spadaccini. Publishes adult and children's books, nonfiction, fiction, regional and national. Children's books are primarily illustrated story books for grades preschool to 6.
Illustration: Uses color artwork only. Illustrations only: Query with samples, photocopies only. Reports back only if interested. Samples returned with SASE.

BLUE SKY PRESS, 555 Broadway, New York NY 10012. (212)343-6100. Website: http://www.scholastic.com. Book publisher. Imprint of Scholastic Inc. **Manuscript Acquisitions:** Bonnie Verberg. **Art Acquisitions:** David Saylor, creative director. Publishes 8 picture books/year; 2 young adult titles/year. 1% of books by first-time authors. Publishes hardcover children's fiction and nonfiction including high-quality novels and picture books by new and established authors.
  • Blue Sky is currently not accepting unsolicited manuscripts.
Fiction: Picture books: adventure, animal, concept, contemporary, fantasy, folktales, history, humor, multicultural, nature/environment, poetry. Young readers: adventure, anthology, contemporary, fantasy, folktales, history, humor, multicultural, nature/environment, poetry. Young adults: adventure, anthology, contemporary, fantasy, history, humor, multicultural, poetry. Multicultural needs include "strong fictional or nonfictional themes featuring non-white characters and cultures." Does not want to see mainstream religious, bibliotherapeutic, adult. Average length : picture books—varies; young adults—150 pages. Recently published *The Sorcerer's Apprentice*, by Nancy Willard, illustrated by Leo and Diane Dillon (ages 7 and up, picture book); *Freak the Mighty*, by Rodman Philbrick (ages 8 and up, young adult, middle readers); and *How Georgie Radbourn Saved Baseball*, by David Shannon (ages 5 and up, picture book).
Nonfiction: Picture books: animal, biography, concept, history, multicultural, nature/environment. Young readers: biography, history, multicultural, nature/environment. Young adults: biography, history, multicultural. Nonfiction multicultural themes "usually best handled in biography format." Average length: picture books—varies; young adults 150 pages. "Often there is a nonfiction element to Blue Sky Press fiction picture books; otherwise we have not yet published nonfiction."
How to Contact/Writers: "Due to large numbers of submissions, we are discouraging unsolicited submissions—send query (don't call!) only if you feel certain we publish the type of book you have written." Fiction: Query (novels), submit complete ms (picture books). Reports on queries/mss in 6 months. Publishes a book 1-3 years after acceptance; depending on chosen illustrator's schedule. Will not consider simultantous submissions.
Illustration: Works with 10 illustrators/year. Uses both b&w and color artwork. Reviews ms/illustration packages "only if illustrator is the author." Submit ms with dummy. Illustrations only: Query with samples, tearsheets. Reports only if interested. Samples returned with SASE. Original artwork returned at job's completion.
Photography: Buys photos from freelancers. Contact: Photo Research Department. Buys stock and assigns work. Uses photos to accompany nonfiction. Model/property releases required. Captions required. Submit cover letter, résumé, client list, stock photo list.
Terms: Author's royalty varies by project—usually standard trade rates. Offers variable advance. Pays illustrators by the project or standard royalty based on retail price. Pays photographers by the project or royalty.
Tips: "Read currently published children's books. Revise—never send a first draft. Find your own voice, style, and subject. With material from new people we look for a theme or style strong enough to overcome the fact that the author/illustrator is unknown in the market. Children's book publishers are becoming more selective, looking for irresistible talent and fairly broad appeal; yet most are still willing to take risks, just to keep the game interesting."

☐**BOINGO BOOKS, INC.**, 12720 Yardley Dr., Boca Raton FL 33428. Book producer. **Acquisitions:** Lisa McCourt, creative director. Packages trade picture books for major children's book publishers. Averages 30 titles/year.
  • Boingo's *I Love You, Stinky Face*, by Lisa McCourt, illustrated by Cyd Moore, was selected as CNN's Best Children's Book of the year in 1997.
Fiction/Nonfiction: "Our specific needs change frequently. Before submitting, please obtain current guidelines by sending a #10 SASE to the address above." Recently published *I Love You, Stinky Face,* by Lisa McCourt,

---

MARKET CONDITIONS are constantly changing! If you're still using this book and it is 1999 or later, buy the newest edition of *Children's Writer's & Illustrator's Market* at your favorite bookstore or order directly from Writer's Digest Books.

Creative Director Lisa McCourt chose Mary O'Keefe Young to illustrate *The Never Forgotten Doll*, part of Boingo Books's *Chicken Soup for Little Souls* series, because of the artist's ability to convey the emotional state of characters. "Mary does that beautifully," says McCourt. "The emotions she paints help move the story along by keeping perfect rhythm with the text." The artist credits her client. "Lisa trusted me to paint in a way I felt would be right for the story. When given a chance to follow my own sense of beauty, painting is a pure joy. I was able to use models I know and love— my niece, Dana, and my mother-in-law—which helped me invest more feeling into the art." When McCourt urged her to "pump up the color," the artist flipped through mail order catalogs for inspiration, substituting a brightly striped quilt for the one her niece was plopped down on in real life. Young credits *Picturebook 97* with helping her land this assignment.

illustrated by Cyd Moore; *The West Texas Chili Monster*, by Judy Cox, illustrated by John O'Brien; *Chocolatina*, by Erik Kraft, illustrated by Denise Brunkus.
How to Contact/Writers: Not accepting unsolicited manuscripts. "To check for a change in our submission status, send a #10 SASE to the above address."
Illustration: Works with 30 illustrators/year. Uses color artwork only. Send samples, résumé, promo sheet, client list. Samples are filed unless illustrator has included a SASE and "requested the return of the materials."
Photography: Buys photos from freelancers. Works on assignment only. Submit résumé, client list, samples or promo pieces.
Terms: All contracts negotiated separately; offers variable advance.
Tips: "Do not submit until you have obtained our most current guidelines."

BOYDS MILLS PRESS, 815 Church St., Honesdale PA 18431. (800)490-5111. Fax: (717)253-0179. Imprint: Wordsong (poetry). Book publisher. **Manuscript Acquisitions:** Beth Troop. **Art Acquisitions:** Tim Gillner, art director. 5% of books from agented writers. Estab. 1990. "We publish a wide range of quality children's books of literary merit, from preschool to young adult."
Fiction: All levels: adventure, contemporary, history, humor. Picture books, young readers, middle readers: animal. Young readers, middle readers, young adult: poetry. Middle readers, young adults: problem novels. Multicultural themes include any story showing a child as an integral part of a culture and which provides children with insight into a culture they otherwise might be unfamiliar with. "Please query us on the appropriateness of suggested topics for middle grade and young adult. For all other submissions send entire manuscript." Does not want to see talking animals, coming-of-age novels, romance and fantasy/science fiction. Recently published *Willie and the Rattlesnake King*, by Clora Gillow Clark (ages 12-up, historical fiction); and *Moon Festival*, by Ching Yeung Russell (ages 6-9, multicultural, picture book).
Nonfiction: All levels: nature/environment. Does not want to see reference/curricular text. Recently published *Everybody Has a Bellybutton*, by Laurence Pringle (ages 4-8, science).
How to Contact/Writers: Fiction/Nonfiction: Submit complete manuscript or submit through agent. Query on middle reader, young adult and nonfiction. Reports on queries/mss in 1 month.
Illustration: Works with 25 illustrators/year. Reviews ms/illustration packages from artists. Submit complete ms with 1 or 2 pieces of art. Illustrations only: Query with samples; send résumé and slides.
Photography: Assigns work.
Terms: Authors paid royalty or work purchased outright. Offers advances. Illustrators paid by the project or

royalties; varies. Photographers paid by the project per photo, or royalties; varies. Mss/artist's guidelines available for #10 SASE.

Tips: "Picture books—with fresh approaches, not work themes—are our strongest need at this time. Check to see what's already on the market before submitting your story. An increasing number of publishers seem to be closing their doors to unsolicited submissions, but at the same time, many new publishing houses are starting. Sometimes a new author can get a foot in the door with a new or small house, then develop credentials for approaching bigger houses. Authors should keep this in mind when looking for a publisher."

‡**BRIGHT LAMB PUBLISHERS**, P.O. Box 844, Evans GA 30809. (706)863-2237. Fax: (706)651-9589. E-mail: brightlamb@aol.com. Website: http://www.brightlamb.com. Book publisher. Estab. 1995. **Manuscript Acquisitions:** Patty Baker. Publishes 3 picture books/year; 3 young readers/year. 50% of books by first-time authors. "We publish books with product concepts or gift items to coincide with the storyline."
Fiction: Picture books, young readers: adventure, concept, contemporary, multicultural. Recently published *Daddy's T-Shirt*; *The Middle is the Best Part*; and *Mommy's Hat*.
How to Contact/Writers: Fiction: Submit complete ms. Reports on queries/mss in 6 weeks. Publishes a book 18 months after acceptance. Will consider simultaneous submissions.
Illustration: Works with 3 illustrators/year. Reviews ms/illustration packages from artists. Send ms with dummy. Illustrations only: Query with samples; send résumé, client list and tearsheets to be kept on file. Reports in 6 weeks. Samples returned with SASE.
Terms: Pays authors royalty based on wholesale price or flat fee. Pays illustrators royalty based on wholesale price or flat fee. Ms guidelines available for SASE.
Tips: "No fairy tales or science fiction. Study our catalog (available on our website) before submitting."

★**BRIGHT RING PUBLISHING, INC**, P.O. Box 31338, Bellingham WA 98228-3338. (360)734-1601 or (800)480-4278. Fax: (360)676-1271. E-mail: brightring@aol.com. Estab. 1985. **Acquisitions:** MaryAnn Kohl. Publishes 1 young reader title/year. 50% of books by first-time authors. "Bright Ring Publishing is *not* looking for picture books, juvenile fiction, poetry, manuals or coloring books. We are highly interested in creative activity/resource books for adults to use with children, or for children to use independently. We prefer books that match our own successful style for pre-school through elementary school (ages 3-12), and must work equally well for a parent and child at home or a teacher and children at school."
Nonfiction: Young readers and middle readers: activity books involving art ideas, hobbies, cooking, how-to, multicultural, music/dance, nature/environment, science. "No picture books, no poetry, no stories of any kind and no coloring books." Average length: "about 125 ideas/book. We are moving into only recipe-style resource books in any variety of subject areas—useful with children 2-12. Interested in integrated art with other subjects." Recently published SCRIBBLE ART: *Independent Creative Art Experiences for Children*; MUDWORKS: *Creative Clay, Dough, and Modeling Experiences*; and SCIENCE ARTS: *Discovering Science Through Art Experiences* (all by Mary Ann Kohl); and *Discovering Great Artists: Hands-on Art for Children in the Styles of the Great Masters* (1997).
How to Contact/Writers: Nonfiction: write for guidelines; submit complete ms. Reports on queries in 2 weeks; mss in 6 weeks. Publishes a book 1 year after acceptance. Will consider simultaneous submissions.
Illustration: Works with 2 illustrators/year. Prefers to review "black line (drawings) for text." Reviews ms/illustration packages from artists. "Query first." Write for guidelines. Illustrations only: Query with samples; send tearsheets and "sample of ideas I request after query." Reports in 6-8 weeks.
Terms: Pays authors in royalties of 3-10% based on net sales. Work purchased outright (range: $500-2,000). Pays illustrators $500-2,000. Also offers "free books and discounts for future books." Book catalog, ms/artist's guidelines for business-size SAE and 32¢ postage.
Tips: "We cannot accept book ideas which require unusual packaging such as attached toys or unique binding or paper."

‡**BROWNDEER PRESS**, 9 Monroe Pkwy., Suite 240, Lake Oswego OR 97035-1487. (503)697-1017. Imprint of Harcourt Brace & Co. **Manuscript Acquisitions:** Linda Zuckerman, editorial director. **Art Acquisitions:** Kaelin Chappell, assistant art director, picture books; Lisa Peters, assistant art director, young adult jackets. Art directors are at Harcourt Brace's San Diego Office: 525 B St., Suite 1900, San Diego CA 92101-4495. Publishes 12 titles/year.
● Browndeer only accepts manuscripts from agents, previously published authors, and SCBWI members.
Fiction: Picture books, young readers, middle readers, young adult: Considers all subject areas.
Nonfiction: Will consider nonfiction for middle readers on a selective basis.
How to Contact/Writers: Fiction: For picture books send complete ms with cover letter listing publishing credits or résumé; for longer fiction and nonfiction, send cover letter, outline/synopsis and 3 sample chapters. Include SASE with all submissions.
Illustration: Send samples with SASE.

Terms: Pays authors royalty. Pays illustrators royalty for books; flat fee for book jackets.

☐**CALLAWAY EDITIONS, INC.**, 70 Bedford St., New York NY 10014. (212)929-5212. Fax: (212)929-8087. Independent book producer/packager. **Acquisitions:** Nicholas Callaway, editor-in-chief. Imprints: Callaway & Kirk Company (Editor-in-Chief: Nicholas Callaway). Publishes 5 picture books/year and 1 middle reader/year. 60% of books by first-time authors. "Callaway Editions is a publishing firm renowned for its innovative and highly successful illustrated books and multimedia products. Callaway titles are released internationally in simultaneous co-editions and have won awards worldwide."
Fiction: All levels: adventure, animal, contemporary, fantasy, folktales, multicultural, nature/environment, science fiction, suspense/mystery. Average word length: picture books—750 words; middle readers—20,000 words. Recently published *Miss Spider's Wedding*, *Miss Spider's Tea Party* and *Miss Spider's New Car*, all written and illustrated by David Kirk (ages 2-10, picture book with rhymes).
How to Contact/Writers: Submit complete ms. Reports on mss in 1-2 months. Publishes a book 10 months after acceptance. Will consider simultaneous submissions.
Illustration: Works with 3 illustrators/year. Uses color artwork only. Reviews ms/illustration packages from artists. Send ms with dummy. Illustration only: Query with samples. Reports back only if interested. Samples returned with SASE; samples filed.
Terms: Original artwork returned at job's completion.
Tips: "The closer to a finished product, with text and illustrations (color photocopies, no originals), the better. Our projects are very high quality, and proposals to us should reflect that quality also. Do not call us—we will be in touch as soon as we can."

CANDLEWICK PRESS, 2067 Massachusetts Ave., Cambridge MA 02140. (617)661-3330. Fax: (617)661-0565. Children's book publisher. Estab. 1991. **Manuscript Acquisitions:** Liz Bicknell, editor-in-chief; Amy Ehrlich, consulting editor; Mary Lee Donovan, senior editor; Gale Pryor, editor; Susan Halperin, editor. **Art Acquisitions:** Ann Stott, senior designer; Anne Moore, senior designer. Publishes 175 picture books/year; 5 middle readers/year; and 5 young adult titles/year. 5% of books by first-time authors. "Our books are truly for children, and we strive for the very highest standards in the writing, illustrating, designing and production of all of our books. And we are not averse to risk." Many of Candlewick's titles are imports from overseas (Candlewick is US component of British Walker Books).
● Candlewick Press is not accepting queries or unsolicited mss at this time.
Fiction: Picture books, young readers: animal, concept, contemporary, fantasy, folktales, history, humor, multicultural, nature/environment, poetry. Middle readers, young adults: animal, anthology, contemporary, fantasy, history, humor, multicultural, poetry, science fiction, sports, suspense/mystery.
Nonfiction: Picture books: activity books, concept, biography, geography, nature/environment. Young readers: activity books, biography, geography, nature/environment.
Illustration: Works with 20 illustrators/year. "We prefer to see a variety of the artist's style." Reviews ms/illustration packages from artists."General samples only please." Illustrations only: Submit résumé and portfolio to the attention of Design Dept. Reports on samples in 4-6 weeks. Samples returned with SASE; samples filed.
Terms: Pays authors royalty of 2.5-10% based on retail price. Offers advances. Pays illustrators 2.5-10% royalty based on retail price. Sends galleys to authors; dummies to illustrators. Photographers paid 2.5-10% royalty. Original artwork returned at job's completion.

CAROLRHODA BOOKS, INC., 241 First Ave. N., Minneapolis MN 55401. (612)332-3344. Website: http://www.lernerbooks.com. Imprint of Lerner. Book publisher. Estab. 1969. **Acquisitions:** Rebecca Poole. Publishes 5 picture books/year; 25 young reader titles/year; and 30 middle reader titles/year. 20% of books by first-time authors; 10% of books from agented writers. "Carolrhoda Books is a children's publisher focused on producing high-quality, socially conscious nonfiction and fiction books for young readers that help them learn about and explore the world around them."
Fiction: Picture books: folktales, multicultural, nature/environment. Young readers, middle readers: historical, special needs. Average word length: picture books—1,000-1,500; young readers—2,000. Recently published *Come Morning*, by Leslie Davis Guccione; and *Fire at the Triangle Factory*, by Holly Littlefield.
Nonfiction: Young readers, middle readers: animal, biography, history, hobbies, multicultural, nature/environment, science, social issues, special needs. Multicultural needs include biographies. Average word length: young readers— 2,000; middle readers—6,000. Recently published *Up in the Air: The Story of Bessie Coleman*, by Philip Hart; and *Bridges Connect*, by Lee Sullivan HIll.
How to Contact/Writers: Fiction/Nonfiction: Submit complete ms. Reports on queries in 3-4 weeks; mss in

THE SUBJECT INDEX, located in the back of this book, lists book publishers and magazines according to the fiction and nonfiction subjects they seek.

3 months. Publishes a book 18 months after acceptance. Will consider simultaneous submissions. Must enclose SASE.

Illustration: Works with 20-30 illustrators/year. "Do not send originals. We like illustrators to send samples we can keep on file." Reviews ms/illustration packages from artists. Submit at least 1 sample illustration (in form of photocopy, slide, duplicate photo) with full ms. Illustrations only: Query with samples; send résumé/slides. Reports on art samples only if interested. Samples kept on file.

Photography: Purchases photos from freelancers. Buys stock and assigns work.

Terms: Pays authors royalty based on wholesale price or work purchased outright. Factors used to determine final payment for illustrations: color vs. b&w, number of illustrations, quality of work. Sends galleys to authors; dummies to illustrators. Book catalog available for 9×12 SAE and 3 first-class stamps; ms guidelines for #10 SAE and 1 first-class stamp.

Tips: Writers: "Research the publishing company to be sure it is in the market for the type of book you're interested in writing. Familiarize yourself with the company's list. We specialize in beginning readers, photo essays and books published in series. We do very few single-title picture books and no novels. For more detailed information about our publishing program, consult our catalog. We do not publish any of the following: textbooks, workbooks, songbooks, puzzles, plays and religious material. In general, we suggest that you steer clear of alphabet books; preachy stories with a moral to convey; stories featuring anthropomorphic protagonists ('Amanda the Amoeba,' 'Frankie the Fire Engine,' 'Tonie the Tornado'); and stories that revolve around trite, unoriginal plots. Be sure to avoid racial and sexual stereotypes in your writing, as well as sexist language." (See also Lerner Publications.)

‡**CARTWHEEL BOOKS**, Imprint of Scholastic Inc., 555 Broadway, New York NY 10012. (212)343-6100. Fax: (212)343-4437. Website: http://www.scholastic.com. Book publisher. **Manuscript Acquisitions:** Bernette G. Ford, vice president/editorial director. **Art Acquisitions:** Edie Weinberg, art director. Publishes 25-30 picture books/year; 30-35 easy readers/year; 15-20 novelty/concept books/year. "With each Cartwheel list, we strive for a pleasing balance among board books and novelty books, hardcover picture books and gift books, nonfiction, paperback storybooks and easy readers. Cartwheel seeks to acquire 'novelties' that are books first; play objects second. Even without its gimmick, a Cartwheel novelty book should stand along as a valid piece of children's literature. We want all our books to be inviting and appealing, and to have inherent educational and social value. We believe that small children who develop personal 'relationships' with books and grow up with a love for reading, become book consumers, and ultimately better human beings."

Fiction: Picture books: adventure, animal, anthology, concept, contemporary, fantasy, folktales, history, humor, multicultural, nature/environment, poetry, science fiction, sports, suspense/mystery. Young readers: adventure, animal, concept, contemporary, fantasy, folktales, history, humor, multicultural, nature/environment, poetry, science fiction. Does not want to see too much of picture books; fantasy; folktales; history; nature. Average work length: picture books—1-3,000; young readers—100-3,000.

Nonfiction: Picture books, young readers: animal, biography, concept, history, multicultural, nature/environment, sports. "Most of our nonfiction is either written on assignment or is within a series. We do not want to see any arts/crafts or cooking." Average word length: picture books—100-3,000; young readers—100-3,000.

How to Contact/Writers: "Author should be previously published." Fiction/nonfiction: Submit complete ms. Reports on queries in 1-2 months; mss in 3-6 months. Publishes a book 18-24 months after acceptance. Will consider simultaneous submissions; electronic submissions via disk or modem; previously published work.

Illustration: Works with 100 illustrators/year. Reviews ms/illustration packages from artists. Send ms with dummy. Illustrations only: Query with samples; arrange personal portfolio review; send promo sheet, tearsheets to be kept on file. Reports in 2 months. Samples returned with SASE; samples filed.

Photography: Buys stock and assigns work. Uses photos of kids, families, vehicles, toys, animals. Submit published samples, color promo piece.

Terms: Pays authors royalty of 2-8% based on retail price or work purchased outright for $600-5,000. Offers advances (Average amount: $3,000). Pays illustrators by the project (range: $2,000-10,000); royalty of 1-3% based on retail price; flat fee; or advance against royalties. Photographers paid by the project (range: $250-10,000); per photo (range: $250-500); or royalty of 1-3% of wholesale price. Sends galley to authors; dummy to illustrators. Originals returned to artist at job's completion. Book catalog available for 9×12 SAE and 2 first-class stamps; ms guidelines for SAE.

Tips: "Know what types of books we do. Check out bookstores or catalogs to see where your work would 'fit' best."

CHARIOT BOOKS, 4050 Lee Vance View, Colorado Springs CO 80918. An imprint of Chariot Family Products and a division of David C. Cook Publishing Co. Book publisher. **Acquisitions:** Liz Duckworth, managing editor. Publishes 15-20 picture books/year; 6-8 young readers/year; and 6-12 middle readers/year. Less than 5% of books by first-time authors; 15% of books from agented authors. "All books have overt Christian values, but there is no primary theme."

● Chariot does not read unsolicited manuscripts. Writers must query.

Illustration: Works with 15 illustrators/year. "Send color material I can keep." Query with samples; send résumé, promo sheet, portfolio, tearsheets. Reports only if interested. Samples returned with SASE; samples filed.

Terms: Pays illustrators by the project, royalty or work purchased outright. Sends dummies to illustrators. Original artwork returned at job's completion. Ms guidelines available for SASE.

CHARLESBRIDGE, 85 Main St., Watertown MA 02172. (617)926-0329. Fax: (617)926-5720. Book publisher. Estab. 1980. Publishes educational programs and supplementary materials as well as trade picture books and board books. Publishes nature, science, multicultural and fiction picture books and board books. **Manuscript Acquisitions:** Harold Underdown, senior editor.

Fiction: Picture books: "Strong, realistic stories with enduring themes." Recently published: *Gifts*, by Phyllis Limbacher Tildes; and *Alice and Greta*, by Steven J. Simmons, illustrated by Cyd Moore.

Nonfiction: Picture books: geography, language arts, math/counting, environment, science, school materials. Average word length: picture books—1,500. Recently published: *The M&M® Brand Chocolate Candies Counting Book*, by Barbara McGrath (picture book); and *COW*, by Jules Older, illustrated by Lyn Severance; and *Domino Addition*, by Lynette Long, Ph.D.

How to Contact/Writers: Submit proposal. Reports on queries/mss in 6 months. Publishes a book 1-2 years after acceptance.

Illustration: Works with 2 illustrators/year. Uses color artwork only. Illustrations only: Query with samples; provide résumé, tearsheets to be kept on file. "Send no original artwork, please." Reports back only if interested.

Terms: Pays authors in royalties or work purchased outright. Pays illustrators by the project. Manuscript/art guidelines available for SASE.

Tips: Wants "books that have humor and are factually correct. Concerning educational material, we want to integrate the reading of good stories with instructional material."

CHICAGO REVIEW PRESS, 814 N. Franklin St., Chicago IL 60610. (312)337-0747. Book publisher. Estab. 1973. **Manuscript Acquisitions:** Cynthia Sherry, editorial director. **Art Acquisitions:** Joan Sommers, art director. Publishes 1 middle reader/year and "about 4" young adult titles/year. 50% of books by first-time authors; 30% of books from agented authors. "We publish activity books for young children. We do not publish fiction."

Nonfiction: Young readers, middle readers and young adults: activity books, arts/crafts. "We're interested in hands-on, educational books; anything else probably will be rejected." Average length: young readers and young adults—175 pages. Recently published *Westward Ho!*, by Laurie Carlson (ages 4-12); *Why Design? Activities & Projects From The National Building Museum*, by Anna Slafer and Kevin Cahill (ages 12 and up); and *Video Cinema: Techniques and Projects for Beginning Filmmakers*, by John Parris Frantz (ages 11 and up).

How to Contact/Writers: Reports on queries/mss in 2 months. Publishes a book 1-2 years after acceptance. Will consider simultaneous submissions and previously published work.

Illustration: Works with 4 illustrators/year. Uses primarily b&w artwork. Reviews ms/illustration packages from artists. Submit 1-2 chapters of ms with corresponding pieces of final art. Illustrations only: Query with samples, résumé. Reports back only if interested. Samples not returned; samples filed.

Photography: Buys photos from freelancers ("but not often"). Buys stock and assigns work. Wants "instructive photos. We consult our files when we know what we're looking for on a book-by-book basis." Uses b&w prints.

Terms: Pays authors royalty of 7½-12½% based on retail price. Offers advances ("but not always") of $500-1,500. Pays illustrators by the project (range varies considerably). Pays photographers by the project (range varies considerably). Sends galleys to authors. Original artwork "usually" returned at job's completion. Book catalog/ms guidelines available for $3.

Tips: "We're looking for original activity books for small children and the adults caring for them—new themes and enticing projects to occupy kids' imaginations and promote their sense of personal creativity. We like activity books that are as much fun as they are constructive. Please write for guidelines so you'll know what we're looking for."

CHILDREN'S BOOK PRESS, 246 First St. #101, San Francisco CA 94105. (415)995-2200. **Acquisitions:** Submissions Editor. Publishes 6-8 picture books/year. 50% of books by first-time authors. "Children's Book Press is a nonprofit publisher of multicultural and bilingual children's literature. We publish folktales and contemporary stories reflecting the traditions and culture of the emerging majority in the United States and from countries around the world. Our goal is to help broaden the base of children's literature in this country to include more

---

"PICTURE BOOKS" are for preschoolers to 8-year-olds; "Young readers" are for 5- to 8-year-olds; "Middle readers" are for 9- to 11-year-olds; and "Young adults" are for those ages 12 and up.

stories from the African-American, Asian-American, Hispanic and Native American communities as well as the diverse Spanish-speaking communities throughout the Americas.''

Fiction: Picture books, middle readers, young adults: contemporary, multicultural. Average word length: picture books—800-1,600.

How to Contact/Writers: Fiction: Submit complete ms to Submissions Editor. Reports on queries in 2-4 months, mss in 1-4 months. Publishes a book 1 year after acceptance. Will consider simultaneous submissions.

Illustration: Works with 4-8 illustrators/year. Uses color artwork only. Reviews ms/illustration packages from artists. Send ms with 3 or 4 color photocopies. Illustrations only: Send slides. Reports in 1-12 months. Samples returned with SASE.

Terms: Pays authors royalty. Pays illustrators by the project. Original artwork returned at job's completion. Book catalog available for SAE; ms guidelines available for SASE.

Tips: "Vocabulary level should be approximately third grade (eight years old) or below. Keep in mind, however, that many of the young people who read our books may be nine, ten, or eleven years old or older. Their life experiences are often more advanced than their reading level, so try to write a story that will appeal to a fairly wide age range. We are especially interested in humorous stories and original stories about contemporary life from the multicultural communities mentioned above by writers *from* those communities.''

‡CHILDREN'S LIBRARY PRESS, P.O. Box 1919, Joshua Tree CA 92252. Book Publisher. Editor-in-Chief: Teresa Bjornson. Publishes 4-5 picture books/year. 80% of books by first-time authors.

Fiction: Picture books: adventure, animal, anthology, concept, contemporary, fantasy, folktales, history, humor, multicultural, nature/environment, science fiction, suspense/mystery.

Nonfiction: Picture books: animal, cooking, geography, history, hobbies, nature/environment, science.

How to Contact/Writers: Fiction/Nonfiction: Submit complete ms. Reports on queries/mss in 6 months. Publishes a book 2 years after acceptance. Will consider simultaneous submissions.

How to Contact/Illustrators: Only interested in agented material.

Terms: Pays authors royalty based on wholesale price (amount determined on a per-book basis). Offers advances (amount varies). Sends galleys to authors.

Tips: Looking for "simple, well-written texts.''

CHILDREN'S WRITER'S & ILLUSTRATOR'S MARKET, 1507 Dana Ave., Cincinnati OH 45207. (513)531-2690, ext. 546. E-mail: aliceb@fwpubs.com. Publication of Writer's Digest Books. Editor: Alice P. Buening.

• *CWIM* needs examples of art sold to listings in this book which we can reproduce.

Illustration: Send samples—photographs, tearsheets or good quality photocopies of artwork. Continuous tone b&w artwork reproduces best. Since *Children's Writer's & Illustrator's Market* is published only once a year, submissions are kept on file for the upcoming edition until selections are made in the summer. Material is then returned by SASE if requested.

Terms: Buys one-time rights to 15-20 illustrations/year. Pays $50 to holder of reproduction rights and free copy of *CWIM* when published.

Tips: "I need examples of art that have been sold to one of the listings in *CWIM*. Thumb through the book for examples. The art must have been freelanced; it cannot have been done as staff work. Include the name of the publisher that purchased the work and what the art was used for.''

‡CHINA BOOKS & PERIODICALS, 2929 24th St., San Francisco CA 94110. (415)282-2994. Fax: (415)282-0994. E-mail: chinabks@sirius.com. Website: http://www.chinabooks.com. Book publisher, distributor, wholesaler. Estab. 1960. **Acquisitions:** Wendy Lee, editor. Publishes 1 picture book/year; 1 middle readers/year; and 1 young adult title/year. 100% of books by first-time authors. Publishes books about China and Chinese culture. Recently published *Sing Chinese! Popular Children's Songs & Lullabies*, by Ma Baolin and Cindy Ma (children—adults/song book); and *The Moon Maiden and Other Asian Folktales*, by Hua Long (children to age 12/folktales). "China Books is the main importer and distributor of books and magazines from China, providing an ever-changing variety of useful tooks for travelers, scholars and others interested in China and Chinese culture.''

Nonfiction: Recently published *West to East: A Young Girl's Journey to China*, by Qian Gao (young adult nonfiction travel journal).

How to Contact/Writers: Fiction/Nonfiction: Query. Reports on queries and mss in 1 month. Publishes a book 1 year after acceptance. Will consider simultaneous submissions, electronic submissions via disk or modem, previously published work.

Illustration: Works with 1-2 illustrators/year. Reviews ms/illustration packages from artists. Query. Illustrations only: Query with samples. Send résumé, promo sheet, tearsheets. Reports in 1 month only if interested. Samples returned with SASE; samples filed.

Photography: Buys stock and assigns work. Submit cover letter, résumé, promo piece. "Include SASE always.''

Terms: Pays authors royalty based on wholesale price or work purchased outright. Pays illustrators by the project or royalty based on wholesale price. Pays photographers by the project or per photo or royalty based on wholesale price. Sends galleys to authors; dummies to illustrators. Originals returned to artist at job's completion. Book catalog for $1; ms and art guidelines available for SASE.

INSIDER REPORT

There's always a place for excellent storytelling

His illustrations are colorful, dramatic and sharply rendered, each paper layer expertly detailed and crisply cut. In his work, author and illustrator David Wisniewski has creatively melded his love for storytelling with his passion for theater in all its forms. He is the first to admit that it's an unusual road he has followed, but the skills he has mastered along the way have yielded great rewards.

David Wisniewski

Wisniewski vowed long ago to make the most of his talents. He then took advantage of every opportunity to sharpen them. The result is the 1997 Caldecott Medal, an honor awarded for *Golem* (Clarion Books), the sixth book he has both authored and illustrated. "If you truly want to do something, you can find ways to do it, regardless of money or education," he says. "God doesn't give you talent and no place to put it."

A former drama student who spent his early childhood wanting to be a scientist, Wisniewski's work experience began at Ringling Brothers and Barnum & Bailey Circus Clown College. After clowning for three years, he worked as an actor and prop designer, then was hired by a puppet theatre troupe. "My job was to cut out the projected scenery, 150 feet of it for each show," he says. Under the tutelage of his future wife he learned the ancient art of shadow puppetry while perfecting the cutting and composition skills he now uses to create intricate cut paper and collage illustrations.

Wisniewski dubs his style "obsessive-compulsive." He begins each illustration with a pencil sketch, followed by a detailed ink sketch. Next, he adds color, makes a more detailed tracing and uses carbon to transfer the tracing to colored papers. He then employs as many as 1,000 X-Acto® blades to cut a single illustration, carefully positioning and assembling each portion to create a rich, layered effect.

Armed with his "dimensional media" signature, a variety of picture books to his credit, and the recent Caldecott honor, Wisniewski admits he is busier than ever, unlike his earlier days in the field. When he first approached publishers, his method was more sweat than savvy. With no published work and an 11×14 portfolio of pieces he "beefed up" with pictures from his clown and puppet work, he spent nearly four months knocking on doors until he acquired a few small assignments. "I wore out a pair of shoes walking around D.C. and Baltimore."

After this initial attempt at marketing, he took another approach. "*Artist's Market* was instrumental in starting me off with basic information," he says, "especially how people want to be contacted." So rather than taking to the streets, Wisniewski next targeted those most likely to be interested in his work. He happily received a 20 percent return on

INSIDER REPORT, *Wisniewski*

his queries. His first children's book, *The Warrior and the Wiseman* (Lothrop) was published in 1989 and is still in print.

"What I learned from having my first sketches rejected is the editing process," he says. "I had the talent, but I needed the technical guidance." For instance, he initially looked at the work of other illustrators, and seeing a plethora of single-page illustrations, he submitted his work in this form only to be told that he had too much of a good thing. His sweeping style simply works better with split text.

Reprinted with permission of Clarion Books. Illustration by David Wisniewski © 1996.

David Wisniewski's *Golem*, his retelling of a Jewish folktale, features amazing illustrations rendered in cut paper. The book was awarded the Caldecott Medal in 1997.

In 1992, 29,000 plastic tub toys (ducks, turtles, frogs and beavers) on a ship sailing from Hong Kong to Washington were washed overboard. Eve Bunting tells the story from the perspective of one worried duck in *Ducky*. Wisniewski's illustrations wonderfully capture the emotions of the scenes as the duck, first surrounded by other floating toys, then all alone, is finally found by a boy in Alaska. Ducky ends up fulfilling his destiny in a tub full of bubbles.

INSIDER REPORT, *Wisniewski*

"Even now, I never assume I know everything," he says. "Not having any formal art education, I didn't have any ego to get over . . . I learned at Ringling Brothers not to get a fat head."

To those just approaching this business he points out that "editors are professionals in their fields." Listen and learn, yet remember that publishing can be a very subjective arena. Working with an editor is easier if you have "common sense in taste and values." His editors appreciate his "meat and potatoes stories." Like *Golem*, the retelling of a Jewish tale about the 16th-century persecution of the Jews of Prague, all of his books have a complexity of plot that make them both appropriate and challenging for his fourth-grade readership.

Believing that "a tidal wave of triviality is directed at children," Wisniewski decided early on that his stories would have a moral point of view and this view would be demonstrated by the story. "The point of the book is the engine that drives it," he states emphatically. The basics of good storytelling apply regardless of the reader's age. "Never dumb a book down," he cautions. Despite the rigors of a dramatically changing market, Wisniewski believes there is always a place for excellent storytelling.

"Even after getting published, [marketing is] still a tough row to hoe," he says. "Most children's book publishers are owned by larger companies and the sales department has control of the book list." Also, merchandise is consolidated into discount chains, knocking out the dwindling number of independent booksellers. Fewer venues remain for selling children's books. Because Wisniewski's books are "well researched and culturally informative," they are popular with library audiences, "which is not a big audience and not a well-financed one," he says.

Consequently, Wisniewski admits that royalty sales are just "gravy" for him. In the field of freelance illustration, "the cash flow will kill ya," he says, revealing that he makes his base income through speaking engagements, primarily school presentations for which he garners $1,000 per diem. Refreshingly frank about his finances and book contracts, he acknowledges that he has easily benefitted beyond the $20,000 advance he received for *Golem*. But he knows that the hype will die down eventually and he will "follow it with more jobs well done."

While publishers, editors, and even some illustrators may look at it as the dramatic end to the creative stuggle for excellence, Wisniewski views the honor of receiving the Caldecott Medal as an opportunity, a sign that it's time to shift his energies once again and try something new. His next books are neither historical epics nor folklorish tales, but humor. *Kid's Guide to the Secret Knowledge of Grown-Ups* is due to be published in Spring 1998. *Tough Cookie*, a story with gangster-style overtones about a cookie who battles evil within the cookie jar will be released in Fall 1999.

Wisniewski has no plans to slow down, and urges novice and veteran illustrators to strive for the same momentum in the search for "alert excellence." He stops working on an illustration only when he can say, "I hope they like this because I can't do any better." A jar of used X-Acto® blades—lovingly labeled "stress relief"—sits on his drawing table as a symbol of the journey that continues.

—Jennifer Hogan-Redmond

★**CHRISTIAN ED. PUBLISHERS**, P.O. Box 26639, San Diego CA 92196. (619)578-4700. Book publisher. Managing Editor: Carol Rogers. Publishes 64 curriculum titles/year. "We publish curriculum for children and youth, including program and student books (for youth) and take-home papers (for children)—all handled by our assigned freelance writers only."

Fiction: Young readers: contemporary. Middle readers: adventure, contemporary, suspense/mystery. "We publish fiction for Bible club take-home papers. All fiction is on assignment only."

Nonfiction: Publishes Bible curriculum and take-home papers for all ages. Recently published *Jet Flight Take-Home Papers*, by Treena Herrington and Letitia Zook, illustrated by Beverly Warren (Bible club curriculum for grades 4-6); and *Honeybees Classroom Activity Sheets*, by Janet Miller and Wanda Pelfrey, illustrated by Aiko Gilson and Terry Walderhaug (Bible club curriculum for ages 2-3).

How to Contact/Writers: Fiction/Nonfiction: Query. Reports on queries in 3-4 weeks. Publishes a book 1 year after acceptance.

Illustration: Works with 4-5 illustrators/year. Uses primarily b&w artwork. Query; include a SASE; we'll send an application form. Contact: Carol Rogers, managing editor. Reports in 3-4 weeks. Samples returned with SASE.

Terms: Work purchased outright from authors for 3¢/word. Pays illustrators by the project (range: $300-400/book). Book catalog available for 9 × 12 SAE and 5 first-class stamps; ms and art guidelines available for SASE.

Tips: "Read our guidelines carefully before sending us a manuscript or illustrations. All writing and illustrating is done on assignment only, and must be age-appropriate (preschool-6th grade)."

CHRISTIAN PUBLICATIONS, INC., 3825 Hartzdale Dr., Camp Hill PA 17011. (717)761-7044. Fax: (717)761-7273. E-mail: editors@cpi-horizon.com. Website: http://cpi-horizon.com. Managing Editor: David Fessenden. **Manuscript Acquisitions:** George McPeek. **Art Acquisitions:** Marilynne Foster. Imprints: Christian Publications, Horizon Books. Publishes 1-2 young readers/year; and 1-2 young adult titles/year. 50% of books by first-time authors. The missions of this press are promoting participation in spreading the gospel worldwide and promoting Christian growth.

Fiction: "Not accepting unsolicited fiction."

Nonfiction: Young adults: religion. Does not want to see evangelistic/new Christian material. "Children and teens are too often assumed to have a shallow faith. We want to encourage a deeper walk with God." Average word length: young adults—25,000-40,000 words. Recently published *Grace and Guts to Live for God*, by Les Morgan (Bible study on Hebrews, 1 and 2 Peter); and *Holy Moses! And other Adventures in Vertical Living*, by Bob Hostetler. (Both are teen books which encourage a deeper commitment to God. Both illustrated by Ron Wheeler.) "Not accepting unsolicited material for age levels lower than teenage."

How to Contact/Writers: Nonfiction: Submit outline/synopsis and 2 sample chapters (including chapter one). Reports on queries in 6 weeks; mss in 2 months. Publishes a book 8-16 months after acceptance. Will consider simultaneous submissions, electronic submissions via disk or modem ("a one page, please").

Illustration: Works with 1-3 illustrators/year. Reviews ms/illustration packages from artists. Query. Contact: David Fessenden, managing editor. Query with samples. Contact: Marilynne Foster, promotions coordinator. Reports back only if interested. Samples returned with SASE; samples filed.

Terms: Pays authors royalty of 5-10% based on retail price. Offers advances. Pays illustrators by the project. Sends galleys to authors; dummies to illustrators (sometimes). Originals returned to artist at job's completion (if requested). Manuscript guidelines available for SASE.

Tips: "Writers: Only opportunity is in teen market, especially if you have experience working with and speaking to teens. Illustrators: Show us a few samples."

CHRONICLE BOOKS, 85 Second St., San Francisco CA 94105. (415)537-3730. Fax: (415)537-4420. Book publisher. **Acquisitions:** Victoria Rock, associate publisher, children's books; Erica Jacobs, editor; Amy Novesky, assistant editor. Publishes 25-50 (both fiction and nonfiction) picture books/year; 2-4 middle readers nonfiction titles/year; 2-4 beginning readers or middle readers fiction/year. 10-50% of books by first-time authors; 10-50% of books from agented writers.

Fiction: Picture books: animal, folktales, history, multicultural, nature/environment. Young readers: animal, folktales, history, multicultural, nature/environment, poetry. Middle readers: animal, history, multicultural, nature/environment, poetry, problem novels. Young adults: multicultural needs include "projects that feature diverse children in everyday situations." Recently published *I Love You the Purplest*, by Barbara M. Joose; and *Hawk Hill*, by Sylvia Long.

Nonfiction: Picture books: animal, history, multicultural, nature/environment, science. Young readers: animal, arts/crafts, cooking, geography, history, multicultural and science. Middle readers: animal, arts/crafts, biography, cooking, geography, history, multicultural and nature/environment. Young adults: biography and multicultural.

THE AGE-LEVEL INDEX, located in the back of this book, lists book publishers and magazines according to the age-groups for which they need material.

Recently published *A Rainbow at Night*, by Bruce Hucko; and *Artist in Overalls: The Life of Grant Wood*, by John Duggleby.

How to Contact/Writers: Fiction/Nonfiction: Submit complete ms (picture books); submit outline/synopsis and 3 sample chapters (for older readers). Reports on queries/mss in 2-18 weeks. Publishes a book 1-3 years after acceptance. Will consider simultaneous submissions, as long as they are marked "multiple submission." Will not consider submissions by fax. Must include SASE.

Illustration: Works with 15-20 illustrators/year. Wants "unusual art, graphically strong, something that will stand out on the shelves. Either bright and modern or very traditional. Fine art, not mass market." Reviews ms/illustration packages from artists. "Indicate if project *must* be considered jointly, or if editor may consider text and art separately." Illustrations only: Submit samples of artist's work (not necessarily from book, but in the envisioned style). Slides, tearsheets and color photocopies OK. (No original art.) Dummies helpful. Résumé helpful. "If samples sent for files, generally no response—unless samples are not suited to list, in which case samples are returned. Queries and project proposals responded to in same time frame as author query/proposals."

Photography: Purchases photos from freelancers. Works on assignment only. Wants nature/natural history photos.

Terms: Generally pays authors in royalties based on retail price "though we do occasionally work on a flat fee basis." Advance varies. Illustrators paid royalty based on retail price or flat fee. Sends proofs to authors and illustrators. Book catalog for 9 × 12 SAE and 8 first-class stamps; manuscript guidelines for #10 SASE.

Tips: "Chronicle Books publishes an eclectic mixture of traditional and innovative children's books. We are interested in taking on projects that have a unique bent to them—be it in subject matter, writing style, or illustrative technique. As a small list, we are looking for books that will lend our list a distinctive flavor. Primarily we are interested in fiction and nonfiction picture books for children ages infant-8 years, and nonfiction books for children ages 8-12 years. We are also interested in developing a middle grade/YA fiction program, and are looking for literary fiction that deals with relevant issues. Our sales reps are witnessing a resistance to alphabet books. And the market has become increasingly competitive. The '80s boom in children's publishing has passed, and the market is demanding high-quality books that work on many different levels."

CLARION BOOKS, 215 Park Ave. S., New York NY 10003. (212)420-5889.Fax: (212)420-5855, Website: http://www.hmco.com/trade/. Imprint of Houghton Mifflin Company. Book publisher. Estab. 1965. **Manuscript Acquisitions:** Dorothy Briley, editor/publisher; Dinah Stevenson, executive editor; Nina Ignatowicz, senior editor. **Art Acquisitions:** Anne Diebel.

● Clarion's title *Golem*, by David Wisniewski, received the 1997 Caldecott Medal. See the Insider Report with Wisniewski in this section. Clarion's list is full through 1999. Do not send timely material.

How to Contact/Writers: Fiction: Send complete mss. Nonfiction: query. Must include SASE. Will accept simultaneous submission if informed.

Illustration: Send samples (no originals).

Terms: Pays authors advance and royalty. Pays illustrators advance and royalty; flat fee for jacket illustration.

CLEAR LIGHT PUBLISHERS, 823 Don Diego, Santa Fe NM 87501. (505)989-9590. Fax: (505)989-9519. Book publisher. **Acquisitions:** Harmon Houghton, publisher. Publishes 3 middle readers/year; and 3 young adult titles/year.

Nonfiction: Middle readers and young adults: multicultural, American Indian only.

How to Contact/Writers: Fiction/Nonfiction: Submit complete ms. Will consider simultaneous submissions. Reports in 3 months.

Illustration: Reviews ms/illustration packages from artists. Submit ms with dummy.

Terms: Pays authors royalty of 10% based on wholesale price. Offers advances (average amount: up to 50% of expected net sales). Sends galleys to authors.

Tips: "We're looking for authentic American Indian art and folklore."

COBBLEHILL BOOKS. This imprint of Penguin was closed down as a result of the Penguin/Putnam merger.

‡□**COMPASS PRODUCTIONS**, 211 E. Ocean Blvd., #360, Long Beach CA 90802. (562)432-7613. Fax: (562)495-0445. **Acquisitions:** Dick Dudley, vice president. Book packager/producer. Produces hardcover originals.

Fiction: Picture books: adventure, fantasy, horror, humor, mystery, plays, religious, science fiction. Recently published *Counting On Angels*, by Ward (pop-up).

Nonfiction: "All our books are pop-up and novelty books." Picture books: Americana, animals, child guidance/parenting, concept, education, recreation, regional, religion, sports, travel. Recent published *Busy Beaver Pond*, by Silver (pop-up).

How to Contact/Writers: Fiction/Nonfiction: Query with SASE. Reports in 6 weeks.

Terms: Pays 2-8% royalty on wholesale price for total amount of books sold to publisher. Offers $2,000 advance for idea/text.

Tips: "Keep in mind our books are *pop-up*, *dimensional*, or novelty *only*! Short verse, couplets or short nonfiction text for 6-7 spreads per book."

★CONCORDIA PUBLISHING HOUSE, 3558 S. Jefferson Ave., St. Louis MO 63118. (314)268-1000. Fax: (314)268-1329. Book publisher. **Manuscript Acquisitions:** Ruth Geisler, creative director; Dawn Weinstock; Rachel Hoyer. **Art Acquisitions:** Ed Luhmann, art director. "Concordia Publishing House produces quality resources which communicate and nurture the Christian faith and ministry of people of all ages, lay and professional. These resources include curriculum, worship aids, books, multimedia products and religious supplies. We publish a number of quality children's books each year. Most are fiction, with some nonfiction, based on a religious subject. We boldly provide Gospel resources that are Christ-centered, Bible-based, and faithful to our heritage."

Fiction: Picture books: concept, religion. Young readers, middle readers, young adults: concept, contemporary, humor, religion, suspense/mystery. "All books must contain explicit Christian content." Published *Laugh & Tickle, Hug & Pray*, by Julaine Kammath (family devotional book); *Stop! It's Christmas*, by Mary Manz Simon (ages 4-7); *Of Spies and Spider Webs*, by Dandi Daley Mackall (grades 2-3, first chapter books); and *Who Kidnapped Jesus?*, by Vicki Berger Erwin (ages 8-12).

Nonfiction: Picture books, young readers, middle readers: activity books, arts/crafts, religion. Young adults: religion.

How to Contact/Writers: Fiction: Submit complete ms (picture books); submit outline/synopsis and sample chapters (novel-length). May also query. Reports on queries in 1 month; mss in 2 months. Publishes a book 1 year after acceptance. Will consider simultaneous submissions. "No phone queries."

Illustration: Illustrations only: Query with samples. Contact: Ed Luhmann, art director.

Terms: Pays authors in royalties based on retail price or work purchased outright (minimum $500). Sends galleys to author. Ms guidelines for 1 first-class stamp and a #10 envelope.

Tips: "Do not send finished artwork with the manuscript. If sketches will help in the presentation of the manuscript, they may be sent. If stories are taken from the Bible, they should follow the Biblical account closely. Liberties should not be taken in fantasizing Biblical stories."

COPPER BEECH BOOKS, Imprint of The Millbrook Press, 2 Old New Milford Rd., Brookfield CT 06804. (203)740-2220. Book publisher. **Manuscript Acquisitions:** Dottie Carlson, manuscript coordinator.

Nonfiction: Picture books, young readers: animal, arts/crafts, concept, cooking, geography, health, history, how-to, music/dance, nature/environment, religion, science, sports. Beginning readers, middle readers: animal, arts/crafts, biography, cooking, geography, history, how-to, music/dance, nature/environment, reference, science, sports.

How to Contact/Writers: Nonfiction: Submit complete ms. Reports on queries in 2 weeks; mss in 1 month. Will consider simultaneous submissions and previously published work.

Illustration: Reviews ms/illustration packages from artists. Query. Reports in 1 month. Samples returned with SASE; samples filed.

Photography: Uses color or b&w prints. Submit cover letter, résumé, published sample, promo piece.

Terms: Pays authors royalty of 4-6%. Manuscript guidelines available for SASE.

❀COTEAU BOOKS LTD., 401-2206 Dewdney Ave., Regina, Sasketchewan S4R 1H3 Canada. (306)777-0170. Thunder Creek Publishing Co-op Ltd. Book publisher. Estab. 1975. **Acquisitions:** Barbara Sapergia, acquisitions editor; Geoffrey Ursell, publisher. Publishes 1-2 juvenile and/or young adult books/year, 12-14 books/year. 10% of books by first-time authors. "Coteau Books publishes the finest Canadian fiction, poetry, drama and children's literature, with an emphasis on western writers."

● Coteau Books publishes Canadian writers and illustrators only; manuscripts from the U.S. are returned unopened.

Fiction: Young readers, middle readers, young adults: adventure, contemporary, fantasy, history, humor, multicultural, nature/environment, science fiction, suspense/mystery. "No didactic, message pieces, nothing religious. No picture books. Material should reflect the diversity of culture, race, religion, creed of humankind—we're looking for fairness and balance." Recently published *Jess and the Runaway Grandpa*, by Mary Woodbury (ages 9-12, adventure novel); and *The Cherry-Pit Princess*, by Lynn Manuel (ages 8-11).

Nonfiction: Young readers, middle readers, young adult: biography, history, multicultural, nature/environment, social issues.

How to Contact/Writers: Fiction: Submit complete ms to acquisitions editor Barbara Sapergia. Reports on queries in 3-4 months; mss in 3-4 months. Publishes a book 1-2 years after acceptance.

Illustration: Works with 1-4 illustrators/year. Illustrations only: Submit nonreturnable samples. Reports only if interested. Samples returned with SASE; samples filed.

Photography: "Very occasionally buys photos from freelancers." Buys stock and assigns work.

Terms: Pays authors in royalties of 5-12½% based on retail price. Pays illustrators and photographers by the project. Sends galleys to authors; dummies to illustrators. Original artwork returned at job's completion. Book catalog free on request with 9×12 SASE.

Tips: "Truthfully, the work speaks for itself! Be bold. Be creative. Be persistent! There is room, at least in the Canadian market, for quality novels for children. Booksellers obviously like series like Goosebumps and The Baby-sitters Club, but they indicate there is room for unique stories. Certainly at Coteau, this is a direction we will continue to take."

★**CRESTWOOD HOUSE**, 299 Jefferson Rd., Parsippany NJ 07054-0480. (201)739-8000. Fax: (201)739-8606. Imprint of Silver Burdett Press, Simon & Schuster Publishing Education Group. Book publisher. **Acquisitions:** Debbie Biber, editor. See listing for Silver Burdett Press.

CROCODILE BOOKS, 46 Crosby St., Northhampton MA 01060. (413)582-7054. Fax: (413)582-7057. E-mail: interpg@aol.com. Imprint of Interlink Publishing Group, Inc. Book publisher. **Acquisitions:** Ruth Moushabeck, vice president. Publishes 6 picture books/year. 25% of books by first-time authors.
● Crocodile does not accept unsolicited manuscripts.
Fiction: Picture books: animal, contemporary, history, spy/mystery/adventure.
Nonfiction: Picture book: history, nature/environment.
Terms: Pays authors in royalties. Sends galleys to author; dummies to illustrator.

CROSSWAY BOOKS, Good News Publishers, 1300 Crescent, Wheaton IL 60187. (630)682-4300. Fax: (630)682-4785. Book Publisher. Estab. 1938. Editorial Director: Leonard Goss. **Acquisitions:** Jill Carter. Publishes 1-2 picture books/year; 1-2 middle readers/year; and 1-2 young adult titles/year. "Crossway Books is committed to publishing books that bring Biblical reality to readers and that examine crucial issues through a Christian world view."
Fiction: Picture books: religion. Middle readers: adventure, contemporary, history, humor, religion, suspense/mystery, Christian realism. Young adults: contemporary, history, humor, religion, suspense/mystery, Christian realism. Does not want to see horror novels, romance or prophecy novels. Not looking for picture book submissions at present time. Published *Tell Me the Secrets*, by Max Lucado, illustrated by Ron DiCianni.
How to Contact/Writers: Fiction: Query with outline/synopsis and up to 2 sample chapters. Reports on queries/mss in 4-6 weeks. Publishes a book 12-18 months after acceptance. Will consider simultaneous submissions.
Illustration: Works with 5 illustrators/year. Reviews ms/illustration packages from artists. Query. Illustrations only: Query with samples; provide résumé, promo sheet and client list.
Terms: Pays authors royalty based on net sales. Pays illustrators by the project. Sends galleys to authors; dummies to illustrators. Book catalog available; ms guidelines available for SASE.

CROWN PUBLISHERS (CROWN BOOKS FOR CHILDREN), 201 E. 50th St., New York NY 10022. (212)940-7742. Imprint of Random House Children's Publishing. Book publisher. Publisher: Simon Boughton. **Manuscript Acquisitions:** Tracy Gates, senior editor; Nancy Siscoe, editor. **Art Acquisitions:** Isabel Warren-Lynch, art director. Publishes 20 picture books/year; 10 nonfiction titles/year. 5% of books by first-time authors; 70% of books from agented writers.
Fiction: Picture books: animal, humor, nature/environment. Young readers: history, nature/environment. Does not want to see fantasy, science fiction, poetry. Average word length: picture books—750. Recently published: *My Little Sister Ate One Hare*, by Bill Grossman; and *Me on the Map*, by Joan Sweeney.
Nonfiction: Picture books, young readers and middle readers: activity books, animal, biography, careers, health, history, hobbies, music/dance, nature/environment, religion, science, sports. Average word length: picture books—750-1,000; young readers—20,000; middle readers—50,000. Does not want to see ABCs. Recently published: *Rosie the Riviter*, by Penny Coleman (ages 9-14); and *Children of the Dust Bowl*, by Jerry Stanley (9-14 years, middle reader).
How to Contact/Writers: Fiction/nonfiction: Submit query letter. Reports on queries/mss in 3-4 months if SASE is included. Publishes book approximately 2 years after acceptance. Will consider simultaneous submissions.
Illustration: Works with 20 illustrators/year. Reviews ms/illustration packages from artists. "Submit double-spaced, continuous manuscripts; do not supply page-by-page breaks. One or two photocopies of art are fine. *Do not send original art.* Dummies are acceptable." Reports in 2 months. Illustrations only: Submit photocopies, portfolio or slides with SASE; provide business card and tearsheets. Contact: Isabel Warren-Lynch, Art Director. Original artwork returned at job's completion.
Terms: Pays authors royalty based on retail price. Advance "varies greatly." Pays illustrators by the project or advance and royalty. Sends galleys to authors; proofs to illustrators. Book catalog for 9×12 SAE and 4 first-class stamps. Ms guidelines for 4½×9½ SASE; art guidelines not available.

 CANADIAN LISTINGS are marked with a maple leaf.

CSS PUBLISHING, 517 S. Main St., P.O. Box 4503, Lima OH 45802-4503. (419)227-1818. Fax: (419)222-4647. E-mail: acquisitions@csspub.com. Book publisher. **Manuscript Acquisitions:** Thomas Lentz. Managing Editor: Teresa Rhoads. Publishes books with religious themes. "We are seeking material for use by clergy, Christian education directors and Sunday school teachers for mainline Protestant churches. Our market is mainline Protestant clergy."
Fiction: Picture books, young readers, middle readers, young adults: religion. Needs children's sermons (object lesson) for Sunday morning worship services; dramas for Advent, Christmas or Epiphany involving children for church services; activity and craft ideas for Sunday school or mid-week services for children (particularly pre-school and first and second grade). Does not want to see secular picture books. Published *That Seeing, They May Believe*, by Kenneth Mortonson (lessons for adults to present during worship services to pre-schoolers-third graders); *What Shall We Do With This Baby?*, by Jan Spence (Christmas Eve worship service involving youngsters from newborn babies-high school youth); and *Miracle in the Bethlehem Inn*, by Mary Lou Warstler (Advent or Christmas drama involving pre-schoolers-high school youth and adult.)
Nonfiction: Picture books, young readers, middle readers, young adults: religion. Needs children's sermons (object lesson) for Sunday morning workship services; dramas for Advent, Christmas or Epiphany involving children for church services; activity and craft ideas for Sunday school or mid-week services for children (particularly pre-school and first and second grade). Does not want to see secular picture books. Published *Mustard Seeds*, by Ellen Humbert (activity/bulletins for pre-schoolers-first graders to use during church); and *This Is The King*, by Cynthia Cowen.
How to Contact/Writers: Reports on queries in 1 month; mss in 4-6 months. Publishes a book 9 months after acceptance. Will consider simultaneous submissions.
Terms: Work purchased outright from authors. Ms guidelines and book catalog available for SASE.

☐★**MAY DAVENPORT, PUBLISHERS**, 26313 Purissima Rd., Los Altos Hills CA 94022-4539. (415)948-6499. Fax: (415)948-6499. Independent book producer/packager. Estab. 1976. **Acquisitions:** May Davenport, editor/publisher. Publishes 1-2 picture books/year and 2-3 young adult titles/year. 99% of books by first-time authors. Seeks books with literary merit. "We like to think that we are selecting talented writers who have something humorous to write about today's unglued generation in 30,000-50,000 words for teens and young adults in junior/senior high school before they become tomorrow's 'functional illiterates.' "
● This publisher is overstocked with picture book/elementary reading material.
Fiction: Young adults: contemporary, humorous fictional literature for use in English courses in junior-senior high schools in US. Average word length: 40,000-60,000. Recently published *Grandpa McKutcheon's Kangaroomatie Rocking Chair*, written and illustrated by Jonathan Middleton (coloring-reading book—the pictures are illustrated drawings to be colored); *The Newman Assignment*, by Kurt Haberl, illustrated by Keith Neely (ages 12 and up, novel with teachers' lesson plans to read/discuss/write); and *Drivers' Ed is Dead*, by Pat Delgado, illustrated by Keith Neely (ages 12 and up, novel with teachers' lesson plans to read/discuss/write).
Nonfiction: Young readers: Special needs including dyslexia, tricks to develop for reading skills. Published *History of Papa Frog*, by William F. Meisburger (Spanish/English, grades 1-2, paper); and *Sumo, The Wrestling Elephant*, by Esther Lee (Spanish/English, grades 1-2, paper).
How to Contact/Writers: Fiction: Query. Reports on queries/mss in 2-3 weeks. "We do not answer queries or manuscripts which do not have SASE attached." Publishes a book 6-12 months after acceptance.
Illustration: Works with 1-2 illustrators/year. "Send samples for our files for future reference."
Terms: Pays authors royalties of 15% based on retail price. Pays "by mutual agreement, no advances." Pays illustrators by the project (range: $175-300). Book catalog, ms guidelines free on request with SASE.
Tips: "Create stories to enrich the non-reading 12-and-up readers. They might not appreciate your similies and metaphors and may find fault with your alliterations with the letters of the alphabet, but show them how you do it with memorable characters in today's society. Just project your humorous talent and entertain with more than two sentences in a paragraph."

DAWN PUBLICATIONS, 14618 Tyler Foote, Nevada City CA 95959. (916)478-7540. Fax: (916)478-7541. Website: http://www.dawnpub.com. Book publisher. Publisher: Muffy Weaver. **Acquisitions:** Glenn J. Hovemann, editor. Publishes works with holistic themes dealing with nature. "Dawn Publications is dedicated to inspiring in children a sense of appreciation for all life on earth."
● Dawn's list includes bilingual and Spanish editions.
Nonfiction: Picture books: animal, nature/environment. Recently published *Places of Power*, by Michael De-Munn, illustrated by Noah Buchanan; and *Dandelion Seed*, by Joseph Anthony, illustrated by Cris Arbo.
How to Contact/Writers: Nonfiction: Query or submit complete ms or submit outline/synopsis and sample chapters. Reports on queries/mss in 2 months maximum. Publishes a book 1 year after acceptance. Will consider simultaneous submissions and previously published work.
Illustration: Works with 4 illustrators/year. Will reviews ms/illustration packages from artists. Query; send ms with dummy. Illustrations only: Query with samples, résumé.
Terms: Pays authors royalty based on wholesale price. Offers advance. Pays illustrators by the project or royalties based on wholesale price. Sends galleys to authors; dummies to illustrators. Book catalog available for 8½×11 SASE; ms guidelines available for SASE.

Tips: Looking for "picture books expressing nature awareness with inspirational quality leading to enhanced self-awareness. Usually no talking or anthropomorphized animals."

DIAL BOOKS FOR YOUNG READERS, Imprint of Penguin Putnam Inc., 375 Hudson St., New York NY 10014. (212)366-2800. President/Publisher: Phyllis J. Fogelman. Editorial Assistant: Victoria Wells. **Acquisitions:** Submissions Editor. Publishes 70 picture books/year; 10 young reader titles/year; 5 middle reader titles/year; and 10 young adult titles/year.
- Dial's title *Minty: A Story of Young Harriet Tubman*, illustrated by Jerry Pinkney, received the 1997 Coretta Scott King Illustrator Award. Dial also publishes a line of paperback reprints called Pied Piper Books. Dial prefers submissions from agents and previously published authors.

Fiction: Picture books: adventure, animal, contemporary, fantasy, folktales, history, nature/environment, poetry, religion, science fiction, sports, suspense/mystery. Young readers: animal, contemporary, easy-to-read, fantasy, folktales, history, nature/environment, poetry, science fiction, sports, mystery/adventure. Middle readers, young adults: animal, contemporary, fantasy, folktales, history, nature/environment, poetry, problem novels, religion, science fiction, sports, spy/mystery/adventure. Published *Brother Eagle, Sister Sky*, illustrated by Susan Jeffers (all ages, picture book); *Amazing Grace*, by Mary Hoffman (ages 4-8, picture book); and *Soul Looks Back in Wonder*, by Tom Feelings, Maya Angelou, et al (ages 7 and up, poetry picture book.)

Nonfiction: Uses very little nonfiction but will consider submissions of outstanding artistic and literary merit. Picture books: animal, biography, history, nature/environment, sports. Young readers: animal, biography, history, nature/environment. Middle readers: biography, history. Young adults: biography. Recently published *Big-Top Circus*, by Neal Porter (ages 4-8, picture book); and *Hand, Heart, and Mind*, by Lou Ann Walker (middle readers).

How to Contact/Writers: Prefers agented material (but will accept queries with a SASE).

Illustration: To arrange a personal interview to show portfolio, send samples and a letter requesting an interview.

A lifetime for an **African crocodile** *is about* **50 years.**

Nile crocodiles are bothered by tiny animals that get on their skin and in their mouths. A bird called the Egyptian plover likes to eat these little animals. The crocodiles let the plovers land on their backs so they can eat the tiny pests. They even seem to open their mouths wider so the plovers, like over-eager dentists, can hop right in. The croc could easily get a quick lunch, but no one has ever seen a crocodile eat a plover.

Nile crocodiles remind us that everyone needs help from others sometimes.

Text © 1997 David L. Rice. Illustrations c 1997 Michael Maydak

Dawn Publishing's editor Glenn Hovemann knew Michael Maydak's illustrations would be just right for *Lifetimes*, David Rice's manuscript about the life spans of plants and animals and cooperative relationships in nature. "Michael's illustrations had the right combination of realism, magic and genuine appreciation for nature," says Hovemann. Like the African crocodile and the Egyptian plover pictured here, Rice and Maydak developed a synergistic relationship. When they discovered a mutual desire to make school visits, they traded on each other's talents to produce promotional brochures. Rice wrote the copy while Maydak and his wife, a designer, provided illustrations and layouts. Rice, a former teacher who has relied on *Children's Writer's & Illustrator's Market* for years, says, "It took almost 25 years and 40 manuscripts before I got my first book published. I am living proof that creativity is 90% perspiration and 10% inspiration."

Photography: Prefers agented material.
Terms: Pays authors and illustrators in royalties based on retail price. Average advance payment "varies."

★**DILLON PRESS, INC.**, 299 Jefferson Rd., P.O. Box 480, Parsippany NJ 07054-0480. (201)739-8000. Fax: (201)739-8606. Imprint of Silver Burdett Press, Simon & Schuster Publishing Education Group. Book Publisher. **Acquisitions:** Debbie Biber, editor. See listing for Silver Burdett Press.

DISNEY JUVENILE PUBLISHING, Subsidiary of Walt Disney Co., 500 S. Buena Vista, Burbank CA 91521. **Art Acquisitions:** Ellen Friedman, creative director. Publishes 35 titles/year based on Disney characters from films and TV.
 ● Disney publishes novelizations, retellings and picture books. All writing is done on a work-for-hire basis. They do not accept unsolicited manuscripts and are not currently accepting queries.
Illustration: Submit samples.
Terms: Pays authors and illustrators flat fee.

‡**DK INK**, 95 Madision Ave., New York NY 10016. (212)213-4800. Fax: (212)213-5240. Imprint of DK Publishing, Inc. Website: http://www.dk.com. Book publisher. Estab. 1997. Will publish 40-50 titles/year; first list included 20 titles. **Acquisitions:** Neal Porter, publisher; Richard Jackson, senior editor; Melanie Kroupa, senior editor. "DK Ink is a distinctive imprint consisting primarily of picture books and fiction for children and adults, created by authors and illustrators you know and respect as well as exciting new talents. The main goal of these books is to edify, entertain and encourage kids to think about the human condition."
Fiction: Looking for picture books, middle readers and young adult material. Recently published: *Jack and the Beanstalk*, told by Rosemary Wells, illustrated by Norman Messenger (retelling of classic story for ages 2-5); *Radiance Descending*, by Paula Fox (a novel for readers ages 9-11); and *Echoes of Elders: The Stories and Paintings of Chief Lelooska* (all ages).
Nonfiction: Nonfiction titles under DK Ink will have a distinctively differnent look from DK Publishing nonfiction titles.
How to Contact/Writers: Fiction: Submit complete manuscript. Nonfiction: Submit outline/sysnopsis and sample chapters. Reports in 8-10 weeks.
Illustration: Submit samples to Art Director.
Terms: Pays authors royalty; offers advance. Pays illustrators advance and royalty or flat fee, depending on assignment.

‡**DK PUBLISHING, INC.**, 95 Madison Ave., New York NY 10016. (212)213-4800. Fax: (212)689-1799. Website: http://www.dk.com. U.S. division of Dorling Kindersley. **Acquistions:** Barbara Minton, editorial coordinator. Imprint: DK Ink. Publishes 30 picture books/year; 30 young readers/year; 30 middle readers/year; and 2 young adult titles/year.
 ● DK works with previously published authors only.
Fiction: Picture books: animal, contemporary, folktales, nature/environment. Young readers: adventure, anthology, contemporary, folktales. Middle readers: adventure, anthology, contemporary, fantasy, folktales, history, humor, sports, suspense/mystery. Young adult: adventure, contemporary, fantasy, problem novels. Average page count: picture books, middle readers: 32 pages; young readers: 128 pages. Recently published: *Eyewitness Classics: Black Beauty*, by Anna Sewell, illustrated by Victor Ambrus (for young readers); and *Cybermania*, by Alexandre Jardin (for middle readers).
Nonfiction: Picture books: animal, concept, nature/environment. Young readers: activity books, animal, arts/craft, nature/environment. Middle readers: activity books, geography, history, nature/environment, reference, science, sports. Young adults: biography, careers, history, reference, science, social issues, sports. Average page count: picture books, middle readers: 32 pages; young readers: 128 pages. Recently published *Children Just Like Me: Our Favorite Stories*, by Jamila Gavin (for all ages); *The Young Swimmer*, by Jeff Rouse (for ages 8 and up); and *Stephen Biesty's Cross-Section Castle* (for ages 8 and up).
How to Contact/Writers: Only interested in agented material. Query with outline/sysnopsis. Reports in 3-5 weeks. Publishes a book 9 months after acceptance. Will consider simultaneous submissions.
Illustration: Only interested in agented material. Uses color artwork only. Reviews manuscript/illustration packages from artists. Query with printed samples. Illustrations only: Query with samples. Send résumé and promo sheet. Reports back only if interested. Samples filed.
Photography: Buys stock and assigns work. Uses color prints. Submit cover letter, résumé, published samples, color promo piece.
Terms: Pays authors royalty. Offers advances. Book catalog available for 10×13 SASE and $3 first-class

---

☐ **BOOK PACKAGERS/PRODUCERS** are marked with an open block.

postage. All imprints included in a single catalog. Manuscript/artist's guidelines available for SASE.
Tips: "Most of our projects are generated in London where authors and illustrators are solicited."

DOVE KIDS BOOKS. This imprint of Dove Entertainment was dissolved as a result of change in management.

DOWN EAST BOOKS, P.O. Box 679, Camden, ME 04843-0679. (207)594-9544. Fax: (207)594-7215. Website: http://www.mainebooks.com. Book publisher. Managing Editor: Karin Womer. **Acquistions:** Alice Devine, associate editor. Publishes 1-2 young middle readers/year. 70% of books by first-time authors. "As a small regional publisher Down East Books specializes in non-fiction books with a Maine or New England theme."
Fiction: Picture books, middle readers: animal, history, nature/environment. Published *Cats in the Dark*, by Kate Rowinski, illustrated by Bonnie Bishop (young-middle readers, animal); and *A Penny for a Hundred*, by Ethel Pochocki, illustrated by Mary Beth Owens (picture book about 9-year-old girl who befriends a German POW boy during WWII).
Nonfiction: Picture books, middle readers, animal, history, nature/environment. Published *Do Whales Ever . . . ? What you Really Want to Know About Whales, Porpoises and Dolphins*, by Nathalie Ward, illustrated by Tessa Morgan (young-middle readers, animal).
How to Contact/Writers: Fiction/Nonfiction: Query. Reports on queries in 4-8 weeks; mss in 4-8 weeks. Publishes a book 6-18 months after acceptance. Will consider simultaneous and previously published submissions.
Illustration: Works with 1-2 illustrators/year. Reviews ms/illustration packages from artists. Query. Illustrations only: Query with samples. Reports in 2-4 weeks. Samples returned with SASE; samples filed sometimes.
Terms: Pays authors royalty (varies widely). Pays illustrators by the project or by royalty (varies widely). Sends galleys to authors; dummies to illustrators. Original artwork returned at job's completion. Book catalog available. Manuscript guidelines available for SASE.

Tessa Morgan received a $1,000 advance on royalties to illustrate *Do Whales Ever . . . ?* for Down East Books. Since she resides in Woods Hole, Massachusetts, a town full of marine biological institutions, natural history assignments are more readily available than other jobs. Though she normally creates whimsical acrylic paintings, Morgan uses a slightly more realistic style to take advantage of regional assignments. Morgan became friends with Nathalie Ward, author of *Do Whales Ever . . . ?*, when both worked on educational coloring books and newletters for Down East Books. Down East has expressed interest in a second book tentatively titled *Do Sharks Ever . . . ?* Both author and illustrator are excited about the possiblity of working together on a series.

DUTTON CHILDREN'S BOOKS, 375 Hudson St., New York NY 10014. (212)366-2600. Imprint of Penguin Putnam Inc. Book publisher. **Manuscript Acquisitions:** Lucia Monfried, editor-in-chief. **Art Acquisitions:** Sara Reynolds, art director. Publishes approximately 60 picture books/year; 4 young reader titles/year; 10 middle reader titles/year; and 8 young adult titles/year. 10% of books by first-time authors. "We publish high-quality trade books and are interested in well-written manuscripts with fresh ideas and child appeal. We have a complete publishing program. Though we publish mostly picture books, we are very interested in acquiring more novels for middle and young adult readers. We are also expanding our list to include more books for preschool-aged children."

● See First Books for an interview with Dutton author/illustrator Nan Parson Rossiter on her book *Rugby & Rosie*.

Fiction: Picture books: adventure, animal, folktales, history, multicultural, nature/environment, poetry. Young readers: adventure, animal, contemporary, easy-to-read, fantasy, pop-up, suspense/mystery. Middle readers: adventure, animal, contemporary, fantasy, history, multicultural, nature/environment, suspense/mystery. Young adults: adventure, animal, anthology, contemporary, fantasy, history, multicultural, nature/environment, poetry, science fiction, suspense/mystery. Recently published *The Puddle Pail*, by Elisa Kleven (picture book); *The Iron Ring*, by Lloyd Alexander (novel); and *HIV Positive*, by Bernard Wolf (photo essay).

Nonfiction: Picture books: animal, history, multicultural, nature/environment. Young readers: animal, history, multicultural, nature/environment. Middle readers: animal, biography, history, multicultural, nature/environment. Young adults: animal, biography, history, multicultural, nature/environment, social issues. Recently published *Chile Fever: A Celebration of Peppers*, by Elizabeth King (ages 7-10, photo essay); and *Part of Me Died, Too: Stories of Creative Survival Among Bereaved Children and Teenagers*, by Virginia Lynn Fry (ages 10 and up).

How to Contact/Writers: Query, or submit complete ms (if picture book). Publishes a book 12-18 months after acceptance. Will consider simultaneous submissions.

Illustration: Works with 40-60 illustrators/year. Reviews ms/illustration packages from artists. Query first. Illustrations only: Query with samples; send résumé, portfolio, slides—no original art please. Reports on art samples in 2 months. Original artwork returned at job's completion.

Photography: Will look at photography samples and photo-essay proposals.

Terms: Pays authors royalties of 4-10% based on retail price. Book catalog, ms guidelines for SASE with 8 first-class stamps. Pays illustrators royalties of 2-10% based on retail price unless jacket illustration—then pays by flat fee.

Tips: Writers: "Avoid topics that appear frequently. In nonfiction, we are looking for history, general biography, science and photo essays for all age groups." Illustrators: "We would like to see samples and portfolios from potential illustrators of picture books (full color), young novels (b&w) and jacket artists (full color)." Foresee "even more multicultural publishing, plus more books published in both Spanish and English."

E.M. PRESS, INC., P.O. Box 4057, Manassas VA 20108. (540)439-0304. Book publisher. **Acquisitions:** Beth Miller, publisher/editor. "E.M. Press has narrowed its focus to manuscripts of local interest (Virginia, Maryland, D.C.); manuscripts by local authors; nonfiction manuscripts; and children's books. We're now publishing illustrated children's books." 50% of books by first-time authors.

Fiction: Recently published *Santa's New Reindeer*, by Judie Schrecker; and *Virginia's Country Stores: A Quiet Passing*, by Joseph E. Morse (illustrated history of the origins of the old community store).

Nonfiction: Young adults: religion, children. Recently published *How Will They Get That Heart Down Your Throat? A Child's View of Transplants*, by Karen Walton (educates children regarding "recycling" life); and *The Relationship*, by John H. Hyman (story of a summer in the lives of two young boys—one white, one "colored"—in rural, 1940s North Carolina).

How to Contact/Writers: Query with outline/synopsis and SASE for novel-length work and complete ms for shorter work. Reports on ms/queries in 3 months. Publishes a book 18 months after acceptance. Will consider simultaneous submissions.

Illustration: Works with 3 children's illustrators/year. Illustration packages should be submitted to Beth Miller, publisher. Reports back in 3 months. Samples returned with SASE; samples kept on file.

Terms: "We've used all means of payment from outright purchase to royalty." Offers varied advances. Sends galleys to authors. Original artwork returned at job's completion. Book catalog for SASE.

Tips: "Present the most professional package possible. The market is glutted, so you must find a new approach."

WM. B. EERDMANS PUBLISHING COMPANY, 255 Jefferson Ave. SE, Grand Rapids MI 49503. (616)459-4591. Book publisher. **Manuscript Acquisitions:** Amy Eerdmans, children's book editor. **Art Acquisitions:** Gayle Brown. Publishes 6 picture books/year; 4 young readers/year; and 4 middle readers/year.

Fiction: All levels: parables, religion, retold Bible stories from a Christian perspective. Picture books: animal, poetry.

Nonfiction: All levels: biography, religion.

How to Contact/Writers: Fiction/Nonfiction: Query or submit complete ms. Reports on queries in 3-6 weeks; mss in 6 weeks.

Illustration: Works with 6-8 illustrators/year. Reviews ms/illustration packages from artists. Reports on ms/art samples in 1 month. Illustrations only: Submit résumé, slides or color photocopies. Samples returned with SASE; samples filed.

Terms: Pays authors and illustrators advance and royalties of 5-10% based on retail price. Sends galleys to authors; dummies to illustrators. Original artwork returned at job's completion. Book catalog free on request; ms and/or artist's guidelines free on request.

Tips: "We are looking for material that will help children build their faith in God. Look at our list. We're interested in a Christian message in novels, picture books and biographies. We accept all genres."

ENSLOW PUBLISHERS INC., 44 Fadem Rd., Box 699, Springfield NJ 07081. Estab. 1978. **Acquisitions:** Brian D. Enslow, vice president. Publishes 50 middle reader titles/year and 75 young adult titles/year. 30% of books by first-time authors.

Nonfiction: Young readers, middle readers, young adults: animal, biography, careers, health, history, hobbies, nature/environment, social issues, sports. Average word length: middle readers—5,000; young adult—18,000. Published *Louis Armstrong*, by Patricia and Fredrick McKissack (grades 2-3, biography); and *Lotteries: Who Wins, Who Loses?*, by Ann E. Weiss (grades 6-12, issues book).

How to Contact/Writers: Nonfiction: Query. Reports on queries/mss in 2 weeks. Publishes a book 18 months after acceptance. Will not consider simultaneous submissions.

Illustration: Submit résumé, business card or tearsheets to be kept on file.

Terms: Pays authors royalties or work purchased outright. Sends galleys to authors. Book catalog/ms guidelines available for $2.

★**EVAN-MOOR EDUCATIONAL PUBLISHERS**, 18 Lower Ragsdale Dr., Monterey CA 93940-5746. (408)649-5901. Fax: (408)649-6256. E-mail: evanmoor@ix.netcom.com. Website: http://www.evan-moor.com. Book publisher. **Manuscript Acquisitions:** Marilyn Evans, editor. **Art Acquisitions:** Joy Evans, production director. Publishes 30-50 books/year. Less than 10% of books by first-time authors. " 'Helping Children Learn' is our motto. Evan-Moor is known for high-quality educational materials written by teachers for use in the classroom and at home. We publish teacher resource and reproducible materials in most all curriculum areas and activity books (language arts, math, science, social studies). No fiction or nonfiction literature books."

Nonfiction: Recently published *How to Make Books with Children, Literature & Writing Connections*, by Joy Evans & Jill Norris, illustrated by Cindy Davis (grades 1-6. Step-by-step directions for making 39 books connected to children's literature topics); *Thinking Skills* (a series of 3 books for grades 1-2, 3-4, 5-6). Authors are Jill Norris, Tekla White and Jeri Nutting, illustrated by Don Robison (problem-solving charts and worksheets); *North America*, by Yvonne Despard; and *Around the World*, by Jill Norris, illustrated by Cindy Davis (grades 1-6, both art projects based on the folk art techniques of many cultural groups). Activity books are 32 pages; teacher resource books are 64-160 pages. Audience: children age 5-11; grades PreK-6.

How to Contact/Writers: Query or submit complete ms. Reports on queries in 1 month; mss in 2 months. Publishes a book 12-18 months after acceptance. Will consider simultaneous submissions if so noted.

Illustration: Works with 6-8 illustrators/year. Uses b&w artwork primarily. Illustrations only: Query with samples; send résumé, tearsheets. Contact: Joy Evans, production director. Reports only if interested. Samples returned with SASE; samples filed.

Terms: Work purchased outright from authors, "dependent solely on size of project and 'track record' of author." Pays illustrators by the project (range: varies). Sends galleys to authors. Artwork is not returned. Book catalog available for 9×12 SAE; ms guidelines available for SASE.

Tips: "Writers—know the supplemental education or parent market. Tell us how your project is unique and what consumer needs it meets. Illustrators—you need to be able to produce quickly, and be able to render realistic and charming children and animals."

★**FACTS ON FILE**, 11 Penn Plaza, New York NY 10001. (212)967-8800. Book publisher. Editorial Director: Laurie Likoff. **Acquisitions:** Eleanora VonDehsen, science and technology/nature; Nicole Bowen, American history and studies; Drew Silver, language and literature; Chris Hollander, world studies; Jim Chambers, arts and entertainment. Estab. 1941. "We produce high-quality reference materials for the school library market and the general nonfiction trade." Publishes 25-30 young adult titles/year. 5% of books by first-time authors; 25% of books from agented writers; additional titles through book packagers, co-publishers and unagented writers.

Nonfiction: Middle readers, young adults: animal, biography, careers, geography, health, history, multicultural, nature/environment, reference, religion, science, social issues and sports. Recently published *Great Women Writers 1900-1950*, by Christina Gombar; *African American Explorers*, by Catherine Reef; and *Modern Mathematics*, by Harry Henderson.

How to Contact/Writers: Nonfiction: Submit outline/synopsis and sample chapters. Reports on queries in 8-10 weeks. Publishes a book 10-12 months after acceptance. Will consider simultaneous submissions. Sends galleys to authors. Book catalog free on request.

 PUBLISHERS PRODUCING educational material are marked with a star.

Tips: "Most projects have high reference value and fit into a series format."

FAIRVIEW PRESS, Imprint of Growing and Reading with Bob Keeshan, 2450 Riverside Ave. S, Minneapolis MN 55454. (612)672-4180, (800)544-8207. Fax: (612)672-4980. Website: http://www.press.fairview.org. Book publisher. Senior Editor: Lane Stiles. **Acquisitions:** Jessica Thoreson, children's book editor. Publishes 9-10 picture books/year. 75% of books by first-time authors. "Fairview Press publishes books and related materials that educate families and individuals about their physical and emotional health, and motivate them to seek positive changes in themselves and their communities."
Fiction: Picture Books: contemporary, health, family issues, special needs. Special needs include any titles specifically for or about physically or mentally challenged children. Average word length: picture books—1,000. Recently published *Clover's Secret*, written and illustrated by Christine M. Winn (ages 5-9, fiction about domestic violence); and *My Dad Has HIV*, by Alexander, Rudin, Sejkova, illustrated by Shipman (ages 4-8, girl deals with father's illness).
Nonfiction: Picture books, young readers: activity books, family issues, health, multicultural, self help, social issues, special needs. Average word length: picture books—1,000. "No children's nonfiction published yet—we're interested in expanding, though."
How to Contact/Writers: Fiction/Nonfiction: Submit complete ms. Reports on queries/ms in 8-10 weeks. Publishes a book 18 months after acceptance. Will consider simultaneous submissions and previously published work.
Illustration: Works with 3-5 illustrators/year. Uses color artwork only. Reviews ms/illustration packages from artists. Submit query. Illustrations only: Query with samples; arrange personal portfolio review. Reports back only if interested. Samples not returned; samples filed.
Terms: Pays authors fee negotiated by project. Offers advances (50% total). Pays illustrators fee negotiated by project. Originals returned at job's completion. Book catalog available; ms guidelines available for SASE.
Tips: "Fairview Press publishes children's books on family issues—virtues, values, coping skills, parental/familial relationships, etc. Submitted work must fit under that 'umbrella.' "

FARRAR, STRAUS & GIROUX INC., 19 Union Square W., New York NY 10003. (212)741-6934. Fax: (212)633-2427. Book publisher. Imprint: Frances Foster Books. Children's Books Editorial Director: Margaret Ferguson. **Acquisitions:** Frances Foster, publisher, Frances Foster Books; Beverly Reingold, executive editor; Wesley Adams, senior editor; Elizabeth Mikesell, associate editor. Estab. 1946. Publishes 21 picture books/year; 6 middle reader titles/year; and 15 young adult titles/year. 10% of books by first-time authors; 20% of books from agented writers.
 • Farrar, Straus & Giroux title *Starry Messenger*, illustrated by Peter Sís, received a Caldecott Honor Book award in 1997.
Fiction: All levels: all categories. "Original and well-written material for all ages." Published *Belle Prater's Boy*, by Ruth White (ages 10 up).
Nonfiction: All levels: all categories. "We publish only literary nonfiction."
How to Contact/Writers: Fiction/Nonfiction: Query with outline/synopsis and sample chapters. Do not fax submissions. Reports on queries in 6-8 weeks; mss in 1-3 months. Publishes a book 18 months after acceptance. Will consider simultaneous submissions.
Illustration: Works with 30-60 illustrators/year. Reviews ms/illustration packages from artists. Submit ms with 1 example of final art, remainder roughs. Illustrations only: Query with tearsheets. Reports back in 1-2 months. Samples returned with SASE; samples sometimes filed.
Terms: "We offer an advance against royalties for both authors and illustrators." Sends galleys to authors; dummies to illustrators. Original artwork returned at job's completion. Book catalog available for 6½×9½ SAE and 64¢ postage; ms guidelines for 1 first-class stamp.
Tips: "Study our catalog before submitting. We will see illustrator's portfolios by appointment. Don't ask for criticism and/or advice—it's just not possible. Never send originals. Always enclose SASE."

FAWCETT JUNIPER, 201 E. 50 St., New York NY 10022. (212)751-2600. Imprint of Ballantine/DelRey/Fawcett Books. Book publisher. Editor-in-Chief/Vice President: Leona Nevler. Executive Administrative Assistant to the Editor-in-Chief: Louis Mendez. Publishes 24 titles/year.
Fiction: Young adults: contemporary, fantasy, romance.
How to Contact/Writers: Fiction: Query.
Terms: Pays authors in royalties.
Tips: "Do not send children's manuscripts—only manuscripts appropriate for young people ages 12 and up!"

THE FEMINIST PRESS AT THE CITY UNIVERSITY OF NEW YORK, 311 E. 94th St., New York NY 10128. (212)360-5790. Estab. 1970. Book publisher. Senior Editor: Jean Casella. **Acquisitions:** Assistant Editor, Children's Books. Publishes 1-2 middle reader, young reader and young adult books/year. "Our primary mission is to publish works of fiction by women which preserve and extend women's literary traditions. We emphasize work by multicultural/international women writers."
Fiction: Young readers: adventure fantasy, contemporary, folktales, history, humor, multicultural. Middle readers:

adventure, fantasy, folktales, history, multicultural. Young adults: concept, contemporary, humor, multicultural, problem novels, suspense/mystery.

Nonfiction: Picture books, young reader: biography, history, multicultural, social issues. Middle reader: biography, history, multicultural, social issues. Young adult: biography, history multicultural, social issues.

How to Contact/Writers: Fiction/Nonfiction: Query. Reports on queries/mss in 6-12 weeks. Publishes a book 1-2 years after acceptance.

Illustration: Works with 1 illustrator/year for covers only. Submit query. Reports back in 1 month only if interested and only if SASE. Samples kept on file.

Terms: Pays authors royalty. Offers advances (average amount: $250). Pays illustrators by the project. Sends galleys to authors. Original artwork returned at job's completion. Book catalog available; ms guidelines available; send 9×12 SASE with $1.01 postage.

❧FIREFLY BOOKS LTD., 3680 Victoria Park Ave., Willowdale, Ontario M2H 3K1 Canada. (416)499-8412. Fax: (416)499-8313. Book publisher and distributor.
- Firefly Books Ltd. does accept unsolicited manuscripts.

‡FIRST STORY, Imprint of J. Pierson Publishing, 1828 Proper St., P.O. Box 38834, Corinth MS 38834. (601)286-0208. Fax: (601)287-1214. Book publisher. Publisher/Editor-in-Chief: Judith Pierson. Publishes 4 picture books/year. 50% of books by first-time authors.

Fiction: Picture books, young readers. Average word length: picture books—700-1,500; young readers—1,500. Recently published *Who's Under Grandma's Quilt*, written by Rachel Waterstone, illustrated by Virginia Esquinaldo; and *Goodnight My Little Chicks/Buenas Noches Mis Dollitos*, written and illustrated by Karen Sharp Foster.

How to Contact/Writers: Fiction: Submit complete ms. Reports on queries/mss in 2 months. Publishes a book 18 months-2 years after acceptance. Will consider simultaneous submissions.

Illustration: Works with 4 illustrators/year. Reviews ms/illustration packages from artists. Send ms with dummy. Contact: Editor. Illustrations only: Send résumé, promo sheet and tearsheets to be kept on file. Contact: Editor. Reports in 2 months. Samples returned with SASE; samples filed.

Terms: Pays authors royalty of 4-5% based on retail price or work purchased outright (negotiable). Offers advances (negotiable). Pays illustrators royalty of 4-5% based on retail price. Sends galleys to authors; dummies to illustrators. Originals returned to artist at job's completion. Book catalog available for 2 first-class stamps; ms guidelines available for SASE.

Tips: "SASE is always required. Do not send original artwork. Guidelines available—send SASE. Take a look at our books."

❧FITZHENRY & WHITESIDE LTD., 195 Allstate Pkwy., Markham, Ontario L3R 4T8 Canada. (905)477-9700. Fax: (905)477-9179. Book publisher. President: Sharon Fitzhenry. Senior Editor: Caroline Walker. 15% of books by first-time authors. Publishes mostly nonfiction—social studies, visual arts, biography, environment. Canadian subject, perspective or authors only.

How to Contact/Writers: Submit outline/synopsis and 1 sample chapter. Reports in 6 months. Will not consider simultaneous submissions.

Terms: Pays authors royalty of 10%. Offers "modest" advances. Pays illustrators by the project and royalty. Pays photographers per photo. Sends galleys to authors; dummies to illustrators.

‡FOCUS PUBLISHING, INC., 1375 Washington Ave. S., Bemidji MN 56601. (218)759-9817. Fax: (218)751-2183. Website: http://www.paulbunyan.net/focus. **Acquisitions:** Jan Haley, vice president. Publishes hardcover and trade paperback originals and reprints. Publishes 4-6 titles/year. 90% of books from first-time authors; 100% from unagented writers. "Focus Publishing is a small press primarily devoted to Christian books and secular titles appropriate to children and home-schooling families."

Fiction: Middle readers, young adult: adventure, suspense/mystery, religion. Recently published *Butch & the Rooster*, by Judy Hess (children's picture book).

Nonfiction: Middle readers, young adults: religion, nature/environment.

How to Contact/Writers: Fiction: Query with synopsis. Nonfiction: Submit proposal package, including marketing ideas with SASE. Reports in 2 months. Publishes book 1 year after acceptance of ms.

Illustration: Reviews ms/illustration packages. Send photocopies.

Photography: Reviews ms/photo packages. Submit photocopies.

Terms: Pays 7-10% royalty on retail price. Book catalog free.

Tips: "I prefer SASE inquiries, synopsis and target markets. Please don't send 5 lbs. of paper with no return

 LISTINGS NEW TO THIS EDITION are marked with a double dagger.

postage."

FORWARD MOVEMENT PUBLICATIONS, 412 Sycamore St., Cincinnati OH 45202. (513)721-6659. Fax: (513)721-0729. E-mail: forward.movement@ecunet.org. Website: http://www.dfms.org/fmp.
Fiction: Religion.
Nonfiction: Religion.
How to Contact/Writers: Fiction/Nonfiction: Query. Reports in 1 month.
Illustration: Query with samples. Samples returned with SASE.
Terms: Pays authors honorarium. Pays illustrators by the project.
Tips: "Forward Movement is now exploring publishing books for children and does not know its niche. We are an agency of the Episcopal Church and most of our market is to mainstream Protestants."

FREE SPIRIT PUBLISHING, 400 First Ave. N., Suite 616, Dept. CWI, Minneapolis MN 55401-1730. (612)338-2068. Fax: (612)337-5050. E-mail: help4kids@freespirit.com. Book publisher. **Acquisitions:** Elizabeth Verdick. Publishes 15-20 titles/year for children and teens, teachers and parents. "We believe passionately in empowering kids to learn to think for themselves and make their own good choices."
 • Free Spirit no longer accepts fiction or picture book submissions.
Nonfiction: "Free Spirit Publishing specializes in SELF-HELP FOR KIDS®, with an emphasis on self-esteem and self awareness, stress management, school success, creativity, friends and family, social action, and special needs (i.e., gifted and talented, children with learning differences). We prefer books written in a natural, friendly style, with little education/psychology jargon. Need books in our areas of emphasis, and prefer titles written by specialists such as teachers, counselors, and other professionals who work with youth." Recently published *The Kid's Guide to Social Action: How to Solve the Social Problems You Choose—and Turn Creative Thinking into Positive Action*, by Barbara A. Lewis; *Stick Up for Yourself! Every Kid's Guide to Personal Power and Positive Self-Esteem*, by Gershen Kaufman, Ph.D. and Lev Raphael, Ph.D.; and *Bringing Up Parents: The Teenager's Handbook*, by Alex J. Packer, Ph.D.
How to Contact/Writers: Send query letter, or outline with sample chapters. Reports on queries/mss in 2 months. "If you'd like materials returned, enclose a SASE with sufficient postage." Write or call for catalog and submission guidelines before sending submission.
Illustration: Submit samples to acquisitions editor for consideration. If appropriate, samples will be kept on file and artist will be contacted if a suitable project comes up. Enclose SASE if you'd like materials returned.
Photography: Submit samples to acquisitions editor for consideration. If appropriate, samples will be kept on file and photographer will be contacted if a suitable project comes up. Enclose SASE if you'd like materials returned.
Terms: Pays authors in royalties of 7-12% based on wholesale price. Offers advance. Pays illustrators by the project. Pays photographers by the project or per photo.
Tips: "Prefer books that help kids help themselves, or that help adults help kids help themselves; that complement our list without duplicating current titles; and that are written in a direct, straightforward manner."

‡FREESTONE, Peachtree Publishers, 494 Armour Circle NE, Atlanta GA 30324. (404)876-8761. Estab. 1997. Publishes 3-4 young adult titles/year. "We look for very good stories that are well-written, and written from the author's experience and heart with a clear application to today's young adults. We feel teens need to read about issues that are relevant to them, rather than reading adult books."
 • Freestone is an imprint of Peachtree Publishers. See the listing for Peachtree for submission information.

FRIENDS UNITED PRESS, 101 Quaker Hill Dr., Richmond IN 47355. (765)962-7573. Fax: (765)966-1293. Estab. 1968. Book publisher. **Acquisitions:** Ardith Talbot, editor. Publishes 1 middle reader/year; and 1 young adult title/year. 90% of books by first-time authors. "Friends United Press commits itself to energise and equip Friends and others through the power of the Holy Spirit to gather people into fellowship where Jesus Christ is known, loved and obeyed as teacher and Lord."
Fiction: Young readers, middle readers and young adults: adventure, history, religion. Recently published *Luke's Summer Secret*, by Randall Wisehart, Jr. (historical fiction); *Stories for Jason*, by Mary Cromer (historical fiction); and *Betsy Ross, Quaker Rebel*, by Ethlyn Walkington (historical fiction for young adults).
Nonfiction: Young readers, middle readers and young adults: history, religion.
How to Contact/Writers: Fiction/Nonfiction: Query or submit outline/synopsis and complete ms. Reports on queries in 2-6 months; on mss in 6 months. Publishes a book 1 year after acceptance. Will consider simultaneous, previously published work.
Terms: Pays authors royalty of 7½% based on wholesale price. Book catalog and ms guidelines available for SASE.
Tips: "Write or call before submitting materials."

‡FRONT STREET BOOKS, P.O. Box 280, Arden NC 28704. (704)681-0811. Website: http://www.frontstreetbooks.com. Book publisher. Estab. 1995. **Acquisitions:** Stephen Roxburgh, publisher. Publishes 10 titles/year. "We are a small independent publisher and have chosen to be out of the corporate loop in the belief that as long as our books are of the highest quality, they will find an audience. We believe that each of the books on our list represents the best of its kind."

● Front Street accepts submissions via e-mail. See their website for details and instructions, as well submission guidelines and their complete catalog. Front Street focuses on fiction, but will publish poetry, anthologies, nonfiction and high-end picture books. They are not currently accepting unsolicited picture book manuscripts.

Fiction: Recently published: *Piggy's Birthday Dream*, by Anke de Vries, illustrated by Jung-Hee Spetter (picture book about a shy pig's first surprise birthday party for ages 2-5); *Apple Island, or The Truth About Teachers*, by Douglas Evans, illustrated by Larry di Fiori (a comic fable about the origins of teachers for ages 8-12); and *Don't Read This! And Other Tales of the Unnatural* (a collection of spooky stories from authors around the world published in a dozen languages for ages 10-14).

How to Contact/Writers: Fiction: Submit cover letter and complete ms if under 100 pages; submit cover letter, one or two sample chapters and plot summary if over 100 pages. Nonfiction: Submit detailed proposal and sample chapters. Poetry: Submit no more than 25 poems. Include SASE with submissions if you want them returned. "It is our policy to consider submissions in the order in which they are received. This is a time-consuming practice and we ask you to be patient in awaiting our response."

Illustration: "If you are the artist or are working with an artist, we will be happy to consider your project." Submit ms, dummy and a sample piece of art "rendered in the manner and style representative of the final artwork."

Terms: Pays advance and royalty.

LAURA GERINGER BOOKS, 10 E. 53rd St., New York NY 10022. (212)207-7554. Fax: (212)207-7192. Imprint of HarperCollins Publishers. **Manuscript Acquisitions:** Laura Geringer, editorial director. **Art Acquisitions:** Harriett Barton, art director. Publishes 10-12 picture books/year; 2 middle readers/year; 2-4 young adult titles/year. 20% of books by first-time authors; 50% of books from agented authors.

Fiction: All levels: adventure, contemporary, folktales, hi-lo, humor, sports, suspense/mystery. Picture books: animal, concept. Young readers: animal, history, poetry, multicultural. Middle readers: animal, poetry, problem novels. Young adults: history, multicultural, problem novels. Average word length: picture books—250-1,200. Recently published *Buz*, by Richard Egielski (ages 3-7, picture book); *Zoe Rising*, by Pam Conrad (ages 10 and up, middle grade fiction); and *The Leaf Men*, by William Joyce (ages 4-8, picture book).

How to Contact/Writers: Submit complete ms. Reports on queries in 2-4 weeks; mss in 3-4 months. Publishes a book 1½-3 years after acceptance. Will consider simultaneous submissions.

Illustration: Works with 15-20 illustrators/year. Reviews ms/illustration packages from artists. Submit complete package. Illustrations only: Query with samples; submit portfolio for review; provide résumé, business card, promotional literature or tearsheets to be kept on file. Reports in 2-3 months. SASE for return of samples; samples kept on file.

Terms: Pays authors royalties of 5-6¼% (picture book) or 10-12½% (novel) based on retail price. Offers advances. Pays illustrators royalties of 5-6¼% based on retail price. Sends galleys to authors; proofs to illustrators. Original artwork returned at job's completion. Book catalog available for 9×11 SASE; ms/artist's guidelines available for SASE.

Tips: "Write about what you *know*. Don't try to guess our needs. And don't forget that children are more clever than we give them credit for!" Wants "artwork that isn't overly 'cutesy' with a strong sense of style and expression."

GIBBS SMITH, PUBLISHER, P.O. Box 667, Layton UT 84041. (801)544-9800. Fax: (801)544-5582. Imprint: Gibbs Smith Junior. Book publisher. Editorial Director: Madge Baird. **Acquisitions:** Theresa Desmond, children's book editor. Publishes 6-8 books/year. 10% of books by first-time authors. 50% of books from agented authors.

Fiction: Picture books: adventure, contemporary, humor, multicultural, nature/environment, suspense/mystery, western. Average word length: picture books—1,000. Published *Once There Was a Bull . . . Frog*, by Rick Walton, illustrated by Greg Hally (ages 4-8, picture book); and *I Know What You Do When I Go to School*, by Ann Edwards Cannon, illustrated by Jennifer Mazzucco (ages 4-8, picture book).

Nonfiction: Middle readers: activity, arts/crafts, cooking, how-to, nature/environment, science. Average word length: up to 10,000. Published *Cooking on a Stick*, by Linda White, illustrated by Fran Lee (ages 7-11, cookbook).

How to Contact/Writers: Fiction/Nonfiction: Submit several chapters or complete ms. Reports on queries and mss in 8-10 weeks. Publishes a book 1-2 years after acceptance. Will consider simultaneous submissions. Ms returned with SASE.

Illustration: Works with 6-8 illustrators/year. Reviews ms/illustration packages from artists. Query. Submit ms with 3-5 pieces of final art. Illustrations only: Query with samples; provide résumé, promo sheet, slides (duplicate slides, not originals). Reports back only if interested. Samples returned with SASE; samples filed.

Terms: Pays authors royalty of 4-7½% based on wholesale price or work purchased outright ($500 minimum). Offers advances (average amount: $2,000). Pays illustrators by the project or royalty of 4-5% based on wholesale price. Sends galleys to authors; color proofs to illustrators. Original artwork returned at job's completion. Book catalog available for 9×12 SAE and postage. Ms guidelines available.

Tips: "We target ages 5-11."

Traci O'Very Covey came up with a clever idea for the cover of *Mapped Out! The Search for Snookums* by Carol Baicker-McKee. Since the reader learns to use maps to solve the case of a pet iguana that has been kidnapped, Covey decided to create excitement by showing Snookums being snatched right off the book cover. Covey has been a graphic designer and illustrator for many years and has designed several books published by Gibbs Smith. Because of the complexity of *Mapped Out!*, it was beneficial to use an artist who could both design and illustrate the book. "I do all of the initial sketches and final drawings by hand and then apply color and create the finished 'painting' on the computer." Covey also writes stories of her own she'd love to see published. In the meantime, projects like *Mapped Out!* generate interest in her work.

DAVID R. GODINE, PUBLISHER, P.O. Box 9103, Lincoln MA 01773. (617)259-0700. Fax: (617)259-9198. Book publisher. Estab. 1970. **Acquisitions:** Mark Polizzotti, editorial director. Publishes 1-3 picture books/year; 1-3 young reader titles/year; 1-3 middle reader titles/year. 10% of books by first-time authors; 75% of books from agented writers. "We publish books that matter for people who care."

● This publisher is no longer considering unsolicited manuscripts of any type.

Fiction: Picture books: adventure, animal, contemporary, folktales, nature/environment. Young readers: adventure, animal, contemporary, folk or fairy tales, history, nature/environment, poetry. Middle readers: adventure, animal, contemporary, folk or fairy tales, history, mystery, nature/environment, poetry. Young adults/teens: adventure, animal, contemporary, history, mystery, nature/environment, poetry. Recently published *The Empty Creel*, by Geraldine Pope (Paterson Prize winning book with vinyl-cut illustrations); and *An Animated Alphabet*, by Marie Angel.

Nonfiction: Picture books: alphabet, animal, nature/environment. Young readers: activity books, animal, history, music/dance, nature/environment. Middle readers: activity books, animal, biography, history, music/dance, nature/environment. Young adults: biography, history, music/dance, nature/environment.
How to Contact/Writers: Query. Reports on queries in 2 weeks. Reports on solicited ms in 2 weeks (if not agented) or 2 months (if agented). Publishes a book 2 years after acceptance.
Illustration: Only interested in agented material. Works with 1-3 illustrators/year. Reviews ms/illustration packages from artists. "Submit roughs and one piece of finished art plus either sample chapters for very long works or whole ms for short works." Illustrations only: "After query, submit slides, with one full-size blow-up of art." Reports on art samples in 2 weeks. Original artwork returned at job's completion. "Almost all of the children's books we accept for publication come to us with the author and illustrator already paired up. Therefore, we rarely use freelance illustrators." Samples returned with SASE; samples filed (if interested).
Terms: Pays authors in royalties based on retail price. Number of illustrations used determines final payment for illustrators. Pay for separate authors and illustrators "differs with each collaboration." Illustrators paid by the project. Sends galleys to authors; dummies to illustrators. Originals returned at job's completion. Book catalog available for SASE.
Tips: "Always enclose a SASE. Keep in mind that we do not accept unsolicited manuscripts and that we rarely use freelance illustrators."

GOLDEN BOOKS, 850 Third Ave., New York NY 10022. (212)583-6700. Fax: (212)371-1091. Imprint of Golden Books Family Entertainment Inc. **Editorial Directors:** Jackie Glasthal, storybooks; Jane Gerver, color/activity; Liz Doyle, novelty. **Art Acquistions:** Paula Darmofal, executive art director; Tracy Tyler, art director. Book publisher. 100% of books from agented authors.
● Golden Books does not accept unsolicited submissions.
Fiction: Board books, novelty books, picture books: adventure, animal, concept, contemporary, folktales, humor, nature/environment, religion. Young readers: adventure, animal, contemporary, history. Middle readers: adventure, animal, nature/environment, suspense/mystery. Young adults: animal, history. "Our Essence line is written and illustrated by African-Americans; the books feature African-Americans." Published *The Easter Bunny's Wish*, by Justine Korman, illustrated by Maggie Swanson (ages 2-5, Wishing Star book, 8×8 die-cut with cardstock); *My First Church Book*, by Beth Hermann, art by Peggy Tagel (ages 1-3 Golden Shaped Naptime Tale, 7½×8, die-cut board book); and Sesame Street: *Elmo Can . . . Taste! Touch! Hear! Smell! See!*, by Michaela Muntean, illustrated by Maggie Swanson (ages 3-5, Golden Little Look-Look, 5½×6).
Nonfiction: All levels: animal, nature/environment, reference, science. Picture books: concept. Young readers: arts/crafts, cooking, geography, music/dance.
How to Contact/Writers: Only interested in agented material.
Illustration: Only interested in agented material. Sometimes reviews ms/illustration packages from artists. Query first. Illustrations only: Will review work for possible future assignments.
Terms: Work purchased outright from authors and illustrators. Book catalog available for SASE.

GRAPEVINE PUBLICATIONS, INC., P.O. Box 2449, Corvallis OR 97339-2449. (541)754-0583. Fax: (541)754-6508. E-mail: gpi@proaxis.com. Book publisher. **Acquisitions:** Chris Coffin, managing editor. Publishes 5 picture books/year; and 5 young readers/year. 50% of books by first-time authors. "Grapevine is looking for fresh, creative fiction for readers aged 4-10. We are also publishing nonfiction in the areas of math, science and technology instruction for ages 10-adult."
● Grapevine's guidelines contain an informative section called "Thoughts and Suggestions on Publishing." Their guidelines are very specific and helpful.
Fiction: Picture books, young readers, middle readers: adventure, animal, concept, contemporary, fantasy, folktales, hi-lo, history, humor, nature/environment, poetry, suspense/mystery. Average length: picture books—16-32 pages; young readers—32 pages; middle readers—64 pages.
Nonfiction: Young adult: computers/electronics, how-to, mathematics.
How to Contact/Writers: Send SASE for guidelines before submitting. Submit complete ms only. Reports only if interested (in 3-6 months). Publishes a book 6-12 months after acceptance. Will consider simultaneous and previously published submissions. No e-mail submissions or inquiries.
Illustration: Works with 3-4 illustrators/year. Reviews ms illustration packages from artists. Submit ms with dummy. Contact: Chris Coffin. Illustrations only: Query with samples; provide tearsheets. Reports only if interested. Samples returned with SASE (please indicate if return is desired); samples filed.
Terms: Pays authors royalty of 9% on wholesale price. Pays illustrators and photographers by the project. Sends galleys to authors; dummies to illustrators. Guidelines available for SASE with 2 oz. postage.
Tips: "Test books on kids other than those who know you. Match the 'look and feel' of text and illustrations to the subject and age level." Wants "early/middle reader fiction with polished writing and 'timeless' feel."

GREENE BARK PRESS, P.O. Box 1108, Bridgeport CT 06601-1108. (203)372-4861. Fax: (203)371-5856. E-mail: greenebark@aol.com. Website: http://www.bookworld.com//greenebark. Book publisher. **Acquisitions:** Michele Hofbauer, associate publisher; Thomas J. Greene, publisher. Publishes 4-6 picture books/year. 40% of books by first-time authors. "We publish quality hardcover picture books for children."
Fiction: Picture books, young readers: adventure, fantasy. Average word length: picture books—650; young

readers—1,400. Recently published *Bug & Slug in the Rug*, by Steve Allen, illustrated by Michele Hofbauer (ages 5-9, young reader); *Cookie for the President*, by Anita Bott, illustrated by Pat Collins (ages 5-9, young reader); and *If Only I Could Whistle Loudly*, by Frank Mellen, illustrated by Ray Dirgo.

How to Contact/Writers: Reports on queries in 1 month; ms in 2-4 months. Publishes a book 18 months after acceptance. Will consider simultaneous submissions.

Illustrations: Works with 2-3 illustrators/year. Uses color artwork only. Reviews ms/illustration packages from artists. Submit ms with 3 pieces of final art (copies only). Illustrations only: Query with samples. Reports in 2 months only if interested. Samples returned with SASE; samples filed.

Terms: Pays authors royalty of 10-15% based on wholesale price. Pays illustrators by the project (range: $1,500-3,000) or 5-7½% royalty based on wholesale price. No advances. Send galleys to authors; dummies to illustrators. Originals returned to artist at job's completion. Book catalog available for 8½×11 SAE. All imprints included in a single catalog. Ms and art guidelines available for SASE.

Tips: "As a guide for future publications do not look to our older backlist. Please no telephone queries."

GREENHAVEN PRESS, 10911 Technology Place, San Diego CA 92127. (619)485-7424. Book publisher. Estab. 1970. **Acquisitions:** Bonnie Szumski, senior editor. Publishes 40-50 young adult titles/year. 35% of books by first-time authors.

● Greenhaven accepts no unsolicited manuscripts. All writing is done on a work-for-hire basis.

Nonfiction: Middle readers: biography, controversial topics, history, issues. Young adults: biography, history, nature/environment. Other titles "to fit our specific series." Average word length: young adults—15,000-25,000.

How to Contact/Writers: Query only.

Terms: Buys ms outright for $1,500-3,000. Offers advances. Sends galleys to authors. Book catalog available for 9×12 SAE and 65¢ postage.

Tips: "Get our guidelines first before submitting anything."

GREENWILLOW BOOKS, 1350 Avenue of the Americas, New York NY 10019. (212)261-6500. Imprint of William Morrow & Co. Book publisher. Editor-in-Chief: Susan Hirschman. **Manuscript Acquisitions:** submit to Editorial Department. **Art Acquisitions:** Ava Weiss, art director. Publishes 50 picture books/year; 5 middle readers books/year; and 5 young adult books/year. "Greenwillow Books publishes picture books, fiction for young readers of all ages, and nonfiction primarily for children under seven years of age. We hope you will read many children's books (especially those on our list), decide what you like or don't like about them, then write the story *you* want to tell (not what you think we want to read), and send it to us!"

Fiction: Will consider all levels of fiction; various categories.

How to Contact/Writers: Submit complete ms. "If your work is illustrated, we ask to see a typed text, rough dummy, and a *copy* of a finished picture. Please do not send original artwork with your submission." Do not call. Reports on mss in 10-12 weeks. Publishes a book 18-24 months after acceptance. Will consider simultaneous submissions.

Illustration: Reviews ms/illustration packages from artists. Illustrations only: Query with samples, résumé.

Terms: Pays authors royalty. Offers advances. Pays illustrators advance and royalty or by the project. Sends galleys to authors. Book catalog available for 9×12 SAE with $2.20 postage; ms guidelines available for SASE.

Tips: "You need not have a literary agent to submit to us. We accept—and encourage—simultaneous submissions to other publishers and ask only that you so inform us. Because we receive thousands of submissions, we do not keep a record of the manuscripts we receive and cannot check the status of your manuscript. We do try to respond within ten weeks' time."

GROLIER CHILDREN'S PUBLISHING, Sherman Turnpike, Danbury CT 06816. (203)797-3500. Book publisher. Creative Director: M. Fiddle. Publishes more than 100 titles/year. 5% of books by first-time authors. Publishes informational (nonfiction) for K-6; picture books for young readers K-3.

Fiction: Picture books, young readers: adventure, animal, concept, contemporary, folktales, multicultural. Middle readers: contemporary, hi-lo, humor, multicultural. Young adults: hi-lo. Does not want to see young adult fiction, romance or science fiction. Average word length: picture book—300; middle readers—4,000.

Nonfiction: Picture books: arts/crafts, biography, concept, geography, hi-lo, history, hobbies, how-to, multicultural, nature/environment, science, special needs. Young readers: animal, arts/crafts, biography, careers, concept, geography, health, hi-lo, history, hobbies, multicultural, nature/environment, science, social issues, sports. Middle readers: hi-lo, history, multicultural, reference, science. Average word length: picture books—400; young readers—2,000; middle readers—8,000; young adult—12,000.

How to Contact/Writers: Fiction: Query; submit outline/synopsis or submit outline/synopsis and 1 sample chapter. Nonfiction: Query; submit outline/synopsis. SASE required for response. Reports in 2-3 months. Publishes book 18 months after acceptance. Will consider simultaneous submissions.

Illustration: Works with 14 illustrators/year. Uses color artwork only. Reviews ms/illustration packages from artists. Illustrations only: Query with samples or arrange personal portfolio review. Contact: V. Fischman, art director. Reports back only if interested. Samples returned with SASE. Samples filed. Originals not returned.

Photography: Purchases photos from freelancers. Contact: Photo Editor. Buys stock and assigns work. Model/property releases and captions required. Uses color and b&w prints; 2¼×2¼, 35mm transparencies. Photographers should send cover letter and stock photo list.

Terms: Pays authors royalty of 5% based on net or work purchased outright (range: $500-1,000). Offers average advances of $1,000. Pays illustrators by the project (range: $1,800-3,500). Photographers paid per photo (range: $50-100). Sends galleys to authors; dummies to illustrators. Book catalog available for SAE; ms guidelines for SASE.

Tips: "Never write down to reader; keep language lively."

‡GROSSET & DUNLAP, INC., 200 Madison Ave., New York NY 10016. (212)951-8700. Imprint of The Putnam & Grosset Group, a division of Penguin Putnam Inc. Book publisher. Estab. 1898. Editor-in-chief: Judy Donnelly. **Manuscript Acquisitions:** Jane O'Connor, president. **Art Acquisitions:** Ronnie Ann Herman. Publishes 80-90 titles/year: picture books; young readers; middle readers; young adult series; board books; novelty books and easy chapter books. 5% of books by first-time authors; 50% of books from agented authors. Publishes fiction and nonfiction for mass market; novelty and board books.

Fiction: Young readers: adventure, animal, concept, history, humor, nature/environment, sports. Most categories will be considered. "We publish series fiction, but not original novels in the young adult category." Sees too many trade picture books. Recently published *Ice Stars*, by S.A. Kramer, illustrations by Jim Campbell (grades 2-3, All Aboard Reading); *Pen Pals*, written and illustrated by Joan Holub.

Nonfiction: Picture books: animal, concept, nature/environment, science. Young readers: activity books, animal, arts/crafts, biography, concept, history, sports. Recently published *Storm Chasers*, by Gail Herman, illustrated by Larry Singer (grades 2-3, All Aboard Reading); *Wing It*, by Steve Tomecek, illustrated by Davy Jones (boomerang and book).

How to Contact/Writers: Fiction/Nonfiction: Query. Reports in 2-4 weeks on queries; 1-2 months on mss. Publishes book 1-2 years after acceptance. Will consider simultaneous submissions.

Illustrations: Works with 50 illustrators/year. Reviews ms/illustration packages from artists. Query. Illustrations only: Query with samples; provide résumé, promo sheet, portfolio, slides, tearsheets. "Portfolio drop-off on Wednesdays." Reports only if interested. Original artwork returned at job's completion.

Photography: Buys photos from freelancers. Uses photos of babies and toddlers, interactive children, animals— full color. Publishes photo concept books. Uses color prints; 35mm, 2¼ × 2¼, 4 × 5 and 8 × 10 transparencies. To contact, photographers should query with samples, send unsolicited photos by mail, submit portfolio, provide promotional literature or tearsheets to be kept on file.

Terms: Pays authors royalty or by outright purchase. Offers advances. Pays illustrators by the project or by royalty. Photographers paid by the project. Book catalog available for 9 × 12 SASE. Ms guidelines available for SASE.

Tips: "We are interested in early chapter books and middle grade series ideas."

★GRYPHON HOUSE, P.O. Box 207, Beltsville MD 20704-0207. (301)595-9500. Fax: (301)595-0051. E-mail: kathyc@ghbooks.com. Book publisher. **Acquisitions:** Kathy Charner, editor-in-chief.

Nonfiction: Parent and teacher resource books—activity books, textbooks. Recently published *500 Five Minute Games*, by Jackie Silberg; *MathArts*, by MaryAnn Kohl and Cindy Gainer; *Never, EVER, Serve Sugary Snacks on Rainy Days*, by Shirley Raines; and *The Complete Learning Center Book*, by Rebecca Isbell.

How to Contact/Writers: Query. Submit outline/synopsis and 2 sample chapters. Reports on queries/mss in 3 months. Publishes a book 18 months after acceptance. Will consider simultaneous submissions, electronic submissions via disk or modem.

Illustration: Works with 3-4 illustrators/year. Uses b&w artwork only. Reviews ms/illustration packages from artists. Submit query letter with table of contents, introduction and sample chapters. Illustrations only: Query with samples, promo sheet. Reports back in 2 months. Samples returned with SASE; samples filed.

Photography: Buys photos from freelancers. Buys stock and assigns work. Submit cover letter, published samples, stock photo list.

Terms: Pays authors royalty based on wholesale price. Offers advances. Pays illustrators by the project. Pay photographers by the project or per photo. Sends galleys to authors. Original artwork returned at job's completion. Book catalog and ms guidelines available for SASE.

Tips: "Send a SASE for our catalog and manuscript guidelines. Look at our books, then submit proposals that complement the books we already publish or supplement our existing books. We are looking for books of creative, participatory learning experiences that have a common conceptual theme to tie them together. The books should be on subjects that teachers want to do on a daily basis in the classroom. If a book caters to a particular market in addition to teachers, that would be a plus."

‡GULLIVER BOOKS, 15 E. 26th St., New York NY 10010. (212)592-1000. Imprint of Harcourt Brace & Co. **Acquisitions:** Elizabeth Van Doren, editorial director. Publishes 25 titles/year.

• Gulliver only accepts manuscripts submitted by agents or previously published authors.

Fiction: Emphasis on picture books and historical fiction; also publishes middle grade and young adult.

Nonfiction: Publishes nonfiction.

How to Contact/Writers: Fiction/Nonfiction: Query.

HACHAI PUBLISHING, 156 Chester Ave., Brooklyn NY 11218. (718)633-0100. Fax: (718)633-0103. Book publisher. **Manuscript Acquisitions:** Devorah Leah Rosenfeld, submissions editor. Publishes 3 picture books/

year; 3 young readers/year; and 1 middle reader/year. 75% of books published by first-time authors. "All books have spiritual/religious themes, specifically traditional Jewish content. We're seeking books about morals and values; the Jewish experience in current and Biblical times; and Jewish observance, Sabbath and holidays."

Fiction: Picture books and young readers: contemporary, history, religion. Middle readers: adventure, contemporary, problem novels, religion. Does not want to see animal stories, romance, problem novels depicting drug use or violence. Recently published *As Big As An Egg*, by Rachel Sandman, illustrated by Chana Zakashanskaya (ages 3-6, picture book); and *Red, Blue, and Yellow Yarn*, by Miriam Kosman, illustrated by Valeri Gorbachev (ages 3-6, picture book).

Nonfiction: Published *My Jewish ABC's*, by Draizy Zelcer, illustrated by Patti Nemeroff (ages 3-6, picture book).

How to Contact/Wrtiers: Fiction/Nonfiction: Submit complete ms.

Illustration: Works with 4 illustrators/year. Uses primary color artwork, some b&w illustration. Reviews ms/illustration packages from authors. Submit ms with 1 piece of final art. Contact: Devorah Leah Rosenfeld, submissions editor. Illustrations only: Query with samples; arrange personal portfolio review. Reports in 2 weeks. Samples returned with SASE.

Terms: Work purchased outright from authors for $1,000. Pays illustrators by the project (range: 2,000). Book catalog, ms/artist's guidelines available for SASE.

Tips: "Write a story that incorporates a moral . . . not a preachy morality tale. Originality is the key. We feel Hachai is going to appeal to a wider readership as parents become more interested in positive values for their children."

HARCOURT BRACE & CO., 525 B St., Suite 1900, San Diego CA 92101-4495. (619)231-6616. Children's Books Division includes: Harcourt Brace Children's Books (Allyn Johnston, editorial director), Gulliver Books (Elizabeth Van Doren, editorial director), Voyager Paperbacks, Odyssey Paperbacks, Browndeer Press (Linda Zuckerman, editorial director), Silver Whistle Books (Paula Wiseman, editorial director) and Red Wagon Books. Book publisher. **Manuscript Acquisitions:** Manuscript Submissions. **Art Acquisitions:** Art Director. Publishes 50 picture books/year; 5-10 middle reader titles/year; 10 young adult titles/year. 20% of books by first-time authors; 50% of books from agented writers. "Harcourt Brace & Company owns some of the world's most prestigious publishing imprints—which distinguish quality products for the juvenile, educational and trade markets worldwide."

● The staff of Harcourt Brace's children's book department is no longer accepting unsolicited manuscripts. Only query letters from previously published authors and manuscripts submitted by agents will be considered.

Fiction: All levels: Considers all categories. Average word length: picture books—"varies greatly"; middle readers—20,000-50,000; young adults—35,000-65,000.

Nonfiction: All levels: Considers all categories. Average word length: picture books—"varies greatly"; middle readers—20,000-50,000; young adults—35,000-65,000.

How to Contact/Writers: Fiction: Query or submit outline/synopsis. Nonfiction: Submit outline/synopsis.

Illustration: Reviews ms/illustration packages from artists. "For picture books ms—complete ms acceptable. Longer books—outline and 2-4 sample chapters." Send one sample of art; no original art with dummy. Illustrations only: Submit résumé, tearsheets, color photocopies, color stats all accepted. "Please DO NOT send original artwork or transparencies. Include SASE for return, please." Reports on art samples in 6-10 weeks.

Photography: Works on assignment only.

Terms: Pays authors and illustrators advance and royalty based on retail price. Pays photographers by the project. Sends galleys to authors; dummies to illustrators. Original artwork returned at job's completion. Book catalog available for 8 × 10 SAE and 4 first-class stamps; all imprints included in a single catalog. Ms/artist's guidelines for business-size SASE.

Tips: "Become acquainted with Harcourt Brace's books in particular if you are interested in submitting proposals to us."

‡HARPERACTIVE, 10 E. 53rd. St., New York NY 10022-5299. Tel: (212)207-7044. Fax: (212)207-7192. Website: http://www.harpercollins.com. Imprint of HarperCollins Children's Books. Book publisher. Estab. 1997. **Acquisitions:** Hope Innelli, editorial director. "Targeting the mass market reader, HarperActive is dedicated to bringing kids the kind of books they read when they just want to have fun. We focus primarily on licensed properties in film, television, music and sports."

● HarperActive welcomes samples from authors with experience in writing novelizations or other tie-in books.

How to Contact/Writers: Query; only send material suited for mass market distribution.

Terms: Because HarperActive focuses on licensed products, the majority of contracts are work-for-hire.

HARPERCOLLINS CHILDREN'S BOOKS, 10 E. 53rd. St., New York NY 10022-5299. (212)207-7044. Fax: (212)207-7192. Website: http://www.harpercollins.com. Book publisher. Editor-in-Chief: Kate Morgan Jackson. **Art Acquisitions:** Harriett Barton, art director. Imprints: Laura Geringer Books, Michael diCapua Books, Joanna Cotler Books, HarperActive, HarperFestival.

● HarperCollins is not accepting unsolicited manuscripts not addressed to a specific editor.

Fiction: Picture books: adventure, animal, anthology, concept, contemporary, fantasy, folktales, hi-lo, history, multicultural, nature/environment, poetry, religion. Middle readers: adventure, hi-lo, history, poetry, suspense/mystery. Young adults/teens: fantasy, science fiction, suspense/mystery. All levels: multicultural. "Artists with diverse backgrounds and settings shown in their work."

Nonfiction: Picture books: animal, arts/crafts, biography, geography, multicultural, nature/environment. Middle readers: how-to.

Illustration: Works with 100 illustrators/year. Reports only if interested. Samples returned with SASE; samples filed only if interested.

How to Contact/Writers: Nonfiction: Query.

Terms: Manuscript and art guidelines available for SASE.

HARVEST HOUSE PUBLISHERS, 1075 Arrowsmith, Eugene OR 97402-9197. (541)343-0123. Fax: (541)342-6410. Book publisher. **Manuscript Acquisitions:** Teresa Burke. **Art Acquisitions:** Design Coordinator. Publishes 1-2 picture books/year; 2 young reader titles/year; and 2 young adult titles/year. 2-5% of books by first-time authors. Books follow a Christian theme.

• Harvest House no longer accepts unsolicited children's manuscripts.

Illustration: Works with 2-3 illustrators/year. Reviews ms/illustration packages from artists. Submit 3 chapters of ms with copies (do not send originals) of art and any approximate rough sketches. Illustrations only: Send résumé, tearsheets. Reports on art samples in 3 weeks. Samples returned with SASE; samples filed.

Terms: Pays authors in royalties of 10-15%. Average advance payment: "negotiable." Pays illustrator: "Sometimes by project." Sends galleys to authors; sometimes sends dummies to illustrators. SASE for book catalog.

★HAYES SCHOOL PUBLISHING CO. INC., 321 Pennwood Ave., Wilkinsburg PA 15221. (412)371-2373. Fax: (412)371-6408. **Acquisitions:** Mr. Clair N. Hayes. Estab. 1940. Produces folders, workbooks, stickers, certificates. Wants to see supplementary teaching aids for grades K-12. Interested in all subject areas. Will consider simultaneous and electronic submissions.

How to Contact/Writers: Query with description or complete ms. Reports in 3-4 weeks. SASE for return of submissions.

Terms: Work purchased outright. Purchases all rights.

HENDRICK-LONG PUBLISHING COMPANY, P.O. Box 25123, Dallas TX 75225. Book publisher. Estab. 1969. **Acquisitions:** Joann Long, vice president. Publishes 1 picture book/year; 4 young reader titles/year; 4 middle reader titles/year. 20% of books by first-time authors.

Fiction: Middle readers: history books on Texas and the Southwest. No fantasy or poetry. Recently published *The Confederate Fiddle*, by Jeanne Williams; *I Know an Old Texan*, by Donna Cooner, illustrated by Hollis Rife.

Nonfiction: Middle, young adults: history books on Texas and the Southwest, biography, multicultural. Recently published *Texas Granite*, by Mary Hoatman.

How to Contact/Writers: Fiction/Nonfiction: Query with outline/synopsis and sample chapter. Reports on queries in 2 weeks; mss in 2 months. Publishes a book 18 months after acceptance. No simultaneous submissions. Include SASE.

Illustration: Works with 3-4 illustrators/year. Uses primarily b&w interior artwork; color covers only. Illustrations only: Query first. Submit résumé or promotional literature or photocopies or tearsheets—no original work sent unsolicited. Material kept on file. No reply sent.

Terms: Pays authors in royalty based on selling price. Advances vary. Pays illustrators by the project or royalty. Sends galleys to authors; dummies to illustrators. Ms guidelines for 1 first-class stamp and #10 SAE.

Tips "Material **must** pertain to Texas or the Southwest. Check all facts about historical firgures and events in both fiction and nonfiction. Be accurate."

★HIGHSMITH PRESS, P.O. Box 800, Ft. Atkinson WI 53538-0800. (414)563-9571. (414)563-4801. E-mail: hpress@highsmith.com. Website: http://www.hpress.highsmith.com. Imprints: Highsmith Press, Alleyside Press. Book publisher. **Acquisitions:** Donald J. Sager, publisher. Highsmith Press publishes library reference and professional books. Alleyside Press publishes reading activity materials, storytelling aids, and skills instructional resources for youth PreK-12 grade.

Nonfiction: All levels: reading activity books, library skills, reference, study skills. Multicultural needs include storytelling resources. Average length: 48-120 pages. Published *Research to Write*, by Maity Schrecengost (ages 8-11, study skills); *An Alphabet of Books, Literature Based Activities for Schools and Libraries*, by Robin Davis (ages 3-7, activity book); and *World Guide to Historical Fiction for Young Adults*, by Lee Gordon (ages 11-17, reference).

How to Contact/Writers: Query or submit complete ms or submit outline/synopsis. Reports on queries in 1 month; mss in 6-8 weeks. Publishes a book 6 months after acceptance. Will consider simultaneous submissions.

Illustration: Works with varying number of illustrators/year. Reports in 1 month. Samples returned with SASE; samples not filed.

Terms: Pays authors royalty of 10-12% based on wholesale price. Pays illustrators by the project; varies considerably. Offers advances. Sends galleys to authors. Book catalog available for 9 × 12 SAE and 2 first-class stamps; ms guidelines available for SASE.

Tips: "Review our catalog and ms guidelines to see what we publish. Our complete catalog and current guidelines can be found at our website on the Internet (address above), as well as a list of projects for which we are seeking authors. It's getting to be a tougher market, with more electronic versions, especially reference."

‡✦**HINTERLAND PUBLISHERS**, Box 198, Sandy Hook, Manitoba R0C 2W0 Canada. (204)389-3842. Fax: (204)339-3635. E-mail: hinterland@gatewest.net. Website: http://www.hinterland.mb.ca. Book publisher. **Acquisitions:** Norma Norton, managing director. Publishes 4 picture books/year. 100% of books by first-time authors.
Fiction: Picture books: adventure, contemporary, multicultural. For multicultural fiction, needs First Nation's contemporary (realistic) fiction. Does not want to see material on legends. Average word length: picture books—1,000-2,000. Recently published *The Moons of Goose Island*, written by Don K. Philpot, illustrated by Margaret Hessian (ages 6-12, contemporary realistic fiction).
How to Contact/Writers: Fiction: Query or submit outline/synopsis. Reports on queries in 6 weeks; ms in 2 months. Publishes a book 18 months after acceptance. Will consider simultaneous submissions.
Illustration: Works with 2 illustrators/year. Reviews ms/illustration packages from artists. Query or send ms with dummy. Illustrations only: Query with samples; send résumé and portfolio to be kept on file. Reports in 6 weeks. Samples returned with SASE.
Terms: Pays authors royalty of 10-25% based on retail price. Pays illustrators royalty of 10-25% based on retail price. Sends galleys to authors; dummies to illustrators. Originals returned to artist at job's completion.
Tips: "Quality is a top consideration at Hinterland Publishers. Stories must be fresh, thoughtful and imaginative. Stylistically, a writer must demonstrate an excellent command on the English language. Stories told in a literary style will receive special attention."

HOLIDAY HOUSE INC., 425 Madison Ave., New York NY 10017. (212)688-0085. Fax: (212)421-6134. Book publisher. Estab. 1935. Vice President/Editor-in-Chief: Regina Griffin. **Acquisitions:** Allison Cunningham, assistant editor. Publishes 30 picture books/year; 3 young reader titles/year; 10 middle reader titles/year; and 3 young adult titles/year. 20% of books by first-time authors; 10% from agented writers.
Fiction: All levels: adventure, contemporary, ghost, historical, humor, school. Picture books, middle readers, young adults: animal, humor. Recently published *The Magic Dreidels*, by Eric A. Kimmel, illustrated by Katya Krenina; *The Golem*, by Barbara Rogasky, illustrated by Trina Schart Hyman; and *The Life and Death of Crazy Horse*, by Russell Freedman, photos by Amos Bad Heart Bull.
Nonfiction: All levels: animal, biography, concept, contemporary, geography, historical, math, nature/environment, science, social studies.
How to Contact/Writers: Send queries and mss to Allison Cunningham. Reports on queries in 3 weeks; mss in 8-10 weeks. Manuscripts returned only with SASE.
Illustration: Works with 15 illustrators/year. Reviews ms illustration packages from artists. Send ms with dummy. Reports back only if interested. Samples returned with SASE or filed.
Terms: Pays authors and illustrators an advance against royalties. Originals returned at job's completion. Book catalog, ms/artist's guidelines available for a SASE.

HENRY HOLT & CO., INC., 115 W. 18th St., New York NY 10011. (212)886-9200. Book publisher. Imprint: Edge Books. **Manuscript Acquisitions:** Laura Godwin, editor-in-chief/associate publisher of Books for Young Readers dept.; Marc Aronson, senior editor; Christy Ottaviano, editor. **Art Acquisitions:** Martha Rago, art director. Publishes 20-40 picture books/year; 4-6 young reader titles/year; 10-15 middle reader titles/year; 10-15 young adult titles/year. 5% of books by first-time authors; 40% of books from agented writers.
  ● See First Books for an interview with Henry Holt author Helen Kim. Her book, *The Long Season of Rain*, was published under Holt's Edge Books young adult imprint.
Fiction: Picture books: concept, history, humor, multicultural, religion, sports. Middle readers: adventure, contemporary, fantasy, history, humor, multicultural, religion, sports, suspense/mystery. Young adults: contemporary, fantasy, history, multicultural, nature/environment, sports.
How to Contact/Writers: Fiction/Nonfiction: Submit complete ms. Reports on queries/mss in 4-6 months. Will consider simultaneous submissions.
Illustration: Reviews ms/illustration packages from artists. Random samples OK. Illustrations only: Submit tearsheets, slides. Do *not* send originals. Reports on art samples in 1-3 months. Samples returned with SASE; samples filed. If accepted, original artwork returned at job's completion.
Terms: Pays authors/illustrators advance and royalty based on retail price. Sends galleys to authors; proofs to illustrators.

HOUGHTON MIFFLIN CO., Children's Trade Books, 222 Berkeley St., Boston MA 02116. (617)351-5000. Fax: (617)351-1111. Website: http://www.hmco.com. Book publisher. Vice President and Publisher: Anita Silvey. **Manuscript Aquisitions:** Sarah Hines-Stephens, submissions coordinator; Matilda Welter, Ann Rider, Margaret Raymo, editors; Amy Thrall, associate editor; Eden Edwards, Sandpiper Paperbooks editor; Walter Lorraine, Walter Lorraine Books, editor. **Art Acquisitions:** Bob Kosturko, art director. Averages 80 titles/year. Publishes hardcover originals and trade paperback reprints and originals. "Houghton Mifflin gives shape to ideas that educate, inform, and above all, delight."

Fiction: All levels: all categories except religion. "We do not rule out any theme, though we do not publish specifically religious material." *Burnt Toast on Davenport Street*, by Tim Egan (ages 4-8, picture book); *Woman in the Wall*, by Patrice Kindl (ages 10-14, novel); and *Three Stories You Can Read to Your Cat*, by Sara Swan Miller, illustrated by True Kelley (ages 7-10, early readers).

Nonfiction: All levels: all categories except religion. Recently published *Animal Dads*, by Sneed B. Collard III, illustrated by Steve Jenkins (ages 4-8, picture book); *Secrets of Animal Flight*, by Nic Bishop (ages 4-8, photo); *Life and Times of the Peanut*, by Charles Micucci (ages 5-8, illustrated).

How to Contact/Writers: Fiction: Submit complete ms. Nonfiction: Submit outline/synopsis and sample chapters. Reports on queries in 2-6 weeks; on mss in 4-10 weeks.

Illustration: Works with 60 illustrators/year. Reviews ms/illustration packages from artists. Ms/illustration packages or illustrations only: Query with samples (colored photocopies are fine); provide tearsheets. Reports in 6-8 weeks. Samples returned with SASE; samples filed if of interest.

Terms: Pays standard royalty based on retail price; offers advance. Illustrators paid by the project and royalty. Ms and artist's guidelines available for SASE.

‡HUCKLEBERRY PRESS, 865 Main St., S. Glastonbury CT 06073. (888)HUCK-FIN. E-mail: huckleberry.press@snet.press. Imprints: Running Start Readers. Book publisher. Estab. 1996. **Acquisitions:** Amanda Robinson, editor. Published 10 picture books/year; 25 young readers/year. 75% of books by first-time authors. Huckleberry Press is known for "its use of first time authors and illustrators, and very diverse styles within a series."

Fiction: Picture books, young readers, middle readers, young adult/teens: history, multicultural. Recently published *Pistachio Peak*, written by Noreen Wise, illustrated by Fred Rawles; *Andrea's Arm*, written by Matt Ryan, illustrated by Krys Denshick; and *Clickity-Clack*, written by Teresa Miller, illustrated by Scott Tao La Bossiere.

Nonfiction: Picture books, young readers: activity books, arts/crafts, biography, history, how-to. Middle readers, young adult/teens: arts/crafts, biography, history, how-to.

How to Contact/Writers: Fiction/Nonfiction: Query or submit outline/synopsis. Reports in queries/mss in 6 months. Publishes a book 1½ years after acceptance. Will consider simultaneous submissions.

Illustration: Works with 7 illustrators/year. Uses primarily b&w artwork. Illustrations only: Arrange personal portfolio review. Reports back only if interested. Samples not returned.

Photography: Works on assignment only. Uses b&w photos. Model/property releases required; captions required. Submit cover letter and published samples.

Terms: Work purchased outright. Pays illustrators by the project. Book catalog; ms, art and photo guidelines available for SASE.

Tips: "Children's authors—keep your story short (two typed pages). No alphabet books. Research your market. Send marketing suggestions for your own book."

★HUMANICS PUBLISHING GROUP, 1482 Mecaslin St. NW, Atlanta GA 30309. (404)874-2176. Fax: (404)874-1976. E-mail: humanics@mindspring.com. Book publisher. **Manuscript Acquisitions:** W. Arthur Bligh, Humanics Learning and Humanics Children's House. **Art Acquisitions:** Chris Korintus. Imprints: Humanics Limited, Humanics Learning (nonfiction), Humanics Children's House (fiction). Publishes 6 picture books/year. 50% of books by first-time authors. "Primary themes include self-esteem, and building the child's awareness of self and others through a multicultural, non-ethnocentric approach. For 20 years, Humanics has and will continue to provide the highest quality Teacher Resource/Activity Guides for young children."

Fiction: Picture books, young readers, middle readers: folktales, health, history, nature/environment, special needs. Multicultural needs include stories dealing with bridging cultural gaps. Average length: picture books—32 pages; young readers—32 pages. Published *The Adventure of Paz in the Land of Numbers*, by Miriam Bowden (English and Spanish counting, picture book); *Planet of the Dinosaurs*, by Dr. Barbara Carr (adventure, picture book); and *Cambio Chameleon*, by Mauro Magellan (self-esteem, picture book), all for ages pre-K to grade 3.

Nonfiction: Picture books, young readers, middle readers: all categories except religion. Average length: activity books—160 pages; young readers—160 pages.

How to Contact/Writers: Fiction: Query. Reports in 3 months. Will consider simultaneous submissions.

Illustration: Works with 4 illustrators/year. Reports on submissions in 3 months. Samples returned with SASE; samples filed. Original artwork returned at job's completion.

Terms: Pays authors 10% royalty based on wholesale price. Pays illustrators by the project ($200-1,200). Sends galleys to authors; dummies to illustrators. Book catalog available for 9×12 SAE and 2 first-class stamps; ms and art guidelines available for SASE.

Tips: "Please send query letters which detail your writing experience and goals, plus a product that is innovative and memorable."

‡□HUNTER HOUSE PUBLISHERS, P.O.Box 2914, Alameda CA 94501-0914. Fax: (510)865-4295. E-mail: editorial@hunterhouse.com. Book publisher. Independent book producer/packager. **Manuscript Acquisitions:** Belinda Breyer. **Art Acquisitions:** Wendy Low, art director. Publishes 0-1 titles for teenage women/year. 50% of books by first-time authors; 5% of books from agented writers.

Nonfiction: Picture books: activity books, social issues, music/dance, self-help. Middle readers: music/dance. Young adults: health, multicultural, self help (self esteem), social issues. "We emphasize that all our books try to take multicultural experiences and concerns into account. We would be interested in a social issues or self-help book on multicultural issues." Books are therapy/personal growth-oriented. Does *not* want to see books for young children; fiction; illustrated picture books; autobiography. Published *Turning Yourself Around: Self-Help Strategies for Troubled Teens*, by Kendall Johnson, Ph.D.; *Safe Dieting for Teens*, by Linda Ojeda, Ph.D.

How to Contact/Writers: Query; submit overview and chapter-by-chapter synopsis, sample chapters and statistics on your subject area, support organizations or networks and marketing ideas. "Testimonials from professionals or well-known authors are crucial." Reports on queries in 1 month; mss in 3 months. Publishes a book 18 months after acceptance. Will consider simultaneous submissions.

Illustration: Works with 1 illustrator/year. Reports back only if interested. Samples returned with SASE; samples filed.

Photography: Purchases photos from freelancers. Buys stock images.

Terms: Payment varies. Sends galleys to authors. Book catalog available for 9 × 12 SAE and 79¢ postage; ms guidelines for standard SAE and 1 first-class stamp.

Tips: Wants therapy/personal growth workbooks; teen books with solid, informative material. "We do few children's books. The ones we do are for a select, therapeutic audience. No fiction! Please, no fiction."

HUNTINGTON HOUSE PUBLISHERS, P.O. Box 53788, Lafayette LA 70505. (318)237-7049. Fax: (318)237-7060. Book publisher. **Acquisitions:** Mark Anthony, editor-in-chief. Publishes 6 young readers/year. 30% of books by first-time authors. "All books have spiritual/religious themes."

Fiction: Picture books, young readers, middle readers, young adults: all subjects. Does not want to see romance, nature/environment, multicultural. Average word length: picture books—12-50; young readers—100-300; middle readers—4,000-15,000; young adults/teens—10,000-40,000. Published *Greatest Star of All*, by Greg Gulley and David Watts (ages 9-11, adventure/religion).

Nonfiction: Picture books: animal, religion. Young readers, middle readers, young adults/teens: biography, history, religion. No nature/environment, multicultural. Average word length: picture books—12-50; young readers—100-300; middle readers—4,000-15,000; young adult/teens—10,000-40,000. Published *To Grow By Storybook Readers*, by Marie Le Doux and Janet Friend (preschool to age 8, textbook) *High on Adventure*, by Steve Arrington (young adult).

How to Contact/Writers: Fiction/Nonfiction: Query. Submit outline/synopsis, table of contents and proposal letter. One or two sample chapters are optional. Send SASE. Reports on queries/mss in 2-3 months. Publishes a book 8 months after acceptance. Will consider simultaneous submissions.

Illustration: Works with 2 illustrators/year. Reviews ms/illustration packages from artists. Query; submit ms with dummy. Reports in 1 month. Illustrations only: Query with samples; send résumé and client list. Reports in 2-3 months. Samples returned with SASE; samples filed. Original artwork returned at job's completion.

Photography: Buys photos from freelancers. Contact: Managing Editor. Buys stock images. Model/property releases required. Submit cover letter and résumé to be kept on file.

Terms: Contracts negotiable. Pays authors royalty of 10% based on wholesale price. Pays illustrators by the project (range: $50-250) or royalty of 10% based on wholesale price. Sends galleys to authors; dummies to illustrators. Book catalog available for #10 SAE and 2 first-class stamps; ms guidelines for SASE.

HYPERION BOOKS FOR CHILDREN, 114 Fifth Ave., New York NY 10011. (212)633-4400. Fax: (212)633-4833. An operating unit of Walt Disney Publishing Group, Inc. Book publisher. **Manuscript Acquisitions:** Lisa Holton, vice president/publisher. **Art Acquisitions:** Ellen Friedman, creative director. 30% of books by first-time authors. Publishes various categories. "The aim of Hyperion Books for Children is to create a dynamic children's program informed by Disney's creative vision, direct connection to children, and unparalleled marketing and distribution."

Fiction: Picture books, young readers, middle readers, young adults: adventure, animal, anthology (short stories), contemporary, fantasy, folktales, history, humor, multicultural, poetry, science fiction, sports, suspense/mystery. Middle readers, young adults: problem novels, romance. Recently published *The Sandy Bottom Orchestra*, by Garrison Keillor (ages 10 and up); McDuff series by Rosemary Wells (ages 2-5); and *Moosetache*, by Margie Palatini (ages 5-9).

Nonfiction: All trade subjects for all levels.

How to Contact/Writers: Only interested in agented material.

Illustration: Works with 100 illustrators/year. "Picture books are fully illustrated throughout. All others depend on individual project." Reviews ms/illustration packages from artists. Submit complete package. Illustrations only: Submit résumé, business card, promotional literature or tearsheets to be kept on file. Reports back only if interested. Original artwork returned at job's completion.

Photography: Works on assignment only. Publishes photo essays and photo concept books. Provide résumé, business card, promotional literature or tearsheets to be kept on file.

☐ **BOOK PACKAGERS/PRODUCERS** are marked with an open block.

Terms: Pays authors royalty based on retail price. Offers advances. Pays illustrators and photographers royalty based on retail price or a flat fee. Sends galleys to authors; dummies to illustrators. Book catalog available for 9×12 SAE and 3 first-class stamps; ms guidelines available for SASE.

✤**HYPERION PRESS LIMITED**, 300 Wales Ave., Winnipeg, Manitoba R2M 2S9 Canada. (204)256-9204. Fax: (204)255-7845. Book Publisher. **Acquisitions:** Dr. M. Tutiah, editor. Publishes authentic-based, retold folktales/legends for ages 4-9. "We are interested in a good story or well researched how-to material."
Fiction: Young readers, middle readers: folktales/legends. Recently published *The Wise Washerman*, by Deborah Froese, illustrated by Wang Kui; *The Cricket's Cage*, written and illustrated by Stefan Czernecki; and *The Peacock's Pride*, by Melissa Kajpust, illustrated by Jo'Anne Kelly.
How to Contact/Writers: Fiction: Query. Reports in 3 months.
Illustration: Reviews ms/illustration packages from artists. Ms/illustration packages and illustration only: Query. Samples returned with SASE.
Terms: Pays authors royalty. Pays illustrators by the project. Sends galleys to authors; dummies to illustrators. Book catalog available for 8 1/2×11 SAE and $2.00 postage (Canadian).

IDEALS CHILDREN'S BOOKS, an imprint of Hambleton-Hill Publishing, Inc., 1501 County Hospital Rd., Nashville TN 37218-2501. Book publisher. **Manuscript Acquisitions:** Suzanne Smith. **Art Acquisitions:** Tama Montgomery. Publishes 30-35 picture books/year; 3-4 young reader titles/year. 10-15% of books by first-time authors; 5-10% of books from agented writers.
● Ideals Children's Books only accepts manuscripts from members of the Society of Children's Book Writers and Illustrators (SCBWI), agented authors, and/or previously published book authors (submit with a list of writing credits). All others will be returned unread provided a SASE has been enclosed.
Fiction: Picture books, young readers: adventure, animal, concept, contemporary, fantasy, folktales, history, humor, multicultural, nature/environment, religion, sports, suspense/mystery. Average word length: picture books—200-1,200. Recently published *If I Were the Wind*, by Lezlie Evans, illustrated by Victoria Lisi (ages 5-8); *The Littlest Tree*, by Charles Tazewell, illustrated by Karen A. Jerome (all ages); and *Sea Maidens of Japan*, by Lili Bell, illustrated by Erin McGonigle Brammer (ages 5-9).
Nonfiction: Picture books, young readers: activity books, animal, arts and crafts, concept, cooking, history, hobbies, nature/environment, religion, science, sports. Does not want "ABC" and counting books of a general nature. "Only interested in them if they incorporate a unique approach or theme." Average word length: picture books—200-1,200; young readers—1,000-2,400. Recently published: *Why Did the Dinosaurs Disappear?* by Melvin and Gilda Berger, illustrated by Susan Harrison (ages 5-9, early reader); *Lunchbox Love Notes*, illustrated by Gary Johnson (ages 4-10, novelty); *The Illustrated Rules of In-Line Hockey*, by Terry Mayo, illustrated by Ned Butterfield (ages 6-9); and *Everyday Magic: The Blackstone Family Magic Shoppe*, by Bellamie Blackstone (ages 6 and up).
How to Contact/Writers: Fiction/Nonfiction: Prefers to see complete manuscript rather than queries. Reports in 3-6 months. Publishes a book 18-24 months after acceptance. Must include SASE for response.
Illustration: Works with 15-20 illustrators/year. Uses color artwork only. Editorial reviews ms/illustration packages from artists. Submit ms with 1 color photocopy of final art and remainder roughs. Illustrations only: Submit résumé and tearsheets showing variety of styles. Reports on art samples only if interested. "No original artwork, please." Samples returned with SASE, but prefers to keep them on file.
Terms: "All terms vary according to individual projects and authors/artists." Ms guidelines, and artist guidelines for business envelope and 1 first-class stamp.
Tips: "Searching for strong storylines with realistic characters as well as 'fun for all kids' kinds of stories. We are not interested in young adult romances, and have little interest in anthropomorphism." Illustrators: "Be flexible in contract terms—and be able to show as much final artwork as possible."

★**INCENTIVE PUBLICATIONS, INC.**, 3835 Cleghorn Ave., Nashville TN 37215-2532. (615)385-2934. Fax: (615)385-2967. E-mail: incentiv@nashville.net. Website: http://www.nashville.net/~incentiv. Estab. 1970. **Manuscript Acquisitions:** Anna Quinn, editor. **Art Acquisitions:** Marta Drayton, art director. Approximately 20% of books by first-time authors. "Incentive publishes developmentally appropriate instructional aids for tots to teens. We publish only teacher resource materials (for teachers of children from pre-school age through the middle grades). We publish *no fiction*."
Nonfiction: Picture books, young reader, middle reader: activity books, arts/craft, biography, geography, health, history, multicultural, nature/environment, science, special needs, supplemental educational materials. "Any manuscripts related to child development or with content-based activities and innovative strategies (K-8) will be reviewed for possible publication." Recently published Basic/Not Boring series, by Imogene Forte and Marjorie Frank (grades 6-8+, basic skills enrichment activity books); and A to Z Active Learning Series, by Imogene Forte and Sandra Schuer (middle grades, exploratory series).
How to Contact/Writers: Nonfiction: Submit outline/synopsis, sample chapters and SASE. Usually reports on queries/mss in 1 month. Reports on queries in 4-6 weeks; mss in 6-8 weeks. Typically publishes a book 18 months after acceptance. Will consider simultaneous submissions.
Illustration: Works with 4-6 illustrators/year. Reports back in 4-6 weeks if reply requested. Samples returned with SASE; samples filed.

Terms: Pays authors in royalties or work purchased outright. Pays illustrators by the project (range: $200-1,500). Pays photographers by the project. Original artwork not returned. Book catalog and ms and artist guidelines for SAE and $1.78 postage.

Tips: Writers: "We buy only teacher resource material. Please do not submit fiction! Incentive Publications looks for a whimsical, warm style of illustration that respects the integrity of the child. We work primarily with local artists, but not exclusively."

★**JALMAR PRESS**, 24426 S. Main St., Suite 702, Carson CA 90745. (310)816-3085. Fax: (310)816-3092. E-mail: blwjalmar@worldnet.att. Website: http://www.ierc.com. Subsidiary of B.L. Winch and Associates. Book publisher. Estab. 1971. **Acquisitions:** Bradley Winch, publisher; Jeanne Iler, publishing assistant. Publishes 3 picture books and young reader titles/year. 10% of books by first-time authors. Publishes self-esteem (curriculum content related), drug and alcohol abuse prevention, peaceful conflict resolution, stress management, whole-brain learning and accelerated learning. "Our goal is to help individuals become personally and socially responsible."
  ● Jalmar's catalog is found on their website.

Fiction: All levels: concept, self-esteem. Does not want to see "children's fiction books that have to do with cognitive learning (as opposed to affective learning) and autobiographical work." Published *Hilde Knows: Some-one Cries for the Children*, by Lisa Kent, illustrated by Mikki Macklen (child abuse); and *Scooter's Tail of Terror: A Fable of Addiction and Hope*, by Larry Shles (ages 5-105). "All submissions must teach (by metaphor) in the areas listed above."

Nonfiction: All levels: activity books, social issues, self-help. Does not want to see autobiographical work. Published *Esteem Builders Program*, by Michele Borba, illustrated by Bob Burchett (for school use—6 books, tapes, posters).

How to Contact/Writers: Only interested in agented material. Fiction/Nonfiction: Submit complete ms. Reports on queries in 1 month; mss in 6 months. Publishes a book 6-12 months after acceptance. Will consider simultaneous submissions.

Illustration: Works with 2 illustrators/year. Reports in 1 week. Samples returned with SASE; samples filed.

Terms: Pays authors 10-15% royalty based on wholesale price. Average advance varies. Pays illustrators by the project ($100-1,000). Pays photographers per photo ($200-800). Book catalog/ms guidelines free on request.

Tips: Wants "thoroughly researched, tested, practical, activity-oriented, curriculum content and grade/level correlated books on self-esteem, peaceful conflict resolution, stress management, drug and alcohol abuse prevention and whole brain learning and books bridging self-esteem to various 'trouble' areas, such as 'at risk,' 'dropout prevention,' etc. Illustrators—make artwork that can be reproduced."

‡**JEWISH LIGHTS PUBLISHING**, P.O. Box 237, Rt. 4, Sunset Farm Offices, Woodstock VT 05091. (802)457-4000. Fax: (802)457-4004. E-mail: editorial@longhillpartners.com. Website: http://www.jewishlights.com. A division of LongHill Partners, Inc. Book publisher. President: Stuart M. Matlins. **Acquisitions:** Jennifer Goneau, editorial assistant. Publishes 1 picture book/year; 1 young reader/year. 50% of books by first-time authors; 50% of books from agented authors. All books have spiritual/religious themes. "Jewish Lights publishes books for people of all faiths and all backgrounds who yearn for books that attract, engage, educate and spiritually inspire. Our authors are at the forefront of spiritual thought and deal with the quest for the self and for meaning in life by drawing on the Jewish wisdom tradition. Our books cover topics including history, spitituality, life cycle, children's, self-help, recovery, theology and philosophy. We do *not* publish autobiography, biography, fiction, *haggadot*, poetry or cookbooks. At this point we plan to do only one book for children annually, and that one will be for younger children (ages 4-10)."

Fiction: Picture books, young readers, middle readers: spirituality. "We are not interested in anything other than spirituality." Recently published: *A Prayer for the Earth: The Story of Naamdh, Noah's Wife*, by Sandy Eisenberg Sasso, illustrated by Bethanne Andersen (ages 4-9, picture book); and *But God Remembered: Stories of Women from Creation to the Promised Land*, by Sandy Eisenberg Sasso, illustrated by Bethanne Andersen (ages 8 and up).

Nonfiction: Picture book, young readers, middle readers: activity books, spirituality. Recently published *When a Grandparent Dies: A Kid's Own Remembering Workbook for Dealing with Shiva and the Year Beyond*, by Nechama Liss-Levinson, Ph.D. (ages 7-11); and *Sharing Blessings: Children's Stories for Exploring the Spirit of the Jewish Holidays*, written by Rabbi Michael Klayman and Rahel Musleah, illustrated by Mary O'Keefe Young (ages 6-10, picture book).

How to Contact/Writers: Fiction/Nonfiction: Query with outline/synopsis and 2 sample chapters; submit complete ms for picture books. Include SASE. Reports on queries/mss in 3-4 months. Publishes a book 6 months after acceptance. Will consider simultaneous submissions and previously published work.

Illustration: Works with 2 illustrators/year. Reviews ms/illustration packages from artists. Query. Illustrations only: Query with samples; provide résumé. Reports in 1 month. Samples returned with SASE; samples filed.

Terms: Pays authors royalty of 10% of revenue received. Offers advances. Pays illustrators by the project or royalty. Pays photographers by the project. Sends galleys to authors; dummies to illustrators. Book catalog available for 6½×9½ SAE and 59¢ postage; ms guidelines available for SASE.

Tips: "Explain in your cover letter why you're submitting your project to *us* in particular. (Make sure you know what we publish.)"

JEWISH PUBLICATION SOCIETY, 1930 Chestnut St., Philadelphia PA 19103. (215)564-5925. Fax: (215)564-6640. Editor-in-Chief: Dr. Ellen Frankel. Children's Editor: Bruce Black. Book publisher. All work must have Jewish content.
Fiction: Picture books, young readers, middle readers and young adults: adventure, contemporary, folktales, history, mystery, problem novels, religion, romance, sports. Recently published *Of Heroes, Hooks and Heirlooms*, by Faye Silton (ages 9 and up, middle reader).
Nonfiction: Picture books: biography, history, religion. Young readers, middle readers, young adults: biography, history, religion, sports. Recently published *God Sent A Rainbow and Other Bible Stories*, retold by Yona Zeldis, paintings by Malcah Zeldis, (ages 5 and up, picture book); and *The Kids' Catalog of Jewish Holidays*, by David A. Adler.
How to Contact/Writers: Fiction/Nonfiction: Query or submit outline/synopsis and sample chapters. Will consider simultaneous submissions (please advise). Reports on queries/mss in 6-8 weeks.
Illustration: Works with 3-4 illustrators/year. Will review ms/illustration packages. Query first or send 3 chapters of ms with 1 photocopy of final art, remainder roughs. Illustrations only: Query with photocopies; arrange a personal interview to show portfolio.
Terms: Pays authors and illustrators flat fees or royalties based on net. Reports back only if interested. Samples returned with SASE. Orginals returned at job's completion.
Tips: Writer/illustrator currently has best chance of selling picture books to this market.

BOB JONES UNIVERSITY PRESS/JOURNEY BOOKS FOR YOUNG READERS, 1500 Wade Hampton Blvd., Greenville SC 29614. (803)242-5100, ext. 4316. Website: http://www.bju.edu/press/freelnce.html. Book publisher. Estab. 1974. **Acquisitions:** Mrs. Gloria Repp, editor. Publishes 4 young reader titles/year; 4 middle reader titles/year; and 4 young adult titles/year. 50% of books by first-time authors. "Our books reflect the highest Christian standards of thought, feeling, and action, are uplifting or instructive and enhance moral purity. Themes advocating secular attitudes of rebellion or materialism are not acceptable. We are looking for books thar present a fully-developed main character, capable of dynamic changes, who experiences the central conflict of the plot, which should have plenty of action and not be didactic in tone."
Fiction: Young readers, middle readers, young adults: adventure, animal, concept, contemporary, easy-to-read, fantasy, history, multicultural, nature/environment, sports, spy/mystery. Average word length: young readers—10,000; middle readers—30,000; young adult/teens—50,000. Published *The Treasure of Pelican Cove*, by Milly Howard (grades 2-4, adventure story); and *Right Hand Man*, by Connie Williams (grades 5-8, contemporary).
Nonfiction: Young readers, middle readers: concept, history, multicultural. Young readers, middle readers, young adults: animal, biography, geography, nature/environment. Young adults/teens: biography, history, nature/environment. Average word length: young readers—10,000; middle readers—30,000; young adult/teens—50,000. Recently published *With Daring Faith*, by Becky Davis (grades 5-8, biography); and *Someday You'll Write*, by Elizabeth Yates (how-to).
How to Contact/Writers: Fiction: "Send the complete manuscript or the first five chapters and synopsis for these genres: Christian biography, modern realism, historical realism, regional realism and mystery/adventure. Query with a synopsis and five sample chapters for these genres: fantasy and science fiction (no extra-terrestrials). Do not send stories with magical elements. We do not publish these genres: romance, poetry and drama." Nonfiction: Query or submit complete manuscript or submit outline/synopsis and sample chapters. Reports on queries in 3 weeks; mss in 2 months. Publishes book "approximately one year" after acceptance. Will consider simultaneous and electronic submissions via IBM-compatible disk or modem.
Illustration: Works with 4 illustrators/year. Reports back only if interested. Samples returned with SASE; samples filed.
Terms: Pays authors royalty of 7-10% based on wholesale price. Or work purchased outright ($800-1,000). Pays illustrators by the project. Originals returned to artist at job's completion. Book catalog and ms guidelines free on request. "Check our web page for guidelines" (address above) or send SASE for book catalog and mss guidelines.
Tips: "Writers—give us original, well-developed characters in a suspenseful plot that has good moral tone. Artists—be good with both color and black & white illustrations. Be willing to take suggestions and follow specific directions. Today's books for children offer a wide variety of well-done nonfiction and rather shallow fiction. With the growing trend toward increased TV viewing, parents may be less interested in good books and less able to distinguish what is worthwhile. We are determined to continue to produce high-quality books for children."

JUST US BOOKS, INC., 356 Glenwood Ave., East Orange NJ 07017. (201)676-4345. Fax: (201)677-7570. Imprint of Afro-Bets Series. Book publisher; "for selected titles" book packager. Estab. 1988. Vice President/Publisher: Cheryl Willis Hudson. **Acquisitions:** Allyson Sherwood, submissions manager. Publishes 4-6 picture books/year; "projected 6" young reader/middle reader titles/year. 33% of books by first-time authors. Looking for "books that reflect a genuinely authentic African or African-American experience. We try to work with authors and illustrators who are from the culture itself."
• Just Us Books is not accepting new manuscripts until further notice.
Fiction: Middle readers: adventure, contemporary, easy-to-read, history, multicultural (African-American themes), romance, suspense/mystery. Average word length: "varies" per picture book; young reader—500-2,000;

middle reader—5,000. Wants African-American themes. Gets too many traditional African folktales. Recently published *Kid Caramel Private Investigator: Case of the Missing Arhk*.

Nonfiction: Middle readers, biography (African-American themes). Recently published *In Praise of Our Fathers and Our Mothers: A Black Family Treasury by Outstanding Authors and Artists*.

How to Contact/Writers: Fiction/Nonfiction: Query or submit outline/synopsis for proposed title. Reports on queries/ms in 3-4 months "or as soon as possible." Publishes a book 12-18 months after acceptance. Will consider simultaneous submissions (with prior notice).

Illustration: Works with 10 illustrators/year. Reviews ms/illustration packages from artists ("but prefers to review them separately"). "Query first." Illustrations only: Query with samples; send résumé, promo sheet, slides, client list, tearsheets; arrange personal portfolio review. Reports in 2-3 weeks. Samples returned with SASE; samples filed. Original artwork returned at job's completion "depending on project."

Photography: Purchases photos from freelancers. Buys stock and assigns work. Wants "African-American and multicultural themes—kids age 10-13 in school, home and social situations."

Terms: Pays authors royalty based on retail price or work purchased outright. Royalties based on retail price. Pays illustrators by the project or royalty based on retail price. Sends galleys to authors; dummies to illustrators. Book catalog for business-size SAE and 78¢ postage; ms/artist's guidelines for business-size SAE and 78¢ postage.

Tips: "Multicultural books are tops as far as trends go. There is a great need for diversity and authenticity here. They will continue to be in the forefront of children's book publishing until there is more balanced treatment on these themes industry wide." Writers: "Keep the subject matter fresh and lively. Avoid 'preachy' stories with stereotyped characters. Rely more on authentic stories with sensitive three-dimensional characters." Illustrators: "Submit 5-10 good, neat samples. Be willing to work with an art director for the type of illustration desired by a specific house and grow into larger projects."

‡KAEDEN BOOKS, P.O. Box 16190, Rocky River OH 44116. (216)356-0030. Fax: (216)356-5081. Book publisher. **Acquisitions:** Dennis Graves, vice president creative. Publishes 100 young readers/year. 50% of books by first-time authors.

Fiction: Young readers: adventure, animal, concept, contemporary, health, history, humor, multicultural, nature/environment, science fiction, sports, suspense/mystery. Average word length: picture books—20-150 words; young readers—20-150 words. Recently published *The Big Fish*, by Joe Yukish, illustated by Kate Salley Palmer; *Sammy Gets A Ride*, by Karen Evans and Kathleen Urmston, illustrated by Gloria Gedeon; and *Hats*, by Deborah Williams, illustrated by Dennis Graves.

Nonfiction: Young readers: activity books, animal, biography, careers, geography, health, history, hobbies, how-to, multicultural, music/dance, nature/environment, religion, science, sports. Multicultural needs include group and character diversity in stories and settings. Average word length: picture books—20-150 words; young readers—20-150 words.

How to Contact/Writers: Fiction/Nonfiction: Query or submit complete ms. Reports on queries/mss in several months. Will consider simultaneous submissions, electronic submissions via disk or modem.

Illustration: Works with 30 illustrators/year. Reviews ms/illustration packages from artists. Query. Submit art samples in color. Can be photocopies or tearsheets. Illustrations only: Query with samples. Send résumé, promo sheet, tearsheets, photocopies of work, preferably in color. Reports only if interested. Samples are filed.

Terms: Work purchased outright from authors. "Royalties to our previous authors." Offers negotiable advances. Pays illustrators by the project (range: $50-150/page). Book catalog available for 8½×11 SAE and 2 first-class stamps.

Tips: "Our books are written for emergent readers to be used in the educational teaching environment. A strong correlation between text and visual is necessary along with creative and colorful juvenile designs."

KAR-BEN COPIES, INC., 6800 Tildenwood Lane, Rockville MD 20852-4371. (301)984-8733. Fax: (301)881-9195. E-mail: karben@aol.com. Website: http://www.karben.com. Book publisher. Estab. 1975. **Manuscript Acquisitions:** Madeline Wikler, vice president. Publishes 5-10 picture books/year; 20% of books by first-time authors. All of Kar-Ben Copies' books are on Jewish themes for young children and families.

Fiction: Picture books, young readers: adventures, concept, contemporary, fantasy, folktales, history, humor, multicultural, religion, special needs, suspense/mystery; *must be* on a Jewish theme. Average word length: picture books—2,000. Published *Kingdom of Singing Birds*, by Miriam Aroner; *Northern Lights*, by Diana Cohen Conway; *Sammy Spider's First Hanukkah*, by Sylvia Rouss; and *Matzah Ball, A Passover Story*, by Mindy Avra Portnoy.

Nonfiction: Picture books, young readers: activity books, arts/crafts, biography, careers, concept, cooking, history, how-to, multicultural, religion, social issues, special needs; must be of Jewish interest. Average word length: picture books—2,000. Published *Jewish Holiday Games for Little Hands*, by Ruth Brinn; *Tell Me a Mitzvah*, by Danny Siegel; and *My First Jewish Word Book*, by Roz Schanzer.

How to Contact/Writers: Fiction/nonfiction: Submit complete ms. Reports on queries in 1 week; ms in 2 weeks. Publishes a book 1 year after acceptance. Will consider simultaneous submissions.

Illustration: Works with 6-10 illustrators/year. Prefers "four-color art to any medium that is scannable." Reviews ms/illustration packages from artists. Submit whole ms and sample of art (no originals). Illustrations only: Submit tearsheets, photocopies, promo sheet or anything representative that does *not* need to be returned. Enclose SASE for response. Reports on art samples in 1 week.

Terms: Pays authors in royalties of 6-8% based on net sales or work purchased outright (range: $500-2,000). Offers advance (average amount: $1,000). Pays illustrators royalty of 6-8% based on net sales or by the project (range: $500-3,000). Sends galleys to authors. Original artwork returned at job's completion. Book catalog free on request. Ms guidelines for 9×12 SAE and 2 first-class stamps.

Tips: Looks for "books for young children with Jewish interest and content, modern, non-sexist, not didactic. Fiction or nonfiction with a *Jewish* theme—can be serious or humorous, life cycle, Bible story, or holiday-related."

‡✺KEY PORTER BOOKS, 70 The Esplanade, Toronto, Ontario M5E 1R2 Canada. (416)862-7777. Fax: (416)862-2304. Book publisher. **Manuscript Acquisitions:** Barbara Berson; Michael Mouland; Susan Renouf, editor-in-chief. Publishes 4 picture books/year; and 4 young readers/year. 30% of books by first-time authors.
Fiction: Young readers, middle readers, young adult: animal, anthology, concept, health, multicultural, nature/environment, science fiction, special needs, sports, suspense/mystery. Does not want to see religious material. Average word length: picture books—1,500; young readers—5,000.
Nonfiction: Picture books: animal, history, nature/environment, reference, science. Middle readers: animal, careers, history, nature/environment, reference, science and sports. Average word length: picture books—1,500; middle readers—15,000. Recently published *How on Earth: A Question and Answer Book About How Animals & Plants Live*, by Ron Orenstein (ages 8-10, nature/environment); *Super Skaters: World Figure Skating Stars*, by Steve Milton (ages 8 and up, sports); and *Underwater Explorers*, by Arlene Moscovitch (ages 9-11, career).
How to Contact/Writers: Only interested in agented material; no unsolicited manuscripts.
Photography: Buys photos from freelancers. Buys stock and assigns work. Captions required. Uses 35mm transparencies. Submit cover letter, résumé, duplicate slides, stock photo list.
Terms: Pays authors royalty of 4-10% based on retail price. Offers advances (average amount: $4,000-20,000, Canadian). Pays illustrators by the project (range: $4,000-20,000, Canadian). Pays photographers by the project (range: $4,000-10,000, Canadian); per photo (range: $50-250, Canadian); royalty (range: 4-10% of retail price). Sends galleys to authors; dummies to illustrators. Book catalog available for 8½×11 SAE and 2 first-class stamps.

*KINGFISHER BOOKS, Imprint of Larousse Kingfisher Chabers, 95 Madison Ave., New York NY 10016. (212)686-1060. Fax: (212)686-1060. Publishes hardcover and trade paperback fiction and nonfiction for preschool through age 14, including novelty, picture books, reference, activity books, and general series and story collections. Publishes 80 titles/year.
• Kingfisher Books is not currently accepting unsolicited manuscripts.

ALFRED A. KNOPF BOOKS FOR YOUNG READERS, 29th Floor, 201 E. 50th St., New York NY 10022. (212)751-2600. Imprint of Random House, Inc. Book publisher. Estab. 1915. Publishing Director: Simon Boughton. Publisher, Apple Soup Books: Anne Schwartz. **Acquisitions:** send mss to Knopf Editorial Department. 90% of books published through agents. "Knopf is known for high quality literary fiction, and is willing to take risks with writing styles. It publishes for children ages 5 and up."
• Knopf only accepts manuscripts from agents and previously published authors.
Fiction: All levels: considers all categories.
Nonfiction: All levels: animal, arts/crafts, biography, history, how to, multicultural, music/dance, nature/environment, science, self help, sports.
How to Contact/Writers: Fiction/Nonfiction: "We read agented material immediately. We will read queries from nonagented authors and then, possibly, request ms." Publishes a book 12-18 months after acceptance. Will consider simultaneous submissions.
Illustration: Reviews ms/illustration packages from artists through agent only. Illustration only: Contact: Art Director. Reports back only if interested. Samples returned with SASE; samples filed.
Terms: Pays authors in royalties. Pays illustrators and photographers by the project or royalties. Original artwork returned at job's completion. Book catalog and ms guidelines free on request with SASE.

★□LAREDO PUBLISHING CO. INC., 8907 Wilshire Blvd., Beverly Hills CA 90211. (310)358-5288. Fax: (310)358-5282. E-mail: laredo@online2000.com. Book publisher. Vice President: Raquel Benatar. Publishes 5 picture books/year; and 15 young readers/year. 10% of books by first-time authors. Spanish language books only.
Fiction: Picture books: adventure, multicultural, suspense/mystery. Young readers: multicultural. Middle readers: multicultural, suspense/mystery. Published *Pregones*, by Alma Flor Ada (middle readers, personal experience in Spanish); *Pajaritos*, by Clarita Kohen (young readers, counting book in Spanish); and *El Conejoyel Coyote*, by Clarita Kohen (young readers, folktale in Spanish).
Nonfiction: All levels: textbooks. Young adults: careers, health. Published *Los Aztecas*, by Robert Nicholson (middle readers, history, culture and traditions of the Aztecs in Spanish); *Los Sioux*, by Robert Nicholson (middle readers; history, culture and traditions of the Sioux in Spanish); and *La Antigua China*, by Robert Nicholson (middle readers; history, culture and traditions of the Chinese in Spanish).
How to Contact/Writers: Fiction: Submit complete ms. Reports in 2 weeks. Publishes a book 1 year after

When she finally got an acceptance for *Brainteasers from Jewish Folklore*, Rosalind Charney Kaye almost couldn't believe it. She had been sending out the manuscript in various forms for over five years. "I never thought I'd say this, but now I'm glad it wasn't accepted earlier because it became a better book," says Kaye. She credits SCBWI conferences and networking groups for keeping her going through the rejection. "Each time I re-submitted the book, it got better. When I first sent it out I included only a few black & white drawings. Later, my skills improved and I painted color illustrations." When the stories were rejected by the book market, Kaye sold one-time rights to *Shofar*, a children's magazine, retaining rights to sell the book later. By the time Judith Groner, editor-in-chief of Kar-Ben Copies, Inc., received the manuscript it had gone through many revisions. "It's rare to receive such a manuscript over the transom," says Groner. "It was 'completely complete.' With just a few minor edits, the book was ready to go."

acceptance. Will consider simultaneous submissions.

Illustration: Works with 20-30 illustrators/year. Uses color artwork only. Reviews ms/illustration packages from artists. Illustrations only: Query with samples, promo sheet. Reports in 2 weeks. Samples returned with SASE. Originals not returned.

Terms: Pays authors royalty of 5-7% based on wholesale price or work purchased outright (range: $1,000-2,000). Offers advances (varies). Pays illustrators by the project (range: $250-500). Sends galleys to authors; dummies to illustrators. Book catalog available for SASE.

Tips: "We specialize in multicultural materials—all languages."

LEARNING TRIANGLE PRESS, Imprint of McGraw-Hill, 13313 Monterey Lane, Blue Ridge Summit PA 17214. Fax: (717)794-5344. Book publisher. Editor-in-Chief: Judith Terrill-Breuer. Publishes 20 young readers and middle readers/year. 10% of books by first-time authors.

Fiction: Picture books, young readers and middle readers: science and math/technology. Average word length: picture books—64; young readers and middle readers—96-122.

Nonfiction: Picture books, young readers and middle readers: nature/environment, science and math/technology.

How to Contact/Writers: Fiction/Nonfiction: Submit complete ms or outline/synopsis and 2 sample chapters. Publishes a book 1 year after acceptance.

LEE & LOW BOOKS, INC., 95 Madison Ave., New York NY 10016-7801. (212)779-4400. Book publisher. Estab. 1991. **Acquisitions:** Elizabeth Szabla, editor-in-chief. Publishes 8-10 picture books/year. 50% of books by first-time authors. Lee & Low publishes only books with multicultural themes.

- Lee & Low's title *The Palm of My Heart: Poetry by African American Children*, illustrated by Gregory Christie, received a 1997 Coretta Scott King Honor Award for illustration.

Fiction: Picture books: Concept. Picture books, young readers: anthology, contemporary, history, multicultural, poetry. "We are not considering folktales, animal stories and chapter books." Average word length: picture books—1,000-1,500 words. Recently published *Sam and the Lucky Money*, by Karen Chinn, illustrated by Cornelius Van Wright and Ying-Hwa Hu (ages 3-9, picture book); and *The Palm of My Heart*; *Poetry by African American Children*, edited by Davida Adedjouna, illustrated by Gregory Christie (ages 4 and up, picture book).

Nonfiction: Picture books: biography, history and multicultural. Average word length: picture books—1,500. Recently published *Dia's Story Cloth: The Hmong People's Journey of Freedom*, by Dia Cha, illustrated by Chue and Nhia Thao Cha (ages 6 and up, picture book).

How to Contact/Writers: Fiction/Nonfiction: Submit complete ms. Reports in 1-4 months. Publishes a book 12-24 months after acceptance. Will consider simultaneous submissions.

Illustration: Works with 8-10 illustrators/year. Uses color artwork only. Reviews ms/illustration packages from artists. Submit ms with dummy. Illustrations only: Query with samples, résumé, promo sheet and tearsheets. Samples returned with SASE; samples filed. Original artwork returned at job's completion.

Photography: Buys photos from freelancers. Works on assignment only. Model/property releases required. Submit cover letter, résumé, promo piece and book dummy.

Terms: Pays authors royalty based on retail price. Offers advances. Pays illustrators royalty based on retail price plus advance against royalty. Photographers paid royalty based on retail price plus advance against royalty. Sends galleys to authors; proofs to illustrators. Book catalog available for 9×12 SAE and $1.01 postage; ms and art guidelines available for SASE.

Tips: "We strongly urge writers to familiarize themselves with our list before submitting. Materials will only be returned with SASE."

‡LEGACY PRESS, Imprint of Rainbow Publishers, P.O. Box 261129, San Diego CA 92196. (619)271-7600. Book publisher. Estab. 1997. **Acquisitions:** Christy Allen, editor. Publishes 1 young reader/year; 1 middle reader/year; 1 young adult title/year. Published nonfiction, Bible-teaching books.

Nonfiction: Young readers, middle readers, young adults: reference, religion. Recently published *My Prayer Journal*, by Mary Davis (ages 10-12, journal); and *The Dickens Family Gospel*, by Robert Hanna (all ages, devotional).

How to Contact/Writers: Nonfiction: Submit outline/synopsis and 3-5 sample chapters. Reports on queries in 6 weeks; on ms in 3 months. Publishes a book 18 months after acceptance. Will consider simultaneous submissions; electronic submissions via disk or modem; previously published work.

Illustration: Works with 5 illustrators/year. Reviews ms/illustration packages from artists. Submit ms with 5-10 pieces of final art. Illustrations only: Query with samples to be kept on file. Reports in 6 weeks. Samples returned with SASE.

Terms: Pays authors royalty or work purchased outright. Offers advances. Pays illustrators by the project. Sends galley to authors. Book catalog available for business size SASE; ms guidelines for SASE.

Tips: "Get to know the Christian bookstore market. We are looking for innovative ways to teach and encourage children about the Christian life. No fiction, please."

LERNER PUBLICATIONS CO., 241 First Ave. N., Minneapolis MN 55401. (612)332-3344. Fax: (612)332-7615. Book publisher. Estab. 1959. **Manuscript Acquisitions:** Jennifer Martin, editor. **Art Acquisitions:** Art Director. Publishes 10-15 young readers/year; 50-70 middle readers/year; and 5 young adults/year. 20% of books

Humor promotes learning for young readers

Brian Cleary

I had a dilemma. I knew that the average white male lives to be about 74. Being a white male approaching my mid-30s and also being about as average as you can get, I became acutely aware that I was marching steadily toward the 50-yard line of my life. I called myself a writer, and, to some extent, I was. I'd written more than 100 gags for cartoons that were published in more than 600 newspapers worldwide. I'd had humor essays and features published in magazines locally and nationally. All of that was very nice, but I was looking to do something, well, huge.

By the time they were in their mid-30s, Bobby Kennedy was U.S. Attorney General, Castro had taken over Cuba, Jefferson authored the Declaration of Independence, Babe Ruth hit more than 500 home runs, and Mozart—well, when he was my age, he was dead. Talk about a wake-up call. It was time for me to do something important—perhaps even more important than those other guys. So I decided I would write books for children.

I picked up a copy of *Children's Writer's & Illustrator's Market.* Figuring it might take me six months or so to find a publisher and year or two to have my book illustrated, bound and distributed, that would put me around age 36, a full year on the sunny side of that half-way mark I mentioned above. I was now ready to set about the business of imparting both my wisdom and insights to the wee folks of the world. Now I had another dilemma. How would I become both wise and insightful in the next few weeks that I'd budgeted for writing?

If Henry Kissinger wanted to write a book, it would probably be about politics, history or diplomacy. Henry Ford could've written the definitive text on assembly line production or how automobiles changed America forever. But what would I write about?

I spent so many years in elementary school, I had my own parking space. As an adult, I've proven to be horrible at home repair, bad at baseball, crummy at cooking and lousy at landscaping. I'm sure my wife and kids could add to this list. I'm not just sub-par in one or two areas—I'm a true renaissance man when it comes to incompetence. I don't have an MBA, CPA or a Ph.D. . . . I'm just a guy with the IQ of a BLT who barely knows his ABCs, and is full of BS on topics from A to Z. Upon examining my myriad of shortcomings, it dawned on me: I'd write a book that was funny.

It's been said that writers are in a constant search for the truth. In my lifelong quest, I've learned two fundamental truths: 1) Humor promotes interest and helps develop intellect; and 2) When a kid says, "Smell my hand," it almost never smells like cinnamon.

Now, while I have no definitive research to back me up on number two, number one

INSIDER REPORT, *Cleary*

can be proven any number of ways. Kids enjoy laughing and are seldom bored when they find something funny. They also ask questions, often of adults, because they understand that the more they can comprehend a funny story or a joke, the more they'll enjoy it.

From my own experience, I remember reading a joke book when I was nine or ten years old, and there was a joke I didn't understand (imagine that). It went like this: A woman goes in to see her doctor and says, "Doc, I've got water on the knee, what should I do?" And the doctor says, "Wear pumps."

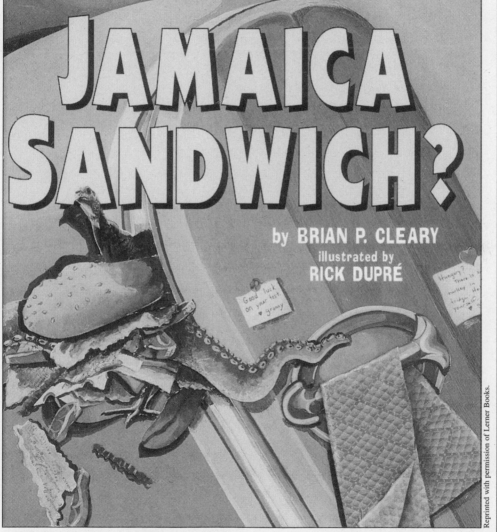

Brian Cleary has penned several books of puns including *Jamaica Sandwich*, which plays on the names of places in verses about food. Here's an example of Cleary's wit: "My brother drank a *Malta* day and dipped his fries in *Greece*. And though his weight was *Dublin*, his *Seoul* seemed quite at peace. He started using *Sweden* low and working off his belly. But then the *Laos* got *Vatican* when they opened that *New Delhi*." One of Cleary's seven books for Lerner, *Give Me Bach my Schubert*, won a Children's Choice Award in 1996.

It's a cute joke, but I didn't know the second meaning of the word "pump," so I asked my mom, who had two things to say to me. *One,* "A pump is a type of women's shoe" and *two,* "I don't care what the other kids are wearing, I'm not going to buy you a pair."

At any rate, knowing both meanings, I was able to get the joke. The same is true for the following little ditty that came from the same joke book. It had a couple of double meanings, and, even though I enjoyed it mostly for its comic value, I could feel my brain expand as I came to understand it fully. It's called "Little Willie."

Little Willie

Little Willie went to the mirror
And sucked the mercury off
Thinking in his childish error
It would cure the whooping cough.

At his funeral, his mother
Smartly said to Mrs. Brown,
"T'was a chilly day for Willie
When the mercury went down."

—Author Unknown

From this, I learned about history, chemistry, biology and English. That may seem like quite a claim, but let's run through it: History—mirrors, once upon a time were made with mercury. Chemistry—mercury is an element, and—apparently like many elements, should not be consumed in any large doses. Biology—'cause if you do that, you'll probably die. English—double meaning of the words, "When the mercury went down" can refer to him drinking it, or the thermometer's mercury dropping because the body has gotten colder. Note the use of internal rhyme with "T'was a chilly day for Willie."

Learning through humor is a fun way to teach and a fun way to learn, but the real reason I wrote a series of funny books is simple—I'm a funny guy. Here's my basic rule for writing, whether it's for children, adults, or puppies: If you're not an expert on Somalia, basket weaving, chess, origami or badminton before you sit down in front of the keyboard, you won't become one at that moment.

The moral? Play to your strengths. Write about stuff you know, or about which you're passionate. This isn't a job, it's a gig. And gigs are supposed to be fun. If writing becomes the same kind of tedious task that the rest of world busies themselves with, you may as well take a side job making widgets in a factory. The pay will be better, there's certainly more security, and you probably won't look at every single widget you make and think the world has never seen anything so loathsome.

Why not take that route? Because you're a writer, that's why. You are a link in a chain that reaches back centuries connecting Socrates, the apostles, Machiavelli, Jefferson, Jane Austen and Joan Collins.

If you've written a book, you've done the hard part. Now do the easy part and put it in front of publishers. When I did, I received so many rejection slips our mail carrier got a hernia. Then I had seven books accepted in the course of four months.

In the words of Shel Silverstein, "Anything can happen child, anything can be."
—Brian P. Cleary

by first-time authors; 5% of books from agented writers. "Most books are nonfiction for children, grades 3-9. "Our goal is to publish books that educate, stimulate and stretch the imagination, foster global awareness, encourage critical thinking and inform, inspire and entertain."

Fiction: Middle readers: adventure, contemporary, hi-lo, multicultural, nature/environment, sports, suspense/mystery. Young adults: hi-lo, multicultural, nature/environment, problem novels, sports, suspense/mystery. "Especially interested in books with ethnic characters." Published the Kerry Hill Casecrackers series, by Joan Warnor and Peggy Nicholson (grades 4-7, mystery).

Nonfiction: Middle readers, young adults: animal, arts/crafts, biography, careers, concept, cooking, geography, health, hi-lo, history, hobbies, how-to, multicultural, music/dance, nature/environment, sports, science/math, social issues, self-help, special needs. Multicultural material must contain authentic details. Does not want to see textbooks, workbooks, song books, audiotapes, puzzles, plays, religious material, books for teachers or parents, picture or alphabet books. Average word length: young readers—3,000; middle readers—7,000; young adults—12,000. Published *Frank Lloyd Wright: Maverick Architect*, by Brad Townsend (grades 5 and up, Lerner Biographies series); and *Shaquille O'Neal: Center of Attention*, by Brad Townsend (grades 4-9, Sports Achievers series).

How to Contact/Writers: Fiction: Submit outline/synopsis and sample chapters. Nonfiction: Query with outline/synopsis and sample chapters. Reports on queries in 3-4 weeks; mss in 3 months. Publishes a book 12-18 months after acceptance. Will consider simultaneous submissions.

Illustration: Works with 1-2 illustrators/year. "We tend to work mostly with local talent." Reviews ms/illustration packages from artists. Ms/illustration packages and illustrations only: Query with samples and résumé. Samples kept on file.

Photography: Contact: Photo Research Department. Buys stock and assigns work. Model/property releases required. Publishes photo essays. Photographers should query with samples.

Terms: Pays authors royalty or work purchased outright. Pays illustrators by the project. Sends galleys to authors. Book catalog available for 9×12 SAE and $1.90 postage; ms guidelines for 4×9 SAE and 1 first-class stamp.

Tips: Wants "straightforward, well-written nonfiction for children in grades 3-9 backed by solid current research or scholarship. Before you send your manuscript to us, you might first take a look at the kinds of books that our company publishes. We specialize in publishing high-quality educational books for children from second grade through high school. Avoid sex stereotypes (e.g., strong, aggressive, unemotional males/weak, submissive, emotional females) in your writing, as well as sexist language." (See also Carolrhoda Books, Inc.)

‡ARTHUR LEVINE BOOKS, 555 Broadway, New York NY 10012. (212)343-6100. Imprint of Scholastic Inc. Book publisher. Estab. 1997. **Acquisitions:** Arthur Levine, publisher. Publishes 8-10 titles/year. "Arthur Levine Books is looking for distinctive literature, for whatever's extraordinary. This is the first year for our list; we plan to focus on fiction. We are willing to work with first-time authors, with or without agent."

Fiction: Recently published: *When She Was Good*, by Norma Fox Mazer (young adult novel).

How to Contact/Writers: Query only. Include SASE.

Terms: Pays royalty on retail price. Advance varies. Book catalog for 9×12 SASE.

LION BOOKS, PUBLISHER, Suite B, 210 Nelson, Scarsdale NY 10583. (914)725-2280. Imprint of Sayre Ross Co. Book publisher. **Acquisitions:** Harriet Ross. Publishes 5 middle readers/year; 10 young adults/year. 50-70% of books by first-time authors. Publishes books "with ethnic and minority accents for young adults, including a variety of craft titles dealing with African and Asian concepts."

Nonfiction: Activity, art/crafts, biography, history, hobbies, how-to, multicultural. Average word length: young adult—30,000-50,000.

How to Contact/Writers: Query, submit complete ms. Reports on queries in 3 weeks; ms in 2 months.

Illustration: Reports in 2 weeks.

Terms: Work purchased outright (range: $500-5,000). Average advance: $1,000-2,500. Illustrators paid $500-1,500. Sends galleys to author. Book catalog free on request.

LITTLE, BROWN AND COMPANY, 34 Beacon St., Boston MA 02108. (617)227-0730. Book publisher. Estab. 1873. Editor-in-Chief: Maria Modugno. Art Director: Sheila Smallwood. **Art Acquisitions:** Dana Guthrie, art assistant. Publishes 5% picture books/year; 50% young reader titles/year; 30% middle reader titles/year; 15% young adult titles/year.

● Little, Brown accepts manuscripts only through agents.

Fiction: Picture books: adventure, animal, contemporary, fantasy, folktales, history, humor, multicultural, nature/environment. Young readers: adventure, animal, contemporary, fantasy, history, humor, multicultural, nature/environment, science fiction, suspense/mystery. Middle readers: adventure, contemporary, fantasy, history, humor,

THE AGE-LEVEL INDEX, located in the back of this book, lists book publishers and magazines according to the age-groups for which they need material.

multicultural, nature/environment, science fiction, suspense/mystery. Young adults: contemporary, health, humor, multicultural, nature/environment, suspense/mystery. Multicultural needs include "any material by, for and about minorities." No "rhyming texts, anthropomorphic animals that learn a lesson, alphabet and counting books, and stories based on an event rather than a character." Average word length: picture books—1,000; young readers—6,000; middle readers—15,000-25,000; young adults—20,000-40,000. Recently published *Edward and the Pirates*, by David McPhail (ages 4-8, picture book); *One of Each*, by Mary Ann Hoberman (ages 4-8, picture book); and *The Tulip Touch*, by Anne Fine (ages 10 and up, young adult fiction).

Nonfiction: Picture books: animal, biography, concept, history, multicultural, nature/environment. Young readers: activity books, biography, multicultural. Middle readers: activity books, arts/crafts, biography, cooking, geography, history, multicultural. Young adults: multicultural, self-help, social issues. Average word length: picture books—2,000; young readers—4,000-6,000; middle readers—15,000-25,000; young adults—20,000-40,000. Recently published *The Tiger's Eye, The Bird's Fist*, by Louise Rafkin (ages 8 and up, middle reader); and *The Girls Guide to Life*, by Catherine Dee (ages 10 and up, middle reader).

Illustration: Works with 40 illustrators/year. Illustrations only: Query art director with samples; provide résumé, promo sheet or tearsheets to be kept on file. Reports on art samples in 6-8 weeks. Original artwork returned at job's completion.

Photography: Works on assignment only. Model/property releases required; captions required. Publishes photo essays and photo concept books. Uses 35mm transparencies. Photographers should provide résumé, promo sheets or tearsheets to be kept on file.

Terms: Pays authors royalties of 3-10% based on retail price. Offers advance (average amount: $2,000-10,000). Pays illustrators and photographers by the project (range: $1,500-5,000) or royalty of 3-10% based on retail price. Sends galleys to authors; dummies to illustrators. Artist's guidelines for SASE.

Tips: "Publishers are cutting back their lists in response to a shrinking market and relying more on big names and known commodities. In order to break into the field these days, authors and illustrators should research their competition and try to come up with something outstandingly different."

‡LITTLE TIGER PRESS, XYZ Group, N16 W23390 Stoneridge Dr., Waukesha WI 53188. (414)544-2001. **Acquisitions:** Amy Mascillino. Publishes hardcover originals. Publishes 12-14 titles/year. 75% of books from first-time authors; 85% from unagented writers.

Fiction: Picture books: animals, humor. "Humorous stories, stories about animals, children's imagination, or realistic fiction are especially sought." Send ms with SASE. Recently published *I Don't Want to Take a Bath!*, by Julie Sykes, illustrated by Tim Warnes; and *Rumble in the Jungle*, by Giles Andreae, illustrated by David Wojtowycz.

How to Contact/Writers: Reports in 2 months on queries and proposals, 3 months on mss. Publishes book 1 year after acceptance. Will consider simultaneous submissions.

Terms: Pays 7½-10% royalty on retail price or for first-time authors, $800-2,500. Offers $2,000 minimum advance. Book catalog for #10 SASE with 3 first-class stamps. Manuscript guidelines for #10 SASE.

Tips: "Audience is children 3-8 years old. We are looking for simple, basic picture books, preferably humorous, that children will enjoy again and again. We do not have a multicultural or social agenda."

LODESTAR BOOKS. This imprint of Penguin was closed down as a result of the Penguin/Putnam merger.

LOLLIPOP POWER BOOKS, 120 Morris St., Durham NC 27701. (919)560-2738. Book publisher. Estab. 1971. Nonprofit, small press. **Manuscript Acquisitions:** Ruth A. Smullin, children's editor. **Art Acquisitions:** Martha Scotford, designer. Publishes an average of 1 picture book/year. "Lollipop Power Books offer alternative points of view to prevailing stereotypes. Our books show children: girls and women who are self-sufficient, with responsibilities beyond those of home and family; boys and men who are emotional and nurturing and involved in domestic responsibilities; families that use day care or alternative child care; families that consist of one parent only, working parents, or extended families; realistic portrayals of children of all races and ethnic groups, who have in common certain universal feelings and experiences."

● Lollipop Power Books is not currently accepting any manuscript or illustration submissions.

Fiction: Picture books: bilingual (English/Spanish), multicultural, multiracial, nonsexist. Average length: 30 pages. Recently published *Puzzles* (picture book), a story about a young girl with sickle cell disease.

Terms: Pays authors and illustrators in royalties of 5% of print-run based on retail price, or cash, if available. Original artwork returned at job's completion.

Tips: "We believe that children must be taken seriously. Our books present their problems honestly and without condescension. Lollipop Power Books must be well-written stories that will appeal to children. We are not interested in preachy tales where message overpowers plot and character. We are looking for good stories told from a child's point of view. Our current publishing priorities are: a) African-American, Hispanic or Native American characters; b) bilingual books (English/Spanish); c) books that show gay men or lesbian women as ordinary people who can raise children. To request a catalog, send a 9×12 envelope with postage sufficient for two ounces."

♦JAMES LORIMER & CO., 35 Britain St., Toronto, Ontario M5A 1R7 Canada. (416)362-4762. Book publisher. **Acquisitions:** Diane Young, senior editor; Jennifer Gillard, editorial assistant. Publishes 3 middle readers/

year; and 2 young adult titles/year. 20% of books by first-time authors. Uses Canadian authors only; wants realistic, contemporary material with Canadian settings.

Fiction: Middle readers: adventure, contemporary, hi-lo, multicultural, problem novels, sports and suspense/mystery. Young adults: contemporary, multicultural, problem novels and sports. Canadian settings featuring characters from ethnic/racial/cultural minorities—prefers author from same background. Does not want to see fantasy, science fiction, verse, drama and short stories. Average word length: middle readers—18,000; young adults—20,000.

How to Contact/Writers: Submit outline/synopsis and 2 sample chapters. Reports on queries in 2 months; mss in 6 months. Publishes a book 8 months after acceptance.

Illustration: Works with 3 illustrators/year. Prefers realistic style. Illustrations only: Submit promo sheet, photocopies OK. Reports only if interested. Samples returned with SASE; samples filed. Original artwork returned at job's completion.

Photography: Buys photos from freelancers. Buys stock and assigns work. Uses color prints and 35mm transparencies. Submit letter.

Terms: Pays authors royalty of 6-10% based on retail price. Pays illustrators and photographers by the project. Sends galleys to authors.

Tips: "Follow submission guidelines and research the market—read current kids' books, talk to kids." Wants realistic novels, set in Canada, dealing with social issues. Recent trends include hi-lo and multicultural.

LOTHROP, LEE & SHEPARD BOOKS, 1350 Avenue of the Americas, New York NY 10019. (212)261-6500. An imprint of William Morrow Co. Inc., Children's Fiction and Nonfiction. **Manuscript Acquisitions:** Susan Pearson, editor-in-chief; Melanie Donovan, senior editor. **Art Acquisitions:** Barbara Fitzsimmons, Morrow Jr. and Lothrop, Lee & Shepard. Publishes 30 total titles/year.

- Lothrop, Lee & Shepard only accepts manuscripts from agents and previously published authors.

Fiction: All levels: adventure, animal, anthology, comtemporary, concept, fantasy, fiction, folktales, health, history, humor, multicultural, nature/environment, poetry, religion, science problem novels, special needs, sports, suspense/mystery. Recently published *My Life with the Wave*, by Catharine Cowan, illustrated by Mark Buehner.

Nonfiction: All levels: animal, biography, concept, history, multicultural, nature/environment, science. Recently published *Celebrate in Central America*, by Joe Viesti; *Komodo Dragon: On Location*, by Kathy Darling, photographs by Tara Darling.

How to Contact/Writers: Fiction/nonfiction: Prefers agented material, but will accept queries; "no unsolicited mss." Reports on queries/mss in 1-6 months (longer for novels).

Illustration: Works with 30 or more illustrators/year. Editorial reviews ms/illustration packages from artists. Write for guidelines first. Illustrations only: Query with samples; submit portfolio for review.

Photography: Purchases photos from freelancers. Buys stock and assigns work.

Terms: Payment terms vary with project. Royalties/advances negotiated. Ms/artist's guidelines free for SASE.

Tips: Currently seeking picture books and young nonfiction. "Multicultural books of all types" are popular right now. Does not want books written to fill a special need instead of from the writer's experience and personal conviction. Also does not want film scripts, cartoon merchandising ideas or pedantic books. Work should come from the heart.

□LOWELL HOUSE JUVENILE/ROXBURY PARK JUVENILE, 2020 Avenue of the Stars, Suite 300, Los Angeles CA 90067. (310)552-7555. Fax: (310)552-7573. Book publisher, independent book producer/packager. **Manuscript Acquisitions:** Michael Artenstein, editor-in-chief, Roxbury Park Juvenile; Amy Downing, editor-in-chief, Lowell House Juvenile. **Art Acquisitions:** Shelly Pomerby, designer. Publishes 1-2 picture books/year; 30 young readers/year; 60 middle readers/year; 5 young adult titles/year. 25% of books by first-time authors.

- Lowell House does not accept manuscripts. Instead they generate ideas inhouse then find writers to work on projects.

Fiction: Middle readers, young adults: adventure, anthology, contemporary, fantasy, humor, nature/environment, science fiction, sports, suspense/mystery. Recently published *Qwan: the Showdown*, by A.L. Kim, cover art by Richard Kirk (ages 13 and up action novel); *Six-Minute Mysteries*, by Don Wulffson, illustrated by Laurel Long (ages 10-12, collection of short mystery stories); and *Classic Ghost Stories*, illustrated by Barbara Kiwak (ages 13 and up, collection of short scary stories).

Nonfiction: Picture books, young readers: activity books, educational. Middle readers: activity books, arts/crafts, concept, cooking, geography, health, history, hobbies, reference, religion, science, self help, sports. Recently published *The 25 Strangest Mysteries in the World*, by Q.L. Pearce, illustrated by Brian W. Dow (ages 10-12, short, strange but true-type stories); *Super Nifty Origami Crafts*, by Andrea Urton and Charlene Olexiewicz, illustrated by Dianne O'Quinn Burke, photos by Ann Bogart (ages 10-12, step-by-step how-to); *Puzzles & Games for Reading and Math: Book Two Workbook for Ages 6-8*, by Martha Cheney, illustrated by Larry Nolte.

Illustration: Works with 75 illustrators/year. Send samples to give a feel for style. Include sample drawings with kids in them. Illustrations only: arrange personal portfolio review; send promo sheet, portfolio, tearsheets. Reports back only if interested. Samples returned with SASE; files samples.

Photography: Buys stock and assigns work. "We're not looking for more photographers at this time."

Terms: Payment decided on project-by-project basis.

Tips: "Send art: lots of drawings of kids, samples to keep on file. Don't be afraid to send b&w art—never see

Concept books: finding the balance between the information and the story

Beyond pretty pictures, fairy tales and dramatic stories of heroism lies a genre of children's literature geared toward those coping with less-than-idyllic circumstances, from divorce or the death of a loved one to cancer, autism and diabetes. Some books deal with common childhood fears, such as the dark, bad dreams, and the first separation from parents, while others delve into bedwetting, wearing glasses, adoption and even mental illness. Although a myriad of subjects have been addressed to children through books, many more need to be explored and new ideas on popular subjects are certainly worth pursuing.

Susan Kent Cakars

Susan Kent Cakars has made a career of publishing self-help books for children, a task she embraced first through Magination Press (formerly a division of Brunner/Mazel, Inc., now owned by the American Psychiatric Association), for which she was editor-in-chief for ten years, and now as a freelance editor. Her publishing experience spans 18 years, during which she has amassed a wealth of knowledge about concept books and writing for children with special needs.

Cakars notes that much of children's self-help literature seems to originate from smaller publishing houses. "My impression is that the big companies aren't doing it that much." Furthermore, "publishing is a very irrational process," she says. "Publishers are often hesitant to publish something that doesn't fit into neat categories."

Many concept books fall into this vague field, particularly ones that deal with difficult subjects. You can approach this market with confidence, however, if you've honed your style and identified your goals clearly. While turning a story or idea into an individualized learning tool is a process Cakars relishes, she is quick to point out the common pitfalls of writing for this purpose. She offers the following guidelines to improve your chances of getting published in this field:

• Use a child's voice and a child's point of view. Children naturally identify with peers. "I love it when it works," Cakars says of this method. But be wary. "Sometimes it sounds like a little adult, like a little therapist" speaking. If you're not skilled using this voice, stick with third person.

• "In every story, the child should in some way be an agent in the solution to the problem," Cakars says. Either the child should solve the problem on his/her own, or seek out someone who can help.

• The classic rule, "Show don't tell," holds with children's self-help books as well. The absence of this is something Cakars sees in what she classifies as "the bad manuscripts." Children and adult characters alike can be good role models in the story, she adds. Parents can learn from the books as well.

• Don't submit illustrations with your story manuscript. "Illustrations [submitted by

INSIDER REPORT, *Cakars*

Luna and the BIG BLUR

A Story for Children Who Wear Glasses

BOOKS TO HELP PARENTS HELP THEIR CHILDREN

by Shirley Day
illustrated by Don Morris

Reprinted with permission

Aimed at ages 4-8, *Luna and the Big Blur* tells of a young girl learning to accept her nearsightedness—and her new glasses.

the author] can kill off your story," Cakars emphasizes. Most publishers prefer to find their own illustrators. However, feel free to give illustration suggestions.

• Don't talk down to your audience, regardless of your readers' age. She cites one of her favorite books, *Putting on the Brakes* (by Patricia O. Quinn, M.D. and Judith M. Stern, M.A.) as a good example of appropriate tone. "I had five manuscripts on this topic, and I chose this one because it was not condescending."

• Do your research. Although many of the books she has published are written by

INSIDER REPORT, *continued*

medical experts or "credential people," Cakars finds that "books by parents are the most interesting." Parents can often look past the medical jargon and therapeautic techniques more easily, because they are personally close to the subject. When in doubt about the factual accuracy of a manuscript, Cakars submits it to an expert in the field for review, a tactic she recommends for any writer before the manuscript reaches the publisher's desk.

When Cakars combines her tips for good writing, they yield a simple formula. "Describe the problem, explain what effects it has, talk about who has the problem, talk about how people who have it feel. Does is make them happy, sad? What can they do about it? What can other people do for them? Do it with a positive attitude, a positive point of view! This can be dealt with. Here's how to do it. Hey, you're OK. This is the problem and here's how you do it."

The trick to a successful fiction manuscript is often finding the balance between the information and the story. "You have to provide something children will like, that will be their friend. The book needs to help them and to comfort them," Cakars says.

Still needed in the children's book arena, and a personal goal for Cakars, are quality books on child abuse, alcoholism and stuttering. She has perused many manuscripts on each topic, but has yet to find "the perfect book," she says. "There are a number of books I didn't publish that I would like to do" on a multitude of other powerful subjects, Cakars says. The field is open to those creative writers who, like Cakars, have a passion for children's literature and a desire to use their knowledge to comfort a child.

—*Jennifer Hogan-Redmond*

With over 100,000 copies in print, *Putting on the Breaks: Young People's Guide to Understanding Attention Deficit Hyperactivity Disorder*, edited by Susan Kent Cakars, is Magination Press' best-selling title. It's success spurred other books on the topics of A.D.D. and A.D.H.D., as well as titles in the same format addressing asthma and learning disabilities. Cakars recommends writers also check out other books like *Gran Gran's Best Trick* (by L. Dwight Holden, M.D.), *Sarah and Puffle* (by Linnea Mulder, R.N.) and *The Case of the Scary Divorce* (by Carl E. Pickhardt, Ph.D.) as good examples of self-help titles for kids.

enough junior-high aged kids! Editorial: We are interested in writing samples to lead to future jobs, but we do not accept manuscripts, preferring to generate ideas ourselves."

LUCAS/EVANS BOOKS INC., 407 Main St., Chatham NJ 07928. Executive Director: Barbara Lucas.
- Lucas/Evans is no longer accepting new clients. The company is downsizing, no longer doing book packaging, only agenting.

★LUCENT BOOKS, P.O. Box 289011, San Diego CA 92128-9009. (619)485-7424. Sister Company to Greenhaven Press. Book publisher. Estab. 1988. **Acquisitions:** Bonnie Szumski, managing editor. 20% of books by first-time authors; 10% of books from agented writers. "Lucent publishes nonfiction for a middle school audience. Our goal is to provide middle grade students with resource material for academic studies and for independent learning."
- This publisher does not accept unsolicited manuscripts.

Nonfiction: Middle readers, young adults: education, health, topical history, nature/environment, sports, "any overviews of specific topics—i.e., political, social, cultural, economic, criminal, moral issues." No fiction. Average word length: 15,000-25,000. Published *The Persian Gulf War*, by Don Nardo (grades 6-12, history); *Photography*, by Brad Steffens (grades 5-8, history); and *Rainforests*, by Lois Warburton (grades 5-8, overview).
How to Contact/Writers: "Writers should query first; we do writing by assignment only. If you want to write for us, send SASE for guidelines."
Illustration: "We use photos, mostly." Uses primarily b&w artwork and prefers 7×9 format—4-color cover. Reviews ms/illustration packages from artists. Query first. Illustrations only: Query with samples; provide résumé, business card, promotional literature or tearsheets to be kept on file.
Terms: "Fee negotiated upon review of manuscript." Sends galleys to authors. Ms guidelines free on request.
Tips: "Books must be written at a 7th-8th-grade reading level. There's a growing market for quality nonfiction. Tentative topics: free speech, tobacco, alcohol, discrimination, immigration, poverty, the homeless in America, space weapons, drug abuse, terrorism, animal experimentation, endangered species, AIDS, pollution, gun control, etc. The above list is presented to give writers an example of the kinds of titles we are seeking. If you are interested in writing about a specific topic, please query us by mail before you begin writing to be sure we have not assigned a particular topic to another author. The author should strive for objectivity. There obviously will be many issues on which a position should be taken—e.g., discrimination, tobacco, alcoholism, etc. However, moralizing, self-righteous condemnations, maligning, lamenting, mocking, etc. should be avoided. Moreover, where a pro/con position is taken, contrasting viewpoints should be presented. Certain moral issues such as abortion and euthanasia, if dealt with at all, should be presented with strict objectivity."

‡THE LUTTERWORTH PRESS, Imprint of James Clarke & Co. Ltd., P.O. Box 60, Cambridge England CB1 2NT. (01223)3350865. Fax: (01223)366951. Book publisher. **Acquisitions:** Adrian Brink, managing director.
Fiction: Picture books, young readers, middle readers and young adults: adventure, animal, folktales, health, history, nature/environment, religion.
Nonfiction: Picture books, young readers, middle readers and young adults: activity books, animal, arts/crafts, history, nature/environment, religion, science.
How to Contact/Writers: Fiction/Nonfiction: Submit outline/synopsis and 1 or 2 sample chapters. Reports on queries in 2 weeks; ms in 6 months.
Illustration: Reviews ms illustration packages from authors. Submit ms with color or b&w copies of illustration. Illustration only: Query with samples. Reports in 2-3 weeks. Samples returned with SASE; samples filed.
Photography: "Occasionally" buys photos from freelancers. Send résumé and samples. Works on assignment only.
Terms: Pays authors royalty of 8%. Offers advances (average amount: $250). Book catalog available for SAE.

McCLANAHAN BOOK COMPANY INC., 23 W. 26th St., New York NY 10010. (212)725-1515. Fax—editorial: (212)684-2785; art: (212)725-5911. Book publisher. CEO: Susan McClanahan. **Manuscript Acquisitions:** Marc Gave, editorial director. **Art Acquisitions:** Dave Werner, creative director. Publishes 60-70 titles/year; 0-11 "affordable, high quality mass market, usually with educational value, including activity books, concept storybooks, workbooks, nonfiction, baby/toddler concept books and novelty books."
Fiction: Mainly baby and toddler concept books; generally no single-title fiction. Recently published: *Baby's First Meal*, by Elizabeth Hathon.
Nonfiction: Activity, concept, novelty, interactive. Recently published: *Pop into Phonics* series by Kent Salisbury; *Presidents Sticker Book*.
How to Contact/Writers: Query only. Ms guidelines available with SASE. Assignments to writers for projects originated inhouse.
Illustration: Works with up to 50 illustrators/photographers a year. Send samples, which will be returned with SASE and/or filed. Reports in 2-4 months.
Terms: Usually pays writers and illustrators/photographers on work-for-hire basis (flat fee by project). May pay small royalty for certain project originated by writer or artist. Artists' originals returned after job's completion.

MARGARET K. McELDERRY BOOKS, 1230 Sixth Ave., New York NY 10020. (212)698-2761. Fax: (212)698-2796. Website: http://www.simonsays.com. Imprint of Simon & Schuster Children's Publishing Division. **Publisher:** Margaret K. McElderry. **Manuscript Acquisitions:** Emma Dryden, editor. **Art Acquisitions:** Ann Bobco, art director. Publishes 10-12 picture books/year; 2-4 young reader titles/year; 8-10 middle reader titles/year; and 5-7 young adult titles/year. 10% of books by first-time authors; 33% of books from agented writers. "Margaret K. McElderry Books publishes original hardcover trade books for children from pre-school age through young adult. This list includes picture books, easy-to-read books, fiction and non-fiction for eight to twelve-year-olds, poetry, science fiction, fantasy and young adult fiction and non-fiction. The style and subject matter of the books we publish is almost unlimited. We do not publish textbooks, coloring and activity books, greeting cards, magazines and pamphlets or religious publications."

• Margaret K. McElderry Books' title *The Moorchild*, by Eloise McGraw, received a 1997 Newberry Honor Book Award. McElderry Books is not currently accepting unsolicited manuscripts. Send queries only.

Fiction: Young readers: adventure, contemporary, fantasy, history. Middle readers: adventure, contemporary, fantasy, mystery. Young adults: contemporary, fantasy, mystery, poetry. "Always interested in publishing humorous picture books and original beginning reader stories. We see too many rhymed picture book manuscripts which are not terribly original or special." Average word length: picture books—500; young readers—2,000; middle readers—10,000-20,000; young adults—45,000-50,000. Recently published *A Summertime Song*, by Irene Haas; *Scaredy Cat*, by Joan Rankin; and *A Boy and His Bear*, by Harriet Graham.

Nonfiction: Young readers, young adult teens, biography, history. Average word length: picture books—500-1,000; young readers—1,500-3,000; middle readers—10,000-20,000; young adults—30,000-45,000. *The Planet Hunters: The Search for Other Worlds*, by Dennis B. Fradin; and *Earthquake Games*, by Mario Salvadore and Matthys Levy.

How to Contact/Writers: Fiction/nonfiction: Submit query only with SASE; may also include brief résumé of previous publishing credits. Reports on queries in 2-3 weeks; mss in 3-4 months. Publishes a book 18 months after contract signing. Will consider simultaneous submissions (only if indicated as such).

Illustration: Works with 20-30 illustrators/year. Query with samples; provide promo sheet or tearsheets; arrange personal portfolio review. Contact: Ann Bobco, art director. Reports on art samples in 2-3 months. Samples returned with SASE or samples filed.

Terms: Pays authors advance and royalty based on retail price. Pay illustrators royalty based on retail price. Pays photographers by the project. Sends galleys to authors; dummies to illustrators. Original artwork returned at job's completion. Ms guidelines free on request with SASE.

Tips: "We're looking for strong, original fiction. We are always interested in picture books for the youngest age reader."

MAGE PUBLISHERS INC., 1032 29th St. NW, Washington DC 20007. (202)342-1642. Book publisher. **Acquisitions:** Amin Sepehri, assistant to publisher. Publishes 2-3 picture books/year.

Fiction: Contemporary/myth, Persian heritage. Average word length: 5,000.

Nonfiction: Average word length: 5,000.

How to Contact/Writers: Fiction/Nonfiction: Query. Reports on queries/ms in 3 months. Will consider simultaneous submissions.

Illustration: Reviews ms/illustration packages from artists. Illustrations only: Submit résumé and slides. Reports in 3 months. Original artwork returned at job's completion.

Terms: Pays authors in royalties. Sends galleys to authors. Book catalog free on request.

★MAGINATION PRESS, 750 First Street NE, Washington DC 20002. Book publisher. Director: Julia Frank-McNeil. Publishes up to 15 picture books and young reader titles/year. "We publish books dealing with the psycho/therapeutic treatment or resolution of children's serious problems and psychological issues, written by mental health professionals."

• Magination Press was acquired by the American Psychological Association; it is now an imprint of the Educational Publishing Foundation of the APA. At press time they were just beginning to develop manuscript and submission guidelines as well as policies and pay structures for authors and illustrators. Permanent staff had not yet been selected.

Fiction: Picture books, young readers: concept, mental health, multicultural, problem novels, special needs. Recently published *Gentle Willow: A Story for Children About Dying*, by Joyce C. Mills, Ph.D. (ages 4-8); *The Case of the Scary Divorce: A Jackson Skye Mystery*, by Carl E. Pickhardt, Ph.D. (ages 8-15); and *You Can Call Me Willy: A Story for Children About AIDS*, by Joan C. Verniero (ages 4-8).

Nonfiction: Picture books, young readers: concept, mental health, how-to, multicultural, psychotherapy, special needs. Recently published *Putting on the Brakes: Young People's Guide to Understanding Attention Deficit Hyperactivity Disorder (ADHD)*, by Patricia O. Quinn, M.D. and Judith M. Stern, M.A. (ages 8-13).

How to Contact/Writers: Fiction/nonfiction: Submit complete ms. Reports on queries/mss: "up to three months (may be only days)." Publishes a book 1 year after acceptance.

Illustration: Works with 4-8 illustrators/year. Reviews ms/illustration packages. Will review artwork for future assignments.

How to Contact/Illustrators: Illustrations only: Query with samples. Original artwork returned at job's completion.

Terms: Pays authors in royalties. Offers vary but low advance. Pays illustrators by the project or royalty. Book catalog and ms guidelines on request with SASE.

‡MARIPOSA, Imprint of Scholastic Inc., 555 Broadway, New York NY 10012. (212)343-6100. Website: http://www.scholastic.com. **Acquisitions:** Susana Pasternac, editor. Publishes trade paperback originals and reprints. Publishes 20-25 titles/year (2-3 original titles/year). "There is a great need for children's Spanish-language literature, work that is well done and authentic, that fills a *need*, not just a space." Book catalog for #10 SASE.
Fiction: Picture books, young adult. "We do Spanish-language translations of the Magic School Bus and Goosebumps series." Recently published *Abuelo and the Three Bears (Abuelo y los tres Osos)*, by Jerry Tello, illustrated by Anna López Escrivá (bilingual picture book).
Nonfiction: "We are introducing more nonfiction; looking for titles that don't have nationalities, that are interesting to everybody."
How to Contact/Writers: Fiction/nonfiction: Query with completed ms and SASE. Reports in 3 months. Publishes book 1 year after acceptance. Will consider simultaneous submissions.
Illustration: Reviews ms/illustration packages "if important to manuscript." Send photocopies.
Photography: Reviews ms/photo packages "if important to manuscript." Send photocopies.
Terms: Pays royalty based on retail price; varies.

MEADOWBROOK PRESS, 5451 Smetana Dr., Minnetonka MN 55343. (612)930-1100. Fax: (612)930-1940. Book publisher. Estab. 1975. **Manuscript Acquisitions:** Jason Sanford, submissions editor. **Art Acquisitions:** Joe Gagne, art director. Publishes 1-2 middle readers/year; and 2-4 young readers/year. 20% of books by first-time authors; 10% of books from agented writers. Publishes children's activity books, gift books, humorous poetry anthologies and story anthologies. "We look for fresh approaches to overcoming traditional problems (e.g., potty training)."
● Meadowbrook does not accept unsolicited children's picture books or novels. The publisher offers specific guidelines for various types of submissions (such as new-fangled fairy tales, poetry and anthologies). Be sure to specify the type of project you have in mind when requesting guidelines.
Fiction: Young readers and middle readers: anthology, folktales, humor, multicultural, poetry. "Poems and short stories representing people of color encouraged." Published *The New Adventures of Mother Goose*; *Girls to the Rescue* (short stories featuring strong girls, for ages 8-12); and *A Bad Case of the Giggles* (children's poetry anthology).
Nonfiction: Young readers, middle readers: activity books, arts/crafts, hobbies, how-to, multicultural, self help. Multicultural needs include activity books representing traditions/cultures from all over the world, and especially fairy tale/folk tale stories with strong, multicultural heroines and diverse settings. "Books which include multicultural activities are encouraged." Average word length: varies. Recently published *Kids' Party Games and Activities*, by Penny Warner; *Free Stuff for Kids* (activity book); and *Kids' Holiday Fun* (activity book).
How to Contact/Writers: Fiction/Nonfiction: Query or submit outline/synopsis and sample chapters or submit complete ms with SASE. Reports on queries/mss in 2-3 months. Publishes a book 1-2 years after acceptance. Send a business-sized SASE and 2 first-class stamps for free writer's guidelines and book catalog before submitting ideas. Will consider simultaneous submissions.
Illustration: Only interested in agented material. Works with 2-3 illustrators/year. Reviews ms/illustration packages from artists. Submit ms with 2-3 pieces of final art. Illustrations only: Submit résumé, promo sheet and tearsheets. Reports back only if interested. Samples not returned; samples filed.
Photography: Buys photos from freelancers. Buys stock and assigns work. Model/property releases required. Submit cover letter.
Terms: Pays authors in royalties of 5-7½% based on retail price. Offers average advance payment of $2,000-4,000. Pays for illustrators: $100-25,000; ¼-¾% of total royalties. Pays photographers per photo ($250). Originals returned at job's completion. Book catalog available for 5 × 11 SASE and 2 first-class stamps; ms guidelines and artists guidelines available for SASE.
Tips: "Illustrators and writers should send away for our free catalog and guidelines before submitting their work to us. Also, illustrators should take a look at the books we publish to determine whether their style is consistent with what we are looking for. Writers should also note the style and content patterns of our books. For instance, our children's poetry anthologies contain primarily humorous, rhyming poems with a strong rhythm; therefore, we would not likely publish a free-verse and/or serious poem. I also recommend that writers, especially poets, have their work read by a critical, objective person before they submit anywhere. Also, please correspond with us by mail before telephoning with questions about your submission. We work with the printed word and will respond more effectively to your questions if we have something in front of us."

‡□★MEGA-BOOKS, INC., 240 E. 60th St., New York NY 10022. (212)355-6200. Fax: (212)355-6303. President: Pat Fortunato. **Acquisitions:** Molly Walsh. Book packager/producer. Produces trade paperback and mass market paperback originals and fiction and nonfiction for the educational market. Produces 95 titles/year. Works with first-time authors, established authors and unagented writers.
● Mega-Books does not accept unsolicited manuscripts.
Fiction: Young adult: mystery. Recently published *Nancy Drew* and *Hardy Boys* series; *Pocahontas* and *The Lion King* (Disney).
How to Contact/Writers: Submit résumé, publishing history and clips.

Terms: Work purchased outright for $3,000 and up. Offers advance: average 50%.

Tips: "Please be sure to obtain a current copy of our writers' guidelines before writing."

MERIWETHER PUBLISHING LTD., 885 Elkton Dr., Colorado Springs CO 80907-3557. Fax: (719)594-9916. E-mail: meriwthpub@aol.com. Book publisher. Estab. 1969. Executive Editor: Arthur L. Zapel. **Manuscript Acquisitions:** Ted Zapel, educational drama; Rhonda Wray, religious drama. **Art Acquisitions:** Tom Myers, art director. "We do most of our artwork in-house; we do not publish for the children's elementary market." 75% of books by first-time authors; 5% of books from agented writers. "Our niche is drama. Our books cover a wide variety of theatre subjects from play anthologies to theatrecraft. We publish books of monologs, duologs, short one-act plays, scenes for students, acting textbooks, how-to speech and theatre textbooks, improvisation and theatre games. We also publish some general humor trade books. Our Christian books cover worship on such topics as clown ministry, storytelling, banner-making, drama ministry, children's worship and more. We also publish anthologies of Christian sketches. We do not publish works of fiction or devotionals."

Fiction: Middle readers, young adults: anthology, contemporary, humor, religion. "We publish plays, not prose-fiction."

Nonfiction: Middle readers: activity books, how-to, religion, textbooks. Young adults: activity books, drama/theater arts, how-to church activities, religion. Average length: 250 pages. Recently published *Perspectives*, by Mary Krell-Oishi (a book of scenes for teenage actors); and *Fool of the Kingdom*, by Philip Noble (a book on clown ministry).

How to Contact/Writers: Nonfiction: Query or submit outline/synopsis and sample chapters. Reports on queries in 3 weeks; mss in 6 weeks. Publishes a book 6-12 months after acceptance. Will consider simultaneous submissions.

Illustration: Works with 3 illustrators/year. Reviews ms/illustration packages from artists. Query first. Illustrations only: Query with samples; send résumé, promo sheet or tearsheets. Reports on art samples in 4 weeks.

Terms: Pays authors in royalties of 10% based on retail or wholesale price. Pays for illustrators by the project (range: $150-3,000); royalties based on retail or wholesale price. Sends galleys to authors. Book catalog for SAE and $2 postage; ms guidelines for SAE and 1 first-class stamp.

Tips: "We are currently interested in finding unique treatments for theater arts subjects: scene books, how-to books, monologs and short plays for teens."

JULIAN MESSNER, 299 Jefferson Rd., Parsippany NJ 07054-0480. (201)739-8000. Fax: (201)739-8606. Imprint of Silver Burdett Press, Simon & Schuster Publishing Education Group. Book publisher. See listing for Silver Burdett Press.

MILKWEED EDITIONS, 430 First Ave. North, Suite 400, Minneapolis MN 55401-1743. (612)332-3192. Fax: (612)332-6248. Book Publisher. Estab. 1980. **Manuscript Acquisitions:** Emilie Buchwald, publisher; Elizabeth Fitz, manuscript coordinator. **Art Acquisitions:** Beth Olson. Publishes 2-3 middle readers/year. 25% of books by first-time authors. "Milkweed Editions publishes with the intention of making a humane impact on society, in the belief that literature is a transformative art uniquely able to convey the essential experiences of the human heart and spirit. To that end, Milkweed Editions publishes distinctive voices of literary merit in handsomely designed, visually dynamic books, exploring the ethical, cultural, and esthetic issues that free societies need continually to address."

Fiction: Middle readers: adventure, animal, contemporary, fantasy, humor, multicultural, nature/environment, suspense/mystery. Does not want to see anthologies, folktales, health, hi-lo, picture books, poetry, religion, romance, sports. Average length: middle readers—90-200 pages. Recently published *The Monkey Thief*, by Aileen Kilgore Henderson, illustrated by Paul Mirccha (middle reader, adventure/nature, comtemporary); *The Gumma Wars*; and *Business as Usual*, by David Haynes (middle reader, adventure/contemporary, multicultural).

How to Contact/Writers: Fiction: Query or submit complete manuscript. Reports on queries in 2 months; mss in 2-6 months. Publishes a book 1-12 months after acceptance. Will consider simultaneous submissions.

Illustration: Works with 1-2 illustrators/year. Reviews ms/illustration packages from artists. Query; submit manuscript with dummy. Illustrations only: Query with samples; provide résumé, promo sheet, slides, tearsheets and client list. Samples filed or returned with SASE; samples filed. Originals returned at job's completion.

Terms: Pays authors royalty of 7½% based on retail price. Offers advance against royalties. Illustrators contracts are decided on an individual basis. Sends galleys to authors. Book catalog available for $1.50 to cover postage; ms guidelines available for SASE. Must include SASE with ms submission for its return.

MARKET CONDITIONS are constantly changing! If you're still using this book and it is 1999 or later, buy the newest edition of *Children's Writer's & Illustrator's Market* at your favorite bookstore or order directly from Writer's Digest Books.

THE MILLBROOK PRESS, 2 Old New Milford Rd., Brookfield CT 06804. (203)740-2220. Fax: (203)775-5643. Website: http://www.neca.com/mall/millbrook. Book publisher. Estab. 1989. **Manuscript Acquisitions:** Colleen Seibert, managing editor; Dottie Carlson, manuscript coordinator. **Art Acquisitions:** Judie Mills, art director. Publishes 20 picture books/year; 40 young readers/year; 50 middle readers/year; and 10 young adult titles/year. 10% of books by first-time authors; 20% of books from agented authors. Publishes nonfiction, concept-oriented/educational books.
Fiction: Picture books: concept. Young adults: history.
Nonfiction: All levels: animal, arts/craft, biography, cooking, geography, how-to, multicultural, music/dance, nature/environment, reference, science. Picture books: activity books, concept, hi-lo. Middle readers: hi-lo, social issues, sports. Young adults: careers, social issues. No poetry. Average word length: picture books—minimal; young readers—5,000; middle readers—10,000; young adult/teens—20,000. Published *Frog Counts to Ten*, by John Liebler (grades K-3, picture book); *The Scopes Trial: Defending the Right to Teach*, by Arthur Blake (grades 4-6, history); and *The U.S. Health Care Crisis*, by Victoria Sherrow (grades 7-up, contemporary issues).
How to Contact/Writers: Query with outline/synopsis and 1 sample chapter. Reports on queries/mss in 1 month.
Illustration: Work with 75 illustrators/year. Reviews ms/illustration packages from artists. Query; submit 1 chapter of ms with 1 photocopy of final art. Illustrations only: Query with samples; provide résumé, business card, promotional literature or tearsheets to be kept on file. Samples returned with SASE; samples filed. Reports back only if interested.
Photography: Buys photos from freelancers. Buys stock and assigns work.
Terms: Pays author royalty of 5-7½% based on wholesale price or work purchased outright. Offers advances. Pays illustrators by the project, royalty of 3-7% based on wholesale price. Sends galleys to authors. Book catalog, ms and artist's guidelines for SASE.

‡MINSTREL BOOKS, Imprint of Pocket Books for Young Readers, Imprint of Simon & Schuster, 1230 Avenue of the Americas, New York NY 10020. (212)698-7000. Fax: (212698-7007. Website: http://www.simonandschuster.com. Editorial director: Patricia McDonald. **Acquisitions:** Attn: Manuscript proposals. Estab. 1986. Publishes hardcover originals and reprints, trade paperback originals. Publishes 125 titles/year. Receives 1,200 queries/year. Less than 25% from first-time authors; less than 25% from unagented writers. "Minstrel publishes fun, kid-oriented books, the kinds kids pick for themselves, for middle grade readers, ages 8-12."
 • Minstrel Books publishes many books in series, such as Nancy Drew and The Hardy Boys. Many are based on TV shows such as "Full House," "Clarissa" and "Star Trek."
Nonfiction: Middle readers: celebrity biographies and books about TV shows. Recently published *Nickelodeon® The Big Help™ Book: 365 Ways You Can Make a Difference Volunteering*, by Alan Goodman; and *My Life with the Chimpanzees*, by Jane Goodall.
Fiction: Middle readers: animal stories, fantasy, humor, suspense/mystery, No picture books. "Thrillers are very popular, and 'humor at school' books." Recently published *R.L. Stine's Ghosts of Fear Street*, by R.L. Stine; and *Aliens Ate My Homework*, by Bruce Coville.
How to Contact/Writers: Fiction/Nonfiction: Query with synopsis/outline, sample chapters and SASE. Reports in 3 months. Publishes book 2 years after acceptance. Will consider simultaneous submissions.
Terms: Pays advance and 6-8% royalty based on retail price. Book catalog and ms guidelines free.
Tips: "Hang out with kids to make sure your dialogue and subject matter are accurate."

‡MIRACLE SOUND PRODUCTIONS, INC., 1560 W. Bay Area Blvd., Suite 110, Friendswood TX 77546-2668. (281)286-4575. Fax: (281)286-0009. E-mail: cdsimsw@ghg.net. Book publisher. Estab. 1997. Publishes 2 young readers/year. 100% of books by first-time authors. Miracle Sound Productions is best known for "positive family values in multimedia products."
Fiction: Young readers. Average word length: young readers—500. Recently published *CoCo's Luck*, by Warren Chaney and Don Boyer (ages 3-8, Read-A-Long book and tape).
Illustration: Only interested in agented material. Works with 1 illustrator/year. Uses color artwork only. Reviews ms/illustration packages from artists. Submit ms with dummy. Contact: Trey W. Boring, director, special projects. Illustrations only: Send résumé and portfolio to be kept on file.
Photography: Works on assignment only. Contact: Trey W. Boring, director, special projects.
Terms: Payment negotiable for authors, illustrators and photographers.

MITCHELL LANE PUBLISHERS, INC., 17 Matthew Bathon Court, Elkton MD 21921-3669. (410)392-5036. Fax: (410)392-4781. E-mail: mitchelllane@hotmail.com. Website: http://www.angelfire.com/biz/mitchelllane/index.html. Book publisher. **Acquisitons:** Barbara Mitchell, president. Publishes 6-12 young adult titles/year. "We publish authorized multicultural biographies of role models for children and young adults."
Nonfiction: Young readers, middle readers, young adults: biography, multicultural. Average word length: 4,000-50,000 words. Recently published *Selena*, by Barbara Marvis; *Robert Rodriguez*; and *Mariah Carey* (all real-life reader biographies for grades K-4); and *Rafael Palmeiro: At Home with the Baltimore Orioles*, by Ed Brandt (ages 11 and up).
How to Contact/Writers: Nonfiction: Query or submit outline/synopsis and 3 sample chapters. Reports on queries/mss in 2-3 months. Publishes a book 18 months after acceptance.

INSIDER REPORT

Literacy movement broadens market for fun-to-read books

Louise May

Many writers and illustrators pass by educational publishers when looking for potential markets. The word "educational" conjures up memories of lackluster textbooks filled with spelling words and boring facts and figures. These days, nothing could be further from the truth. There's a growing trend toward educational titles that are well written, beautifully illustrated, and fun to read. If you're interested in a burgeoning, relatively untapped market, check out what's happening in today's literacy programs. It will blow away all your preconceptions.

The early literacy movement started as a grassroots crusade supported by librarians, teachers, tutors, parents, grandparents, educational theorists, booksellers, scientists and medical professionals worldwide who believe early literacy is key in preventing society's gravest problems. Though its proponents take their mission seriously, the heart of this innovative movement is fun and games. For in recent years, science has determined unquestionably that the chemistry of growing brains responds more positively to books that are fun to read.

Backed by scientific research, teachers campaigned to abandon dreary (if nostalgic) textbooks featuring Dick and Jane and their dog, Spot, in favor of lavishly illustrated folktales, mysteries, biographies, science books and funny yarns. They added affordable trade books to literacy programs, because studies show children respond more enthusiastically to books they choose themselves.

Mondo Publishing is the perfect example of an educational publisher whose books garner praise and awards from educators while eliciting oohs and ahs and hearty gaffaws from tiny readers. One look at their catalog or a quick visit to their website (http://www.mondopub.com) will convince you learning has never been this fun.

Though founded in 1990, a year when children's book publishing was seeing a downswing, Mondo's sales climbed. Their secret? This small Greenvale, N.Y.-based publisher, which has ties to education, was riding the crest of the literacy movement. Mondo president Mark Vineis and Diane Snowball, an Australian educator, regularly visited classrooms so they knew what children and teachers needed. In a 1995 article in *Publishers Weekly*, Vineis described their mission. "Our objective is to create beautiful books children can read on their own and find so enjoyable they'll want to come back to them time and time again." Mondo also creates support materials for teachers, providing a framework for literacy teaching.

"The best advice I can give to children's writers and illustrators is 'Know your audience,' " says Louise May, senior editor of Mondo Publishing. "Think about the age group

ZOO-LOOKING

Mem Fox

illustrated by
Candace Whitman

When planning a picture book, art directors strive to choose illustrations that match the writer's style. Candace Whitman's torn paper collages in *Zoo-looking* resonate with Mem Fox's simple, lyrical sentences.

you want to appeal to." What reading skills do they have? What can they read independently?"

That doesn't mean you should eliminate or include certain words, says May. "The littlest kids can read the word 'dinosaur,' yet it's a very difficult word. Vocabulary isn't the only factor that makes a book easy or difficult for a child. It's also concepts expressed and the background knowledge a child brings to the story."

Science now understands literacy begins at birth. Babies who are read to in their first year later learn to read with ease. Two-year-olds make strides in their skills just by holding books and turning pages. Four-year-olds constantly ask "Why?" So books for that age group should capitalize on that natural curiosity. "At age six children are still mastering the basics of getting meaning from words," says May. "Surrounding text with supportive illustrations help them figure out difficult words."

INSIDER REPORT, *continued*

Number of words does not always indicate ease or readibility, says May. Rhyme, repetition and other factors enter in. "If there's a pattern to the language, if there's a phrase that gets repeated on every page or every other page, that makes even a book with difficult words easier to read. Once they get that phrase they can get through the book. The rhythm or repeated phrase ties pages together."

To explain how good writers employ this strategy, May points to a sentence in *Zoo-looking* by Mem Fox: "She looked at the tiger, and the tiger looked back." Variations on that rhythm are repeated throughout the book. Good picture book writing is deceptively simple, says May. "A book like *Zoo-looking* can take years to write. Mem Fox has written many times that she agonizes over each word. She takes days, weeks to write a sentence. The sparseness of it does not necessarily mean it's easy to write."

Picture book illustrations must do more than captivate. They help children get the most meaning from their books. Art for picture books for children who are just beginning to read is often chosen with different criteria than for books destined to read by more fluent readers. "Sometimes a great deal of a story can be told by the pictures, thus fleshing out a brief text," says May. "For older children, the pictures expand the text and bring more meaning and interest to the story." To explain this concept, May points out how the illustrations for *Thinking About Ants* expanded on Barbara Brenner's simplified, poetic exploration of the life cycle of ants. "We definitely needed a realistic style, so we chose an illustrator who specializes in natural science illustrations. Carol Schwartz did a lot of research to get the ants' bodies and colors just right." For all their meticulous detail, Schwartz's ants charm and fascinate, while bringing children age five to ten as much information as each is ready to understand.

"We feel the book dictates what the illustrations should be," says May. She first envisioned realistic illustrations for *Zoo-looking*, but they didn't enhance the text. The glowing colors of Candace Whitman's torn paper collages—a simpler style—brought the animals to life and resonated with the author's simple sentences.

May also uses a variety of art styles because children like variety and it helps expose them to different kinds of art. "There are a lot of unusual and very graphic styles that work well in children's books." *The Straight Line Wonder*, also by Mem Fox, for ages six to ten, incorporates very sophisticated, innovative design in a fun way. Finding the right illustrator for a story about three straight lines was a challenge, says May. After considering several illustrators and animators, May picked Marc Rosenthal, a designer/illustrator better known for magazine illustration than children's books. Rosenthal's exuberant characters and bold layouts fit perfectly with Mem Fox's delightful tale. An added bonus is that the humorous, sophisticated drawings also appeal to adults who read it to their children.

May occasionally finds quality manuscripts and illustrations through submissions, but she finds it easier to approach writers and illustrators whose work she has seen and admired. Too often, freelancers send inappropriate material, or present it unprofessionally. If you want to appear professional, don't submit a picture book as a stack of pages with one sentence to a page. "I think it's a wasteful approach," says May. And stay away from rhymes unless you're sure you can pull it off. "If you're not careful, it can come out sounding forced." Don't boast in your cover letter "I read this to my child's class and they begged for more." May invariably finds the story is not up to par. "They don't realize that what they interpret as enthusiasm for their work is often the children's positive response to being read to with enthusiasm by a loving adult. It doesn't always follow that the story will hold up on its own, or that it will appeal to other children."

INSIDER REPORT, *continued*

When choosing illustrators, May tends to consult sourcebooks and agents. But sometimes she'll take a chance on a newcomer based on impressive samples. She prefers receiving three or four non-returnable color copies sent in one envelope rather than a spread-out mailing of postcards.

Though 75% of books Mondo publishes are marketed to schools, an increasing number of their titles appeal to the trade market (bookstores and libraries). And in a decade where large children's book publishers are decreasing their lists, Mondo—a relatively small company—continues to expand. "We don't fit the mold of the big publishers that have been around for years." When larger publishers gobble up smaller companies and imprints, it leaves a gap for smaller publishers to rise up from the bottom. Since smaller publishers can work more quickly in smaller print runs they can afford to take more risks.

The risks Mondo took in the early '90s now seem like a sure thing. As of last July, it's clear the literacy movement is destined to grow. Congress passed legislation (and appropriated over two billion dollars) to launch the "America Reads" program, which will employ early literacy tenets to make sure every American child can read independently by the end of third grade. Booksellers predict the additional funding will create a ripple effect that's bound to increase children's educational book sales in the next five years. It's not a market to ignore anymore.

—*Mary Cox*

The Straight Line Wonder by Mem Fox, a quirky tale about three straight lines, called for equally quirky illustrations and layouts. Marc Rosenthal's humorous, sophisticated style fit the bill.

Illustration: Works with 2-3 illustrators/year. Reviews ms/illustration packages from artists. Query; arrange portfolio review, including color copies of work. Illustration only: query with samples; arrange personal portfolio review; send résumé, portfolio, slides, tearsheets. Reports back only if interested. Samples not returned; samples filed.

Photography: Buys stock images. Needs photos of famous and prominent minority figures. Captions required. Uses b&w prints. Submit cover letter, résumé, published samples, stock photo list.

Terms: Pays authors 5-10% royalty based on wholesale price or work purchased outright for $250-2,000. Pays illustrators by the project (range: $40-250). Sends galleys to authors.

Tips: "Most of our assignments are work-for-hire. Submit résumé and samples of work to be considered for future assignments."

★MONDO PUBLISHING, One Plaza Rd., Greenvale NY 11548. (516)484-7812. Fax: (516)484-7813. Book publisher. **Acquisitions:** Louise May, senior editor. Publishes 60 picture and chapter books/year. 10% of books by first-time authors. Publishes various categories. "Our motto is 'creative minds creating ways to create lifelong readers.' We publish for both educational and trade markets, aiming for the highest quality books for both."

Fiction: Picture books, young readers, middle readers: adventure, animal, contemporary, fantasy, folktales, history, humor, multicultural, nature/environment, poetry, sports. Multicultural needs include: stories about children in different cultures or about children of different backgrounds in a U.S. setting. Recently published *The Straight Line Wonder*, by Mem Fox (ages 5-10); and *Twiddle Twins* series by Howard Goldsmith (ages 6-10, adventure chapter books).

Nonfiction: Young readers, middle readers: animal, biography, geography, how-to, multicultural, nature/environment, science, sports. Recently published *Up and Away!*, by Meredith Davis (ages 6-10, technology); and *Thinking About Ants*, by Barbara Brenner (ages 5-10, animals).

How to Contact/Writers: Fiction/Nonfiction: Query or submit complete ms. Reports on queries in 1 month; mss in 4-5 months. Will consider simultaneous submissions and previously published work. Mss returned with SASE. Queries must also have SASE.

Illustration: Works with 40 illustrators/year. Reviews ms/illustration packages from illustrators. Illustration only: Query with samples, résumé, portfolio. Reports only if interested. Samples returned with SASE; samples filed.

Photography: Occasionally uses freelance photographers. Buys stock images. Uses mostly nature photos. Uses color prints, transparencies.

Terms: Pays authors royalty of 2-5% based on wholesale/retail price. Offers advance based on project. Pays illustrators by the project (range: $3,000-9,000), royalty of 2-5% based on wholesale/retail price. Pays photographers by the project or per photo. Sends galleys to authors depending on project. Originals returned to artists at job's completion. Book catalog available for 9×12 SASE.

Tips: "Prefer illustrators with book experience or a good deal of experience in illustration projects requiring consistency of characters and/or setting over several illustrations. Prefer manuscripts targeted to trade market plus crossover to educational market."

MOREHOUSE PUBLISHING CO., P.O. Box 1321, Harrisburg PA 17105. (717)671-4500. Fax: (717)541-8128. Book publisher. Estab. 1884. Publisher: E. Allen Kelley. **Manuscript Acquisitions:** Debra Farrington, editorial director; Deborah Grahame, senior editor. **Art Acquisitions:** Corey Kent. Publishes 4 picture books/year. 25% of books by first-time authors. "Morehouse is a publisher and provider of books, church curricula, church resources materials and communications services for the Episcopal Church and other church groups and organizations."

Fiction: All levels: history, religion. Does not want to see "anything other than traditional Christian values." Recently published *Elizabeth's Beauty*, by Nancy Markham Alberts, illustrated by Pat Skiles.

Nonfiction: All levels: multicultural, religion, self help, social issues. Recently published *Make Five Bible Models*, by Gordon and Charlotte Stowell.

How to Contact/Writers: Fiction/nonfiction: Submit outline/synopsis and sample chapters. Reports on queries in 4-6 weeks; mss in 2-3 months. Publishes a book 1 year after acceptance. "Agented manuscripts are preferred."

Illustration: Works with 2-3 illustrators/year. Reviews ms/illustration packages from artists. Submit 3 chapters of ms with 1 piece of final art. Illustrations only: Submit résumé, tearsheets. Reports on art samples in 2 weeks. Samples returned with SASE; samples filed.

Photography: Buys photos from freelancers. Buys stock images. Uses photos of children/youth in everyday life experiences.

Terms: Pays authors royalty of 7-12% based on retail price. Offers modest advance payment. Pay illustrators royalty of 7-12%. Pays photographers by the project (range: $100-350). Sends galleys to authors. Original artwork returned at job's completion. Book catalog free on request if SASE ($2 postage) is supplied.

Tips: Writers: "Prefer authors who can do their own illustrations. Be fresh, be fun, not pedantic, but let your work have a message." Illustrators: "Work hard to develop an original style." Looks for ms/illustration packages "with a religious or moral value while remaining fun and entertaining."

MORGAN REYNOLDS PUBLISHING, 620 S. Elm St., Suite 384, Greensboro NC 27406. (910)275-1311. Fax: (910)274-3705. **Acquisitions:** John Riley, editor. Book publisher. Publishes 12 young adult titles/year. 50% of books by first-time authors.
 • Morgan Reynolds has added a new series called Great Athletes—8,000-10,000 word, contemporary or historical biographies of mail and female athletes for middle readers.
Fiction: Middle readers, young adults/teens: history, religion, sports.
Nonfiction: Middle readers, young adults/teens: biography, history, multicultural, social issues, sports. Multicultural needs include Native American, African-American and Latino subjects. Average word length: 12,000-20,000. Recently published *Tiger Woods*, by Aorn Boyd; *Myra Brodwell: First Woman Lawyer*, by Nancy Whitelaw; and *The Ordeal of Olive Oatman: A True Story of the American West*, by Margaret Rau.
How to Contact/Writers: Query; submit outline/synopsis with 3 sample chapters. Reports on queries in 1 month; mss in 1-2 months. Publishes a book 6 months after acceptance. Will consider simultaneous submissions or electronic submissions via disk.
Terms: Pays authors royalty of 8-12% based on wholesale price. Offers advances. Sends galleys to authors. Book catalog available for business-size SAE with 1 first-class stamp; ms guidelines available for SASE.
Tips: "We are open to suggestions—if you have an idea that excites you send it along. Recent trends suggest that the field is open for younger, smaller companies. Writers, especially ones starting out, should search us out."

JOSHUA MORRIS PUBLISHING, 221 Danbury Rd., Wilton CT 06897. (203)761-9999. Fax: (203)761-5655. Subsidiary of Reader's Digest, Inc. **Contact:** Acquisition Editor. **Art Director:** Julia Sabbagh. "We publish mostly early concept books and books for beginning readers. Most are in series and contain some kind of novelty element (i.e., lift the flap, die cut holes, book and soft toy, etc.). We publish approximately 200 books per year." 5% of books by first-time authors; 5% of books from agented authors; 90% of books published on commission (Book packaging).
Fiction: Picture books and young readers: activity books, adventure, animal, concept, nature/environment, reference, religion. Middle readers: animal, nature/environment, religion. Does not want to see poetry, short stories, science fiction. Average word length: picture books—300-400. Published *Whooo's There?*, by Lily Jones (ages 3-7, sound and light); *Ghostly Games*, by John Speirs, with additional text by Gill Speirs (ages 8-12, puzzle).
Nonfiction: Picture books, young readers and middle readers: activity books, animal, nature/environment, religion. Average word length: varies. Published *Alan Snow Complete Books (Dictionary, Atlas* and *Encyclopedia)*, by Alan Snow (ages 3-7, first reference); *Rain Forest Nature Search*, by Paul Sterry (ages 7-12, puzzle/activity).
How to Contact/Writers: Fiction/Nonfiction: Query. Nonfiction: Query. Reports on queries/mss in 3-4 months. Publishes a book 12-18 months after acceptance. Will consider simultaneous submissions and previously published work.
Illustration: Reviews ms/illustration packages from artists. Query. Illustrations only: Query with samples (nonreturnable). Provide résumé, promo sheet or tearsheets to be kept on file. Contact: Julia Sabbagh, art director and Ira Teichberg, creative director. Reports back only if interested. Original artwork returned (only if requested).
Photography: Buys stock and assigns work. Contact: Ira Teichberg, creative director. Uses photos of animals and children. Model/property releases required. Publishes photo concept books. Uses 4×6 glossy, color prints and 4×5 transparencies. Submit résumé, promo sheet or tearsheets to be kept on file.
Terms: Pays authors royalty or work purchased outright. Offers advances. Pays illustrators by the project or royalty. Photographers paid per photo.
Tips: Best bets with this market are "innovative concept and books that have a novelty element."

WILLIAM MORROW AND CO., 1350 Avenue of the Americas, New York NY 10019. (212)261-6500. See listings for Beech Tree Books, Greenwillow Books, Lothrop, Lee & Shepard Books and Morrow Junior Books.

MORROW JUNIOR BOOKS, 1350 Avenue of the Americas, New York NY 10019. "Morrow is one of the nation's leading publishers of books for children, including bestselling fiction and nonfiction." **Acquisitions**: David L. Reuther, editor-in-chief; Meredith Carpenter, executive editor; Andrea Curley, senior editor. Publishes 50 titles/year.
 • Morrow Junior accepts only manuscripts from agents or previously published authors.
Fiction: Recently published *Rumpelstiltskin's Daughter*, by Diane Stanley; *Engelbert Joins the Circus*, by Tom Paxton, illustrated by Roberta Wilson; and *Flood*, by Mary Calhoun, illustrated by Erick Ingraham.
Nonfiction: Recently published *I'm a Big Brother, I'm a Big Sister*, by Joanna Cole, illustrated by Maxie Chambliss; and *The Honey Makers*, by Gail Gibbons (nature).
How to Contact/Writers: Query.
Terms: Offers variable advance and royalty. All contracts negotiated individually. Book catalog and guidelines available for 9×12 SAE with 3 first-class stamps.

MULTNOMAH PUBLISHERS, INC., (formerly Questar Publishers, Inc.), 204 W. Adams Ave., P.O. Box 1720, Sisters OR 97759. (541)549-1144. E-mail: mcarlson@questarpubl.com. Imprint: Gold 'n' Honey. Book publisher. **Manuscript Acquisitions:** Melody Carlson, editorial coordinator. **Art Acquisitions:** Martin French. Publishes 3-5 picture books/year; 5-8 young readers/year; 6-9 middle readers/year; and 4-6 adult titles/year. Less than 10% of books by first-time authors. Publishes spiritual/religious titles. "Our goal is to be a Christian publishing company that glorifies God by creating products that change and enrich lives. We will distinguish ourselves from other publishers: 1) In the way we treat people; 2) In the quality of products and services we provide; and 3) In the stewardship of the resources God has given to Multnomah Publishers, Inc.''

Fiction: Picture books: animals. Picture books, young readers: concept, folktales, history, humor, nature/environment, religion. Recently published *Tupsu The Squirrel Who Was Afraid*, by Melody Carlson, illustrated by Alexander Reichstein (ages 3-8, lesson about what it means to trust God instead of being afraid).

Nonfiction Picture books, young readers: activity books, animal, arts/craft, concept, history, multicultural, nature/environment, religion, science. Recently published *Someday Heaven*, by Larry Libby, illustrated by Tim Jonke (children of all ages, answers questions and thoughts about Heaven).

How to Contact/Writers: Multnomah Publishers, Inc. accepts unsolicited mss.

Illustration: Works with 10-15 illustrators/year. Uses color artwork only. Reviews ms/illustration packages from artists. Query. Illustrations only: Query with samples, résumé, promo sheet. Reports back only if interested. Samples filed.

Photography: Buys photos from freelancers. Contact: art director. Buys stock and assigns work. Uses children, animals and nature photos. Model/property releases required; captions required. Uses 35mm, $2\frac{1}{4} \times 2\frac{1}{4}$, 4×5 transparencies. Submit cover letter, résumé, published samples, color promo piece.

Terms: Pays royalty based on wholesale price. Pays illustrators by the project or royalty. Pays photographers by the project or per photo. Sends galleys to authors. Originals returned to artists at job's completion.

‡**TOMMY NELSON**, Imprint of Thomas Nelson, Inc., 404 BNA Dr., Bldg. 200, Suite 508, Nashville TN 37206. (615)889-9000. Fax: (615)902-2415. Book publisher. **Acquisitions Editor:** Laura Minchew. Publishes 15 picture books/year; 20 young readers/year; and 25 middle readers/year. 5% of books by first-time authors. Evangelical Christian publisher.

Fiction: Picture books: concept, humor, religion. Young readers: adventure, concept, humor, religion. Middle readers: adventure, humor, religion, sports, suspense/mystery. Young adults: adventure, problem novels, religion, sports, suspense/mystery. Recently published *The Younguns of Mansfield*, by Thomas L. Tedrow (ages 10-14); *The Parable of the Lily*, by Liz Curtis Higgs, illustrated by Nancy Murger (picture book for ages 3-7); and *Stage Fright*, by C. Archer (part of Christy series for ages 10-14).

Nonfiction: Picture books, young readers: activity books, religion, self help. Middle readers, young adults: reference, religion, self help. Recently published *Angels in Action*, by Helen Haidle, illustrated by David Haidle (ages 3-7); *Tiny Talks*, by Robert J. Morgan, illustrated by Ann Hogue (ages 3-7); and *The Toddler's ABC Book*, by Andy and Sandra Stanley (ages 1-3).

How to Contact/Writers: Submit outline/synopsis and 3 sample chapters. Reports on queries in 1 month; mss in 3 months. Publishes a book 12-18 months after acceptance.

Illustration: Reviews ms/illustration packages from artists. Query with samples. Reports in 1 month. Samples filed.

Terms: Pays authors royalty of 5% based on wholesale price or work purchased outright. Offers advances of $1,000 and up. Pays illustrators by the project or royalty. Sends galleys to authors. Manuscript guidelines for SASE.

Tips: "Know the CBA market—and avoid preachiness."

‡**NEW CANAAN PUBLISHING COMPANY INC.**, P.O. Box 752, New Canaan CT 06840. Phone/Fax: (203)966-3408. E-mail: newcan@sprynet.com. Website: http://ourworld.compuserve.com/homepages/New_Canaan. Book publisher. Vice President: Kathy Mittelstadt. Publishes 1 picture book/year; 3 young readers/year; 5 middle readers/year; and 1 young adult title/year. 50% of books by first-time authors. "We seek books with strong educational or traditional moral content."

Fiction: All levels: adventure, history, religion (Christianity), suspense/mystery. Picture books: phonics readers. "Stories about disfunctional families are not encouraged." Average word length: picture books—1,000-3,000; young readers—8,000-20,000; middle readers—8,000-30,000; young adults—15,000-40,000. Recently published *My Daddy is a Soldier*, written and illustrated by Kirk and Sharon Hibrecht (picture book for military kids); *Indian Gold*, by Steve Givens, cover by Lorraine Heokel (first of an adventure series); and *Levi Dust*, by Steve Givens, illustrated by Lorraine Heokel (historical fiction).

Nonfiction: All levels: geography, history, how-to, reference, religion (Christian only), textbooks. Average word length: picture books—1,000-3,000; young readers—8,000-20,000; middle readers—8,000-30,000; young adults—15,000-40,000.

How to Contact/Writers: Submit outline/synopsis or complete ms. Reports on queries in 1-2 months; mss in 2 months. Publishes a book 6-12 months after acceptance. Will consider electronic submissions via disk or modem.

Illustration: Works with 3-5 illustrators/year. Reviews ms/illustration packages from artists. Query or send ms with dummy. Illustrations only: Query with samples; send résumé, promo sheet. Reports in 1-2 months. Samples returned with SASE.

Terms: Pays authors royalty of 7-12% based on wholesale price. Royalty may be shared with illustrator where relevant. Pays illustrators royalty of 4-6% as share of total royalties. Book catalog available for SAE; ms guidelines available for SASE.

Tips: "We are a small be growing startup company. Writers and illustrators will be coming to us very close to our beginning. We believe based on sampling of our initial products that there is a very strong demand for fiction works with strong, traditional values content.

‡THE NEW DAWN PUBLISHING CO., 608 Huntington St., Waterton NY 13601. (315)779-2268. E-mail: newdawnmcnet.net. Website: http://www.imcnet/~newdawn/index.html. Book publisher. Estab. 1991. Published 3 young readers/year; 2 young adult titles/year. 60% of books by first-time authors. "We publish children's spiritual self-help book, unique 'one-of-a-kind' practical stories developing love of self and others."
● New Dawn's catalog and guidelines are available on their website.
Fiction: All levels: adventure, health, humor, multicultural, nature/environment, special needs. Picture books: concept. Young readers: anthology, concept, science fiction. Middle readers, young adults: problem novels, science fiction. Recently published *Monkey See, Monkey Do*, by G.M.P. Bennett, illustrated by Tye Poe.
Nonfiction: All levels: how-to, mulitcultural, nature/environment, self help, social issues, special needs. Young readers: concept. Middle readers: health. Young adults: concept, health. Recenlty published *Syncronizing Yourself* and *Who Am I? Getting it together*, both by G.M.P. Bennett.
How to Contact/Writers: Fiction/Nonfiction: Submit complete ms. Reports in 3 weeks. Publishes a ms 1 year after acceptance. Will consider electronic submissions via disk or modem.
Terms: Pays authors 5-12% royalty or work purchased outright for $350-2,000. Offers advance. (Average amount: $600.) Sends galleys to authors. Book catalog available for $2.50. Writer's/artist's guidelines available for SASE.

NEW DISCOVERY BOOKS, 299 Jefferson Rd., P.O. Box 480, Parsippany NJ 07054-0480. (201)739-8000. Fax: (201)739-8606. Imprint of Silver Burdett Press, Simon & Schuster Publishing Education Group. Book publisher. **Acquisitions:** Debbie Biber, editor. See Silver Burdett Press listing.

‡NEW HOPE, Imprint of Woman's Missionary Union, P.O. Box 12065, Birmingham AL 35202-2065. (205)991-8100. Website: http://www.wmu.com/wmu. Book publisher. **Acquisitions:** Cindy McClain, editorial director. Publishes 2-3 picture books/year; 1-2 young readers/year; and 1-2 middle readers/year. 25% of books by first-time authors. "Our goal is to provide missions-related programs, information, resources and training to motivate and enable churches and believers to meet spiritual, physical and social needs, locally and globally."
Fiction: All levels: multicultural, religion. Multicultural fiction must be related to Christian concepts, particularly Christian missions. Recently published *The Elephant Path*, by Judy Langley, illustrated by Wendy Kikugawa (picture book, preschool).
Nonfiction: All levels: multicultural, religion. Multicultural nonfiction must be related to Christian concepts, particularly Christian missions.
How to Contact/Writers: Submit complete ms. Reports on queries in 3 months; mss in 3-6 months. Publishes a book 2 years after acceptance. Will consider simultaneous submissions.
Illustration: Works with 2-3 illustrators/year. Reviews ms/illustration packages from artists. Send ms with dummy. Illustrations only: query with samples (color copies). Reports back only if interested. Samples not returned; samples filed.
Photography: Buy stock already on file. Model/property releases required.
Terms: Pays authors royalty of 7-10% based on retail price or work purchased outright (depends on length). Pays illustrators by the project. Sends galleys to author. Originals returned to artist at job's completion. Book catalog available for 10×12 SAE and 3 first-class stamps; ms guidelines for SASE.
Tips: "Obtain the catalog first to see the kinds of material we publish."

NORTHLAND PUBLISHING, P.O. Box 1389, Flagstaff AZ 86002-1389. (520)774-5251. Fax: (520)774-0592. E-mail: info@northlandpub.com. Website: http://www.northlandpub.com. Book publisher. Estab. 1958. **Manuscript Acquisitions:** Erin Murphy, editor-in-chief. **Art Acquisitions:** David Janney, art director. Publishes 6 picture books/year; 2 young readers/year; 7 young adult titles/year. 75% of books by first-time authors. Primary theme is West and Southwest regionals, Native American stories. "We seek authoritative manuscripts on our specialty subjects; no mainstream, general fiction or nonfiction."
Fiction: Picture books, young readers and middle readers: animal. Picture books, young readers: folktales, humor. Middle readers: adventure. Middle readers, young adults: suspense/mystery. All levels: history, nature/environment, multicultural. "Multicultural needs include stories with characters/plots that have to do with multicultural aspects of the Southwest; i.e., Hispanic and Native American. Our Native American folktales are enjoyed by readers of all ages, child through adult." No religion, science fiction, anthology. Average word length: picture books—800; young readers—1,500; middle readers—20,000. Recently published *A Campfire for Cowboy Billy*, by Wendy K. Ulmer, illustrated by Kenneth S. Spengler (picture book, (ages 5-8); *Jack and the Giant: A Story Full of Beans*, by Jim Harris (picture book, ages 5-8).
Nonfiction: Picture books, young readers and middle readers: animal, multicultural, historical. Average word length: picture books—800; young readers—1,500; middle readers—20,000.
How to Contact/Writers: Reports on queries/mss in 2-3 months. "Acknowledgment sent immediately upon receipt." If ms and art are complete at time of acceptance, publication usually takes 18 months. Will consider simultaneous submissions if labelled as such.
Illustration: Works with 6-8 illustrators/year. Uses color artwork only. Reviews ms/illustration packages from

INSIDER REPORT

Growing Christian market offers unexpected outlet for writers

If you think Christian children's publishers produce only kids' Bible story books, Christmas stories and parables, you'll be surprised paging through a Tommy Nelson catalog. A Division of Thomas Nelson, Inc. (resulting from a marriage of Nelson's children's line to Word Kids), Tommy Nelson offers a diverse list including a series of scary mysteries, a book of money-making ideas for kids, and an adventure series of futuristic fiction including virtual reality and time travel, along with traditional Biblical tales.

Laura Minchew

"Bible stories are very important to Christians," says Laura Minchew, vice president of editorial acquisitions for Tommy Nelson. "They also live the rest of the day just like everyone else, so we're trying to offer Bible story books along with adventure books and fun books for casual reading."

An adventure story from a Christian publisher does differ somewhat from an adventure story from a general children's publisher. "Our books have a take-away value," explains Minchew. "There are some delightful stories in trade bookstores that are simply fun to read, but there's nothing really to take away at the end of the day. In the inspirational market, readers come away with something they've learned about life, a value, something that inspires them, a moral."

For example, the Tommy Nelson title *50 Money Making Ideas for Kids*, by Larry Burkett, "actually teaches some stewardship principles such as 'with ownership comes responsibility' found in other financial books, but actually based in the Bible."

Writers may wonder how Tommy Nelson's SpineChillers Mysteries line of scary stories could fit the needs of an inspirational publisher. These titles certainly are not clones of R.L. Stine's books. "There are mystery elements to these books; there are scary things, but the difference is that by the end of our books, everything is explained rationally or scientifically—there's no supernatural. These are not nightmare books."

These "kinder, gentler Goosebumps" books may be just what some parents seek for their children's bookshelves. "We're trying to offer an alternative to parents, so they don't have to say, 'You can't read anything scary.' SpineChillers offer a nice combination of elements that a child is looking for and the things a parent is going to feel good about them reading," says Minchew.

There is one pitfall writers should avoid when submitting to the Christian children's market—preachiness. Books can have a spiritual bent without talking down to kids, pointing fingers at them, or shoving lessons down their throats. "As an adult, I don't like someone telling me, 'This is what you will think and this is what you will do.' To me that's really offensive. We see kids in a lot of our books for whom Christianity is a way of life. They act as Christians would act, they talk as Christians would talk. They don't

INSIDER REPORT, *Minchew*

go around preaching to everyone they see—it's more natural," says Minchew.

This light touch may explain why sales of books from inspirational publishers are not limited to the Christian market. One humorous Tommy Nelson series, The Incredible Worlds of Wally MacDoogle, written by Bill Myers, has sold over a quarter million units in CBA (Christian Booksellers Association), ABA (American Booksellers Association) and mass market outlets. "I think the sales figures of some of our books would be surprising to people," says Minchew. In fact, a recent consumer research study shows, out of all book categories, juvenile religious fiction has had the second highest growth in market share in recent years.

Sales potential is certainly an important factor for writers to consider when preparing a submission package. "When I present a book to a sales rep, I have to have a hook," says Minchew. "I was talking to an author today, and I said, 'What differentiates your series from these other two series that sound very similar?' He said, 'I'm a better writer.' Okay, good. You are a better writer. That will help sell book number six in your series. But tell me—when I'm going to sell book number one, what's the marketing hook? What's the angle? What differentiates this book from everything else?

"I get submissions from authors that say, 'I've always wanted to write a children's book, and this is a nice little story.' Well, am I supposed to say to a sales rep, 'Hey look—here's a nice little story'; then they're supposed say that to the bookseller; and the bookseller is supposed to say that to the customer? There has to be something to motivate the buyer. There's either a felt need, or something really unique about the book. I know

Tommy Nelson's SpineChillers series offers an alternative to horror stories so popular among middle readers. SpineChillers books give scientific and logical explanations for weird occurrences, with no inclusion of supernatural elements.

INSIDER REPORT, *continued*

Reprinted with permission of Tommy Nelson.

A great marketing plan along with the hip concept of virtual reality have made Sigmund Brouwer's CyberQuest series a success for Tommy Nelson. Brouwer's books follow the travels of his hero Mok through virtual time. "This person from the future is seeing how Jesus impacted people's lives and thinking in every time period and throughout every part of history," says Laura Minchew, Tommy Nelson editor.

writers feel very strongly about their books, and it's amazing how often they don't tell me why they feel strongly. They expect me to dig through 200 pages to figure out why."

Another Tommy Nelson series, CyberQuest, is a perfect example of an author with a great marketing concept. The first book in this series by Sigmund Brouwer is selling for 99 cents, "seeding the market." Each book in the six-book series is an independent story, but the end of each book teases the next one, and they're all a serial—at the end, kids can read them all through as a straight story. Brouwer has also taken an ultra-hip element—virtual reality—and woven it into a series of adventures following a futuristic hero as he travels through time to save his race from annihilation by the evil Technocrats. "Sigmund Brouwer is one of our most fun authors," says Minchew. "He is in schools constantly, so he really knows where kids are, what they like and what they're thinking."

For Minchew, this audience familiarity is important. But more important is knowing the companies you're submitting to and targeting manuscripts appropriately. "We get about 50 manuscripts a week right now—it's unbelievable to try to get through them. The vast majority are not what we're looking for. If you don't have something that's inspirational in nature, don't send it to us saying, 'This isn't really what you want, but here's a nice story.'"

—*Alice P. Buening*

© 1997 Kenneth Spengler

Though Ken Spengler, whose gouaches bring color and feeling to *Campfire for Cowboy Billy*, has been a successful illustrator for ten years, he worked mainly in advertising, editorial and adult trade book publishing. When he discovered the children's market five years ago, he found it suited him well. "I like children's books because they give me something to play with that's whimsical, that I can be freer with as opposed to advertising assignments or murder mystery covers." Long term projects like children's picture books allow him to spend more time on each illustration, a luxury he misses on assignments in markets with tighter deadlines. This is Spengler's second picture book for Northland. He got his first assignment, *How Jack Rabbit Got His Very Long Ears*, after he sent the publisher tearsheets from work he had done for other markets.

artists. Submit ms with samples; slides or color photocopies. Illustrations only: Query art director with samples, promo sheet, slides, tearsheets. Reports only if interested. Samples returned with SASE; samples filed.
Terms: Pays authors/illustrators royalty of 4-7% based on wholesale price. Pays photographers by the project (range $1,500-3,000). Offers advances. "This depends so much on quality of work and quantity needed." Original artwork returned at job's completion. Book catalog, artists' and ms guidelines available for SASE.
Tips: Receptive to "Native American folktales (must be retold by a Native American author). Please research our company (look at our catalog) before submitting your work. No phone queries, please."

‡NORTH-SOUTH BOOKS, 1123 Broadway, Suite 800, New York NY 10010. (212)463-9736. **Acquisitions:** Marc Cheshire, president, publisher and art director. U.S. office of Nord-Süd Verlag, Switzerland. Publishes 75 titles/year; 25 acquired through U.S. office.
Fiction: Picture books.
Nonfiction: Publishes nonfiction occasionally.
How to Contact/Writers: Only interested in agented material.
Illustration: Use artists for picture book illustration.
Terms: Pays authors and illustrators advance and royalties.

THE OLIVER PRESS, INC., Charlotte Square, 5707 W. 36th St., Minneapolis MN 55416. Phone: (612)926-8981. Fax: (612)926-8965. Book publisher. **Acquisitions:** Denise Sterling, Teresa Faden, Jason Richie. Publishes 8 young adult titles/year. 10% of books by first-time authors. "We publish collective biographies of people who made an impact in one area of history, including science, government, archaeology, business and crime. Titles from The Oliver Press can connect young adult readers with their history to give them the confidence that only knowledge can provide. Such confidence will prepare them for the lifelong responsibilities of citizenship. Our books will introduce students to people who made important discoveries and great decisions."

Nonfiction: Middle reader, young adults: biography, geography, history, multicultural, science, history of science and technology. "Authors should only suggest ideas that fit into one of our existing series. We would like to add to our Innovators series on the history of technology." Average word length: young adult—20,000 words. Recently published *America's Third-Party Presidential Candidates*, by Nathan Aaseng (ages 10 and up, collective biography); *Women Business Leaders*, by Robert B. Pile (ages 10 and up, collective biography); *Diseases: Finding the Cure*, by Robert Mulcahy (ages 10 and up, collective biography); and *Aviation: Reaching for the Sky*, by Don Berliner (ages 10 and up, collective biography).

How to Contact/Writers: Nonfiction: Query with outline/synopsis. Reports in 6 months. Publishes a book approximately 1 year after acceptance.

Photography: Buys photos from freelancers. Buys stock images. Looks primarily for photos of people in the news. Captions required. Uses 8 × 10 b&w prints. Submit cover letter, résumé and stock photo list.

Terms: Work purchased outright from authors ($750 and up). Sends galleys to authors upon request. Book catalog and ms guidelines available for SASE.

Tips: "Authors should read some of the books we have already published before sending a query to The Oliver Press. Authors should propose collective biographies for one of our existing series."

OPEN HAND PUBLISHING INC., P.O. Box 22048, Seattle WA 98122. (206)447-0597. Book publisher. **Acquisitions Editor:** Pat Andrus. Publishes 1-3 children's books/year. 50% of books by first-time authors. Multicultural books: African-American theme or bilingual.

• Open Hand is not currently accepting manuscripts.

Fiction: Picture books, young readers and middle readers: history and African-American. Young adult/teens: African-American. Average length: picture books—32-64 pages; young readers—64 pages; middle readers—64 pages; young adult/teens—120 pages.

Nonfiction: All levels: history and African-American. Average length: picture books—32-64 pages; young readers—64 pages; middle readers—64 pages; young adult/teens: 64-120 pages.

Terms: Pays authors royalty of 5-10% based on wholesale price. Offers advances. Pays illustrators by the project; commission for the work. Sends galleys to authors. Book catalog available for SAE and 2 first-class stamps; ms guidelines available for SAE and 1 first-class stamp.

✦ORCA BOOK PUBLISHERS, P.O. Box 5626 Station B, Victoria, British Columbia V8R 6S4 Canada. (604)380-1229. Fax: (604)380-1892. Book publisher. Estab. 1984. Publisher: R. Tyrell. **Acquisitions:** Ann Featherstone, children's book editor. Publishes 10 picture books/year; 4 middle readers/year; and 4 young adult titles/year. 25% of books by first time authors. "We only consider authors and illustrators who are Canadian or who live in Canada."

• Orca no longer considers nonfiction.

Fiction: Picture books: animals, contemporary, history, nature/environment. Middle readers: adventure, contemporary, history, nature/environment, problem novels, suspense/mystery. Young adults: adventure, contemporary, history, multicultural, nature/environment, problem novels, suspense/mystery. Average word length: picture books—500-2,000; middle readers—20,000-35,000; young adult—25,000-45,000. Published *The Lighthouse Dog*, by Betty Waterton, illustrated by Dean Griffiths (picture book, ages 4-8); *Cougar Cove*, by Julie Lawson (juvenile novel); and *The Tuesday Cafe*, by Don Trembath (young adult novel).

How to Contact/Writers: Fiction: Submit complete ms if picture book; submit outline/synopsis and 3 sample chapters. Nonfiction: Query with SASE. "All queries or unsolicited submissions should be accompanied by a SASE." Reports on queries in 6-8 weeks; mss in 1-3 months. Publishes a book 18-24 months after acceptance.

Illustration: Works with 8-10 illustrators/year. Reviews ms/illustration packages from artists. Submit ms with 3-4 photocopies of final art. "Reproductions only, no original art please." Illustrations only: Query with samples; provide résumé, slides. Reports in 6-8 weeks. Samples returned with SASE; samples filed.

Terms: Pays authors royalty of 5% for picture books, 10% for novels, based on retail price. Offers advances (average amount: $2,000). Pays illustrators royalty of 5% minimum based on retail price and advance against royalties. Sends galleys to authors. Original artwork returned at job's completion if picture books. Book catalog available for legal or 8½ × 11 manila SAE and $2 first-class postage. Ms guidelines available for SASE. Art guidelines not available.

Tips: "American authors and illustrators should remember that the U.S. stamps on their reply envelopes cannot be posted in any country outside of the U.S."

ORCHARD BOOKS, 95 Madison Ave., New York NY 10016. (212)951-2600. Imprint of Grolier, Inc. Book publisher. President and Publisher: Judy V. Wilson. **Manuscript Acquisitions:** Sarah Caguiat, editor. **Art Acquisitionis:** Art Director. "We publish between 60 and 70 books yearly including fiction, poetry, picture books, and some non-fiction." 10-25% of books by first-time authors.

• Orchard's books won several awards in 1997. *A Girl Named Disater*, by Nancy Farmer, received a Newbery Honor Book award. Three titles received Caldecott Honor Book awards: *Hush!*, illustrated by Holly Meade; *The Graphic Alphabet*, illustrated by David Pelletier; and *The Paper Boy*, illustrated by Dav Pilkey. Orchard is not accepting unsolicited manuscripts.

Fiction: All levels: animal, anthology, contemporary, fantasy, folktales, history, humor, multicultural, nature/environment, poetry, science fiction, sports, suspense/mystery.

Nonfiction: Picture books, young readers: animal, history, multicultural, nature/environment, science, social issues. "We publish nonfiction on a very selective basis."
How to Contact/Writers: Query only with SASE.
Illustration: Works with 40 illustrators/year. Art director reviews ms/illustration portfolios. Submit "tearsheets or photocopies or photostats of the work." Reports on art samples in 1 month. Samples returned with SASE. No disks or slides, please.
Terms: Most commonly an advance against list royalties. Sends galleys to authors; dummies to illustrators. Original artwork returned at job's completion. Book catalog free on request with 8½×11 SASE with 4 oz. postage.
Tips: "Read some of our books to determine first whether your manuscript is suited to our list."

‡□OTTENHEIMER PUBLISHERS, 5 Park Center Court, Suite 300, Owings Mills MD 21117-5001. (410)902-9100. Fax: (410)902-7210. Imprints: Dream House, Halo Press. Independent book producer/packager. Estab. 1896. **Manuscript Acquisitions:** Laura J. Wallace, editorial director. **Art Acquisitions:** Michael Young, art director. Publishes 2 picture books/year; 30 early readers/year. 20% of books by first-time authors. "We publish series; rarely single-title ideas. Early learning, religious, Beatrix Potter, activity books. We do lots of novelty formats and always want more ideas for inexpensive and creative packaging concepts. We are sticker book and pop-up book experts."
Nonfiction: Picture books: activity books, animal, concept, early learning novelty formats, geography, nature/environment, reference, religion. Recently published *My Bible Alphabet Block Pop-Up Book* (ages 3-6); *Wonders of Nature* (ages 3-6); and *Christmas Stocking Stuffer Activity Books* (ages 3-6).
How to Contact/Writers: Fiction (very rarely): Query. Nonfiction: Submit complete ms. Reports on queries in 3 weeks; on ms in 2-3 months. Publishes a book 6 months to 1 year after acceptance. Will consider simultaneous submissions; previously published work.
Illustration: Works with 8 illustrators/year. Reviews ms/illustration packages from artists. Query. Illustrations only: Send promo sheet and tearsheets to be kept on file. Reports back only if interested. Samples not returned; samples kept on file.
Photography: Buys stock images.
Terms: Pays authors royalty of 5-10% based on wholesale price or work purchased outright for $200-1,000. Offers advances. Pays illustrators by the project (range: $200-16,000). Sends galleys to authors. Originals returned to artist at job's completion. Ms guidelines for SASE.
Tips: "Don't submit single stories; we want series concepts for early learners, ages three to seven."

‡OTTER CREEK PUBLISHING, P.O. Box 126, 104 W. Main, Mulvane KS 67110-0126. (800)447-9099. Book publisher. Estab. 1994. **Manuscript Acquisitions:** John D. Loeb, acquisitions editor. **Art Acquisitions:** Brad A. Steventon, art director. Publishes 2 picture books/year; 2 middle readers/year. 25% of books are by first-time authors. "We are best known for our author/illustrator programs presented at Kansas elementary schools."
Fiction: Picture books, middle readers: adventure, animal, humor, nature/environment, suspense/mystery. Average word length: picture books—1,000; middle readers—15,000. Recently published *Secret Jealousy*, written by Misty A. Henson, illustrated by Nanetta Bananto (ages 9-11, mystery); *Messy Tessie Takes a Bath*, written by Julie Brown, illustrated by Brad Steventon (ages pre-8, humor); and *Mandy's Backyard*, written by John D. Loeb, illustrated by Jean Thomson (pre-8, animal/pet).
Nonfiction: Picture books, middle readers: activity books, animal, nature/environment. Average word length: picture books—1,000; middle readers—15,000. Recently published *The Long and the Short of It—Fun with Phonics*, written by Denise Schoemer, illustrated by Brad Steventon (ages pre-8, activity book).
How to Contact/Writers: Fiction/Nonfiction: Submit complete ms. Reports on ms in 2 months. Publishes a book 1 year after acceptance. Will consider simultaneous submissions; electronic submissions via disk or modem.
Illustration: Works with 3 illustrators/year. Reviews ms/illustration packages from artists. Send ms with dummy or submit ms with 3 pieces of final art. Illustrations only: Arrange personal portfolio review. Reports in 2 months. Samples returned with SASE; samples filed.
Terms: Pays authors royalty of 5-15% based on wholesale and retail price. Pays illustrators by the project (range: $500-1,500). Sends galleys to authors; dummies to illustrators. Book catalog available for #10 SAE and 1 first-class stamp; ms guidelines available for SASE.
Tips: "We have a small distribution base. We have sold books all over the world; most of our sales are in Kansas, but we are not a regional publisher."

OUR CHILD PRESS, P.O. Box 74, Wayne PA 19087-0074. (610)964-0606. Fax: (610)293-9038. Book publisher. **Acquisitions:** Carol Hallenbeck, president. 90% of books by first-time authors.
Fiction/Nonfiction: All levels: adoption, multicultural, special needs. Published *Don't Call Me Marda*, written and illustrated by Sheila Kelly Welch; *Is That Your Sister?* by Catherine and Sherry Burin; and *Oliver: A Story About Adoption*, by Lois Wichstrom.
How to Contact/Writers: Fiction/Nonfiction: Query or submit complete ms. Reports on queries/mss in 6 months. Publishes a book 6-12 months after acceptance.
Illustration: Works with 1 illustrator/year. Uses primarily b&w artwork. Reviews ms/illustration packages from artists. Ms/illustration packages and illustration only: Query first. Submit résumé, tearsheets and photocopies.

Contact: Carol Hallenbeck, president. Reports on art samples in 2 months. Samples returned with SASE; samples kept on file.
Terms: Pays authors in royalties of 5-10% based on wholesale price. Pays illustrators royalties of 5-10% based on wholesale price. Original artwork returned at job's completion. Book catalog for business-size SAE and 52¢ postage.
Tips: Won't consider anything not related to adoption.

★OUR SUNDAY VISITOR, INC., 200 Noll Plaza, Huntington IN 46750. (219)356-8400. Fax: (219)356-8472. Book publisher. **Acquisitions:** Jacquelyn M. Lindsey, James Manney. Publishes primarily religious, educational, parenting, reference and biographies.
  ● Our Sunday Visitor, Inc., is publishing only those children's books that tie in to sacramental preparation. Contact the acquisitions editor for manuscript guidelines and a book catalog.
How to Contact/Writers: Nonfiction: Query, submit complete ms, or submit outline/synopsis, and 2-3 sample chapters. Reports on queries in 2 months. Publishes a book 18-24 months after acceptance. Will consider simultaneous submissions, electronic submissions via disk or modem, previously published work.
Illustration: Reviews ms/illustration packages from artists. Contact: Jacquelyn Lindsey or James Manney, acquisitions editors. Illustration only: Query with samples. Contact: Aquisitions Editor. Reports in 2 weeks. Original artwork returned at job's completion.
Photography: Buys photos from freelancers. Contact: Jacquelyn Lindsey, acquisitions editor.
Terms: Pays authors based on net receipts. Offers royalty. Sends galleys to authors; dummies to illustrators. Book catalog available for SAE; ms guidelines available for SASE.
Tips: "Stay in accordance with our guidelines."

RICHARD C. OWEN PUBLISHERS, INC., P.O. Box 585, Katonah NY 10536. (914)232-3903. Fax: (914)232-3977. Website: http://www.rcowen.com. Book publisher. **Acquisitions:** Janice Boland, children's books editor/art director. Publishes 20 picture story books/year. 90% of books by first-time authors. We publish "child-focused books about characters and situations with which five-, six-, and seven-year-old children can identify—books that can be read for meaning, entertainment, enjoyment and information. We include multicultural stories that present minorities in a positive and natural way. Our stories show the diversity in America."
Fiction: Picture books for young readers: adventure, animal, anthology, contemporary, folktales, humor, multicultural, nature/environment, poetry, science fiction, sports, suspense/mystery. Does not want to see holiday, religious themes, moral teaching stories. "No talking animals with personified human characteristics, jingles and rhymes, holiday stories, alphabet books, stories without plots, stories with nostalgic views of childhood, soft or sugar-coated tales. No stereotyping." Average word length: 40-100 words. Recently published *Spiders Everywhere*, by Betty Baker, illustrated by Judith Pfeiffer; and *Jump the Broom*, by Candy Grant Helmso, illustrated by Joanne Friar (folktale).
Nonfiction: Picture books for young readers: animals, careers, geography, multicultural, nature/environment, science, sports. Multicultural needs include: "Good stories respectful of all heritages, races, cultural—African-American, Hispanic, American Indian." Wants lively stories. No "encyclopedic" type of information stories. Average word length: 40-100 words. Recently published *New York City Buildings*, by Ann Mace, photos by Tim Holmstron.
How to Contact/Writers: Fiction/nonfiction: Submit complete ms. "*Must* request guidelines first with #10 SASE." Reports on mss in 1-8 months. Publishes a book 2-3 years after acceptance. Will consider simultaneous submissions.
Illustration: Works with 15-20 illustrators/year. Uses color artwork only. Illustration only: Send color copies/reproductions or photos of art or provide tearsheets; do not send slides. Must request guidelines first. Reports in 4-6 months only if interested. Samples returned with SASE; samples filed.
Photography: Buys photos from freelancers. Wants photos that are child-oriented; candid shots; not interested in portraits. "Natural, bright, crisp and colorful—of children and of interesting subjects and compositions attractive to children. If photos are assigned, we buy outright—retain ownership and all rights to photos taken in the project." Sometimes interested in stock photos for special projects. Uses 35mm, 2¼×2¼, color transparencies.
Terms: Pays authors royalties of 5% based on retail price. Offers no advances. Pays illustrators by the project (range: $800-2,500). Pays photographers by the project (range: $800-1,500) or per photo ($100-150). Original artwork returned 12-18 months after job's completion. Book brochure, ms/artists guidelines available for SASE.
Tips: Seeking "stories (both fiction and nonfiction) that have charm, magic, impact and appeal; that children living in today's society will want to read and reread; books with strong storylines, child-appealing language, action and interesting, vivid characters. Write from your heart—for the ears and eyes and heart of your readers—use an economy of words. Visit the children's room at public library."

‡♥OWL BOOKS, Imprint of Grey de Pencier Books, 179 John St., Suite 500, Toronto, Ontario M5T 3G5 Canada. Book publisher. Estab. 1976. Publishing Director: Sheba Meland. **Manuscript Acquisitions:** Submissions Editor. **Art Acquisitions:** Art Director; Photo Editor. Publishes 2 picture books/year; 3 young readers, middle readers/year. 10% of books by first-time authors. Publishes nature, science and children's crafts and hobbies. "We give preference to work by Canadian writers living in Canada or the U.S.; please let us know if you are Canadian."

© Joanne Friar

Joanne Friar received an assignment to illustrate *Jump the Broom*, a story about an African-American wedding custom, after sending samples of her color pencil style to Janice Boland, editor/art director at Richard C. Owen Publishers, Inc. "Joanne sent us a really attractive mailer," says Boland, whose publishing company is always on the lookout for artists who can portray multicultural characters. "Joanne's samples showed her ability to portray African-American and Hispanic characters with dignity, freshness and charm. She sent us several pieces in one envelope with a very brief cover letter. That's helpful to us, because it's easier to see what artists can do when they send several samples at once rather than one at a time. Joanne's colors are beautiful and she really has a voice. We hope to work with her on several projects in the future."

Fiction: Picture books, young readers: animal, concept, humor, nature/environment. Does not want to see "clichéd environmental stories." Average word length: picture books—1,000; young readers—2,000. Recently published *Wild in the City*, written and illustrated by Jan Thornhill (ages 5-10, picturebook/nature); and *Dragon in the Rocks*, written and illustrated by Marie Day (ages 5-10, picturebook/biography).
Nonfiction: Picture books, young readers, middle readers: animal, arts/crafts, concept, hobbies, how-to, nature/environment, science. Average word length: picture books—1,000-1,500; young readers—2,000-3,500; middle readers—7,500-10,000. Recently published *Crime Science: How Investigators Use Science to Track Down the Bad Guys* (ages 8-12, science/tech); *Little Wonders: Animal Babies and their Families*, by Marilyn Baillie (ages 5 and up, nature); and *I Can Make Art*, by Mary Wallace (ages 4 and up, crafts).
How to Contact/Writers: Fiction: Submit complete ms. Nonfiction: Submit outline/synopsis and 2 sample chapters. Reports on queries/mss in 3 months. Publishes a book 18 months after acceptance.

Illustration: Uses color artwork only. Reviews ms/illustration packages from artists. Send ms with dummy and 3 photocopies of final art.

Photography: Buys stock images. Uses photos of nature, science, children. Model/property release required; captions required. Uses 35mm, 2¼×2¼, color transparencies. Submit cover letter, résumé, published samples, client list, stock photo list.

Terms: Pays authors royalties based on retail price, outright purchase. Offers advances. Pays illustrators royalty or by the project. Pays photographers by the project or per photo. Sends galleys to authors; dummies to illustrators. Book catalog available for SAE and first-class postage; IRCs outside Canada.

Tips: "We are affiliated with *Owl* and *Chickadee* magazines. We publish mainly nonfiction, and look for innovative ideas, top-notch research, and an understanding of what children want in an information or activity book. Read some Owl Books for an appreciation of our approach!"

PACIFIC VIEW PRESS, P.O. Box 2657, Berkeley CA 94702. (510)849-4213. Fax: (510)843-5835. Book publisher. **Acquisitions:** Pam Zumwalt, president. Publishes 1-2 picture books/year. 50% of books by first-time authors. "We publish unique, high-quality introductions to Asian cultures and history for children 8-12, for schools, libraries and families. Our children's books focus on hardcover illustrated nonfiction. We look for titles on aspects of the history and culture of the countries and peoples of the Pacific Rim, especially China, presented in an engaging, informative and respectful manner. We are interested in books that all children will enjoy reading and using, and that parents and teachers will want to buy."

Nonfiction: Young readers, middle readers: Asia-related multicultural only. Recently published *Kneeling Carabao and Dancing Giants: Celebrating Filipino Festivals*, by Rena Krasno, illustrated by Ileana C. Lee (ages 8-12, nonfiction on festivals and history of Philippines); and *Made in China: Ideas and Inventions from Ancient China*, by Suzanne Williams, illustrated by Andrea Fong (ages 10-12, nonfiction on history of China and Chinese inventions).

How to Contact/Writers: Query with outline and sample chapter. Reports in 3 months.

Illustration: Works with 2 illustrators/year. Reports back only if interested. Samples returned with SASE.

Terms: Pays authors royalty of 8-12% based on wholesale price. Pays illustrators by the project (range: $2,000-5,000).

Tips: "We welcome proposals from persons with expertise, either academic or personal, in their area of interest. While we do accept proposals from previously unpublished authors, we would expect submitters to have considerable experience presenting their interests to children in classroom or other public settings, and to have skill in writing for children."

PAGES PUBLISHING GROUP, (formerly Willowisp Press), 801 94th Ave. N., St. Petersburg FL 33702-2426. A division of PAGES, Books Fairs, Inc. Imprints: Willowisp Press, Worthington Press, Riverbank Press, Hamburger Press. Book publisher. **Writers contact:** Acquisitions Editor. **Illustrators contact:** Art Director. Publishes 4-8 picture books/year; 10-20 young readers/year; and 10-20 middle readers/year. 25% of books by first-time authors. "Our market is exclusively the school book fair market; *kids* are our customers, not adults usually. Our books are intended for children to be able to read *themselves*. Language, length and sentence structure are age-appropriate, and the adult voice is kept out."

Fiction: Picture books: adventure, animal, contemporary, folktales, history, humor, multicultural, nature. Young readers: adventure, animal, contemporary, fantasy, folktales, history, humor, multicultural, nature, sports, suspense/mystery. Middle readers: adventure, animal, anthology, contemporary, folktales, history, humor, multicultural, nature, problem novels, romance, sports, suspense/mystery. Young adults: adventure, animal, anthology, contemporary, folktales, history, humor, multicultural, nature, problem novels, romance, sports, suspense/mystery. No horror or violence. Average word length: picture books—350-1,000; beginning chapter books—2,000-6,000; middle readers—14,000-18,000; young adult—20,000-24,000. Recently published *Mixed-Up Michael*, by Rick Rossiter, illustrted by Michael Martchenko (grades K-3, picture book); *Marty the Millionaire*, by Debbie Dadey (grades 2-4, beginning chapter book); and *Innocent Victim*, by Karle Dickerson (grades 6-8, novel).

Nonfiction: Picture books: activity books, animal, biography, geography, history, how-to, multicultural, nature, reference, science. Young readers: activity books, animal, arts/crafts, biography, geography, history, how-to, multicultural, nature, reference, science, sports. Middle readers: activity books, animal, biography, geography, history, hobbies, how-to, multicultural, nature, reference, science, social issues, sports. Young adults: animal, biography, careers, concept, geography, history, hobbies, how-to, multicultural, nature, reference, science, social issues, sports. No religious. Recently published *Big Bad Bugs*, by Tracey E. Dils (ages K-3, science); *Our American Presidents*, by Joan Bumann and John Patterson (grades 4-8, history); and *Tiger Woods*, by Carol Perry (grades 3-5, biography).

How to Contact/Writers: Novels: Query or submit outline/synopsis and 3 sample chapters. Nonfiction: Query with outline/synopsis and 1 sample chapter. "Only *one* manuscript at a time! Do *not* send original work when querying." Reports on queries/mss in 6-8 weeks. Publishes a book 6-12 months after acceptance. Will consider simultaneous submissions (if so noted). "SASE a must."

Illustration: Works with 10-12 illustrators/year. Reviews ms/illustration packages from artists "though almost all art is assigned independent of manuscript." Query; submit ms with dummy. Query with samples that can be kept on file; provide résumé. Reports in 2-3 months. Samples returned with SASE (and on request). Original artwork not returned at job's completion.

Photography: Purchases few photos from freelancers. Contact: Acquisitions Editor. Buys stock and assigns work. Seeking photos related to sports and animals. Photo captions required. Uses color slides. Submit cover letter, résumé, published samples, stock photo list.

Terms: Pays authors royalty or work purchased outright. Offers advance. Pays illustrators by the project. Photographers paid by the project or per photo. "Our terms are highly variable, both in reference to royalties and outright purchase." Ms and art guidelines each available for SASE.

PAPERSTAR BOOKS, Imprint of The Putnam & Grosset Group, 200 Madison Ave., New York NY 10016. Book publisher. **Manuscript Acquisitions:** Susan Kochan, associate editor. **Art Acquisitions:** Cecilia Yung, art director. Publishes 50 picture books/year; 20 middle readers/year.

● PaperStar does not publish original fiction in paperback, only reprint picture books that were first hardcovers and middle grade novels from Putnam, Philomel and other publishers.

Fiction: Middle readers: adventure, contemporary, humor, multicultural, sports, suspense/mystery. Recently published *The Big Bazoohley*, by Peter Carey; *Ribbons*, by Laurence Yep; and *Rimwalkers*, by Vicki Grove.

Illustration: Works with 20 illustrators/year. Send samples of cover art (tearsheets). Reports back only if interested. Samples returned with SASE.

Terms: Pays illustrators by the project. Originals returned to artist at job's completion. Book catalog available for 9×11 SAE and 2 first-class stamps.

‡□**PARACHUTE PRESS, INC.**, 156 Fifth Ave., New York NY 10010. (212)691-1421. President: Joan Waricha. Director of Development: Susan Knopf. Book packager. Produces 70 titles/year.

● Parachutes current series include Goosebumps, Fear Street, Full House, Silver Blades, No Stars and Junior Gymnasts. They are not currently accepting unsolicited submissions.

★**PARENTING PRESS, INC.**, P.O. Box 75267, Seattle WA 98125. (206)364-2900. Fax: (206)364-0702. E-mail: fcrary@parentbooks.com. Website: http://www.parentbooks.com. Book publisher. Estab. 1979. Publisher: Carolyn Threadgill. Publishes 4-5 books/year for parents or/and children and those who work with them. 40% of books by first-time authors. "Parenting Press publishes educational books for children in story format—no straight fiction. We publish books that help build competence in parents and children. We are interested in books that help people feel good about themselves and gain skills needed in dealing with others. We are particularly interested in material that provides 'options' rather than 'shoulds.' "

● Parenting Press's guidelines are available on their website.

Fiction: Publishes social skills books, problem-solving books, safety books, dealing-with-feelings books that use a "fictional" vehicle for the information. "We rarely publish straight fiction." Recently published *I Can't Wait, I Want It, My Name Is Not Dummy*, by Elizabeth Crary, illustrations by Marina Megale (ages 3-8, social skill building); *Telling Isn't Tattling*, by Kathryn Hammerseng, illustrations by Dave Garbot (ages 4-12, personal safety); and 4 toddler board books on expressing feelings.

Nonfiction: Picture books: health, social skills building. Young readers: health, social skills building books. Middle readers: health, social skills building. No books on "new baby; coping with a new sibling; cookbooks; manners; books about disabilities (which we don't publish at present); animal characters in anything; books that tell children what they should do, instead of giving options." Average word length: picture books—500-800; young readers—1,000-2,000; middle readers—up to 10,000. Published *Kids to the Rescue*, by Maribeth and Darwin Boelts (ages 4-12).

How to Contact/Writers: Query. Reports on queries/mss in 3 months, "after requested." Publishes a book 18 months after acceptance. Will consider simultaneous submissions.

Illustrations: Works with 3 illustrators/year. Reviews ms/illustration packages from artists. "We do reserve the right to find our own illustrator, however." Query. Illustrations only: Submit "résumé, samples of art/drawings (no original art); photocopies or color photocopies okay." Reports in 3 weeks. Samples returned with SASE; samples filed.

Terms: Pays authors royalties of 3-4% based on wholesale price. Outright purchase of ms, "negotiated on a case-by-case basis. Not common for us." Offers average advance of $150. Pays illustrators (for text) by the project; 3-4% royalty based on wholesale price. Pays illustrators (for covers) by the project ($300-800). Pays photographers royalty of 3-4%. Sends galleys to authors; dummies to illustrators. Book catalog/ms/artist's guidelines for #10 SAE and 1 first-class stamp.

Tips: "Make sure you are familiar with unique nature of our books. All are aimed at building certain 'people' skills in adults or children. Our publishing for children follows no trend that we find appropriate. Children need

 SPECIAL COMMENTS by the editor of *Children's Writer's & Illustrator's Market* are set off by a bullet.

nonfiction social skill-building books that help them think through problems and make their own informed decisions."

‡PAULINE (ST. PAUL) BOOKS AND MEDIA, 50 St. Paul's Ave., Jamaica Plain MA 02130. (617)522-8911. Daughters of St. Paul. Book publisher. Estab. 1934. **Manuscript Acquisitions:** Sister Mary Mark, FSP., editor. **Art Acquisitions:** Sister Helen Rita, design director. Publishes 1-2 picture books/year; 1-2 young reader titles/year. 20% of books by first-time authors. "As a Catholic publishing house, Pauline Books & Media communicates the Gospel message through all available forms of media. We serve the Church by responding to the hopes and needs of all people with The Word of God, in the spirit of St. Paul."

Fiction: All levels: moral values, religion. Average word length: picture books—150-300; young readers—1,500-5,000.

Nonfiction: All levels: biography (saints), devotionals, religion. Average word length: picture books—200; young readers—1,500-5,000; middle readers—10,000; young adults—20,000-50,000.

How to Contact/Writers: Fiction/Nonfiction: Submit outline/synopsis and sample chapters. Reports on queries in 3-8 weeks; on mss in 3 months. Publishes a book 2-3 years after acceptance. No simultaneous submissions.

Illustration: Works with 20 illustrators/year. Style/size of illustration "varies according to the title." Reviews ms/illustration packages from artists. "Submit outline first with art samples." Illustrations only: Query with samples; send promo sheets or tearsheets. Reports on art samples in 3-8 weeks.

Photography: Buys photos from freelancers. Buys stock. Looking for children, animals—active interaction. Uses 4×5 or 8×10 b&w prints; 35mm or 4×5 transparencies.

Terms: Pays authors in royalties of 4-12% based on gross sales. Illustrations paid by the project. Photographers paid by the project, $15-200. Book catalog for 9×12 SAE and 5 first-class stamps. Manuscript guidelines for legal-size SAE and 1 first-class stamp.

Tips: "We are a Roman Catholic publishing house looking for devotional material for all ages (traditional and contemporary prayer-forms); obviously, material should be consonant with Catholic doctrine and spirituality!"

PAULIST PRESS, 997 Macarthur Blvd., Mahwah NJ 07430. (201)825-7300. Fax: (201)825-8345. Website: http://paulistpress.com. Book publisher. Estab. 1865. **Acquisitions:** Karen Scialabba, editor. Publishes 9-11 picture books/year; 8-10 young reader titles/year; and 3-4 middle reader titles/year. 80% of books by first-time authors; 30% of books from agented writers. "Our goal is to produce books that 'heal with kid-appeal' and that 'share the goodness.' "

Fiction: Picture books, young readers, middle readers and young adults: interested mainly in books providing an accessible introduction to basic religious and family values, but not preachy. Recently published *I Hate Goodbyes*, by Kathleen Szaj, illustrated by Mark A. Hicks; Walking With God board book series: *Spirit!*, *Yes, I Can!*, *Imagine!* and *Where Is God?*, by Heidi Bratton; *Elizabeth, Who is NOT a Saint*, by Kathleen Szaj, illustrated by Mark A. Hicks; and *Little Blessings*, by Sally Ann Conan, illustrated by Kathy Rogers.

Nonfiction: All levels: biography, concept, multicultural, religion, self help, social issues.

How to Contact/Writers: Fiction/nonfiction: Submit complete ms. Reports on queries/mss in 6-8 months. Publishes a book 12-16 months after acceptance.

Illustration: Works with 10-12 illustrators/year. Editorial reviews all varieties of ms/illustration packages from artists. Submit complete ms with 1 piece of final art (photocopy only) remainder roughs. Illustrations only: Submit résumé, tearsheets. Reports on art samples in 6-8 months.

Photography: Buys photos from freelancers. Works on assignment only. Uses inspirational photos.

Terms: Pays authors royalty of 6-8% based on retail price. Offers average advance payment of $500. Pays illustrators by the project (range: $50-100) or royalty of 2-6% based on retail price. Pays photographers by the project (range: $25-150; negotiable). Factors used to determine final payment: color art, b&w, number of illustrations, complexity of work. Pay for separate authors and illustrators: Author paid by royalty rate; illustrator paid by flat fee, sometimes by royalty. Sends galleys to authors; dummies to illustrators. Original artwork returned at job's completion, "if requested by illustrator."

Tips: "We cannot be responsible for unsolicited manuscripts. Please send copies, not originals. We try to respond to all manuscripts we receive—please understand if you have not received a response within six months the manuscript does not fit our current publishing plan. We look for authors who diligently promote their work."

PAWS IV PUBLISHING, P.O. Box 2364, Homer AK 99603. (907)235-7697. Fax: (907)235-7698. E-mail: pawsiv@ptialaska.net. Book publisher. **Art Acquisitions:** Celeste Fenger, marketing director. Publishes 1 young reader/year; 1 young adult/year. 20% of books by first-time authors.

Fiction: Picture books, young readers: adventure, animal, concept, contemporary. Middle readers, young adult/teens: adventure, animal, contemporary. Sees too much non-Alaskan material. Recently published *Storm Run*, by Libby Riddles, illustrated by Shannon Cartwright (tale of a young girl's dream and eventual win of the Iditarod for gardes 5-7); *Swimmer*, by Gill/Cartwright (ages 9-11, journey of a salmon); and *Alaska Mother Goose*, by Gill/Cartwright (ages preschool-8 years, nursery rhymes).

Nonfiction: All levels: activity books, animal, arts/crafts, biography, nature/environment. Sees too much non-Alaskan material. Recently published *Count Alaska's Colors*, by Gill/Cartwright (primary level book teaching math and colors the Alaskan way); *Adventure at the Bottom of the World*, by Gill (ages young adult, mountain

climbing); and *Iditarod Curriculum*, by Gill/Cartwright (ages 9 and up, Iditarod-related activities).
How to Contact/Writers: Fiction/Nonfiction: Submit outline/synopsis. Reports on queries/mss in 1 month. Publishes a book 6 months after acceptance.
Illustration: Works with 1-2 illustrators/year. Reviews ms/illustration packages from artists. Query. Contact C. Fenger, marketing director. Illustrations only: Query with samples. Reports in 1 month. Samples returned with SASE; samples filed.
Photography: Buys stock and assigns work. "Subject matter depends on current project, i.e., mountaineering, rainforests, etc." Uses 35mm transparencies. Submit cover letter.
Terms: Pays authors royalty of 5% based on wholesale price. Illustrators and photographers paid by the project. Sends galleys to authors; dummies to illustrators. Originals returned to artist at job's completion. Book catalog for SASE.
Tips: "We are looking for Alaskan children's/young adult material."

PEACHTREE PUBLISHERS, LTD., 494 Armour Circle NE, Atlanta GA 30324. (404)876-8761. Fax: (404)875-2578. Book publisher. Imprints: Peachtree Jr. and Freestone. Estab. 1977. **Acquisitions:** Helen Harriss. Publishes 10 titles/year.
Fiction: Picture books: adventure, animal, concept, history, nature/environment. Young readers: adventure, animal, concept, history, nature/environment, poetry. Middle readers: adventure, animal, history, nature/environment, sports. Young adults: history, humor, nature/environment. Does not want to see science fiction, romance.
Nonfiction: Picture books: animal, history, nature/environment. Young readers, middle readers, young adults: animal, biography, history, nature/environment. Does not want to see religion.
How to Contact/Writers: Fiction/Nonfiction: Submit complete manuscript. Reports on queries in 2-3 months; mss in 4 months. Publishes a book 1-1½ years after acceptance. Will consider simultaneous and previously published submissions.
Illustration: Works with 4 illustrators/year. Illustrations only: Query with samples, résumé, slides, color copies to keep on file. Reports back only if interested. Samples returned with SASE; samples filed.
Terms: Manuscript guidelines for SASE, or call for a recorded message.

‡**PEEL PRODUCTIONS**, P.O. Box 546, Columbus NC 28722. (704)894-8838. Fax: (704)894-8839. E-mail: peelbks@aol.com. Book publisher. **Acquisitions:** Susan Dubosque, editor. Publishes 1 picture book/year; and 5 how to draw books/year. 25% of books by first-time authors.
Fiction: Peel Productions will not publish fiction for children until 1999.
Nonfiction: Young readers, middle readers: activity books (how to draw).
How to Contact/Writers: Fiction/Nonfiction: Submit outline/synopsis and 2 sample chapters. Reports on queries in 2-3 weeks; mss in 6 weeks. Publishes a book 1 year after acceptance. Will consider simultaneous submissions.
Terms: Pays authors royalty. Offers advances. Sends galleys to authors. Book catalog available for SAE and 2 first-class stamps. Ms guidelines available for SASE.

PELICAN PUBLISHING CO. INC., P.O. Box 3110, Gretna LA 70054-3110. (504)368-1175. Website: http://www.pelicanpub.com. Book publisher. Estab. 1926. **Manuscript Acquisitions:** Nina Kooij, editor-in-chief. **Art Acquisitions:** Tracey Clements, production manager. Publishes 15 young readers/year and 4 middle reader titles/year. 5% of books from agented writers. "Pelican publishes hardcover and trade paperback originals and reprints. Our children's books (illustrated and otherwise) include humor, social commentary, folklore, and textbooks."
Fiction: Young readers: folktales, history, multicultural, religion. Middle readers: folktales, history, multicultural. Multicultural needs include stories about Native Americans, African-Americans, Irish-Americans, Jews and Hispanics. Does not want animal stories, general Christmas stories, "day at school" or "accept yourself" stories. Average word length: "when printed" young readers—32 pages; middle readers—160 pages. Recently published *A Leprechaun's St. Patrick's Day*, by Sarah Kirwan Blazek.
Nonfiction: Young readers: biography, history, religion. Middle readers: biography, cooking. Published *Jim Thorpe, the Legend Remembered*, by Rosemary K. Updyke (ages 8-12, biography).
How to Contact/Writers: Fiction/Nonfiction: Query. Reports on queries in 1 month; mss in 3 months. Publishes a book 12-18 months after acceptance.
Illustration: Works with 15 illustrators/year. Reviews ms/illustration packages from artists. Query first. Illustrations only: Query with samples (no originals). Reports only if interested. Samples returned with SASE; samples kept on file.
Terms: Pays authors in royalties; buys ms outright "rarely." Sends galleys to authors. Illustrators paid by "various arrangements." Book catalog and ms guidelines available for SASE.
Tips: "No anthropomorphic stories, pet stories (fiction or nonfiction), fantasy, poetry, science fiction or romance. Writers: Be as original as possible. Develop characters that lend themselves to series and always be thinking of new and interesting situations for those series. Give your story a strong hook—something that will appeal to a well-defined audience. There is a lot of competition out there for general themes. We look for stories with specific 'hooks' and audiences, and writers who actively promote their work."

□★**PERFECTION LEARNING CORPORATION**, Cover to Cover, 10520 New York, Des Moines IA 50322. (515)278-0133. Fax: (515)278-2980. E-mail: perflern@netins.net. Book publisher, independent book producer/packager. **Manuscript Acquisitions:** S. Thies/T. Ofner (K-6). **Art Acquisitions:** Randy Messer, art director. Publishes 5-10 early chapter books/year; 10 middle readers/year; 10 young adult titles/year.
  ● Perfection Learning Corp. publishes all hi-lo children's books on a variety of subjects.
Fiction: Picture books: concept. All levels: adventure, animal, contemporary, fantasy, folktales, hi-lo, history, humor, multicultural, nature/environment, poetry, problem novels, science fiction, special needs, sports, suspense/mystery. Average word length: early chapter books—2,000-4,000; middle readers—10,000-14,000; young adults: 10,000-30,000. Recently published *Holding the Yellow Rabbit*; and *Prairie Meeting*.
Nonfiction: All levels: activity, animal, biography, careers, geography, health, hi-lo, history, hobbies, multicultural, nature/environment, science, self-help, social issues, special needs, sports. Multicultural needs include stories, legends and other oral tradition narratives by authors who are of the culture. Does not want to see ABC books. Average word length: early chapter books—3,000; middle readers—10,000; young adults—10,000.
How to Contact/Writers: Fiction/Nonfiction: Submit complete ms. Reports on queries in 2 weeks; mss in 3 months. Publishes a book 18 months after acceptance.
Illustration: Works with 10-15 illustrators/year. Illustration only: Query with samples; send résumé, promo sheet, client list, tearsheets. Contact: Randy Messer, art director. Reports only if interested. Samples returned with SASE; samples filed.
Photography: Buys photos from freelancers. Contact: Randy Messer, art director. Buys stock and assigns work. Uses children. Uses color or up to 8×10 b&w glossy prints; 2¼×2¼, 4×5 transparencies. Submit cover letter, client list, stock photo list, promo piece (color or b&w).
Terms: Pays authors "depending on going rate for industry." Offers advances, Pays illustrators by the project. Pays photographers by the project. Original artwork returned on a "case by case basis."
Tips: "Our materials are sold through schools for use in the classroom. Talk to a teacher about his/her needs."

PERSPECTIVES PRESS, P.O. Box 90318, Indianapolis IN 46290-0318. (317)872-3055. Book publisher. Estab. 1982. **Acquisitions:** Pat Johnston, publisher. Publishes 1-3 picture books/year; 1-3 young reader titles/year. 95% of books by first-time authors. "Our purpose is to promote understanding of infertility issues and alternatives, adoption and closely-related child welfare issues, and to educate and sensitize those personally experiencing these life situations, professionals who with such clients, and the public at large."
Fiction/Nonfiction: Picture books, young readers: adoption, foster care, donor insemination or surrogacy. Does not want young adult material. Published *Lucy's Feet*, by Stephanie Stein, illustrated by Kathryn A. Imler, *Two Birthdays for Beth*, by Gay Lynn Cronin, illustrated Joanne Bowring, *Let Me Explain: A Story about Donor Insemination*, by Jane Schnitter, illustrated by Joanne Bowring and *The Mulberry Bird* (revised), by Anne Brodzinsky, illustrated by Diana L. Stanley.
How to Contact/Writers: Fiction/nonfiction: Query or submit outline/synopsis and sample chapters. "No query necessary on subject appropriate picture books." SASE required for reply. Reports on queries in 2 weeks; mss in 6 weeks. Publishes a book 10-12 months after acceptance.
Illustration: Works with 1-2 illustrators/year. Illustrations only: Submit promo sheet and client list. Reports in 2-6 weeks. Samples returned with SASE.
Terms: Pays authors royalties on a sliding scale based on net sales or by work purchased outright. Pays illustrators royalty or by the project. Sends galleys to authors; dummies to illustrators. Book catalog, ms guidelines available for #10 SAE and 2 first-class stamps.
Tips: "Do your homework! I'm amazed at the number of authors who don't bother to check that we have a very limited interest area and subsequently submit unsolicited material that is completely inappropriate for us. For children, we focus *exclusively* on issues of adoption and interim (foster) care plus families built by donor insemination or surrogacy; for adults we also include infertility issues."

PHILOMEL BOOKS, 200 Madison Ave., New York NY 10016. (212)951-8700. Imprint of The Putnam & Grosset Group, a division of Penguin Putnam Inc. Book publisher. Estab. 1980. **Manuscript Acquisitions:** Patricia Gauch, editorial director; Michael Green, editor. **Art Acquisitions:** Cecilia Yung, art director. Publishes 20 picture books/year; 5 middle-grade/young adult novels. 20% of books by first-time authors; 80% of books from agented writers. "We look for beautifully written, engaging manuscripts for children and young adults."
Fiction: All levels: adventure, animal, fantasy, folktales, history, nature/environment, special needs, multicultural. Middle readers, young adults: problem novels. No concept picture books, mass-market "character" books, or series.
Nonfiction: All levels: arts/crafts, biography, history, multicultural, music/dance. "Creative nonfiction on any subject." Average length: "not to exceed 150 pages."
How to Contact/Writers: Fiction/Nonfiction: Query; submit outline/synopsis and first three chapters. Reports on queries in 4-6 weeks. Publishes a book 2 years after acceptance.
Illustration: Works with 20-25 illustrators/year. Reviews ms/illustration packages from artists. Query first. Illustrations only: Query with samples. Send resume, promo sheet, portfolio, slides, client list, tearsheets or arrange personal portfolio review. Reports on art samples in 2 months. Original artwork returned at job's completion.

Terms: Pays authors in royalties. Average advance payment "varies." Illustrators paid by advance and in royalties. Sends galleys to authors; dummies to illustrators. Book catalog, ms/artist's guidelines free on request with SASE (9×12 envelope for catalog).
Tips: Wants "unique fiction or nonfiction with a strong voice and lasting quality. Discover your own voice and own story—and persevere." Looks for "something unusual, original, well-written. Fine art. The genre (fantasy, contemporary, or historical fiction) is not so important as the story itself, and the spirited life the story allows its main character. We are also interested in receiving adolescent novels, particularly novels that contain regional spirit, such as a story about a young boy or girl written from a Southern, Southwestern or Northwestern perspective."

★**PHOENIX LEARNING RESOURCES**, 12 W. 31st St., New York NY 10001. (212)629-3887. (212)629-5648. Book publisher. Executive Vice President: John A. Rothermich. Publishes 10 textbooks/year.
Nonfiction: All levels: textbooks. Published *New Practice Readers*, Third Edition.
How to Contact/Writers: Nonfiction: Submit outline/synopsis. Reports on queries in 2 weeks; mss in 1 month. Will consider simultaneous submissions and previously published work.
Photography: Buys stock. Contact: John A. Rothermich, executive vice president. Uses color prints and 35mm, $2\frac{1}{4} \times 2\frac{1}{4}$, 4×5 transparencies. Submit cover letter.
Terms: Pays authors royalty based on wholesale price or work purchased outright. Pays illustrators and photographers by the project. Sends galleys to authors. Book catalog available for SASE.
Tips: "We look for classroom tested and proven materials."

***PIÑATA BOOKS**, Imprint of Arte Publico Press, University of Houston, Houston TX 77204-2090. (713)743-2841. (713)743-2847. Book publisher. Estab. 1994. **Acquisitions:** Nicolas Kanellos, director. Russell William, managing editor (illustrations). Publishes 2-4 picture books, middle (ms/illustration packages)readers/year; 8-10 young adult/year. 60% of books by first-time authors. "Piñata Books specializes in publication of children's and young adult literature that authentically portray themes, characters and customs unique to U.S.-Hispanic culture."
Fiction: Picture books, young readers: adventure, contemporary, folktales, multicultural, poetry. Middle readers, young adult/teens: adventure, anthology, contemporary, folktales, multicultural, poetry, problem novels. Recently published *Walking Stars*, by Victor Villaseñor; *The Desert Is My Mother/El desierto es mi madre*, by Pat Mora; and *Pepita Talks Twice/Pepita habla dos veces*, by Ofelia Dumas Lachtman, illustrated by Alex Pardo DeLange.
Nonfiction: All levels: Biography, multicultural.
How to Contact/Writers: Fiction/Nonfiction: Query; submit complete ms; outline/synopsis and 2 sample chapters. Reports on queries in 2-4 weeks; ms in 3-6 months. Publishes a book 2 years after acceptance. Will consider electronic submissions via disk or modem and previously published work.
Illustration: Works with 2-4 illustrators/year. Reviews ms/illustration packages from artists. Query. Send ms with dummy; submit ms with 2-4 photocopies of final art. Illustrations only: Query with samples. Send resume, promo sheet, slides, client list, tearsheets or arrange personal portfolio review. Samples returned with SASE; samples filed.
Terms: Pays authors royalty of 10% based on wholesale price. Offers advances (average amount: $1,000-3,000). Pays illustrators by the project or royalty of 10% based on wholesale price. Sends galleys to authors; dummies to illustrators. Book catalog free; ms guidelines available for SASE.
Tips: "Include cover letter explaining why your manuscript is unique and important, why we should publish it, who will buy it, etc."

THE PLACE IN THE WOODS, "Different" Books. 3900 Glenwood Ave., Golden Valley MN 55422. (612)374-2120. Book publisher. **Acquisitions:** Roger Hammer, publisher/editor. Publishes 4 elementary-age titles/year and 2 middle readers/year; 2 young adult titles/year. 100% of books by first-time authors. Books feature primarily diversity/multicultural storyline and illustration.
Fiction: Picture books and young adults: adventure, multicultural, suspense/mystery. Young readers: adventure, animal, fantasy, folktales, hi-lo, humor, multicultural, sports, suspense/mystery. Middle readers: adventure, animal, fantasy, folktales, hi-lo, humor, multicultural, problem novels, sports, suspense/mystery. Average word length: young readers—no limits; middle readers—no limits.
Nonfiction: Picture books and young adults: history, multicultural, special needs. Young readers and middle readers: activity books, animal, hi-lo, history, hobbies, how-to, multicultural, self help, social issues, special needs. sports. Multicultural themes must avoid negative stereo types. Average word length: young readers—no limits; middle readers—no limits.
How to Contact/Writers: Fiction/Nonfiction: Submit complete ms. Reports on queries/mss in 1 week with SASE. "No multiple or simultaneous submissions. Please indicate a time frame for response."
Illustration: Works with 2 illustrators/year. Uses primarily b&w artwork only. Reviews ms/illustration packages from authors. Query; submit ms with dummy. Contact: Roger Hammer, editor. Illustration only: Query with samples. Reports in 1 week. Include SASE. "We buy all rights."
Photography: Buys photos from freelancers. Works on assignment only. Uses photos that appeal to children. Model/property releases required; captions required. Uses any b&w prints. Submit cover letter and samples with SASE.

Terms: Work purchased outright from authors ($10-250). Pays illustrators by the project (range: $10-250). Pays photographers by project (range $10-250). For all contracts, "initial payment repeated with each printing." Original artwork not returned at job's completion. Guidelines available for SASE.

PLANET DEXTER, One Jacob Way, Reading MA 01867. (617)944-3700. Imprint of Addison Wesley Longman Publishing Co. Book publisher. **Acquisitions:** Beth Wolfensberger, editor; Kaesmere Harrison, assistant editor. Publishes 10-15 young readers, middle readers/year. 25% of books by first-time authors. Publishes nonfiction interactive books—mainly math and science. No fiction, poetry, whole language or early readers at all. "Looking for inventive, smart, quirky takes on any educational topic."
Nonfiction: Young readers, middle readers: how-to, nature/environment, science, math. No curriculum-oriented or textbook-style manuscripts; no characters or narratives. Average word length: middle readers—15,000; young readers—10,000. Published *Planet Dexter's Calculator Mania* (comes with calculator); *Grossology*, by Sylvia Branzei (comes with fake vomit on the cover); and *Planet Dexter's Planet Ant*.
How to Contact/Writers: Query with outline/synopsis and 2 sample chapters with SASE. Reports in 8-12 weeks. Publishes a book 18 months after acceptance.
Illustration: Works with 1-2 illustrators/year. Uses color artwork only.
Terms: Pay authors royalty, or work purchased outright from authors. Offers advances. Pays illustrators/photographers by the project. Ms guidelines available for SASE.
Tips: "The more thorough a proposal, the better. Include outline, competition analysis, marketing 'hooks,' etc. Children's publishing is as competitive as adult's, so preparation on the author's part is key. We want fun, hip, irreverent, educational titles—books that kids learn from without realizing it (we call it 'stealth learning')."

PLAYERS PRESS, INC., P.O. Box 1132, Studio City CA 91614-0132. (818)789-4980. Book publisher. Estab. 1965. Vice President/Editorial: Robert W. Gordon. **Manuscript Acquisitions:** Attention: Editor. **Art Acquisitions:** Attention: Art Director. Publishes 7-25 young readers dramatic plays and musicals/year; 2-10 middle readers dramatic plays and musicals/year; and 4-20 young adults dramatic plays and musicals/year. 35% of books by first-time authors; 1% of books from agented writers.
Fiction: "We use all categories (young readers, middle readers, young adults) but only for dramatic plays and/or musicals. No novels or storybooks." Multicultural needs include plays and musicals. Recently published *Tower of London*, a play by William Hezlep; *Punch and Judy*, a play by William-Alan Landes; and *Silly Soup!*, by Carol Kerty (a collection of short plays with music and dance).
Nonfiction: "Any children's nonfiction pertaining to the entertainment industry, performing arts and how-to for the theatrical arts only." Needs include act and activity, arts/crafts, careers, history, how-to, multicultural, music/dance, reference and textbook. Published *Stagecrafter's Handbook*, by I.E. Clark; and *New Monologues for Readers Theatre*, by Steven Porter. Recently published *Assignments in Musical Theatre Acting & Directing*, by Jacque Wheeler and Halle Laughlin (how-to on teaching or learning to a musical theater actor or director); and *Theatre for Children in the United States: A History*, by nellie McCaslin (complete history of children's theater from the turn of the century through 1996).
How to Contact/Writers: Fiction/nonfiction: Submit plays or outline/synopsis and sample chapters of entertainment books. Reports on queries in 1 week; mss in 1-12 months. Publishes a book 10 months after acceptance. No simultaneous submissions.
Illustration: Works with 1-5 illustrators/year. Use primarily b&w artwork. Illustrations only: Submit résumé, tearsheets. Reports on art samples in 1-6 weeks only if interested. Samples returned with SASE; samples filed.
Terms: Pays authors in royalties of 6-12% based on wholesale price or by outright purchase. Pay illustrators by the project; royalties range from 2-5%. Sends galleys to authors; dummies to illustrators. Book catalog and ms guidelines available for SASE.
Tips: Looks for "plays/musicals and books pertaining to the performing arts only. Illustrators: send samples that can be kept for our files."

‡PLAYSKOOL BOOKS, 375 Hudson St., New York NY 10014. (212)366-2600. Fax: (212)366-2011. Website: http://www.penguin.com. Book publisher. Division of Dutton Children's Books/Penguin Putnam. **Manuscript Acquisitions:** Lucia Monfried, editor-in-chief. **Manuscript/illustration packages:** Susan Van Metre, editor. **Art Acquisitions:** Rick Farely, art director. Published 20 picture books/year. 5% by first-time authors. "We publish books for preschoolers that emphasize play and learning."
Fiction: Picture books: animal, concept, contemporary, humor, multicultural, novelty. Does not want to see folktales. Recently published: *My First Toolbox*; *My Red Book*, illustrated by Angie Sage; and *Mr. Potato Head's Costume Party: A Mix and Match Book* (all novelty books for ages 2-5).
Nonfiction: Picture Books: activity books, animal, concept, social issues. Recently published: *Seeing Shapes*, photographed by Sandra Lousada (concept board book for ages 2-5).
How to Contact/Writers: Submit complete ms. Reports in 2 months. Published a book 1 year after acceptance. Will consider simultaneous submissions.
Illustration: Works with 12-20 illustrators/year. Uses color artwork only. Reviews ms/illustration packages from artists. Send ms with dummy. Illustrations only: send tearsheets. Reports in 1 month. Samples returned with SASE; samples filed.
Photography: Buys stock images. Contact: Rick Farley, art director or Susan Van Metre, editor. Looking for

photos of animals and children. Uses color prints and 35mm transparencies. Send color promo piece.
Terms: Work purchased outright from authors; fee negotiable. Pays illustrators and photographers by the project; negotiable. Sends galleys to authors; dummies to illustrators. Original artwork returned at job's completion. Book catalog available for 9 × 12 SAE with 3 first-class stamps. All imprints included in a single catalog. Ms guidelines available for SASE.
Tips: "We are only interested in manuscripts and art appropriate for preschool age children."

PLEASANT COMPANY PUBLICATIONS, 8400 Fairway Place, Middleton WI 53562-0998. (608)836-4848. Fax: (608)836-1999. Website: http://www.americangirl.com. Book publisher. Editorial Director: Judi Woodburn. **Manuscript Acquisitions:** Jennifer Hirsch, submissions editor; Jodi Evert, senior editor, The American Girls Collection; Michelle Watkins, senior editor, American Girl Library. **Art Acquisitions:** Jane Varda, art director. Imprints: The American Girls Collection, American Girl Library, Bitty Baby Collection. Publishes 3 picture books/year; and 8-10 middle readers/year. 10% of books by first-time authors. Publishes fiction and nonfiction for girls 7 and up. "Pleasant Company's mission is to educate and entertain girls with high-quality products and experiences that build self-esteem and reinforce positive social and moral values."
● Pleasant Company publishes *American Girl* magazine. They are sponsoring a contest for writers—see listing in Contests & Awards section for Pleasant T. Rowland Prize for Fiction for Girls.
Fiction: Middle readers: adventure, animal, contemporary, history, suspense/mystery. Recently published *Meet Josefina*, by Valerie Tripp, illustrated by Jean-Paul Tibbles (ages 7-12, historical fiction); *Meet Felicity*, by Valerie Tripp, illustrated by Dan Andreasen (ages 7-12, historical fiction); and *Meet Addy*, by Connie Porter, illustrated by Melodye Rosales (ages 7-12, historical fiction).
Nonfiction: Middle readers: activity books, arts/crafts, cooking, history, hobbies, how-to, self help, sports. Recently published *Ooops! The Manners Guide for Girls*, by Nancy Holyoke, illustrated by Debbie Tilley (ages 8 and up, self help); *Super Slumber Parties*, by Brooks Whitney, illustrated by Nadine Westcott (ages 8 and up, how-to); and *Felicity's Cookbook, Pleasant Company* (ages 7-12, cooking).
How to Contact/Writers: Fiction/nonfiction: Query. Reports on queries/mss in 2 months. Will consider simultaneous submissions, previously published work.
Illustration: Works with 8 illustrators/year. Reviews ms/illustration packages from artists. Illustrations only: Query with samples. Reports back only if interested. Samples returned with SASE; samples filed.
Photography: Buys stock and assigns work. Submit cover letter, published samples, promo piece.
Terms: Pays authors royalty or work purchased outright. Pays illustrators by the project. Pays photographers by the project. Sends galleys to authors; dummies to illustrators. Originals returned to artist at job's completion. Book catalog available for 8½ × 11 SAE and 4 first-class stamps. All imprints included in a single catalog.

‡**PRESS-TIGE PUBLISHING INC.**, 291 Main St., Catskill NY 12414. (518)943-1440. Fax: (518)943-0702. Imprints: Grave Yard, God Send, Love Garden. **Manuscript Acquisitions:** Martha Ivery, publisher. **Art Acquisitions:** Pam Muzoleski, designer. Imprints: M. Reidda, editor, Grave Yard; J. Ferrar, assistant editor, Godsend; Paula Heath, editor, Love Garden. Publishes 60 picture books/year; 40 young readers/year; 190 middle readers/year; and 300 young adult titles/year.
Fiction: All levels: Considers all categories of fiction. Young adult: Also considers romance. Multicultural needs include African-American experiences. Special needs include work dealing with disabilities to benefit the young reader. Does not want to see first-person accounts. Average word length: picture books—100; young readers—50; middle readers—400; young adults—30,000. *Grandmother Mary*, by Elizabeth Uhlig (ages 7-10); *Jelly on My Knee*, by Toni Ingram (ages 2-5); and *Pickles & Peanuts*, by Martha Ivery (ages 10-13).
Nonfiction: All levels: considers all categories on nonfiction. Multicultural needs include: nonfiction dealing with how to get along better with others of a different race. Does not want to see autobiography or first-person accounts. Recently published *ABC Bible Coloring Book*, by Marge Palmer; *The Crime Solving Adventures of Sgt. Dillon & Max*, by Steve Turner (computers); and *Life's a Bowl of Soup*, by Steve Young (dealing with school problems).
How to Contact/Writers: Fiction/Nonfiction: Query or submit complete ms. Reports on queries in 3-4 weeks; mss in 1-2 months. Publishes a book 18 months after acceptance. Will consider simultaneous submissions.
Illustration: Only interested in agented material. Works with 16 illustrators/year. Query or send ms with dummy. Reports in 1 month. Samples returned with SASE.
Photography: Buys stock. Needs vary; include environmental, animals. Uses color prints; 4 × 5, 8 × 10 transparencies. Submit résumé, published samples, portfolio.
Terms: Pays authors royalty of 8-15% based on retail price. Offers advance of $2,000. Pays illustrators royalty

MARKET CONDITIONS are constantly changing! If you're still using this book and it is 1999 or later, buy the newest edition of *Children's Writer's & Illustrator's Market* at your favorite bookstore or order directly from Writer's Digest Books.

of 12-18% based on wholesale price. Pays photographers 20-30% based on wholesale price. Sends galleys to authors. Originals returned to artist at job's completion. Book catalog available for 6×9 SAE and 3 first-class stamps; ms guidelines available for SASE.

Tips: "Be descriptive when writing. Publishing a book takes time and my 'client from hell' would be described as someone who thinks we slipped into a black hole. Be patient. Think positive. Do your best. Look forward in receiving an acceptance. Remember, all things are possible with God!"

PRICE STERN SLOAN, INC., 200 Madison Ave., New York NY 10016. A Member of The Putnam & Grosset Group, a division of Penguin Putnam, Inc. Imprints: Mad Libs, Crazy Games, Serendipity, Doodle Art, Troubador Press, Cybersurfers, Mad Mysteries, Funstations, Workstations, Sliding Surprise, Wee Sing. Book publisher. Publisher: Jane O'Connor. Editorial Director: Lara Bergen. Estab. 1963. **Manuscript Acquisitions:** Daniel Weizmann, editor. **Art Acquisitions:** Ronnie Herman, art director. Publishes 20-40 young reader titles/year; 10-20 middle reader titles/year; 0-6 young adult titles/year. 35% of books by first-time authors; 65% of books from agented writers; 10% from packagers.
Fiction: Young readers, middle readers: novelty, graphic readers. Recently published *Giant Animal Fold-outs, Scary Mysteries for Sleep-Overs, I'm Sick of It* and *Bang on the Door*.
Nonfiction: Novelty, activity books, important issues for young adults, computer, topical subjects. Recently published *Internet for Kids, Tattoo You!, Take a Stand!, Marco! Polo!* and *Quest Role-Playing Games*.
How to Contact/Writers: Fiction/nonfiction: Query with SASE for guidelines. "Absolutely no multiple submissions."
Illustration: Reviews ms/illustration packages from artists. "Please *do not* send original artwork." Query; submit 1-3 chapters of ms with 1-2 pieces of final art (color copies—no original work). Illustrations only: Query with samples; provide résumé, promo sheet, portfolio, tearsheets to be kept on file. Reports in 2-3 months.
Photography: Buys stock and assigns work. Model/property releases required.
Terms: Pays authors royalty or work purchased outright. Offers advances. Pays photographers by the project or per photo. Book catalog available for 9×12 SAE and 5 first-class stamps. Ms/artist's guidelines available.

‡**PRIDE PUBLICATIONS**, P.O. Box 148, Radnor OH 43066. E-mail: pridepblsh@aol.com. Website: http://members.aol.com/pridepblsh/pride.html. **Acquisitions:** Cris Newport, senior editor. Publishes trade paperback originals and reprints. Publishes 10 titles/year. 50% of books from first-time authors; 50% from unagented writers.
Fiction: All levels: adventure, animal, contemporary, fantasy, history, humor, multicultural, nature/environment, problem novels, science fiction, special needs, suspense/mystery. Recently published *The Magical Child*, by Carol DiMarco, illustrated by Connie Wurm (magical fantasy, ready to color, for ages 8 and under); and *The Best Thing*. by Kemmofer Anna, illustrated by Joey Marsocci (contemporary fantasy for ages 10 and under).
Nonfiction: All levels: activity books, social issues, history, multcultural, science.
How to Contact/Writers: Submit synopsis and sample chapters with SASE. Reports in 3 months. Publishes book 1 year after acceptance of ms.
Illustration: Works with 10 illustrators/year. Reports in 2 weeks. Samples are filed.
Photography: Buys photos from freelancers. Query first.
Terms: Pays 10-15% royalty based on wholesale price. Will consider simultaneous submissions. Book catalog and ms guidelines for #10 SASE.

‡**PROMETHEUS BOOKS**, 59 John Glenn Dr., Amherst NY 14228-2197. Fax: (716)564-2711. E-mail: slmpbbooks@aol.com. Website: http://www.PrometheusBooks.com. Book publisher. Estab. 1969. **Acquisitions:** Steven L. Mitchell, editorial director. **Art Acquisitions:** Jacqueline Cook. Publishes 1-2 titles/year. 40% of books by first-time authors; 50% of books from agented writers. "Our primary focus is to publish books with alternative viewpoints: humanism, free thought and skepticism in regards to the paranormal. Our goal is to provide thought-provoking works that are based upon science and rational philosophy. In order to achieve our goals, we have entered into other areas to provide profitability. These areas include education, current events, young readers, health, gerontology, social science and more. Prometheus publishes both trade and academic titles. We are dedicated to offering its customers the highest-quality books. We are also committed to the development of new markets both in North America and throughout the world."
Nonfiction: All levels: sex education, moral education, critical thinking, nature/environment, science, self help, skepticism, social issues. Average word length: picture books—2,000; young readers—10,000; middle readers—20,000; young adult/teens—60,000. Recently published *If You Had to Choose What Would You Do?*, by S.M. Humphrey (ethics, ages 6-12); *Bringing UFOs Down to Earth*, by P. Klass (skepticism, ages 9 and up); and *Little Feelings*, by J.S. Bartan (self-help, ages 3-8).
How to Contact/Writers: Submit complete ms with sample illustrations (b&w). Reports on queries in 1-2 months; mss in 2-3 months. Publishes a book 12-18 months after acceptance. SASE required for return of ms/proposal.
Illustration: Works with 1-2 illustrators/year. "We will keep samples in a freelance file, but freelancers are rarely used." Reviews ms/illustration packages from artists. "Prefer to have full work (manuscript and illustrations); will consider any proposal." Include résumé, photocopies.
Terms: Pays authors royalty of 5-15% based on wholesale price. "Author hires illustrator; we do not contract

with illustrators." Pays photographers per photo (range: $50-100). Sends galleys to author. Book catalog is free on request.

Tips: "Book should reflect secular humanist values, stressing nonreligious moral education, critical thinking, logic, and skepticism. Authors should examine our book catalog to learn what sort of manuscripts we're looking for."

PUFFIN BOOKS, 375 Hudson St., New York NY 10014-3657. (212)366-2000. Website: http://www.penguin. com/childrens. Imprint of Penguin Putnam Inc. **Acquisitions:** Sharyn November, senior editor; Joy Peskin, editorial assistant. Publishes trade paperback originals and reprints. Publishes 175-200 titles/year. Receives 300 queries and mss/year. 1% of books by first-time authors; 5% from unagented writers. "Puffin Books publishes high-end trade paperbacks and paperback originals and reprints for preschool children, beginning and middle readers, and young adults."

Fiction: Picture books, young adult novels, middle grade and easy-to-read grades 1-3. "We publish mostly paperback reprints. We do few original titles." Recently published *A Gift for Mama*, by Esther Hautzig (Puffin chapter book).

Nonfiction: Biography, children's/juvenile, illustrated book, young children's concept books (counting, shapes, colors). Subjects include education (for teaching concepts and colors, not academic), women in history. "'Women in history' books interest us." Reviews artwork/photos. Send color photocopies. Recently published *Rachel Carson: Pioneer of Ecology*, by "Fadlinski" (history); *Grandma Moses*, by O'Neill Ruff (history).

How to Contact/Writers: Fiction: Submit complete picture book ms or 3 sample chapters with SASE. Nonfiction: Submit 5 pages of ms with SASE. Reports on mss in 1 month. Publishes book 1 year after acceptance. Will consider simultaneous submissions, if so noted.

Terms: Pays royalty. Offers advance (varies). Book catalog for 9×12 SASE with 7 first-class stamps; send request to Marketing Department.

G.P. PUTNAM'S SONS, 200 Madison Ave., New York NY 10016. (212)951-8700. Imprint of The Putnam & Grosset Group, a division of Penguin Putnam Inc. Book publisher. **Manuscript Acquisitions:** Refna Wilkin, executive editor; Kathy Dawson, editor. **Art Acquisitions:** Cecilia Yung, art director, Putnam and Philomel. Publishes 17 picture books/year; 7 middle readers/year; and 6 young adult titles/year. 5% of books by first-time authors; 50% of books from agented authors.

Fiction: Picture books: animal, concept, contemporary, humor, multicultural, special needs. Young readers: adventure, contemporary, history, humor, multicultural, special needs, suspense/mystery. Middle readers: adventure, contemporary, history, humor, multicultural, problem novels, special needs, sports, suspense/mystery. Young adults: contemporary, history, problem novels, special needs. "Multicultural books should reflect different cultures accurately but unobtrusively." Regarding special needs, "stories about physically or mentally challenged children should portray them accurately and without condescension." Does not want to see series, romances. Very little fantasy. Average word length: picture books—200-1,500; middle readers—10,000-30,000; young adults—40,000-50,000. Recently published *Saving Sweetness*, by Diane Stanley, illustrated by Brian Karas (ages 4-8); and *Amber Brown Sees Red*, by Paula Danziger (ages 7-10).

Nonfiction: Picture books: animal, concept, nature/environment. Young readers: biography, history, multicultural, nature/environment, social issues, special needs. Middle readers: biography, history, social issues, special needs. Young adults: history, social issues, special needs. No hard science, series. Average word length: picture books—200-1,500; middle readers: 10,000-30,000; young adults: 30,000-50,000. Recently published *Irresistible Spirit*, by Susan Kuklin (ages 11 up); and *The Case of Roe vs. Wade*, by Leonard Stevens (ages 11 up).

How to Contact/Writers: Fiction/nonfiction: Query with outline/synopsis and 3 sample chapters. Unsolicited picture book mss only. Reports on queries in 2-3 weeks; mss in 4-10 weeks. Publishes a book 2 years after acceptance. Will consider simultaneous submissions on queries only.

Illustration: Works with 40 illustrators/year. Reviews ms/illustration packages from artists. Ms/illustration packages and illustration only: Query. Reports back only if interested. Samples returned with SASE; samples filed.

Terms: Pays authors advance and royalty based on retail price. Pays illustrators by the project or advance and royalty based on retail price. Sends galleys to authors. Original artwork returned at job's completion. Books catalog and ms and artist's guidelines available for SASE.

Tips: "Study our catalogs and get a sense of the kind of books we publish, so that you know whether your project is likely to be right for us. Putnam publishes high-quality books with child appeal as well as outstanding design and text. We have published two Caldecott Medal winners, *Mirette on the High Wire*, by Emily Arnold McCully and *Officer Buckle and Gloria*, by Peggy Rathmann. Our books are frequently nominated for state awards, and we have also won several awards such as the Christopher Award, the Carter G. Woodwon Award and the Jane Addams Peace Award, for our nonfiction books on social issues."

RAINBOW PUBLISHERS, P.O. Box 261129, San Diego CA 92196. (619)271-7600. Book publisher. Estab. 1979. Imprints: Rainbow Books; Legacy Press. **Acquisitions:** Christy Allen, editor. Publishes 5 young readers/ year; 5 middle readers/year; and 5 young adult titles/year. 50% of books by first-time authors. "Our mission is to publish Bible-based, Christ-centered materials that contribute to and inspire spiritual growth and development."

Nonfiction: Young readers, middle readers, young adult/teens: activity books, arts/crafts, how-to, reference, religion. Does not want to see traditional puzzles. Recently published (Rainbow): *Instant Bible Lessons*, by

Pamela Kuhn, illustrated by Joel Ryan and Roger Johnson (series of 4; Christian lessons and activities for ages 5-10); *Make & Learn Bible Toys*, by Linda Adams, illustrated by Joel Ryan (craft book for age 2-grade 4). Legacy: *The Dickens Family Gospel*, by Robert C. Hanna, illustrated by Terry J. Walderhaug (all ages; family devotions); and *My Prayer Journal*, by Mary Davis, illustrated by Joel Ryan (upper elementary; journal).

How to Contact/Writers: Nonfiction: Submit outline/synopsis and 3-5 sample chapters. Reports on queries in 6 weeks; mss in 3 months. Publishes a book 18 months after acceptance. Will consider simultaneous submissions, electronic submissions via disk and previously published work.

Illustration: Works with 2-5 illustrators/year. Reviews ms/illustration packages from artists. Submit ms with 2-5 pieces of final art. Illustrations only: Query with samples. Reports in 6 weeks. Samples returned with SASE; samples filed.

Photography: Works on assignment only. Contact: Dan Miley, general manager. Uses scenes suitable for greeting cards. Model/property releases required. Uses color prints. Submit cover letter, color promo piece.

Terms: Pays authors royalty of 4% based on wholesale price or work purchased outright (range: $500 and up). Pays illustrators by the project (range: $300 and up). Pays photographers per photo. Sends galleys to authors. Original artwork returned at job's completion. Book catalog available for 10×13 SAE and 2 first-class stamps; ms guidelines available for SASE.

Tips: "Our Rainbow imprint carries reproducible books for teachers of children in Christian ministries, including crafts, activities, games and puzzles. Our Legacy imprint (new in '97) handles nonfiction titles for children and adults in the Christian realm, such as Bible story books, devotional books, and so on. Please write for guidelines and study the market before submitting material."

★RAINTREE STECK-VAUGHN, Imprint of Steck-Vaughn, 466 Southern Blvd., Chatham NJ 07928. (201)514-1525. Fax: (201)514-1612. Book publisher. Publishing Directors: Frank Sloan and Walter Kossmann. Art Director: Joyce Spicer (Steck-Vaughn, 4515 Seton Center Pkwy., Suite 30, Austin TX 78759.) Publishes 30 young readers/year; 30 middle readers/year; 20 young adults/year.

• Raintree Steck-Vaughn publishes strictly nonfiction titles.

Nonfiction: Picture books, young readers, middle readers: animal, biography, geography, health, history, multicultural, nature/environment, science, sports. Young adults: biography, careers, geography, health, history, sports. Multicultural needs include: biographies. Average word length: young readers—48; middle readers—32; young adults: 64-100. Recently published: Innovative Mind series (about famous scientists);World's Top Ten series (about famous geographical sites); and contemporary Hispanic and African-American biographies.

How to Contact/Writers: Nonfiction: query. Reports on queries/mss in 3-4 months.

Illustration: Contact Joyce Spicer at above Texas address.

Photography: Contact Joyce Spicer at above Texas address.

Terms: Pays authors royalty. Offers advance. Sends galleys to authors. Book catalog available for 9×12 SAE and $3 first-class postage. Ms guidelines available for SASE.

Tips: "Request a catalog so you're not proposing books similar to those we've already done. Always include SASE."

RANDOM HOUSE BOOKS FOR YOUNG READERS, 201 E. 50th St., New York NY 10022. (212)572-2600. Random House, Inc. Book publisher. Estab. 1935. Vice President/Publishing Director: Kate Klimo. Vice President/Associate Publishing Director: Cathy Goldsmith. **Acquisitions:** Easy-to-Read Books (step-into-reading): Lori Haskins, associate editor. Nonfiction: Alice Torcutis, editor. Picture Books: Mallory Loehr, assistant publishing director. First Stepping Stones: Linda Hayward, creative director. Middle Grade Fiction: Lisa Banim, creative director. Fantasy & Science Fiction: Alice Alfonsi, senior editor. Young Adult: Ruth Koeppel, senior editor. Baby & Toddler Books: Elizabeth Rivlin, associate editor. 100% of books published through agents; 2% of books by first-time authors. "Random House Books aims to create books that nurture the hearts and minds of children, providing and promoting quality books and a rich variety of media that entertain and educate readers from 6 months to 12 years."

• Random House accepts only agented material.

Fiction: Picture books: animal, easy-to-read, history, sports. Young readers: adventure, animal, easy-to-read, history, sports, suspense/mystery. Middle readers: adventure, history, science, sports, suspense/mystery.

Nonfiction: Picture books: animal. Young readers: animal, biography, hobbies. Middle readers: biography, history, hobbies, sports.

How to Contact/Writers: Fiction/Nonfiction: **Submit through agent only.** Publishes a book 12-18 months after acceptance. Will consider simultaneous submissions.

A SELF-ADDRESSED, STAMPED ENVELOPE (SASE) should always be included with submissions within your own country. When sending material to other countries, include a self-addressed envelope (SAE) and International Reply Coupons (IRCs).

Illustration: Reviews ms/illustration packages from artists through agent only.

Terms: Pays authors in royalties; sometimes buys mss outright. Sends galleys to authors. Book catalog free on request.

‡RED DEER COLLEGE PRESS, 56th Ave. and 32nd St., Box 5005, Red Deer, Alberta T4N 5H5 Canada. (403)342-3321. Fax: (403)357-3639. E-mail: vmix@admin.rdc.ab.ca. Imprints: Northern Lights Books for Children, Northern Lights Young Novels. Book publisher. Estab. 1975. **Acquisitions:** Peter Carver, children's editor. Publishes 3 picture books/year; 4 young adult titles/year. 70% of books by first-time authors. Red Deer College Press is known for their "high-quality international children's program that tackles risky and/or serious issues for kids."

Fiction: Picture books, young readers: adventure, animal, contemporary, fantasy, folktales, history, humor, multicultural, nature/environment, poetry; middle readers, young adult/teens: adventure, animal, contemporary, fantasy, folktales, hi-lo, history, humor, multicultural, nature/environment, problem novels, suspense/mystery. Recently published *How Smudge Came*, written by Nan Gregory, illustrated by Ron Lightburn (ages 5 and up, children's illustrated); *Tiger's New Cowboy Boots*, written by Irene Morck, illustrated by Georgia Graham (ages 5 and up, children's illustrated); and *Vanishing Act*, written by Cora Taylor (ages 9 and up, ya novel).

How to Contact/Writers: Fiction/Nonfiction: Query or submit outline/synopsis. Reports on queries in 6 months; ms in 6-8 months. Publishes a book 18 months after acceptance. Will consider simultaneous submissions.

Illustration: Works with 3-5 illustrators/year. Illustrations only: Query with samples. Reports back only if interested. Samples not returned; samples filed.

Photography: Buys stock and assigns work. Model/property releases required. Submit cover letter, résumé and color promo piece.

Terms: Pays authors royalty (negotiated). Offers advances (negotiated). Pays illustrators and photographers by the project or royalty (depends on the project). Sends galleys to authors. Originals returned to artist at job's completion. Guidelines not available.

Tips: "Red Deer College Press is currently not accepting children's manuscripts unless the writer is an established Canadian children's writer with an original project that fits its publishing program. Writers, illustrators and photographers should familiarize themselves with RDC Press's children's publishing program."

❀★REIDMORE BOOKS INC., 10109-106 St., 1200, Edmonton, Alberta T5J 3L7 Canada. (403)424-4420. Fax: (403)441-9919. E-mail: reidmore@compusmart.ab.ca. Website: http://www.reidmore.com. Book publisher. **Acquisitions:** Leah-Ann Lymer, editor-in-chief. Publishes 4 textbooks/year (grades 2-12). 25% of books by first-time authors.

● Reidmore Books is not looking at fiction titles this year. See their listing in the Multimedia Section.

Nonfiction: Young readers: history. Middle readers, young adults/teens: geography, history, multicultural, nature/environment, science, textbooks. Does not want or use "material that is not directly tied to social studies, science or math curricula. No picture books, please." Recently published: *Beginnings: From the First Nations to the Great Migration*, by Marshall Jamieson (grades 5-6, history textbook).

How to Contact/Writers: Nonfiction: Query, submit complete ms, submit outline/synopsis. Reports on queries in 1 month, mss in 2 months. Publishes a book 18 months after acceptance. Will consider simultaneous submissions.

Illustration: Works with 1 illustrator/year. Uses color artwork only. Illustration only: Query with samples. Contact: Leah-Ann Lymer, editor-in-chief. Samples returned with SASE; samples filed.

Photography: Buys photos from freelancers. Buys stock images. Uses "content-rich photos, often geography-related." Photo captions required. Uses color prints and 35mm transparencies. Submit cover letter.

Terms: Pays authors royalty. Pays illustrators by the project. Pays photographers by the project or per photo. Sends galleys to authors. Book catalog available for 9×12 SAE and 2 first-class stamps.

Tips: "There are fewer titles being published in Canada. Call before submitting—it tends to speed up the process and saves everyone time, money and effort."

RHACHE PUBLISHERS, LTD., 9 Orchard Dr., Gardiner NY 12525. (914)883-5884. E-mail: chedlund@aol.com, rhadin@aol.com, rhache@aol.com. Book publisher. Publisher: Richard H. Adin. **Acquisitions:** Carolyn H. Edlund, associate publisher. Publishes 1-5 middle readers/year; 1-5 young adult titles/year. 90% of books by first-time authors. "We are looking for books for children 10 and up. They need to be primarily nonfiction. By that, we mean the story line can be fiction (e.g., a mystery) but the story must teach and not too subtly why a 'clue' in the mystery can't be correct because it defies a natural law, with a good solid exploration of that natural law. We are not looking for stories of the 'Little Engine That Could' or the Peter Cottontail type. No books for very young or that are primarily illustration."

Nonfiction: Middle readers, young adults: activity books, animal, arts/crafts, careers, concept, cooking, computer, health, history, hobbies, how-to, music/dance, nature/environment, reference, science, self help, special needs. Interested in books for (not about) challenged children in any of the above areas, especially self help and computers. Average word length: middle readers—50,000 (minimum); young adults—50,000 (minimum).

How to Contact/Writers: Nonfiction: Query with résumé first. Submit outline/synopsis and 2-4 sample chapters. Reports on queries in 3-4 weeks; mss in 45-60 days. Anticipates publishing a book 6 months after acceptance.

Illustration: Uses both b&w and color artwork. Reviews ms/illustration packages from authors. Query. Submit ms with 4-5 photocopies of final art. associate publisher. Illustration only: Query with samples, résumé. Reports in 4-5 weeks. Samples returned with SASE; samples filed.

Photography: Buys photos from freelancers. Buys stock and assigns work. Model/property releases required; captions required. Uses 3×5, 4×5 glossy, color or b&w prints; or 35mm, 4×5 transparencies. Submit cover letter, résumé, samples.

Terms: Pays authors royalty of 10-17.5% based on wholesale price. Pays illustrators royalty of 5-10% based on wholesale price. Pays photographers per photo. Sends galleys to authors. Original artwork is not returned. Ms guidelines available for SASE only with topic query and résumé.

Tips: "Do not send a form request for guidelines; do not send handwritten queries; be sure any correspondence is grammatically correct and spelling error-free; be sure query is targeted and clearly stated; always include a résumé."

RIZZOLI BOOKS FOR CHILDREN, 300 Park Ave. S., New York NY 10010. (212)387-3653. Fax: (212)387-3535. Book publisher.
• Rizzoli Books For Children has suspended publishing indefinitely.

‡RONSDALE PRESS, 3350 W. 21st Ave., Vancouver BC V6AS 1G7 Canada. (604)738-1195. Fax: (604)731-4548. E-mail: ronhatch@pinc.com. Website: http://ronsdalepress.com. Book publisher. Estab. 1988. **Manuscript/Art Acquisitions:** Veronica Hatch, children's editor. Publishes 1 young reader/year. 100% of titles by first-time authors. Publishes children's novels with b&w illustrations.

Fiction: Young readers, middle readers: adventure, animal, contemporary, folktales, history, multicultural, nature/environment, poetry. Average word length: young readers—90; middle readers—90. Recently published *Willobe of Wuzz*, written by Sondra Glaze, illustrated by Pamela Breeze Currie (ages 3-12); *Long Long Ago*, written by Robin Skelton, illustrated by Pamela Breeze Currie (ages 3-12); and *Molly Brown Is Not a Clown*, written by Linda Rogus, illustrated by Rick Von Krugel (ages 5-11).

Nonfiction: Young readers, middle readers: animal, biography, history, multicultural, nature/environment, social issues; young adult/teens: animal, biography, history, multicultural, nature/environment. Average word length: young readers—90; middle readers—90.

How to Contact/Writers: Fiction/Nonfiction: Submit complete ms. Reports on queries in 2 weeks; ms in 2 months. Publishes a book 1 year after acceptance. Will consider simultaneous submissions.

Illustrations: Works with 1 illustrator/year. Reviews ms/illustration packages from artists. Submit ms with dummy. Reports back in 2 weeks. Samples returned with SASE.

Terms: "We prefer author and illustrator to share royalties of 5% each." Sends galleys to authors; dummies to illustrators. Originals returned to artist at job's completion. Book catalog available for 8½×11 SAE and $1 postage; ms and art guidelines available for SASE.

Tips: "We publish at present only Canadian authors. We prefer authors to approach us with illustrators already chosen."

THE ROSEN PUBLISHING GROUP, 29 E. 21st St., New York NY 10010. (212)777-3017. Book publisher. Estab. 1950. Publisher: Roger Rosen. **Manuscript Acquisitions:** Patra Sevastiades, young adult; Helen Packard, juvenile. Publishes 144 juvenile readers/year; 75 middle readers/year; and 100 young adults/year. 35% of books by first-time authors; 1% of books from agented writers. "We publish quality self-help/guidance books for children and young adults."

Nonfiction: Young readers: animal, concept, cooking, history, how-to, nature/environment, religion, science, sports. Middle readers: hi-lo. Young adult: careers, hi-lo, religion. All levels: biography, health, multicultural, self-help, social issues, special needs. No fiction. Average word length: juvenile—800; middle readers—8,000; young adults—40,000. Published *Black Bears* (juvenile, Bears of the World series); *Everything You Need to Know About the Dangers of Tattooing and Body Piercing* (hi-lo, young adult, The Need to Know Library); *Coping with Asthma* (young adult, The Coping Series); and *Careers in Cyberspace* (young adult, The Career Series).

How to Contact/Writers: Submit outline/synopsis and sample chapters. Reports on queries in 2 months; mss in 1-2 months. Publishes a book 9 months after acceptance.

Photography: Buys photos from freelancers. Contact: Roger Rosen. Works on assignment only.

Terms: Pays authors in royalties or work purchased outright. Pays illustrators and photographers by the project. Book catalog free on request.

Tips: "Target your manuscript to a specific age group and reading level and write for established series published by the house you are approaching."

ROUSSAN PUBLISHERS INC., P.O. Box 321, Prairie du Chien WI 53821. Fax: (608)326-8404. Book publisher. **Acquisitions:** Judy Frydenlund, editor-in-chief. Publishes 2 middle readers/year; 4 young adults/year. 25% of books by first-time authors.

Fiction: Middle readers: adventure, fantasy, history, science fiction, sports. Young adult/teens: adventure, contemporary, fantasy, history, problem novels, science fiction, sports, suspense/mystery. Does not want to see picture books. Average word length: middle readers—20,000; young adult/teens—30,000. Recently published *Parents*

From Space, by George Bowering (young adult fiction); *Dark of the Moon*, by Barbara Haworth-Attard (middle reader, contemporary/time travel); and *Night of the Aliens*, by Dayle Campbell Gaetz (middle reader, hi-lo/science fiction).

How to Contact/Writers: Submit outline/synopsis and 3 sample chapters with SASE. Publishes a book 1 year after acceptance. Will consider simultaneous submissions.

Terms: Pays authors royalty of 8-10% based on retail price. Pays illustrators by the project. Sends galleys to authors. Book catalog; ms guidelines available for SASE.

‡★**WILLIAM H. SADLIER, INC.**, 9 Pine St., New York NY 10005. (212)227-2120. Textbook publisher. **Manuscript Acquisitions:** William S. Dinger, president. **Art Acquisitions:** Joe Svadlenka, art director. "We publish texts for Roman Catholic religious studies. We are looking for writers whose stories might be used in our religious education programs."

Fiction: All levels: religion. "Multicultural themes are important."

Nonfiction: All levels: religious education textbooks. Average word length: 25-30 words per lesson in each text for all age levels.

Illustration: Works with 50-75 illustrators/year. Reports on samples only if interested. Samples are not returned; samples filed.

Terms: Pays authors "fee for stories" (authors are work for hire). Pays illustrators by the project ($400/full page). Pays photographers per photo (depends on size used). Original artwork returned at job's completion.

Tips: "We are looking for engaging stories that will involve the child especially primary grades, ages 3-8."

ST. ANTHONY MESSENGER PRESS, 1615 Republic St., Cincinnati OH 45210-1298. (513)241-5615. Fax: (513)241-0399. E-mail: stanthony@americancatholic.org. Website: http://www.AmericanCatholic.org. Book publisher. Managing Editor: Lisa Biedenbach. 25% of books by first-time authors. "Through print and electronic media marketed in North America and worldwide, we endeavor to evangelize, inspire and inform those who search for God and seek a richer Catholic, Christian, human life. We also look for books for parents and religious educators."

● St. Anthony Messenger Press book *Can You Find Jesus*, by Philip Gallery and Janet Horlow was named best children's book by the 1997 Catholic Book Awards.

Nonfiction: Young readers, middle readers, young adults: religion. "We like all our resources to include anecdotes, examples, etc., that appeal to a wide audience. All of our products try to reflect cultural and racial diversity." Does not want to see fiction, story books, picture books for preschoolers. Recently published *The Wind Harp and Other Angel Tales*, by Ethel Pochocki (middle to adult readers); and *Can You Find Jesus? Introducing Your Child to the Gospel*, by Philip Gallery and Janet Harlow (ages 5-10).

How to Contact/Writers: Query or submit outline/synopsis and sample chapters. Reports on queries in 2-4 weeks; mss in 4-6 weeks. Publishes a book 12-18 months after acceptance.

Illustration: Works with 1 illustrator/year. "We design all covers and do most illustrations in-house, unless illustrations are submitted with text." Uses primarily b&w artwork. Reviews ms/illustration packages from artists. Query with samples, résumé. Contact: Mary Alfieri, art director. Reports on queries in 2-4 weeks. Samples returned with SASE; or samples filed.

Photography: Purchases photos from freelancers. Contact: Mary Alfieri, art director. Buys stock and assigns work.

Terms: Pays authors royalties of 10-12% based on net receipts. Offers average advance payment of $600. Pays illustrators by the project. Pays photographers by the project. Sends galleys to authors. Book catalog and ms guidelines free on request.

Tips: "Know our audience—Catholic. We seek popularly written manuscripts that include the best of current Catholic scholarship. Parents, especially baby boomers, want resources for teaching children about the Catholic faith for passing on values. We try to publish items that reflect strong Catholic Christian values."

‡✦**SCHOLASTIC CANADA LTD.**, 123 Newkirk Rd., Richmond Hill, Ontario L4C 3G5 Canada. Imprints: North Winds Press (contact Joanne Richter); Les Éditions Scholastic (contact Sylvie Andrews, French editor). **Acquisitions**: Diane Kerner, Sandra Bogart Johnston, editors, children's books. Publishes hardcover and trade paperback originals. Publishes 30 titles/year; imprint publishes 4 titles/year. 3% of books from first-time authors; 50% from unagented writers.

Fiction: Children's/juvenile, young adult. Recently published *After the War*, by Carol Matas (novel).

Nonfiction: Animals, history, hobbies, nature, recreation, science, sports. Reviews artwork/photos as part of ms package. Send photocopies. Recently published *Take a Hike*, by Sharon Mackay and David Macleod (informal guide to hiking for kids).

How to Contact/Writers: Query with synopsis, 3 sample chapters and SASE. Nonfiction: Query with outline, 1-2 sample chapters and SASE. Reports on queries in 1 month; on proposals in 3 months. Publishes book 1 year after acceptance.

Terms: Pays 5-10% royalty on retail price. Offers advance: $1,000-5,000 (Canadian). Book catalog for 8½ × 11 SAE with 2 first-class stamps (IRC or Canadian stamps only).

Shoot what you love—the rest will follow

Putting together an effective portfolio is often as puzzling as solving a riddle. How many images should you include? Should you use big-name assignments or choose the pieces you like best? Should you mail a promotional postcard before you contact an art director for a portfolio review? Unfortunately, there isn't one right answer. But, as children's book photographer Walter Wick discovered, some answers are more right than others.

Walter Wick

Wick, who began his career as a general commercial photographer in New York, never dreamed that his inventive, colorful photographs would become the centerpiece of a top-selling series of children's books for Scholastic. He certainly had big name clients, shooting covers for magazines like *Psychology Today*, *Fortune* and *Newsweek*. He even thought he'd probably do a book one day—a compilation of the visual logic puzzles he created for *Games Magazine*. "It never occurred to me to pursue children's publishing," he says. But it did occur to Jean Marzollo, then editor of a Scholastic children's magazine called *Let's Find Out*.

Wick sent her the reprint of an image he created for *American Showcase*. He took the picture almost by accident one day when he was organizing a collection of odds and ends—screws and nuts and springs—on his lightboard. "I was always very lazy about mailing those reprints out but apparently I managed to get some of them out anyway. So I got a call based on that photograph to do a poster for Scholastic's *Let's Find Out*. At that point Scholastic was just another one of my many magazine clients."

Wick had also shot for Scholastic's *Super Science* and *Home Computing* magazines. "So I had a lot of ins at Scholastic," he says, "but none of them were really connected with the book division. The poster somehow floated into the offices of one of the book editors and became a favorite. It was sort of an inspiration to think about photography in children's books for that editor. And the editor got in touch with Jean and Jean got in touch with me and we all got together and came up with the I Spy series."

The first book, *I Spy: A Book of Picture Riddles*, is challenging for the sheer number of objects in each photograph. Yet it is certainly the most simple book of the series. The book combines Wick's images, chock full of the trappings of childhood, with Jean Marzollo's musical riddles. "I spy a snake, a three-letter word./ And flying underneath, a great white bird;/ Nine gold stars, a blue tube of glitter,/ One clay cat, and a six-legged critter."

Published in 1992, *I Spy* was so successful that Wick started to think about children's books as an outlet for his passions—combining photography with puzzles and games. Seven books later the series will soon include an anthology of the best and hardest photo-

Photographer Walter Wick's I Spy series, such as the book of picture riddles shown above, was so popular with older children that Scholastic released several titles in mini-book versions for a younger audience.

graphs with new riddles by Marzollo, a mini-book for younger children, board books and a CD-ROM. Wick's relationship with Scholastic has also allowed him to create a science picture book called *A Drop of Water* and a book of optical illusions that will be published next year. "I'm fully ensconced in the book world right now. I turn down all the commercial assignments that come my way and I'm happier doing this work, at least for now."

But Wick says he's always been happy with his photography career. "I always enjoyed doing assignments because most of them were right up my alley." Of course there were more difficult shots. "I never really turned down work," he says, "but about ten percent were like getting root canals because my heart wasn't in it." Even if Wick got stuck with boring assignments to pay the bills, he could always create interesting work for himself.

"Whenever I did a self-promotional piece I would do sort of an epic thing—it was really heavily conceived and planned—with model-making and all kinds of production put into it. I would only do one or two a year, whereas some photographers would take a week and shoot like 10 or 12 new shots, maybe even a whole new portfolio. I always gravitated toward the complex and high-concept type of images." Even so, Wick had to learn how to win assignments through trial and error.

"My first portfolio was what I thought people would like and I got no work whatsoever and then I did seven or eight shots of what I wanted to do and I started getting work." Wick says that, especially in New York, photographers are chosen for their specialties and if they are doing work they don't love it will show. "It shows in the personal interviews you have with people. It shows in your enthusiasm and it shows, perhaps, even in your work. There are a few people who can choose a particular area like packaging or something like that and do it primarily as a business, but that's not me. I was never able to do that."

Wick can always choose the subject he wants to shoot now. "But I couldn't have done that when I started out. I didn't have the power to do that. But because I chose to cultivate my passions into my work, to fold it in together, when I'm hired for a job I'm hired for more than my ability as a photographer. I'm hired for my expertise as a photographer and my expertise in the subject matter. That is a very, very powerful reason to be hired." For example, Wick explains, if an underwater photographer doesn't become an expert in fish and underwater plant life, he'll never be as good a photographer as he could be.

"The other things that I bring to photography are sometimes intangible." he says. "I wouldn't pin them down as an expertise necessarily, but I have an affinity for puzzles and games. For instance, I have a sense of how to make the hidden objects interesting and have variety to them rather than just looking for one Waldo or something. I devise different ways to hide objects and I have kids looking for not only objects, but shadows of objects and reflections of objects. So I involve a lot of optical games. I also put in a lot of things that hold your interest beyond the act of finding things."

Wick has certainly found his niche in photography and in children's book publishing but he wouldn't advise anyone to necessarily follow the same path. He believes people should allow their careers to be directed by their passions and desires. "I think my natural ability comes from the past—a sense of play I had as a child and I never lost. I've always had a sense of discovery and invention."

—*Megan Lane*

SCHOLASTIC INC., 555 Broadway, New York NY 10012. (212)343-6100. Website: http://www.scholastic.c om. Estab. 1920. Vice President, Editor-in-Chief: Jean Feiwel. **Manuscript Acquisitions:** Scholastic Press: Brenda Bowen, editorial director; Blue Sky Press: Bonnie Verberg, editorial director; Trade Paperback Craig Walker, editorial director; Scholastic Trade: Ann Reit, executive editor; Scholastic Press: Dianne Hess, executive editor; Cartwheel Books, Grace Maccarone; Arthur Levine Books: Arthur Levine. **Art Acquisitions:** Trade Hardcover: David Saylor, creative director; Trade Paperback: David Tammasino, creative director; Cartwheel Books: Edie Weinberg, art director. "We are proud of the many fine, innovative materials we have created—such as classroom magazines, book clubs, book fairs, and our new literacy and technology programs. But we are most proud of our reputation as 'The Most Trusted Name in Learning.' "

  • Scholastic's title *Slam!*, by Walter Dean Myers, received the 1997 Coretta Scott King Award. Their title *Rebels Against Slavery: American Slave Revolts*, by Patricia C. and Frederick L. McKissack, received a 1997 Coretta Scott King Honor Award. Scholastic is not interested in receiving ideas for more fiction paperback series. They do not accept unsolicited manuscripts.

Illustration: Works with 50 illustrators/year. Does not review ms/illustration packages. Illustrations only: send promo sheet and tearsheets.Reports back only if interested. Samples not returned. Original artwork returned at job's completion.

Terms: All contracts negotiated individually; pays royalty. Sends galleys to author; dummies to illustrators.

‡SCHOLASTIC PRESS, 555 Broadway, New York NY 10012. (212)343-6100. Website: http://www.scholastic .com. Imprint of Scholastic Inc., **Acquisitions:** Brenda Bowen, editorial director. Publishes 60 titles/year. 5% of books from first-time authors. Scholastic Press publishes a range of picture books, middle grade and young adult novels. Publishes hardcover originals.

  • Scholastic Press only accepts agented submissions.

Fiction: Juvenile, picture books. Recently published *Slam*, by Walter Dean Myers (ages 12 and up); *Harlem*, by Walter Dean Myers, illustrated by Christopher Myers (all ages); and *The Music of Dolphins*, by Karen Hesse (for ages 11-13).

Nonfiction: Children's/juvenile, general interest. Recent published *The Great Fire*, by Jim Murphy (history); *A Drop of Water*, by Walter Wick (science); and *Girls Speak Out*, by Andrea Johnston (for ages 9-14).

How to Contact Writers: Only interested in agented material. Reports on queries in 6 months. Publishes book 18 months after acceptance.

Terms: Pays royalty based on retail price. Royalty and advance vary.

SEEDLING PUBLICATIONS, INC., 4079 Overlook Dr. E., Columbus OH 43214-2931. Phone/fax: (614)451-2412 or (614)792-0796. E-mail: sales@seedlingpub.com. Website: http://www.SeedlingPub.com. **Acquisitions:** Josie Stewart, vice president. Publishes 5-10 young readers/year. 20% of books by first-time authors. Publishes books for the beginning reader in English and Spanish. "Natural language and predictable text are requisite to our publications. Patterned text acceptable, but must have a unique storyline. Poetry, books in rhyme, full-length picture books or chapter books are not being accepted at this time. Illustrations are not necessary."

Fiction: Picture books: adventure, animal, fantasy, hi-lo, humor, multicultural, nature/environment, special needs. Multicultural needs include stories which include children from many cultures and Hispanic centered storylines. Does not want to see texts longer than 16 pages or over 150-200 words or stories in rhyme. Averge word length: young readers—100. Recently published *Bumpity, Bumpity, Bump*, by Carol Parker; and *A Birthday in the Woods*, by L. Salem and J. Stewart (ages 3-7, paperback early reader).

Nonfiction: Picture books: animal, concept, hi-lo, multicultural, music/dance, nature/environment, science, special needs, sports. Does not want to see texts longer than 16 pages or over 150-200 words. Average word length: young readers—100. Recently published *Free to Fly*, by K. Gibson (ages 3-7, early reader).

How to Contact/Writers: Fiction/Nonfiction: Submit complete ms. Reports in 4-5 months. Publishes a book 1 year after acceptance. Will consider simultaneous submissions.

Illustration: Works with 4-5 illustrators/year. Uses color artwork only. Reviews ms/illustration packages from artists. Submit ms with dummy. Illustrations only: Send color copies. Reports back only if interested. Samples returned with SASE only; samples filed if interested.

Photography: Buys photos from freelancers. Works on assignment only. Model/property releases required. Uses color prints and 35mm transparencies. Submit cover letter and color promo piece.

Terms: Pays authors royalty of 5% based on retail price or work purchased outright. Pays illustrators and photographers by the project. Original artwork returned at job's completion. Book catalog available for 2 first-class stamps.

Tips: "Follow our guidelines carefully and test your story with children and educators."

‡SHAMROCK PUBLISHING, INC. OF ST. PAUL, 1490 Sherbourne Ave., St. Paul MN 55104. (612)646-0276. Fax: (612)645-9859. E-mail: shmrckpub@aol.com. Website: http://members.aol.com/shmrckpub/. Book publisher. Estab. 1994. **Manuscript/Art Acquisitions:** Stefany Cruze, editor. Publishes 1 picture book/year; 1 young reader/year; 1 middle reader/year. 95% of books by first-time authors. "Our goal is to help first-time authors and illustrators break into the publishing industry."

Fiction: Picture books, young readers: adventure, animal, contemporary, fantasy, humor, multicultural, nature/environment; middle readers: adventure, animal, contemporary, fantasy, humor, multicultural, nature/environment, science fiction, sports, suspense/mystery. Average word length: picture books—100-1,000; young readers—5,000-10,000; middle readers—1,000-5,000. Recently published *The Special One*, by Trish Keating (picture book); *Monsters Make Me Giggle*, by J. Fashingbauer (picture book); and *The Tiny String of Pearls*, by R. Barbara Fay (chapter book).

How to Contact/Writers: Fiction: Query. Reports on queries/mss in 6-10 weeks. Publishes a book 1-2 years after acceptance. Will consider simultaneous submissions.

Illustration: Works with 1-2 illustrators/year. Reviews ms/illustration packages from artists. Query. Illustrations only: Query with samples. Reports back only if interested. Samples filed.

Terms: Pays authors and illustrators royalty of 5% based on wholesale price. Send galleys to authors; dummies to illustrators. Originals returned to artist at job's completion. Ms and art guidelines available for SASE.

‡SIERRA CLUB BOOKS FOR CHILDREN, 85 Second St., San Francisco CA 94105. (415)977-5500. Imprint of Sierra Club Books. **Acquisitions:** Helen Sweetland, director. Publishes hardcover originals and trade paperback originals and reprints. Publishes 15 titles/year. Receives 100 queries/year. 2% of books from first-time authors; 10% from unagented writers. "Sierra Club Books for Children publishes books that offer responsible information about the environment to young readers, with attention to the poetry and magic in nature that so fascinated and inspired John Muir, the poet-philosopher who was the Sierra Club's founder."

• Sierra Club Books for Children prefers agented submissions.

Nonfiction: Subjects include nature/environment. Recently published *Squishy, Misty, Damp & Muddy: The In Between World of Wetlands*, by Molly Cone (science); *In the Heart of the Village: The World of the Indian Banyan Tree*, by Barbara Bash.

Fiction: Subjects include nature/environment. Recently published *Desert Trip*, by Barbara A. Steiner; *The Empty Lot*, by Dale H. Fife; *The Snow Whale*, by Caroline Pitcher.

How to Contact/Writers: Query. All unsolicited mss returned unopened. Reports in up to 1 year on queries. Publishes book an average of 2 years after acceptance of ms; works waiting for illustrators may take significantly longer.

Terms: Pays 8-10% royalty on retail price. Advance varies. Book catalog for 9 × 12 SASE.

★SILVER BURDETT PRESS, 299 Jefferson Rd., Parsippany NJ 07054-0480. (201)739-8000. Fax: (201)739-8606. Simon & Schuster Publishing Education Group. Imprints: Crestwood House, Dillon Press, Julian Messner, New Discovery, Silver Press. Book publisher. Executive Editor: Susan Eddy. **Manuscript Acquisitions:** Debbie Biber, editor, Crestwood House, Dillon Press, New Discover Books; Dorothy Goeller, editor, Silver Burdett Press, Silver Press. **Art Acquisitions:** Michele Farinella, art director. Publishes 40 young readers/year and 40 young titles/year. 1% of books by first-time authors.

Fiction/Nonfiction: "Our list ranges from pre-school to young adult books, both fiction and nonfiction. This also includes Crestwood House which is a hi-lo nonfiction imprint." Considers all fiction and nonfiction categories. Recently published *Riddle by the River*, *The United States Holocaust Memorial Museum*, *The White Stallions* and *Insects*.

How to Contact/Writers: Fiction/Nonfiction: Submit outline/synopsis and 1 sample chapter. Reports on queries in 6 months; mss in 12 months. Publishes a book 1 year after acceptance. Will consider simultaneous and electronic submissions via disk or modem. Only interested in agented material.

Illustration: Only interested in agented material. Works with 40 illustrators/year. Reviews ms/illustration packages from artists. Submit ms with dummy. Illustrations only: Submit résumé and portfolio. Reports only if interested. Samples returned with SASE.

Photography: Buys photos from freelancers. Buys stock and assigns work. Captions required. Uses color or b&w prints, ½-full page. Submit published samples and client list.

Terms: Pays authors royalty of 3-7½% based on wholesale or retail price or work purchased outright from authors. Offers advances (average amount: $4,000). Pays illustrators by the project (range: $500-10,000) or royalty of 3-7½% based on wholesale or retail price. Sends galleys to authors; dummies to illustrators. Book catalog available for 9 × 11 SAE and $2.60 postage.

SILVER MOON PRESS, 160 Fifth Ave., New York NY 10010. (212)242-6499. Publisher: David Katz. Book publisher. Publishes 2 books for grades 1-3; 10 books for grades 4-6. 25% of books by first-time authors; 10% books from agented authors. "We publish books of entertainment and educational value and develop books which fit neatly into curriculum for grades 4-6."

Fiction: All levels: historical and mystery. Average word length: varies. Recently published *The Conspiracy of the Secret Nine*, by Celia Bland (ages 10-12, historical fiction); and *Told Tales*, by Jo Sepha Sherman (ages 10-12, folktales).

Nonfiction: All levels. Recently published *Techno Lab*, by Robert Sheely (ages 8-12, science).

How to Contact/Writers: Fiction/Nonfiction: Query. Reports on queries in 2-4 weeks; mss in 1-2 months. Publishes a book 1-2 years after acceptance. Will consider simultaneous submissions, electronic submissions via disk or moden, previously published work.

Illustration: Reviews ms/illustration packages from artists. Query. Illustrations only: Query with samples, résumé, client list; arrange personal portfolio review. Reports only if interested. Samples returned with SASE. Original artwork returned at job's completion.

Photography: Buys photos from freelancers. Buys stock and assigns work. Uses archival, historical, sports photos. Captions required. Uses color, b&w prints; 35mm, 2¼×2¼, 4×5, 8×10 transparencies. Submit cover letter, résumé, published samples, client list, promo piece.

Terms: Pays authors royalty or work purchased outright. Pays illustrators by the project, royalty. Pays photographers by the project, per photo, royalty. Sends galleys to authors; dummies to illustrators. Book catalog available for SAE.

‡**SILVER PRESS**, 299 Jefferson Rd., Parsippany NJ 07054-0480. (201)739-8000. Fax: (201)739-8606. Imprint of Silver Burdett Press, Simon & Schuster Publishing Education Group. Book Publisher. **Acquisitions:** Dorothy Goeller, editor. See Silver Burdett Press listing.

SIMON & SCHUSTER BOOKS FOR YOUNG READERS, 1230 Avenue of the Americas, New York NY 10022. (212)698-7200. Website: http://www.simonsays.com. Imprint of Simon & Schuster Children's Publishing Division. Vice President/Editorial Director: Stephanie Owens Lurie. **Manuscript Acquisitions:** Virginia Duncan, executive editor (picture books, nonfiction, fiction); David Gale, senior editor (middle grade and YA fiction); Andrea Davis Pinkney, editor (picture books, fiction); Rebecca Davis, editor (picture books, poetry, fiction). **Art Acquisitions:** Lucille Chomowicz, senior art director and Paul Zakris. Publishes 80 books/year. "We publish high-quality fiction and nonfiction for a variety of age groups and a variety of markets. Above all we strive to publish books that will offer kids a fresh perspective on their world."
- Simon & Schuster's title *Running the Road to ABC*, illustrated by Reynold Ruffins, received a 1997 Coretta Scott King Honor Award for illustration.

Fiction: Picture books: animal, concept. Middle readers, young adult: adventure, suspense/mystery. All levels: anthology, contemporary, history, humor, poetry, nature/environment. Recently published *The Adventures of Sparrowboy*, by Brian Pinkney; *The Dog in the Freezer*, by Harry Mazer; and *Slave Day*, by Rob Thomas.

Nonfiction: All levels: biography, nature/environment. Picture books: concept. Young readers, young adult: reference. "We're looking for innovative and accessible nonfiction for all age levels." Recently published *Food Fight*, by Janet Bode; and *I Have Lived a Thousand Years*, by Livia Bitton-Jackson.

How to Contact/Writers: Accepting query letters only. Reports in 1-2 months. Publishes a book 2-4 years after acceptance. Will consider simultaneous submissions.

Illustration: Works with 70 illustrators/year. Do not submit original artwork. Editorial reviews ms/illustration packages from artists. Submit query letter to Submissions Editor. Illustrations only: Query with samples; provide promo sheet, tearsheets. Reports only if interested.

Terms: Pays authors advance and royalty (varies) based on retail price. Pays illustrators by the project or advance and royalty (varies) based on retail price. Photographers paid royalty. Original artwork returned at job's completion. Ms/artist's guidelines free on request.

Tips: "We're looking for picture books centered on a strong, fully-developed protagonist who grows or changes during the course of the story; YA novels that are challenging and psychologically complex; also imaginative and humorous middle-grade fiction. And we want nonfiction that is as engaging as fiction. Send a query letter only. Take a look at what we're publishing to see if your work would fit in. The hardcover market is shrinking and so it is more difficult than ever to break in for the first time. Your work must sparkle with humor, imagination, wit and creativity."

‡**SOMERVILLE HOUSE, INC.**, 3080 Yonge St., Suite 5000, Toronto, Ontario M4N 3N1 Canada. (416)488-5938. International book packager. **Acquisitions:** Jane Somerville, president and publisher. Produces 10-15 titles/year in multimedia formats and for the religious/spiritual marketplace.
- Somerville is currently accepting unsolicited manuscripts.

SOUNDPRINTS, 353 Main Ave., Norwalk CT 06851-1552. (203)846-2274. Fax: (203)846-1776. E-mail: sndprnts@ix.netcom.com. Book publisher. Lines: Smithsonian Backyard, Smithsonian Oceanic Collection, Smithsonian Odyssey and The Nature Conservancy Habitat series. **Manuscript Acquisitions:** Cassia Farkas, editor. **Art Acquisitions:** Diane Hinze Kanzler, graphic designer. Publishes 16 picture books/year. 10% of books by first-time authors; 10% of books from agented authors. "Soundprints publishes books about wildlife (including oceanic and backyard wildlife and habitats) and history created to educate while entertaining. Each book communicates information about its subject through an exciting storyline. At the same time, each book is based solidly in fact and all aspects must be supported by careful research. All titles are published with an audio and toy component. Each book is illustrated in full-color and contains a glossary and 'about the subject' paragraph to further explain to young children information in the text. All materials in Soundprints' books require the approval of curators and reviewers at the Smithsonian Institution and The Nature Conservancy. This curatorial review is

‡ **LISTINGS NEW TO THIS EDITION** are marked with a double dagger.

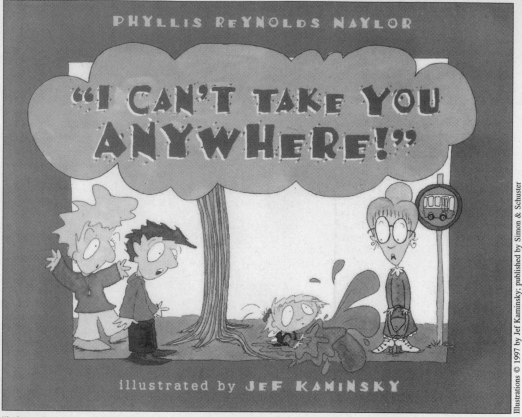

Illustrations © 1997 by Jef Kaminsky; published by Simon & Schuster

"I always have wanted to make picture books, I mean *always*! After sending my portfolio around for about four years, I finally got the chance to make one!," says Jef Kaminsky, whose eccentric, endearing pen and ink drawings bring poor klutzy Amy Audrey Perkins and her aunts and uncles to life in *I Can't Take You Anywhere*. During the course of the assignment for Atheneum Books for Young Readers, a division of Simon & Schuster, Kaminsky learned how to manage deadlines and "just keep drawing—even when it wasn't going well for a few days." The business of making a book is hard work, says Kaminsky. "But when you finally hold the finished copy, all bound and ready to read, it feels totally fantastic!"

a careful scrutiny that frequently necessitates changes in the text before approval will be granted."

Fiction: Picture books, young readers: animal, history, nature/environment. *No* fantasy or anthropomorphic animals. Average word length: picture books (grades PS-2)—800-1,000; (grades 1-4)—1,800-2,200. Recently published *Opossum at Sycamore Road*, by Sally Walker, illustrated by Joel Snyder (grades PS-2, picture book); *Octopus' Den*, by Deirdre Langeland, illustrated by Steven Petruccio (grades PS-2, picture book); *Thar She Blows!*, by Sue Kassirer, illustrated by Pat Fridell (grades 2-5, picture book); and *Bamboo Valley*, by Ann Whitehead Nagda, illustrated by Jim Effler (grades 1-4, picture book).

Nonfiction: Picture books, young readers: animal, history. "Soundprints books are fiction, but based in research, with an intent to teach."

How to Contact/Writers: Query. Reports on queries/mss in 6-8 weeks. Publishing time approximately 2 years. Will consider simultaneous submissions. "Do not send manuscripts without reading our guidelines first."

Illustration: Works with 10-12 illustrators/year. Uses color artwork only. Illustrations are usually full bleed 2-page spreads. Reviews ms/illustration packages from artists "if subject matter is appropriate." Query. Illustrations only: Query with samples; provide résumé, portfolio, promo sheet, slides. "If interest is generated, additional material will be requested." Reports back only if interested. Samples returned with SASE.

Terms: Authors and illustrators used on a work-for-hire basis. Original artwork returned at job's completion. Book catalog for 8½×11 SAE and $1.05 postage; ms guidelines and artist guidelines for #10 SASE. "It's best to request both guidelines and catalog. Both can be sent in self-addressed envelope at least 8½×11 with $1.05 postage."

Tips: "We want books that educate children about the subject while capturing the interest of the reader/listener through an entertaining storyline. As of Spring 1997, Soundprints offers 16 titles in the Smithsonian Wild heritage collection, 13 titles in the Smithsonian's Backyard series, 13 titles in the Smithsonian Oceanic Collection and 6 titles in the Smithsonian Odyssey series. Authors should read a few of the titles in the relevant series before submitting a manuscript. Soundprints has very specific guidelines for each line and it is unlikely that a manuscript written by an author who is not familiar with our books will be acceptable. It is also a good idea to verify in advance that Soundprints has not already published, or is not currently working on, a book on your chosen topic."

SOUTHWEST PARKS & MONUMENTS ASSOCIATION, 221 N. Court St., Tucson AZ 85701. (520)622-1999. Fax: (520)623-9519. E-mail: dgallagher@spma.org. Nonprofit association. Publishes 10 picture books/year; and 2 middle readers/year. 50% of books by first-time authors. Publishes books to help children understand and appreciate national parks in the Southwest.
Nonfiction: Middle readers: animal, geography, history, nature/environment. Average word length: middle readers—2,000. Recently published *101 Questions About Desert Life*; and *101 Questions About Ancient Southwest Cultures*.
How to Contact/Writers: Nonfiction: Query. Reports on queries in 6 weeks; mss in 3 months. Publishes a book 1 year after acceptance. Will consider simultaneous submissions and electronic submissions via disk or modem.
Illustration: Works with 2 illustrators/year. Reviews ms/illustration packages from artists. Query. Contact: Derek Gallagher, director of publishing. Illustrations only: Query with samples. Contact: Derek Gallagher, director of publishing. Reports in 6 weeks. Samples returned with SASE; samples filed.
Photography: Buys stock and assigns work. Contact: Laura Symms-Wallace, production editor. Uses photographs of sites in national parks and monuments in the Southwest. General natural history photographs (for example, animals). Model/property releases required; captions required. Uses $2\frac{1}{4} \times 2\frac{1}{4}$, 4×5 or 8×10 transparencies. Submit published samples, promo piece or other nonreturnable samples.
Terms: Work purchased outright from authors ($1,000-2,500). Pays illustrators by the project (range: $500-2,500). Pays photographers by the project (range: $1,000-5,000) or per photo (range: $50-250). Sends galleys to authors. Book catalog available for SAE and 55¢ postage. All imprints included in a single catalog.
Tips: "We are a nonprofit association (private) working with 53 national parks in the Southwest. Any work submitted to us should advance the understanding of visitors to the parks as to the resources the parks preserve and protect."

★**THE SPEECH BIN, INC.**, 1965 25th Ave., Vero Beach FL 32960. (561)770-0007. Fax: (561)770-0006. Book publisher. Estab. 1984. **Acquisitions:** Jan J. Binney, senior editor. Publishes 10-12 books/year. 50% of books by first-time authors; less than 15% of books from agented writers. "Nearly all our books deal with treatment of children (as well as adults) who have communication disorders of speech or hearing or children who deal with family members who have such disorders (e.g., a grandparent with Alzheimer's disease or stroke)."
  ● The Speech Bin is currently overstocked with fiction.
Fiction: Picture books: animal, easy-to-read, fantasy, health, special needs. Young readers, middle readers, young adult: health, special needs.
Nonfiction: Picture books, young readers, middle readers, young adults: activity books, health, textbooks, special needs. Published *Chatty Hats and Other Props*, by Denise Mantione; *Holiday Hoopla: Holiday Games for Language & Speech*, by Michele Rost; and *Speech Sports*, by Janet M. Shaw.
How to Contact/Writers: Fiction/Nonfiction: Query. Reports on queries in 4-6 weeks; mss in 2-3 months. Publishes a book 10-12 months after acceptance. "Will consider simultaneous submissions *only* if notified; too many authors fail to let us know if manuscript is simultaneously submitted to other publishers! We *strongly* prefer sole submissions."
Illustration: Works with 4-5 illustrators/year ("usually inhouse"). Reviews ms/illustration packages from artists. Ms/illustration packages and illustration only: "Query first!" Submit tearsheets (no original art). SASE required for reply or return of material.
Photography: Buys stock and assigns work. Looking for scenic shots. Model/property releases required. Uses glossy b&w prints, 35mm or $2\frac{1}{4} \times 2\frac{1}{4}$ transparencies. Submit résumé, business card, promotional literature or tearsheets to be kept on file.
Terms: Pays authors in royalties based on selling price. Pay illustrators by the project. Photographers paid by the project or per photo. Sends galleys to authors. Original artwork returned at job's completion. Book catalog for 4 first-class stamps and 9×12 SAE; ms guidelines for #10 SASE.
Tips: "No calls, please."

‡**SRI RAMA PUBLISHING**, Box 2550, Santa Cruz CA 95063. (408)426-5098. Book publisher. Estab. 1975. Publishes 1 or fewer young reader titles/year.
  ● Sri Rama is not accepting manuscripts for the 1998 book year.
Illustration: Illustrations used for fiction, design, diagrams. Will review artwork for possible future assignments. Contact: James "Dharni" McElheron, graphic design director.
Terms: "We are a nonprofit organization. Proceeds from our sales support an orphanage in India. We encourage donated and partially donated labor. Each case is looked at individually." Pays illustrators. Sends galleys to authors; dummies to illustrators. Book catalog free on request.

Steven Petruccio enjoys a successful career balancing his time between illustration, fine art and teaching. *Octopus' Den*, for Soundprints is typical of his assignments. Petruccio "fell into" the natural history niche after working on an outdoor science series. When he began getting offers from art directors who had seen his work, he discovered a steady market for children's illustration that's inviting to look at but also conveys a technical message. But it takes research. "Children should not be spoken down to in illustration, " he says. "There's always that smart kid who will catch you if a fin is out of place." Petruccio, who works from a home studio, says his eight-year-old daughter and four-year-old son are his best critics. "If they don't get it, the other kids won't either." Diane Hinze Kanzler, art director for Soundprints, is a big fan. "Our books are curated by the Smithsonian so they have to be technically excellent. Steve knows when to make the ocean water sunny and jewel-like or murky, depending on each animal's habitat. He's just awesome. Plus, he's an all-around swell guy to work with!"

STANDARD PUBLISHING, 8121 Hamilton Ave., Cincinnati OH 45231. (513)931-4050. Fax: (513)931-0950. Book publisher. Estab. 1866. Director, New Products: Diane Stortz. **Manuscript Acquisitions:** Greg Holder, children's editor. **Art Acquisitions:** Coleen Davis, creative director. Number and type of books varies yearly. Many projects are written inhouse. No juvenile or young adult novels. 25-40% of books by first-time authors; 1% of books from agented writers. "We publish well-written, upbeat books with a Christian perspective. Books are fun with relevancy in Christian education."
   ● Standard publishes *LiveWire*, *R-A-D-A-R* and *Straight*. Also see listing for Standard Publishing in the Greeting Cards, Puzzles & Games section.
Fiction: Adventure, animal, contemporary, Bible stories. Average word length: board/picture books—400-1,000.
Nonfiction: Bible background, nature/environment, sports devotions. Average word length: 400-1,000. Recently published *The Bible Time Travelers On the Scene With Jesus*, by Mikal Keefer, illustrated by Carl Moore (picture book); and *Some Kind of Journey: On the Road With Audio/Adrenaline* (teens).
How to Contact/Writers: Fiction/Nonfiction: Send proposals only. Reports in 3 months. Publishes a book 18 months after acceptance. Will consider simultaneous submissions.
Illustration: Works with 15-20 new illustrators/year. Illustrations only: Submit cover letter and photocopies. Reports on art samples only if interested. Samples returned with SASE; samples filed.
Terms: Pays authors royalties based on net price or work purchased outright (range varies by project). Pays illustrators (mostly) by project. Pays photographers by the photo. Sends galleys to authors on most projects. Book catalog available for $2 and 8½ × 11 SAE; ms guidelines for letter-size SASE.

Tips: "We look for manuscripts that help draw children into a relationship with Jesus Christ; help children develop insights about what the Bible teaches; make reading an appealing and pleasurable activity."

STEMMER HOUSE PUBLISHERS, INC., 2627 Caves Rd., Owings Mills MD 21117-9919. (410)363-3690. Fax: (410)363-8459. Book publisher. Estab. 1975. **Acquisitions:** Barbara Holdridge, president. Publishes 1-3 picture books/year. "Sporadic" numbers of young reader, middle reader and young adult titles/year. 60% of books by first-time authors. "Stemmer House is best known for its commitment to fine illustrated books, excellently produced."
Fiction: Picture books: animal, folktales, multicultural, nature/environment. Middle readers: folktales, nature/environment. Does not want to see anthropomorphic characters. Published *How Pleasant to Know Mr. Lear: Poems by Edward Lear*, illustrated by Bohdan Butenko; and *The Marvelous Maze*, by Maxine Rose Schur, illustrated by Robin DeWitt and Patricia DeWitt-Grush.
Nonfiction: Picture books: multicultural. All level: animals, nature/environment. Multicultural needs include Native American, African. Recently published *A Duck in a Tree*, by Jennifer A. Loomis, photographs by the author; *The Hawaiian Coral Reef Coloring Book*, by Katherine Orr; and *The First Teddy Bear*, by Helen Kay, illustrations by Susan Kronz.
How to Contact/Writers: Fiction/Nonfiction: Query or submit outline/synopsis and sample chapters. Reports on queries/mss in 2 weeks. Publishes a book 18 months after acceptance. Will consider simultaneous submissions.
Illustration: Works with 2 illustrators/year. Uses color artwork only. Reviews ms/illustration packages from artists. Query first with several photocopied illustrations. Illustrations only: Submit tearsheets and/or slides (with SASE for return). Reports in 2 weeks. Samples returned with SASE; samples filed "if noteworthy."
Terms: Pays authors royalties of 5-10% based on wholesale price. Offers average advance payment of $300. Pays illustrators royalty of 4-5% based on wholesale price. Pays photographers 4-5% royalty based on wholesale price. Sends galleys to authors. Original artwork returned at job's completion. Book catalog and ms guidelines for 9 × 12 SASE.
Tips: Writers: "Simplicity, literary quality and originality are the keys." Illustrators: "We want to see ms/illustration packages—don't forget the SASE!"

STERLING PUBLISHING CO., INC., 387 Park Ave. S., New York NY 10016. (212)532-7160. Fax: (212)213-2495. Book publisher. Estab. 1949. **Manuscript Acquisitions:** Sheila Anne Barry, acquisitions director. **Art Acquisitions:** Karen Nelson. Publishes 30 middle readers/year. 10% of books by first-time authors. "We publish books in the following categories: Science experiments and activities; math puzzles and activities; other puzzles; interactive books on natural history or science; ghost stories (true and very short); tricks and games, mini-mysteries; optical illusions; chess; magic; mazes; dot-to-dot books; papercrafts and other crafts, riddles and jokes. We are not publishing any children's picture books or fiction."
Nonfiction: Middle readers: activity books, animal, arts/crafts, geography, ghosts, hobbies, how-to, humor, mini-mystery, true mystery, multicultural, music, nature/environment, puzzles, reference, science, sports, supernatural incidents. "Since our books are highly illustrated, word length is seldom the point. Most are 96-128 pages." Does not want to see fiction, poetry, story books or personal narratives. Published *Awesome Jokes*, by Charles Keller, illustrated by Jeff Sinclair (ages 8-12, riddle and joke book); and *Reptiles & Amphibians: Birth & Growth*, by Andres Llamas Ruiz, illustrated by Ali Garousi (ages 8-12, nature/animals).
How to Contact/Writers: Reports on queries in 4 months. "If we are interested it may take longer." Publishes a book 12-18 months after acceptance. Will consider simultaneous submissions.
Illustration: Works with 12 illustrators/year. Reviews ms/illustration packages from artists. "Query first." Illustrations only: "Send sample photocopies of line drawings; also examples of some color work." Reports only if interested. Samples returned with SASE; samples kept on file.
Terms: Pays authors in royalties of up to 10%; "standard terms, no sliding scale, varies according to edition." Usually pays illustrators and photographers flat fee/project or royalty. Sends galleys to authors. Original artwork returned at job's completion "if possible, but sometimes held for future needs." Ms guidelines for SASE.
Tips: Looks for "humor, hobbies, science books for middle-school children." Also, "mysterious occurrences, activities and fun and games books."

✤**STODDART KIDS,** *A Division of Stoddart Publishing Co. Ltd.* 34 Lesmill Rd., North York, Ontario M3B 2T6 Canada. (416)445-3333. Fax: (416)445-5967. E-mail: kelly.jones@ccmailgw.genpub.com. Book publisher. **Manuscript Acquisitions:** Donald G. Bastian, managing editor. **Art Acquisitions:** Kathryn Cole, publisher. Publishes 15 picture books/year; 6 young readers/year; 6 young adults/year. 20% of books by first-time authors.
Fiction: Picture books: adventure, animal, contemporary, folktales, history, humor, multicultural. Young readers:

THE SUBJECT INDEX, located in the back of this book, lists book publishers and magazines according to the fiction and nonfiction subjects they seek.

contemporary, folktales, history. Young adult: contemporary, history, multicultural, suspense/mystery. Does not want to see science fiction. Average word length: picture books—800; young readers—38,000; young adult/teens—70,000. Recently published *Emma's Eggs*, by Margriet Ruurs (picture book); *Vision Seeker*, by James Whetung (picture book, historical fiction); *Breath of a Ghost*, by Anita Horrocks (young reader fiction); and *Stranger on the Line*, by Marilyn Halvorson (young adult fiction).

How to Contact/Writers: Fiction: submit outline/synopsis and 2 sample chapters. Reports on queries in 3 weeks; mss in 3 months. Publishes a book 18 months after acceptance. Will consider simultaneous submissions.

Illustration: Works with 18 illustrators/year. Reviews ms/illustration packages from artists. Submit ms and photocopied artwork (no originals) and SASE. Illustrations only: Send photocopied artwork, SASE and query. Reports in 2 months. Samples returned with SASE; samples filed "if desirable."

Terms: Author and illustrator payments vary with project size and type. Sends galleys to authors. Originals returned to artist at job's completion. Book catalog available for large SAE and 2 first-class stamps. Ms guidelines available to SASE.

Tips: "Stoddart Kids is interested in developing a strong Canadian publishing program and therefore encourages the submission of Canadian materials. However, topics that cover both American and Canadian markets are also welcome."

STOREY COMMUNICATIONS, INC., Imprint of Storey Publishing, Garden Way Publishing, Schoolhouse Rd., Pownal VT 05261. (802)823-5200. Fax: (802)823-5819. Book publisher. Estab. 1983. **Acquisitions:** Gwen Steege, editorial director; Deborah Bremuth (crafts); Elizabeth McHale (animals); Pamela Lappies; Charly Smith (gardening). Publishes 2-4 young readers/year. 7% of books by first-time authors. "We publish practical information that encourages personal independence in harmony with the environment."

Nonfiction: Young readers, middle readers: animal, arts/crafts, gardening, hobbies, how-to, nature/environment. Does not want to see cooking or nonfiction with a story line. Recently published *Your Pony/Your Horse*, by Cherry Hill (ages 9+, guide to care of horses); *Tooth Truth* and *Puddle Jumpers*, by Jennifer Storey Gillis (ages 5-10, projects); and *Everything You Never Knew About Birds*, by Rebecca Rupp (ages 9 and up science).

How to Contact/Writers: Nonfiction: Query. Submit outline/synopsis and 1 sample chapter. Reports on queries/mss in 2 months. Publishes a book 1 year after acceptance. Will consider simultaneous and electronic submissions via disk or modem.

Illustration: Works with 24 illustrators/year. Reviews ms/illustration packages from artists. Send ms with dummy. Illustrations only: Query with samples, résumé and portfolio. Reports in 2 months. Samples returned with SASE; samples filed. "Return of originals subject to negotiation."

Photography: Buys stock and assigns work. Contact: Cathy Gee Graney, managing editor. Uses animals and children. Model/property releases required. Uses b&w glossy prints and 35mm, 2¼×2¼, 4×5 transparencies. Submit cover letter, résumé, published samples, stock photo list.

Terms: Offers advances. Sends galleys to authors. Book catalog available for 8½×11 SAE. Ms guidelines available for SASE.

Tips: "Review our catalog."

‡STORM PEAK PRESS, 157 Yesler Way, Suite 413, Seattle WA 98104. (206)223-0162. Publishes trade paperback originals and reprints. Publishes 3 books/year.

Fiction: Juvenile adventure. Recently published *The Ballad of Big Ben's Boots & Other Tales for Telling*, by John Dashney.

Terms: Pays royalty on retail price or net revenues.

Tips: "Get editorial help before sending a manuscript. Be confident the material is well-written."

‡THE SUMMIT PUBLISHING GROUP, Suite 500, 1227 W. Magnolia, Fort Worth TX 76104. Book publisher. **Manuscript Acquisitions:** Mike Towle, managing editor. **Art Acquisitions:** David Sims, art director (illustrations); Mike Towle (ms/illustration packages).

Nonfiction: All levels: activity books, arts/crafts, careers, health, hobbies, how-to, self help. Average word length: picture books—5,000; young readers—5,000. Recently published *You Can Do it!*; series includes cheerleading, ballet, balloon, baloon animals, card tricks, painting T-shirts, sock puppets.

How to Contact/Writers: Submit complete ms. Reports in 1-3 months. Publishes a book 4-6 months after acceptance. Will consider simultaneous and previously published submissions. Prefers no agents.

Illustration: Works with 4-6 illustrators/year. Uses primarily b&w artwork (some color). Reviews ms/illustration packages from artists. Submit with 4-5 pieces of final art. Contact: Mike Towle, managing editor. Illustrations only: Query with samples, résumé, portfolio, slides, client list and tearsheets. Reports back only if interested in 3 months. Samples filed.

Photography: Model/property release required; captions required. Uses 5×7, 8×10 b&w prints; 35mm, 4×5 transparencies. Submit cover letter, résumé, published samples, slides, client list.

Terms: Pays authors royalty of 5-12% based on wholesale price. Work purchased outright from authors. Rarely offers advances. Sends galleys to authors; dummies to illustrators. Ms guidelines available for SASE.

‡SWORD OF THE LORD PUBLISHERS, 224 Bridge Ave., Murfreesboro TN 37129. (800)24-SWORD. Book publisher. Estab. 1934. **Manuscript/Art Acquisitions:** Guy King, director of publishing operations. Publishes 2 picture books/year; 2 young readers/year; 3 middle readers/year; 3 young adult titles/year. 40% of books are by first-time authors.

Fiction: Picture books, young readers, middle readers: adventure, animal, religion; young adult/teens: adventure, religion, suspense/mystery. Recently published *Scamper Squirrel Goes to Camp*, by Pyle (ages 7-8); and *Flight of Terror*, by Handford (ages 13-14).

Nonfiction: Picture books: activity books, religion; young readers: activity books, animal, biography, religion; middle readers: animal, biography, history, religion; young adult/teens: biography, history, reference, religion. Recently published *Family Portraits*, by Barber; *Great Preaching of Revival*, by Smith; and *Diamonds in the Rough*.

How to Contact/Writers: Fiction/Nonfiction: Submit complete ms. Reports on ms in 6-9 months. Publishes a book 1 year after acceptance. Will consider simultaneous submissions; electronic submissions via disk or modem; previously published work.

Illustration: Works with 3 illustrators/year. Reviews ms/illustration packages from artists. Submit ms with 1-4 photocopies of final art. Illustrations only: Send résumé and portfolio to be kept on file. Reports in 6-9 months. Samples returned with SASE.

Photography: Buys stock and assigns work. Model/property releases required. Uses color prints. Submit résumé, portfolio and color promo piece.

Terms: Pays author royalty of 10% based on retail price. Pays illustrators by the project. Book catalog available for $1.25; ms, art and photography guidelines available for SASE.

✿THISTLEDOWN PRESS LTD., 633 Main St., Saskatoon, Saskatchewan S7H 0J8 Canada. (306)244-1722. Fax: (306)244-1762. E-mail: thistle@sk.sympatico.ca. Website: http://www.thistledown.sk.ca. Book publisher. **Manuscript Acquisitions:** Patrick O'Rourke, editor-in-chief; Jesse Strothers. **Art Acquisitions:** A.M. Forrie, art director. Publishes numerous middle reader and young adult titles/year. "Thistledown originates books by Canadian authors only, although we have co-published titles by authors outside Canada. We do not publish children's picture books."

Fiction: Middle readers, young adults: adventure, anthology, contemporary, fantasy, humor, poetry, romance, science fiction, suspense/mystery. Average word length: middle readers—35,000; young adults—40,000. Recently published *The Blue Jean Collection*, and *Notes Across the Aisle*, edited by Peter Carver (young adult, short story anthologies); *Takes: Stories for Young Adults*, edited by R.P. MacIntyre (anthology); *Fish House Secrets*, by Kathy Stinson (YA novel) and *The Blue Camaro*, by R.P. MacIntyre (YA short fiction).

How to Contact/Writers: Prefers agented writers but "not mandatory." Submit outline/synopsis and sample chapters. Reports on queries in 3-4 weeks, mss in 3-6 months. Publishes a book about one year after acceptance. No simultaneous submissions.

Illustration: Prefers agented illustrators but "not mandatory." Works with few illustrators. Illustrations only: Query with samples, promo sheet, slides, tearsheets. Reports back only if interested. Samples returned with SASE; samples filed.

Terms: Pays authors royalty of 10-15% based on retail price. Pays illustrators and photographers by the project (range: $250-750). Sends galleys to authors. Original artwork returned at job's completion. Book catalog free on request. Ms guidelines for #10 envelope and IRC.

Tips: "Send cover letter including publishing history and SASE."

TILBURY HOUSE, PUBLISHERS, 132 Water St., Gardiner ME 04345. (207)582-1899. Fax: (207)582-8227. Book publisher. Publisher: Jennifer Elliott. Publishes 1-3 young readers/year.

Fiction: Young readers and middle readers: multicultural, nature/environment. Special needs include books that teach children about tolerance and honoring diversity.

Nonfiction: Young readers and middle readers: multicultural, nature/environment. Recently published *Talking Walls: The Stories Continue* and *Project Puffin* both by Margy Burns Knight, illustrated by Anne Sibley O'Brien (grades 3-8).

How to Contact/Writers: Fiction/Nonfiction: Submit outline/synopsis. Reports on queries/mss in 1 month. Publishes a book 1-2 years after acceptance. Will consider simultaneous submissions "with notification."

Illustration: Works with 1-2 illustrators/year. Illustrations only: Query with samples. Contact: J. Elliott, associate publisher. Reports in 1 month Samples returned with SASE. Original artwork returned at job's completion.

Photography: Buys photos from freelancers. Contact: J. Elliott, associate publisher. Works on assignment only.

Terms: Pays authors royalty. Pays illustrators/photographers by the project; royalty. Sends galleys to authors. Book catalog available for 9×12 SAE and 78¢ postage.

Tips: "We are primarily interested in children's books that teach children about tolerance in a multicultural society and honoring diversity. We are also interested in books that teach children about environmental issues."

TIME-LIFE FOR CHILDREN, subsidiary of Time Life, Inc., 777 Duke St., Alexandria VA 22314.
● Time-Life no longer accepts unsolicited manuscripts. All books produced by them are conceived and developed inhouse.

TREASURE PUBLISHING, 829 S. Shields St., MSC 1000, Fort Collins CO 80521. (970)484-8483. Fax: (970)495-6700. Book publisher. **Acquisitions:** Mark Steiner, editor. "Treasure Publishing exists to assist the

Church of Jesus Christ in fulfilling the Great Commission. We create, market and distribute Christian education resouces which feature excellence in biblical content, educational methodology and product presentation. Our primary responsibility is to serve the local and international Church. We began in 1935 as *Through the Bible Publishers* and developed into an established publishing ministry with a reputation for solid, biblical curriculum. The company was later renamed Roper Press. In 1987, Roper introduced Me Too! books for young children. They have won the loyalty and admiration of parents throughout the world. This series was awarded "1996 Children's Book Series of the Year" by the British Christian Booksellers Association. In 1995, after proclaiming God's Word for 60 years, Roper Press changed ownership and moved from Texas to Colorado. Our new name, Treasure!, reflects the central value we shall continue to place on the Scriptures. With the Lord's guidance, our team anticipates creating many new resources and making many new friends in the coming months and years."

Nonfiction: Picture books, young readers: Bible stories. Recently published *Faith to Win*; *More than Beautiful*; *Nobody Knew but God*; *Big Enemy, Bigger God*, all by Marilyn Lashbrook, illustrated by Stephanie McFetridge Britt.

How to Contact/Writers: Submit complete ms with SASE. Reports in 1 month. Publishes a book 1 year after acceptance.

Illustration: Works with 3 illustrators/year. Uses color artwork only. Reviews ms/illustration packages from artists. Send ms with dummy. Illustrations only: Send résumé, promo sheet. Reports in 1 month if interested. Samples returned with SASE; samples filed.

Terms: Work purchased outright from authors (average: $1,000). Illustrators paid by the project. Original artwork returned at job's completion. Book catalog for 9×12 SAE and 2 first-class stamps. Manuscript guidelines for SASE.

Tips: "Our present interests include: children's material; topical and exegetical Bible study resources; freelance editors—to revise children's Bible curriculum. No fiction, please."

TRICYCLE PRESS, Imprint of Ten Speed Press, P.O. Box 7123, Berkeley CA 94707. **Acquisitions:** Nicole Geiger, editor. Publishes 7 picture books/year; and 4 activity books/year. 30% of books by first-time authors. "Tricycle Press looks for something outside the mainstream; books that encourage children to look at the world from a possibly different angle."

Fiction: Picture books: concept, health, nature/environment. Average word length: picture books—1,200. Recently published *Amelia Hits the Road*, by Marissa Moss (ages 7-12, picture book); and *Arm in Arm*, by Remy Charlip (ages 7 and up, picture book).

Nonfiction: Picture books: activity books, arts/crafts, concept, geography, health, how-to, nature/environment, science, self help, social issues. Young readers: activity books, arts/crafts, health, how-to, nature/environment, science, self help, social issues. Recently published *Splash! A Penguin Counting Book*, by Jonathan Chester and Kirsty Melville (ages 2-4, picture book); *Mousetracks: A Kid's Computer Idea Book*, by Peggy Steinhauser (ages 5-10, activity book); and *Divorce is Not the End of the World: Zoe's and Evan's Coping Guide for Kids*, by Zoe, Evan and Ellen Sue Stein.

How to Contact/Writers: Fiction: Submit complete ms for picture books and activity books. "No queries!" Nonfiction: Submit complete ms. Reports on mss in 10-12 weeks. Publishes a book 1 year after acceptance. Will consider simultaneous submissions.

Illustration: Works with 6 illustrators/year. Reviews ms/illustration package from artists. Submit ms with dummy. Illustrations only: Query with samples, promo sheet, tearsheets. Reports back only if interested. Samples returned with SASE; samples filed. Original artwork returned at job's completion unless work for hire.

Terms: Pays authors 15% royalty (but lower if illustrated ms) based on wholesale price with escalator. Offers advances. Pays illustrators by the project or royalty. Sends galleys to authors. Book catalog for 9×12 SASE ($1.01). Ms guidelines for SASE.

Tips: "We are looking for something a bit outside the mainstream and with lasting appeal (no one-shot-wonders). Lately we've noticed a sacrifice of quality writing for the sake of illustration."

TROLL COMMUNICATIONS, 100 Corporate Dr., Mahwah NJ 07430. Book publisher. **Acquisitions:** Marian Frances, editor.
● Troll Communications is not accepting unsolicited manuscripts. Writers must query.

Fiction: Picture books: animal, contemporary, folktales, history, nature/environment, poetry, sports, suspense/mystery. Young readers: adventure, animal, contemporary, folktales, history, nature/environment, poetry, science fiction, sports, suspense/mystery. Middle readers: adventure, anthology, animal, contemporary, fantasy, folktales, health-related, history, nature/environment, poetry, problem novels, romance, science fiction, sports, suspense/mystery. Young adults: problem novels, romance and suspense/mystery.

● **SPECIAL COMMENTS** by the editor of *Children's Writer's & Illustrator's Market* are set off by a bullet.

Nonfiction: Picture books: activity books, animal, biography, careers, history, hobbies, nature/environment, sports. Young readers: activity books, animal, biography, careers, health, history, hobbies, music/dance, nature/environment, sports. Middle readers: activity books, animal, biography, careers, health, history, hobbies, music/dance, nature/environment, sports. Young adults: health, music/dance.

How to Contact/Writers: Fiction: Query or submit outline/synopsis and 3 sample chapters. Nonfiction: Query. Reports in 4 weeks.

Illustration: Reviews ms/illustration packages from artists. Contact: Marian Frances, editor. Illustrations only: Query with samples; provide résumé, promotional literature or tearsheets to be kept on file. Reports in 4 weeks.

Photography: Interested in stock photos. Model/property releases required.

Terms: Pays authors royalty or work purchased outright. Pays illustrators by the project or royalty. Photographers paid by the project.

TROPHY BOOKS, 10 E. 53rd St., New York NY 10022. Fax: (212)207-7915. Subsidiary of HarperCollins Children's Books Group. Book publisher. Publishes 6-9 chapter books/year, 25-30 middle grade titles/year, 30 reprint picture books/year, 25-30 young adult titles/year.

- Trophy is primarily a paperback reprint imprint. They do not publish original illustrated manuscripts.

‡TUNDRA BOOKS, P.O. Box 1030, Plattsburgh NY 12901. (416)598-4786. Fax: (416)598-0247. E-mail: mail@mcclelland.com. Book publisher. Estab. 1967. **Acquisitions:** Kathy Lowinger, publisher. Publishes 12 picture books/year; 4 young adult titles/year. 10% of books are by first-time authors. Publishes quality picture books and YA novels.

Fiction: "Please study catalog and submit accordingly." Recently published *Promise Song*, written by Linda Holeman (ages 11-14, ya novel); and *Dippers*, written by Barbara Nichol, illustrated by Barry Moser (ages 8 and up, picture book).

Nonfiction: "Please study catalog and submit accordingly." Recently published *Amazing Grace*, written by Linda Granfield, illustrated by Janet Wilson (ages 9 and up, picture book).

How to Contact/Writers: Fiction/Nonfiction: Query. Reports on queries/mss in 3 months. Publishes a book 2 years after acceptance. Will consider simultaneous submissions.

Illustration: Works with 10 illustrators/year. Uses color artwork only. Submit ms with 1 photocopy of final art. Illustrations only: Query with samples; send résumé, portfolio, slides and tearsheets to be kept on file. Reports in 3 months. Samples returned with SASE; samples kept on file.

Terms: Pays authors royalty. Offers advances. Pays illustrators royalty. Sends galleys to authors. Originals returned to artist at job's completion. Book catalog available for 8½ × 11 SASE and sufficient Canadian postage; ms and art guidelines for SASE.

Tips: "For faster response, please send to our editorial office in Canada at 481 University Ave., Suite 802, Toronto, Ontario M5G 2E9. Please note that American postage is not acceptable."

‡TURTLE BOOKS, 866 United Nations Plaza, New York NY 10017. (212)644-2020. Book Publisher. Estab. 1997. **Acquisitions:** John Whitman. "Turtle Books publishes only picture books for very young readers. We plan to bring all our titles out in hardcover, in both English and Spanish at the same time."

Fiction: Recently published: *La Cucaracha Martina: A Carribbean Folktale*, retold and illustrated by Daniel Moreton (the story of a cockroach and a menagerie of animals that woo her with their noises); and *The Lady in the Box*, by Ann McGovern, illustrated by Marni Backer (the story of a boy and girl who discover a homeless woman living in their neighborhood).

How to Contact/Writers: Send complete manuscript. Response time varies.

Terms: Pays royalty. Offers advances.

TYNDALE HOUSE PUBLISHERS, INC., 351 Executive Dr., P.O. Box 80, Wheaton IL 60189. (630)668-8300. Book publisher. Estab. 1962. **Manuscript Acquisitions:** Karen Watson. **Art Acquisitions:** Beth Sparkman. Publishes approximately 20 children's titles/year.

- Tyndale House no longer reviews unsolicited manuscripts.

Fiction: Middle readers: adventure, religion, suspense/mystery.

Nonfiction: Picture books: religion. Young readers: Christian living, Bible.

How to Contact/Writers: "Request children's writer guidelines from (630)668-8310 ext. 836 for more information."

Illustration: Uses full-color for book covers, b&w or color spot illustrations for some nonfiction. Illustrations only: Query with photocopies (color or b&w) of samples, résumé.

Photography: Buys photos from freelancers. Works on assignment only.

Terms: Pay rates for authors and illustrators vary.

Tips: "All accepted manuscripts will appeal to Evangelical Christian children and parents."

‡UAHC PRESS, 838 Fifth Ave., New York NY 10021-7064. (212)650-4120. Fax: (212)650-4119. E-mail: press@uahc.org. Website: http://www.uahc.press.org. Book publisher. Estab. 1876. **Manuscript/Art Acquisitions:** Greg Sanders, managing editor. Publishes 4 picture books/year; 4 young readers/year; 4 middle readers/year; 2 young adult titles/year. "The Union of American Hebrew Congregations Press publishes textbooks for the religious classroom, children's tradebooks and scholarly work of Jewish education import—no adult fiction."

Fiction: Picture books, young readers, middle readers, young adult/teens: religion.Average word length: picture books—150; young readers—500; middle readers—3,000; young adult/teens—20,000. Recently published *A Thousand and One Chickens*, written by Seymour Rosser, illustrated by Vlad Guzner (ages 10 and up, Jewish folktales); *The Mystery of the Coins*, written and illustrated by Chara Burnstein (ages 10 and up, juvenile Jewish fiction); and *Rooftop Secrets*, by Lawrence Bush (ya, stories of anti-semitism).

Nonfiction: Picture books, young readers, middle readers, young adult/teens: religion. Average word length: picture books—150; young readers—500; middle readers—3,000; young adult/teens—20,000. Recently published *Tot Shabbat*, illustrated by Camille Kress (toddlers' board book); *Book of the Jewish Year*, by Stephen Wylen (ages 12 and up, Jewish holidays); and *The Number on My Grandfather's Arm*, by David Adler (ages 6 and up, Holocaust survival).

How to Contact/Writers: Fiction: Submit outline/synopsis and 2 sample chapters. Nonfiction: Submit complete ms. Reports of queries/ms in 1-2 months. Publishes a book 18 months after acceptance. Will consider simultaneous submissions.

Illustration: Works with 10 illustrators/year. Reviews ms/illustration packages from artists. Send ms with dummy. Illustrations only: Send portfolio to be kept on file. reports in 2 months. Samples returned with SASE.

Photography: Buys stock and assigns work. Uses photos with Jewish content. Prefer modern settings. Submit cover letter and promo piece.

Terms: Offers advances. Pays photographers by the project (range: $200-3,000) or per photo (range:$20-100). Book catalog free; ms guidelines for SASE.

Tips: "Look at some of our books. Have an understanding of the reform Jewish community. We sell mostly to Jewish congregations and day schools.' "

UNIVERSITY CLASSICS, LTD. PUBLISHERS, One Bryan Rd., P.O. Box 2301, Athens OH 45701-5101. (614)592-4543. Website: http://www.bookworld.com/university_classics. Book publisher. President: Albert H. Shuster. **Acquisitions:** Katherine Dana. Publishes 1 young readers/year; 1 middle readers/year; 1 young adult title/year. 50% of books by first-time authors.

●	This publisher is "booked for the next two years" in children's fiction and nonfiction. Do not submit work (manuscripts or illustrations) to them at this time.

Fiction: Picture books: animal, concept, health, nature/environment. Young readers: concept, health, nature/environment, special needs. Middle readers: health, nature/environment, problem novels, special needs. Young adults: health, nature/environment, special needs. Average word length: young readers—1,200; middle readers—5,000. Published *Toodle D. Poodle*, by Katherine Dana and Dorathyre Shuster (grades 4-6, ages 10-12); *The Day My Dad and I Got Mugged*, by Howard Goldsmith (grades 5-8, ages 12-15).

Nonfiction: Picture books: activity books, animal, arts/crafts, concept, health, nature/environment, self help, special needs. Young readers: activity books, animal, arts/crafts, concept, health, nature/environment, self help, special needs, textbooks. Middle readers, young adults: arts/crafts, concept, health, nature/environment, self help, special needs, textbooks. Average word length: young readers—1,200; middle readers—5,000. Published *Fitness and Nutrition: The Winning Combination*, by Jane Buch (ages 13-17, textbook); *The Way We Live: Practical Economics*, by John Shaw (ages 13-adult, textbook); *Ride Across America: An Environmental Commitment*, by Lucian Spataro (ages 13-17, trade).

How to Contact: Reports on queries/mss in 1 month.

Terms: Pays authors royalty of 4-12% based on retail price. Book catalog available for #10 SAE and 2 first-class stamps.

Tips: "Consumers are looking more for educational than fictional books, and this will continue."

‡VIKING CHILDREN'S BOOKS, 375 Huron St., New York NY 10014. (212)366-2000. Imprint of Penguin Putnam Inc. **Acquisitions:** Elizabeth Law, editor-in-chief. Publishes hardcover originals. Publishes 80 books/year. 25% of books from first-time authors; 33% from unagented writers. "Viking Children's Books publishes the highest quality trade books for children including fiction, nonfiction, and novelty books for pre-schoolers through young adults."

Fiction: Picture books submit entire ms. Recently published *The Awful Aardvarks Go to School*, by Reeve Lindbergh (picture book); *Virtual World*, by Chris Westwood (young adult novel).

Nonfiction: Query with outline, one sample chapter and SASE. Reports on queries in 2 months. Publishes book 1 year after acceptance. Will consider simultaneous submissions.

How to Contact/Writers: Fiction: Query with synopsis, one sample chapter and SASE.

"PICTURE BOOKS" are for preschoolers to 8-year-olds; "Young readers" are for 5- to 8-year-olds; "Middle readers" are for 9- to 11-year-olds; and "Young adults" are for those ages 12 and up.

Terms: Pays 10% royalty on retail price. Advance negotiable.
Tips: Mistake often made is that "authors disguise nonfiction in a fictional format."

VOLCANO PRESS, Box 270, Volcano CA 95689. (209)296-3345. Fax: (209)296-4515. E-mail: sales@volcano press.com. Website: http://www.volcanopress.com. Book publisher. **Acquisitions:** Ruth Gottstein, president/publisher. "We believe that the books we are producing today are of even greater value than the gold of yesteryear, and that the symbolism of the term 'Mother Lode' is still relevant to our work."
Fiction: All levels: animals, folktales, multicultural, nature/environment, poetry, history.
Nonfiction: Young readers, middle readers, young adult: self help, social issues, special needs. Sees too much "fiction, trite fantasy, didactic and moralistic material, bad fairy tales, anthropomorphic male animal heroes."
How to Contact/Writers: Nonfiction: Submit outline/synopsis and sample chapters. Reports on queries in 2-3 weeks; mss in 4-6 weeks. Publishes a book 1 year after acceptance. "Please always enclose SASE."
Terms: Pays authors royalty. Book catalog for #10 SASE.
Tips: Considers "non-racist, non-sexist types of books that are empowering to women and girls."

WALKER AND CO., 435 Hudson St., New York NY 10014. (212)727-8300. Division of Walker Publishing Co. Inc. Book publisher. Estab. 1959. **Acquisitions:** Emily Easton, editorial director; Soyung Pak, editor. Publishes 12 picture books/year; 10 middle readers/year; 2-4 young adult titles/year. 5% of books by first-time authors; 65% of books from agented writers.
Fiction: Picture books: animal, history, multicultural. Young readers: contemporary, history, humor, multicultural. Middle readers: animal, contemporary, history, multicultural, humor. Young adults: contemporary and historical fiction. Recently published *Shooting Star*, by D. Dadey; *These Are The Rules*, by P. Many (young adult); *The Keeping Room*, by A. Myers (middle grade).
Nonfiction: Young readers: science, history. Middle readers: animal, history, multicultural. Young adults: biography, careers, health, history, multicultural, reference, social issues, sports. Published *Grand Canyon*, by L. Viera (picture book history); and *Where Will This Shoe Take You?*, by L. Lawlor (young adult history). Multicultural needs include "contemporary, literary fiction and historical fiction written in an authentic voice. Also high interest nonfiction with trade appeal."
How to Contact/Writers: Fiction/nonfiction: Submit outline/synopsis and sample chapters. Reports on queries/mss in 2-3 months. Will consider simultaneous submissions.
Illustration: Works with 10-12 illustrators/year. Uses color artwork only. Editorial reviews ms/illustration packages from artists. Query or submit ms with 4-8 samples. Illustrations only: Tearsheets. "Please do not send original artwork." Reports on art samples only if interested. Samples returned with SASE.
Terms: Pays authors in royalties of 5-10% based on wholesale price "depends on contract." Offers advance payment against royalties. Original artwork returned at job's completion. Pays illustrators by the project (range: $500-5,000); royalties from 50%. Sends galleys to authors. Book catalog available for 9×12 SASE; ms guidelines for SASE.
Tips: Writers: "Make sure you study our catalog before submitting. We are a small house with a tightly focused list." Illustrators: "Have a well-rounded portfolio with different styles." Does not want to see folktales, ABC books, genre fiction (mysteries, science fiction, fantasy).

‡WARD HILL PRESS, P.O. Box 04-0424, Staten Island NY 10304-0008. (718)816-9449. Fax: (718)816-4056. E-mail: wardhill@interport.net. Website: http://bookzone.com/wardhill. Estab. 1989. **Acquisitions:** Elizabeth Davis, editorial director. Publishes 3-6 middle readers/year; 3-6 young adults/year. 90% of books by first-time authors. "Our books focus on some aspect of U.S. history (1860 to present) or multiculturalism in a U.S. context. They include biographies of little-known historical figures, nonfiction books about particular historical events and peoples, and fiction that explores relations between different cultures in America or personalizes a historical event."
Fiction: Middle readers, young adults: multicultural novels. Young adults: contemporary. Average word length: middle readers—20,000; young adults—30,000.
Nonfiction: Middle readers, young adults: biography, history, multicultural, social issues. Multicultural needs include biographies of figures from diverse cultures. Does not want to see biographies of mainstream personalities or pop entertainers. Average word length: middle readers—20,000; young adults—30,000. Recently published *Flatboating on the Yellowstone, 1877*, by Fred G. Bond; *My Best Defense*, by Bob Riggs; and *Woody Guthrie: American Balladeer*, by Janelle Yates.
How to Contact/Writers: Fiction/Nonfiction: Query with outline or outline and sample chapters. "In your query letter, please describe the subject of your book, your reasons for choosing that subject, your particular 'angle' or orientation, your writing qualifications and a review of similar books on the market (or a lack thereof). We prefer books that personalize the subject matter in some way, not dry accumulations of fact. This, in fact, is our trademark." Reports on queries in 6-8 weeks. Publishes a book 1 year after acceptance. Will consider previously published work.
Illustration: Works with 3-6 illustrators/year. Reviews ms/illustration packages from artists. Query. Illustrations only: Query with samples; provide résumé. Reports in 1-2 months. Samples returned with SASE; samples filed. Originals not returned.
Terms: Pays authors royalty of 5-8% based on retail price. Offers advances (average amount: $800). Pays

illustrators royalty of 3-5% based on retail price or by the project. Sends galleys to authors; dummies to illustrators. Book catalog available for 4×9½ SAE and 1 first-class stamp. "We send manuscript guidelines only after seeing query."

♣★WEIGL EDUCATIONAL PUBLISHERS, 1902 11th St. SE., Calgary, Alberta T2G 3G2 Canada. (403)233-7747. Fax: (403)233-7769. E-mail: weigl@mail.telusplanet.net. Website: http://www.weigl.com. Book publisher. Publisher and President: Linda Weigl. **Acquisitions:** L. Seidlitz, editor. "Weigl is a publisher of high-quality education materials, including books, teacher guides, library series, and multimedia kits for social studies, language arts, environmental science, and career studies for the K-12 educational market."
Nonfiction: Young reader, middle reader, young adult: textbooks. Young reader, middle reader: careers, multicultural. Average length: young reader, middle reader, young adult—64 pages. Recently published *Career Connections Series III*, (grades 4-6); *Career Connections*, Teacher Resource Banks (grades 7-9); *Untamed World* series I and II (grades 4-6); and *Outstanding African Americans* series (grades 4-6).
How to Contact/Writers: Nonfiction: Submit query and résumé. Reports on queries in 6 months; mss in 6 months. Publishes a book 2 years after acceptance. Will consider simultaneous submissions.
Illustration: Works with 1 illustrator/year. Reviews ms/illustration packages from artists. Query first. Illustrations only: Query with samples. Reports back only if interested or when appropriate project comes in. Samples returned with SASE; samples filed.
Photography: Buys photos from freelancers. Buys stock and assigns work. Wants political, juvenile, multicultural, animals and nature, historical figures, well-known women, art, culture and history, and Order of Canada winners photos.
Terms: Pays authors royalty or work purchased outright. Pays illustrators/photographers by the project. Sends galleys to author; dummies to illustrator. Original artwork returned at job's completion. Book catalog for SASE.
Tips: Looks for "a manuscript that answers a specific curriculum need, or can be applied to a curriculum topic with multiple applications (e.g. career education)."

☐DANIEL WEISS ASSOCIATES, INC., 11th Floor, 33 W. 17th St., New York NY 10011. (212)645-3865. Fax: (212)633-1236. Independent book producer/packager. Estab. 1987. **Manuscript Acquisitions:** Kieran Scott, editorial assistant. **Art Acquisitions:** Paul Matarazzo, art director (illustrations); Mike Rivilis, assistant art director (ms/illustration packages). Publishes 30 young readers/year; 40 middle readers/year; and 70 young adults/year. 25% of books by first-time authors. "We do mostly series!"
Fiction: Middle readers: sports. Young adults: fantasy, romance.
Nonfiction: Young adults: history.
readers, young adults: adventure, anthology, contemporary, problem novels, romance, sports, suspense/mystery.
How to Contact/Writers: Submit outline/synopsis and 2 sample chapters. Reports on queries in 1-2 months; mss in 2 months. Publishes a book 1 year after acceptance. Will consider simultaneous submissions.
Illustration: Works with 20 illustrators/year. Reviews ms/illustration packages from artists. Submit query. Illustrations only: Provide promo sheet. Reports in 2 months. Samples returned with SASE. Original artwork returned at job's completion.
Terms: Pays authors royalty of 4%. Work purchased outright from authors, $1,000 minimum. Offers advances (average amount: $3,000). Pays illustrators by the project. Ms guidelines available if SASE sent.

WHISPERING COYOTE PRESS, INC., 300 Crescent Court, Suite 860, Dallas TX 75201. **Acquisitions:** Mrs. Lou Alpert, editor/publisher. Publishes 8 picture books/year. 40% of books from first-time authors.
Fiction: Picture books: adventure, animal, contemporary, fantasy, hi-lo, history, humor, poetry. Does not want to see number, alphabet, death, handicap and holiday books. Average word length: picture books—under 1,200. Recently published *How Much Is That Doggie in the Window?*, written and illustrated by Iza Trapani (4-8, picture book); and *The Red Shoes*, by Barbara Bazilian.
How to Contact/Writers: Submit complete ms. Reports in 3 months. Publishes a book 1½-3 years after acceptance. Will consider simultaneous submissions. "Include SASE. If no SASE is included manuscript is destroyed *without* reading."
Illustration: Works with 6-8 illustrators/year. Uses color artwork only. Reviews ms/illustration packages from artists. Submit ms with dummy or 3-4 photocopies of final art. Illustrations only: Submit color copies or a half dozen pieces for file. "Do not send originals." Reports back only if SASE is included. Samples returned with SASE; samples filed if instructed to do so by illustrator.
Terms: Pays authors royalty of 4-5% based on retail price. Offers advances. Pays illustrators royalty of 4-5%. Book catalog available for #10 SASE and 55¢ first-class postage. Manuscript and art guidelines available for SASE.

 ★ PUBLISHERS PRODUCING educational material are marked with a star.

Tips: "Look at what we do before submitting. Follow the guidelines. I think publishers are doing fewer books and are therefore more selective in what they agree to publish. We are having more luck with shorter books with a sense of humor."

✤**WHITECAP BOOKS**, 351 Lynn Ave., North Vancouver, British Columbia V7J 2C4 Canada. (604)980-9852. E-mail: whitecap@pinc.com. Book publisher. **Acquisitions:** Colleen MacMillan, publisher. Publishes 4 young readers/year; and 2 middle readers/year.
● Whitecap is just entering the children's picture book market this fall.
Fiction: Picture books for children 3-7.
Nonfiction: Young readers, middle readers: animal, nature/environment. Does not want to see text that writes down to children. Recently published *Welcome to the World of Wolves*, by Diane Swanson (ages 5-7); *Buffalo Sunrise*, by Diane Swanson (ages 9-11); and *The Day of the Twelve-Story Wave*, illustrated by Laura Cook (ages 9-11).
How to Contact/Writers: Nonfiction: Query. Reports on queries in 1 month; ms in 3 months. Publishes a book 6 months after acceptance. Will consider simultaneous submissions.
Illustration: Works with 1-2 illustrators/year. Reviews ms/illustration packages from artists. Query. Illustrations only: Query with samples—"never send original art." Contact: Colleen MacMillan, publisher. Samples returned with SASE with international postal voucher for Canada if requested.
Photography: Buys stock. "We are always looking for outstanding wildlife photographs." Uses 35mm transparencies. Submit cover letter, client list, stock photo list.
Terms: Pays authors a negotiated royalty or purchases work outright. Offers advances. Pays illustrators by the project or royalty (depends on project). Pays photographers per photo (depends on project). Originals returned to artist at job's completion unless discussed in advance. Ms guidelines available for SASE with international postal voucher for Canada.
Tips: "Writers and illustrators should spend time researching what's already available on the market. Whitecap specializes in nonfiction for children and adults."

ALBERT WHITMAN & COMPANY, 6340 Oakton St., Morton Grove IL 60053-2723. (708)581-0033. Fax: (847)581-0039. Book publisher. Estab. 1919. **Acquisitions:** Kathleen Tucker, editor-in-chief. Publishes 30 books/year. 15% of books by first-time authors; 15% of books from agented authors.
Fiction: Picture books, young readers, middle readers: adventure, animal, concept, contemporary, folktales, health, history, humor, multicultural, nature/environment, special needs. Middle readers: problem novels, suspense/mystery. "We are mostly interested in contemporary multicultural stories, set both in the U.S. and in other countries. We publish a wide variety of topics, and are interested in stories that will help children deal with their problems and concerns. Does not want to see "religion-oriented, ABCs, pop-up, romance, counting or any book that is supposed to be written in." Published *Turkey Pox*, by Laurie Halse Anderson, illustrated by Dorothy Donohue; *The Dog Who Lost His Bob*, by Tom and Laura McNeal, illustrated by John Sandford; and *The Borrowed Hanukkah Latkes*, by Linda Glaser, illustrated by Nancy Cote.
Nonfiction: Picture books, young readers, middle readers: animal, biography, concept, geography, health, history, hobbies, multicultural, music/dance, nature/environment, special needs. Middle readers: careers. Middle readers, young adults: biography, social issues. Does not want to see "religion, any books that have to be written in, biographies of living people." Recently published *The Fragile Frog*, by William P. Mara, illustrated by John R. Quinn; *Small Steps: The Year I Got Polio*, by Peg Kehret; and *I'm Tougher Than Asthma*, by Siri M. Carter and Alden R. Carter, photographs by Dan Young.
How to Contact/Writers: Fiction/Nonfiction: Submit complete ms. Reports on queries in 4-6 weeks; mss in 2 months. Publishes a book 18 months after acceptance. Will consider simultaneous submissions "but let us know if it is one." Samples returned with SASE; samples filed.
Illustration: Works with 30 illustrators/year. Uses more color art than b&w. Reviews ms/illustration packages from artists. Illustrations only: Query with samples. Send slides or tearsheets. Reports back in 2 months.
Photography: Publishes books illustrated with photos but not stock photos—desires photos all taken for project. "Our books are for children and cover many topics; photos must be taken to match text. Books often show a child in a particular situation (e.g., kids being home-schooled, a sister whose brother is born prematurely)." Photographers should query with samples; send unsolicited photos by mail.
Terms: Pays authors royalty. Offers advances. Pays illustrators and photographers royalty. Sends galleys to authors; dummies to illustrators. Original artwork returned at job's completion. Ms/artist's guidelines available for SASE.
Tips: "In both picture books and nonfiction, we are seeking stories showing life in other cultures and the variety of multicultural life in the U.S. We also want fiction and nonfiction about mentally or physically challenged children—some recent topics have been AIDS, asthma, cerebral palsy. Look up some of our books first, to be sure your submission is appropriate for Albert Whitman & Co."

JOHN WILEY & SONS, INC., 605 Third Ave., New York NY 10158. (212)850-6206. Fax: (212)850-6095. E-mail: writers@cyberhighway.net. Website: http://www.writerspress.com. Book publisher. **Acquisitions:** Kate Bradford, editor. Publishes 18 middle readers/year; 2 young adult titles/year. 10% of books by first-time authors. Publishes educational, nonfiction primarily science, and other activities. "We publish books, journals, and electronic products for the scientific, technical, eductional, professional and consumer markets. We are committed to providing information in those formats most accessible to our readers and are taking advantage of the rapid advances in digital information technology to our print publications and develop a range of offerings in electronic formats."

Fiction: Picture books: humor, poetry, special needs. Young readers: adventure, special needs. Middle readers: adventure, history.

Nonfiction: Middle readers: activity books, animal, arts/crafts, biography, cooking, geography, health, history, hobbies, how-to, nature/environment, reference, science, self help. Young adults: activity books, arts/crafts, health, hobbies, how-to, nature/environment, reference, science, self help. Average word length middle readers—20,000-40,000. Recently published: *Can It Really Rain Frogs*, by Spencer Christian (ages 8-12).

How to Contact/Writers: Query. Submit outline/synopsis and 2 sample chapters. Reports on queries in 1 month; mss in 3 months. Publishes a book 1 year after acceptance. Will consider simultaneous and previously published submissions.

Illustration: Works with 6 illustrators/year. Uses primarily black & white artwork. Reviews ms/illustration packages from artists. Query. Illustrations only: Query with samples, résumé, client list. Reports back only if interested. Samples filed. Original artwork returned at job's completion.

Photography: Buys photos from freelancers.

Terms: Pays authors royalty of 4-10% based on wholesale price, or by outright purchase ($700-2,500). Offers advances. Pays illustrators by the project ($350-2,000). Photographers pay negotiable. Sends galleys to authors. Book catalog available for SAE.

Tips: "We're looking for topics and writers that can really engage kids' interest—plus we're always interested in a new twist on time-tested subjects."

WILLIAMSON PUBLISHING CO., Box 185, Charlotte VT 05445. (802)425-2102. Fax: (802)425-2199. Website: http://williamsonbooks.com. Book publisher. Estab. 1983. **Manuscript Acquisitions:** Susan Williamson, editorial director. **Art Acquisitions:** Jack Williamson, publisher. Publishes 12-15 young readers titles/year. 50% of books by first-time authors; 10% of books from agented authors. Publishes "very successful nonfiction series (Kids Can!® Series—2,000,000 sold) on subjects such as nature, creative play, arts/crafts, geography. Successfully launched *Little Hands*® series for ages 2-6 and *Tales Alive*® series and recently introduced the new *Kaleidoscope Kids*™ series (tales plus activities)." Our mission is to help every child fulfill his/her potential and experience personal growth.

• Williamson won Benjamin Franklin Awards for Best Nonfiction, juvenile; Best Fiction, juvenile; Best Multicultural. Also winner of Oppenheim Toy Award, Parent's Choice Awards.

Fiction: Young readers, middle readers: folktales, multicultural.

Nonfiction: Young readers: activity books, animal, arts/crafts, career, cooking, health, history, how-to, multicultural, music/dance, nature/environment, science, self-help, social issues. Does not want to see textbooks, picture books, fiction. "We are looking for books in which learning and doing are inseparable." Published *Super Science Concoctions*, by Jill Hauser, illustrated by Michael Kline (ages 6-12, exploring science); *Shapes, Sizes and More Surprises*, by Mary Tomczyk, illustrated by Loretta Trezzo Braren (ages 2-6, early learning skills); and *Tales of the Shimmering Sky*, retold by Susan Milord, illustrated by JoAnn Kitchel (ages 4 and up, multicultural tales with activities).

How to Contact/Writers: Query with outline/synopsis and 2 sample chapters. Reports on queries in 4 months; mss in 6 months. Publishes book, "depending on graphics, about 1 year" after acceptance.

Illustration: Works with 6 illustrator and 6 designers/year. "We're interested in expanding our illustrator and design freelancers." Uses primarily b&w artwork; some 2-color and 4-color.

Photography: Buys photos from freelancers

Terms: Pays authors royalty based on wholesale price. Offers advances. Pays illustrators by the project. Pays photographers by the project or per photo. Sends galleys to authors. Book catalog available for 8½×11 SAE and 4 first-class stamps; ms guidelines available for SASE.

Tips: "We're interested in interactive learning books with a creative approach packed with interesting information, written for young readers ages 2-6 and 4-10. In nonfiction children's publishing, we are looking for authors with a depth of knowledge shared with children through a warm, embracing style. Our publishing philosophy is based on the idea that all children can succeed and have positive learning experiences. Children's lasting learning experiences involve participation."

WOMAN'S MISSIONARY UNION, P.O. Box 830010, Birmingham AL 35283-0010. (205)991-8100. Fax: (205)995-4841. Website: http://www.wmu.com/wmu. Imprint: New Hope. **Acquisitions:** Cindy McClain, editorial director. Publishes 2 picture books/year; 5 young readers/year; 10 middle readers/year; and 20 young adult titles/year. 25% of books by first-time authors.

Fiction: All levels: multicultural, religion. Multicultural fiction must be related to mission/ministry.

Nonfiction: All levels: multicultural, religion. Multicultural nonfiction must be related to Christian concepts, particularly Christian missions.

How to Contact/Writers: Fiction/nonfiction: Submit complete ms. Reports on queries in 3 months; mss in 3-6 months. Publishes a book 2 years after acceptance. Will consider simultaneous submissions.

Illustration: Works with 2-3 illustrators/year. Reviews ms/illustration packages from artists. Send ms with

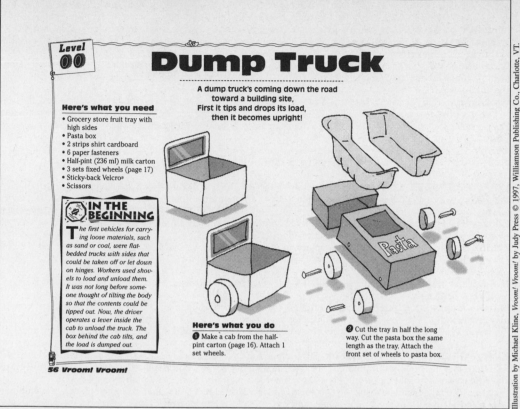

Level 00

Dump Truck

A dump truck's coming down the road
toward a building site.
First it tips and drops its load,
then it becomes upright!

Here's what you need
- Grocery store fruit tray with high sides
- Pasta box
- 2 strips shirt cardboard
- 6 paper fasteners
- Half-pint (236 ml) milk carton
- 3 sets fixed wheels (page 17)
- Sticky-back Velcro®
- Scissors

IN THE BEGINNING

The first vehicles for carrying loose materials, such as sand or coal, were flat-bedded trucks with sides that could be taken off or let down on hinges. Workers used shovels to load and unload them. It was not long before someone thought of tilting the body so that the contents could be tipped out. Now, the driver operates a lever inside the cab to unload the truck. The box behind the cab tilts, and the load is dumped out.

Here's what you do
❶ Make a cab from the half-pint carton (page 16). Attach 1 set wheels.

❷ Cut the tray in half the long way. Cut the pasta box the same length as the tray. Attach the front set of wheels to pasta box.

56 Vroom! Vroom!

Illustration by Michael Kline, *Vroom! Vroom!* by Judy Press © 1997, Williamson Publishing Co., Charlotte, VT.

As the craft fad continues to be popular and spreads to the children's market, there is a growing need for writers and illustrators for children's activity and crafts books. *Vroom! Vroom! Making 'dozers, 'copters, trucks & more*, published by Williamson Publishing, not only taps into every kid's fascination with earth and people movers, but it helps kids build them. With simple instructions written by author Judy Press and using recycled materials like empty milk cartons, cereal boxes and cardboard toilet tissue tubes, kids can build everything from backhoes to double-decker buses, fire engines to helicopters. Williamson Publishing's designer chose illustrator Michael Kline for the difficult task of making the projects look playful and fun, yet clear enough for kids to understand.

dummy. Illustrations only: Query with samples (color copies). Reports back only if interested. Samples filed.
Photography: Buys stock already on file. Model/property releases required.
Terms: Pays authors royalty of 7-10% (depends on length). Pays illustrators by the project. Sends galleys to authors. Originals returned to artist at job's completion. Book catalog available for 10×12 SAE and 3 first-class stamps. Manuscript guidelines available for SASE.
Tips: "Obtain the catalog first to see the kinds of material we publish."

WORLD BOOK, INC., 525 W. Monroe St., Chicago IL 60661. (312)258-3700. Fax: (312)258-3950. Website: http://www.worldbook.com. Book publisher. **Manuscript Acquisitions:** Paul A. Kobasa, product development director. **Art Acquisitions:** Roberta Dimmer, executive art director. Publishes 6-10 picture books/year; 6-10 young readers/year; 6-10 middle readers/year; and 15-20 young adult titles/year. 20% of books by first-time authors. "World Book Trade, a division of World Book, Inc. (publisher of *The World Book Encyclopedia*), publishes reference sources and nonfiction series for children in the areas of science, mathematics, English-language skills, basic academic and social skills, social studies, history, and health and fitness. We publish print and nonprint material appropriate for children ages 3 to 14. WBT does not publish fiction, poetry, or wordless picture books."
Nonfiction: Picture books: animal, concept, reference. Young readers: activity books, animal, arts/crafts, careers, concept, geography, health, reference. Middle readers: activity books, animal, arts/crafts, careers, geography, health, history, hobbies, how-to, nature/environment, reference, science. Young adult: arts/crafts, careers, geography, health, history, hobbies, how-to, nature/environment, reference, science. Average word length: picture books—10-20 words; young readers—20-100 words; middle readers—100-400 words; young adults—500-2,000

words. Recently published *World Book Looks at Insects and Spiders* (ages 8-12); *World Book Children's Illustrated Atlas* (ages 7-12); and *Me and My Pet Cat* (ages 6-10).

How to Contact/Writers: Nonfiction: Submit outline/synopsis only; no mss. Reports on queries/mss in 1-2 months. Unsolicited mss will not be returned. Publishes a book 18 months after acceptance. Will consider simultaneous submissions.

Illustration: Works with 10-30 illustrators/year. Illustrations only: Query with samples. Contact: Roberta Dimmer, executive art director. Reports only if interested. Samples returned with SASE; samples filed "if extra copies and if interested."

Photography: Buys stock and assigns work. Needs broad spectrum; editorial concept, specific natural, physical and social science spectrum. Model/property releases required; captions required. Uses color 8×10 gloss and matte prints, 35mm, $2\frac{1}{4} \times 2\frac{1}{4}$, 4×5, 8×10 transparencies. Submit cover letter, résumé, promo piece (color and b&w).

Terms: Payment negotiated on project-by-project basis. Sends galleys to authors. Book catalog available for 9×12 SAE. Manuscript and art guidelines for SASE.

‡WRITERS PRESS, 5278 Chinden Blvd., Boise ID 83714. (208)327-0566. Fax: (208)327-3477. E-mail: writers @cyberhighway.net. Website: www.writerspress.com. **Acquisitions:** John Ybarra, editor. Publishes hardcover and trade paperback originals. Publishes 6 titles/year. 60% of books from first-time authors; 100% from unagented writers. "Our philosophy is to publish educational literature that equally represents all children, including children with disabilities, as a natural part of our environment."

Fiction: Picture books, young adult: adventure, historical, inclusion, special education. Recently published *Eagle Feather*, by Sonia Gardner, illustrated by James Spurlock (picture book); and *Hodgepodge*, by Kevin Boos (poetry).

Nonfiction: Education, history, inclusion, special education. Reviews artwork/photos as part of ms package. Send photocopies.

How to Contact/Writers: Fiction/Nonfiction: Query. Reports on queries in 1 month; proposals in 2 months; mss in 4 months. Publishes book 6 months after acceptance.

Terms: Pays 4-12% royalty or work purchased outright for up to $1,500. Catalog and guidelines free.

ZINO PRESS CHILDREN'S BOOK, Division of Knowledge Unlimited, 2348 Pinehurst Dr., Middleton WI 53562. (608)836-6660. Fax: (608)831-1570. Website: http://www.ku.com. Book publisher. **Acquisitions Editor:** Dave Schreiner. Publishes 2 picture books/year. Publishes rhyming stories and multicultural books.

Fiction: Rhyming picture books, young readers, middle readers: adventure, animal, contemporary, multicultural. "Text and art that is original and unique, and not a retold folktale. Works must reflect a range of lifestyles accurately and without stereotyping, and should express values that lead to tolerance, greater awareness of self and others, kindness and compassion." Does not want to see folktales; books about colors, vegetables, the alphabet, etc. or books without a plot. Average length: picture books—32 pages. Recently published *The Contrary Kid*, by Matt Cibula, illustrated by Brian Strassburg; and *Slumgullion, the Executive Pig*, by Matt Cibala, illustrated by Tamara Boudreau.

Nonfiction: Picture books, young readers: history, multicultural, special needs. For multicultural work, author should be of culture written about or author should work with consultant of that culture. Does not want to see biographies of famous people. Average length: picture books—32-48 pages. Recently published *Sweet Words So Brave: The Story of African-American Literature*, by Barbara Curry and James Brodie, illustrated by Jerry Butler.

How to Contact/Writers: Fiction/Nonfiction: Submit complete ms. Reports in 16 weeks. Publishes a book 12-16 months after acceptance. Will consider simultaneous submissions. Must enclose SASE.

Illustration: Works with 2-3 illustrators/yearly. Uses color artwork only. Reviews ms/illustration packages from artists. Submit ms with dummy. Illustrations only: Query with samples. Reports in 1 month. Samples returned with SASE; some samples filed.

Photography: Buys stock images.

Terms: Pays authors royalty based on wholesale price or work purchased outright. Pays illustrators by the project. Pays photographers per photo. Sends galleys to authors; dummies to illustrators. Ms and artist's guidelines available for SASE.

Tips: "Take a fresh approach in submitting rhyming material. We are *not* looking for familiar stories or whimsical lines. We *are* looking for offbeat humor."

‡ZONDERVAN PUBLISHING HOUSE, Division of HarperCollins, 5300 Patterson S.E., Grand Rapids MI 49530. (616)698-6900. Website: http://www.zondervan.com. Book publisher. Estab. 1931. **Manuscript Acquisitions:** Manuscript Review Editor. Publishes 2-3 picture books/year; 2 young readers/year; 2-4 middle readers/year; 2 young adult titles/year. 20% of books are by first-time authors. Zondervan is an "evangelical Christian publisher. Best known for publishing the most popular English translation of the Bible: the New International Version. Publishes best-selling children's Bibles and Bible story books. Zondervan Publishing House seeks to be the leading Christian communications company meeting the needs of people with resources that glorify Jesus Christ and promote biblical principles."

Fiction: Picture books, young readers, middle readers, young adult/teens: religion. Recently published *Legend of the Candy Cane*, written by Lori Walberg, illustrated by James Bernardin (ages 4-8, picture book).

Nonfiction: Picture books, young readers, middle readers, young adult/teens: religion. Recently published *Completely Alive*, written by Rick Christian (ages 12-18, devotional with b&w photos); *Beginner's Bible* (ages 2-9, Bible storybook); and *The Read with Me Bible Series: "Angels of the Bible,"* illustrated by Dennis Jones (Bible stories).

How to Contact/Writers: Fiction/Nonfiction: Submit outline/synopsis and 3-4 sample chapters. Reports on queries in 2 months; ms in 3 months. Publishes a book 9-12 months after acceptance. Will consider simultaneous submissions.

Illustration: Works with 4 illustrators/year.

Terms: Pays authors 6-14% royalty based on retail price. Offers advances. Pays illustrators by the project (range: $80-800) or 6-8% royalty based on retail price. Pays photographers per photo. Sends galleys to authors; dummies to illustrators. Originals returned to artist when job is completed. Ms guidelines for SASE.

Tips: "You should be familiar with the Christian bookstore market, and should be a practicing, evangelical Christian interested in writing or illustrating explicitly or implicitly Christian material."

MARKET CONDITIONS are constantly changing! If you're still using this book and it is 1999 or later, buy the newest edition of *Children's Writer's & Illustrator's Market* at your favorite bookstore or order directly from Writer's Digest Books.

Magazines

Children's magazines are great places for unpublished writers and illustrators to break into the market. Illustrators, photographers and writers alike may find it easier to get book assignments if they have tearsheets from magazines. Having magazine work under your belt shows you're professional and have experience working with editors and art directors and meeting deadlines.

But magazines aren't merely a breaking-in point. Writing, illustration and photo assignments for magazines let you see your work in print quickly, and the magazine market can offer steady work and regular paychecks (a number of them pay on acceptance). Book authors, illustrators and photographers may have to wait a year or two before receiving royalties from a project.

The magazine market is also a good place to use research material that didn't make it into a book project you're working on. Or what you thought was just an article idea could blossom into a book project. Elaine Marie Alphin wrote an article on vacuum cleaners that appeared in *Cricket*, but she had enough great information to write *Vacuum Cleaners* for Carolrhoda. Accomplished writer Alphin shares tips on writing for both the book and magazine markets in an Insider Report on page 220.

AN ARRAY OF OFFERINGS

There are now a couple hundred kids' magazines found in homes, libraries and classrooms, about 120 of which are listed in this section. Magazines devoted to licensed characters (such as Barney, Barbie or Batman), or publications that serve as promotions for toys or movies (which are primarily produced inhouse) are not included. You will find diverse magazines aimed at children of all ages and interests.

Some of the listings in this section are religion-oriented or special interest publications; others are general interest magazines. Though large circulation, ad-driven publications generally offer better pay rates than religious or nonprofit magazines, smaller magazines are more open to reviewing the work of newcomers and can provide an excellent source for clips and tearsheets as you work your way toward more lucrative markets.

Children's magazine publishers know that young readers have varying interests just as adult readers do. In this section you'll find magazines targeting boys (such as *Boys' Life* and *Boys' Quest*) and magazines targeting girls (like *American Girl* and *YM*) just as you might find news-stand publications specifically for men or women.

Magazines for young people affiliated with almost every religious denomination are listed. You'll also notice specialized magazines devoted to certain sports, such as *Blackbelt for Kids*. Publications addressing various world cultures like *Skipping Stones* and *Faces* supply readers with ethnically diverse stories and artwork. The need for multicultural material is also present in general interest magazines (many editors have indicated specific multicultural needs within their listings). If you're not a member of the group you're interested in writing about, make sure to thoroughly research your subject to insure authenticity. Better yet, pass your work by an expert on the culture before submitting it.

Another plus for the children's magazine industry is that teachers are using fact-based educational publications—such as those teaching history, math or science—as supplements in their classrooms. As a result, it's not unusual for children to want their own personal subscriptions after initially being exposed to the magazines at school.

More and more informational adult magazines (like *Time*, *Sports Illustrated*, *People* and *Consumer Reports*) are publishing versions for kids. Since magazines have the advantage of

MINDING YOUR AGE-LEVEL

The big word in children's magazines is specialization. Publications for children are becoming more narrowly focused in subject matter, gender and especially age-level. It's more important than ever for writers to research and read the magazine they are interested in writing for before submitting to get a feel for the reading level of the publications. Here are some examples of the age-specific magazines from some well known publishers, including some new offerings (which you'll find listed in this section):

• *Boy's Life* is now published in two editions—one for the older Boy Scout and one for the younger Scout.

• Added to the roster of The Cricket Magazine Group, publisher of *Cricket* (for ages 9-14), *Spider* (for ages 6-9), *Ladybug* (for ages 2-6), and *Babybug* (for ages 6 months-2 years) are *Muse* for ages 6-14 and *Click* for ages 2-6, both published in cooperation wtih the Smithsonian Institution. In the fall, they began experimenting with a new teen magazine for ages 14-18.

• Standard publishing, producers of *R-A-D-A-R* (for grades 3-4) and *Straight* (for teens) also publishes *Livewire* for 5th- and 6th-grade readers.

• OWL Communications, publishers of *OWL* (for ages 8-14) and *Chickadee* (for ages 3-8) have added *Chirp* to their lineup, a publication for readers ages 2-6.

• The publisher of *Guideposts for Kids* (for ages 7-12) recently launched *Guideposts for Teens*. (See Insider Report with Mary Lou Carney, *Guideposts* editor, on page 214.)

timeliness, they can relay information about current events or interests much more quickly and cheaply than books. The average one-year subscription costs about the same as one hardcover picture book.

TARGETING YOUR SUBMISSIONS

While it's important to know the current interests of children, you must also know the topics typically covered by different children's magazines. To help you match your work with the right publications, a Subject Index is included at the back of this book. This index lists both book and magazine publishers by the fiction and nonfiction subjects they're seeking.

A Photography Index listing all the children's magazines that use photos from freelancers is also found in the back of this book. Use this in combination with the Subject Index, and you can quickly narrow your search of markets that suit your work. For instance, if you photograph sports, compare the Magazine list in the Photography Index with the lists under Sports in the Subject Index. Highlight the markets that appear on both lists, then read those listings to decide which are best for you.

Writers can use the Subject Index in conjunction with the Age-Level Index to narrow their list of markets. Targeting the correct age-group with your submission is an important consideration. The majority of rejection slips are sent because the writer has not targeted a manuscript to the correct age. Few magazines are aimed at children of all ages, so you must be certain your manuscript is written for the audience level of the particular magazine you're submitting to.

Each magazine has a different editorial philosophy. Language usage also varies between periodicals, as does the length of feature articles and the use of artwork and photographs. Reading the magazines you're considering submitting to is the best way to determine if your material is appropriate. Also, because magazines targeted to specific age-groups have a natural turnover in readership every few years, old topics (with a new slant) can be recycled.

Since many kids' magazines sell subscriptions through direct mail or schools, you may not be able to find a particular publication at bookstores or newsstands. Check your local library, or send for copies of the magazines you're interested in. Most magazines in this section have sample copies available and will send them for a SASE or small fee.

It's not uncommon for juvenile magazines to purchase all rights to both stories and artwork. Though work for hire is generally frowned upon among freelancers, well-respected magazines like *Highlights* and the magazines published by the Children's Better Health Institute buy all rights. But any clips acquired through these reputable magazines will be valuable. Other publications, such as those produced by The Cricket Magazine Group, purchase only first rights, allowing writers and illustrators to sell the work again, perhaps to a book publisher. Writers, illustrators and photographers must decide for themselves whether it's worth it to sell all rights to a piece.

It's important to carefully review the listings of markets you wish to target for their preferred method of receiving submissions. Some editors may wish to see an entire manuscript; others prefer a query letter and outline, especially for nonfiction articles (with which accompanying photographs are generally welcome). If you're an artist or photographer, review the listing for the types of samples the art director wants to see. Following a magazine's guidelines, and sending only your best work improves your chances of having work accepted in this competitive market. For expert advice on writing for magazines, read the Insider Report with Mary Lou Carney, editor of *Guideposts for Kids* on page 214.

Information on publications listed in the previous edition but not included in this edition of *Children's Writer's & Illustrator's Market* may be found in the General Index.

ADVOCATE, PKA'S PUBLICATION, PKA Publication, 301A Rolling Hills Park, Prattsville NY 12468. (518)299-3103. **Articles/Fiction Editor**: Remington Wright. **Art Director/Photo Editor**: CJ Karlie. Bimonthly tabloid. Estab. 1987. Circ. 12,000. "*Advocate* advocates good writers and quality writings. We publish art, fiction, photos and poetry. *Advocate*'s submitters are talented people of all ages who do not earn their livings as writers. We wish to promote the arts and to give those we publish the opportunity to be published through a for-profit means rather than in a not-for-profit way. We do this by selling advertising and offering reading entertainment."
Fiction: Middle readers and young adults/teens: adventure, animal, contemporary, fantasy, folktales, health, humorous, nature/environment, problem-solving, romance, science fiction, sports, suspense/mystery. Looks for "well written, entertaining work, whether fiction or nonfiction." Buys approximately 42 mss/year. Average word length: 1,500. Byline given. Wants to see more humorous material, nature/environment and romantic comedy.
Nonfiction: Middle readers and young adults/teens: animal, arts/crafts, biography, careers, concept, cooking, fashion, games/puzzles, geography, history, hobbies, how-to, humorous, interview/profile, nature/environment, problem-solving, science, social issues, sports, travel. Buys 10 mss/year. Average word length: 1,500. Byline given.
Poetry: Reviews poetry any length.
How to Contact/Writers: Fiction/nonfiction: send complete ms. Reports on queries in 4-6 weeks/mss in 6-8 weeks. Publishes ms 2-18 months after acceptance.
Illustration: Uses b&w artwork only. Uses cartoons. Reviews ms/illustration packages from artists. Submit a photo print (b&w or color), an excellent copy of work (no larger than 8×10) or original. Illustrations only: "Send previous unpublished art with SASE, please." Reports in 2 months. Samples returned with SASE; samples not filed. Credit line given.
Photography: Buys photos from freelancers. Model/property releases required. Uses color and b&w prints. Send unsolicited photos by mail with SASE. Reports in 2 months. Wants nature, artistic and humorous photos.
Terms: Pays on publication. Acquires first rights for mss, artwork and photographs. Pays in copies. Original work returned upon job's completion. Sample copies for $4. Writer's/illustrator/photo guidelines for SASE.
Tips: "Artists and photographers should keep in mind that we are a b&w paper."

AIM MAGAZINE, America's Intercultural Magazine, P.O. Box 20554, Chicago IL 60620. (312)874-6184. **Contact:** Ruth Apilado (nonfiction), Mark Boone (fiction). **Photo Editor:** Betty Lewis. Quarterly magazine. Circ. 8,000. Readers are high school and college students, teachers, adults interested in helping, through the written word, to create a more equitable world. 15% of material aimed at juvenile audience.
Fiction: Young adults/teens: history, multicultural, "stories with social significance." Wants stories that teach children that people are more alike than they are different. Does not want to see religious fiction. Buys 20 mss/ year. Average word length: 1,000-4,000. Byline given.
Nonfiction: Young adults/teens: interview/profile, multicultural, "stuff with social significance." Does not want to see religious nonfiction. Buys 20 mss/year. Average word length: 500-2,000. Byline given.
How to Contact/Writers: Fiction: Send complete ms. Nonfiction: Query with published clips. Reports on

queries/mss in 1 month. Will consider simultaneous submissions.

Illustration: Buys 20 illustrations/issue. Preferred theme: Overcoming social injustices through nonviolent means. Reviews ms/illustration packages from artists. Query first. Illustrations only: Query with tearsheets. Reports on art samples in 2 months. Original artwork returned at job's completion "if desired." Credit line given.

Photography: Wants "photos of activists who are trying to contribute to social improvement."

Terms: Pays on publication. Buys first North American serial rights. Pays $15-25 for stories/articles. Pays in contributor copies if copies are requested. Pays $5-25 for b&w cover illustration. Photographers paid by the project (range: $10-15). Sample copies for $4.

Tips: "We need material of social significance, stuff that will help promote racial harmony and peace and illustrate the stupidity of racism."

‡ALL ABOUT YOU, Petersen Publishing Co., L.L.C., 6420 Wilshire Blvd., 15th Floor, Los Angeles CA 90048. (213)782-2950. Fax: (213)782-2660. **Articles Editor:** Beth Mayall. **Art Director:** Diana Quarry. Magazine published 10 times/year. Estab. 1994. "Teen fashion and beauty magazine with a focus on self-esteem. Quizzes and self-help pieces. Fun, hip voice. Informative yet entertaining."

Nonfiction: Young adults/teens: careers, health, humorous, interview/profile, problem-solving. Does not want to see anything sex related; or anything written in a voice/language that a teen wouldn't relate to. Buys 100 mss/year. Average word length: 1,700-4,000. Byline given.

How to Contact/Writers: Nonfiction: Query with published clips. Reports on queries/mss in 1 month. Publishes ms 4 months after acceptance. Will consider electronic submissions via disk or modem.

Illustration: Buys 4 illustrations/issue; 32 illustrations/year. Uses color artwork only. Works on assignment only. Reviews ms/illustration packages from artists. Contact: Dianna Quarry, art director. Illustrations only: Send promo sheet, tearsheets. Reports back only if interested. Samples are not returned. Credit line given.

Photography: Query with samples. Reports back only if interested.

Terms: Pays on publication. Buys all rights. Buys one-time rights for artwork. Pays $150-600 for articles. Pays illustrators $150-500 for color (inside). Writer's guidelines for SASE.

Tips: "Talk to readers in a voice they'll listen to—honest, young, not preachy or condescending. Keep it fun but informational."

AMERICAN CHEERLEADER, Lifestyle Publications LLC, 350 W. 50th St., Suite 2AA, New York NY 10019. (212)265-8890. Fax: (212)265-8908. **Editor:** Julie Davis. Bimonthly magazine. Estab. 1995. Circ. 125,000. Special interest teen magazine for kids who cheer.

Nonfiction: Young adults: careers, fashion, health, how-to, problem-solving, sports, cheerleading specific material. "We're looking for authors who know cheerleading." Buys 50 mss/year. Average word length: 200-1,000. Byline given.

How to Contact/Writers: Query with published clips. Reports on queries/mss in 3 months. Publishes ms 3 months after acceptance. Will consider electronic submission via disk or modem.

Illustration: Buys 6 illustrations/issue; 30-50 illustrations/year. Works on assignment only. Reviews ms/illustration packages from artists. Illustrations only: Query with samples; arrange portfolio review. Reports only if interested. Samples filed. Originals not returned at job's completion. Credit line given.

Photography: Buys photos from freelancers. Looking for cheerleading at different sports games, events, etc. Uses 35mm, 2¼ × 2¼ transparencies. Query with samples; provide résumé, business card, tearsheets to be kept on file. "After sending query, we'll set up an interview." Reports only if interested.

Terms: Pays on publication. Buy all rights for mss, artwork and photographs. Pays $100-1,000 for stories. Pays illustrators $50-200 for b&w inside, $100-300 for color inside. Pays photographers by the project $300-800; per photo (range: $25-100). Sample copies for $5.

Tips: "Authors: Absolutely must have cheerleading background. Photographers and illustrators must have teen magazine experience or high profile experience."

‡AMERICAN GIRL, Pleasant Company, 8400 Fairway Place, P.O. Box 620986, Middleton WI 53562-0984. (608)836-4848. Fiction Editor: Harriet Brown. Editor-in-Chief: Judith Woodburn. **Submissions:** attn: Editorial Dept. Assistant. Bimonthly magazine. Estab. 1992. Circ. 500,000. "For girls ages 7-12. We run fiction and nonfiction, historical and contemporary."

• Pleasant Company, publisher, of *American Girl* is sponsoring a contest for writers. See listing in Contests & Awards section for Pleasant T. Rowland Prize for Fiction for Girls.

Fiction: Middle readers: contemporary, historical, multicultural, suspense/mystery, good fiction about anything. No preachy, moralistic tales or stories with animals as protagonists. Only a girl or girls as characters—no boys. Buys approximately 6 mss/year. Average word length: 1,000-2,300. Byline given.

---

‡ **LISTINGS NEW TO THIS EDITION** are marked with a double dagger.

Nonfiction: Any articles aimed at girls ages 8-12. Buys 3-10 mss/year. Average word length: 600. Byline sometimes given.

How to Contact/Writers: Fiction: Send complete ms. Nonfiction: Query with published clips. Reports on queries/mss in 6-12 weeks. Will consider simultaneous submissions.

Illustration: Works on assignment only.

Terms: Pays on acceptance. Buys first North American serial rights. Pays $500 minimum for stories; $300 minimum for articles. Sample copies for $3.95 and 9 × 12 SAE with $1.93 in postage (send to Editorial Department Assistant). Writer's guidelines free for SASE.

Tips: "Keep (stories and articles) simple but interesting. Kids are discriminating readers, too. They won't read a boring or pretentious story. We're looking for short (maximum 175 words) how-to stories and short profiles of girls for 'Girls Express' section, as well as word games, puzzles and mazes."

ASPCA ANIMAL WATCH, ASPCA, 424 E. 92nd St., New York NY 10128. (212)876-7700, ext. 4441. Fax: (212)410-0087. E-mail: caadams1@aol.com. Website: http://www.aspca.org. **Art Director:** Sibylle von Fischer. Quarterly magazine. Estab. 1951. Circ. 210,000. "The American Society for the Prevention of Cruelty to Animals publishes *Animal Watch*, a four-color magazine for its members. We cover many different topics related to animals, including companion and domestic animals, endangered species, animal abuse, lab animals and animal testing, animals in entertainment and environmental issues related to animals." 10% of publication aimed at juvenile market.

Fiction: Young readers, middle readers: adventure, folktales, multicultural, animal, nature/environment, history, problem-solving.

Nonfiction: Young readers, middle readers: animal, geography, how-to, multicultural, science, arts/crafts, nature/environment, social issues, history, interview/profile, problem-solving, careers, games/puzzles, hobbies.

Illustration: Buys 5 illustrations/issue; 12 illustrations/year. Works on assignment only. Reviews ms/illustration packages from artists. Send ms with dummy. Illustrations only: "Please send a photocopy or tearsheet sample that we can hold on file for reference. We need dynamic, endearing, descriptive and imaginative images which communicate ideas or emotions. Off-beat, alternative techniques are always welcome. We are always in need of heart-warming portraits of cats (and kittens), dogs (and puppies). We have plenty of 'realistic wildlife' as well as single-cell pen and ink cartoons and do not need any of these." Reports in 1-3 months. Samples returned with SASE or kept on file. Originals returned upon job's completion. Credit line given.

Photography: Looking for animal care and animal protection. Model/property releases required. Uses 8 × 10, glossy color/b&w prints; 35mm, 2¼ × 2¼ and 4 × 5 transparencies. "If you are interested in joining our Photographers File: please send dupes (35mm slides or any larger format transparency) of your work, a brief statement of the kind of photography you do or a résumé as well as a properly posted SASE. We keep our photographers on file for approximately three to four years. You may submit anywhere from 10 to 100 slides of various images or all of the same subject." Reports in 2 months.

Terms: Pays on publication. Buys one-time rights for artwork/photographs. Original artwork returned at job's completion. Pays illustrators $200-250 for color cover; $100-125 for b&w, $100-200 for color inside. Pays photographer per photo (range: $50-200). Sample copies for 9 × 12 SASE with $2 postage. Writer's guidelines not available. Illustrator's/photo guidelines for SASE.

Tips: Trends include "more educational, more interactive" material. Children's section is "Eye on Animals."

BABYBUG, Carus Publishing Company, P.O. Box 300, Peru IL 61354. (815)224-6656. **Editor:** Paula Morrow. **Art Director:** Suzanne Beck. Published 9 times/year (every 6 weeks). Estab. 1994. "A listening and looking magazine for infants and toddlers ages 6 to 24 months, *Babybug* is 6 ¼ × 7, 24 pages long, printed in large type (26-point) on high-quality cardboard stock with rounded corners and no staples."

Fiction: Looking for very simple and concrete stories, 4-6 short sentences maximum.

Nonfiction: Must use very basic words and concepts, 10 words maximum.

Poetry: Maximum length 8 lines. Looking for rhythmic, rhyming poems.

How to Contact/Writers: "Please do not query first." Send complete ms with SASE. "Submissions without SASE will be discarded." Reports in 6-8 weeks.

Illustration: Uses color artwork only. Works on assignment only. Reviews ms/illustration packages from artists. "The manuscripts will be evaluated for quality of concept and text before the art is considered." Contact: Paula Morrow, editor. Illustrations only: Send tearsheets or photo prints/photocopies with SASE. "Submissions without SASE will be discarded." Reports in 12 weeks. Samples filed.

Terms: Pays on publication for mss; after delivery of completed assignment for illustrators. Buys first rights with reprint option or (in some cases) all rights. Original artwork returned at job's completion. Rates vary ($25 minimum for mss; $250 minimum for art). Sample copy for $5. Guidelines free for SASE.

Tips: "*Babybug* would like to reach as many children's authors and artists as possible for original contributions, but our standards are very high, and we will accept only top-quality material. Before attempting to write for *Babybug*, be sure to familiarize yourself with this age child." (See listings for *Click, Cricket, Ladybug, Muse* and *Spider*.)

BECKETT PUBLICATIONS, 15850 Dallas Parkway, Dallas TX 75248. (972)991-6657. Fax: (972)991-8930. Website: http://www.beckett.com. **Articles Editors:** Mike Payne and Mike McAllister. **Art Director:** Judi Small-

from the publishers of Ladybug

© 1997 Jon Goodell

Jon Goodell received $500 for creating these ice skating polar bears for the cover of *Babybug* magazine. The art director of *Babybug* saw Goodell's illustrations in another publication and called him to request samples. "But it was at least one year before they contacted me to do an assignment," says Goodell, who used oil paint and acrylic paint on canvas to create the image which conveys both fun and a feeling of parental guidance. The assignment was worth the wait. "The response to this illustration has been very good. To me, the most encouraging aspect of working with *Babybug* is the freedom to create images I personally choose."

ing. **Photo Editor:** Doug Williams. Monthly magazines. Estab. 1984. "Articles in Beckett® are hobby-related and deal with the sports world's hottest superstars."

- Beckett Publications' magazines include *Beckett Baseball Card Monthly*, *Beckett Basketball Card Monthly*, *Beckett Football Card Monthly*, *Beckett Future Stars & Sports Collectibles*, *Beckett Hockey Monthly* and *Beckett Racing & Motorsports Marketplace*.

Nonfiction: Picture-oriented material: humorous, sports. Young readers, middle readers: hobbies, humorous, sports. Young adults/teens: history, hobbies, humorous, sports. Buys 8-10 mss/year. Average word length: 500-2,000. Byline given.

How to Contact/Writers: Nonfiction: Query. Reports on queries/mss in 1 month. Publishes ms 2 months after acceptance. Will consider simultaneous submissions, electronic submissions via disk or modem and some previously published work.

Illustration: Buys 2 illustrations/issue; 24 illustrations/year. Illustrations only: Query with samples in 35mm slide or 4×5 professional color transparency format. Reports in 1 month. Originals returned to artist at job's completion. Credit line given.

Photography: Looks for action sports photos (popular league players). Uses color prints and 35mm, 2¼×2¼ transparencies. Query with samples. Reports in 4-6 weeks.

Terms: Pays on acceptance. Buys first North American serial rights for mss. Buys one-time North American serial rights for photos. Pays $150-250 for stories and articles. Pays illustrators $150-200. Pays photographers per photo (range: $50-300). Writer's/illustrator's/photo guidelines free for SASE.

BLACK BELT FOR KIDS, Rainbow Publications, P.O. Box 918, Santa Clarita CA 91380. (805)257-4066. Fax: (805)257-3028. **Articles Editor:** Robert Young. Bimonthly. Special insert in *Karate/Kung Fu Illustrated* magazine. Estab. 1995. Circ. 35,000. "We publish instructional, inspirational and philosophical pieces written for children who study martial arts."

Nonfiction: Picture-oriented material: health, history, humorous, sports, travel. Young readers: health, history, humorous, interview/profile, sports, travel. Middle readers, young adults/teens: health, history, how-to, humorous, interview/profile, sports, travel. Does not want to see profiles written by parents about their own kid. Buys 10-15 mss/year. Average word length: 800-1,500. Byline given.

How to Contact/Writers: Nonfiction: Query. Reports on queries/mss in 1 month. Publishes ms 6 months after acceptance. Will consider electronic submissions via disk or modem.

Terms: Pays on publication. Buys all rights for mss. Pays $100-200 for articles. Sample copies free for 9×12 SAE and 6 first-class stamps. Writer's guidelines free for SASE.

Tips: "Make it fun."

‡BLUE JEAN MAGAZINE, Blue Jean Magazine Inc., P.O. Box 90856, Rochester NY 14609-0856. (716)654-5070. Fax: (716)654-6785. E-mail: editors@bluejeanmag.com. Website: http://www.bluejeanmag.com. **Articles Editor:** Victoria E. Nam. Bimonthly magazine. Estab. 1996. "*blue jean magazine* publishes teen-produced artwork, poetry, fiction and nonfiction. *bjm* provides young women (ages 12-19) with the opportunity to gain national recognition for their work." 90% of publication aimed at juvenile market. Considers all types of fiction, especially contemporary, fantasy, folktales, multicultural, nature/environment, romance. "We love multicultural fiction—fiction that's written in the voice of a woman of color about her experiences interacting with society." Byline given.

Nonfiction: Young adults/teens: Considers all categories of nonfiction, especially arts/crafts, careers, fashion, health, how-to, multicultural and social issues. Multicultural needs include: "Any writings by women of color!" Buys 6-10 mss/year. Average word length: 700 (1 page) to 1,400 (2 pages). Byline given.

Poetry: Reviews poetry. Unlimited submissions.

How to Contact/Writers: Fiction/nonfiction: Send complete ms. Reports on queries in 3 weeks; mss in 2 months. Publishes ms 3 months or more after acceptance. Will consider simultaneous submissions, electronic submissions via disk or modem, previously published work.

Terms: Pays on publication. Buys one-time rights. Pays $75 flat rate. Writer's guidelines for SASE.

Tips: "Request submission guidelines!"

THE BLUFTON NEWS PUBLISHING AND PRINTING COMPANY, 103 N. Main St., Blufton OH 45817. See listings for *Boys' Quest* and *Hopscotch*.

BOY SCOUTS OF AMERICA, 1325 W. Walnut Lane, P.O. Box 152079, Irving TX 75015-2079. See listings for *Boys' Life* and *Exploring*.

BOYS' LIFE, Boy Scouts of America, 1325 W. Walnut Hill Lane, P.O. Box 152079, Irving TX 75015-2079. (214)580-2000. Website: http://www.bsa.scouting.org. **Editor-in-Chief:** J.D. Owen. **Managing Editor:** W.E. Butterworth, IV. **Articles Editor:** Michael Goldman. **Fiction Editor:** Shannon Lowry. **Director of Design:** Joseph P. Connolly. **Art Director:** Elizabeth Hardaway Morgan. Monthly magazine. Estab. 1911. Circ. 1,300,000. *Boys' Life* is "a general interest magazine for boys 8 to 18 who are members of the Cub Scouts, Boy Scouts or Explorers; a general interest magazine for all boys."

"PICTURE-ORIENTED MATERIAL" is for preschoolers to 8-year-olds; "Young readers" are for 5- to 8-year-olds; "Middle readers" are for 9- to 11-year-olds; and "Young adults" are for those ages 12 and up.

• *Boys' Life* is now published in two editions—one for the younger Scout and one for the older Scout.
Fiction: Middle readers: adventure, animal, contemporary, fantasy, history, humor, problem-solving, science-fiction, sports, spy/mystery. Does not want to see "talking animals and adult reminiscence." Buys 12 mss/year. Average word length: 1,000-1,500. Byline given.
Nonfiction: "Subject matter is broad. We cover everything from professional sports to American history to how to pack a canoe. A look at a current list of the BSA's more than 100 merit badge pamphlets gives an idea of the wide range of subjects possible. Even better, look at a year's worth of recent issues. Column headings are science, nature, earth, health, sports, space and aviation, cars, computers, entertainment, pets, history, music and others." Average word length: 500-1,500. Columns 300-750 words. Byline given.
How to Contact/Writers: Fiction: Send complete ms with SASE. Nonfiction: query with SASE for response. Reports on queries/mss in 6-8 weeks.
Illustration: Buys 5-7 illustrations/issue; 23-50 illustrations/year. Works on assignment only. Reviews ms/illustration packages from artists. "Query first." Illustrations only: Send tearsheets. Reports on art samples only if interested. Original artwork returned at job's completion.
Terms: Buys first rights. Pays $750 and up for fiction; $400-1,500 for major articles; $150-400 for columns; $250-300 for how-to features. Sample copies for $3 plus 9×12 SASE. Writer's/illustrator's/photo guidelines available for SASE.
Tips: "I strongly urge you to study at least a year's issues to better understand type of material published. Articles for *Boys' Life* must interest and entertain boys ages 8 to 18. Write for a boy you know who is 12. Our readers demand crisp, punchy writing in relatively short, straightforward sentences. The editors demand well-reported articles that demonstrate high standards of journalism. We follow *The New York Times* manual of style and usage. All submissions must be accompanied by SASE with adequate postage." (See listing for *Exploring*.)

BOYS' QUEST, The Bluffton News Publishing and Printing Co., 103 N. Main St., Bluffton OH 45817. (419)358-4610. Fax: (419)358-5027. **Articles Editor:** Marilyn Edwards. **Art Submissions:** Becky Jackman. Bimonthly magazine. Estab. 1995. "*Boys' Quest* is a magazine created for boys from 6 to 13 years, with youngsters 8, 9 and 10 the specific target age. Our point of view is that every young boy deserves the right to be a young boy for a number of years before he becomes a young adult. As a result, *Boys' Quest* looks for articles, fiction, nonfiction, and poetry that deal with timeless topics, such as pets, nature, hobbies, science, games, sports, careers, simple cooking, and anything else likely to interest a young boy."
Fiction: Young readers, middle readers: adventure, animal, history, humorous, nature/environment, problem-solving, sports, jokes, building, cooking, cartoons, riddles. Does not want to see violence, teenage themes. Buys 30 mss/year. Average word length: 200-500. Byline given.
Nonfiction: Young readers, middle readers: animal, arts/crafts, biography, cooking, games/puzzles, history, how-to, humorous, math, problem-solving, science. No nonfiction with photos. Buys 30 mss/year. Average word length: 200-500. Byline given.
Poetry: Reviews poetry. Maximum length: 21 lines. Limit submissions to 6 poems.
How to Contact/Writers: Fiction/Nonfiction: Query or send complete ms (preferred). Send SASE with correct postage. No faxed material. Reports on queries in 1-2 weeks; mss in 3 weeks (if rejected); 3-4 months (if scheduled). Publishes ms 3 months-3 years after acceptance. Will consider simultaneous submissions and previously published work.
Illustration: Buys 6 illustrations/issue; 36-45 illustrations/year. Uses b&w artwork only. Works on assignment only. Reviews ms/illustration packages from artists. Send ms with dummy. Illustrations only: Query with samples, arrange portfolio review. Send portfolio, tearsheets. Reports in 2 weeks. Samples returned with SASE; samples filed. Credit line given.
Photography: Looks mostly for animal and sport photos. Model/property releases required. Uses b&w, 5×7 or 3×5 prints. Query with samples; send unsolicited photos by mail. Reports in 2-3 weeks.
Terms: Pays on publication. Buys first North American serial rights for mss. Buys first rights for artwork. Pays 5¢/word for stories and articles. Additional payment for ms/illustration packages and for photos accompanying articles. Pays $150-200 for color cover. Pays photographers per photo (range: $5-10). "*Boys' Quest*, as a new publication, is aware that its rates of payment are modest at this time. But we pledge to increase those rewards in direct proportion to our success. Meanwhile, we will strive to treat our contributors and their work with respect and fairness. That treatment, incidentally, will include quick decision on all submissions." Originals returned to artist at job's completion. Sample copies for $3. Writer's/illustrator's/photo guidelines free for SASE.
Tips: "We are looking for lively writing, most of it from a young boy's point of view—with the boy or boys directly involved in an activity that is both wholesome and unusual. We need nonfiction with photos and fiction stories—around 500 words—puzzle, poems, cooking, carpentry projects, jokes and riddles. Nonfiction pieces that are accompanied by black and white photos are far more likely to be accepted than those that need illustrations. We will entertain simultaneous submissions as long as that fact is noted on the manuscript."

BREAD FOR GOD'S CHILDREN, Bread Ministries, Inc., P.O. Box 1017, Arcadia FL 34265-1017. (941)494-6214. Fax: (941)993-0154. **Editor:** Judith M. Gibbs. Monthly magazine. Estab. 1972. Circ. 10,000 (US and Canada). "*Bread* is designed as a teaching tool for Christian families." 85% of publication aimed at juvenile market.
Fiction: All levels: adventure, history, problem-solving, sports. Looks for "teaching stories that portray Christian

When Hatch, the band's songwriter, comes down with a bad case of writer's block, can his buddy Barney convince him it's all in his mind?

Double-Talk

BOYS' LIFE ✦ FEBRUARY 1997

Bill Basso's style is a perfect match for the fiction series featured in *Boys' Life*. "The characters Bill has developed for this series have a life of their own that gives the written fiction a greater dimension and richness," says Joseph P. Connolly, *Boys' Life*'s director of design. Connolly likes Basso's varied approach and the fact that the artist handles humorous situations well. To keep up with the latest haircuts and headphones, Basso regularly browses through Sears, JC Penney and Sharper Image catalogs, and sketches characters he sees at malls. He doesn't render fads exactly. "Drawings have more oomph and verve if you just give an impression of what's going on today."

lifestyles without preaching." Buys approximately 20 mss/year. Average word length: 900-1,500 (for teens); 600-900 (for young children). Byline given.

Nonfiction: Young readers, middle readers: animal. All levels: how-to. "We do not want anything detrimental of solid family values. Most topics would fit if they are slanted to our basic needs." Buys 3-4 mss/year. Average word length: 500-800. Byline given.

Illustration: "The only illustrations we purchase are those occasional good ones coming with a story we accept."

How to Contact/Writers: Fiction/nonfiction: Send complete ms. Reports on mss in 3 weeks-6 months "if considered for use." Will consider simultaneous submissions and previously published work.

Terms: Pays on publication. Pays $30-50 for stories; $10-20 for articles. Sample copies free for 9 × 12 SAE and 6 first-class stamps (for 3 copies).

Tips: "We want stories or articles that illustrate overcoming by faith and living solid, Christian lives. Know our publication and what we have used in the past . . . know the readership . . . know the publisher's guidelines. Stories should teach the value of morality and honesty without preaching. Edit carefully for content and grammar."

CALLIOPE, World History for Kids, Cobblestone Publishing, Inc., 7 School St., Peterborough NH 03458. (603)924-7209. **Managing Editor:** Denise L. Babcock. **Art Director:** Ann Dillon. Magazine published 9 times/year. "*Calliope* covers world history (East/West) and lively, original approaches to the subject are the primary concerns of the editors in choosing material."

Fiction: Middle readers and young adults: adventure, folktales, history, biographical fiction. Material must relate to forthcoming themes. Word length: up to 800.

Nonfiction: Middle readers and young adults: arts/crafts, biography, cooking, games/puzzles, history. Material must relate to forthcoming themes. Word length: 300-800.

Poetry: Maximum line length: 100. Wants "clear, objective imagery. Serious and light verse considered."

How to Contact/Writers: "A query must consist of the following to be considered (please use nonerasable paper): a brief cover letter stating subject and word length of the proposed article; a detailed one-page outline explaining the information to be presented in the article; an extensive bibliography of materials the author intends to use in preparing the article; a self-addressed stamped envelope. Writers new to *Calliope* should send a writing sample with query. If you would like to know if your query has been received, please also include a stamped postcard that requests acknowledgment of receipt. In all correspondence, please include your complete address as well as a telephone number where you can be reached. A writer may send as many queries for one issue as he or she wishes, but each query must have a separate cover letter, outline, bibliography and SASE. Telephone queries are not accepted. Handwritten queries will not be considered. Queries may be submitted at any time, but queries sent well in advance of deadline *may not be answered for several months*. Go-aheads requesting material proposed in queries are usually sent five months prior to publication date. Unused queries will be returned approximately three to four months prior to publication date."

Illustration: Illustrations only: Send tearsheets, photocopies. Original work returned upon job's completion (upon written request).

Photography: Buys photos from freelancers. Wants photos pertaining to any forthcoming themes. Uses b&w/color prints, 35mm transparencies. Send unsolicited photos by mail (on speculation).

Terms: Buys all rights for mss and artwork. Pays 20-25¢/word for stories/articles. Pays on an individual basis for poetry, activities, games/puzzles. "Covers are assigned and paid on an individual basis." Pays photographers per photo ($15-100 for b&w; $25-100 for color). Sample copy for $3.95 and SAE with $1.05 postage. Writer's/illustrator's/photo guidelines for SASE. (See listings for *Cobblestone, The History Magazine for Young People; Faces, The Magazine About People*; and *Odyssey, Science That's Out of This World*.)

‡CAREER WORLD, Curriculum Innovations Group, 900 Skokie Blvd., Suite 200, Northbrook IL 60062-4028. (847)205-3000. Fax: (847)564-8197. **Articles Editor:** Carole Rubenstein. **Art Director:** Kristi Simkins. Monthly (school year) magazine. Estab. 1972. A guide to careers, for students grades 7-12.

Nonfiction: Young adults/teens: education, how-to, interview/profile, career information. Byline given.

How to Contact/Writers: Nonfiction: Query with published clips and résumé. "We do not want any unsolicited manuscripts." Reports on queries in 2 weeks.

Illustration: Buys 5-10 illustrations/year. Works on assignment only. Reviews ms/illustration packages from artists. Ms/illustration packages and illustration only: Query; send promo sheet and tearsheets. Credit line given.

Photography: Purchases photos from freelancers.

Terms: Pays on publication. Buys all rights. Pays $75-250 for articles. Pays illustrators $100-250 for color cover; $25-35 for b&w inside; $50-75 for color inside. Writer's guidelines free, but only on assignment.

‡CAREERS & COLLEGES, E.M. Guild, 989 Avenue of the Americas, New York NY 10018. (212)563-4688. (212)967-2531. Website: http://www.careersandcolleges.com. **Editor-in-Chief:** Sue Macy. **Senior Editor:** Don Rauf. **Art Director:** Leah Bossio. Magazine published 4 times during school year (September, November, January, March). Circ. 100,000. "*Careers & Colleges* provides juniors and seniors in high school with useful, thought-provoking, and hopefully entertaining reading on career choices, higher education and other topics that will help prepare them for life after high school. Content of the magazine includes career features, colleges (or other post-secondary education) features, coming-of-age columns, career profiles and celebrity interviews."

• *Careers & Colleges* has recently been redesigned.

Nonfiction: Young adults/teens: careers, college, health, how-to, humorous, interview/profile, personal development, problem-solving, social issues, sports, travel. Wants more celebrity profiles. Buys 20-30 mss/year. Average word length: 1,000-1,500. Byline given.

How to Contact/Writers: Nonfiction: Query. Reports on queries in 3 weeks. Will consider electronic submissions via disk or modem.

Illustration: Buys 8 illustrations/issue; buys 32 illustrations/year. Works on assignment only. Reviews ms/ illustration packages from artists. Query first. Illustrations only: Send tearsheets, cards. Reports on art samples in 3 weeks if interested. Original artwork returned at job's completion. Credit line given.

Terms: Pays on acceptance plus 30 days. Buys first North American serial rights. Pays $100-600 for assigned/ unsolicited articles. Additional payment for ms/illustration packages "must be negotiated." Pays $300-1,000 for color illustration; $200-700 for b&w/color inside illustration. Pays photographers by the project. Sample copy $2.50 with SAE and $1.25 postage; writer's guidelines free with SASE.

Tips: "We look for articles with great quotes, good reporting, good writing. Articles must be rich with examples and anecdotes, and must tie in with our mandate to help our teenaged readers plan their futures."

CARUS PUBLISHING COMPANY, P.O. Box 300, Peru IL 61354. See listing for *Babybug*, *Click*, *Cricket*, *Ladybug*, *Muse* and *Spider*.
- Carus is experimenting with a new magazine for ages 14-18. For information contact "Teen Materials" at the above address.

CAT FANCY, The Magazine for Responsible Cat Owners, Fancy Publications, P.O. Box 6050, Mission Viejo CA 92690. (714)855-8822. Fax: (714)855-3045. **Articles Editor:** Jane Calloway. Monthly magazine. Estab. 1965. Circ. 300,000. "Our magazine is for cat owners who want to know more about how to care for their pets in a responsible manner. We want to see stories and articles showing children relating to or learning about cats in a positive, responsible way. We'd love to see more craft projects for children." 3% of material aimed at juvenile audience.

Fiction: Middle readers, young adults/teens: animal (all cat-related). Does not want to see stories in which cats talk. Buys 3-9 mss/year. Average word length: 750-1,000. Byline given. Never wants to see work showing cats being treated abusively or irresponsibly or work that puts cats in a negative light. Never use mss written from cats' point of view.

Nonfiction: Middle readers, young adults/teens: animal, arts/crafts (all cat-related). Buys 3-9 mss/year. Average word length: 450-1,000. Byline given. Would like to see more crafts and how-to pieces for children.

Poetry: Reviews short poems only. "No more than ten poems per submission please."

How To Contact/Writers: Fiction/nonfiction: Send query only. Reports on queries in 1-2 months; mss in 2-3 months. Publishes ms (juvenile) 4 months after acceptance.

Illustration: Buys 10-12 illustrations/year. "Most of our illustrations are assigned or submitted with a story. We look for realistic images of cats done with pen and ink (no pencil)." Illustration only: "Submit photocopies of work; samples of spot art possibilities." Reports in 1-2 months. Credit line given.

Photography: "Cats only, in excellent focus and properly lit. Send SASE for photo needs and submit according to them."

Terms: Pays on publication. Buys first North American serial rights. Buys one-time rights for artwork and photos. Originals returned to artist at job's completion. Pays $50-200 for stories; $100-400 for articles. Pays illustrators $20 for b&w inside; $50-200 for color inside. Photographers paid per photo (range: $35-200). Sample copies for $5.50. Writer's/artist's/photo guidelines free for #10 SAE and 1 first-class stamp.

Tips: "Our 'Kids for Cats' department is most open. Perhaps the most important tip I can give is: Consider what 9- to 11-year-olds want to know about cats and what they enjoy most about cats, and address that topic in a style appropriate for them. Writers, keep your writing concise, and don't be afraid to try again after a rejection. Illustrators, we use illustrations mainly as spot art; occasionally we make assignments to illustrators whose spot art we've used before."

CHALLENGE, North American Mission Board, 4200 N. Point Pkwy., Alpharetta GA 30022. (770)410-6288. Fax: (770)410-6018. E-mail: 70423.2340@compuserve.com. **Articles Editor:** Jor Conway. **Art Director:** Aubree Elliot. Monthly magazine. Circ. 30,000. Magazine contains youth interests, sports, crafts, sports personalities, religious.

Fiction: Young adults/teens: adventure, animal, contemporary, health, history, nature/environment, problem-solving, religious, sports.

Nonfiction: young adults/teens: animal, arts/crafts, biography, games/puzzles, history, interview/profile, problem-solving. Young men: career, geography, health, hobbies, how-to, humorous, multicultural, nature/environment, religion, science, social issues, sports, travel, youth issues. Looking for stories on sports heroes with Christian testimony. Buys 36 mss/year. Average word length: 700-900. Byline given.

How to Contact/Writers: Nonfiction: Send complete ms. Reports on queries/mss in 3-5 weeks. Will consider simultaneous submissions.

Illustration: Buys 1-2 illustrations/issue; 12-24 illustrations/year. Reports in 3-5 weeks. Samples returned with SASE; samples filed. Credit line given.

Photography: Purchases photography from freelancers. Wants b&w photos with youth appeal.

Terms: Pays on publication. Buys one-time and reprint rights. Pays $20-100 for articles and stories. $5-20 for b&w, $10-35 for color inside. Photographers paid per photo (range: $5-100) or by project (range: $20-200). Originals returned to artist at job's completion. Sample copies for $4. Writer's guidelines for SAE and 1 first-class stamp.

Tips: "We prefer photo essays and articles about teenagers and teen activities, interests and issues (sports, nature, health, hobbies). Most open to new writers are features on sports figures who offer good moral guidelines to youth, especially those with an effective Christian testimony. We appreciate articles that encourage Christ-like character."

♣**CHICKADEE**, Owl Communications, 179 John St., Suite 500, Toronto, Ontario M5T 3G5 Canada. (416)340-2700. Fax: (416)340-9769. E-mail: owlcom@owlkids.com. Website: http://www.owlkids.com. **Editor-in-Chief:** Nyla Ahmad. **Editor:** Susan Petersiel Berg. **Art Director:** Tim Davin. Magazine published 9 times/year. Estab. 1979. Circ. 100,000. "*Chickadee* is a hands-on publication designed to interest 6- to 9-year-olds in science, nature and the world around them. It features games, stories, crafts, experiments. Every effort is made to provide *Chickadee* readers with fresh ideas that are offered in an innovative and surprising way. Lively writing and a strong visual component are necessary strengths in any piece written for *Chickadee*."

Fiction: Picture-oriented material, new readers: animal, humorous, nature/environment. Does not want to see religious, anthropomorphic animal, romance material, material that talks down to kids. Buys 8 mss/year. Average word length: 800-900. Byline given.

Nonfiction: Picture-oriented material, new readers: animal (facts/characteristics), arts/crafts, games/puzzles, humorous, nature/environment, science. Does not want to see religious material. Buys 2-5 mss/year. Average word length: 300-800. Byline given.

Poetry: Limit submissions to 5 poems at a time.

How to Contact/Writers: Fiction/nonfiction: Send complete ms. SAE and international postage coupon for answer and return of ms. Reports on mss in 3 months unless return postage is missing. Will consider simultaneous submissions. "We prefer to read complete manuscript on speculation."

Illustration: Buys 3-5 illustrations/issue; 40 illustrations/year. Preferred theme or style: realism/humor (but not cartoons). Works on assignment only. Illustration only: Send promo sheet. Reports on art samples only if interested. Samples returned with SASE. Credit line given.

Photography: Looking for animal (mammal, insect, reptile, fish, etc.) and nature photos. Uses 35mm and 2¼ × 2¼ transparencies. Write to request photo package for $1 money order, attention Ekaterina Gitlin, researcher.

Terms: Pays on publication. Buys all rights for mss. Buys one-time rights for photos. Original artwork returned at job's completion. Pays $10-250 for stories. Pays illustrators $100-650 for color inside, pays photographers per photo (range: $100-350). Sample copies for $4. Writer's guidelines free. All requests must include SAE and international postage coupon.

Tips: "The magazine publishes fiction and nonfiction that encourages kids to read and learn more about the world around them. The majority of *Chickadee*'s content is stories, puzzles, activities and observation games for young kids to enjoy on their own. Each issue also includes a longer story or poem that can be enjoyed by older kids." (See listings for *Chirp* and *OWL*.)

CHILD LIFE, Children's Better Health Institute, 1100 Waterway Blvd., P.O. Box 567, Indianapolis IN 46206. Parcels and packages: please send to 1100 Waterway Blvd., 46202. (317)636-8881. **Editor:** Lise Hoffman. **Art Directors:** Phyllis Lybarger, Penny Rasdall. Magazine published 8 times/year. Estab. 1921. Circ. 80,000. Targeted toward kids ages 9-11. Focuses on health, sports, fitness, nutrition, safety, general interests, and the nostalgia of *Child Life*'s early days.

 • *Child Life* is no longer accepting manuscripts for publication. The content will consist mostly of reprinted stories and artwork.

Tips: See listings for *Children's Digest*, *Children's Playmate*, *Humpty Dumpty's Magazine*, *Jack And Jill*, *Turtle Magazine* and *U*S*Kids*.

CHILDREN'S BETTER HEALTH INSTITUTE, 1100 Waterway Blvd., P.O. Box 567, Indianapolis IN 46206. See listings for *Child Life*, *Children's Digest*, *Children's Playmate*, *Humpty Dumpty's Magazine*, *Jack And Jill*, *Turtle* and *U*S* Kids*.

CHILDREN'S DIGEST, Children's Better Health Institute, 1100 Waterway Blvd., Box 567, Indianapolis IN 46206. (317)636-8881. **Editors:** Danny Lee and Jeff Ayers. Art Director: Mary Stropoli. Magazine published 8 times/year. Estab. 1950. Circ. 125,000. For preteens; approximately 33% of content is health-related.

 • *Children's Digest* is no longer accepting manuscripts for publication. The magazine will now include

---

♣ **CANADIAN LISTINGS** are marked with a maple leaf.

book reviews, book excerpts and other previously published material. See listings for *Child Life*, *Children's Playmate*, *Humpty Dumpty's Magazine*, *Jack And Jill*, *Turtle Magazine* and *U*S* Kids*.

CHILDREN'S PLAYMATE, Children's Better Health Institute, 1100 Waterway Blvd., Box 567, Indianapolis IN 46206. (317)636-8881. **Editor:** Terry Harshman. **Art Director:** Chuck Horsman. Magazine published 8 times/year. Estab. 1929. Circ. 135,000. For children ages 6-8 years; approximately 50% of content is health-related.
Fiction: Young readers: animal, contemporary, fantasy, folktales, history, humorous, science fiction, sports, suspense/mystery/adventure. Buys 25 mss/year. Average word length: 300-700. Byline given.
Nonfiction: Young readers: animal, arts/crafts, biography, cooking, games/puzzles, health, history, how-to, humorous, sports, travel. Buys 16-20 mss/year. Average word length: 300-700. Byline given.
Poetry: Maximum length: 20-25 lines.
How to Contact/Writers: Fiction/nonfiction: Send complete ms. Reports on mss in 8-10 weeks.
Illustration: Works on assignment only. Reviews ms/illustration packages from artists. Query first.
Photography: Buys photos with accompanying ms only. Model/property releases required; captions required. Uses 35mm transparencies. Send completed ms with transparencies.
Terms: Pays on publication for illustrators and writers. Buys all rights for mss and artwork; one-time rights for photos. Pays 17¢/word for assigned articles. Pays $275 for color cover illustration; $35-90 for b&w inside; $70-155 for color inside. Pays photographers per photo (range: $10-75). Sample copy $1.25. Writer's/illustrator's guidelines for SASE. (See listings for *Child Life*, *Children's Digest*, *Humpty Dumpty's Magazine*, *Jack And Jill Turtle Magazine* and *U*S* Kids*.)

‡CHIRP, Owl Communications, 179 John St., Suite 500, Toronto, Ontario M5T 3G5 Canada. **Editor-in-chief:** Nyla Ahmad. **Creative Director:** Tim Davin. Published monthly during school year. Nature magazine for children ages 2-6. "*Chirp* aims to introduce preschool non-readers to reading for pleasure about the world around them."
Fiction: Picture-oriented material: nature/environment. Word length: 250 maximum.
Nonfiction: Picture-oriented materil: fun, easy craft ideas.
Poetry: Wants rhymes and poetry. Maximum length: 8 lines.
How to Contact/Writers: Query. Reports in 6-8 weeks.
Terms: Pays on acceptance. buys all rights. Pays $50-300.
Tips: See listings for *Chicadee* and *OWL*.

CLASS ACT, Class Act, Inc., P.O. Box 802, Henderson KY 42420. E-mail: mthurman@hccuky.campus.mci.net. **Articles Editor:** Susan Thurman. Monthly, September-May. Newsletter. Estab. 1993. Circ. 300. "We are looking for practical, ready-to-use ideas for the English/language arts classroom (grades 5-12)."
Nonfiction: Middle readers and young adults/teens: games/puzzles, how-to. Does not want to see esoteric material; no master's theses; no poetry (except articles about how to write poetry). Buys 35 mss/year. Average word length: 200-4,000. Byline given.
How to Contact/Writers: Send complete ms. Reports in 10-12 weeks. Usually publishes ms 3-12 months after acceptance. Will consider simultaneous submissions. Must send SASE.
Terms: Pays on acceptance. Pays $10-30 per article. Buys all rights. Sample copy for $3 and SASE.
Tips: "We're only interested in language arts-related articles for teachers and students. Writers need to realize teens often need humor in classroom assignments. In addition, we are looking for teacher-tested ideas that have already worked in the classroom. If sending puzzles, we usually need at least 20 entries per puzzle to fit our format."

COBBLESTONE, American History For Kids, Cobblestone Publishing Co., 7 School St., Peterborough NH 03458. (603)924-7209. Fax: (603)924-7380. **Editor:** Meg Chorlian. **Art Director:** Ann Dillon. **Managing Editor:** Denise L. Babcock. Magazine published 10 times/year. Circ. 38,000. "*Cobblestone* is theme-related. Writers should request editorial guidelines which explain procedure and list upcoming themes. Queries must relate to an upcoming theme. It is recommended that writers become familiar with the magazine (sample copies available)."
Nonfiction: Middle readers (school ages 10-15): activities, biography, games/puzzles (no word finds), history (world and American), interview/profile, science, travel. All articles must relate to the issue's theme. Buys 120 mss/year. Average word length: 800. Byline given.
Poetry: Up to 100 lines. "Clear, objective imagery. Serious and light verse considered." Pays on an individual basis. Must relate to theme.
How to Contact/Writers: Fiction/nonfiction: Query. "A query must consist of all of the following to be considered (please use nonerasable paper): a brief cover letter stating the subject and word length of the proposed article; a detailed one-page outline explaining the information to be presented in the article; an extensive bibliography of materials the author intends to use in preparing the article; a self-addressed stamped envelope. Writers new to *Cobblestone* should send a writing sample with query. If you would like to know if your query has been received, please also include a stamped postcard that requests acknowledgment of receipt. In all correspondence, please include your complete address as well as a telephone number where you can be reached. A writer may send as many queries for one issue as he or she wishes, but each query must have a separate cover letter, outline, bibliography and SASE. Telephone queries are not accepted. Handwritten queries will not be considered. Queries

may be submitted at any time, but queries sent well in advance of deadline *may not be answered for several months*. Go-aheads requesting material proposed in queries are usually sent five months prior to publication date. Reports on queries/mss in two weeks. Unused queries will be returned approximately three to four months prior to publication date."

Illustration: Buys 3 illustrations/issue; 27 illustrations/year. Preferred theme or style: Material that is simple, clear and accurate but not too juvenile. Sophisticated sources are a must. Works on assignment only. Reviews ms/illustration packages from artists. Query. Illustrations only: Send photocopies, tearsheets, or other nonreturnable samples. "Illustrators should consult issues of *Cobblestone* to familiarize themselves with our needs." Reports on art samples in 2 weeks. Samples returned with SASE; samples not filed. Original artwork returned at job's completion (upon written request). Credit line given.

Photography: Photos must relate to upcoming themes. Send transparencies and/or color/b&w prints. Submit on speculation.

Terms: Pays on publication. Buys all rights to articles and artwork. Pays 20-25¢/word for articles/stories. Pays on an individual basis for poetry, activities, games/puzzles. Pays photographers per photo ($15-100 for b&w; $25-100 for color). Sample copy $3.95 with 7½×10½ SAE and 5 first-class stamps; writer's/illustrator's/photo guidelines free with SAE and 1 first-class stamp.

Tips: Writers: "Submit detailed queries which show attention to historical accuracy and which offer interesting and entertaining information. Be true to your own style. Study past issues to know what we look for. All feature articles, recipes, activities, fiction and supplemental nonfiction are freelance contributions." Illustrators: "Submit b&w samples, not too juvenile. Study past issues to know what we look for. The illustration we use is generally for stories, recipes and activities." (See listings for *Calliope, World History for Kids*; *Faces, Places & Cultures*; and *Adventures in Science*.)

COBBLESTONE PUBLISHING, INC., 7 School St., Peterborough NH 03458. See listings for *Calliope, Cobblestone, Faces* and *Odyssey*.

COUNSELOR, Cook Communications Ministries, P.O. Box 36640, Colorado Springs CO 80936. (719)536-0100 or (800)708-5550. **Editor:** Janice K. Burton. **Art Director:** Randy Maid. Newspaper distributed weekly; published quarterly. Estab. 1940. "Audience: children 8-12 years. Papers designed to present everyday living stories showing the difference Christ can make in a child's life. Must have a true Christian slant, not just a moral implication. Correlated with Scripture Press Sunday School curriculum."

Fiction: Middle readers: adventure, history, multicultural, nature/environment, problem-solving, sports (all with Christian context). "Appreciate well-written fiction that shows knowledge of our product. Suggest people write for samples." Buys approximately 12 mss/year. Average word length: 900. Byline given.

Nonfiction: Middle readers: arts/crafts, biography, games/puzzles, history, interview/profile, nature/environment, problem-solving, religion, science, social issues, sports (all with Christian context). Buys approximately 12 mss/year. Average word length: 900. Byline given.

How to Contact/Writers: Fiction/nonfiction: Send complete ms. Reports on mss in 3 months. Publishes ms 1-2 years after acceptance ("we work a year in advance"). Will consider previously published work.

Terms: Pays on acceptance. Buys second (reprint) rights, one-time rights, or all rights for mss. Pays 7-10¢/word for stories or articles, depending on amount of editing required. Sample copies for #10 SAE and 1 first-class stamp. Writers/photo guidelines for SASE.

Tips: "Send copy that is as polished as possible. Indicate if story is true. Indicate rights offered. Stick to required word lengths. Include Social Security number on manuscript. Write for tips for writers, sample copies and theme lists."

CRAYOLA KIDS, Family Time Fun, Meredith Custom Publishing, 1912 Grand Ave., Des Moines IA 50309-3379. (515)284-2170. Fax: (515)284-2064. **Articles Editor:** Mary Heaton. **Art Director:** Bob Riley. Bimonthly magazine. Estab. 1994. Circ. 400,000. "The mission of *Crayola Kids, Family Time Fun*, is to enrich the lives of families with young children (ages 3-8) by encouraging creative fun and the joy of discovery."

Nonfiction: Picture-oriented material, young readers: animal, arts/crafts, games/puzzles, how-to, multicultural, science, travel. "Seasonal tie-ins are a plus." Does not want to see biographies. Buys 20-30 mss/year. Average word length: 250. Byline given.

How to Contact/Writers: Nonfiction: Query. Reports on queries in 6-8 weeks.

Illustration: Only interested in agented material.

Terms: Pays on acceptance. Buys all rights for mss. Pays $15-400 for articles. "Depends on subject, length, complexity, originality." Sample copies for $2.95 plus SASE.

Tips: "We are interested in highly creative multicultural, nonsexist activities, visual puzzles, games and craft ideas. We also publish brief interviews with children's book authors and illustrators. Tell us your story or activity idea and what's unique and fun about it. Convince us that kids will love reading it, doing it, or making it. Study the magazine. Query."

CRICKET MAGAZINE, Carus Publishing, Company, P.O. Box 300, Peru IL 61354. (815)224-6656. **Articles/Fiction Editor-in-Chief:** Marianne Carus. **Editor:** Deborah Vetter. **Art Director:** Ron McCutchan. Monthly magazine. Estab. 1973. Circ. 83,000. Children's literary magazine for ages 9-14.

Did you know that Jell-O was first made in Delaware? Or that the world's largest tire is in Dearborn, Michigan? Or that the sweatshirt capital of the world is in Martinsville, Virginia? This colorful map points out such interesting facts and more. Maps are a great way to make geography fun, which is why they're frequently featured in kids' magazines. This one, created by Joe Lacey, was used as the center spread for *Crayola Kids* June/July '97 issue. Lacey's illustrations of Elvis in his birthplace of Tupelo, Mississippi and a boisterous duck in Stuttgart, Arkansas (a town that holds a yearly duck-calling contest) were generated electronically.

Fiction: Middle readers, young adults/teens: adventure, animal, contemporary, fantasy, folk and fairy tales, history, humorous, multicultural, nature/environment, science fiction, sports, suspense/mystery. Buys 180 mss/year. Maximum word length: 2,000. Byline given.

Nonfiction: Middle readers, young adults/teens: animal, arts/crafts, biography, environment, experiments, games/puzzles, history, how-to, interview/profile, natural science, problem-solving, science and technology, space, sports, travel. Multicultural needs include articles on customs and cultures. Requests bibliography with submissions. Buys 180 mss/year. Average word length: 1,200. Byline given.

Poetry: Reviews poems, 1-page maximum length. Limit submissions to 5 poems or less.

How to Contact/Writers: Send complete ms. Do not query first. Reports on mss in 2-3 months. Does not like but will consider simultaneous submissions. SASE required for response.

Illustration: Buys 35 illustrations (14 separate commissions)/issue; 425 illustrations/year. Uses b&w and full-color work. Preferred theme or style: "strong realism; strong people, especially kids; good action illustration; no cartoons. All media, but prefer other than pencil." Reviews ms/illustration packages from artists "but reserves option to re-illustrate." Send complete ms with sample and query. Illustrations only: Provide tearsheets or good quality photocopies to be kept on file. SASE required for response/return of samples. Reports on art samples in 2 months.

Photography: Purchases photos with accompanying ms only. Model/property releases required. Uses color transparencies, b&w glossy prints.

Terms: Pays on publication. Buys first publication rights in the English language. Buys first publication rights plus promotional rights for artwork. Original artwork returned at job's completion. Pays up to 25¢/word for unsolicited articles; up to $3/line for poetry. Pays $750 for color cover; $75-150 for b&w, $150-250 for color inside. Pays $750 for color cover; $75-150 for b&w, $150-250 for color inside. Writer's/illustrator's guidelines for SASE.

Tips: Writers: "Read copies of back issues and current issues. Adhere to specified word limits. *Please* do not query." Illustrators: "Edit your samples. Send only your best work and be able to reproduce that quality in assignments. Put name and address on *all* samples. Know a publication before you submit—is your style appropriate?" (See listings for *Babybug, Click, Ladybug, Muse* and *Spider*.)

CRUSADER, Calvinist Cadet Corps, P.O. Box 7259, Grand Rapids MI 49510. (616)241-5616. Fax: (616)241-5558. **Editor:** G. Richard Broene. **Art Director:** Robert DeJonge. Magazine published 7 times/year. Circ. 13,000. "Our magazine is for members of the Calvinist Cadet Corps—boys aged 9-14. Our purpose is to show how God is at work in their lives and in the world around them. Our magazine offers nonfiction articles and fast-moving fiction—everything to appeal to interests and concerns of boys, teaching Christian values subtly."

• *Crusader*'s 1997-1998 theme list includes issues on prejudice, sportsmanship and careers. Send SASE for current list of themes before submitting.

Fiction: Middle readers, young adults/teens: adventure, animal, contemporary, humorous, multicultural, nature/environment, problem-solving, religious, sports. Wants to see more adventure, nature and sports. Buys 12 mss/year. Average word length: 900-1,500.

Nonfiction: Middle readers, young adults/teens: animal, arts/crafts, biography, careers, games/puzzles, hobbies, how-to, humorous, interview/profile, nature/environment, problem-solving, religion, science, social issues, sports. Buys 6 mss/year. Average word length: 400-900.

How to Contact/Writers: Fiction/nonfiction: Send complete ms. Reports on queries/mss in 3-5 weeks. Will consider simultaneous submissions.

Illustration: Buys 1 illustration/issue; buys 6 illustrations/year. Works on assignment only. Reviews ms/illustration packages from artists. Reports in 3-5 weeks. Credit line given.

Photography: Buys photos from freelancers. Wants nature photos and photos of boys.

Terms: Pays on acceptance. Buys first North American serial rights; reprint rights. Pays $10-100 for stories/articles. Pays illustrators $50-200 for b&w cover or inside. Sample copy free with 9×12 SAE and 3 first-class stamps.

Tips: "Our publication is most open to fiction; write for a list of themes (available yearly in January). We use mostly fast-moving fiction that appeals to a boy's sense of adventure or sense of humor. Avoid preachiness; avoid simplistic answers to complicated problems; avoid long dialogue with little action. Articles on sports, outdoor activities, bike riding, science, crafts, etc. should emphasize a Christian perspective, but avoid simplistic moralisms."

‡**THE CRYSTAL BALL**, The Starwind Press, P.O. Box 98, Ripley OH 45167-0098. (937)392-4549. Articles Editor: Susannah West. Fiction Editor and Art Director: Marlene Powell. Quarterly magazine. Estab. 1997. "We present well-written, high-quality science fiction and fantasy for the young adult reader, as well as science-related nonfiction that may interest this age range."

Fiction: Middle readers, young adult: fantasy, folktale, science fiction. Buys 8-10 mss/year. Average word length: 1,000-4,000. Byline given.

Nonfiction: Middle readers, young adult: biography, how-to, interview/profile, science. Buys 4-8 mss/year. Average word length: 900-1,200. Byline given.

Poetry: Reviews poetry with a science fiction or fantasy theme.

How to Contact/Writers: Fiction: send complete manuscript. Nonfiction: query. Reports on queries/mss in 4-6 weeks. Publishes ms 6 months to 1 year after acceptance. Will consider previously published work "by a non-competing market."

Illustration: Buys 4-6 illustrations/issue; 8-12 illustrations/year. Uses b&w artwork only. Works on assignment only. Reviews ms/illustration packages from artists. Query. Contact: Marlene Powell, editor. Illustrations only: query with samples. Contact: Marlene Powell, editor. Reports in 1-2 months if requested. Samples returned with SASE; samples kept on file. Credit line given.

Terms: Pays on publication. Buys first North American serial rights. Original artwork returned at job's completion if requested. Pays $5-20 for stories/articles. Additional payment for ms/illustration packages and for photos accompanying articles. Pays illustrators $5-20 for b&w. Sample copies for $3. Writer's/illustrators guidelines for SASE.

Tips: "Writers: don't 'write down' to your audience just because they're kids. We want to see real three-dimensional characters, not the 'cardboard' stereotyped characters found in some of the series books popular with kids. Artists: be familiar with the science fiction/fantasy genre. If you don't enjoy or feel uncomfortable with portraying it, perhaps we're not the magazine you should approach. Get a good handle on what kids are reading today: novels, nonfiction, magazines, etc. Above all, be true to yourself."

‡**CURIOCITY FOR KIDS**, Thomson Target Media, 730 N. Franklin St., #706, Chicago IL 60610. (312)573-3800. Fax: (312)573-3810. Website: http://freezone.com. **Articles Acquisitions:** Andrew Scott. **Art Acquisitions:** Art Director. Monthly magazine. Estab. 1994. Circ. 250,000. *"Curiocity* takes a lighthearted approach to inform and entertain kids 8-12."

THE SUBJECT INDEX, located in the back of this book, lists book publishers and magazines according to the fiction and nonfiction subjects they seek.

Fiction: Middle readers, young adults/teens: adventure, contemporary, fantasy, humorous, science fiction, suspense/mystery. Does not want to see anything with talking animals or anything with a predictable ending. Buys 8-9 mss/year. Average word length: 600-700. Byline given.

Nonfiction: Middle readers, young adult/teens: animal, arts/crafts, biography, cooking, geography, hobbies, how-to, interview/profile, nature/environment, science, social issues, sports, travel. Buys 96 mss/year. Average word length: 300-800. Byline given.

How to Contact/Writers: Fiction/nonfiction: Query with published clips. "We do not review unsolicited manuscripts." Reports on queries in 6 weeks. Publishes ms 10 weeks after acceptance.

Illustration: Buys 7 illustrations/issue; 84 illustrations/year. Works on assignment only. Reviews ms/illustration packages from artists. Query. Contact: Design Director, Thomson Target Media. Query with samples. Send promo sheet and tearsheets. Contact: Design Director, Thompson Target Media. Reports back only if interested. Samples filed. Credit line given.

Photography: Looks for color-peak action, emotions—fun angles. Model/property release required; captions required. Uses color, b&w up to 11×17 prints and 35mm, $2\frac{1}{2} \times 2\frac{1}{2}$, 4×5, 8×10 transparencies. Query with samples, provide promotional literature; tearsheets to be kept on file. Reports back only if interested.

Terms: Pays on acceptance. Buys all rights. Buys first time print and Web rights for artwork/photos. Original artwork returned at job's completion. Pays $100-450. Additional payment for ms/illustration packages and for photos accompanying articles. Pays illustrators $700-1,000 for color cover; $125-500 for b&w inside, $350-750 for color inside. Pays photographers by the project (range: $500-1,200). Sample copies for $5. Writer's guidelines for SASE.

Tips: "Make sure you know our audience. Be familiar with the magazine, its departments and style. We prefer to work with published authors."

CURRENT HEALTH I, The Beginning Guide to Health Education, 900 Skokie Blvd., Suite 200, Northbrook IL 60062. (847)205-3000. **Editor:** Carole Rubenstein. Published 8 times/year; monthly during school year September-May magazine. "For classroom use by students, this magazine is curriculum-specific and requires experienced educators who can write clearly and well at fifth grade reading level."

Nonfiction: Middle-grade readers: health, nature/environment. Buys 60-70 mss/year. Average word length: 1,000. "Credit given in staff box."

How to Contact/Writers: Nonfiction: Query with published clips and résumé. Publishes ms 6-7 months after acceptance.

Illustration: Works on assignments only. Query with samples. Samples returned with SASE; samples filed. Originals returned at job's completion. Credit line given.

Terms: Pays on publication. Buys all rights. Pays $100-150, "more for longer features."

Tips: Needs material about drug education, nutrition, fitness and exercise, first aid and safety, and environment. Articles are assigned to freelance writers on specific topics.

CURRENT HEALTH II, The Continuing Guide to Health Education, 900 Skokie Blvd., Suite 200, Northbrook IL 60062-1563. (847)205-3000. Fax: (847)564-8197. **Editor**: Carole Rubenstein. **Supervisor of Art Direction**: Jill Sherman. Monthly (during school year September-May). "For classroom use by students, this magazine is curriculum specific and requires experienced writers who can write in a clear, informative and interesting style and at a ninth grade reading level."

Nonfiction: Young adults/teens: psychology, disease, nutrition, first-aid and safety, drugs, conflict resolution, fitness and exercise. Buys 70-90 mss/year. Average word length: 1,000-2,500. Byline given.

How to Contact/Writers: Nonfiction: Query with published clips and résumé. Does not accept unsolicited mss. Reports on queries in 2 months. Publishes ms 5-6 months after acceptance.

Illustration: Buys 2-4 illustrations/issue; 20-40 illustrations/year. Works on assignment only. Query with samples, promo sheet, slides, tearsheets. Reports only if interested. Samples not returned; samples filed. Originals returned at job's completion. Credit line given.

Terms: Pays on publication. Buys all rights. Pays average $150 for assigned article, "more for longer features." Pays illustrators $200-300 for color cover; $50 for b&w inside; $75-125 for color inside. Sample copies for 9×12 SAE with 3 first-class stamps. Writer's guidelines available only if writers are given an assignment; photo guidelines for SASE.

Tips: Needs writers with background in drug education, first aid and safety.

‡DINOSAURUS, 826 Broadway, New York NY 10003. (212)979-1333. **Managing Editor:** Vanessa Etherington. **Art Director:** Wendy Palitz. Bimonthly magazine for 6- to 12-year-olds. Estab. 1994. Circ. 100,000.
   • *Dinosaurus* buys 80 manuscripts and 72 illustrations/year from freelancers. Contact them for complete guidelines.

‡DISCOVERIES, Children's Ministries, 6401 The Paseo, Kansas City MO 64131. (816)333-7000. Fax: (816)333-4439. E-mail: rraleigh@nazarene.com. **Editor**: Rebecca Raleigh. **Executive Editor**: Mark York. **Assistant Editor:** Kathleen M. Johnson. Weekly tabloid. "*Discoveries* is a leisure-reading piece for third and fourth graders. It is published weekly by WordAction Publishing. The major purpose of the magazine is to provide a leisure-reading piece which will build Christian behavior and values and provide reinforcement for Biblical concepts taught in the Sunday School curriculum. The focus of the reinforcement will be life-related, with some historical appreciation. *Discoveries'* target audience is children ages eight to ten in grades three and four. The readability goal is third to fourth grade."

Fiction: Young readers, middle readers: adventure, contemporary, problem-solving, religious. "Fiction—stories should vividly portray definite Christian emphasis or character-building values, without being preachy. The setting, plot and action should be realistic." 500 word maximum. Byline given.

Nonfiction: Game/puzzles, history (all Bible-related) and Bible "trivia."

How to Contact/Writers: Fiction: Send complete ms. Reports on mss in 6-8 weeks.

Illustration: Buys 1 illustration/issue; 53 illustrations/year. "*Discoveries* publishes a wide variety of artistic styles, i.e., cartoon, realistic, montage, etc., but whatever the style, artwork must appeal to eight- to ten-year-old children. It should not simply be child-related from an adult viewpoint. All artwork for *Discoveries* is assigned on a work-for-hire basis. Samples of art may be sent for review. Illustrations only: send résumé, portfolio, client list, tearsheets. Reports back only if interested. Samples returned with SASE. Credit line given.

Terms: Pays "approximately one year before the date of issue." Buys multi-use rights. For illustration, buys all rights. Pays 5¢/word. Pays illustrators $75 for color cover. Contributor receives 4 complimentary copies of publication. Sample copy free for #10 SASE with 1 first-class stamp. Writer's/artist's guidelines free with #10 SAE.

Tips: "*Discoveries* is committed to reinforcement of the Biblical concepts taught in the Sunday School curriculum. Because of this, the themes needed are mainly as follows: faith in God, obedience to God, putting God first, choosing to please God, accepting Jesus as Savior, finding God's will, choosing to do right, trusting God in hard times, prayer, trusting God to answer, importance of Bible memorization, appreciation of Bible as God's Word to man, Christians working together, showing kindness to others, witnessing." (See listing for *Power and Light*.)

DISCOVERY, The John Milton Society for the Blind, 475 Riverside Dr., Room 455, New York NY 10115. (212)870-3335. Fax: (212)870-3229. **Assistant Editor**: Ingrid Peck. **Editor**: Darcy Quigley. Quarterly braille magazine. Estab. 1935. Circ. 2,000. "*Discovery* is a free braille magazine for blind and visually impaired youth ages 8-18. 95% of material is stories, poems, quizzes and educational articles, reprinted from 20 Christian and other magazines for youth. Original pieces from individual authors must be ready to print with little or no editing involved. We cannot offer reprint fees. Christian focus."

Fiction: Middle readers, young adults/teens: all categories and issues pertaining to blind. Does not want stories in which blindness is described as a novelty. It should be part of a story with a larger focus. Buys less than 10 mss/year. Average word length: 1,500 words (maximum). Byline given.

Nonfiction: Middle readers, young adults/teens: all categories. Buys less than 10 mss/year. Average word length: 1,500 words (maximum). Byline given.

Poetry: Reviews poetry. Maximum length: 500 words.

How to Contact/Writers: Fiction/nonfiction: Send complete ms. Reports on queries/mss in 6 weeks. Publishes ms 3-12 months after acceptance. Will consider simultaneous submissions, previously published work.

Terms: Acquires reprint rights. Authors do not receive payment.

Tips: "95% of the material in *Discovery* is reprinted previously unpublished material must therefore be ready to print with little or no editing involved. Please send complete manuscripts or request our 'Writers' Guidelines' which includes a list of periodicals we reprint from."

DISNEY ADVENTURES, The Walt Disney Company, 114 Fifth Ave., New York NY 10011-9060. Monthly magazine. Estab. 1990. Circ. 1 million.

• *Disney Adventures* does not accept freelance material.

DOLPHIN LOG, The Cousteau Society, 777 United Nations Plaza, 5th Floor, New York NY 10017-3585. (212)949-6290. Fax: (212)949-6296. **Editor:** Lisa Rao. Bimonthly magazine for children ages 7-13. Circ. 80,000. Entirely nonfiction subject matter encompasses all areas of science, natural history, marine biology, ecology and the environment as they relate to our global water system. The philosophy of the magazine is to delight, instruct and instill an environmental ethic and understanding of the interconnectedness of living organisms, including people. Of special interest are articles on ocean- or water-related themes which develop reading and comprehension skills.

Nonfiction: Middle readers, young adult: animal, games/puzzles, geography, interview/profile, nature/environment, science, ocean. Multicultural needs include indigenous peoples, lifestyles of ancient people, etc. Does not want to see talking animals. No dark or religious themes. Buys 10 mss/year. Average word length: 500-700. Byline given.

How to Contact/Writers: Nonfiction: Query first. Reports on queries in 3 months; mss in 6 months.

Illustration: Buys 1 illustration/issue; buys 6 illustrations/year. Preferred theme: Biological illustration. Reviews ms/illustration packages from artists. Illustrations only: Query; send résumé, promo sheet, slides. Reports on art samples in 8 weeks only if interested. Credit line given to illustrators.

Photography: Wants "sharp, colorful pictures of sea creatures. The more unusual the creature, the better." Submit duplicate slides only.

Terms: Pays on publication. Buys first North American serial rights; reprint rights. Pays $75-250 for articles.

'Wow' factor helps kids appreciate the natural world

Lisa Rao

Lisa Rao, editor of the award-winning children's magazine *Dolphin Log*, has a personal goal for the magazine—to make sure kids don't lose their sense of wonder. "I try to include at least one article per issue that I feel should make a reader gasp and say, 'Wow! That's cool!' The 'wow' factor is extremely important to me."

Part of that 'wow' factor comes from writing that gets children excited about the natural world that surrounds them. *Dolphin Log* is a publication of the Cousteau Society, the nonprofit organization dedicated to the protection and improvement of the quality of life for present and future generations. The Society was founded in 1973 by the late Captain Jacques-Yves Cousteau, and *Dolphin Log* follows the same principles, focusing on all areas of science, natural history, marine biology, ecology and the environment as they relate to the global water system. The philosophy of the magazine is to "delight, instruct, and instill in children an environmental ethic, including an understanding of the interconnectedness of living organisms," Rao says. "Captain Cousteau believed that children should learn to appreciate the beauty of the real world, not a fantasy place where sharks tap-dance or tunafish sing!"

There's no room for fiction in the pages of *Dolphin Log*, nor is there room for stories featuring wise-cracking sea creatures with human features. "I can't tell you how many submissions I get that start, 'When little Johnny went swimming one day he met Dolly the Dolphin . . .' Remember the kids you're writing for have grown up watching MTV and playing Nintendo. Don't be overly sweet or cutesy. Nothing turns them off more."

Writers for *Dolphin Log* also need to know the topic they're writing about, and know it well. "Don't hand in something that you basically copied out of a book about fish," Rao says. "Nothing turns me off more than a writer who hasn't done his or her homework, who hands in an article with very little 'meat' to it.

"I never worry when a freelancer warns me that a story is running long—we can always find places to cut. But if I've assigned an article and you're having problems with it, I'd much prefer you call me and either resolve the problem, or we can assign a new story. Just because we initially thought an idea would work, doesn't necessarily mean it will! If a freelancer hands in a flimsy piece and I call to question it and he says, 'Oh, I had a difficult time tracking down any information,' or 'the person I wanted to interview was never home,' that's the last assignment he will ever receive from me."

Articles must be informative, realistic and funny, with an easygoing tone that will appeal to young readers. "If you write about something you're comfortable with," Rao says, "your tone will be more casual, and that's what we're looking for."

With only two freelance articles published per issue, and 15-20 submissions coming

INSIDER REPORT, *Rao*

Dolphin Log editor Lisa Rao strives to nurture an appreciation of nature in her young readers. This issue's cover features an underwater shot of a sea turtle and a diver, typical of the beautiful and often amazing photos found in the award-winning magazine.

across her desk each month, Rao has to be selective about the articles she chooses for *Dolphin Log*. But she's very open to hearing from new writers. "Every query letter I receive gets the same consideration. I don't care who you are or where you are coming from, as long as I think you can get the job done, that's good enough for me." And getting the job done involves writing that doesn't talk down to kids, that deals with subjects interesting to both boys and girls.

"For example, we ran an article explaining why fish travel in schools," Rao says. "One of the main reasons is for protection. So we ran the cover line, 'Why Do Fish Love Schools?' It was a cover line that made both our male and female readers curious to read the story." *Dolphin Log* also features one story in each issue written by a Cousteau explorer for the "Expedition News" section.

Testing out your ideas on kids *before* writing an article is something Rao advocates. "Writers should think of the story idea they would like to submit, and present it to a child in a 'Did you know?' format. For example, 'Did you know that in the marine world, it is the *father* sea horse who carries the babies?' If the child seems interested and wants to hear more, you've got an idea worth submitting. If the conversation immediately turns to something else, so should you." The "father sea horse" idea actually turned into an article on "Moms and Dads in the Animal World," a three-page feature story in the May 1997 issue of *Dolphin Log*.

Illustrators also need to adhere to *Dolphin Log*'s policy of showcasing real creatures of nature. "As cute as your drawing of a dancing penguin may be, it's not getting in *Dolphin Log*," Rao says. "An artist who wants to be hired by us should study some books on marine biology, and be able to draw a shark that really looks like a shark. As far as photography goes, that's even trickier, because you have to compete with the photo library of Captain Jacques Cousteau! So we don't use freelance photographers that often. But the same basic rules apply to a photographer as well as a writer: show me something unique. Don't go to Sea World and take a picture of a seal balancing a ball on its nose and send it to us."

Rao certainly knows the children's magazine market, having worked on various children's publications for over ten years. After spending four years with Scholastic Magazines and six years with the Children's Television Workshop, Rao came to *Dolphin Log* with a clear sense of what kids like—and want—to read. "When the idea of working at *Dolphin Log* was first presented to me," she says, "I examined some back issues of the publication. I realized this was a wonderful magazine that needed a strong children's editor to give it some kid appeal. With the addition of more interactive features, puzzles, games, jokes, riddles and contests, I think I've helped give the magazine a brighter, fresher new look, and made it more exciting for our readers."

Getting children excited about nature and ecology is what *Dolphin Log* is all about, and Rao's reward comes in the mail she receives from children, reflecting the love of nature and sense of wonder that the magazine instills in its young readers. "After an afternoon of editing articles, my favorite way to end the day is to go through reader mail, picking out the poetry and jokes they send in. Chuckling over 'Why did the eel cross the road? To get to the other *tide*!' is a nice way to end the day."

—Cindy Laufenberg

Pays $100-400 for illustrations. Pays $75-200/color photos. Sample copy $2.50 with 9×12 SAE and 3 first-class stamps. Writer's/illustrator's guidelines free with #10 SASE.

Tips: Writers: "Write simply and clearly and don't anthropomorphize." Illustrators: "Be scientifically accurate and don't anthropomorphize. Some background in biology is helpful, as our needs range from simple line drawings to scientific illustrations which must be researched for biological and technical accuracy."

‡**DRAMATICS**, Educational Theatre Association, 3368 Central Pkwy., Cincinnati OH 45225. (513)559-1996. (513)559-0012. E-mail: pubs@one.net. Website: http://www.etassoc.org. **Articles Editor:** Don Corathers. **Art Director:** William Johnston. Published monthly September-May. Estab. 1929. Circ. 38,000. "Dramatics is for students (mainly high school age) and teachers of theater. Mix includes how-to (tech theater, acting, directing, etc.), informational, interview, photo feature, humorous, profile, technical, We want our student readers to become a more discerning and appreciative audience. Material is directed to both theater students and their teachers, with strong student slant."

Fiction: Young adults: drama (one-act and full-length plays.) Does not want to see plays that show no understanding of the conventions of the theater. No plays for children, no Christmas or didactic "message" plays. "We prefer unpublished scripts that have been produced at least once." Buys 5-9 plays/year. Emerging playwrights have better chances with short plays, 10 minute or one-act.

Nonfiction: Young adults: arts/crafts, careers, how-to, interview/profile, multicultural (all theater-related). "We try to portray the theater community in all its diversity." Does not want to see academic treatises. Buys 50 mss/year. Average word length: 750-3,000. Byline given.

How to Contact/Writers: Send complete ms. Reports in 2-3 months (longer for plays). Published ms 3 months after acceptance. Will consider simultaneous submissions and previously published work occasionally.

Illustration: Buys 0-2 illustrations/year. Works on assignment only. Arrange portfolio review; send résumé, promo sheets and tearsheets. Reports back only if interested. Samples returned with SASE; sample not filed. Credit line given.

Photography: Buys photos with accompanying ms only. Looking for "good-quality production or candid photography to accompany article. We very occasionally publish photo essays." Model/property release and captions required. Uses 5×7 or 8×10 b&w glossy prints and 35mm transparencies. Query with résumé of credits. Reports back only if interested.

Terms: Pays on acceptanct. Buys one-time rights, occasionally reprint rights. Buys one-time rights for artwork and photos. Original artwork returned at job's completion. Pays $100-400 for plays; $50-300 for articles; up to $100 for illustrations. Pays photographers by the project or per photo. Sometimes offers additional payment for ms/illustration packages and photos accompanying a ms. Sample copy available for $3 and 9×12 SAE. Writer's and photo guidelines available for SASE.

Tips: "Obtain our writer's guidelines and look at recent back issues. The best way to break in is to know our audience—drama students, teachers and others interested in theater—and write for them. Writers who have some practical experience in theater, especially in technical areas, have an advantage, but we'll work with anybody who has a good idea. Some freelancers have become regular contributors."

DYNAMATH, Scholastic Inc., 555 Broadway, New York NY 10012-3999. (212)343-6432. **Editor:** Joe D'Agnese. **Art Director:** Joan Michael. Monthly magazine. Estab. 1981. Circ. 300,000. Purpose is "to make learning math fun, challenging and uncomplicated for young minds in a very complex world."

Nonfiction: All levels: animal, arts/crafts, cooking, fashion, games/puzzles, health, history, hobbies, how-to, humorous, math, multicultural, nature/environment, problem-solving, science, social issues, sports—all must relate to math and science topics.

How to Contact/Writers: Nonfiction: Query with published clips, send ms. Reports on queries in 1 month; mss in 6 weeks. Publishes ms 4 months after acceptance. Will consider simultaneous submissions.

Illustration: Buys 4 illustrations/issue. Illustration only: Query first; send résumé and tearsheets. Reports back on submissions only if interested. Credit line given.

Terms: Pays on acceptance. Buys all rights for mss, artwork, photographs. Originals returned to artist at job's completion. Pays $50-300 for stories. Pays artists $800-1,000 for color cover illustration; $100-800 for color inside illustration. Pays photographers $300-1,000 per project.

Tips: See listings for *Junior Scholastic*, *Scholastic Math Magazine*, *Science World* and *Superscience Blue*.

EXPLORING, Boy Scouts of America, 1325 W. Walnut Hill Lane, P.O. Box 152079, Irving TX 75015-2079. (972)580-2365. **Executive Editor:** Scott Daniels. **Editor:** Joe Halter. **Art Director:** Joe Connally. **Photo Editor:** Stephen Seeger. Magazine published "four times a year (January, April, June and November)." *Exploring* is a 20-page, 4-color magazine published for Exploring program members of the Boy Scouts of America. These members are young men and women between the ages of 14-21. Interests include careers, computers, life skills (money management, parent/peer relationships, study habits), college, camping, hiking, canoeing.

Nonfiction: Young adults: interview/profile, outdoor adventure (hiking, camping, white water boating), problem-solving, travel. Buys 12 mss/year. Average word length: 600-1,200. Byline given.

How to Contact/Writers: Nonfiction: Query with published clips. Reports on queries/mss in 1 week.

Illustration: Buys 3 illustrations/issue; 12 illustrations/year. Works on assignment only. Illustration only: Reports on art samples in 2 weeks. Original artwork returned at job's completion.

Terms: Pays on acceptance. Buys first North American serial rights. Pays $350-800 for assigned/unsolicited articles. Pays $1,000 for color illustrated cover; $250-500 for b&w inside; $500-800 for color inside. Sample copy with 8½×11 SAE and 5 first-class stamps. Free writer's/illustrator's guidelines.
Tips: Looks for "short, crisp career profiles of 1,000 words with plenty of information to break out into graphics." (See listing for *Boys' Life*.)

FACES, People, Places & Cultures, Cobblestone Publishing, Inc., 7 School St., Peterborough NH 03458. (603)924-7209. Fax: (603)924-7380. **Editor**: Lynn Sloneker. **Managing Editor**: Denise L. Babcock. **Art Director**: Ann Dillon. Magazine published 9 times/year (September-May). Circ. 15,000. *Faces* is a theme-related magazine; writers should send for theme list before submitting ideas/queries."
Fiction: Middle readers: anthropology. Young adults/teens: contemporary, folktales, history, multi.cultural, religious. Does not want to see material that does not relate to a specific upcoming theme. Buys 9 mss/year. Maximum word length: 800. Byline given.
Nonfiction: Middle readers and young adults/teens: anthropology, arts/crafts, games/puzzles, history, interview/profile, religious, travel. Does not want to see material not related to a specific upcoming theme. Buys 63 mss/year. Average word length: 300-800. Byline given.
How to Contact/Writers: Fiction/nonfiction: Query with published clips and 2-3 line biographical sketch. "Ideas should be submitted six to nine months prior to the publication date. Responses to ideas are usually sent approximately four months before the publication date."
Illustration: Buys 3 illustrations/issue; buys 27 illustrations/year. Preferred theme or style: Material that is meticulously researched (most articles are written by professional anthropologists); simple, direct style preferred, but not too juvenile. Works on assignment only. Roughs required. Reviews ms/illustration packages from artists. Illustrations only: Send samples of b&w work. "Illustrators should consult issues of *Faces* to familiarize themselves with our needs." Reports on art samples in 1-2 months. Original artwork returned at job's completion (upon written request).
Photography: Wants photos relating to forthcoming themes.
Terms: Pays on publication. Buys all rights for mss and artwork. Pays 20-25¢/word for articles/stories. Covers are assigned and paid on an individual basis. Pays photographers per photo ($15-100 for b&w; $25-100 for color). Sample copy $3.95 with 7½×10½ SAE and 5 first-class stamps. Writer's/illustrator's/photo guidelines free with SAE and 1 first-class stamp.
Tips: "Writers are encouraged to study past issues of the magazine to become familiar with our style and content. Writers with anthropological and/or travel experience are particularly encouraged; *Faces* is about world cultures. All feature articles, recipes and activities are freelance contributions." Illustrators: "Submit b&w samples, not too juvenile. Study past issues to know what we look for. The illustration we use is generally for retold legends, recipes and activities." (See listing for *Calliope*, *Cobblestone* and *Odyssey*.)

‡FIRST OPPORTUNITY, The Notebook Mentor, CPG, Inc., 660 Penn Tower, 3100 Broadway, Kansas City MO 64111-2413. (816)960-1988. Fax: (816)960-1989. **Contact**: Amy Schiska, assistant editor. Magazine published twice in spring, twice in fall. Estab. 1986. Circ. 500,000. "Targeted to African-American and Hispanic high school students bound for post-high school training in math, science and vo-tech fields."
Fiction: Young adults/teens: multicultural. Multicultural needs include: personal experience as it relates to education or careers. Does not want to see those that are unsophisticated, overly ponderous or "cute." Buys 5 mss/year. Average word length: 500-1,000. Byline given.
Nonfiction: Young adults/teens: careers, health, how-to, interview/profile, math, multicultural, problem-solving, science. Multicultural needs include: profiles of outstanding students. Does not want to see articles with lots of lists or common-sense information. Buys 15 mss/year. Average word length: 800-2,000. Byline given.
How to Contact/Writers: Fiction/nonfiction: Send complete ms. Reports on queries/mss in 6-8 weeks. Publishes ms 6 months after acceptance. Will consider simultaneous submissions and electronic submission via disk or modem.
Illustration: Buys 1 illustration/issue; 5 illustrations/year. Uses color artwork only. Works on assignment only. Reviews ms/illustration packages from artists. Send ms with dummy. Illustrations only: Send résumé, client list and tearsheets. Reports in 6-8 weeks. Samples returned with SASE. Credit line sometimes given.
Photography: Buys photos with accompanying ms only. Looking for photos of minorities in occupational/career situations. Model/property release required. Uses color 5×7, 8×10 prints and 8×10 transparencies. Provide résumé; business card; promotional literature; tearsheets. Reports in 6-8 weeks.
Terms: Pays on publication. Buys one-time rights for mss. Buys one-time rights for artwork and photographs. Original artwork returned at job's completion. Pays 10¢-$400/word for stories and articles. Pays illustrators $20 for b&w, $20 for color cover; $25 for b&w, $25 for color inside. Pays photographers per photo (range: $20-25). Samples copies for $3. Writer's/illustrator's/photo guidelines free for SASE.
Tips: "Remember, we are targeted to a multicultural audience. While there are some 'soft' pieces and entertainment sections, this is not a leisure magazine."

*THE FLICKER MAGAZINE, Hillview Publishing, P.O. Box 660544, Birmingham AL 35266-0544. (205)324-7111. Fax: (205)324-4035. E-mail: yellowhamr@aol.com. **Associate Editor:** Ann Dorer. **Art Director:** Jimmy Bass. Bimonthly magazine. Estab. 1994. Circ. 7,000. "*The Flicker Magazine* is a publication that promotes balanced growth in all areas of life—physical, spiritual, social, mental and emotional. It includes nonfiction, fiction, poetry, interviews, etc."

Fiction: Middle readers: adventure, animal, folktale, health, history, humorous, multicultural, nature/environment, problem-solving, religious, sports. Does not want to see science fiction, fantasy or romance. Sees too much fantasy and didactic materials. Wants more adventure, humorous and multicultural submissions. Buys 75-80 mss/year. Average word length: 400-800. Byline given.

Nonfiction: Middle readers: animal, arts/crafts, biography, careers, concept, cooking, games/puzzles, geography, health, history, hobbies, how-to, humorous, interview/profile, multicultural, nature/environment, problem-solving, religion, science, social issues, sports, travel. Does not want to see fashion oriented submissions. See too many how-to articles. Would like more arts/crafts, multicultural, science and nature articles. Buys 15-25 mss/year. Average word length: 400-600. Byline given.

Poetry: Reviews poetry. Maximum length: 4-24 lines.

How to Contact/Writers: Fiction/Nonfiction: Send complete ms. Reports on queries/mss in 1-2 months. Publishes ms 2-12 months after acceptance. Will consider simultaneous submissions and sometimes previously published work.

Illustration: Only interested in agented material. Buys 5 illustrations/issue; 30 illustrations/year. Uses color artwork only. Works on assignment only. Reviews ms/illustration packages from artists. Send ms with dummy. Contact: Jimmy Bass, art director. Illustrations only: send promo sheet and tearsheets. Samples returned with SASE; samples filed. Credit line sometimes given.

Photography: Buys photos from freelancers. Looking for action photos. Model/property releases required; captions required. Uses color, 8½×11 matte prints and 35mm transparencies, 2¼×2¼ transparencies. Send unsolicited photos by mail. Reports only if interested.

Terms: Pays on acceptance. Buys all rights for mss, artwork and photos. Pays 10¢/word for stories; 10¢/word for articles; $25 for poems; $10 for jokes. Pays illustrators $50-250 for color inside. Pays photographers by the project (range: $50-200). Sample copies for $2.95. Writer's/illustrator guidelines free for SASE.

Tips: "If you are submitting photos or illustrations, please do not send originals unless otherwise specified. Call and inquire about future issues. The magazine usually has a central theme. Also call for guidelines."

FLORIDA LEADER, for high school students, Oxendine Publishing, Inc., P.O. Box 14081, Gainesville FL 32604-2081. (352)373-6907. Fax: (352)373-8120. E-mail: 75143.2043@compuserve.com. Website: http://www.studentleader.com. **Articles Editor:** Kay Quinn. **Art Director:** Jeff Riemersma. Quarterly magazine. Estab. 1992. Circ. 25,000. "Magazine features academic-major and career articles, current financial aid and admissions information, and stories on other aspects of college life for prospective college students." Audience includes ages 14-17. Aimed at the juvenile market.

Nonfiction: Young adult/teens: biography, careers, how-to, humorous, interview/profile, problem-solving, social issues, travel. Looking for "more advanced pieces on college preparation—academic skills, career exploration and general motivation for college." Buys 6-8 mss/year. Average word length: 800-1,000. 200-300 for columns.

How to Contact/Writers: Nonfiction: Query with published clips. Reports on queries in 3-5 weeks; mss in 3-5 weeks. Publishes ms 3-5 months after acceptance. Will consider simultaneous submissions, electronic submissions, previously published work.

Illustration: Buys 5 illustrations/issue; 20 illustrations/year. Uses color artwork only. Works on assignment only. Reviews ms/illustration packages from artists. Query. Illustrations only: query with samples; send résumé, promo sheet, tearsheets. Reports only if interested. Samples returned with SASE; samples filed. Credit line given.

Photography: Buys photos from freelancers. Buys photos separately. Works on assignment only. Model/property release required. Uses color prints and 35mm, 2¼×2¼, 4×5 transparencies. Query with samples. Reports only if interested.

Terms: Pays on publication. Buys first North American serial rights, reprint rights for mss. Buys first time rights for artwork and photos. Originals returned at job's completion. Pays $35-75 for articles. Pays first-time or less experienced writers or for shorter items with contribution copies or other premiums. Pays illustrators $75 for color inside. Pays photographers by the project (range: $150-300). Sample copies for $3.50. Writer's guidelines for SASE.

Tips: "Query first and review past issues for style and topics."

FOCUS ON THE FAMILY CLUBHOUSE; FOCUS ON THE FAMILY CLUBHOUSE JR., Focus on the Family, 8605 Explorer Dr., Colorado Springs CO 80920. (719)531-3400. **Editor:** Annette Bourland. **Art Director:** Timothy Jones. Monthly magazine. Estab. 1987. Combined circulation is 250,000. "*Focus on the*

MARKET CONDITIONS are constantly changing! If you're still using this book and it is 1999 or later, buy the newest edition of *Children's Writer's & Illustrator's Market* at your favorite bookstore or order directly from Writer's Digest Books.

Family Clubhouse is a 16-page Christian magazine, published monthly, for children ages 8-12. Similarly, *Focus on the Family Clubhouse Jr.* is published for children ages 4-8. We want fresh, exciting literature that promotes biblical thinking, values and behavior in every area of life."

Fiction: Picture-oriented material, young readers, middle readers: adventure, animal, health, nature/environment, religious, sports. Picture-oriented material, young readers: multicultural. Multicultural needs include: "interesting, informative, accurate information about other cultures to teach children appreciation for the world around them." Buys approximately 6-10 mss/year. Average word length: *Clubhouse*, 500-1,400; *Clubhouse Jr.*, 250-1,100. Byline given on all fiction; not on puzzles.

Nonfiction: Picture-oriented material, young readers, middle readers: animal, arts/crafts, cooking, games/puzzles, health, hobbies, how-to, multicultural, nature/environment, science. Middle readers: humorous, interview/profile, sports. Buys 3-5 mss/year. Average word length: 200-1,000. Byline given.

Poetry: Wants to see "humorous or biblical" poetry. Maximum length: 25 lines.

How to Contact/Writers: Fiction/nonfiction: send complete ms. Reports on queries/mss in 4-6 weeks. Publishes ms 6-8 months after acceptance.

Illustration: Buys 8 illustrations/issue. Uses color artwork only. Works on assignment only. Reviews ms/illustration packages from artists. Submit ms with rough sketches. Contact: Tim Jones, art director. Illustrations only: Query with samples, arrange portfolio review or send tearsheets. Contact: Tim Jones, art director. Reports in 2-3 months. Samples returned with SASE; samples kept on file. Credit line given.

Photography: Buys photos from freelancers. Uses 35mm transparencies. Photographers should query with samples; provide résumé and promotional literature or tearsheets. Reports in 2 months.

Terms: Pays on acceptance. Buys first North American serial rights for mss. Buys first rights or reprint rights for artwork and photographs. Original artwork returned at job's completion. Additional payment for ms/illustration packages. Pays writers $100-300 for stories; $50-150 for articles. Pays illustrators $300-700 for color cover; $200-700 for color inside. Pays photographers by the project or per photo. Sample copies for 9 × 12 SAE and 3 first-class stamps. Writer's/illustrators/photo guidelines for SASE.

Tips: "Test your writing on children. The best stories avoid moralizing or preachiness and are not written *down* to children. They are the products of writers who share in the adventure with their readers, exploring the characters they have created without knowing for certain where the story will lead. And they are not always explicitly Christian, but are built upon a Christian foundation (and, at the very least, do not contradict biblical views or values)."

FOR SENIORS ONLY, Campus Communications, Inc., 339 N. Main St., New York NY 10956. (914)638-0333. **Publisher:** Darryl Elberg. **Articles/Fiction Editor:** Judi Oliff. **Art Director:** David Miller. Semiannual magazine. Estab. 1971. Circ. 350,000. Publishes career-oriented articles for high school students, college-related articles, and feature articles on travel, etc.

Fiction: Young adults: health, humorous, sports, travel. Byline given.

Nonfiction: Young adults: careers, games/puzzles, health, how-to, humorous, interview/profile, social issues, sports, travel. Buys 4-6 mss/year. Average word length: 1,000-2,500. Byline given.

How to Contact/Writers: Fiction/nonfiction: Send complete ms. Publishes ms 2-4 months after acceptance. Will consider simultaneous submissions, electronic submissions via disk or modem and previously published work.

Illustration: Reviews ms/illustration packages from artists. Query; submit complete package with final art; submit ms with rough sketches. Illustrations only: Query; send slides. Reports back only if interested. Samples not returned; samples kept on file. Original work returned upon job's completion. Credit line given.

Photography: Model/property release required. Uses 5½ × 8½ and 4⅞ × 7⅜ color prints; 35mm and 8 × 10 transparencies. Query with samples; send unsolicited photos by mail. Reports back only if interested.

Terms: Pays on publication. Buys exclusive magazine rights. Payment is byline credit. Writer's/illustrator's/photo guidelines for SASE.

THE FRIEND MAGAZINE, The Church of Jesus Christ of Latter-day Saints, 50 E. North Temple, 23rd Floor, Salt Lake City UT 84150. (801)240-2210. **Editor:** Vivian Paulsen. **Art Director:** Richard Brown. Monthly magazine for 3-11 year olds. Estab. 1971. Circ. 350,000.

Fiction: Picture material, young readers, middle readers: adventure, animal, contemporary, folktales, history, humorous, problem-solving, religious, ethnic, sports, suspense/mystery. Does not want to see controversial issues, political, horror, fantasy. Average word length: 400-1,000. Byline given.

Nonfiction: Picture material, young readers, middle readers: animal, arts/crafts, biography, cooking, games/puzzles, history, how-to, humorous, problem-solving, religious, sports. Does not want to see controversial issues, political, horror, fantasy. Average word length: 400-1,000. Byline given.

Poetry: Reviews poetry. Maximum length: 20 lines.

How to Contact/Writers: Fiction/nonfiction: Send complete ms. Reports on mss in 2 months.

Illustration: Illustrations only: Query with samples; arrange personal interview to show portfolio; provide résumé and tearsheets for files.

Terms: Pays on acceptance. Buys all rights for mss. Pays 9-11¢/word for unsolicited fiction articles; $25 and up for poems; $10 for recipes, activities and games. Contributors are encouraged to send for sample copy for $1.50, 9 × 11 envelope and $1 postage. Free writer's guidelines.

Tips: "*The Friend* is published by The Church of Jesus Christ of Latter-day Saints for boys and girls up to 12 years of age. All submissions are carefully read by the *Friend* staff, and those not accepted are returned within two months when a self-addressed, stamped envelope is enclosed. Submit seasonal material at least eight months in advance. Query letters and simultaneous submissions are not encouraged. Authors may request rights to have their work reprinted after their manuscript is published."

GIRLS' LIFE, Monarch Avalon, 4517 Harford Rd., Baltimore MD 21214. (410)254-9200. Fax: (410)254-0991. Website: http://www.girlslife.com. **Articles Editor**: Kelly White. **Art Director**: Chun Kim. Bimonthy magazine. Estab. 1994. General interest magazine for girls, ages 7-14.
Nonfiction: Animal, arts/crafts, biography, careers, cooking, health, history, hobbies, humorous, interview/profile, multicultural, nature/environment, science, social issues, sports, travel. Buys appoximately 25 mss/year. Word length varies. Byline given. "No fiction!"
How to Contact/Writers: Nonfiction: Query with published clips or send complete ms on spec only. Reports in 2 weeks. Publishes ms 3 months after acceptance. Will consider simultaneous submissions.
Illustration: Buys 40 illustrations/issue. Uses color artwork only. Works on assignment only. Reviews ms/illustration packages from artists. Send ms with dummy. Contact: Kelly White, senior editor. Illustration only: Query with samples; send tearsheets. Contact: Chun Kim, art director. Reports back only if interested. Samples returned with SASE; samples filed. Credit line given.
Photography: Buys photos from freelancers. Uses 35mm transparencies. Provide samples. Reports back only if interested.
Terms: Pays on publication. Original artwork returned at job's completion. Pays $500-800 for features; $150-350 for departments. Sample copies available for $2.95. Writer's guidelines for SASE.
Tips: "Don't call with queries. Make query short and punchy."

THE GOLDFINCH, Iowa History for Young People, State Historical Society of Iowa, 402 Iowa Ave., Iowa City IA 52240. (319)335-3916. Fax: (319)335-3935. **Editor**: Amy Ruth. Quarterly magazine. Estab. 1975. Circ. 2,500. "The award-winning *Goldfinch* consists of 10-12 nonfiction articles, short fiction, poetry and activities per issue. Each magazine focuses on an aspect or theme of history that occurred in or affected Iowa."
Fiction: Middle readers: historical fiction only. "Study past issues for structure and content. Most manuscripts written inhouse." Average word length: 500-1,500. Byline given.
Nonfiction: Middle readers: arts/crafts, biography, games/puzzles, history, interview/profile, "all tied to an Iowa theme." Uses about 10 freelance mss/year. Average word length: 500-800. Byline given.
Poetry: Reviews poetry. No minimum or maximum word length; no maximum number of submissions. "All poetry must reflect an Iowa theme."
How to Contact/Writers: Fiction/nonfiction: Query with published clips. Reports on queries/mss in up to 2 months. Publishes ms 1 month-1 year after acceptance. Will consider electronic submissions via disk or modem.
Illustration: Buys 8 illustrations/issue; 32 illustrations/year. Works on assignment only. Prefers cartoon, line drawing. Illustrations only: Query with samples. Reports in up to 2 months. Samples returned with SASE.
Photography: Types of photos used vary with subject. Model/property releases required with submissions. Uses b&w prints; 35mm transparencies. Query with samples. Reports in 2-4 weeks.
Terms: Pays on publication. Buys all rights. Payment begins at $25 per article. Pays illustrators $10-150. Sample copy for $4. Writer's/illustrator's guidelines free for SASE.
Tips: "The editor researches the topics and determines the articles. Writers, most of whom live in Iowa, work from primary and secondary research materials to write pieces. The presentation is aimed at children 8-14. All submissions must relate to an upcoming Iowa theme. Please send SASE for our writer's guidelines and theme lists before submitting manuscripts."

GUIDE MAGAZINE, Review and Herald Publishing Association, 55 W. Oak Ridge Dr., Hagerstown MD 21740. (301)791-7000. **Articles Editor**: Carolyn Rathbun. **Art Director**: Bill Kirstein. Weekly magazine. Estab. 1953. Circ. 34,000. "Ours is a weekly Christian journal written for middle readers and young adults, presenting true stories relevant to the needs of today's young person, emphasizing positive aspects of Christian living."
Nonfiction: Middle readers, young adults/teens: adventure, animal, character-building, contemporary, games/puzzles, humorous, multicultural, problem-solving, religious. "We need true, or based on true, happenings, not merely true-to-life. Our stories and puzzles must have a spiritual emphasis." No violence. No articles. "We always need humorous adventure stories." Buys 150 mss/year. Average word length: 500-600 minimum, 1,000-1,200 maximum. Byline given.
How to Contact/Writers: Nonfiction: Send complete ms. Reports in 3-4 weeks. Will consider simultaneous submissions. "We can only pay half of the regular amount for simultaneous submissions." Reports on queries/mss in 1 week. Credit line given.
Terms: Pays on acceptance. Buys first North American serial rights; first rights; one-time rights; second serial (reprint rights); simultaneous rights. Pays 3-6¢/word for stories and articles. "Writer receives several complimentary copies of issue in which work appears." Sample copy free with 5×9 SAE and 2 first-class stamps. Writer's guidelines for SASE.
Tips: "Children's magazines want mystery, action, discovery, suspense and humor—no matter what the topic. For us, truth is stronger than fiction."

Tenacity is the true mark of a professional

It happens to all of us: A critic steps on our dream. For author and *Guideposts for Kids* Editor Mary Lou Carney, it was a fifth-grade teacher. "I wrote my first poem and my teacher gave me a 'D'. I made a mental note never to try this anymore!" But she was not down for long.

How did she go from throwing in the pen and paper to being a successful author? She rediscovered her dream while teaching high school. While at a young authors' conference with her class, she met her first real-life author. "Listening to that man speak, something almost spiritual happened to me. I thought, 'Wow, I wonder if I can do this?' "

On that last Saturday of April, 1977, Carney turned to a colleague and said, " 'I'd like to write.' She laughed in my face and said, 'Carney, what would you write?' " While Car-ney wasn't sure what she'd write, she was confident in her

Mary Lou Carney

abilities. Keeping in mind that old adage "write what you know," she began her 20-year career as a successful author. "When I started writing, there were two things inside of me: scripture and poetry."

The poetry came from Carney's mother reciting poems as the family did their chores around their Indiana farm. "We'd be hoeing corn and my mother would say, 'Listen my children and you shall hear of the midnight ride of Paul Revere . . .' " This special time set a foundation for Carney. "I memorized lots of poetry as a child."

The scripture part also came from Carney's mother. She declared that Carney and her sister read two chapters of the Bible every day except Sunday. "I cut my teeth on the King James Bible," she jokes. Carney would read a verse to her mother and then ask for clarification if the meaning wasn't clear. A ravenous learner, she loved the language of the Bible and, as a result, Carney says, "I committed huge portions of scripture to memory. So when I came to write, it was all in place. I was ready. I had things to say, and I had the skills to say them.

"I was smart about the marketing, targeting things and doing my research," she says. After careful thought, she came up with a direction—her first book, *Bubble Gum and Chalkdust: Prayers and Poems for Teachers.* "I decided I wanted to do a book for teachers because I kept going to buy this book and it wasn't there." Fifteen years later, the book is still in print. Laughing, Carney says, "That has to be an act of God."

Ideas continued to blossom. After publishing four books for adults, Carney created a new niche for herself—writing for kids. Although that didn't meet with instant success, Carney's tenacity came in handy. "*Angel in My Locker* was rejected 21 times before it sold, and when it was finally published, the first printing sold out in one day!" Tenacity also took Carney to magazine success. Having more ideas than she could execute in books,

INSIDER REPORT, *Carney*

Editor Mary Lou Carney began publishing *Faith'n Stuff* magazine out of her home in 1989, after writing for Guideposts' adult publications. *Faith'n Stuff* eventually became *Guideposts for Kids*. The cover story of this issue is about young people who race horses and use them to work on their families' ranches.

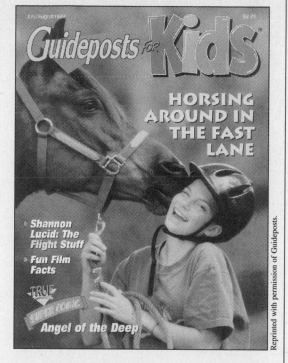

Carney became excited about magazine writing—particularly for *Guideposts* (writing for the hardcover edition, *Daily Guideposts*, was her dream). But then rejection reared its head again. Meeting Terri Castillo, editor for *Guideposts*, Carney expressed her interest in writing for them. "She gave this smile that said, 'You and the rest of the world.' But she said, 'We have a regular stable of writers.' "

Carney knew how to create opportunity. "Every time I had a book come out, I'd send it to Terri. Every time I had something published, I'd send it to Terri. She'd send me back these form letters that would say, 'Thank you for your interest in *Daily Guideposts*. We have a regular stable of writers.' I would wait a week and send her back a note that would say, 'This is just a reminder that I'm chomping outside the barn door in case there's an opening in the stable.' "

This exchange continued for a couple of years. "Then I got a letter that said, 'We'd like to invite you to audition for *Daily Guideposts*.' Requested to write 15 pieces, Carney was accepted. After writing for *Daily Guideposts* for several years, Carney was approached by Castillo to create a product for kids similar to what *Daily Guideposts* is to adults. Carney responded with a successful four-book series, Faith 'n Stuff. Kids wanted more, and in 1989, Carney was asked to create a bimonthly product.

She wrote and edited *Faith 'n Stuff* magazine out of her home for five years. In 1994, the name changed to *Guideposts for Kids*. In 1995, Carney moved the project out of her house (along with five employees) into a downtown business office. The same year, *Guideposts for Kids* earned the honor of "Distinguished Achievement in Educational Publishing, 1995 EdPress Award Winner." With a half million readers, Carney rejoices in being able to reach so many kids. "I feel that this is my mission in life. This is what I've been called to do."

INSIDER REPORT, *continued*

Today, Carney has 20 books published and a poetry anthology, *Absolutely Angels*, due out in the fall of '98 by Boyds Mill Press. She's in her tenth year of writing for *Daily Guideposts*. Her enthusiastic approach to life keeps her in constant demand to speak at conferences and seminars.

Having "walked the walk" she knows what it takes to sell your writing and what it takes to buy an article. "To me the purpose of writing is to be read." Here's her best advice for children's writers:

• Show, don't tell. Lead a child to a conclusion. Show the kids the facts and they'll reach the right conclusion.

• Remember all kids are listening to the same station: WIFM—What's In It For Me? Write to them, not down to them.

• Study the market. See what's not there and write it.

• Push the edges, not only in your topic, but of yourself as well. Accept and solicit new challenges. "Every kind of writing benefits every kind of writing."

• Use humor.

• Always offer kids hope.

• Be careful of your research. An editor remembers when you are wrong.

• Be available for additional questions and rewrites.

• Don't have a spirit of fear. Be bold in your queries and projects.

• Publish something short before publishing something long.

• Do your homework! Know the editorial bias of the magazine and know the name of the editor.

Here's Carney's list of what makes a good magazine piece:

• Find fresh ideas. If it's an overworked topic, approach it in a way no one else has.

• Have a clear kid's voice. Don't write the way you remember them or the way you wish they were.

• Be objective. Show both sides of an issue. "I want to teach kids how to think, instead of what to think."

• Use expert testimony. Do the primary research.

• Know the word length. "If you know my word length is 1,400 words, don't send me 3,000."

• Be aware of lead time. "Almost any magazine will look at stuff six months in advance."

• Be persistent and don't give up. "Tenacity is the one true mark of a professional. People that succeed as writers are a diverse group, but we all have one thing in common: We didn't give up."

—Tricia Branson

GUIDEPOSTS FOR KIDS, P.O. Box 638, Chesterton IN 46304. **Editor**: Mary Lou Carney. **Fiction Editor**: Lurlene McDaniel. **Art Director**: Mike Lyons. **Photo Editor**: Wendy Marciniak. Bimonthly magazine. Estab. 1990. Circ. 200,000. "*Guideposts for Kids* is published bimonthly by Guideposts for kids 7-12 years old (emphasis on upper end of that age bracket). It is a value-centered, direct mail magazine that is *fun* to read. It is *not* a Sunday school take-home paper or a miniature *Guideposts*."
  • The premiere issue of *Guideposts for Teens* will be available in January/February 1998. Contact the publisher for guidelines.
Fiction: Middle readers: adventure, animal, contemporary, fantasy, folktales, health, historical, humorous, multi-cultural, nature/environment, problem-solving, religious, romance, science fiction, sports, suspense/mystery, travel. Multicultural needs include: Kids in other cultures—school, sports, families. Does not want to see preachy fiction. "We want real stories about real kids doing real things—conflicts our readers will respect; resolutions our readers will accept. Problematic. Tight. Filled with realistic dialogue and sharp imagery. No stories about 'good' children always making the right decision. If present at all, adults are minor characters and *do not* solve kids' problems for them." Buys approximately 10 mss/year. Average word length: 500-1,300. Byline given.
Nonfiction: Middle readers: animal, biography, careers, concept, cooking, current events, fashion, games/puzzles, geography, health, history, how-to, humorous, interview/profile, math, multicultural, nature/environment, problem-solving, profiles of kids, religious, science, seasonal, social issues, sports, travel. "Make nonfiction issue-oriented, controversial, thought-provoking. Something kids not only *need* to know, but *want* to know as well." Buys 20 mss/year. Average word length: 200-1,300. Byline usually given.
How to Contact/Writers: Fiction: Send complete ms. Nonfiction: Query. Reports on queries/mss in 6 weeks.
Illustration: Buys 10 illustrations/issue; 60 illustrations/year. Uses color artwork only. Works on assignment only. Reviews ms/illustration packages from artists. Contact: Mike Lyons, art director. Illustration only: Query; send résumé, tearsheets. Reports only if interested. Credit line given.
Photography: Looks for "spontaneous, *real* kids in action shots."
Terms: Pays on acceptance. Buys all rights for mss. Buys first rights for artwork. "Features range in payment from $250-600; fiction from $250-600. We pay higher rates for stories exceptionally well-written or well-researched. Regular contributors get bigger bucks, too." Additional payment for ms/illustration packages "but we prefer to acquire our own illustrations." Pays illustrators $400-800/page. Pays photographers by the project (range: $300-1,000) or per photo (range: $100-500). Sample copies for $3.25. Writer's guidelines free for SASE.
Tips: "Make your manuscript good, relevant and playful. No preachy stories about Bible-toting children. *Guideposts for Kids* is not a beginner's market. Study our magazine. (Sure, you've heard that before—but it's *necessary*!) Neatness *does* count. So do creativity and professionalism. SASE essential."

‡HIGH ADVENTURE, Assemblies of God, 1445 Boonville Ave., Springfield MO 65802. (417)862-2781, Ext. 4181. Fax: (417)862-0416. **Editor**: Marshall Bruner. Quarterly magazine. Circ. 86,000. Estab. 1971. Magazine is designed to provide boys ages 5-7 with worthwhile, enjoyable, leisure reading; to challenge them in narrative form to higher ideals and greater spiritual dedication; and to perpetuate the spirit of Royal Rangers through stories, ideas and illustrations. 75% of material aimed at juvenile audience.
Fiction: Buys 100 mss/year. Average word length: 1,000. Byline given.
Nonfiction: Articles: Christian living, devotional, Holy Spirit, salvation, self-help; biography; missionary stories; news items; testimonies, inspirational stories based on true-life experiences.
How to Contact/Writers: Fiction/nonfiction: Send complete ms. Reports on queries in 6-8 weeks. Will consider simultaneous submissions. Will review ms/illustration packages.
How to Contact/Illustrators: Ms/illustration packages: Send complete ms with final art. Illustrations only: "Most of our artwork is done in-house."
Terms: Pays on acceptance. Buys first or all rights. Pays 2-3¢/word for articles; $12-20 for cartoons; $12 for puzzles, $2-3 for jokes. Sample copy free with 9 × 12 SASE. Free writer's/illustrator's guidelines for SASE.

HIGHLIGHTS FOR CHILDREN, 803 Church St., Honesdale PA 18431. (717)253-1080. **Manuscript Coordinator**: Beth Troop. **Art Director**: Janet Moir. Monthly magazine. Estab. 1946. Circ. 2.8 million. "Our motto is 'Fun With a Purpose.' We are looking for quality fiction and nonfiction that appeals to children, encourages them to read, and reinforces positive values. All art is done on assignment."
Fiction: Picture-oriented material, young readers, middle readers: adventure, animal, contemporary, fantasy, folktales, history, humorous, multicultural, nature/environment, science fiction, sports. Multicultural needs include first person accounts of children from other cultures and first-person accounts of children from other countries. Does not want to see war, crime, violence. "We see too many stories with overt morals." Would like to see more suspense/stories/articles with world culture settings, sports pieces, action/adventure. Buys 150 mss/year. Average word length: 400-800. Byline given.
Nonfiction: Picture-oriented material, young readers, middle readers: animal, arts/crafts, biography, careers, games/puzzles, geography, health, history, hobbies, humorous, interview/profile, multicultural, nature/environment, problem solving, religion, science, sports, travel. Young readers, middle readers: careers, foreign, geography, interview/profile, problem-solving, social issues. Multicultural needs include articles set in a country *about* the people of the country. "We have plenty of articles with Asian and Spanish settings. We also have plenty of holiday articles." Does not want to see trendy topics, fads, personalities who would not be good role models for children, guns, war, crime, violence. "We'd like to see more nonfiction for younger readers—maximum of

600 words. We still need older-reader material, too—600-900 words." Buys 75 mss/year. Maximum word length: 900. Byline given.

How to Contact/Writers: Send complete ms. Reports on queries in 4-6 weeks; mss in 2 months.

Illustration: Buys 25-30 illustrations/issue. Preferred theme or style: Realistic, some stylization, cartoon style acceptable. Works on assignment only. Reviews ms/illustration packages from artists. Illustrations only: photocopies, promo sheet, tearsheets, or slides. Résumé optional. Portfolio only if requested. Contact: Janet Moir, art director. Reports on art samples in 4-6 weeks. Samples returned with SASE; samples filed. Credit line given.

Terms: Pays on acceptance. Buys all rights for mss. Pays 14¢/word and up for unsolicited articles. Pays illustrators $1,000 for color cover; $25-200 for b&w, $100-500 for color inside. Sample copies $3.95 and 9 × 11 SASE with 4 first-class stamps. Writer's/illustrator's guidelines free on request.

Tips: "Know the magazine's style before submitting. Send for guidelines and sample issue if necessary." Writers: "At *Highlights* we're paying closer attention to acquiring more nonfiction for young readers than we have in the past." Illustrators: "Fresh, imaginative work encouraged. Flexibility in working relationships a plus. Illustrators presenting their work need not confine themselves to just children's illustrations as long as work can translate to our needs. We also use animal illustrations, real and imaginary. We need party plans, crafts and puzzles—any activity that will stimulate children mentally and creatively. We are always looking for imaginative cover subjects."

HOBSON'S CHOICE, P.O. Box 98, Ripley OH 45167. (513)392-4549. **Editor**: Susannah C. West. Quarterly magazine. Estab. 1974. Circ. 2,000. "*Hobson's Choice* is a science fiction magazine which also publishes science and technology-related nonfiction along with stories. Although the magazine is not specifically aimed at children, we do number teenagers among our readers. Such readers are the type who might enjoy reading science fiction (both young adult and adult), attending science fiction conventions, using computers, and be interested in such things as astronomy, the space program, etc."

Fiction: Young adults/teens: fantasy, science fiction. "I'm really not interested in seeing fiction other than science fiction and fantasy. Nor am I interested in horror and cyberpunk, although these can be considered subgenres of fantasy and science fiction. I also see too much hackneyed science fiction and fantasy." Buys 12-15 mss/year. Average word length 2,000-10,000.

Nonfiction: Young adults/teens: how-to (science), interview/profile, science. Does not want to see crafts. Buys 8-10 mss/year. Average word length: 1,500-5,000. Byline given.

How to Contact/Writers: Fiction: Send complete ms. Nonfiction: Query first. Reports on queries/mss in 4 months maximum. ("After four months, author should feel free to withdraw manuscript from consideration.") Will consider submissions via disk (Macintosh MacWrite, WriteNow, IBM PC or compatible on 3½ disks).

Illustration: Buys 5-8 illustrations/issue; 20-30 illustrations/year. Uses b&w artwork only. Prefers to review "science fiction, fantasy or technical illustration." Reviews ms/illustration packages; "would like to see clips to keep on file (b&w only, preferably photocopies)." Illustrations only: Query with samples to be kept on file. "If we have an assignment for an artist, we will contact him/her with the manuscript we want illustrated. We like to see roughs before giving the go-ahead for final artwork." Reports in 4 months "if requested and if request accompanied by SASE." Credit line given.

Photography: Purchases photos with accompanying ms only. Uses b&w prints. Wants photos for nonfiction.

Terms: Pays 50% on acceptance, 50% on publication. Buys first North American serial rights for mss, artwork and photographs. Pays $20-100 for stories/articles. Pay illustrators $25-50 for b&w cover; $5-25 for b&w inside. Pays photographers per photo (range: $5-25). Original artwork returned at job's completion, "sometimes, if requested. We prefer to retain originals, but a high-quality PMT or Velox is fine if artist wants to keep artwork." Sample copies for $2.75. Writer's/illustrator's guidelines free with business-size SAE and 1 first-class stamp. "Specify fiction or nonfiction guidelines, or both." Tip sheet package for $1.25 and business-size envelope with 1 first-class stamp (includes all guidelines and tips on writing science fiction and nonfiction).

Tips: "If you think *Hobson's* would be a good place for your work, keep letting us see your stuff! Don't give up! Take critiques you may receive to heart—they tell you about what we look for in sf stories, and give you information about making your writing the best it can be. Give editors credit; they *do* care about you, the writer."

HOLIDAYS & SEASONAL CELEBRATIONS, Teaching & Learning Company, 1204 Buchanan, P.O. Box 10, Carthage IL 62321. (217)357-2591. Fax: (217)357-6789. **Contact:** Articles Editor or Art Director. Quarterly magazine. Estab. 1995. "Every submission must be seasonal or holiday-related. Materials need to be educational and consistent with grades pre-K through 3 development and curriculum."

Fiction: Young readers: health, multicultural, nature/environment; must be holiday or seasonal-related. Buys 8 mss/year. Byline given.

Nonfiction: Young readers: arts/crafts, cooking, games/puzzles, geography, how-to, math, multicultural, nature/environment, science. "We need holiday and seasonally related ideas from all cultures that can be used in the classroom." Buys 150 mss/year. Byline given.

Poetry: Reviews holiday or seasonal poetry.

How to Contact/Writers: Fiction: Query. Nonfiction: Send complete ms. Reports on queries in 2 months; mss in 3 months. Publishes ms 4-12 months after acceptance. Will consider electronic submissions via disk or modem.

Illustration: Buys 70 illustrations/issue; 300 illustrations/year. Uses b&w and color artwork. Works on assignment only. "Prefers school settings with lots of children; b&w sketches at this time." Reviews ms/illustration packages from artists. Submit ms with rough sketches. Illustrations only: submit résumé, promo sheet, tearsheets, sketches of children. Reports in 1 month. Samples returned with SASE; samples filed. Credit line sometimes given.

Photography: Buys photos from freelancers. Looking for photos of children. Model/property releases required. Uses 35mm transparencies. Send unsolicited photos by mail or submit portfolio for review. Reports in 2 months.

Terms: Pays on publication. Buys all rights. Pays $20-75 for stories; $10-125 for articles. Additional payment for ms/illustration packages. Pays illustrators $150-300 for color cover; $10-15 for b&w inside. Pays photographers per photo. Sample copy available for $4.95. Writer's/illustrator's guidelines for SASE.

Tips: "95% of our magazine is written by freelancers. Writers must know that this magazine goes to teachers for use in the classroom, grades pre-K through 3. Also 90% of our magazine is illustrated by freelancers. We need illustrators who can provide us with 'cute' kids grades pre-K through 3. Representation of ethnic children is a must. Because our magazine is seasonal, it is essential that we receive manuscripts approximately 8-12 months prior to the publication of that magazine. Too often we receive a holiday-related article way past the deadline."

HOPSCOTCH, The Magazine for Girls, The Bluffton News Publishing and Printing Company, 103 N. Main St., Bluffton OH 45817. (419)358-4610. **Editor**: Marilyn Edwards. Bimonthly magazine. Estab. 1989. Circ. 10,000. For girls from ages 6-12, featuring traditional subjects—pets, games, hobbies, nature, science, sports, etc.—with an emphasis on articles that show girls actively involved in unusual and/or worthwhile activities."

● The publishers of *Hopscotch* now publish *Hopscotch Plus*, a bimonthly appearing alternate months to *Hopscotch. Plus* will offer similar material for the same audience and age group. Send SASE for theme list.

Fiction: Picture-oriented material, young readers, middle readers: adventure, animal, history, humorous, nature/environment, science fiction, sports, suspense/mystery. Does not want to see stories dealing with dating, sex, fashion, hard rock music. Buys 30 mss/year. Average word length: 300-700. Byline given.

Nonfiction: Picture-oriented material, young readers, middle readers: animal, arts/crafts, biography, cooking, games/puzzles, geography, hobbies, how-to, humorous, math, nature/environment, science. Does not want to see pieces dealing with dating, sex, fashion, hard rock music. "Need more nonfiction with quality photos about a *Hopscotch*-age girl involved in a worthwhile activity." Buys 46 mss/year. Average word length: 400-700. Byline given.

Poetry: Reviews traditional, wholesome, humorous poems. Maximum word length: 300; maximum line length: 20. Will accept 6 submissions/author.

How to Contact/Writers: Fiction: Send complete ms. Nonfiction: Query, send complete ms. Reports on queries in 2 weeks; on mss in 2 months. Will consider simultaneous submissions.

Illustration: Buys illustrations for 6-8 articles/issue; buys 50-60 articles/year. "Generally, the illustrations are assigned after we have purchased a piece (usually fiction). Occasionally, we will use a painting—in any given medium—for the cover, and these are usually seasonal." Uses b&w artwork only for inside; color for cover. Review ms/illustration packages from artists. Query first or send complete ms with final art. Illustrations only: Send résumé, portfolio, client list and tearsheets. Reports on art samples with SASE in 2 weeks. Credit line given.

Photography: Purchases photos separately (cover only) and with accompanying ms only. Looking for photos to accompany article. Model/property releases required. Uses 5×7, b&w prints; 35mm transparencies. Black and white photos should go with ms. Should have girl or girls ages 6-12.

Terms: For manuscripts, pays a few months ahead of publication. For mss, artwork and photos, buys first North American serial rights; second serial (reprint rights). Original artwork returned at job's completion. Pays 5¢/word and $5-10/photo. "We always send a copy of the issue to the writer or illustrator." Text and art are treated separately. Pays $150-200 for color cover. Photographers paid per photo (range: $5-15). Sample copy for $3. Writer's/illustrator's/photo guidelines free for #10 SASE.

Tips: "Remember we publish only six issues a year, which means our editorial needs are extremely limited. Please look at our guidelines and our magazine . . . and remember, we use far more nonfiction than fiction. If decent photos accompany the piece, it stands an even better chance of being accepted. We believe it is the responsibility of the contributor to come up with photos. Please remember, our readers are 6-12 years—most are 7-10—and your text should reflect that. Many magazines try to entertain first and educate second. We try to do the reverse of that. Our magazine is more simplistic like a book, to be read from cover to cover. We are looking for wholesome, non-dated material." (See listing for *Boys' Quest*.)

HUMPTY DUMPTY'S MAGAZINE, Children's Better Health Institute, 1100 Waterway Blvd., P.O. Box 567, Indianapolis IN 46206. (317)636-8881. Fax: (317)684-8094. **Editor:** Lise Hoffman. **Art Director:** Rebecca Ray. Magazine published 8 times/year—Jan/Feb; Mar; April/May; June; July/Aug; Sept; Oct/Nov; Dec. *HDM* is edited for children approximately ages 4-6. It includes fiction (easy-to-reads; read alouds; rhyming stories; rebus stories), nonfiction articles (some with photo illustrations), poems, crafts, recipes and puzzles. Much of the content encourages development of better health habits.

● *Humpty Dumpty's* especially needs material promoting fitness, as well as sports stories, including profiles of famous and amateur and pro athletes, and athletes who have overcome obstacles.

INSIDER REPORT

Make the most of your ideas in the magazine market

Elaine Marie Alphin

Elaine Marie Alphin enjoys talking about writing—and with good reason. Writing is something she's loved since she was a little girl. She writes both children's fiction and nonfiction for various age-groups in both book and magazine form, speaks at writers conferences, is an instructor for the Institute of Children's Literature, and writes a column for *Children's Writer*, their monthly newsletter. Alphin's articles for children have appeared in *Cricket*, *Highlights*, *Humpty Dumpty*, *Straight* and *On the Line*. Her books include *A Bear for Miguel*, *The Ghost Cadet*, *The Proving Ground*, and *Vacuum Cleaners*, part of a Household History series for Carolrhoda Books. Here she shares some of her extensive knowledge on writing for children.

How much magazine work do you do?
I've had over a hundred magazine pieces in print. I'd say in an average year, maybe 15-20 pieces and sometimes less. I like doing magazine work as opposed to only writing books because I get a lot of ideas that are magazine ideas and not book ideas.

The idea for *Vacuum Cleaners* was neat, but it's unusual. I envisioned it in the beginning as a magazine piece. But in doing the research for the history of the vacuum cleaner, I was fascinated by all of the developments and what a quirky machine it was.

There were all these other stories about it, too, and I had to try to cram them into this article for *Cricket*. When Carolrhoda came to me and said, "Do you have enough that you could consider expanding this into a book?" I said, "Yes!" There was just such a wealth of weird and wonderful information.

Normally an idea either has the depth for a book or not. And there's a lot of good magazine stuff that is satisfying to young readers, it helps them grow, it makes them think about their lives—but then they move on. It's not something they will go back and read over and over again. A book needs staying power. You can have a good idea, capture it and realize it very effectively in a magazine story, but it doesn't have the staying power that a book does.

So many people who want to write picture books may have ideas better suited for magazines?
Yes, much. Because it's not a bad idea, but it's not deep enough to be a book.

Is it less competitive? Is it easier to get magazine articles published than books?
It depends on what you're writing. I've got a friend who's a scientist, and he gets a lot of science articles published. He's both an expert and skilled at expressing complicated thoughts clearly for young readers. It's almost at some point a genre thing. If you have an

INSIDER REPORT, *Alphin*

Elaine Marie Alphin's *Vacuum Cleaners* is part of Carolrhoda's Household History series. Alphin researched a story on vacuums for *Cricket* and had found so many interesting tidbits on the history of the machine she was excited to put together the book when approached by Carolrhoda.

area of expertise, it's very easy to get repeatedly published.

The magazine market is certainly wide-open and hungry, but they're also suffering the same slush pile glut that the book market is—at least the big names. Everyone wants to write for the big name magazines.

So these large magazines are being innundated with a lot of things that are simply not appropriate. If you're in a critique group, and tell the group "I want to send this to *Highlights*," and somebody in the group says, "This is just not *Highlights* material," that's a good piece of advice to listen to. We all want to sell to *Highlights* and some things are good for them and other things just aren't. And that doesn't mean it's not a good manuscript, but it's better suited for someone else.

I think being successful in the magazine market is really having a strong sense of where

INSIDER REPORT, *continued*

you as a writer fit in interest-wise with the different magazines. And you probably won't be limited to just one interest and one magazine—you'll probably have a lot of them, because as a writer, hopefully, you have many different interests, so you can sell to many different magazines.

How realistic is it for somebody who wants to make a living writing for children? Obviously, if you have a book a year published . . .

. . . It's not enough to pay the mortgage and support a family. Forget it. I think that's what so many people forget: Writing is a job. It's a joy, also. If you want to be able to make a living at it, you need to work very hard. I know some writers who actually publish 100 magazine pieces a year.

It's really funny explaining it to kids, because they think all writers are rich and famous, and as soon as you explain the royalty routine and you hold up the books and say, "This is a paperback; it sells for $3.25. Now, for most books, I get 10 percent. So how much is that?" The kids say, "32½ cents." I say, "But, since it's a paperback reprint, I only get half of that." And the kids go "Ewwww!" And I say, "You've got to buy an awful lot of these before I can even go to lunch!"

The nicest thing about writing is that it's never boring. And I think this is probably much more true writing for children than for adults. You have such a wide diversity of topics. You get to go to schools, you get to go to conferences. Everything you do that is part of your professional life is exciting, and therefore it's energizing.

You're always working, but that's just part of the drill. All of us in our adult lives are working. The nice thing is if you can get paid to do what you enjoy. Whether it's the writing itself, or teaching other people, or talking to kids and sharing what you know with them and getting a lot out of it. Kids are very generous and giving, they just don't know it. All of this is delightful—just to be able to sit back and think, "Wow, this is what I want to do, this is what I love doing, and I'm able to do it—people want me to do it."

For me, writing is very intense. I do a lot of free writing, I do a lot of thinking, and I do a lot of planning. So when I sit down and write, I literally have a day where I can write three or four chapters. The rest of the world just stops, grinds to a halt, forget it. We get pizza, I'm not cooking.

Let's talk about nonfiction a little bit. You mentioned that you've been doing more and more of that lately. Is that because of you, because of the market, or is it a combination of both?

The market is very welcoming to nonfiction and I like writing nonfiction. I thought I wouldn't, because I started out originally writing journalism for adults, which is not like nonfiction for kids, although they are both loosely termed nonfiction. I stopped writing journalism for adults because I didn't like the slant that editors impose on adult journalists. I got very hostile about it in fact. And I decided that if I felt that strongly I should not be doing it, so that was an easy decision.

Nonfiction if fun; nonfiction is me as a writer discovering something weird and neat and quirky that I love and then introducing it to kids, because they'll like it as much as I do. And I find that if it's quirky enough and weird enough that I like it, usually the kids will too.

Why do you think ficiton is so much more appealing to many writers?

Most people think nonfiction and they think of the boring textbooks they read as kids. If

INSIDER REPORT, *Alphin*

they're going to write about the dermestid beetle, they will tell you its Latin name and they will tell you how long it is and how long its lifespan is . . . You've got to transcend that and say, "Well what's fun about this? What appeals to me?" And in a sense, you use the same skills that you use in writing fiction—making the scene come alive for your reader. You want to pull the reader in. Whether it's in a museum preparation room, or in the middle of a tribal council, you want to excite them about it. Strong active writing goes into successful nonfiction.

Most people think they want to write a picture book because they believe it's easy to write because it's small and it's short, and children love it. There's no question, it's a wonderful thing to see that look of delight on a child's face as they sit there poring over the pictures in a picture book. A writer wants to be an active part of this delight a child gets from reading. It's not neccesary to do it in a picture book and quite honestly, picture books are the hardest things to write because they have to be so perfect. You have to have a crystal clear idea of the road you're going to travel in the book and you have to express it without a single word out of place. And that's hard. The nice thing about a novel is you can have a few words out of place, because you've got so many of them, and you'll be forgiven if the road is still true.

My feeling when I started writing was that I wanted to write things that would make people question their assumptions, think about who they were and where they were going. And I discovered that most readers don't want to think about who they are and where they're going—they are there. They may not like it, but they're stuck with it, and they feel that. You find very few grown-ups who are willing to chuck things and say, "Oh, forget this—this isn't going well," and then take another path in life. They've got mortgages; they've got children; they've got expenses; they've got commitments. They're stuck with their path.

But children do it all the time. Children are constantly trying something out to see if it works, and if they don't like it, moving on to something else. When you write for children, you're part of that experience. They read your book and they think about it. They don't neccessarily write a paper about it, but it becomes part of their spirit. If it's designed to make them question their assumptions, they do. They may come up with an entirely new game plan to move forward into the next year of their life or so.

You can have a profound impact on a child that you can't have on a bored adult who is locked into place. It's a wonderful thought. I get letters from kids from all over the country, some from other countries, from kids who've read *The Ghost Cadet*. They write to tell me about the way it made them feel about history or about their family, and that's a wonderful benefit.

It's marvelous and it's very inspiring because it makes you know that you are in fact shaping the future. You are having an impact on this world. We look at so many things we're unhappy with in the world, and we say, "Well, I can't do anything about it." No, you can't really do anything about what the president is going to do tomorrow. But you may change what the president does 30 years from now, if the kid you had an impact on grows up to be President.

—*Alice P. Buening*

Fiction: Picture-oriented material: adventure, animal, contemporary, fantasy, folktales, health, history, humorous, multicultural, nature/environment, problem-solving, sports. Does not want to see "bunny-rabbits-with-carrot-pies stories! Also, talking inanimate objects are very difficult to do well. Beginners (and maybe everyone) should avoid these." Buys 25-40 mss/year. Maximum word length: 500. Byline given.

Nonfiction: Picture-oriented material: animal, arts/crafts, concept, cooking, games/puzzles, health, hobbies, how-to, humorous, nature/environment, science, sports, health-related. Does not want to see long, boring, encyclopedia rehashes. "We're open to almost any subject (although most of our nonfiction has a health angle), but it must be presented creatively. Don't just string together some facts." Looks for a fresh approach. Buys 6-10 mss/year. Prefers very short nonfiction pieces—350 words maximum. Byline given.

How to Contact/Writers: Send complete ms. Nonfiction: Send complete ms with bibliography if applicable. "No queries, please!" Reports on mss in 3 months.

Illustration: Buys 13-16 illustrations/issue; 90-120 illustrations/year. Preferred theme or style: Realistic or cartoon. Works on assignment only. Illustrations only. Query with slides, printed pieces or photocopies. Contact: Rebecca Ray, art director. Samples are not returned; samples filed. Reports on art samples only if interested. Credit line given.

Terms: Writers: Pays on publication. Artists: Pays within 1-2 months. Buys all rights. "One-time book rights may be returned if author can provide name of interested book publisher and tentative date of publication." Pays up to 22¢/word for stories/articles; payment varies for poems and activities. 10 complimentary issues are provided to author with check. Pays $250 for color cover illustration; $35-90 per page b&w inside; $70-155 for color inside. Sample copies for $1.25. Writer's/illustrator's guidelines free with SASE.

Tips: Writers: "Study current issues and guidelines. Observe, especially, word lengths and adhere to requirements. It's sometimes easier to break in with recipe or craft ideas, but submit what you do best. Don't send your first, second, or even third drafts. Polish your piece until it's as perfect as you can make it." Illustrators: "Please study the magazine before contacting us. Your art must have appeal to three- to seven-year-olds." (See listings for *Child Life, Children's Digest, Children's Playmate, Jack And Jill, Turtle Magazine* and *U*S* Kids*.)

‡I.D., David C. Cook Publishing Co., 4050 Lee Vance View, Colorado Springs CO 80918. **Editor**: Frieda Nossaman. **Senior Designer**: Jeffrey P. Barnes. **Designer**: Rebekah J. Lyon. Weekly magazine. Estab. 1991. Circ. 100,000. "*I.D.* is a class-and-home paper for senior high Sunday school students. Stories relate to Bible study."

Fiction: Young adults/teens: adventure, animal, contemporary, folktales, history, humorous, multicultural, nature/environment, religious, science fiction, sports, suspense/mystery. "All must have religious, redeeming qualities." Buys approx. 12 mss/year. Average word length: 600-1,000.

Nonfiction: Young adults/teens: animal, arts/crafts, biography, careers, concept, geography, health, history, how-to, humorous, interview/profile, multicultural, nature/environment, problem solving, religion, science, social issues, sports. "Sometimes material sent to us is too 'preachy.' " Buys 12 mss/year. Average word length: 600-1,000. Byline sometimes given if written in the first person.

How to Contact/Writers: Send complete ms. Reports in 2 months. Publishes ms 15 months after acceptance. Will consider simultaneous submissions.

Illustrations: Buys 3 illustrations/issue; 30 illustrations/year. Uses b&w and color artwork. Reviews ms/illustration packages from artists. Submit ms with rough sketches. Illustrations only: Query. Works on assignment only. Reports back only if interested.

Terms: Pays on acceptance. Pays $50-300 for stories and articles.

JACK AND JILL, Children's Better Health Institute, 1100 Waterway Blvd., P.O. Box 567, Indianapolis IN 46206. (317)636-8881. **Editor**: Daniel Lee. **Art Director**: Mary Rivers. Magazine published 8 times/year. Estab. 1938. Circ. 360,000. "Write entertaining and imaginative stories *for* kids, not just *about* them. Writers should understand what is funny to kids, what's important to them, what excites them. Don't write from an adult 'kids are so cute' perspective. We're also looking for health and healthful lifestyle stories and articles, but don't be preachy."

Fiction: Young readers: animal, contemporary, folktales, health, history, humorous, problem-solving, sports. Middle readers: adventure, animal, contemporary, folktales, health, history, humorous, problem-solving, sports. Buys 30-35 mss/year. Average word length: 700. Byline given.

Nonfiction: Young readers: animal, arts/crafts, cooking, history, hobbies, how-to, humorous, interview/profile, problem-solving, science, sports. Buys 8-10 mss/year. Average word length: 500. Byline given.

Poetry: Reviews poetry.

How to Contact/Writers: Fiction/nonfiction: Send complete ms. Reports on mss in 3 months.

Illustration: Buys 18 illustrations/issue; 216 illustrations/year. Reports back only if interested. Samples not

---

● **SPECIAL COMMENTS** by the editor of *Children's Writer's & Illustrator's Market* are set off by a bullet.

returned; samples filed. Credit line given.
Terms: Pays on publication; minimum 17¢/word. Pays illustrators $275 for color cover; $35-90 fr b&w, $70-155 for color inside. Pays photographers negotiated rate. Sample copies $1.25. Buys all rights.
Tips: See listings for *Child Life*, *Children's Digest*, *Children's Playmate*, *Humpty Dumpty's Magazine*, *Turtle Magazine* and *U*S* Kids*. Publishes writing/art/photos by children.

JUNIOR SCHOLASTIC, Scholastic Inc., 555 Broadway, New York NY 10012-3999. (212)343-6295. **Articles Editor:** Lee Baier. **Art Director:** Holly Grundum. **Photo Editor:** Moya McAllister. Magazine published biweekly during school year. Estab. 1937. Circ. 587,000. Social studies and current events classroom magazine for students in grades 6-8.
Nonfiction: Middle readers, young adults/teens: geography, history, interview/profile, multicultural, nature/environment, social issues, foreign countries. "We mainly buy stories on countries in the news, that include interviews and profiles of kids 11-14." Buys 20 mss/year. Average word length: 1,000. Byline given.
How to Contact/Writers: Nonfiction: Query with published clips. Reports on queries in 2 months; mss in 6 months. Publishes ms 2 months after acceptance.
Illustration: Buys 1 illustration/issue; 20 illustrations/year. Works on assignment only. Reviews ms/illustration packages from artists. Illustrations only: send portfolio. Reports back only if interested. Samples returned with SASE; samples filed. Credit line given.
Photography: Buys photos from freelancers. Wants "photos of young teens in foreign countries; teens relating to national issues." Uses b&w/color prints and 35mm transparencies. Query with samples. Reports back only if interested.
Terms: Pays on publication. Buys all rights. Pays $300-600 for articles. Additional payment for photos accompanying articles. Pays illustrators $800 for color cover; $600 for color inside. Sample copies for 9×11 SAE and $1.75. Writers/photo guidelines for SASE.
Tips: See listings for *Dynamath*, *Scholastic Math Magazine*, *Science World* and *Superscience Blue*.

KEYNOTER, Key Club International, 3636 Woodview Trace, Indianapolis IN 46268. (317)875-8755. **Articles Editor:** Julie A. Carson. **Art Director:** James Patterson. Monthly magazine. Estab. 1915. Circ. 133,000. "As the official magazine of the world's largest high school service organization, we publish nonfiction articles that interest teenagers and will help our readers become better students, better citizens, better leaders."
Nonfiction: Young adults/teens: careers, health, hobbies, how-to, humorous, nature/environment, problem-solving, social issues. Does not want to see first-person accounts; short stories. Buys 15 mss/year. Average word length: 1,500-1,800. Byline given.
How to Contact/Writers: Nonfiction: Query. Reports on queries/mss in 1 month. Will consider simultaneous submissions.
Illustration: Buys 2-3 illustrations/issue; 15 illustrations/year. Works on assignment only. Reviews ms/illustration packages from artists. Ms/illustration packages and illustration only: "Because of our publishing schedule, we prefer to work with illustrators/photographers within Indianapolis market." Reports on art samples only if interested. Samples returned with SASE. Credit line given.
Terms: Pays on acceptance. Buys first North American serial rights. Pays $150-350 for assigned/unsolicited articles. Original artwork returned at job's completion if requested. Sample copy for 8½×11 SAE and 65¢ postage. Writer's guidelines for SAE and 1 first-class stamp.
Tips: "Review a sample copy of the magazine before querying. Write a strong query, complete with persons to be interviewed, angle, lead paragraph, etc."

KIDS AT HOME, the magazine written by and for homeschoolers, Kids at Home, Inc., P.O. Box 363, Astoria OR 97103-0363. E-mail: kidshome@transport.com. **Contact:** Joann Lum, editor. Bimonthly magazine. Estab. 1995. Circ. 5,000. "We are dedicated to publishing a quality magazine that gives homeschoolers a purpose for writing—not just self-expression, but for sharing their works with others across the country."
Fiction: Picture-oriented material, young readers, middle readers, young adults/teens: adventure, animal, contemporary, folktales, history, multicultural, nature/environment, science fiction, sports, suspense/mystery. "We accept works, writing and art, from homeschoolers, ages 4-13." Name, age, city state given.
Nonfiction: Picture-oriented material, young readers, middle readers, young adults/teens (up to age 13): animal, arts/crafts, careers, geography, history, hobbies, multicultural, nature/environment, science, sports, travel. Looks for nonfiction contributions from home schoolers ages 4-13. Average word length: 35-1,500.
Poetry: Reviews all poetry. Maximum length: 20 lines.
How to Contact/Writers: Fiction/Nonfiction: Send complete ms. Reports on mss in 1 week. Publishes ms 1-6 months after acceptance. Will consider simultaneous submissions and electronic submission via disk or modem.
Illustration: Uses b&w artwork only. Illustration only: Query with samples. Send résumé. Reports in 1 week. Samples returned with SASE; samples filed.
Terms: Pays on publication. Originals returned to artist at job's completion. Sample copy $4. Writer's/illustrator's/photo guidelines free with SASE.
Tips: "We feature a published children's author or illustrator in every issue. We also have an author contest which enables homeschoolers to win an autographed copy of the featured author! We *only* publish writing/art/photos by homeschooled children, ages 4-13. Payment is issue of *Kids at Home*."

‡**KIDS' WALL STREET NEWS**, Kids' Wall Street News, Inc., P.O. Box 1207, Rancho Santa Fe CA 92067. (760)591-7681. Fax: (760)591-3731. E-mail: info@kwsnews.com. Website: http://www.kwsnews.com. **Contact**: Kate Allen, editor-in-chief. Bimonthly magazine. Estab. 1996. *"Kids' Wall Street News* hopes to empower and educate America's youth so they will be better prepared for today and their future. This bimonthly magazine covers world and business news, financial information, computer updates, the environment, adventure and much more."

Nonfiction: Young adults/teens: animal, biography, careers, finance, geography, health, history, interview/profile, nature/environment, science, social issues, sports, travel. Buys 130 mss/year. Average word length: 250-550. Byline given.

How to Contact/Writers: Nonfiction: Query with published clips. Reports on queries in 2-3 months. Will consider simultaneous submissions and electronic submission via disk or modem.

Terms: Pays on publication. Buys exclusive magazine rights for mss. Samples copies for 9 × 12 SAE and $1.70 postage (6 first-class stamps).

Tips: *"Kids' Wall Street News* generally assigns specific subject matter for articles. There is a heavy financial slant to the magazine."

*❋KIDS WORLD MAGAZINE, MIR Communications Inc., 108-93 Lombard Ave., Winnipeg, Manitoba R3B 3B1 Canada. (204)942-2214. Fax: (204)943-8991. E-mail: kidsworld@kidsworld~online.com. Website: http://www.kidsworld~online.com. **Articles Editor:** Stuart Slayen. **Fiction Editor:** Leslie Malkin. **Art Director:** Brian Kauste. Magazine published 6 times/year. Estab. 1993. Circ. 225,000. *Kids World Magazine* aims to give its 9-12-year-old readers an entertaining, interactive and empowering publication with a global perspective.

Fiction: Middle readers: adventure, contemporary, folktale, humorous, multicultural, nature/environment, problem-solving, science fiction, sports, suspense/mystery, relationships. Multicultural needs include relationships/learning between kids of different backgrounds. "I get too many serious submissions." Buys 8 mss/year. Average word length: 550-1,000. Byline given.

Nonfiction: Middle readers: animal, biography, careers, concept, games/puzzles, history, hobbies, how-to, humorous, interview/profile, multicultural, nature/environment, problem-solving, science, social issues, sports. Multicultural needs include stories of an international nature—kids relating with schools/kids in other countries. Buys 12 mss/year. Average word length: 550-1,200. Byline given.

How to Contact/Writers: Fiction: Send complete ms. Nonfiction: Query with published clips. Reports on queries/mss in 2 months. Publishes ms 2 months after acceptance.

Terms: Pays on publication plus 30 days. Buys first rights for mss. Pays $100-200 (Canadian) for stories; $100-400 (Canadian) for articles. Sample copies when available for 9 × 12 SAE and $1.45 (Canadian). Writer's guidelines for SASE.

Tips: "We're beginning to run stories with an international flavor. We want our readers to feel part of the world and we encourage them to interact with kids in other countries via the Internet. We treat our readers with respect and dignity. We avoid cliché and we try to create a fun and responsible publication." (See listing for *What! A Magazine*.)

LADYBUG, THE MAGAZINE FOR YOUNG CHILDREN, Carus Publishing Company, P.O. Box 300, Peru IL 61354. (815)224-6656. **Editor-in-Chief**: Marianne Carus. **Editor**: Paula Morrow. **Art Director**: Suzanne Beck. Monthly magazine. Estab. 1990. Circ. 130,000. Literary magazine for children 2-6, with stories, poems, activities, songs and picture stories.

Fiction: Picture-oriented material: adventure, animal, fantasy, folktales, humorous, multicultural, nature/environment, problem-solving, science fiction, sports, suspense/mystery. "Open to any easy fiction stories." Buys 50 mss/year. Average word length 300-850 words. Byline given.

Nonfiction: Picture-oriented material: activities, animal, arts/crafts, concept, cooking, humorous, math, nature/environment, problem-solving, science. Buys 35 mss/year.

Poetry: Reviews poems, 20-line maximum length; limit submissions to 5 poems. Uses lyrical, humorous, simple language.

How to Contact/Writers: Fiction/nonfiction: Send complete ms. Queries not accepted. Reports on mss in 3 months. Publishes ms up to 2 years after acceptance. Does not like, but will consider simultaneous submissions.

Illustration: Buys 12 illustrations/issue; 145 illustrations/year. Prefers "bright colors; all media, but use watercolor and acrylics most often; same size as magazine is preferred but not required." To be considered for future assignments: Submit promo sheet, slides, tearsheets, color and b&w photocopies. Reports on art samples in 3 months.

Terms: Pays on publication for mss; after delivery of completed assignment for illustrators. For mss, buys first publication rights; second serial (reprint rights). Buys first publication rights plus promotional rights for artwork. Original artwork returned at job's completion. Pays up to 25¢/word for prose; $3/line for poetry; $25 minimum for articles. Pays $750 for color (cover) illustration, $50-100 for b&w (inside) illustration, $250/page for color (inside). Sample copy for $4. Writer's/illustrator's guidelines free for SASE.

Tips: Writers: "Get to know several young children on an individual basis. Respect your audience. Wants less cute, condescending or 'preach-teachy' material. Less gratuitous anthropomorphism. More rich, evocative language, sense of joy or wonder. Set your manuscript aside for at least a month, then reread critically." Illustrators: "Include examples, where possible, of children, animals, and—most important—action and narrative (i.e., several scenes from a story, showing continuity and an ability to maintain interest). Keep in mind that people come in all colors, sizes, physical conditions. Be inclusive in creating characters." (See listings for *Babybug*, *Cricket* and *Spider*.)

‡LISTEN, Drug-Free Possibilities for Teens, 55 West Oak Ridge Dr., Hagerstown MD 21740. (301)791-7000, ext. 2535. **Editor:** Lincoln Steed. Monthly magazine. Circ. 50,000. *Listen* offers positive alternatives to drug use for its teenage readers.

Fiction: Young adults: contemporary, health, humorous, nature/environment, problem solving activities, sports. Buys 12 mss/year. Average word length: 1,000-1,200. Byline given.

Nonfiction: Young adults: arts/crafts, hobbies, health, nature/environment, problem solving activities, sports. Wants to see more factual articles on drug abuse. Buys 50 mss/year. Average word length: 1,000-1,200. Byline given.

How to Contact/Writers: Fiction/nonfiction: Send complete ms. Reports on queries/mss in 2 months.

Illustration: Reviews ms/illustration packages from artists. Ms/illustration packages and illustration only:Query, send promo sheet and slides. Reports in 1 month. Credit line given.

Photography: Purchases photos from freelancers. Looks for "youth oriented—action (sports, outdoors), personality photos."

Terms: Pays on acceptance. Buys exclusive magazine rights for ms. Buys one-time rights for artwork and photographs. Pays $50-250 for stories/articles. Pays illustrators $150-300 for b&w cover; $250-600 for color cover; $75-150 for b&w inside; $100-300 for color inside. Pays photographers by the project (range: $200-500) or per photo (range: $50-500). Sample copy for $1 and SASE. Writer's guidelines free with SASE.

Tips: "*Listen* is a magazine for teenagers. It encourages development of good habits and high ideals of physical, social and mental health. It bases its editorial philosophy of primary drug prevention on total abstinence from alcohol and other drugs. Because it is used extensively in public high school classes, it does not accept articles and stories with overt religious emphasis. Four specific purposes guide the editors in selecting materials for *Listen*: (1) To portray a positive lifestyle and to foster skills and values that will help teenagers deal with contemporary problems, including smoking, drinking and using drugs. This is *Listen*'s primary purpose. (2) To offer positive alternatives to a lifestyle of drug use of any kind. (3) To present scientifically accurate information about the nature and effects of tobacco, alcohol and other drugs. (4) To report medical research, community programs and educational efforts which are solving problems connected with smoking, alcohol and other drugs. Articles should offer their readers activities that increase one's sense of self-worth through achievement and/or involvement in helping others. They are often categorized by three kinds of focus: (1) Hobbies. (2) Recreation. (3) Community Service.

‡LIVEWIRE, Standard Publishing, 1821 Hamilton Ave., Cincinnati OH 45231. (513)931-4050. Editors: Marjorie Redford and Karen Roth. Senior Editor: Barbara Cottrell. Art Director: Sandra S. Wimmer. Weekly magazine. "*LiveWire* is a weekly Sunday school newspaper for preteens in grades 5 and 6. Our goal is to reach these youth with the good news of God's word and to help them apply that news to the everyday situations they encounter."

Nonfiction: Middle readers: animals, arts/crafts, humor, interview/profile, multicultural, sports, science. "Articles should be news briefs that deal with current topics of interest to preteens such as school, church youth groups, family life, recreation, friends and music. They should have a religious emphasis." Average word length: 100-250.

Poetry: "Only poetry by preteens is accepted."

How to Contact/Writers: Submit complete manuscript, "including name, address, daytime telephone number, social security number and approximate word count on cover sheet." Those under age 20 must include birthdate. Reports on submissions in 1-2 weeks. SASE.

Illustration: Works on assignment only. Needs "devotions, puzzles, cartoons."

Photography: Buys photos with accompanying ms only. Model/property releases required. Uses professional quality, high contrast b&w glossy and color transparencies. SASE.

Terms: Pays on acceptance. Buys first rights and reprint rights. Pays 3-7¢/word and 2 contributors copies for articles. Rates for preteen submissions vary. Quarterly theme list available for SASE. Send seasonal material 9-12 months in advance."

Tips: "We buy submissions to fit in with specific themes. Also, get to know preteens before you write for them. Many manuscripts are rejected simply because the vocabulary is outdated for modern preteens. Send seasonal material 9-12 months in advance.

‡MUSE, Carus Publishing, 332 S. Michigan Ave, Suite 2000, Chicago IL 60604. E-mail: muse@caruspub.com. Website: http://www.musemag.com **Art Director:** John Grandits. **Photo Editor:** Carol Parden. Estab. 1996. Circ. 100,000. "The goal of *Muse* is to give as many children as possible access to the most important ideas and concepts underlying the principal areas of human knowledge. It will take children seriously as developing intellects by assuming that, if explains clearly, the ideas and concepts of an article will be of interest to them. Articles should meet the highest possible standards of clarity and transparency aided, wherever possible, by a tone of skepticism, humor, and irreverence."

● *Muse* is published in cooperation of the Cricket Magazine Group and *Smithsonian* magazine.

Nonfiction: Work on commision only. "Each article must be about a topic that children can understand. the topic must be a 'large' one that somehow connects with a fundamental tenet of some discipline or area of practical knowledge. The topic and presentation must lead to further questioning and exploration; it must be open-ended rather than closed. The treatment of the topic must be of the competence one would expect of an expert in the field in which the topic resides. It must be interesting and hold the reader's attention, not because of the way it is written, but because of the compelling presentation of the ideas it describes."

How to Contact/Writers: Nonfiction: Query with résumé, writing samples, detailed story ideas and SASE. Will consider simultaneous submissions, electronic submissions via disk or modem or previously published work.
Illustration: Buys 3 illustrations/issue; 25 illustrations/year. Uses color artwork only. Works on assignment only. Reviews ms/illustration packages. Query. Illustrations only: Query with samples. Send résumé and tearsheets. Reports back only if interested. Samples returned with SASE. Credit line given.
Photography: Needs vary. Query with samples. Reports back only if interested.
Terms; Pays within 60 days of acceptance. Buys first publications rights; all rights for feature articles. Pays 50¢/word for assigned articles; 25¢/word for unsolicited manuscripts. Writer's guidelines and sample copy available for $5.
Tips: "*Muse* many on occasion publish unsolicited manuscripts, but the easiest way to be printed in *Muse* is to send a query. However, manuscripts may be submitted to the Cricket Magazine Group fro review, and any that are considered suitable for *Muse* will be forwarded. Such manuscripts will also be considered for publication in *Cricket, Spider* or *Ladybug.*" (See listing for *Babybug, Cricket, Ladybug* and *Spider.*

MY FRIEND, The Catholic Magazine for Kids, Pauline Books & Media, 50 St. Paul's Ave., Jamaica Plain, Boston MA 02130. (617)522-8911. Website: http://www.pauline.org. **Articles/Fiction Editor:** Sr. Kathryn James, FSP. **Art Director:** Sister Helen Rita Lane, FSP. Monthly magazine. Estab. 1979. Circ. 12,000. "*My Friend* is a 32-page monthly Catholic magazine for boys and girls. Its' goal is to celebrate the Catholic Faith—as it is lived by today's children and as it has been lived for centuries. Its pages are packed with fun, learning, new experiences, information, crafts, global awareness, friendships and inspiration. Together with it's web-page KidStuff. *My Friend* provides kids and their families a wealth of information and contacts on every aspect of the Faith."
Fiction: Young readers, middle readers: adventure, animal, Christmas, contemporary, humorous, nature/environment, religious. Does not want to see poetry, animals as main characters in religious stories, stories whose basic thrust would be incompatible with Catholic values. Buys 50 mss/year. Average word length: 450-750. Byline given.
Nonfiction: Young readers: arts/crafts, games/puzzles, health, history, hobbies, humorous, problem-solving, religious, science. Middle readers: arts/crafts, games/puzzles, health, history, hobbies, how-to, humorous, interview/profile, media literacy, nature/environment, problem-solving, religion, science, sports. Does not want to see material that is not compatible with Catholic values; no "New Age" material. Buys 10 mss/year. Average word length: 450-750. Byline given.
How to Contact/Writers: Fiction/nonfiction: Send complete ms. Reports on queries/mss in 2 months.
Illustration: Buys 8 illustrations/issue; buys 60-80 illustrations/year. Preferred theme or style: Realistic depictions of children, but open to variety! "We'd just like to hear from more illustrators who can do *humans*! (We see enough of funny cats, mice, etc.)" Looking for a "Bible stories" and comic book style artist, too. Reviews ms/illustration packages from artists. Send complete ms with copy of final art. Contact: Sister Helen Rita Lane, art director. Illustrations only: Query with samples. Send résumé, promo sheet and tearsheets. Contact: Sister Helen Rita Lane. Reports only if interested. Credit line given.
Photography: Wants photos of "children at play or alone; school scenes; also, sports."
Terms: Pays on acceptance for mss. Buys first rights for mss; variable for artwork. Original artwork returned at job's completion. Pays $20-150 for stories/articles. Pays illustrators $50-150/b&w (inside); $50-200/color (inside). Sample copy $2 with 9×12 SAE and 4 first-class stamps. Writer's guidelines free with SAE and 1 first-class stamp.
Tips: Writers: "We are looking for fresh perspectives into a child's world that are imaginative, unique, challenging, informative, current and fun. We prefer articles that are visual, not necessarily text-based—articles written in "windows" style with multiple points entry. Biographies are accepted if they emphasize the childhood of the subject and are written from a slant that emphasizes a theme or a particular issue. A biography should be written by someone who shows a rich mastery in the field in question. It should not be re-written from an encyclopedia. Please accompany biographies with a bibliography. Fiction can entertain, inspire, or teach. Fiction stories do not have to do all three. We have a need for each of these types at different times. Illustrators: "Please contact us! For the most part, we need illustrations for fiction stories." In the future, sees children's magazines "getting

---

A SELF-ADDRESSED, STAMPED ENVELOPE (SASE) should always be included with submissions within your own country. When sending material to other countries, include a self-addressed envelope (SAE) and International Reply Coupons (IRCs).

more savvy, less sappy. Suspect that electronic media styles will penetrate a greater number of magazines for kids and adults alike; literary or intellectual publications would be less affected."

*NATIONAL GEOGRAPHIC WORLD, National Geographic Society, 1145 17th St. NW, Washington DC 20036-4688. (202)857-7000. Fax: (202)425-5712. **Editor:** Susan Tejada. **Art Director:** Ursula Vosseler. **Photo Editor:** Chuck Herron. Monthly magazine. Estab. 1975. Circ. 1.1 million.
Nonfiction: Young readers, middle readers, young adult/teens: animal, arts/crafts, biography, cooking, games/puzzles, geography, history, hobbies, how-to, interview/profile, multicultural, nature/environment, science, sports, travel. Middle readers, young adult/teens: social issues. "We do not review or buy unsolicited manuscripts, but do use freelance writers."
Illustration: Buys 100% of illustrations from freelancers. Works on assignment only. Query. Illustrations only: Query with samples. Reports in 2 months. Samples returned with SASE; samples filed. Credit line given.
Photography: Buys photos separately. Looking for active shots, funny, strange animal close-ups. Uses 35mm transparencies. Query with samples. Reports in 2 months.
Terms: Pays on acceptance. Buys all rights for mss and artwork. Originals returned to artist at job's completion. Writers get 3 copies of issue their work appears in. Pays photographers by the project. Sample copies for 9×12 SAE and 2 first-class stamps; photo guidelines available free for SASE.
Tips: "Most story ideas are generated in-house and assigned to freelance writers. Query with cover letter and samples of your writing for children or young adults. Keep in mind that *World* is a visual magazine. A story will work best if it has a very tight focus and if the photos show children interacting with their surroundings as well as with each other."

NATURE FRIEND MAGAZINE, Pilgrim Publishers, 22777 State Road 119, Goshen IN 46527-0073. (219)534-2245. **Articles Editor:** Stanley Brubaker. Monthly magazine. Estab. 1983. Circ. 9,000.
Nonfiction: Picture-oriented material, young readers, middle readers, young adults: animal, nature. Does not want to see evolutionary material. Buys 50-80 mss/year. Average word length: 350-1,500. Byline given.
How to Contact/Writers: Nonfiction: Send complete ms. Reports on mss in 1-4 months. Will consider simultaneous submissions.
Illustration: Works on assignment only.
Terms: Pays on publication. Buys one-time rights. Pays $15-75. Payment for illustrations: $15-80/b&w; $50-100/color inside. Two sample copies and writer's guidelines for $5 with $7\frac{1}{2} \times 10\frac{1}{2}$ SAE and $1.47 postage. Writer's/illustrator's guidelines for $2.50.
Tips: Looks for "main articles, puzzles and simple nature and science projects. Please examine samples and writer's guide before submitting."

NEW ERA MAGAZINE, Official Publication for Youth of the Church of Jesus Christ of Latter-Day Saints, 50 E. North Temple St., Salt Lake City UT 84150. (801)240-2951. **Articles/Fiction Editor:** Richard M. Romney. **Art Director:** B. Lee Shaw. Monthly magazine. Estab. 1971. Circ. 230,000. General interest religious publication for youth ages 12-18 who are members of The Church of Jesus Christ of Latter-Day Saints (Mormons).
Fiction: Young adults: contemporary, humorous, religious, romance, science fiction, sports. "All material must relate to Mormon point of view." Does not want to see "formula pieces, stories not sensitive to an LDS audience." Buys 20 mss/year. Average word length: 250-2,500. Byline given.
Nonfiction: Young adults: biography, games/puzzles, history, religion, social issues, travel, sports; "general interest articles by, about and for young Mormons. Would like more about Mormon youth worldwide." Does not want to see "formula pieces, articles not adapted to our specific voice and our audience." Buys 150-200 mss/year. Average word length: 250-2,000. Byline given.
Poetry: Reviews poems, 30-line maximum. Limit submissions to 10 poems.
How to Contact/Writers: Fiction/nonfiction: Query. Reports on queries/mss in 2 months. Publishes ms 1 year or more after acceptance. Will consider electronic submissions via disk.
Illustration: Buys 5 illustrations/issue; 50-60 illustrations/year. "We buy only from our pool of illustrators. We use all styles and mediums." Works on assignment only. Illustrations only: Query with samples or to arrange portfolio review. Send résumé, promo sheet, slides and tearsheets. Samples returned with SASE; samples filed. Originals returned at job's completion. Reports only if interested. Original artwork returned at job's completion. Credit line given.
Terms: Pays on acceptance. For mss, buys first rights; right to publish again in other church usage (rights reassigned on written request). Buys all or one-time rights for artwork and photos. Pays $25-375 for stories; $25-350 for articles. Pays illustrators and photographers "by specific arrangements." Sample copies for $1.50. Writer's guidelines free for #10 SASE.
Tips: Open to "first-person and true-life experiences. Tell what happened in a conversational style. Teen magazines are becoming more brash and sassy. We shy away from the outlandish and trendy, but still need a contemporary look."

NEW MOON: The Magazine For Girls & Their Dreams, New Moon Publishing, Inc., P.O. Box 3620, Duluth MN 55803-3620. (218)728-5507. Fax: (218)728-0314. E-mail: newmoon@newmoon.duluth.mn.us. Website: http://newmoon.org. **Articles Editor/Art Director:** Barbara Stretchberry. Bimonthly magazine. Estab. 1992.

This magical ink and colored pencil work on textured scratchboard was illustrator Theresa Brandon's first professional sale in the children's market. Brandon was paid $60 for this freelance assignment which she found through *Children's Writer's & Illustrator's Market*. The piece appeared in the March/April 1997 issue of *New Moon Magazine* to accompany a story called *Dream Catcher*. Brandon describes herself as "a full-time mom with two kids, two cats, two dogs (and a very understanding husband)." She's a member of SCBWI and uses the internet to stay in touch with other illustrators. Check out her website at http://members.aol.com/TheBrandon.

Circ. 25,000. *New Moon* is for every girl who wants her voice heard and her dreams taken seriously. *New Moon* portrays strong female role models of all ages, backgrounds and cultures now and in the past. 100% of publication aimed at juvenile market.

Fiction: Middle readers, young adults: adventure, animal, contemporary, fantasy, folktales, health, history, humorous, multicultural, nature/environment, problem-solving, science fiction, sports, suspense/mystery, travel. Buys 6 mss/year. Average word length: 300-1,200. Byline given.

Nonfiction: Middle readers, young adults: animal, arts/crafts, biography, careers, concept, games/puzzles, health, history, hobbies, humorous, interview/profile, math, multicultural, nature/environment, problem-solving, science, social issues, sports, travel, stories about real girls. Does not want to see how-to stories. Wants more stories about real girls doing real things. Buys 6 mss/year. Average word length: 300-900. Byline given.

How to Contact/Writers: Fiction/Nonfiction: send complete ms. Reports on queries/mss in 4-6 months. Will consider simultaneous submissions, electronic submissions via disk or modem, previously published work.

Illustration: Buys 15 illustrations/year from freelancers. *New Moon* seeks 4-color cover illustrations as well as b&w illustrations for inside. They also seek small graphics, borders and other illustrations which are multicultural, whimsical and positively portray girls. Reviews ms/illustrations packages from artists. Query. Submit ms with rough sketches. Illustration only: Query; send résumé. Samples returned with SASE; samples filed. Reports only if interested. Credit line given.

Photography: Buys photos from freelancers. Model/property releases required; captions required. Uses color, b&w, glossy prints. Query with samples. Reports only if interested.

Terms: Pays on publication. Buys first rights, one-time rights, reprint rights for mss. Buys one-time rights, reprint rights, first rights for artwork and photographs. Original artwork returned at job's completion. Pays 4-8¢/word for stories; 4-8¢/word for articles. Pays in contributor's copies. Additional payment for ms/illustration packages and for photos accompanying articles. Pays illustrators $400 for color cover; $50-100 for b&w inside. Pays photographers $15-25 per photo. Sample copies for $6.50. Writer's/illustrator's/photo/cover art guidelines for SASE.

Tips: "Please refer to a copy of *New Moon* to understand the style and philosophy of the magazine. Writers and artists who comprehend our goals have the best chance of publication. We're looking for stories about real girls; women's careers, and articles for our Global Village feature on the lives of girls from other countries." Publishes writing/art/photos by children.

ODYSSEY, Adventures in Science, Cobblestone Publishing, Inc., 7 School St., Peterborough NH 03458. (603)924-7209. **Editor:** Elizabeth E. Lindstrom. **Managing Editor:** Denise L. Babcock. **Art Director**: Ann Dillon. Magazine published 10 times/year. Estab. 1979. Circ. 35,000. Magazine covers astronomy and space exploration for children ages 8-14. All material must relate to the theme of a specific upcoming issue in order to be considered.

Fiction: Middle readers and young adults/teens: adventure, folktales, history, biographical fiction. Does not want to see anything not theme-related. Average word length: 750 maximum.

Nonfiction: Middle readers and young adults/teens: arts/crafts, biography, cooking, games/puzzles (no word finds), science (space). Don't send anything not theme-related. Average word length: 200-750, depending on section article is used in.

How to Contact/Writers: "A query must consist of all of the following to be considered (please use nonerasable paper): a brief cover letter stating the subject and word length of the proposed article; a detailed one-page outline explaining the information to be presented in the article; an extensive bibliography of materials the author intends to use in preparing the article; a SASE. Writers new to *Odyssey* should send a writing sample with query. If you would like to know if your query has been received, please also include a stamped postcard that requests acknowledgment of receipt. In all correspondence, please include your complete address as well as a telephone number where you can be reached. A writer may send as many queries for one issue as he or she wishes, but each query must have a separate cover letter, outline, bibliography, and SASE. Telephone queries are not accepted. Handwritten queries will not be considered. Queries may be submitted at any time, but queries sent well in advance of deadline *may not be answered for several months*. Go-aheads requesting material proposed in queries are usually sent five months prior to publication date. Unused queries will be returned approximately three to four months prior to publication date."

Illustration: Buys 3 illustrations/issue; 27 illustrations/year. Works on assignment only. Reviews ms/illustration packages from artists. Query. Contact: Beth Lindstrom, editor. Illustration only: Query with samples. Send tearsheets, photocopies. Reports in 2 weeks. Samples returned with SASE; samples not filed. Original artwork returned upon job's completion (upon written request).

Photography: Wants photos pertaining to any of our forthcoming themes. Uses b&w and color prints; 35mm transparencies. Photographers should send unsolicited photos by mail on speculation.

Terms: Pays on publication. Buys all rights for mss and artwork. Pays 20-25¢/word for stories/articles. Covers are assigned and paid on an individual basis. Pays photographers per photo ($15-100 for b&w; $25-100 for color). Sample copy for $3.95 and SASE with $1.05 postage. Writer's/illustrator's/photo guidelines for SASE. (See listings for *Calliope, World History for Kids*; *Cobblestone, American History for Kids*; and *Faces, People, Places & Cultures*.)

ON COURSE, A Magazine for Teens, General Council of the Assemblies of God, 1445 Boonville Ave., Springfield MO 65802-1894. (417)862-2781. Fax: (417)866-1146. E-mail: oncourse@ag.org. **Editor:** Melinda Booze. **Art Director:** Richard Harman. Quarterly magazine. Estab. 1991. Circ. 162,000. *On Course* is a religious quarterly for teens "to encourage Christian, biblical discipleship; to promote denominational post-secondary schools; to nurture loyalty to the denomination."

● *On Course* works on assignment only. Each issue focuses on a theme. Send for theme list along with writer's guidelines.

Fiction: Young adults: adventure, contemporary, history, humorous, religious, Christian discipleship, sports. Average word length: 1,000. Byline given.

Nonfiction: Young adults: careers, hobbies, humorous, interview/profile, religion, social issues, sports, college life, Christian discipleship.

How to Contact/Writers: Reports on mss in 2 months. Publishes ms 6-24 months after acceptance. Will consider simultaneous submissions, electronic submissions via disk or modem and previously published work.

Illustration: Buys 4 illustrations/issue; 16 illustrations/year. Uses color artwork only. Reviews ms/illustration packages from artists. Query. Illustration only: Query with samples or send résumé, promo sheet, slides, client list and tearsheets. Contact Melinda Booze, editor. Reports in 2 months. Samples returned with SASE; samples filed. Originals not returned at job's completion. Credit line given.

Photography: Buys photos from freelancers. "Teen life, church life, college life; unposed; often used for illustrative purposes." Model/property releases required. Uses color glossy prints and 35mm or 2¼ × 2¼ transparencies. Query with samples; send business card, promotional literature, tearsheets or catalog. Reports only if interested.

Terms: Pays on acceptance. Buys first or reprint rights for mss. Buys one-time rights for photographs. Pays 6¢/word for stories/articles. Pays illustrators and photographers "as negotiated." Sample copies free for 9 × 11 SAE. Writer's guidelines for SASE.

ON THE LINE, Mennonite Publishing House, 616 Walnut Ave., Scottdale PA 15683. (412)887-8500. Fax: (412)887-3111. E-mail: otl%mph@mcimail.com. **Editor:** Mary Clemens Meyer. Magazine published monthly. Estab. 1970. Circ. 6,000. "*On The Line* is a children's magazine for ages 9-14, emphasizing self-esteem and Christian values. Also emphasizes multicultural awareness, care of the earth and accepting others with differences."

Fiction: Middle readers, young adults: contemporary, history, humorous, nature/environment, problem-solving, religious, science fiction, sports. "No fantasy or fiction with animal characters." Buys 50 mss/year. Average word length: 1,000-1,800. Byline given.

Nonfiction: Middle readers, young adults: arts/crafts, biography, cooking, games/puzzles, health, history, hobbies, how-to, humorous, sports. Does not want to see articles written from an adult perspective. Average word length: 200-600. Byline given.

Poetry: Wants to see light verse, humorous poetry.

How to Contact/Writers: Fiction/nonfiction: Send complete ms. "No queries, please." Reports on queries/mss in 1 month. Will consider simultaneous submissions.

Illustration: Buys 5-6 illustrations/issue; buys 60 illustrations/year. "Inside illustrations are done on assignment only, to accompany our stories and articles—our need for new artists is very limited." Looking for new artists for cover illustrations—full-color work. Illustrations only: "Prefer samples they do not want returned; these stay in our files." Reports on art samples only if interested.

Terms: Pays on acceptance. For mss buys one-time rights; second serial (reprint rights). Buys one-time rights for artwork and photos. Pays 2-5¢/word for assigned/unsolicited articles ($60 maximum for stories, $35 maximum for articles). Pays $40-50 for 2- or 3-color inside illustration; $150 for full-color cover illustration. Photographers are paid per photo, $25-50. Original artwork returned at job's completion. Sample copy free with 7 × 10 SAE. Free writer's guidelines.

Tips: "We will be focusing on the age 12-13 group of our age 9-14 audience. (Focus was somewhat younger before.)" Publishes writing/art/photos by children.

♣OWL COMMUNICATIONS, 179 John St., Suite 500, Toronto, Ontario M5T 3G5 Canada. See listings for *Chickadee*, *Chirp* and *OWL*.

♣OWL, The Discovery Magazine for Children, Owl Communications, 179 John St., Suite 500, Toronto, Ontario M5T 3G5 Canada. (416)340-2700. Fax: (416)340-9769. E-mail: owl@owlkids.com. Website: http://www.owlkids.com. **Editor:** Keltie Thomas. **Creative Director:** Tim Davin. **Photo Editor:** Ekaterina Gitlin. Monthly magazine. Circ. 110,000. "*OWL* helps children over eight discover and enjoy the world of science, nature and technology. We look for articles that are fun to read, that inform from a child's perspective, and that motivate hands-on interaction. *OWL* explores the reader's many interests in the natural world in a scientific, but always entertaining, way."

Nonfiction: Middle readers: animal, biology, games/puzzles, high-tech, humor, nature/environment, science, social issues, sports, travel. Especially interested in puzzles and game ideas: logic, math, visual puzzles. Does not want to see religious topics, anthropomorphizing. Buys 20 mss/year. Average word length: 500-1,500. Byline given.

How to Contact/Writers: Nonfiction: Query with published clips. Reports on queries in 3 months.
Illustration: Buys 3-5 illustrations/issue; 40-50 illustrations/year. Uses color artwork only. Preferred theme or style: lively, involving, fun, with emotional impact and appeal. "We use a range of styles." Works on assignment only. Illustrations only: Send tearsheets and slides. Reports on art samples only if interested. Original artwork returned at job's completion.
Photography: Looking for shots of animals and nature. "Label the photos." Uses 2¼ × 2¼ and 35mm transparencies. Photographers should query with samples.
Terms: Pays on publication. Buys first North American and world rights for mss, artwork and photos. Pays $200-500 (Canadian) for assigned/unsolicited articles. Pays up to $650 (Canadian) for illustrations. Photographers are paid per photo. Sample copies for $4. Free writer's guidelines.
Tips: Writers: "*OWL* is dedicated to entertaining kids with contemporary and accurate information about the world around them. *OWL* is intellectually challenging but is never preachy. Ideas should be original and convey a spirit of humor and liveliness." (See listings for *Chickadee Magazine* and *Chirp*.)

*PARENTS AND CHILDREN TOGETHER ONLINE, A magazine for parents and children on the World Wide Web, EDINFO Press/Family Literary Centers, 2805 East 10th St., Suite 150, Bloomington IN 47408. (800)759-4723. E-mail: disted@indiana.edu. Website: http://www.indiana.edu/~eric_rec/fl/pcto/menu.html. **Editor-in-Chief:** Christopher Essex. Quarterly online magazine. Estab. 1990 (in print format). Circ. 9,000 via World Wide Web. "Our magazine seeks to promote family literacy by providing original articles and stories for parents and children via the World Wide Web." 50% of publication aimed at juvenile market.
Fiction: "We accept all categories except the overtly religious. Would like to see more humorous stories. We welcome stories from all cultural backgrounds." Buys 32 mss/year. Byline given.
Nonfiction: All categories are looked at and considered. "We especially look for articles with photographs and/or illustrations included. We welcome articles about children and subjects that children will find interesting, that reflect diverse cultural backgrounds. We like articles about animals, but we do get quite a few of them." Buys 24 mss/year. Byline given.
Poetry: Reviews poetry. Limit submissions to 3 poems. "We accept poems written for children that children will enjoy—not poems about childhood by an adult looking back nostalgically. Humorous, but not just silly, poems especially appreciated."
How to Contact/Writers: Fiction/nonfiction: Send complete ms. Reports on queries in 1 week; mss in 3 months. Publishes ms 3-6 months after acceptance. Will consider simultaneous submissions, electronic submissions via disk or modem and previously published work.
Illustration: Buys 12 illustrations/issue; 48 illustrations/year. Uses color artwork only. Reviews ms/illustration packages from artists. Query with ms dummy. Contact: Christopher Essex, editor. Illustrations only: Query with samples. Contact: Christopher Essex, editor. Reports on art samples in 1 month. Samples returned with SASE. Credit line given.
Photography: Looking for children and parents together, either reading together or involved in other interesting activities. Also, children with grandparents. Uses color prints and 35mm transparencies. Query with samples. Send unsolicited photos by mail. Reports in 1 month.
Terms: Buys first North American serial rights for mss. Art/photos use on Web with copyright retained by artist/photographer. "We are a free online publication, and cannot afford to pay our contributors at present." Sample copies for $9. Writer's guidelines free for SASE.
Tips: "We are a good market for writers, artists and photographers who want their material to reach a wide audience. Since we are a free publication, available without charge to anyone with a Web browser, we cannot offer our contributors anything more than a large, enthusiastic audience for their work. Our stories and articles are read by thousands of children and parents every month via their families' Internet-connected computer."

POCKETS, Devotional Magazine for Children, The Upper Room, 1908 Grand, P.O. Box 189, Nashville TN 37202-0189. (615)340-7333. Fax: (615)340-7006. E-mail: pockets@upperroom.org. Website: http://www.upperroom.org. **Articles/Fiction Editor:** Lynn W. Gilliam. **Art Director**: Chris Schechner, Suite 207, 3100 Carlisle Plaza, Dallas TX 75204. Magazine published 11 times/year. Estab. 1981. Circ. 96,000. "*Pockets* is a Christian devotional magazine for children ages 6-12. Stories should help children experience a Christian lifestyle that is not always a neatly wrapped moral package but is open to the continuing revelation of God's will."
Fiction: Picture-oriented, young readers, middle readers: adventure, contemporary, folktales, multicultural, nature/environment, problem-solving, religious. Does not want to see violence or talking animal stories. Buys 40-45 mss/year. Average word length: 800-1,600. Byline given.
Nonfiction: Picture-oriented, young readers, middle readers: cooking, games/puzzles, interview/profile, religion.

THE AGE-LEVEL INDEX, located in the back of this book, lists book publishers and magazines according to the age-groups for which they need material.

Does not want to see how-to articles. "Our nonfiction reads like a story." Multicultural needs include: stories that feature children of various racial/ethnic groups and do so in a way that is true to those depicted. Buys 10 mss/year. Average word length: 800-1,600. Byline given.

How to Contact/Writers: Fiction/nonfiction: Send complete ms. "Prefer not to deal with queries." Reports on mss in 6 weeks. Will consider simultaneous submissions.

Illustration: Buys 40-50 illustrations/issue. Preferred theme or style: varied; both 4-color and 2-color. Works on assignment only. Illustrations only: Send promo sheet, tearsheets and slides to Chris Schechner, Suite 207, 3100 Carlisle Plaza, Dallas TX 75204. "Include samples of both 2-color and 4-color, if you have them." Reports on art samples in 3 months. Samples returned with SASE; samples filed. Credit line given.

Photography: Purchases photography from freelancers. Buys photos with accompanying ms only.

Terms: Pays on acceptance. Buys first North American serial rights for mss; one-time rights for artwork and photos. Original artwork returned at job's completion. Pays 14¢/word for stories/articles. Pays $600 for color cover illustration; $50-400 for color inside; $50-250 (2-color). Pays $25 for color transparencies accompanying articles; $500 for cover photos. Sample copy free with 8×10 SAE and 4 first-class stamps. Writer's/illustrator's guidelines free with SASE.

Tips: "Ask for our themes first. They are set yearly in the fall. Also, we are looking for articles about real children involved in environment, peace or similar activities. We have added a 2-page story, about 600 words, for beginning readers. Become familiar with *Pockets* before submitting. So much of what we receive is not appropriate for our publication."

POWER AND LIGHT, Children's Ministries, 6401 The Paseo, Kansas City MO 64131. (816)333-7000. Fax: (816)333-4439. E-mail: mhammer@nazarene.org. Website: http://www.nazarene.org. **Editor:** Beula Postlewait. **Associate Editor:** Melissa Hammer. Weekly story paper. "*Power and Light* is a leisure-reading piece for fifth and sixth graders. It is published weekly by the Department of Children's Ministries of the Church of the Nazarene. The major purposes of *Power and Light* are to provide a leisure-reading piece which will build Christian behavior and values; provide reinforcement for Biblical concepts taught in the Sunday School curriculum. The focus of the reinforcement will be life-related, with some historical appreciation. *Power and Light*'s target audience is children ages 11-12 in grades 5 and 6."

Fiction: Middle readers, young adults: adventure, contemporary, humorous, multicultural, preteen issues, problem solving, religious. "Avoid fantasy, science fiction, abnormally mature or precocious children, personification of animals. Also avoid extensive cultural or holiday references, especially those with a distinctly American frame of reference. Our paper has an international audience. We need stories involving multicultural preteens in realistic settings dealing with realistic problems with God's help." Average word length: 500-700. Byline given.

Nonfiction: Middle readers, young adults: archaeological religions, games/puzzles, how-to, interview/profile, problem-solving, multicultural, religion, social issues, travel. Multicultural needs include: ethnics and cultures—other world areas especially English-speaking.

How to Contact/Writers: Send complete ms. Reports on queries/mss in 2 months. Publishes ms 2 years after acceptance.

Illustration: Buys 1 illustration/issue; 14 illustrations/year. *Power and Light* publishes a wide variety of artistic styles, i.e., cartoon, realistic, montage, etc., but whatever the style, artwork must appeal to 11- to 12-year-old children. Illustrations only: Query; send résumé, promo sheet and portfolio. Reports back only if interested. Credit line given.

Photography: Buys "b&w archaeological/Biblical for inside use and color preteen/contemporary/action for cover use."

Terms: Pays on publication. "Payment is made approximately one year before the date of issue." Buys multiple use rights for mss. Purchases all rights for artwork and first/one-time rights for photographs. Pays 5¢/word for stories/articles. Pays illustrators $40 for b&w, $75 for color cover; $40 for b&w, $50-75 for color inside. Photographers paid per photo (range: $35-45; $200 maximum for cover color photo). Writer's/illustrator's guidelines for SASE.

Tips: Writers: "Themes and outcomes should conform to the theology and practices of the Church of the Nazarene, Evangelical Friends, Free Methodist, Wesleyan and other Bible-believing Evangelical churches." We look for bright, colorful illustrations; concise, short articles and stories. Keep it realistic and contemporary. Request guidelines first!" (See listing for *Discoveries*.)

‡RACING FOR KIDS, Griggs Publishing Company Inc., P.O. Box 588, Concord NC 28026. (704)455-5111. Fax: (704)455-2227. **Editor:** Gary McCredie. Monthly magazine. Estab. 1990. Circ. 17,000. Publication caters to kids ages 8-12 ;nterested in racing.

Fiction: Middle readers, young adults: sports (motor sports).

Nonfiction: Young readers: auto racing, sports. Middle readers and young adults: sports (motor sports). Multicultural needs include: sensitivity to minorities in racing—women and African-Americans; with foreign drivers, tell a little about their home country. Buys 12-20 mss/year. Average word length: 400-1,200. Byline given.

How to Contact/Writers: Nonfiction: Query. Reports on queries in 2-4 weeks only if interested. Publishes ms 6-12 months after acceptance.

Illustration: Works on assignment only. Reviews ms/illustration packages from artists. Query. Contact: Gary McCredie, editor. Illustrations only: Query with samples and tearsheets. Contact: Bob Vlasich, art director.

Reports in 2-4 weeks. Samples not returned. Originals returned at job's completion if requested. Credit line given.
Terms: Pays on publication. Buys exclusive magazine rights for mss. Pays $50-150 for stories; $50-150 for articles. Additional payment for photos that accompany article ($10-125).
Tips: "Know the subject matter, study publication. All stories are racing-related. We like stories about NASCAR, NHRA and Monster Truck drivers. No fiction please."

R-A-D-A-R, Standard Publishing, 8121 Hamilton Ave., Cincinnati OH 45231. (513)931-4050. **Editor:** Elaina Meyers. Weekly magazine. Circ. 80,000. *R-A-D-A-R* is a weekly take-home paper for boys and girls who are in grades 3 and 4. "Our goal is to reach these children with the truth of God's Word, and to help them make it the guide of their lives. Most of our features, including our stories, correlate with the Sunday school lesson themes. Send SASE for a quarterly theme list and sample copies of *R-A-D-A-R*."
Fiction: Young readers, middle readers: adventure, animal, humorous, nature/environment, sports, suspense/mystery, travel. Does not want to see fantasy or science fiction. Buys 52 mss/year. Average word length: 400-1,000. Byline given.
Nonfiction: Young readers, middle readers: animal, arts/crafts, games/puzzles, health, how-to, humorous, nature/environment, science, social issues. Buys 50 mss/year. Average word length: 400-500. Byline given.
Poetry: Reviews poetry. Maximum length: 16 lines.
How to Contact/Writers: Fiction/nonfiction: Send complete ms. Reports on mss in 2-3 weeks. Will consider simultaneous submissions (but prefers not to). "No queries or manuscript submissions via fax, please."
Illustration: Buys 2-3 illustrations/issue; 156 illustrations/year. Works on assignment only. Illustrations only: Send résumé, tearsheets or promo sheets; samples of art can be photocopied. Reports in 2-3 weeks. Samples returned with SASE; samples filed. Credit line given. Send SASE for artists' guidelines.
Terms: Pays on acceptance. Buys first rights, one-time rights, second serial, first North American rights for mss. Purchases all rights for artwork. Originals not returned at job's completion. Pays 3-7¢/word for unsolicited articles. Contributor copies given not as payment, but all contributors receive copies of their art/articles. Pays $150 for color (cover); $70-100 for color (inside). Sample copy and writer's guidelines free with business SASE and 1 first-class stamp.
Tips: "Write about current topics, issues that elementary-age children are dealing with. Keep illustrations/photos current. Children are growing up much more quickly these days than ever before. This is seen in illustrations and stories. Send an SASE for sample copies, guidelines, and theme sheet. Be familiar with the publication for which you wish to write." (See listing for *LiveWire* and *Straight*.)

RANGER RICK, National Wildlife Federation, 8925 Leesburg Pike, Vienna VA 22184. (703)790-4000. Website: http://www.nwf.org. **Editor:** Gerald Bishop. **Design Director:** Donna Miller. Monthly magazine. Circ. 650,000. "Our audience ranges from ages 7 to 12, though we aim the reading level of most material at 9-year-olds or fourth graders."
Fiction: Middle readers: animal (wildlife), fantasy, humorous, science fiction. Buys 3-4 mss/year. Average word length: 900. Byline given.
Nonfiction: Middle readers: animal (wildlife), conservation, humorous, nature/environment, outdoor adventure, science fiction, travel. Buys 15-20 mss/year. Average word length: 900. Byline given.
How to Contact/Writers: Fiction: Send complete ms. Nonfiction: Query with published clips. Reports on queries/mss in 6 weeks.
Illustration: Buys 5-7 illustrations/issue. Preferred theme: nature, wildlife. Works on assignment only. Illustrations only: Send résumé, tearsheets. Reports on art samples in 2 months.
Terms: Pays on acceptance. Buys exclusive first-time worldwide rights and non-exclusive worldwide rights thereafter to reprint, transmit, and distribute the work in any form or medium. Original artwork returned at job's completion. Pays up to $600 for full-length of best quality. For illustrations, buys one-time rights. Pays $150-250 for b&w; $250-1,200 for color (inside, per page) illustration. Sample copies for $2. Writer's guidelines for SASE.
Tips: "Fiction and nonfiction articles may be written on any aspect of wildlife, nature, outdoor adventure and discovery, domestic animals with a 'wild' connection (such as domestic pigs and wild boars), science, conservation or related subjects. To find out what subjects have been covered recently, consult our cumulative index on our website and the *Children's Magazine Guide*, which is available in many libraries. The National Wildlife Federation (NWF) discourages the keeping of wildlife as pets, so the keeping of such pets should not be featured in your copy. Avoid stereotyping of any group. For instance, girls can enjoy nature and the outdoors as much as boys can, and mothers can be just as knowledgeable as fathers. The only way you can write successfully for *Ranger Rick* is to know the kinds of subjects and approaches we like. And the only way you can do that is to read the magazine. Recent issues can be found in most libraries or are available from our office for $2 a copy."

REACT MAGAZINE, The magazine that raises voices, Parade Publications, 711 Third Ave., New York NY 10017. (212)450-0900. Fax: (212)450-0978. **Editor:** Lee Kravitz. **Art Director:** Linda Rubes. **Photo Editor:** Nancy Iacoi. Weekly magazine. Estab. 1995. Circ. 4.6 million. 100% publication aimed at teen market.
Nonfiction: Young adult: animal, entertainment, games/puzzles, health, hobbies, interview/profile, nature/environment, news, science, social issues, sports. Average word length: 250-600. Byline given.
How to Contact/Writers: Query with published clips.

Illustration: Works on assignment only. Illustration only: arrange portfolio review. Contact: Lynda Rubes, art director. Credit given.

Photography: Query with résumé or credits. Arrange portfolio review. Reports only if interested.

Terms: Pays on acceptance. Buys all rights for mss, artwork and photographs. Pays writers by the project. Additional payment for photos accompanying articles. Pays photographers by the project. Writer's guidelines and sample issue for SAE and 80¢ postage.

Tips: "Do not submit work. Query with clips only."

‡READ, Weekly Reader Corporation, 200 First Stamford Place, P.O. Box 120023, Stamford CT 06912-0023. (203)705-3406. Fax: (203)705-1661. E-mail: edread@weeklyreader.com. Website: http://www.weeklyreader.com. **Editor:** Kate Davis. **Art Director:** Jeffrey Talbot. **Photo Editor:** Julie Wolf-Alissi. Magazine published 18 times during the school year. Estab. 1951. Circ. 1 million. Language arts periodical for use in classrooms for students grades 6-10.

Fiction: Young adults: adaptations of classics, adventure, animal, contemporary, fantasy, folktale, health, history, humorous, multicultural, nature/environment, problem-solving, romance, science fiction, sports, suspense/mystery. Wants plays, short stories and narratives to be used for classroom discussions. Average word length: 1,000-3,000.

Nonfiction: Young adults: animal, biography, careers, concept, games/puzzles, history, humorous, interview/profile, nature/environment, problem solving, science, social issues, sports, travel. Does not want to see religious, sexual or overly controversial material.

How to Contact/Writers: Send complete ms. Reports in 4-6 weeks.

Illustration: Buys 2-3 illustrations/issue; 40-45/year. Works on assignment only. Reviews ms/illustration packages from artists. Query with samples; send promo sheets, portfolio, slides or tearsheets. Reports back only if interested. Samples returned with SASE; samples sometimes filed.

Photography: Needs a large range of subject matter from news to historical. Uses 35mm, $2\frac{1}{4} \times 2\frac{1}{4}$, 4×5 and 8×10 transparencies.

Terms: Pays on publication. Rights purchased varies. Pays $300-500 for stories.

Tips: "We especially like plot twists and surprise endings. Plays should have at least eight speaking parts for classroom reading. Avoid formula plots, trite themes, underage material, stilted or profane language, and sexual suggestion."

SCHOLASTIC INC., 555 Broadway, New York NY 10012-3999. See listings for *Dynamath*, *Junior Scholastic*, *Scholastic Math Magazine*, *Science World* and *Superscience Blue*. Scholastic publishes a number of other children's magazines. Contact them for more information.

SCHOLASTIC MATH MAGAZINE, Scholastic Inc., 555 Broadway, New York NY 10012-3999. (212)343-6100. Fax: (212)343-6333. E-mail: mathmag@scholastic.com. **Editor:** Jack Silbert. **Art Director:** Joan Michael. Magazine published 14 times/year, September-May. Estab. 1980. Circ. 230,000. "We are a math magazine for seventh, eighth and ninth-grade classrooms. We present math in current, relevant, high-interest (to teens) topics. Math skills we focus on include whole number, fraction and decimal computation, percentages, ratios, proportions, geometry."

Nonfiction: Young adults: animal, arts/crafts, careers, games/puzzles, health, history, hobbies, how-to, humorous, interview/profile, math, multicultural, nature/environment, problem solving, science, sports. No fiction. Does not want to see "anything dealing with *very* controversial issues—e.g., teenage pregnancy, etc. Multicultural submissions must feature a math application, such as math games from around the world." Buys 20 mss/year. Byline given.

How to Contact/Writers: Query. Reports on queries/mss in 6 weeks. Will consider simultaneous submissions. Please include clips of previously published writing for teenagers.

Illustration: Buys 3 illustrations/issue; 42 illustrations/year. Prefers to review "humorous, young adult sophistication" types of art. Works on assignment only. Reviews ms/illustration packages from artists. Query first. Illustrations only: Query with samples; submit portfolio for review. Reports back only if interested. Credit line given.

Terms: Pays on publication. Buys all rights for mss. Original artwork returned at job's completion. Pays $25 for puzzles and riddles; maximum of $300 for stories/articles. Photographers are paid by the project. Samples copies are free for $8\frac{1}{2} \times 11$ SASE.

Tips: "For our magazine, stories dealing with math concepts and applications in the real world are sought. We are a unique magazine with extremely specific needs. Most of the submissions we receive are wildly inappropriate because the freelancer who has sent the submission has never seen the magazine. Writers should get a copy of the magazine first, and then send a query rather than a complete article." (See listings for *Dynamath*, *Junior Scholastic*, *Science World* and *Superscience Blue*.)

SCHOOL MATES, USCF's Magazine for Beginning Chess Players, United States Chess Federation, 186 Rt. 9W, New Windsor NY 12553. (914)562-8350. Fax: (914)561-CHES. **Editor:** Beatrice Marivello. **Graphic Designer:** Tammy Steinman. Bimonthly magazine. Estab. 1987. Circ. 30,000. Magazine for beginning chess players. Offers instructional articles, features on famous players, scholastic chess coverage, games, puzzles, occasional fiction, listing of chess tournaments.

Fiction: Young readers, middle readers, young adults: chess. Middle readers: humorous (chess-related). Average word length: 500-2,500 words.

Nonfiction: Young readers, middle readers, young adults: games/puzzles, chess. Middle readers, young adults: interview/profile (chess-related). "No *Mad Magazine* type humor. No sex, no drugs, no alcohol, no tobacco. No stereotypes. We want to see chess presented as a wholesome, non-nerdy activity that's fun for all. Good sportsmanship, fair play, and 'thinking ahead' are extremely desirable in chess articles. Also, celebrities who play chess."

Poetry: Infrequently published. Must be chess related.

How to Contact/Writers: Send complete ms. Reports on queries/mss in 5 weeks.

Illustration: Buys 10-25 illustrations/year. Prefers b&w and ink; cartoons OK. Illustration only: Query first. Reports back only if interested. Credit line sometimes given. "Typically, a cover is credited while an illustration inside gets only the artist's signature in the work itself."

Photography: Purchases photos from freelancers. Wants "action shots of chess games (at tournament competitions), well-done portraits of popular chess players."

Terms: Pays on publication. Buys one-time rights for mss, artwork and photos. For stories/articles, pays $20-100. Pays illustrators $50-75 for b&w cover; $20-50 for b&w inside. Pays photographers per photo (range: $25-75). Sample copies free for 9×12 SAE and 2 first-class stamps. Writer's guidelines free on request.

Tips: Writers: "Lively prose that grabs and sustains kids' attention is desirable. Don't talk down to kids or over their heads. Don't be overly 'cute.' " Illustration/photography: "Whimsical shots are often desirable."

SCIENCE WEEKLY, Science Weekly Inc., P.O. Box 70638, Chevy Chase MD 20813. (301)680-8804. Fax: (301)680-9240. **Editor:** Deborah Lazar. Magazine published 16 times/year. Estab. 1984. Circ. 200,000.

● *Science Weekly* uses freelance writers to develop and write an entire issue on a single science topic. Send résumé only, not submissions. Authors must be within the greater DC, Virginia, Maryland area. *Science Weekly* works on assignment only.

Nonfiction: Young readers, middle readers, (K-8th grade): science/math education, education, problem-solving.

Terms: Pays on publication. Prefers people with education, science and children's writing background.

SCIENCE WORLD, Scholastic Inc., 555 Broadway, New York NY 10012-3999. (212)343-6456. Fax: (212)343-6333. E-mail: scienceworld@scholastic.com. **Articles Editor:** Rex Roberts. **Art Director:** Susan Kass. **Photo Editor**: Daniella Jo Nilva. Magazine published biweekly during the school year. Estab. 1959. Circ. 350,000. Publishes articles in Life Science/Health, Physical Science/Technology, Earth Science/Environment/Astronomy for students in grades 7-10. The goal is to make science relevant for teens.

● *Science World* publishes a separate teacher's edition with lesson plans and skills pages to accompany feature articles.

Nonfiction: Young adults/teens: animal, concept, geography, health, nature/environment, science. Multicultural needs include: minority scientists as role models. Does not want to see stories without a clear news hook. Buys 20 mss/year. Average word length: 500-1,000. Byline sometimes given.

How to Contact/Writers: Nonfiction: Query with published clips. Reports on queries/mss in 2 weeks. Publishes ms 2 months after acceptance.

Illustration: Buys 2 illustrations/issue; 28 illustrations/year. Works on assignment only. Illustration only: Query with samples, tearsheets. Contact: Susan Kass, art director. Reports back only if interested. Samples returned with SASE; samples filed "if we use them." Credit line sometimes given.

Photography: Model/property releases required; captions required including background information. Provide résumé, business card, promotional literature or tearsheets to be kept on file. Reports back only if interested.

Terms: Pays on acceptance. Buys all right for mss/artwork. Originals returned to artist at job's completion. For stories/articles, pays $200. Pays photographers per photo. Sample copies free for 9×12 SAE and 2 first-class stamps. Writer's guidelines for SASE.

Tips: See listings for *Dynamath, Junior Scholastic, Scholastic Math Magazine* and *Superscience Blue.*

SCIENCELAND, To Nurture Scientific Thinking, Scienceland Inc., 501 Fifth Ave., #2108, New York NY 10017-6165. (212)490-2180. Fax: (212)490-2187. **Editor/Art Director:** Al Matano. Magazine published 8 times/year. Estab. 1977. Circ. 16,000. This is "a content reading picture-book for the preschool youngster being read to, the first-grader learning to read and for the second and third grader beginning to read independently."

Nonfiction: Picture-oriented material, young readers: animal, art/crafts, biography, careers, cooking, education, games/puzzles, health, history, how-to, nature/environment, problem-solving. Does not want to see unillustrated material; all material must be illustrated in full color.

How to Contact/Writers: *Must* be picture or full-color illustrated stories.

Illustration: Uses color artwork only. Prefers to review "detailed, realistic, full color art. No abstracts or fantasy." Reviews captioned/illustration packages from artists. "Query first." Illustrations only: Send unsolicited art by mail; provide résumé, promotional literature or tearsheets to be kept on file. Reports back in 3-4 weeks. "Exclusively contracted original artwork retained at our option for exhibits, etc. Others returned at job's completion."

Photography: Wants to see "physical and natural science photos with children in scenes whenever possible."

Model/property release and photo captions required where applicable. Uses 35mm transparencies. Photographer should submit portfolio for review; provide résumé, promotional literature or tearsheets to be kept on file.

Terms: Pays on publication. Buys nonexclusive rights to artwork and photos. Payment for captioned/illustration packages: $50-500 and up. Payment for illustrations: $25-300 and up for color cover; $25-300 and up for color inside. Photographers paid by the project. Sample copy free with 9×12 SASE.

Tips: "Must be top notch illustrator or photographer. No amateurs."

SEVENTEEN MAGAZINE, K-III Magazines, 850 Third Ave., New York NY 10022. (212)407-9700. **Editor-in-Chief:** Caroline Miller. **Fiction Editor:** Susan Brenna. **Senior Editor:** Heidi Parker. **Art Director:** Florence Sicard. Monthly magazine. Estab. 1944. Circ. 2 million. "General interest magazine for teenage girls."

Fiction: Young adults: animal, contemporary, fantasy, folktales, health, history, humorous, religious, romance, science fiction, sports, spy/mystery/adventure. "We consider all good literary short fiction." Buys 12-20 mss/year. Average word length: 800-2,500. Byline given.

Nonfiction: Young adults: animal, fashion, careers, health, hobbies, how-to, humorous, interview/profile, multicultural, religion, social issues, sports. Buys 150 mss/year. Word length: Varies from 800-1,000 words for short features and monthly columns to 800-2,500 words for major articles. Byline given.

How to Contact/Writers: Fiction: Send complete ms. Nonfiction: Query with published clips or send complete ms. "Do not call." Reports on queries/mss in 6-12 weeks. Will consider simultaneous submissions.

Terms: Pays on acceptance. Writer's guidelines available for SASE.

‡SHADOW MAGAZINE, Between Parallels, Shadow Publications, P.O. Box 5464, Santa Rosa CA 95402. E-mail: brianwts@aol.com. Website: http://www.metro.net/shadow/. **Articles Editor:** Brian P. Murphy. Quarterly magazine. Estab. 1995. Circ. 3,000. "A publication aimed at providing well-written and inspiring fiction to teens."

Fiction: Young adults/teens: adventure, animal, contemporary, fantasy, folktales, health, history, humorous, multicultural, nature/environment, problem-solving, religious, romance, science fiction, sports, suspense/mystery. Does not want to see poorly thought-out work. Buys 15-20 mss/year. Average word length: 1,000-5,000. Byline given.

Nonfiction: Young adults/teens: animal, arts/crafts, biography, careers, concept, cooking, fashion, games/puzzles, geography, health, history, hobbies, how-to, humorous, interview/profile, math, multicultural, nature/environment, problem-solving, religion, science, social issues, sports, travel. Does not want to see nonfiction written for people younger than teens. Buys 3-5 mss/year. Average word length: 500-3,000. Byline given.

How to Contact/Writers: Fiction/nonfiction: Send complete ms. Reports on queries in 3-5 weeks; mss in 1-2 months. Publishes ms 2 months after acceptance. Will consider simultaneous submissions, electronic submissions via disk or modem, previously published work.

Illustration: Uses b&w artwork only. Works on assignment only. Reviews ms/illustration packages from artists. Send ms with dummy. Contact: Brian P. Murphy, editor. Illustrations only: Query with samples; send résumé. Contact: Brian P. Murphy, editor. Reports in 4-6 weeks. Samples kept on file.

Terms: Pays on publication. Buys one-time rights for mss. Buys exclusive rights for artwork. Pays in sample copies. Pays illustrators copies. Sample copies for $2.50. Writer's guidelines for SASE.

Tips: "We're looking for exciting fiction that will engage the reader. The characters don't have to be teens, but the stories should be of particular interest to teens."

‡SHARING THE VICTORY, Fellowship of Christian Athletes, 8701 Leeds, Kansas City MO 64129. (816)921-0909. Fax: (816)921-8755. **Articles/Photo Editor:** John Dodderidge. **Art Director:** Frank Grey. Monthly magazine. Estab. 1982. Circ. 60,000. "Purpose is to present to coaches and athletes, and all whom they influence, the challenge and adventure of receiving Jesus Christ as Savior and Lord."

Nonfiction: Young adults/teens: interview/profile, sports. Buys 15-20 mss/year. Average word length: 500-1,000. Byline given.

Poetry: Reviews poetry. Maximum length: 50-75 words.

How to Contact/Writers: Nonfiction: Query with published clips. Reports in 3 weeks. Publishes ms 3 months after acceptance. Will consider simultaneous submissions, electronic submissions via disk or modem and previously published work.

Photography: Purchases photos separately. Looking for photos of sports action. Uses color, b&w prints and 35mm transparencies.

Terms: Pays on publication. Buys first rights and second serial (reprint) rights. Pays $50-200 for assigned and unsolicited articles. Photographers paid per photo (range: $50-100). Sample copies for 9×12 SASE and $1. Writer's/photo guidelines for SASE.

Tips: "Be specific—write short. Take quality photos that are useable." Wants interviews and features. Interested in colorful sports photos.

SHOFAR, 43 Northcote Dr., Melville NY 11747. (516)643-4598. **Managing Editor:** Gerald H. Grayson. Magazine published monthly October through May—double issues December/January and April/May. Circ. 17,000. For Jewish children ages 9-13.

Fiction: Middle readers: cartoons, contemporary, humorous, poetry, religious, sports. All material must be on a

Jewish theme. Buys 10-20 mss/year. Average word length: 500-700. Byline given.
Nonfiction: Middle readers: history, humorous, interview/profile, puzzles, religious. Buys 10-20 mss/year. Average word length: 600-1,000. Byline given.
How to Contact/Writers: Fiction/nonfiction: Send complete ms (preferred) with SASE. Queries welcome. Publishes special holiday issues. Submit holiday theme pieces at least 4 months in advance. Reports on queries/ mss in 1 month. Will consider simultaneous submissions.
Illustration: Buys 3-4 illustrations/issue; buys 15-20 illustrations/year. Works on assignment only. Reviews ms/ illustration packages from artists. Query first. Illustrations only: Send tearsheets. Works on assignment only. Reports on art samples only if interested. Original artwork returned at job's completion.
Terms: Buys first North American serial rights or first serial rights for mss and artwork. Pays on publication. Pays 10¢/word plus 5 contributor's copies. Photos purchased with mss at additional fees. Pays $25-100/b&w cover illustration; $50-150/color (cover). Sample copy free with 9×12 SAE and 98¢ postage. Free writer's/ illustrator's guidelines.
Tips: Submit holiday material at least 4 months in advance.

SKIPPING STONES, A Multicultural Children's Magazine, P.O. Box 3939, Eugene OR 97403. (541)342-4956. Website: http://www.nonviolence.org/~nvweb/skipping/. **Articles/Photo/Fiction Editor:** Arun N. Toké. Bimonthly magazine. Estab. 1988. Circ. 3,000. "*Skipping Stones* is a multicultural, nonprofit children's magazine designed to encourage cooperation, creativity and celebration of cultural and environmental richness. We encourage submissions by minorities and under-represented populations."
  • Send for *Skipping Stones* guidelines and theme list for detailed descriptions of the topics they're looking for.
Fiction: Middle readers, young adult/teens: animal, contemporary, humorous. All levels: folktales, multicultural, nature/environment. Multicultural needs include: bilingual or multilingual pieces; use of words from other languages; settings in other countries, cultures or multi-ethnic communities.
Nonfiction: All levels: animal, biography, cooking, games/puzzles, history, humorous, interview/profile, multicultural, nature/environment, creative problem-solving, religion and cultural celebrations, sports, travel, multicultural and environmental awareness. Does not want to see preaching or abusive language; no poems by authors over 18 years old; no suspense or romance stories for the sake of the same. Average word length: 500-750. Byline given.
How to Contact/Writers: Fiction: Query. Nonfiction: Send complete ms. Reports on queries in 1 month; mss in 4 months. Will consider simultaneous submissions; reviews artwork for future assignments. Please include your name on each page.
Illustration: Prefers b&w drawings especially by young adults. Will consider all illustration packages. Ms/ illustration packages: Query; submit complete ms with final art; submit tearsheets. Reports back in 4 months. Credit line given.
Photography: Black & white photos preferred, but color photos will be considered. Children 7-15, international, nature, celebration.
Terms: Pays on publication. Buys first or reprint rights for mss and artwork; reprint rights for photographs. Pays in copies for authors, photographers and illustrators. Sample copies for $5 with SAE and 4 first-class stamps. Writer's/illustrator's guidelines for 4×9 SASE.
Tips: "We want material meant for children and young adults/teenagers with multicultural or environmental awareness themes. Think, live and write as if you were a child. Let the 'inner child' within you speak out— naturally, uninhibited." Wants "material that gives insight on cultural celebrations, lifestyle, custom and tradition, glimpse of daily life in other countries and cultures. Photos, songs, artwork are most welcome if they illustrate/ highlight the points. Translations are welcome if your submission is in a language other than English. In 1998, our themes will include cultural celebrations, living abroad, challenging disability, rewards and punishments, hospitality customs of various cultures, modern technology and its impact on human societies, cross-cultural communications, African, Asian and Latin American cultures, indigenous architecture of your region or country, photo essays, creative problem solving and changing times, changing families."

SOCCER JR., The Soccer Magazine for Kids, Triplepoint Inc., 27 Unquowa Rd., Fairfield CT 06430. (203)259-5766. Fax: (203)256-1119. E-mail: soccerjrol@aol.com. **Articles/Fiction Editor:** Jill Schoff. Bimonthly magazine. Estab. 1992. Circ. 120,000. *Soccer Jr.* is for soccer players 8-16 years old. "The editorial focus of *Soccer Jr.* is on the fun and challenge of the sport. Every issue contains star interviews, how-to tips, lively graphics, action photos, comics, games, puzzles and contests. Fair play and teamwork are emphasized in a format that provides an off-the-field way for kids to enjoy the sport."
Fiction: Middle readers, young adults/teens: sports (soccer). Does not want to see "cute," preachy or "moralizing" stories. Buys 3-4 mss/year. Average word length: 1,000-2,000. Byline given.
Nonfiction: Young readers, middle readers, young adults/teens: sports (soccer). Buys 10-12 mss/year.
How to Contact/Writers: Fiction/nonfiction: Send complete ms. Reports on mss in 4-6 weeks. Publishes ms 3-12 months after acceptance. Will consider simultaneous submissions.
Illustration: Buys 2 illustrations/issue; 20 illustrations/year. Uses color artwork only. Works on assignment only. Illustrations only: Send samples to be filed. Samples not returned; samples kept on file. "We have a small pool

of artists we work from, but look for new freelancers occasionally, and accept samples for consideration." Credit line given.

Terms: Pays on acceptance. Buys first rights for mss. Pays $50-600 for stories and articles. Pays illustrators $250-300 for color cover; $50-200 for b&w, $75-300 for color inside. Pays photographers per photo (range: $75-125). Sample copies for 9×12 SAE and 5 first-class stamps.

Tips: "We ask all potential writers to understand *Soccer Jr.*'s voice. We write to kids, not to adults. We request a query for any feature ideas, but any fiction pieces can be sent complete. All submissions, unless specifically requested, are on a speculative basis. Please indicate if a manuscript has been submitted elsewhere or previously published. Please give us a brief personal bio, including your involvement in soccer, if any, and a listing of any work you've had published. We prefer manuscripts in Microsoft Word, along with an attached hard copy." The magazine also accepts stories written by children.

SPIDER, The Magazine for Children, Carus Publishing Company, P.O. Box 300, Peru IL 61354. **Editor-in-Chief:** Marianne Carus. **Associate Editor:** Laura Tillotson. **Art Director**: Tony Jacobson. Monthly magazine. Estab. 1994. Circ. 85,000. *Spider* publishes high-quality literature for beginning readers, primarily ages 6-9.

Fiction: Young readers: adventure, animal, contemporary, fantasy, folktales, history, humorous, multicultural, nature/environment, problem-solving, science fiction, sports, suspense/mystery. "Authentic, well-researched stories from all cultures are welcome. We would like to see more multicultural material. No didactic, religious, or violent stories, or anything that talks down to children." Average word length: 300-1,000. Byline given.

Nonfiction: Young readers: animal, arts/crafts, cooking, games/puzzles, geography, history, math, multicultural, nature/environment, problem-solving, science. "Well-researched articles on all cultures are welcome. Would like to see more games, puzzles and activities, especially ones adaptable to *Spider*'s takeout pages. No encyclopedic or overtly educational articles." Average word length: 300-800. Byline given.

Poetry: Serious, humorous, nonsense rhymes. Maximum length: 20 lines.

How to Contact/Writers: Fiction/nonfiction: Send complete ms. Reports on mss in 3 months. Publishes ms 1-2 years after acceptance. Will consider simultaneous submissions and previously published work.

Illustration: Buys 20 illustrations/issue; 240 illustrations/year. Uses color artwork only. "Any medium—preferably one that can wrap on a laser scanner—no larger than 20×24. We use more realism than cartoon-style art." Works on assignment only. Reviews ms/illustration packages from artists. Submit ms with rough sketches. Illustrations only: Send promo sheet and tearsheets. Reports in 6 weeks. Samples returned with SASE; samples filed. Credit line given.

Photography: Buys photos from freelancers. Buys photos with accompanying ms only. Model/property releases required; captions required. Uses 35mm or 2¼×2¼ transparencies. Send unsolicited photos by mail; provide résumé and tearsheets. Reports in 6 weeks.

Terms: Pays on publication for text; within 45 days from acceptance for art. Buys first, one-time or reprint rights for mss. Buys first and promotional rights for artwork; one-time rights for photographs. Original artwork returned at job's completion. Pays 25¢/word for stories/articles. Authors also receive 2 complimentary copies of the issue in which work appears. Additional payment for ms/illustration packages and for photos accompanying articles. Pays illustrators $750 for color cover; $200-300 for color inside. Pays photographers per photo (range: $25-75). Sample copies for $4. Writer's/illustrator's guidelines for SASE.

Tips: Writers: "Read back issues before submitting." (See listings for *Babybug*, *Cricket*, and *Ladybug*.)

STANDARD PUBLISHING, 8121 Hamilton Ave., Cincinnati OH 45231. See listings for *R-A-D-A-R*, *LiveWire* and *Straight*.

STORY FRIENDS, Mennonite Publishing House, 616 Walnut Ave., Scottdale PA 15683. (412)887-8500. Fax: (412)887-3111. E-mail: rstutz%mph@mcimail.com. **Editor:** Rose Mary Stutzman. **Art Director:** Jim Butti. Magazine published monthly in weekly issues. Estab. 1905. Circ. 7,000. Story paper that reinforces Christian values for children ages 4-9.

Fiction: Picture-oriented material: contemporary, humorous, multicultural, nature/environment, problem-solving, religious, relationships. Multicultural needs include fiction or nonfiction pieces which help children be aware of cultural diversity and celebrate differences while recognizing similarities. Buys 45 mss/year. Average word length: 300-800. Byline given.

Nonfiction: Picture-oriented: animal, humorous, interview/profile, multicultural, nature/environment. Buys 10 mss/year. Average word length: 300-800. Byline given.

Poetry: "I like variety—some long story poems and some four-lines."

How to Contact/Writers: Fiction/nonfiction: Send complete ms. Reports on mss in 5-6 weeks. Will consider simultaneous submissions.

Illustration: Works on assignment only. Send tearsheets with SASE. Reports in 2 months. Samples returned with SASE; samples filed. Credit line given.

Photography: Occasionally buys photos from freelancers. Wants photos of children ages 4-8.

Terms: Pays on acceptance. Buys one-time rights or reprint rights for mss and artwork. Original artwork returned at job's completion. Pays 3-5¢/word for stories and articles. Pays $20-30 for b&w cover; $50 for color cover; $20-30 for b&w inside; $50 for color inside. Writer's guidelines free with SAE and 2 first-class stamps.

Tips: "Become immersed in high quality children's literature."

STRAIGHT, Standard Publishing, 8121 Hamilton Ave., Cincinnati OH 45231. (513)931-4050. Fax: (513)931-0950. **Articles/Fiction Editor:** Heather Wallace. Magazine published quarterly in weekly parts. Circ. 40,000. *Straight* is a magazine designed for today's Christian teenagers.

Fiction: Young adults/teens: contemporary, health, humorous, problem solving, religious, sports. Does not want to see science fiction, fantasy, historical. "All should have religious perspective." Buys 100-115 mss/year. Average word length: 1,100-1,500. Byline given.

Nonfiction: Young adults/teens: health, hobbies, humorous, interview/profile, problem-solving, religion, social issues, sports. Does not want to see devotionals. Buys 24-30 mss/year. Average word length: 500-1,000. Byline given.

Poetry: Reviews poetry from teenagers only.

How to Contact/Writers: Fiction/nonfiction: Query or send complete ms. Reports on queries in 1-2 weeks; mss in 1-2 months. Will consider simultaneous submissions.

Illustration: Buys 40-45 illustrations/year. Uses color artwork only. Preferred theme or style: Realistic, cartoon (full-color only). Works on assignment only. Reviews ms/illustration packages from artists. Query first. Illustrations only: Submit promo sheets or tearsheets. Samples kept on file. Reports back only if interested. Credit line given.

Photography: Buys photos from freelancers. Looking for photos of contemporary, modestly dressed teenagers. Model/property release required. Uses 35mm transparencies. Photographer should send unsolicited photos by mail.

Terms: Pays on acceptance. Buys first rights and second serial (reprint rights) for mss. Buys full rights for artwork; one-time rights for photos. Pays 5-7¢ per word for stories/articles. Pays illustrators $150-325/color inside. Pays photographers per photo (range: $75-125). Sample copy free with business SASE. Writer's/illustrator's guidelines for business SASE.

Tips: "Remember we are a publication for Christian teenagers. Each fiction or nonfiction piece should address modern-day issues from a religious perspective. We are trying to become more racially diverse. Writers, illustrators and photographers should keep this in mind and submit more material with African-Americans, Hispanics, Asian-Americans, etc. as the focus. The main characters of all pieces should be contemporary teens who cope with modern-day problems using Christian principles. Stories should be uplifting, positive and character-building, but not preachy. Conflicts must be resolved realistically, with thought-provoking and honest endings. Accepted length is 1,100 to 1,500 words. Nonfiction is accepted. We use articles on current issues from a Christian point of view and humor. Nonfiction pieces should concern topics of interest to teens, including school, family life, recreation, friends, part-time jobs, dating and music." This magazine publishes writing/art/photos by children. (See listings for *LiveWire* and *R-A-D-A-R*.)

STREET TIMES, Outside In, 1236 SW Salmon, Portland OR 97205. (503)223-4121, ext. 31. Fax: (503)223-6837. **Editor:** Deborah Abela Chauvin. Monthly newsletter. Estab. 1987. Circ. 800. Contains "resources, street-life stories, poetry and art—designed as a pre-employment training tool for Portland street youth." 70% of publication aimed at juvenile market.

Fiction: Young adult/teens: adventure, contemporary, fantasy, folktales, history, humorous, multicultural, problem-solving.

Nonfiction: Young adult/teens: arts/crafts, careers, concepts, history, interview/profile, multicultural, problem-solving. Wants experiences of "other street youth or former street youth; difficulties of getting off the street."

Poetry: Reviews poetry.

How to Contact/Writers: Nonfiction: Send complete ms. Reports on queries/mss in 6 months. Will consider simultaneous submissions and previously published work.

Terms: Sample copies free for SASE.

Tips: "Authors should have had some street experience or currently be on the streets. Preferred age of authors 0-23 years."

STUDENT LEADERSHIP JOURNAL, InterVarsity Christian Fellowship, P.O. Box 7895, Madison WI 53707. (608)274-9001, ext. 425. **Editor:** Jeff Yourison. Quarterly magazine. Estab. 1988. Circ. 10,000.

Fiction: Young adults (collegiate): multicultural, religious. Multicultural themes include: Forming campus fellowships that reflect the ethnic makeup of the campus and demonstrating *reconciliation* beyond celebrating difference. "I see too much aimed at young teens. Our age group is 18-30 years old." Buys 4 mss/year. Average word length: 300-1,800. Byline given.

Nonfiction: Young adults: history, interview/profile, multicultural, nature/environment, religion, social issues. Multicultural themes include: Affirming the need for ethnic validation and reconciliation. "We don't affirm all lifestyles—therefore we are promoting multi-ethnicity but not full-orbed multiculturalism. We prefer articles on issues, leadership, spiritual growth, sexual healing, campus ministry, etc." Buys 6-8 mss/year. Average word length: 1,100-2,200. Byline given.

Poetry: Wants to see free verse; lots of good imagery. Maximum length: 18 lines. Limit submissions to 5 poems.

How to Contact/Writers: Fiction/nonfiction: Send complete ms. Reports on queries/mss in 6 months. Publishes ms 1-2 years after acceptance. Accepts IBM-compatible word processing files on diskettes.

Illustration: Buys 5 illustrations/issue; 20 illustrations/year. Uses b&w line art only. Prefers cartoon pen & ink 5×7 or 8×10 stand alone campus/religious humor. Illustrations only: Send promo sheet, portfolio and tearsheets.

Reports only if interested. Samples not returned; samples kept on file. Credit line given.

Photography: Looks for campus shots—all types: single faces, studying, thinking, "mood"—pairs and groups: praying, studying, talking, playing. 18-22 year old subjects or professor-types. Model/property release preferred. Uses color and b&w 5×7 glossy prints; $2\frac{1}{4} \times 2\frac{1}{4}$, 4×5 or 35mm transparencies. Photographers should query with samples; send unsolicited photos by mail; provide business card, promotional literature or tearsheets. "Send photocopies I can keep. I'll call for the print." Reports only if interested.

Terms: Pays on acceptance for ms; on publication for photos and cartoons. Buys first North American serial rights, first rights and reprint rights for ms. Purchases first rights for artwork; one-time rights for photographs. Original work returned at job's completion. Pays $50-75 for stories; $50-125 for articles; and contributor's copies. Pays illustrators $50-100 for b&w cover; $25-75 for b&w inside. Photographers paid per photo (range: $25-50). Sample copies for $3. Writer's guidelines for SASE.

Tips: "Please write and photograph according to the audience. Research the age group and the subculture. Older teens are really sensitive to tokenism and condescension toward their generation. They want to be treated as sophisticated even though they are frequently uninformed and hurting. To reach this audience requires credibility, vulnerability, transparency and confidence!"

SUPERSCIENCE BLUE, Scholastic Inc., 555 Broadway, New York NY 10012-3999. (212)343-6100. **Editor:** Kathy Burkett. **Art Director:** Susan Kass. Monthly (during school year) magazine. Estab. 1989. Circ. 375,000. "News and hands-on science for children in grades 4-6. Designed for use in a class setting; distributed by teacher. Articles make science fun and interesting for a broad audience of children. Issues are theme-based."
  ● *Superscience Blue* is not currently accepting submissions.

Nonfiction: Middle readers: animal, how-to (science experiments), nature/environment, problem-solving, science topics. Does not want to see "general nature stories. Our focus is science with a *news* or *hands-on* slant. To date we have never purchased an unsolicited manuscript. Instead, we assign articles based on clips—and sometimes queries." Average word length: 250-800. Byline sometimes given.

How to Contact/Writers: Nonfiction: Query with published clips. (Most freelance articles are assigned.)

Illustration: Buys 2-3 illustrations/issue; 10-12 illustrations/year. Works on assignment only.Illustrations only: Send résumé and tearsheets. Reports on art samples only if interested. Original artwork returned at job's completion.

Tips: Looks for "news articles and photo essays. Good journalism means always going to *primary* sources—interview scientists in the field, for example, and *quote* them for a more lively article." (See listings for *Dynamath, Junior Scholastic, Scholastic Math Magazine* and *Science World.*)

‡SURPRISES, The Publishing Group, 1200 N. Seventh St., Minneapolis MN 55411. (612)522-1200. Fax: (612)522-1182. E-mail: editor@surprises.com. Website: http://www.surprises.com. **Acquisitions:** Tim Drake. Bimonthly magazine. Estab. 1984. Circ. 41,000. "*Surprises* is an activity-oriented publication for children ages 5-12."

How to Contact/Writers: Nonfiction: Query. Reports on queries in 1 month. Publishes ms 2 months after acceptance. Will consider simultaneous submissions, electronic submission via disk or modem and previously published work.

Illustration: Buys 10-12 illustrations/issue; 60 illustrations/year. Uses color artwork only. Works on assignment only. Reviews ms/illustration packages from artists. Query. Illustrations only: Query with samples; send résumé, promo sheet. Reports in 1 month. Samples returned with SASE. Credit line given.

Photography: Looking for animals, cultural, realistic photos. Model/property release required. Uses color prints; 35mm, $2\frac{1}{4} \times 2\frac{1}{4}$, 4×5, 8×10 transparencies. Query with samples; provide résumé. Reports in 1 month.

Terms: Pays on publication. Buys one-time rights. Original artwork returned at job's completion. Pays $10-200 for articles. Additional payment for ms/illustration packages and for photos accompanying articles. Pays illustrators $50-150 for color cover; $50-100 for color inside. Pays photographers per photo (range: $50-100). Sample copies for $3.95.

Tips: "*Surprises* primarily works with inhouse artists, writers and photogrpahers."

TEEN LIFE, Gospel Publishing House, 1445 Boonville Ave., Springfield MO 65802-1894. (417)862-2781, ext. 4370. Fax: (417)862-6059. E-mail: tbicket@publishing.ag.org. **Articles/Fiction Editor:** Tammy Bicket. **Art Director:** Sonny Carder. Quarterly magazine. Estab. 1920. Circ. 50,000. "Slant articles toward the 15- to 19-year-old teen. We are a Christian publication, so all articles should focus on the Christian's responses to life. Fiction should be realistic, not syrupy nor too graphic. Fiction should have a Christian slant also."

Fiction: Young adults/teens: adventure, contemporary, history, humorous, multicultural, problem-solving, religious, romance, science fiction, sports (all with Christian slant). Also wants fiction based on true stories. Buys 50 mss/year. Average word length 700-1,500. Byline given.

Nonfiction: Young adults/teens: biography, careers, games/puzzles, history, how-to, humorous, interview/profile, multicultural, problem-solving, religion, social issues, sports, "thoughtful treatment of contemporary issues (i.e., racism, preparing for the future); interviews with famous Christians who have noteworthy stories to tell." Multicultural needs include: material on missions. Buys 50 mss/year. "Looking for more articles and fewer stories." Average word length: 1,000. Byline given.

How to Contact/Writers: Fiction/nonfiction: Send complete ms. Do *not* send query letters. Reports on mss in 2-3 months. Will consider simultaneous submissions.

Illustration: Buys 50-100 illustrations/issue, 200 illustrations/year. Uses color artwork only. Prefers to review youth-oriented styles. Art director will assign freelance art. Works on assignment only. Reviews ms/illustration packages from artists. Send portfolio. "We are Mac literate." Illustration only: arrange portfolio review or send promo sheet, slides, client list, tearsheets or on disk (Mac). Illustrations and design: "We are interested in looking at portfolios consisting of illustration and design work that is teen-oriented." Reports in 3-4 weeks. Samples returned with SASE. Originals returned to artist at job's completion. Credit line given.

Photography: Buys photos from freelancers. Wants "teen photos that look spontaneous. Ethnic and urban photos urgently needed." Uses color prints, 35mm, 2¼×2¼, 4×5 transparencies. Send unsolicited photos by mail.

Terms: Pays on acceptance. For mss, buys first North American serial rights, first rights, one-time rights, second serial (reprint rights), simultaneous rights. For artwork, buys one-time rights for cartoons; one-time rights for photos. Rights for illustrations negotiable. Pays $25-75 for stories; $25-100 for articles. Pays illustrators: $75-100 for color cover or $50-60 for color inside. Pays photographers $25-100. Sample copy free with 9×12 SASE for 3 first-class stamps. Writer's/photo guidelines for SASE.

Tips: "We want contemporary, real life articles, or fiction that has the same feel. Try to keep it teen-oriented—trendy, hip, interesting perspectives; current, topical situations that revolve around teens. We work on specific themes for each quarter, so interested writers should request current writers guidelines and topic list."

‡'**TEEN MAGAZINE**, Petersen Publishing Co., 6420 Wilshire Blvd., Los Angeles CA 90048-5515. (213)782-2950. **Editor:** Roxanne Camron. **Managing/Fiction Editor:** Amy Diamond. **Art Director:** Laurel Finnerty. Monthly magazine. Estab. 1957. Circ. 1,100,000. "We are a pure junior high and senior high female audience. '*TEEN* teens are upbeat and want to be informed."

Fiction: Young adults: contemporary, humorous, problem-solving, romance, suspense/mystery. Does not want to see "that which does not apply to our market—i.e., science fiction, history, religious, adult-oriented." Buys 12 mss/year. Length for fiction: 10-15 pages typewritten, double-spaced.

Nonfiction: Young adults: careers, cooking, health, multicultural, problem-solving, social issues, travel. Does not want to see adult-oriented, adult point of view." Buys 25 mss/year. Length for articles: 10-20 pages typewritten, double-spaced. Byline given.

How to Contact/Writers: Fiction/nonfiction: Query. Reports on queries in 3 weeks; mss in 3-4 weeks. Prefer submissions hard copy and disk.

Illustration: Buys 0-4 illustrations/issue. Uses various styles for variation. Uses a lot of b&w illustration. "Light, upbeat." Reviews ms/illustration packages from artists. "Query first." Illustrations only: "Want to see samples whether it be tearsheets, slides, finished pieces showing the style." Reports back only if interested. Credit line given.

Terms: Pays on acceptance. Buys all rights. Pays $100-400 for stories; $50-500 for articles. Pays $25-250/b&w inside; $100-400/color inside. Writer's/illustrator's guidelines free with SASE.

Tips: Illustrators: "Present professional finished work. Get familiar with magazine and send samples that would be compatible with the style of publication." There is a need for artwork with "fiction/specialty articles. Send samples or promotional materials on a regular basis."

TEEN PEOPLE, Time & Life Building, Rockefeller Center, New York NY 10020. **Editor:** Christian Ferrari.
● This publication from the editors of *People* is for 12- to 19-year old readers and features celebrity profiles, fashion and beauty articles, and stories about real teens and their schools. Fashion articles will feature real kids, not models. Features like "local hero," "success story" and "cool school," about everyday teenagers, are most open to freelancers. The magazine will also appear online.

‡**TEENAGE CHRISTIAN MAGAZINE**, Christian Publishing Inc., P.O. Box 549, Murray KY 42071. **Editor:** James G. Pounders. **Submissions Editor:** Shana Curtis (179 Wimbledon Court, Gallatin TN 37066). Bimonthly magazine. Circ. 13,000. "We publish articles that challenge Christian teenagers to grow in their Christian faith."

Fiction: Young adults/teens: adventure, contemporary, humorous, problem-solving, religious, sports, suspense/mystery. We get too many articles about perfect people where everything works out in the end. We like to see real-life stories." Buys 15-20 mss/year. Average word length: 1,000-1,750. Byline sometimes given.

Nonfiction: Young adults/teens: animal, arts/crafts, biography, careers, games/puzzles, health, history, hobbies, how-to, humorous, interview/profile, problem-solving, religion, social issues, sports, travel. Work needs to be in touch with Christian teen perspective." Buys 20 mss/year. Average word length: 500-1,500. Byline given.

Poetry: Reviews religious teen-oriented poetry. Maximum length: 20-25 lines. Limit submissions to 3 poems.

How to Contact/Writers: Fiction: Query. Nonfiction: Send complete ms. Reports on queries in 1 month/mss in 2 months. Publishes ms 4-6 months after acceptance. Will consider simultaneous and previously published submissions.

Terms: Pays on publication. Buys one-time rights for ms. Pays $15-25 (occasionally more) for stories/articles. Sample copies for 9×12 SAE and 98¢ postage.

Tips: "We look at anything that would help our audience. It is obvious when writers have read the magazine and when they have not. We use freelance writers almost exclusively for fiction. We use well-written pieces on nonfiction topics such as dating, alcohol, finding jobs, etc."

‡**3-2-1 CONTACT**, Children's Television Workshop, One Lincoln Plaza, New York NY 10023. (212)595-3456. **Articles Editor:** Curtis Slepian. **Art Director:** Gretchen Grace. Magazine published 10 times/year. Estab. 1979. Circ. 440,000. This is a science and technology magazine for 8-14 year olds. Features all areas of science and nature.

  ● *3-2-1 Contact* uses a small amount of freelance material. They do not accept unsolicited manuscripts.

Fiction: "Our fiction piece is an on-going series called 'The Time Team.' It is written in-house."

Nonfiction: Middle readers, young adults: animal, health, how-to, interview/profile, multicultural, nature/environment, science. Multicultural needs include: how kids live in other countries (with a science hook; profiles of minority scientists). Does not want to see religion, travel or history. "We see too many research reports on the life of a toad. We'd like to see more articles about scientists doing exciting work (in the field) with lots of quotes." Buys 20 mss/year. Average word length: 750-1,000. Byline given.

How to Contact/Writers: Nonfiction: Query with published clips. Reports on queries in 3 weeks.

Illustration: Buys 15 illustrations/issue; buys 150 illustrations/year. Works on assignment only. Illustrations only: Send tearsheets, portfolio. Reports on art samples only if interested. Original artwork returned at job's completion. Credit line given.

Photography: Buys photos from freelancers.

Terms: Pays on acceptance. Buys all rights for mss (negotiable). Buys one-time rights for photos unless on assignment. Pays $500-600 for assigned/unsolicited articles. Pays $500-1,000 for color cover illustration; $150-300 for b&w inside; $175-500 for color inside. Pays photographers per photo (range: $150-750). Sample copy for $1.75 and 8×14 SASE; writer's/illustrator's guidelines free with 8½×11 SASE.

Tips: Looks for "features. We do not want articles based on library research. We want on-the-spot interviews about what's happening in science now."

TIME FOR KIDS, 1271 Avenue of the Americas, 23rd Floor, New York NY 10020-1393. (212)522-1212. Estab. 1995. News magazine for kids from the publishers of TIME.

  ● This magazine no longer uses freelancers.

‡**TOGETHER TIME**, WordAction Publishing Co., 6401 The Paseo, Kansas City MO 64131. (816)333-7000. Fax: (816)333-4439. **Contact:** Lynda T. Boardman. Weekly magazine. Estab. 1981. Circ. 27,000. *"Together Time* is a story paper that correlates with the WordAction Sunday School Curriculum. Each paper contains a story, a poem, an activity, and an article directed to the parents. It is designed to connect Sunday School learning with the daily living experiences and growth of children three and four years old.'"

Fiction: Picture-oriented material: religious. "We would like to see more realistic stories. We don't like them to seem staged. We also do not purchase stories that give life and feeling to inanimate objects." Buys 50 mss/year. Average word length: 100-150. Byline given.

Nonfiction: Picture-oriented material: arts/crafts.

Poetry: Reviews poetry. Maximum length: 8 lines. Limit submissions to 10 poems.

How to Contact/Writers: Fiction: Send complete ms. Reports on queries in 6-8 weeks; mss in 2 months. Publishes ms 1 year after acceptance.

Illustration: Buys 52 illustrations/year. "We do assignment only and like both realistic and cartoon. Must be age-appropriate." Works on assignment. Reviews ms/illustration packages from artists. Illustration only: Query with samples. Send résumé slides and tearsheets. Reports in 2 months. Sample returned with SASE. Credit line given.

Photography: Buys photos from freelancers. Looks for outdoor or indoor pictures of 3- and 4-year-old children. Uses color and b&w prints; 35mm transparencies. Query with samples. Reports in 1 month.

Terms: Pays on acceptance. Buys all rights for mss. Buys all rights for artwork; multi-use rights for photographs. Original artwork returned at job's completion. Pays 5¢/word minimum for stories. "Writers receive payment and contributor copies." Pays illustrators $40 for b&w, $75 for color cover; $40 for b&w, $75 for color inside. Pays photographers per photo (range $30-75). Sample copies for #10. Writer's/illustrator's/photo guidelines for SASE.

Tips: "Make sure the material you submit is geared to three- and four-year-old children. Request a theme list with the guidelines and try to submit things that apply."

TOTALLY FOX KIDS MAGAZINE, Peter Green Design/Fox Kids Network, 4219 W. Burbank Blvd., Burbank CA 91505. (818)953-2210. E-mail: bananadog@aol.com. **Articles Editor:** Scott Russell. **Art Director:** Debra Hintz. Quarterly magazine. Estab. 1990. Circ. 4 million. Features "fun and hip articles, games and activities for Fox Kids Club members ages 6-13, promoting Fox Kids shows."

Nonfiction: Picture-oriented material, young readers, middle readers: Any material tied in to a Fox Kids Network show or one of our other features (no religious material). Buys 16 mss/year. Average word length: 200-500.

---

‡ **LISTINGS NEW TO THIS EDITION** are marked with a double dagger.

How to Contact/Writers: Nonfiction only: Query with published clips. Reports on queries/mss in 2-3 months. Publishes mss 2-6 months after acceptance. Will consider simultaneous submissions and electronic submissions via disk or modem.

Illustration: Buys 5 illustrations/issue. Uses color artwork only. Works on assignment only. Prefers "cartoon character work, must be *on model*." Reviews ms/illustration packages from artists. Query. Illustrations only: Send résumé, promo sheet, tearsheets. Reports only if interested. Samples returned with SASE; samples filed. Original work returned at job's completion. Credit line given.

Photography: Buys photos from freelancers. Uses a variety of subjects, depending on articles. Model/property release required. Uses color prints and 4×5 or 35mm transparencies. Query with résumé, business card, tearsheets. Reports only if interested.

Terms: Pays 30 days from acceptance. Buys all rights. Pays $100-400 for stories/articles. Additional payment for ms/illustration packages and for photos accompanying articles. Sample writer's guidelines for SASE.

Tips: "Practice. Read. Come up with some new and creative ideas. Our articles are almost always humorous. We try to give kids cutting-edge information. All of our articles are tied into Fox Kids shows."

TOUCH, GEMS Girls' Clubs, Box 7259, Grand Rapids MI 49510. (616)241-5616. Fax: (616)241-5558. **Managing Editor:** Carol Smith. **Art Director:** Joan Hall. Monthly (with combined issues May/June, July/August) magazine. Circ. 16,000. "*Touch* is designed to help girls ages 9-14 see how God is at work in their lives and in the world around them."

Fiction: Middle readers, young adults/teens: adventure, animal, contemporary, fantasy, folktales, health, history, humorous, multicultural, nature/environment, problem-solving, religious, romance. Does not want to see unrealistic stories and those with trite, easy endings. Buys 30 mss/year. Average word length: 400-1,000. Byline given.

Nonfiction: Middle readers, young adults/teens: animal, careers, fashion, games/puzzles, hobbies, how-to, humorous, interview/profile, multicultural, problem-solving, religious, social issues, sports, travel. Buys 9 mss/year. Average word length: 200-800. Byline given.

How to Contact/Writers: Send for annual update for publication themes. Fiction/nonfiction: Send complete ms. Reports on mss in 1 month. Will consider simultaneous submissions.

Illustration: Buys 3 illustrations/year. Prefers ms/illustration packages. Works on assignment only. Reports on submissions in 3 weeks. Samples returned with SASE. Credit line given.

Terms: Pays on publication. Buys first North American serial rights, first rights, second serial (reprint rights) or simultaneous rights. Original artwork not returned at job's completion. Pays $5-50 for stories; $20-50 for assigned articles; $5-30 for unsolicited articles. "We send complimentary copies in addition to pay." Pays $25-75 for color cover illustration; $25-50 for color inside illustration. Pays photographers by the project ($25-75 per photo). Writer's guidelines for SASE.

Tips: Writers: "The stories should be current, deal with adolescent problems and joys, and help girls see God at work in their lives through humor as well as problem-solving."

TURTLE MAGAZINE, For Preschool Kids, Children's Better Health Institute, 1100 Waterway Blvd., P.O. Box 567, Indianapolis IN 46206. (317)636-8881. **Editor:** Terry Harshman. **Art Director:** Bart Rivers. Monthly/bimonthly magazine published January/February, March, April/May, June, July/August, September, October/November, December. Circ. 300,000. *Turtle* uses read-aloud stories, especially suitable for bedtime or naptime reading, for children ages 2-5. Also uses poems, simple science experiments, and health-related articles. All but 2 pages aimed at juvenile audience.

Fiction: Picture-oriented material: adventure, animal, contemporary, fantasy, folktales, health-related, history, holiday themes, humorous, multicultural, nature/environment, problem-solving, sports, suspense/mystery. "Need very simple experiments illustrating basic science concepts. Also needs action rhymes to foster creative movement." Do not want stories about monsters or scary things. Avoid stories in which the characters indulge in unhealthy activities like eating junk food. Buys 50 mss/year. Average word length: 150-300. Byline given.

Nonfiction: Picture-oriented material: animal, arts/crafts, cooking, games/puzzles, geography, health, multicultural, nature/environment, science, sports. Buys 20 mss/year. Average word length: 150-300. Byline given.

How to Contact/Writers: Fiction/nonfiction: "Prefer complete manuscript to queries." Reports on mss in 8-10 weeks.

Photography: Buys photos from freelancers with accompanying ms only.

Terms: Pays on publication. Buys all rights for mss/artwork; one-time rights for photographs. Pays up to 22¢/word for stories and articles (depending upon length and quality) and 10 complimentary copies. Pays $30-70 for b&w inside. Sample copy $1.25. Writer's guidelines free with SASE.

Tips: "We're beginning to edit *Turtle* more for the very young preschooler, so we're looking for stories and articles that are written more simply than those we've used in the past. Our need for health-related material, especially features that encourage fitness, is ongoing. Health subjects must be age-appropriate. When writing about them, think creatively and lighten up! Fight the tendency to become boringly pedantic. Nobody—not even young kids—likes to be lectured. Always keep in mind that in order for a story or article to educate preschoolers, it first must be entertaining—warm and engaging, exciting, or genuinely funny. Understand that writing for *Turtle* is a difficult challenge. Study the magazine to see if your manuscript is right for *Turtle*. Magazines have distinct personalities which can't be understood by only reading market listings. Here the trend is toward leaner, lighter writing. There will be a growing need for interactive activities. Writers might want to consider developing an

KITTEN LOVE

Faith L. Rice

Gloria Oostema used marker and colored pencil to create three characters, Jeremy, Hope and May, who learn a lesson about love and prejudice from a mother cat named Inkspot and her three kittens of different colors. Oostema received $60 to illustrate this story by Faith Rice featured in *Touch*. *Touch*, published by the Calvinettes, is a religious magazine for girls ages 9 to 14. Oostema has been involved with the GEMS/Calvinettes organization as a counselor for a number of years and began doing freelance artwork for them about five years ago.

activity to accompany their concise manuscripts." (See listings for *Child Life*, *Children's Digest*, *Children's Playmate*, *Humpty Dumpty's Magazine*, *Jack And Jill* and *U*S* Kids*.)

‡**TWIST**, Bauer Publishing Company, 270 Sylvan Ave., Englewood Cliffs NJ 07632. (201)569-6699. Fax: (201)569-4458. E-mail: twistmail@aol.com. **Articles Editor:** Jeannie Kim. **Art Director:** Robin Zachary. Monthly magazine. Estab. 1997. Circ. 700,000. "We capture the energy, attitude and interests of young women today. We stress reality over fantasy and serve as a forum for the concerns and passions of our 14- to 19-year-old readers."

Nonfiction: Young teens: careers, health, humorous, interview/profile, social issues, relationships/dating, "real life" experiences, quizzes, college. Average word length: 100-1,800. Byline given.

How to Contact/Writers: Nonfiction: query with published clips. Reports on queries in 1-4 weeks. Will consider simultaneous submissions, electronic submission via disk or modem and previously published work.

Illustration: Buys 4 illustrations/issue. Uses color artwork only. Works on assignment only. Query; send promo sheet and tearsheets; "follow with a phone call." Contact: Robin Zachary, creative director. Reports only if interested. Samples not returned; samples not filed.

Photography: Uses 35mm, 2¼×2¼ transparencies. Query with samples; provide promotional literature or tearsheets.

Terms: Pays on acceptance. Buys first North American serial rights. Pays $50 minimum and up to $1/word for articles. Pays illustrators $100-500 for color inside. Pays photographers by the project (range: $30/day up to $400); or per photo (range: $75 minimum). Sample copies not available. Writer's guidelines free for SASE.

U*S* KIDS, Children's Better Health Institute, 1100 Waterway Blvd., P.O. Box 567, Indianapolis IN 46206. (317)636-8881. **Editor:** Jeff Ayres. **Art Director:** Matthew Brinkman. Magazine published 8 times a year. Estab. 1987. Circ. 250,000.

Fiction: Young readers and middle readers: adventure, animal, contemporary, health, history, humorous, multicultural, nature/environment, problem-solving, sports, suspense/mystery. "We see too many stories with no real story line. We'd like to see more mysteries and contemporary humor stories." Buys approximately 8-16 mss/year. Average word length: 500-800. Byline given.

Nonfiction: Young readers and middle readers: animal, arts/crafts, cooking, games/puzzles, health, history, hobbies, how-to, humorous, interview/profile, multicultural, nature/environment, science, social issues, sports, travel. Wants to see interviews with kids ages 5-10, who have done something unusual or different. Buys 30-40 mss/year. Average word length: 500-600. Byline given.

Poetry: Maximum length: 32 lines.

How to Contact/Writers: Fiction: Send complete ms. Nonfiction: Query or submit complete ms. Reports on queries and mss in 1 month. Publishes ms 6 months after acceptance. Will consider simultaneous submissions, electronic submissions via disk or modem and previously published work.

Illustration: Buys 8 illustrations/issue; 70 illustrations/year. Color artwork only. Works on assignment only. Reviews ms/illustration packages from artists. Query. Illustrations only: Send résumé and tearsheets. Reports back only if interested. Samples returned with SASE; samples kept on file. Does not return originals. Credit line given.

Photography: Purchases photography from freelancers. Looking for photos that pertain to children ages 5-10. Model/property release required. Uses color and b&w prints; 35mm, 2¼×2¼, 4×5 and 8×10 transparencies. Photographers should provide résumé, business card, promotional literature or tearsheets to be kept on file. Reports back only if interested.

Terms: Pays on publication. Buys all rights for mss. Purchases all rights for artwork. Purchases one-time rights for photographs. Pays 10¢/word minimum. Additional payment for ms/illustration packages. Pays illustrators $140/page for color inside. Photographers paid by the project or per photo (negotiable). Sample copies for $2.50. Writer's/illustrator/photo guidelines for SASE.

Tips: "Write clearly and concisely without preaching or being obvious." (See listings for *Child Life*, *Children's Digest*, *Children's Playmate*, *Humpty Dumpty's Magazine*, *Jack And Jill* and *Turtle Magazine*.)

W.O.W. (Wild Outdoor World), (formerly *Falcon*), 4 N. Last Chance Gulch, Suites 16-18, P.O. Box 1249, Helena MT 59624. (406)449-1335. Fax: (406)442-2995. E-mail: graphicb@aol.com. **Editorial Director:** Carolyn Zieg Cunningham. **Executive Editor:** Kay Morton Ellerhoff. **Design Editor:** Bryan Knaff. Bimonthly magazine. Estab. 1993. Circ. 100,000. "A magazine for young conservationists (age 8-12)."

● *W.O.W.* is distributed in fourth grade classes in Montana, North Dakota, Colorado, Michigan and Nevada. The publisher is working on distribution in New England as well.

Nonfiction: Middle readers: adventure (outdoor), animal, nature/environment, sports (outdoor recreation), travel (to parks, wildlife refuges, etc.). Average word length: 800 maximum. Byline given.

How to Contact/Writers: Fiction/nonfiction: Query. Reports in 6 months.

Illustration: Buys 2 illustrations/issue; 12-15 illustrations/year. Prefers work on assignment. Reviews ms/illustration packages from artists. Illustrations only: Query; send slides, tearsheets. Reports in 2 months. Samples returned with SASE; samples sometimes filed. Credit line given.

Photography: *Must* be submitted in 20-slide sheets and individual protectors, such as KYMAC. Looks for "children outdoors—camping, fishing, doing 'nature' projects." Model/property releases required. Photo captions required. Uses 35mm transparencies. Should query with samples. Contact: Theresa Morrow Rush, photo editor. Reports in 2 months.

Terms: Pays 30-60 days after publication. Buys one-time rights for mss. Purchases one-time rights for photographs. Original work returned at job's completion. Pays $100-500 for articles; $50 for fillers. Pays illustrators variable rate for b&w inside; $250 color cover; $35-100 color inside. Pays photographers by the project ($35 minimum); per photo (range: $35-100); $250 for cover photo. Sample copies for $3.95 and 8½×11 SAE. Writer's/illustrator's/photo guidelines for SASE.

Tips: "We are seriously overloaded with manuscripts and do not plan to buy very much new material in the next year."

*❧WHAT! A MAGAZINE, What! Publishers Inc. 108-93 Lombard Ave., Winnipeg, Manitoba R3B 3B1 Canada. (204)942-2214. Fax: (204)943-8991. E-mail: what@fox.nstn.ca. **Articles Editor:** Stuart Slayen. **Art Director:** Brian Kauste. Magazine published 5 times/year. Estab. 1987. Circ. 200,000. "Informative and entertaining teen magazine for both genders. Articles deal with issues and ideas of relevance to Canadian teens. The magazine is distributed through schools so we aim to be cool and responsible at the same time."

Nonfiction: Young adults (14 and up): biography, careers, concept, health, how-to, humorous, interview/profile, nature/environment, science, social issues, sports. "No cliché teen stuff. Also, we're getting too many heavy pitches lately on teen pregnancy, AIDS, etc." Buys 8 mss/year. Average word length: 675-2,100. Byline given.

How to Contact/Writers: Nonfiction: Query with published clips. Reports on queries/mss in 2 months. Publishes ms 2 months after acceptance.

Terms: Pays on publication plus 30 days. Buys first rights for mss. Pays $100-500 (Canadian) for articles. Sample copies when available for 9×12 and $1.45 (Canadian). Writer's guidelines free for SASE.

Tips: "Teens are smarter today than ever before. Respect that intelligence in queries and articles. Aim for the older end of our age-range (14-19) and avoid cliché. Humor works for us almost all the time." (See listing for *Kids World Magazine*.)

WITH, The Magazine for Radical Christian Youth, Faith & Life Press, 722 Main, P.O. Box 347, Newton KS 67114. (316)283-5100. Fax: (316)283-0454. **Editors:** Eddy Hall, Carol Duerksen. Published 8 times a year. Circ. 6,100. Magazine published for teenagers, ages 15-18, in Mennonite, Brethren and Mennonite Brethren congregations. "We deal with issues affecting teens and try to help them make choices reflecting a radical Christian faith."

Fiction: Young adults/teens: contemporary, fantasy, humorous, multicultural, problem-solving, religious, romance, science fiction, sports. Multicultural needs include race relations, first-person stories featuring teens of ethnic minorities. Buys 15 mss/year. Average word length: 1,000-2,000. Byline given.

Nonfiction: Young adults/teens: first-person teen personal experience (as-told-to), how-to, humorous, multicultural, problem-solving, religion, social issues. Buys 15-20 mss/year. Average word length: 1,000-2,000. Byline given.

Poetry: Wants to see religious, humorous, nature. "Buys 1-2 poems/year." Maximum length: 50 lines.

How to Contact/Writers: Send complete ms. Query on first-person teen personal experience stories and how-to articles. (Detailed guidelines for first-person stories, how-tos, and fiction available for SASE.) Reports on queries in 2-3 weeks; mss in 2-4 weeks. Will consider simultaneous submissions.

Illustration: Buys 6-8 illustrations/issue; buys 50-60 illustrations/year. Uses b&w and 2-color artwork only. Preferred theme or style: candids/interracial. Reviews ms/illustration packages from artists. Query first. Illustrations only: Query with portfolio (photocopies only) or tearsheets. Reports back only if interested. Credit line given.

Photography: Buys photos from freelancers. Looking for candid photos of teens (ages 15-18), especially ethnic minorities. Uses 8×10 b&w glossy prints. Photographers should send unsolicited photos by mail.

Terms: Pays on acceptance. For mss buys first rights, one-time rights; second serial (reprint rights). Buys one-time rights for artwork and photos. Original artwork returned at job's completion upon request. Pays 5¢/word for unpublished manuscripts; 3¢/word for reprints. Will pay more for assigned as-told-to stories. Pays $50-60 for b&w cover illustration and b&w inside illustration. Pays photographers per photo (range: $25-50, cover only). Sample copy for 9×12 SAE and 5 first-class stamps. Writer's/illustrator's guidelines for SASE.

Tips: "We want stories, fiction or nonfiction, in which high-school-age youth of various cultures/ethnic groups are the protaganist. Stories may or may not focus on cross-cultural relationships. We're hungry for stuff that makes teens laugh—fiction, nonfiction and cartoons. It doesn't have to be religious, but must be wholesome. Most of our stories would not be accepted by other Christian youth magazines. They would be considered too gritty, too controversial, or too painful. Our regular writers are on the *With* wavelength. Most writers for Christian youth magazines aren't."

WONDER TIME, WordAction Publications, 6401 The Paseo, Kansas City MO 64131. (816)333-7000. **Editor:** Donna Fillmore. Weekly magazine. Circ. 45,000. "*Wonder Time* is a full-color story paper for first and second graders. It is designed to connect Sunday School learning with the daily living experiences and growth of the primary child. Since *Wonder Time*'s target audience is children ages six to eight, the readability goal is to encourage beginning readers to read for themselves. The major purposes of *Wonder Time* are to: Provide a life-related paper that will build Christian values, encourage ethical behavior and provide reinforcement for the biblical concepts taught in the WordAction Sunday School curriculum.''

Fiction: Picture-oriented material: adventure, contemporary, multicultural, nature/environment, religious. ''We need ethnic balance—stories and illustrations from a variety of ethnic experiences.'' Buys 52 mss/year. Average word length: 300-400. Byline given.

Nonfiction: Picture-oriented material: problem solving, religious, social issues.

How to Contact/Writers: Fiction/nonfiction: Send complete ms. Reports on queries/mss in 6 weeks. Will consider simultaneous submissions.

Illustration: Buys 50 illustrations/year. Works on assignment only. Reviews ms/illustration packages from artists. Illustrations only: Submit samples of work. Reports on art samples in 6 weeks. Samples returned with SASE; samples kept on file. Credit line given.

Terms: Pays on acceptance. Original artwork not returned. Pays $25 per story for rights which allow the publisher to print the story multiple times without repayment. Pays illustrators $40 for b&w cover or inside; $75 for color cover or inside. Photographers paid per photo (range: $25-75). Sends complimentary contributor's copies of publication. Sample copy and writer's guidelines with 9½×12 SAE and 2 first-class stamps.

Tips: ''Basic themes reappear regularly. Please write for a theme list. Also be familiar with what *Wonder Time* is all about. Ask for guidelines, sample copies, theme list *before* submitting.''

WRITER'S INTERNATIONAL FORUM, "For Those Who Write to Sell," Bristol Services International, P.O. Box 516, Tracyton WA 98393-0516. **Editor:** Sandra E. Huren. Monthly (10 times/year, excluding December and August) newsletter. Estab. 1990. Up to 25% aimed at writers of juvenile literature. ''We offer authors the unique chance of having a short story or essay published plus receiving a free professional critique. If published, author must agree to allow both the manuscript and our professional critique to be published in our Featured Manuscript section. Each issue includes writing lessons and markets information.''

Fiction: Young readers, middle readers, young adults/teens: adventure, contemporary, fantasy, humorous, nature/environment, problem-solving, religious, romance, science fiction, suspense/mystery. ''No experimental formats; no picture books; no poetry. No stories for children under age eight. We see too many anthropomorphic characters. We would like to see more mysteries, problem-solving and adventures.'' Buys approximately 20 mss/year. Maximum word length: 1,000. Byline and bio information given.

How to Contact/Writers: Fiction: Reports on mss in 2 months. Publishes ms 4-6 months after acceptance.

Terms: Pays on acceptance. Buys first North American serial rights. Pays $30, 2 contributor copies plus a written professional critique for stories and essays. Sample copy for $3.

Tips: ''We want well-crafted stories with traditional plots which are written in clear language, have fully developed characters and an interesting storyline. Essays must have a tight focus, make a distinct point, and back up that point with specific facts and/or experiences. Always state the age group for which the children's manuscript is intended and be certain your material is suitable specifically for that audience.''

‡YM, 685 Third Ave., New York NY 10017. **Editor:** Lesley Seymour. ''*YM* is a national magazine for young women ages 15-24 to help guide them through the many exciting and often rough aspects of young adulthood.''

Nonfiction: ''We buy articles on topics of interest to young women. All articles should be lively and informative. In the past year, we have tackled everything from interracial dating to sexual abuse to eating disorders. Expert opinions should be included as a supplement to the feelings and experiences of young women. We do not publish fiction or poetry.'' Word length: up to 2,500 words.

How to Contact/Writers: Nonfiction: Query with SASE. (Write ''query''on envelope.)

Terms: Pays on acceptance. Rates vary.

*YOUNG JUDAEAN, Young Judaea-Hadassah Zionist Youth Commission, 50 West 58th St., New York NY 10019. (212)303-4575. Fax: (212)303-4572. **Articles Editor:** Deborah Newfield. Quarterly magazine. Circ. 5,000. Children's magazine with Jewish/Zionist theme.

Fiction: Middle readers: religious; any subject with Jewish relevance. Does not want to see preachy/moral stories. Buys 4 mss/year. Average word length: 600-1,200. Byline given.

Nonfiction: Middle readers: history, religion, social issues; any subject with Jewish theme. Buys 2-3 mss/year. Average word length: 1,000-1,500. Byline given.

How to Contact/Writers: Fiction/nonfiction: send complete ms. Reports on queries in 1 month; mss in 6 months. Publishes ms 2-3 months after acceptance. Will consider simultaneous submissions and previously published work.

Illustrations: Uses b&w artwork only. Illustrations only: Query with samples. Contact: Jonathan Mayo, editor. Reports back only if interested. Samples returned with SASE. Credit line given.

Photography: Reports back only if interested.

Terms: ''No payment—just copies of publication.'' Sample copies free for SAE. Writer's guidelines free for SASE.

YOUNG SALVATIONIST, The Salvation Army, 615 Slaters Lane, P.O. Box 269, Alexandria VA 22313. (703)684-5500. Published 10 times/year. Estab. 1984. Circ. 50,000. **Managing Editor:** Lesa Davis. ''We accept material with clear Christian content written for high school age teenagers. *Young Salvationist* is published for

Cory has wandered off. Can you help him swim safely back to mom?

Mazes are popular features in many children's magazines. Lyn Martin was paid $900 for this this two-page spread featured in *Your Big Backyard*, a magazine published by the National Wildlife Federation. The Knoxville, Tennessee illustrator believes strongly that freelancers in small communities should tap larger markets for work. "*Children's Writer's & Illustrator's Market* and *Artist's & Graphic Designer's Market* are both valuable resources for this purpose." Martin received this assignment through her rep, Cliff Knecht, who she found through a Writer's Digest Books publication. "*Your Big Backyard* is a fun publication to work for—they offer lots of creative freedom. Art Director Tammy Tylenda always has insightful comments."

teenage members of The Salvation Army, an evangelical part of the Christian Church."
Fiction: Young adults/teens: contemporary religious. Buys 12-20 mss/year. Average word length: 750-1,200. Byline given.
Nonfiction: Young adults/teens: religious—careers, health, interview/profile, social issues, sports. Buys 40-50 mss/year. Average word length: 750-1,200. Byline given.
How to Contact/Writers: Fiction/nonfiction: Query with published clips or send complete ms. Reports on queries/mss in 1 month. Will consider simultaneous submissions.
Illustrations: Buys 3-5 illustrations/issue; 20-30 illustrations/year. Reviews ms/illustration packages from artists. Send ms with art. Illustrations only: Query; send résumé, promo sheet, portfolio, tearsheets. Reports back only if interested. Samples returned with SASE; samples filed. Credit line given.
Photography: Purchases photography from freelancers. Looking for teens in action.
Terms: Pays on acceptance. Buys first North American serial rights, first rights, one-time rights or second serial (reprint) rights for mss. Purchases one-time rights for artwork and photographs. Original artwork returned at job's completion "if requested." For mss, pays 15¢/word; 10¢/word for reprints. Pays $100-150 color (cover) illustration; $50-100 b&w (inside) illustration; $100-150 color (inside) illustration. Sample copy for 9×12 SAE and 4 first-class stamps. Writer's guidelines for #10 SASE.
Tips: "Ask for theme list/sample copy! Write 'up,' not down to teens. Aim at young *adults*, not children." Wants "less fiction, more 'journalistic' nonfiction."

*YOUR BIG BACKYARD, National Wildlife Federation, 8925 Leesburg Pike, Vienna VA 22184. (703)790-4515. Fax: (703)827-2585. E-mail: johnsond@nwf.org. **Articles/Fiction Editor:** Donna Johnson. **Art Director:** Tamara Tylenda. **Photo Editor:** Stephen B. Freligh. Monthly magazine (includes a parents newsletter bound into the center to be pulled out.) Estab. 1980. Circ. 400,000. Purpose of the magazine is to educate young children (ages 3-6) about nature and wildlife in a fun, interactive and entertaining way. 90% of publication aimed at juvenile market (10% is parents' newsletter).
Fiction: Picture-oriented material: animal, fantasy, humorous, multicultural, nature/environment. Young readers: adventure, animal, humorous, multicultural, nature/environment. "We do not want fiction that does not involve

animals or nature in some way." Buys 12 mss/year. Average word length: 200-1,000. Byline given.

Nonfiction: Picture-oriented material, young readers: animal, arts/crafts, games/puzzles, nature/environment. Wants no articles that deal with subjects other than nature. Buys 2 mss/year. Average word length: 50-100.

Poetry: Reviews poetry. Buys 5-6 poems/year. Maximum length: 15 words or 25 lines.

How to Contact/Writers: Fiction: send complete ms. Nonfiction: Query with published clips; send complete ms. Reports on queries/mss in 2 weeks. Publishes ms 4 months after acceptance. Will consider simultaneous submissions, electronic submission via disk or modem and previously published work.

Illustration: Buys 5 illustrations/issue 60 illustrations/year. Uses color artwork only. Reviews ms/illustration packages from artists. Send ms with dummy. Contact: Donna Johnson, art director. Illustrations only: Send promo sheet, portfolio, slides, tearsheets. Contact: Tammy Tylenda, art director. Reports back only if interested. Samples not returned; filed. Credit line given.

Photography: Wants animal photos. Uses 35mm transparencies. Send unsolicited photos by mail ("professional photographers only"). Reports in 2 months.

Terms: Pays on acceptance. Buys one-time rights, reprint rights for mss. Buys one-time rights for artwork and photographs. Original artwork returned at job's completion. Pays $250-750 for stories; $50-200 for articles. Additional payment for ms/illustration packages and for photos accompanying articles. Pays illustrators $200-500 for color inside. Pays photographers per photo (range: $200-600). Sample copies for $1.

Tips: "With regard to fiction, we accept stories in which the main characters can be talking animals; however, the storyline should deal with some aspect of the animal's natural history or habitat. The book *Stellaluna* is an example of the type or good fiction we want to see more of."

ZILLIONS For Kids From Consumer Reports, Consumers Union, 101 Truman Ave., Yonkers NY 10703-1057. (914)378-2551. Fax: (914)378-2904. **Articles Editor:** Karen McNulty. **Art Director:** Rob Jenter. Bimonthly magazine. Estab. 1980. Circ. 300,000. "*Zillions* is the consumer reports for kids (with heavy emphasis on fun!) We cover products, advertising, money matters, etc."

• *ZILLIONS* works on assignment only. They do not accept unsolicited manuscripts; query first.

Nonfiction: Young adults/teens: arts/crafts, careers, games/puzzles, health, hobbies, how-to, humorous, nature/environment, problem-solving, social issues, sports. "Will consider story ideas on kid money matters, marketing to kids and anything that educates kids to be smart consumers." Buys 10 mss/year. Average word length: 800-2,000.

How to Contact/Writers: Nonfiction: Query with résumé and published clips. "We'll contact if interested (within a few months probably)." Publishes ms 2 months after acceptance.

Terms: Pays on publication. Buys all rights for ms. Pays $1,000 for articles. Writer's guidelines for SASE.

Tips: "Read the magazine!"

Electronic Publishing

Welcome to the world of electronic publishing. This section is devoted to producers and developers of CD-ROMs and software for children. The companies listed here operate in different ways. Reidmore Books, for example, is an offshoot of a print publisher, and many of the electronic items they produce relate to the books they publish. Companies like Creative Wonders, producer of *Sesame Street*- and Mr. Potato Head-related titles, among others, only develop material that ties in with licensed characters. Other companies, such as Girl Games, produce licensed material but also create original products. Girl Games' titles include their original CD-ROM *Let's Talk About ME!*, along with Sabrina the Teenage Witch tie-ins. (See the Insider Report interview with Girl Games producer Jan Bozarth on page 256.)

All of the companies listed here need freelance illustration and writing. Some companies accept project proposals, but it's difficult to get original ideas published in electronic form. It's more common for companies to take already-established ideas and develop them into products, using the talents of writers and illustrators in the creation process. Writers and illustrators should submit samples to these companies in much the same way they submit to book publishers. A difference is that they may want samples of previous multimedia work submitted on disk. It's not always necessary, however, that writers and illustrators have experience working on CD-ROM or software titles. Companies state preferences within their listings. Also, be sure to visit companies' websites, if listed, for more information on their products and submissions policies.

The companies in this section are just the tip of the iceberg in a sea of multimedia producers. There are hundreds of companies that produce CD-ROMs and software for kids. Hopefully, the number of listings in this section will grow as the industry expands and stabilizes in years to come. There's been speculation that CD-ROMs are on the way out to be replaced by online products. But CD-ROMs are still making money, especially in the children's area. There are still far more consumers with CD-ROM drives than are online, although the online numbers grow daily. Companies have found that it's difficult to make money online with children's products because of the problems selling to consumers not old enough to have credit cards.

There are a number of sources available if you'd like to find additional multimedia producers to query. The Society of Children's Book Writers and Illustrators has a "Guide to Multimedia Markets" compiled by Bruce Balan, available for an 8½×11 SAE and $1.01 postage. You can also consult the sixth edition of *The Multimedia Directory*. It's published by The Corronade Group, 2355 Francisco St., Suite 6, San Francisco CA 94123. (800)529-3501. Website: http://www.carronade.com. A trade show is also a great place to learn about an industry—Digital Kids, held annually by Jupiter Communications, is devoted solely to electronically published products for kids. Their '98 conference will be in Los Angeles April 1-3. For information see their website—http://www.jup.com/conference.

Information on electronic publishers listed in the previous edition but not included in this edition of *Children's Writer's & Illustrator's Market* may be found in the General Index.

‡**ABBY LOU ENTERTAINMENT**, 1411 Edgehill Place, Pasadena CA 91103. (626)795-7334. Fax: (626)795-4013. E-mail: ale@full-moon.com. Estab. 1987. Produced 0 titles last year; 0 titles currently in distribution; 3 titles currently in production.
Software: Produces interactive storybooks software in Mac and Windows on CD-ROM for preschool and ages 5-8. Games: produces action/adventure in Mac and Windows for ages 5-8. Recently produced *World of Whispering Gardens* (age 5-8).
Writing: Submit cover letter, résumé, writing samples (hard copy) and demo disk of previous projects (Mac).

Contact: George Le Fave, president. Submissions returned with SASE. Reports in 1 month. Does not require previous multimedia experience, "however, must be accomplished prose writer." Requires writers be available for on-site consultations. "Know character development, story breakdown and be able to write literate story—beginning, middle and end."

Illustration: Needs freelancers for storyboarding, animation and backgrounds. Submit cover letter, résumé, samples (color copies, original art, on disk, Mac), demo disk of previous projects (Mac) or demo real. Contact: George Le Fave, president. Samples not returned; samples filed. Reports in 1 month. Does not require previous multimedia experience. Requires artists be available for on-site consultation. "Be able to illustrate!"

Proposals: Accepts proposals directly from individuals, from agents and from book publishers. Submission guidelines for proposals not available. Requires signed submission before reviewing proposal. Submission agreement free on request. Submit résumé, submission agreement, storyboard (hard copy), script (hard copy) and original book (if based on published work). Contact: Cheryl Pestor, vice president of development. Prefers project proposal presented by regular mail. Reports back in 1 month. Product development varies.

Terms: Work purchased outright for variable amount. Creators paid royalty of variable amount. Offers advance to creators ($5,000). Product catalogs not available.

Tips: "The children's market will always welcome a good solid story with creative characters. Market is growing but will be hurt with inferior product, copycat philosophy! There must be market support in different categories to enhance the brand name. Be flexible and keep pushing your talents."

‡COMPU-TEACH, 16541 Redmond Way, Suite 137-C, Redmond WA 98052. (425)885-0517. Fax: (425)883-9169. E-mail: cmpteach@compu-teach.com. Website: http://www.wafenet.com/~cmpteach. Estab. 1983. Produced 1 title last year; 10 titles currently in distribution; 2 titles currently in production.

Software: Produces early learning, reading/language arts, science and geography software in Mac and Windows on floppy and CD-ROM for all ages. Recently produced *Once Upon a Time . . .* (writing/creativity, ages 6-12); *Code: Europe* (geography/history, ages 10 to adult).

Writing: Submit cover letter, résumé, writing samples (hard copy) and demo disk of previous projects. Contact: David Urban, president. Submission returned with SASE; submissions filed. Reports only if interested. Requires previous multimedia experience. Does not require writers be available for on-site consultation.

Illustration: Submit cover letter, résumé, samples (website, original art, on disk), computer presentation or demo disk of previous projects. Samples returned with SASE; samples filed. Reports only if interested. Requires previous multimedia experience. Does not require artists to be available for on-site consultation.

Proposals: Accepts proposals directly from individuals, from agents and from book publishers. Submission guidelines for proposals not available. Requires signed submission before reviewing proposal. Submission agreement free on request. Submit résumé, submission agreement, storyboard (hard copy), computer presentation or demo of product (Mac or Windows). Prefers project proposal by phone, in person or by regular mail. Reports back only if interested. Product development varies.

Terms: Writers and artists paid royalty of 5-15%. Creators paid royalty of 10-20%. Product catalogs free on request.

CREATIVE WONDERS, 595 Penobscot Dr., Redwood City CA 94063. (415)482-2300. Fax: (415)482-2301. Website: http://www.cwonders.com. Estab. 1994. 23 titles currently in distribution.

Software: Produces early learning, creativity tools, problem solving, math, social studies, language arts and science software (for grades pre-K and up). Recently produced *Sesame Street: Elmo's Preschool* (preschool, ages 3-6); and *School House Rock: Grammar Rock* (ages 6-10).

Writing: Submit cover letter, résumé, writing samples: hard copy, on disk (Mac, Windows); demo disk of previous projects. Submissions not returned; submissions filed. Reports only if interested. Requires previous multimedia experience. Does not require writers be available for on-site consultation.

Illustration: Needs freelancers for various assignments. Submit cover letter, résumé and demo disk of previous projects (Mac, Windows). Samples not returned; samples filed. Does not require artist to be available for on-site consultation.

Proposals: Accepts proposals directly from individuals, from agents and from book publishers. Contact: Maryann Duringer, product submissions. Submission guidelines free on request. Requires signed submission before reviewing proposal. Submission agreement free on request. Submit résumé, submission agreement, storyboard (hardcopy), script (hard copy), videotape, original book (if based on published work), computer presentation, demo of product, complete product, all available materials relevant to proposal. Prefers project proposal presented by regular mail. Reports back only if interested. Product development varies.

Terms: Payment determined on individual basis. Product catalogs free on request.

Tips: "Be knowledgeable about the market you are trying to serve: look at and be familiar with all current software 'hits.' Don't 'hound' publishers. Persistence can be irritating."

DYNACOMP, INC., 4560 E. Lake Rd., Livonia NY 14487. (716)346-9788. Estab. 1978. 800 titles currently in distribution; 800 titles currently in production.

Software: Produces interactive storybooks in Mac, MS-DOS on floppy (for ages preschool and up); produces early learning, reading/language arts, science, math and reference software in MS-DOS on floppy (for ages preschool and up). Games: produces mystery/puzzle and horror software in Mac, MS-DOS on floppy (for ages preschool and up). Recently produced *Children's Carrousel* (early learning, ages 2-6); and *Hodge Podge* (early learning, ages 2-6).

Writing: "Submit full documentation with software—no partial products or 'ideas.' " Contact: Marketing Director. Submissions returned with SASE; submissions filed. Reports in 1 week.

Terms: Writers paid royalty of 5-15%. Product catalogs available for 9×12 SAE with $1.93 postage.

‡**DYNAMIC SOFTWARE**, P.O. Box 13991, Berkeley CA 94701. (510)644-0139. E-mail: wahl@dnac.com. Website: http://www.wahl.org/dynamic. Produced 4 titles last year; 4 titles currently in distribution.

Software: Produces interactive storybooks, science, math, creativity tools and online content in Mac and Windows for floppy and CD-ROM for ages 10 to adult. Recently produced *Fracta Sketch* (math, age 10 to adult); and *Mandel Movie* (math, age 10 to adult).

Proposals: Accepts proposals directly from individual and from book publishers. Submission guidelines for proposals not available. Contact: Kristina Wahl, CPO. Submit script (hard copy), videotape, demo of product or complete product (Mac or Windows). Prefers project proposal by e-mail or by regular mail. Reports back only if interested. "Be creative."

Terms: Creators paid royalty of 5-20%. Product catalogs not available.

ELECTROPIX™, **INC.**, 28631 S. Western Ave. #101, Rancho Palos Verdes CA 90275. (310)521-5967. Estab. 1990 Live Wire Productions, 1994 ElectroPix, Inc.

Software: Produces interactive storybooks, early learning, reading/language arts, creativity tools and reference software in Mac, Windows and Set Top on CD-ROM for ages 9 and up. Games: produces action/adventure, mystery/puzzle, horror, simulation and arcade software in Mac, Windows and Set Top on CD-ROM for ages 12 and up.

Writing: Submit résumé, titles of recent work and the age group/market the work is designed for. Reports only in interested.

Illustration: Needs freelancers for animation, 3-D modeling, special effects animators and programmers. Submit résumé, b&w photocopy of work or demo reel. Samples not returned. Requires artists be available for on-site consultation "depending on the project." Contact: Production Manager.

Proposals: Accepts proposals directly from agents and from book publishers. "We do not accept proposals from unrepresented individuals not known to the company or unsolicited proposals from individuals without company's prior approval of letter of inquiry and request for proposal." Requires signed submission before reviewing proposal. Submission agreement "only available to individuals when the company responds to a letter of inquiry and sends a request for a proposal. Letters of inquiry should be one paragraph and include the target age group/market, the broad category of the software and the current state of the project without describing specifics with regard to storyline or high concept ideas." Contact: Janet Donaldson/Product Development.

Terms: Pay is determined on an individual basis.

Tips: "Be able to tell us the strengths and weaknesses of currently available games from your point of view as a game player."

‡**GIRL GAMES INC.**, 221 E. Ninth St., Suite 302, Austin TX 78701. (512)478-1158. Fax: (512)478-2957. E-mail: info@girlgamesinc.com. Website: http://www.planetgirl.com. Contact: General Manager. Estab. 1994. Produced 1 title last year; 1 title currently in distribution; 2 titles currently in production.

Software: Produces hybrid CD-ROMs for girls for ages 9-11 ages and up. Recently produced *Let's Talk About ME!* (ages 8-14).

Writing: Submit cover letter, résumé and writing samples (hard copy); writing samples on disk (Mac); demo disk of previous projects (Mac). Submissions not returned; submissions filed. Reports only if interested. Does not require previous multimedia experience. Does not require writers be available for on-site consutation.

Illustration: Needs freelancersss for storyboarding, animation, backgrounds and textures. Submit cover letter, résumé, samples (color copies, website, Mac), demo disk of previous projects (Mac). Samples not returned; samples filed. Reports only if interested. Does not require previous multimedia experience. Requires artists be available for on-site consultation.

Proposals: Accepts proposals directly from individuals and from book publishers. Submission guidelines for proposals not available. Requires signed submission agreement before reviewing proposal. Submission agreement free on request. Submit résumé, submission agreement, storyboard, script, original book or demo of product (Mac or Windows). Contact: Jane Stavinoha, associate producer. Prefers project proposal presented by fax or regular mail. Reports back only if interested. Product development varies.

---

‡ **LISTINGS NEW TO THIS EDITION** are marked with a double dagger.

Terms: Product catalogs not available.

HEARTSOFT, INC., 3101 N. Hemlock, Broken Arrow OK 74012. (918)251-1066. Fax: (918)251-4018. Website: http://www.heartsoft.com. Estab. 1986. 50 titles currently in distribution; 50 titles currently in production.
Software: Produces early learning, reading/language arts, science, math, creativity tools software in Mac and Windows on floppy (for ages preschool and up). Games: produces mystery/puzzle in Mac and Windows on floppy for ages preschool and up. Produced *Tommy the Time Turtle* (math, grades 2-4); *Reading Rodeo* (early learning, grades K-2).
Illustration: Needs freelancers for storyboarding, animation, backgrounds and textures. Submit cover letter, résumé, samples (color copies, website, original art, Mac), demo disk of previous projects (Mac). Contact: Jimmy Butler, vice president of development. Samples filed; samples returned. Reports only if interested. Requires previous multimedia experience. Requires artists to be available for on-site consultation.
Terms: Work purchased outright.

LAREDO PUBLISHING CO., 8907 Wilshire Blvd., Beverly Hills CA 90211. (310)358-5288. Fax: (310)358-5282. E-mail: laredo@online2000.com. Estab. 1991. Produced 15 titles last year; 150 titles currently in distribution; 20 titles currently in production.
Software: Produces interactive storybooks, early learning and reading/language arts software.
Writing: Submit writing samples (Mac) and demo disk of previous projects (Mac). Contact: Sam Laredo, president. Submissions returned with SASE; submissions filed. Reports in 2 weeks. Requires previous multimedia experience. "We specialize in language development tools and English as a second language (ESL) material."
Illustration: Needs storyboarding, animation and 3-D modeling, "all kinds of illustration for children." Submit samples (color copies) or demo disk of previous projects (Mac). Contact: Sam Laredo, president. Samples returned with SASE; submissions filed. Reports on submissions in 2 weeks.
Proposals: Accepts proposals directly from individuals. Submission guidelines not available. Contact: Sam Laredo, president.
Terms: Writers paid royalty of 7-10% or work purchased outright for $1,000-5,000. Artists paid royalty or work purchased outright for $1,000-5,000. Work purchased outright for $1,000-5,000 from creators. Offers advance (depends on project).

‡MEDIA SPHERE, INC., 250 Mercer St., Suite D803, New York NY 10012. (212)529-6954. Fax: (212)529-1203. President: Lori Laubich. Estab. 1993. 1 title currently in production. Produces online content and edutainment software in Mac and Windows on CD-ROM for ages 9 and up. Games: produces mystery/puzzle software in Mac or Windows on CD-ROM for ages 9 and up.
Writing: Submit cover letter and résumé. "Do not submit writing samples (submissions release required for writing samples)." Contact: Lori Laubich, president. Submissions not returned; submissions filed. Reports in 1 month. Requires previous multimedia experience. Requires writers be available for on-site consultations. Requires willingness to revise work and "sense of humor, ability to meet deadlines."
Illustration: Needs freelancers for storyboarding, animation, 3-D modeling and overall art design/interface design. Submit cover letter, résumé or samples (color copies). Samples filed; samples returned with SASE. Reports in 4-6 weeks. Requires previous multimedia experience. Requires artists be available for on-site consultation. Requires "sense of humor, ability to meet deadlines and willingness to revise work and work within designed parameters."
Terms: Work purchased outright.

MEMOREX SOFTWARE N-TK ENTERTAINMENT TECHNOLOGY, 18000 Studebaker Rd., #200, Cerritos CA 90703. (310)403-0039. Fax: (310)403-0049. Estab. 1995. Produced 150 titles last year; 125 titles currently in distribution; 12 titles currently in production.
Software: Produces interactive storybooks, early learning, reference software in Windows on CD-ROM (for ages preschool and up). Games: produces action/adventure, fantasy, mystery/puzzle and arcade software in Windows on CD-ROM (for ages preschool and up). Recently produced *Bug Explorers* (entertainment, ages 4 and up); *Aladdin & His Wonderful Lamp* (storybook, 6 and up).
Writing: Submit demo disk of previous projects (Windows, hybrid) or finished product (previously published). Submissions returned with SASE; submissions filed. Reports in 2 months. Requires previous multimedia experience. Requires writers to be available for on-site consultations.
Proposals: Accepts proposals directly from individuals, from agents and from book publishers. Submission guidelines not available. Submit storyboard (hardcopy), videotape, original book (if based on published work), demo of product (Windows, hybrid), complete product (Windows, hybrid). Contact: Olivier Vabois, acquisition coordinator. Prefers project proposal presented by fax or by regular mail. Reports in 2 months. Development of product varies.

INSIDER REPORT

Creating unique multimedia for a neglected audience—girls

Girl Games, Inc., the Austin, Texas-based multimedia company, does exactly what its name implies—produces CD-ROM games targeted exclusively to girls. Laura Groppe, a Hollywood veteran with an Academy Award to her credit (for Best Short Film) as well as experience producing award-winning music videos, noticed that most CD-ROM games on the market were made specifically for young boys. With the philosophy to create games and products for girls and young women which encourage them to incorporate technology into their lives, Girl Games was launched in 1994, with Jan Bozarth as executive producer.

Jan Bozarth

Bozarth started her career in the entertainment industry by working in the record business, moved on to the home video business, and left the corporate world behind in 1986 to write and perform her original songs and stories. After writing and producing an award-winning musical for kids, she helped develop a new multimedia format for music called CD-EXTRA (the original version of the enhanced CDs that are now so common throughout the music industry). She was then asked to write the music for Girl Games' first CD-ROM project, *Let's Talk About ME!* Now as executive producer at Girl Games, "I write and produce the music (with my son and boyfriend) for Girl Games and I develop and produce their products," she says. "This is a great combination of my skills!"

Entering a market saturated with blood-and-gore shoot 'em up games targeted to adolescent boys, *Let's Talk About ME!* hit the shelves and was an instant hit. An interactive handbook for girls ages 8-18, the bright, fast-moving graphics and hip music guide girls through various activities, letting them keep a diary, choose a wardrobe from the "ultimate closet," change hairstyles and colors via the "Hairmaster 2000," take personality quizzes and join in activities that explore self-image and relationships. The CD-ROM, which was looked at skeptically by many in the industry because of the false belief that "girls don't buy computer software," was an instant best-seller, becoming almost as hard to find as a Tickle Me Elmo at Christmas. Obviously girls do buy software, and *Let's Talk About ME!* became one of the top-selling titles for girls. "Sales started out strong and have continued to grow since other girl titles have hit the market," says Bozarth. "There is more of an awareness of the need for girls' titles now so we can only get stronger."

To reach the girl market, Girl Games needed to take its product not only to computer stores but to places where girls shop and hang out. Bookstores, toy stores, girls' clothing and accessory stores, major retailers such as Target and Wal-Mart, and even the Avon catalog have become girl-friendly retailers. Girl Games' products are primarily marketed through publishers Simon & Schuster Interactive and Mattel Interactive, and are also sold through the Girl Games Club, an 800 number, and their website.

INSIDER REPORT, *Bozarth*

With so many publishers closing down their CD-ROM departments, and the recent glut of CD-ROM products hitting store shelves, how does Girl Games manage to thrive? Bozarth believes it's because they targeted one of the last untapped markets—young girls. "Fortunately we were one of the first to recognize this opening and are well positioned to be leaders now. We have evangelized the market, done major research on girls with the National Science Foundation, and are led by one of the brightest and most charismatic women in this field, Laura Groppe. I think we have a great chance at success."

The key to that success lies in the attention paid to the audience they're courting. "Our constant relationship with real girls sets us apart," says Bozarth. "We never lose sight of who this product is for and what they are into. We have to keep our ears and eyes to the streets for ideas. The kids tell us what they do and don't like. We are very interested in edgy products with a new twist. We do look at traditional stuff but we lean more towards the edge."

Creating a Girl Games product is an involved process, and takes a lot of creative teamwork from researchers, writers, illustrators and songwriters. An idea for a product begins with extensive research to see if young girls would be interested. "Each of our products begins with a constant review of our market research," Bozarth says. "We are intent on knowing what girls want and need so we are always checking in with them by doing focus groups three times a week and referring back to our larger research project with the National Science Foundation, where we have data on girls' preferred play patterns and such."

If the idea is based on a licensed product, "We we must first know what the licensor has in mind, study their style guides, read all the scripts, books, see video footage—in

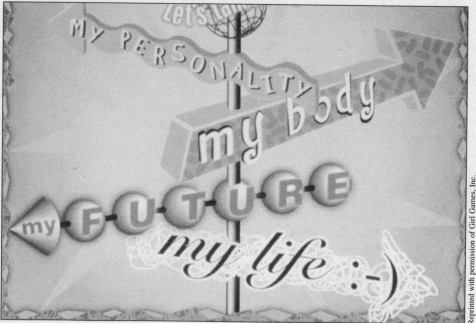

One of the first stops in Girl Games' CD-ROM, *Let's Talk About ME!*, is this screen pointing users in some of the many directions of "ME" the CD-ROM explores.

short, become one with the property. We spend a lot of hours brainstorming. We create the structure, the flow, the sections or modules of play, and then finally, the individual games, activities or experiences."

Then come storyboards, flow charts, budgets and target market information, as well as artwork for the project. "We might assign three artists to do a single illustration for three different sections," says Bozarth. "To identify the look and feel of a project, all the elements must work together. A writer is brought in to do some sample writing and we will locate 'look and feel' music as well." Once everything is approved by the licensor (if applicable) and publisher, a complete design document is created, which includes technical specifications, storyboards, budgets, breakdowns, script samples, music samples and digital art. The whole process can take anywhere from three to six months.

Two new Girl Games CD-ROMs, *Sabrina the Teenage Witch* and *Clueless*, are based on characters from top-rated television shows, and this influx of licenced product may seem to limit the role for writers and illustrators. But Bozarth still sees a need for creative input. "Licensed products still provide a need for writers and illustrators," she says, "but maybe they will be fewer in number. We have to be very creative even with these. The multimedia experience of the licensed character should be different than the television or book experience. This year we have done more with licensed characters, but we are also interested in original works."

In the search for new ideas, Girl Games does not accept unsolicited submissions, but an interested writer or illustrator with an original idea can fill out a submissions form, which can be obtained by calling the company. "We will not accept original concepts without that form," Bozarth says. After filling out a submission form, a writer or illustrator can submit a résumé accompanied by sample works (scripts, stories or digital art and flat illustrations are accepted).

"Make your submissions short and send your best work only with a good résumé, some screen shots or color art, and then a brief summary or a storyline. We can usually see what we like in the first ten seconds. It takes us a while, but we do review all submissions. If you don't hear back, we have filed it for a later reference. If we're interested immediately, we'll call. I'm always looking for awesome designers, illustrators, writers, programmers and other producers who can make Girl Games' vision a reality."

For those with little or no experience in multimedia, Bozarth emphasizes the importance of learning all you can about the most recent, cutting-edge products available. "Look at everything," she advises. "Go out on the web and surf. There is some really creative stuff out there. Also look at CDs. Learn how they are set up and what kinds of interfaces are most fun and most functional. This is a non-linear format so just writing a story will not be enough. You must be able to convey all aspects and iterations of an idea. Learn about programming to be familiar with the tools you will be relying on. Pay attention to how video, animation, the script and the music work together to create an entirely new art form. Read books on how people relate to their computers. Demo your own original work so you can convey your understanding of the medium. I can't express how important it will be for those aspiring writers and illustrators who wish to break into the multimedia area to educate themselves with the tools used to create multimedia. Try creating a little demo on your own or with an associate to see how the experience of moving through this kind of program is. It is an interactive experience, not a passive one like TV or reading. The way the eyes see and the ears hear what come through a computer is different."

INSIDER REPORT, *Bozarth*

"The Ultimate Closet," offering girls the chance to mix and match hundreds of outfits, is just one of the cool activities in *Let's Talk About ME!*

Along with their CD-ROM projects, Girl Games has branched out into other media as well. A book version of *Let's Talk About ME!* has recently been published; *Girl-illa World*, a half-hour TV variety show, is in development; there's a membership club girls can join called Club Girl Games; and an ultra-hip website, planetgirl.com, can be found on the Internet (http://www.planetgirl.com). This integration of various media is where Bozarth sees the future of multimedia publishing heading.

"It works best when you have a CD-ROM, a book, a record, a TV show and a website," she says, "and maybe even a school curriculum or a radio show. Children are media savvy and can bore easily with one dimension. They will become brand builders by allowing beloved characters and trusted experts to talk to them, teach them, entertain them and play with them in a variety of media. One kind of media supports another and possibly speaks to some other part of a child's needs. The market is definitely changing.

"There was a glut of product this year, but these things are cyclical. There will be the year of licensed products and then I expect a year of original products making it through somehow. Content is still king so there will always be a need for writers and artists. Many designers and developers will have the same ideas; the way those ideas are put together is what will set them apart. Great writing, art and music working together to form a completely unique experience is what we hope for and what we think will survive into the new age of products."

—*Cindy Laufenberg*

Terms: Writers paid royalty or work purchased outright. Creators paid royalty of 50% or purchased outright. Advance amount varies. Product catalogs free on request.

NORDIC SOFTWARE, P.O. Box 83499, Lincoln NE 68506. (402)455-5300. Fax: (402)475-5310. Website: http://www.nordicsoftware.com. Estab. 1983. Produced 6 titles last year; 12 titles currently in distribution; 5 titles currently in production.
Software: Produces early learning, reading/language arts and math software in Mac or Windows on floppy or CD-ROM (for ages preschool and up). Recently produced *Turbo Math Facts 3.0* (math, ages 5-8); *Noah's Ark* (early learning, preschool).
Writing: Submit cover letter, résumé, writing samples (Mac), demo disk of previous projects (Mac). Contact: Kent Porter, director of development. Submissions returned with SASE; submissions filed. Reports back only if interested. Does not require writers to be available for on-site consultation.
Illustration: Needs freelancers for storyboarding, animation and 3-D modeling. Submit cover letter, résumé, samples (Mac), demo disk of previous projects (Mac). Contact: Kent Porter, director of development. Samples returned with SASE; samples filed. Reports only if interested. Does not require previous multimedia experience. Requires artists to be available for on-site consultation.
Terms: Writers/artists paid royalty of 1-10% or work purchased outright (varies from project to project). Advance amount varies.

‡ORGANA, 105 Reade St. #3E, New York NY 10013. (212)233-5161. Fax: (212)233-5160. E-mail: info@organ a.com. Website: http://www.organa.com. Vice President of Development: Julia Jones. CEO: Aleen Stein. Estab. 1995. Produced 5 titles last year; 5 titles currently in distribution; 4 titles currently in production.
Software: Produces interactive storybook and other software in Mac and Windows on CD-ROM for ages 5 and up. Games: produces mystery/puzzle software in Mac and Windows on CD-ROM for ages 5 and up. Recently produced *The Book of Lulu* (interactive story, ages 8-12); and *The Snow Queen* (interactive story, ages 8-12).
Writing: Submit cover letter, résumé, writing samples (hard copy, website, Mac) or demo disk of previous projects (Mac). Contact: Aleen Stein, CEO. Submissions not returned; submissions filed. Reports only if interested. Does not require previous multimedia experience. Requires writers be available for on-site consultations.
Illustration: Needs freelancers for storyboarding, animation, 3-D modeling, backgrounds, textures and box design. Submit cover letter, résumé, samples (color copies, website or Mac) or demo disk of previous projects (Mac). Contact: Julia Jones, vice president of development. Samples not returned; samples filed. Reports only if interested. Does not require previous multimedia experience. Requires artists be available for on-site consultation.
Proposals: Accepts proposals directly from individuals. Submission guidelines for proposals not available. Submit demo of product (Mac) or complete product (Mac). Contact: Aleen Stein, CEO. Prefers project proposal presented by fax, e-mail or regular mail. Reports back only if interested. Product developed inhouse with the input of the creator. "Call first."
Terms: Pay determined on an individual basis. Product brochures available for SASE.

POWER INDUSTRIES, INC., 37 Walnut St., Wellesley Hills MA 02181. (617)235-7733. Fax: (617)235-0084. E-mail: 71107.1111@compuserve.com. Estab. 1990. Produced 1 title last year; 20 titles currently in distribution; 1 title currently in production.
Software: Produces interactive storybooks, early learning, reading/language arts, science, math, creativity tools, reference software in Mac and Windows on floppy and CD-ROM (for ages 4-12).
Proposals: Accepts proposals directly from individuals, from agents and from book publishers. Submit demo of product (Mac or Windows) and complete product (Mac or Windows). Contact: New Product Submission Department. Prefers project proposal presented by regular mail. Reports back only if interested. Product developed by the creator.
Terms: Creators paid royalty or work purchased outright. Product catalogs not available.

✦REIDMORE BOOKS INC., 1200, 10109-106th St., Edmonton, Alberta T5J 3L7 Canada. (403)424-4420. Fax: (403)441-9919. E-mail: reidmore@compusmart.ab.ca. Website: http://www.reidmore.com. Estab. 1979. Produced 1 title last year; 1 title currently in distribution; 2 titles currently in production.
Software: Produces reference software in Mac and Windows on CD-ROM (for ages 10-adult). Recently produced *From Mountain to Plain* (reference, middle readers to teens).
Writing: "We don't subcontract writing. We're looking for authors with experience in developing software packages. Contact for this is Suzanne Moquin-Vani, director of marketing/sales." Query. Submissions returned

---

MARKET CONDITIONS are constantly changing! If you're still using this book and it is 1999 or later, buy the newest edition of *Children's Writer's & Illustrator's Market* at your favorite bookstore or order directly from Writer's Digest Books.

with SASE; submissions filed (if worthwhile). Requires previous multimedia experience. Does not require writers to be available for on-site consultation. "We're looking for people to come to us with ideas for nonfiction works, preferably saleable to elementary or junior high schools for use in social studies programs. Call first. We definitely are not interested in trade titles, fiction or children's 'picture book' style products."

Illustration: Needs storyboarding, animation, 3-D modeling, backgrounds, textures, box design and C++ programmers. Submit cover letter, and samples (Mac or Windows). "Any format for submission, other than original art, is acceptable." Contact: Pat Reid, manager, production and design. Samples returned with SASE; samples filed. Reports only if interested. Requires previous multimedia experience. "We prefer to work with local artists due to convenience, but will sometimes work long distance. We need to work with artists willing to make revisions based on feedback from editors and reviewers. We sell to the educational (nonfiction) market, and accuracy is essential. We do very little work with new artists, but are always interested in learning about who is out there and their work. Don't have high expectations!"

Proposals: Accepts proposals directly from individuals, from agents and from book publishers. Call first to discuss project and how material should be submitted. Contact: Suzanne Moquin-Vani, director of marketing/sales. Prefers project proposal presented by phone, e-mail or regular mail. Reports back in 2 months. Product development varies. "We prefer that project personnel be experienced in the field; previously published is best. Call first."

Terms: Writers paid royalty or work purchased outright. Artists paid royalty or work purchased outright. Creators paid royalty. Product catalogs free on request.

‡SNOW LION INTERACTIVE MEDIA, 1119 Colorado Ave., Santa Monica CA 90401. (310)319-6226. Fax: (310)319-6227. E-mail: snowlion@ix.netcom.com. President: Carol Plone. COO: Allen Plone. Estab. 1992. Produced 4 titles last year; 2 titles currently in distribution; 4 titles currently in production.

Software: Produces interactive storybooks and reading/language arts (ages preschool-8) and early learning (ages 5-8) software for Mac and Windows on CD-ROM. Games: produces action/adventure and fantasy software for ages 12 and up for Mac and Windows on CD-ROM. Recently produced *Alphabet Adventure* (language arts/early learning, ages 4-6).

Writing: Submit cover letter, résumé and writing samples (hard copy, Mac or Windows). Contact: Carol Plone, president. Submissions filed or returned with SASE. Reports in 4-6 weeks. Requires previous multimedia experience. Requires writers be available for on-site consultations. They require "quality. Be innovative, literary and skilled."

Proposals: Accepts proposals directly from individuals and from book publishers. Submission guidelines for proposals not available. Submit script (hard copy), storyboard (hard copy) or original book (if based on published work). Contact: Allen Plone, COO. Prefers project proposal presented in person or by regular mail. Reports back in 4-6 weeks only if interested. Product development varies.

Terms: Pay varies. Product catalog not available.

‡TEXAS CAVIAR INC., 3933 Steck Ave., Suite B-115, Austin, TX 78759. (512)346-7887. Fax: (512)346-1393. President: Carolyn Kuhn. Estab. 1990. Produced 2 titles last year; 4 titles currently in distribution; 1 title currently in production.

Software: Produces interactive storybooks (for ages 6-13), reading/language arts, reference and social studies (ages 6-adult) software in Mac or Windows on CD-ROM. Recently produced *Annabel's Dream of Medieval England* (children's education, ages 6-13); and *Vital Signs: The Good Health Resource* (reference, all ages).

Writing: Submit cover letter and résumé. Contact: Carolyn Kuhn, president. Submissions returned with SASE. Reports ASAP. "Know what subjects you are particularly able to address, resource and communicate."

Illustration: Needs freelancers for backgrounds and characters. Submit cover letter and résumé. Samples returned with SASE. Reports ASAP. "You must understand palette and other cross platform issues, specs" and have computer experience.

Proposals: Accepts proposals directly from agents and from book publishers. Requires signed submission agreement before reviewing proposal. Reports ASAP.

♣TIMEBOX INC., P.O. Box 3060, Station D, Ottawa, Ontario K1P 6H6 Canada. (613)256-7338. Fax: (613)256-7340. E-mail: timebox@magi.com. Website: http://www.infoweb.magi.com/~timebox/. **Submissions:** Colette Dionne, president. Estab. 1992. Produced 1 title last year; 5 titles currently in distribution; 2 titles currently in production.

Software: Produces interactive storybooks, science and reference software in Mac on CD-ROM (for ages 7-adult). Games: produces fantasy software in Mac on CD-ROM (for ages 7-adult). Recently produced *Adventure Book of Christopher Columbus* (education, ages 7-14); and *Dreambuilders* (reference, 8 and up).

Writing: Submit cover letter, résumé, writing samples: website and on disk (Mac). Submissions not returned; submissions filed. Reports only if interested. Does not require previous multimedia experience. Usually requires writers to be available for on-site consultations. "Just do it! And don't try to find a recipe on how to do it. There isn't any—(yet!)"

Illustration: Needs freelancers for animation, 3-D modeling and box design. Submit cover letter, résumé, samples (color copies), website or on disk (Mac) or demo disk (1 or 2 of the above). Samples not returned; samples filed. Reports only if interested. Requires previous multimedia experience. Does not require artists to be available for on-site consultation.

Proposals: Accepts proposals directly from individuals. Submission guidelines for proposals not available. Submit résumé, script (hard copy) and computer presentation (PowerPoint) ("one or two samples"). Prefers project proposal presented by regular mail. Reports only if interested. Product developed in house with the input of the creator (varies).

Terms: Writers paid royalty of 15-25%. Artist's work purchased outright. Creators paid royalty of 15-25%. Product catalogs available on website listed above.

Tips: "To be successful in multimedia, do the same things you do to be successful elsewhere—work and be creative. Ideas are not as valuable as you think. The market needs to have distribution ideas. Creative ones are not lacking."

‡UNIVERSAL MARKETING PUBLICATIONS, P.O. Box 36347—Miracle Mile, Los Angeles CA 90036. (310)281-8574. E-mail: russmc@cheerful.com. Website: http://www.geocites.com/RodeoDrive5905. Estab. 1987. Produced 9 titles last year; 4 titles currently in distribution; 14 titles currently in production.

Software: Produces interactive storybooks and reading/language arts in Mac and Windows for floppy and CD-ROM for ages 5 and up; math and online content in Mac and Windows for CD-ROM for ages 5 and up. Games: Produces mystery/puzzles in Mac and Windows for floppy and CD-ROM for ages 5 and up. Recently produced *Think and Do with O.Z. Bookworm* (English/reading for ages 6-12); and *Jenny Marbol* (reading for ages 8-12).

Writing: Submit cover letter, writing samples (hardcopy, website, or on disk for Windows). Contact: Steven McCormick, vice president multimedia programming. Submissions returned with SASE. Requires writers be available for on-site consultations. "Work must be original and belong to artist."

Illustraion: Needs freelancers for storyboarding, animation, 3-D modeling, backgrounds, textures, box design. Submit samples (color copies, website or on disk for Windows), demo reel of previous projects. Reports in 2 weeks. Requires previous multimedia experience. Requires artists be available for on-site consultation.

Tips: "The market will grow. It will grow toward Internet and online publications; CD-ROM will level off, but will still be an active, vital market."

Audiovisual & Audiotape

The business of kids' audio and video has gained respectability in the past few years. *Billboard* magazine now features Billboard's Top Kid Audio Chart. The National Academy of Recording Arts and Sciences created separate categories for children's music and spoken work. And children's audio and video are enjoying healthy sales.

Just as in the children's book industry, the use of licensed characters in children's audio and video is commonplace. The sales charts are littered with Disney characters from Mickey Mouse to the Hunchback of Notre Dame to Winnie the Pooh. Barney the dinosaur is still enjoying popularity. TV tie-ins like Thomas the Tank Engine and Sesame Street-related products also sell well.

Sales of character-driven products help the sales of other audio and video titles. Stocking hundreds of items on store shelves featuring the Hunchback, for example, brings consumers into the stores who will ultimately buy other audio and video products.

Producers and publishers also offer an array of educational materials. Kids can learn about colors and shapes, or counting; animals, art or geography. You'll also find products that tie into books like *Stellaluna* and *Walk Two Moons*, as well as not-so-famous titles.

With a lot happening in the world of children's entertainment, there are growing opportunities for a great many talents. In the Audiovisual and Audiotape sections that follow, you'll find record companies, book publishers, video production houses and more. Many of the companies listed work with a variety of projects and may need anything from songs and short stories to illustration and clay animation.

To keep up on the dynamic world of children's entertainment, read "Child's Play," Moira McCormick's *Billboard* magazine column, as well as *Publishers Weekly*, which often covers and reviews audio and video in its children's section. Industry publications such as *Variety* and *Hollywood Reporter* may also offer useful information on kids' video.

AUDIOVISUAL

The production houses listed here don't produce just video cassettes. Many also create filmstrips, slide sets, multimedia productions—even television shows. These studios and production houses are in need of illustration, video graphics, special effects, and a variety of animation techniques, including stop motion, cell, clay and computer animation. They also need the work of writers for everything from animation scripts to educational filmstrips, but be aware that audiovisual media rely more on the "visual" to tell the story.

Also note that technology in the world of video production is advancing. Many companies are producing CD-ROM and interactive titles for kids, and computer imaging is becoming the norm in kids' video, so illustrators must stay up-to-date on high-tech techniques. (For a list of CD-ROM and software producers, see our Electronic Publishing section on page 252.)

Information on audiovisual companies listed in the previous edition but not included in this edition of *Children's Writer's & Illustrator's Market* may be found in the General Index.

‡**AIMS MULTIMEDIA**, (formerly Aims Media), 9710 DeSoto Ave., Chatsworth CA 91311. (818)773-4300. Fax: (818)341-6700. Vice President Production: Michael Wright. Estab. 1956. Producer/Distributor. Audience: ages 6-adult. Produces multimedia productions, films and videotapes. Uses 5 freelance writers/year; buys 5 writing projects per year. Uses 1 freelance artist/year.
Children's Writing: Needs: Grade school picture books K-3 level. Query. Submissions returned with proper SASE. Reports in 2 weeks. Guidelines/catalog free on request. Pays royalty or buys material outright.

Illustration: Hires for background plates. Types of animation produced: cel animation, clay animation, stop motion, computer animation and video graphics. Submit cover letter, résumé and demo tape (VHS or ¾″). Art samples returned with proper SASE; art samples not filed. Reports in 2 weeks.

BRIDGESTONE MULTIMEDIA GROUP, 300 North McKerny Ave., Chandler AZ 85226-2618. (602)438-2717. Fax: (602)940-8924. Estab. 1986. Video management, license and distribution, software publisher. Audience: Family, children. Produces multimedia productions.
Illustration: Submit demo tape (VHS). Guidelines/catalog free on request.

BROADCAST QUALITY, INC., 2334 Ponce de Leon Blvd., #200, Coral Gables FL 33143. (305)461-5416. Fax: (305)446-7746. E-mail: bqiaix.netcom.com. President: Diana Udel. Estab. 1978. Video production and post production house. Produces videotapes. Children's productions: "It's Ours to Save—Biscayne National Park," written by Diana Udel, produced by Diana Udel/BQI, Betacam SP/1″ Master, (Environmental awareness for grades 4-7); and "The Wildlife Show at Parrot Jungle," written by Amy Smith, produced by BQI, Betacam SP/1″ Master, (Hands on to Florida's Wildlife for K-8th grade). Uses 2-5 freelance writers/year. "All work is on a for-hire basis only."
Tips: "Send a résumé and demo reel. Seeks variety, knowledge of subject and audience."

‡**DIMENSION FILMS**, 15007 Gault St., Van Nuys CA 91405. (818)997-8065. President: Gary Goldsmith. Estab. 1962. Production house. Audience: schools and libraries. Uses film strips, interactive media, films, videotapes. 10% of writing is by freelancers; 100% of illustrating/animating is by freelancers.
Children's Writing: Needs: educational material and documentaries for kindergarten-12th-grade audience. To submit, query. Submissions filed. Reports "in a matter of weeks. Call for guidelines." Pays in accordance with Writer's Guild standards.
Illustration/Animation: Hires illustrators for storyboarding, comprehensives. Types of animation produced: cel animation, video graphics, live action. To submit, send cover letter and résumé. Reports "in a matter of weeks. Call for guidelines." Pays $30-60/frame.
Tips: Illustrators/animators: looking for "imagination, clarity and purpose." Portfolio should show "strong composition; action in stillness."

EDUCATIONAL VIDEO NETWORK, 1401 19th St., Huntsville TX 77340. (409)291-2860. Fax: (409)295-4360. E-mail: evn@edvidnet.com. Website: http://www.edvidnet.com. Production Manager: Anne Russell. Estab. 1954. Production house. Audience: educational (school). Uses videotapes. 20% of writing by freelancers; 20% of illustrating/animating is by freelancers. Recent children's productions: "How a Bill Becomes a Law," written and illustrated by Tom Zilis (government cartoon for grades 4-college); and "Teenage Marijuana Abuse," written by Dr. Christopher Wilson, Kenneth T. Hill and Rachel Phelps, illustrated by Jeff Dates (drug abuse live action and computer graphics for grades 6-college). Uses 1-2 freelance artists/year; buys 2-3 art projects/year.
Children's Writing: Needs: "Curriculum-oriented educational material" for junior high through college audiences. Query. Submissions returned with proper SASE. Reports in 2-6 months. Guidelines/catalog free. Pays writers royalties of 3% or buys material outright.
Illustration/Animation: Hires illustrators for animation. Types of animation produced: video graphics, extensive computer animation. To submit, send cover letter and VHS demo tape. Art samples returned with proper SASE. Reports in 2-6 months. Guidelines/catalog free. Pays $10-30/cel for animation work.
Tips: "Materials should fill a curriculum need for junior high to college. We seldom assign projects to freelancers. We want to be approached by people who know a particular subject and who have a plan for getting that information across to students. Programs should feature professional production techniques and involve the viewers in the message."

FILM CLASSIC EXCHANGE, 143 Hickory Hill Circle, Osterville MA 02655. (508)428-7198. Fax: (508)420-0121. President: J.H. Aikman. Estab. 1916. Distribution/production house. Audience: pre-school through college. Produces films, videotapes. Children's productions: "The Good Deed," written by William P. Pounder, illustrated by Karen Losaq (film on family values aimed at preschool); "Willie McDuff's Big Day," written and illustrated by Joe Fleming (anti-drug film aimed at ages 12 and up). Uses 6 freelance writers and artists/year. Purchases 6 writing and 6 art projects/year.
Children's Writing: Needs: preschool. Subjects include: anti-drug. Query with synopsis or submit completed script. Submissions are returned with proper SASE. Reports back only if interested. Buys material outright.
Illustration/Animation: Hires illustrators for cel/video animation, storyboarding, character development, live action, comprehensives, pencil testing. Types of animation produced: cel animation, clay animation, stop motion,

---

‡ **LISTINGS NEW TO THIS EDITION** are marked with a double dagger.

special effects, computer animation, video graphics, motion control, live action. To submit, send cover letter, résumé, demo tape (VHS), color print samples. Art samples returned with proper SASE. Reports back only if interested.

Tips: "Keep sending updated résumés/samples of work."

‡FINE ART PRODUCTIONS, 67 Maple St., Newburgh NY 12550. (914)561-5866. Director: Richie Suraci. Estab. 1989. "We cover every aspect of the film, video, publishing and entertainment industry." Audience: All viewers. Uses filmstrips, films, slide sets, videotapes, multimedia productions, any format needed. Children's productions: "1991 Great Hudson River Revival," illustrated by various artists (35mm film and print on environment, clearwater sailing ship); and "Wheel and Rock to Woodstock Bike Tour," written and illustrated by various artists (film, print, video on exercise, health, music and volunteerism). Percent of freelance illustrators/animators used varies.

Children's Writing: Query with synopsis, or submit synopsis/outline, completed script, résumé. Submissions are filed, or returned with proper SASE. Reports in 1 month if interested. Pay is negotiated.

Illustration/Animation: Hires illustrators for animation, storyboarding, character development, live action, comprehensives, pencil testing. Types of animation produced: cel animation, clay animation, stop motion, special effects, computer animation, video graphics, motion control, live action. To submit, send cover letter, résumé, demo tape (VHS or ¾"), b&w print samples, color print samples, tearsheets, business card. Art samples are filed, or returned with proper SASE. Reports in 1 month if interested. Guidelines/catalog for SASE. Pay is negotiated.

‡HOME, INC., 731 Harrison Ave., Boston MA 02118. (617)266-1386. Director: Alan Michel. Estab. 1974. Nonprofit video production and postproduction facility which produces some teen television programming for the local Boston market. Audience: teenagers, teachers, instructors, education administrators, parents, social workers and court intervention professionals. Uses videotapes. Children's productions: "Going to Court," written by Ken Cheeseman, graphics by Alan Michel (¾" videotape puppet drama explaining the court for ages 3 through teens); and "Stand Back from Crack," written by Young Nation, graphics by Alan Michel (¾" videotape, anti-drug public service video for teen and pre-teen). 90% of writing is by freelancers; 15% of illustrating/animating is by freelancers.

Children's Writing: Needs: scripts, curriculum, educational support material for videos, proposal writing for elementary through high school. Subjects include social or cultural content/sometimes career or health care oriented. To submit, send synopsis/outline and résumé. Submissions are filed and cannot be returned. Reports back only if interested. Payment negotiated/commissioned.

Illustration/Animation: Hires illustrators for storyboarding and graphics. Types of animation produced: special effects, computer animation and video graphics. To submit send cover letter, résumé, VHS demo tape, b&w and color print samples. Samples are filed and not returned. Reports back only if interested. Payment negotiated. Pays $250-4,000/project for specialized animation.

Tips: "We look for cooperative associates who have a commitment to quality and to their profession. This includes their presentation and follow-through in their dealings with us prior to project engagement."

KIDVIDZ: Special Interest Video for Children, 618 Centre St., Newton MA 02158. (617)965-3345. Fax: (617)965-3640. Website: http://www.kidvidz.com. Partner: Jane Murphy. Estab. 1987. Home video publisher and family media consultants. Audience: pre-school and primary-age children, 2-12 years. Produces videotapes. Children's productions: "Paws, Claws, Feathers & Fins" (a kid's video guide to pets); "Piggy Banks to Money Markets" (a kid's video guide to dollars and sense); "Hey, Whay About Me?" (a video guide for brothers and sisters of new babies); and "Kids Get Cooking" (a kid's video guide to food and cooking). Uses 2 freelance writers/year. Uses 3 freelance artists/year. Submissions filed.

• Kidvidz has just published the book, *Stay Tuned! Raising Media Savvy Kids in the Age of the Channel-surfing Couch Potato* (Doubleday).

Tips: "Submit material strong on dialogue using a child-centered approach. Be able to write shooting scripts."

KJD TELEPRODUCTIONS, 30 Whyte Dr., Voorhees NJ 08043. (609)751-3500. Fax: (609)751-7729. President: Larry Scott. Creative Director: Kim Davis. Estab. 1989. Location production services (Betacam SP) plus interformat edit and computer animation. Audience: industrial and broadcast. Uses slide sets, multimedia productions, videotapes. Recent children's productions: "Aluminations," (about recycling superheroes). 10% of writing is by freelancers; 25% of animating/illustrating by freelancers.

Children's Writing: Needs: animation. To submit, query. Submissions are filed. Reports in 3 months. Pays royalty or buys material outright.

Illustration/Animation: Hires illustrators for animation. Types of animation produced: computer animation. To submit, send cover letter, résumé, demo tape (VHS or ¾"), b&w print samples, tearsheets, business card. Art samples are filed. Reports in 3 months. Pay varies.

Tips: "Keep us up to date with work; we inquire on projects. Stay diligent."

NEW & UNIQUE VIDEOS, 2336 Sumac Dr., San Diego CA 92105-4651. (619)282-6126. Fax: (619)283-8264. E-mail: videos@concentric.net. Website: http://www.concentric.net/~videos. Acquisitions Managers: Candy Love, Mark Schulze. Estab. 1985. Video production and distribution services. "Audience varies with each title." Uses films and videotapes. Children's productions: "Full Cycle: A World Odyssey," written by Patty Mooney, animated by Bob Ocegueda ('endless summer' with mountain bicycles); and "John Howard's Lessons in Cycling," written by John Howard, direction and camera by Mark Schulze (VHS video on cycling for 12 and over). 50% of writing is by freelancers; 85% of illustrating/animating is by freelancers.

Children's Writing: Needs: Completed and packaged videotape productions (45 minutes to 1 hour in length) whose intended audiences may range from 1 and older. "No scripts or treatments, please. Any subject matter focusing on a special interest that can be considered 'new and unique.' " Query. Submissions are returned with proper SASE. Reports in 2-3 weeks. Payment negotiable.

Illustration/Animation: Hires illustrators for film or video animation. Types of animation produced: computer animation and video graphics. To submit, send cover letter. Art samples returned with proper SASE. Reports back in 2-3 weeks. Payment negotiable.

Tips: "As more and more video players appear in homes across the world, and as the interest in special interest videos climbs, the demand for more original productions is rising meteorically."

ST. ANTHONY MESSENGER PRESS AND FRANCISCAN COMMUNICATIONS, 1615 Republic St., Cincinnati OH 45210. (513)241-5615. Fax: (513)241-0399. E-mail: gregf@americancatholic.org. Website: http://wwwamericancatholic.org. Executive Producer: Greg Friedman, OFM. Estab. 1893. Supplier of resources (print, audio and video) for education within the Catholic Church. Audience: Catholic religious educators and Catholics at large. Produces videotapes. "We are just beginning our video department productions in this area." Uses 1-2 freelance writers/year. Uses 1-2 freelance artists/year.

Children's Writing: Needs: short dramatic stories (maximum 10 minutes). Subjects include: life issues told in dramatic/story form. Query. Submissions are returned with proper SASE. Submissions are filed. Reports in 2 weeks. Guidelines/catalog free on request. Buys material outright; pays $100-250.

Illustration: Hires illustrators for animation (limited—"photomation" from stills). Types of animation produced: motion control. Send cover letter, résumé, b&w print samples, color print samples. Art samples returned with proper SASE. Reports in 2 weeks. Guidelines/catalog free on request.

Tips: "We are a very specialized producer, so would be interested in writers willing to work with our direction and goals. For artists, we are more flexible, and are interested to build a file of potential illustrators to work with."

SEA STUDIOS, INC., 810 Cannery Row, Monterey CA 93940. (408)649-5152. Fax: (408)649-1380. E-mail: seastudios@seastudios.com. Website: http://www.seastudios.com. Office Manager: Melissa Lewington. Estab. 1985. Natural history video production company. Audience: general. Recent children's productions: "Jellies & Other Ocean Drifters," written by Robin Burnett, illustrated by Heather Weyers (general video on jellyfish). Uses multimedia productions, videotapes. 50% of writing is by freelancers; 50% of illustrating/animating is by freelancers.

Children's Writing: Needs: educational material—target age dependent on project. Send résumé (no phone calls, please). Submissions returned with proper SASE. Reports back in 3 months. Pay negotiable.

Illustration/Animation: Send cover letter, résumé (no phone calls please). Art samples returned with proper SASE. Reports back in 3 months.

‡SISU HOME ENTERTAINMENT, 10th Floor, 18 W. 27th St., New York NY 10001. (212)779-1559. Fax: (212)779-7115. President: Haim Scheininger. Estab. 1988. Video and audio manufacturers (production, distribution). Audience: Children (educational videos and entertainment videos). Uses videotapes and audio. Children's productions: "Lovely Butterfly—Chanuka," written by IETV (Israel Educational TV), illustrated by IETV (Jewish holiday-program for ages 2-5); and "Shalom Sesame" co-production with CTW (Children's Television Workshop). 25% of writing is by freelancers.

Children's Writing: Needs: publicity writing—all ages. To submit, arrange interview.

Illustration/Animation: Types of animation produced: clay animation, video graphics illustrations for video box covers. To submit, send résumé. Art samples filed. Reports back only if interested.

CHIP TAYLOR COMMUNICATIONS, 15 Spollett Dr., Derry NH 03038. (603)434-9262. Fax: (603)432-2723. E-mail: chip@chiptaylor.com. President: Chip Taylor. Estab. 1985. Production house. Audience: all ages. Produces multimedia productions, videotapes. Recent children's productions: "I've Got Your Nose," written by Nancy Bentley, illustrated by Don Madden (video on values aimed at preschool to 3rd-grade audience); and "Picking Pens for a Penny," written by Angela Shelf Medearis, illustrated by Charles Shaw (video about growing

---

MARKET CONDITIONS are constantly changing! If you're still using this book and it is 1999 or later, buy the newest edition of *Children's Writer's & Illustrator's Market* at your favorite bookstore or order directly from Writer's Digest Books.

up during the depression for 2nd- to 5th-grade audience). Uses 5-10 freelance writers/year; buys 20-50 writing projects/year. Uses 1-2 freelance artists/year; buys 10-20 art projects/year.

Children's Writing: Needs: scripts and already-written picture books. Subjects include educational content—values. Submit sample of books. Submissions returned with proper SASE; submissions filed. Reports in 3 weeks. Guidelines/catalog for 9 × 12 SAE and 3 first-class stamps. Pays royalty of 2-10%.

Illustration: Hires illustrators for character development, live action. Types of animation produced: computer animation, video graphics, live action. Send color print samples, demo tape. Art samples returned with proper SASE; art samples filed. Reports in 3 weeks. Guidelines/catalog for 9 × 12 SAE and 3 first-class stamps. Payment varies with project.

TREEHAUS COMMUNICATIONS, INC., 906 W. Loveland Ave., P.O. Box 249, Loveland OH 45140. (513)683-5716. Fax: (513)683-2882. President: Gerard A. Pottebaum. Estab. 1968. Production house. Audience: preschool through adults. Produces film strips, multimedia productions, videotapes. Recent children's production: "The Little Grain of Wheat," written by Gerard Pottebaum, illustrated by Robert Strobridge (Biblical parable video, for ages 4-9). 30% of writing is by freelancers; 30% of illustrating/animating is by freelancers.

Children's Writing: Needs: educational material/documentaries, for all ages. Subjects include: "social studies, religious education, documentaries on all subjects, but primarily about people who live ordinary lives in extraordinary ways." Query with synopsis. Submissions returned with proper SASE. Reports in 1 month. Guidelines/catalog for SASE. Pays writers in accordance with Writer's Guild standards.

Tips: Illustrators/animators: "Be informed about movements and needs in education, multi-cultural sensitivity." Looks for "social values, originality, competency in subject, global awareness."

‡VIDEO AIDED INSTRUCTION, INC., 182 Village Rd., Roslyn Heights NY 11577. (800)238-1512. Fax: (516)484-8785. E-mail: melanzer@videoaidedinstruction.com. Contact: Mona E. Lanzer, president. Estab. 1983. Video publisher. Audience: grade 5 through adult. Uses videotapes. Recent children's productions: "GED" series written by Peter Lanzer, M.B.A. and Karl Weber, M.A. (High School Equivalency Test—grade high school to adult); and "SAT" series written by Karl Weber, M.A. and Dr. Harold Shane (grade high school).

Children's Writing: Needs: educational material for all age levels on all school subjects. Query. Submissions are filed. Reports in 1 month. Guidelines/catalog free on request. Pays royalty; buys material outright.

Illustration/Animation: Types of animation produced: video graphic, live action. Guidelines/catalog free on request.

Tips: "If you have an academic subject you can teach, call us!"

‡BILL WADSWORTH PRODUCTIONS, 1913 W. 37th St., Austin TX 78731-6012. (512)452-4243. Fax: (512)206-0606. E-mail: bwp@mindspring.com Website: http://www.mindspring.com/~bwp. Producer/Director: Bill Wadsworth. Estab. 1978. Production/animation company. Audience: youth/adult. Produces films, multimedia productions, videotapes. Recent children's productions: "Tailypo," written by Bill Wadsworth (live action folktale for elementary-aged children); and "Porfirio Salinas," Bill Wadsworth (live action biography for ages 12-adult).

  • Bill Wadsworth Productions is looking only for illustrators at this time.

Illustration: Hires illustrators for animation, storyboarding, character development, comprehensives, rotoscope. Types of animation produced: computer animation, video graphics, rotoscope. Send cover letter, résumé. Samples not returned; art samples not filed. Reports only if interested. Pay scale provided on request.

AUDIOTAPE

Among these listings you'll find companies with a range of offerings. Some publish exclusively story tapes; more often the companies listed publish and produce music as well as stories. In either case, these companies provide opportunities for songwriters and writers to showcase their work on tape or compact disk.

Among the record companies listed you'll find both large producers and distributors, and smaller independent studios. For more information about the children's entertainment industry, see the Audiovisual & Audiotape introduction on page 263.

Information on audiotape producers listed in the previous edition but not included in this edition of *Children's Writer's & Illustrator's Market* **may be found in the General Index.**

AMERICATONE INTERNATIONAL—USA, 1817 Loch Lomond, Las Vegas NV 89102-4437. (702)384-0030. Fax: (702)382-1926. President/CEO: Joe Jan Jaros. Music publisher, record company. Record labels include Americatone Records International and Christy Records International. Estab. 1983.

Music: Releases 5-10 singles/year (CDs and cassettes). Member of BMI. Hires staff writers for children's music. For music published, pays standard royalty of 50%; for songs recorded, pays musicians on salary for inhouse studio work, and songwriters on royalty contract (10%). Submit demo tape by mail; unsolicited submissions OK. Submit demo cassette. Submissions returned with SASE.

‡**AUDIO-FORUM**, 96 Broad St., Guilford CT 06437. (203)453-9794 or (800)243-1234. Fax: (203)453-9774. Publicity & Reviews: Nancy Grant. Estab. 1972.
Stories: "We publish children's educational materials on audio and video cassettes on the following subjects: foreign languages, music, English as a second language, history, math, reading, grammar, spelling, touch typing, astronomy and games." Recently published story tapes: *Winko Teddy Bear: Flash cards with cassette in French, German, and Spanish* (ages 5-12 language teaching program). Free children's catalog available.

BARRON'S EDUCATIONAL SERIES, 250 Wireless Blvd., Hauppauge NY 11788. (516)434-3311. Fax: (516)434-3723. Managing Editor/Director of Acquisitions: Grace Freedson. Book publisher. Estab. 1940.
Stories: Publishes 1 book/cassette package/year. 100% of stories are fiction. For fiction, will consider foreign language. Pays authors royalty. Query. Catalog free for SAE. Ms guidelines free for SASE. Recently recorded story tapes: *Un, Deux, Trois—My First French Rhymes*, by Opal Dunn, illustrated by Patricia Aggs (ages 4-8 foreign language).

‡**BLACK ROSE PRODUCTIONS INC.**, P.O. Box 216, Cold Spring Harbor NY 11724. (516)367-8544. Fax: (516)692-4709. Vice President/A&R: Mr. Daniel Batista. Music publisher, record company. Record labels include Reiter Records Ltd. Estab. 1969.
Music: Releases 20 singles/year; 50 LPs/year; 100 CDs/year. Member of BMI. Publishes 50 and records 10 children's songs/year. Hires staff writers for children's music. Works with composers, lyricists and teams collaborators. For music published, pays standard royalty of 50%; for songs recorded, pays musicians/artists on record contract, musicians on salary for inhouse studio work, and songwriters on royalty contract (50%). Submit demo tape by mail; unsolicited submissions OK. Submit demo cassette with 3 songs, lyric and lead sheet. Reports in 2 weeks. Recently recorded songs: "The Song," written and recorded by Denny Sant on Black Rose Records (pop for ages 10-24); and "Children," written and recorded by Cindy Richards on Reiter Records Ltd. (pop for ages 5-10).
Music Tips: "Give us the best work you have."
Stories: Publishes 5 book/cassette packages/year; 10 cassettes/CDs/year. 3% of stories are fiction; 7% nonfiction. For fiction will consider animal, fantasy (ages 5-10). For nonfiction will consider biography, education, history (ages 5-15). Pays authors 50% royalties based on wholesale price; or work purchased outright. Submit complete ms; outline/synopsis and sample chapters; cassette tape of story. Reports on queries/mss in 2 weeks. Catalog available. Manuscript guidelines available. Recently recorded story tapes: "The Boy and His Dog, " by Daniel Oliverio, narrated by Dr. Reiter Ann (ages 8-13, love); and "My Toy Car," by Jane Barr, narrated by Daniel Oliverio (ages 5-10, work and fun).
Tips: "Give us the best work."

‡**DUTTON CHILDREN'S BOOKS**, 375 Hudson St., New York NY 10014. (212)366-2600. President and Publisher: Christopher Franceschelli. Book publisher.
Stories: Publishes fiction and nonfiction. Will consider animal and fantasy. Authors are paid 5-10% royalties based on retail price; outright purchase of $2,000-20,000; royalty inclusive. Average advance $3,000. Submit outline/synopsis and sample chapters through agent. Reports on queries in 3 weeks; on mss in 6 months. Catalog is available for 8×11 SAE and 8 first-class stamps. Ms guidelines available for #10 SASE.
Tips: "Do not call publisher. Get agent. Celebrity readers sell."

‡**EMERALD RECORDS**, 159 Village Green Dr., Nashville TN 37217. (615)361-7902. President: Cliff Ayers. Music publisher, record company (Emerald, American Sound). Estab. 1951.
Music: Releases 7 singles/year; 20 LPs-cassettes/year; 12 CDs/year. Member of ASCAP. Publishes 20 children's songs/year; records 10 children's songs/year. Works with composers, lyricists and team collaborators. For music published, pays standard royalty of 50%; for songs recorded, pays musicians/artists on royalty contract. Submit demo tape by mail; unsolicited submissions OK. Submit demo cassette with 2 songs and lyric sheet. Cannot return submissions. Reports in 2 weeks. Recently recorded "Birds of a Feather," by Miss Marti, recorded by Cathy Lemmon on Emerald Records (for ages 4-7); and "All God's Children," written and recorded by M. Jeffries on Emerald Records (ages 3-6).
Music Tips: "Keep the lyrics simple."
Stories: 70% of stories are fiction; 30% nonfiction. For fiction, will consider animal, fantasy (ages 2-7). For nonfiction, will consider animal and sports (ages 3-7). Pays authors royalty (no set rate). Submit both cassette tape and ms. Reports on queries in 2 weeks. Ms guidelines free for SASE.

‡**MARTIN EZRA & ASSOCIATES**, 45 Fairview Ave., Lansdowne PA 19050. (610)622-1600. President: Martin Ezra. Producer. Estab. 1968.

---

‡   **LISTINGS NEW TO THIS EDITION** are marked with a double dagger.

Music: Submit demo tape by mail; unsolicited submissions OK. Submit demo cassette (VHS videocassette if available). Lyric or lead sheets not necessary.
Stories: Will consider all types of fiction and nonfiction. Submit cassette tape of story.

FINE ART PRODUCTIONS, 67 Maple St., Newburgh NY 12550-4034. (914)561-5866. E-mail: rs7.fap@mhv.net. Websites: http://www.audionet.com/pub/books/fineart/fineart.htm or http://www.geocites.com/Hollywood/1077. Contact: Richie Suraci. Music publisher, record company, book publisher. Estab. 1989.
Music: Member of ASCAP and BMI. Publishes and records 1-2 children's songs/year. Hires staff writers for children's music. Works with composers, lyricists and team collaborators. For music published, pays standard royalty of 50% or other amount; for songs recorded, pays musicians/artists on record contract, musicians on salary for inhouse studio work, songwriters on varying royalty contract. Submit ½″ demo tape by mail; unsolicited submissions OK. Submit demo cassette. Not neccessary to include lyric or lead sheets. Submissions returned with SASE. Reports in 3-4 months. Include SASE with all submissions.
Stories: Publishes 1 book/cassette package and 1 audio tape/year. 50% of stories are fiction; 50% nonfiction. Will consider all genres for all age groups. Authors are paid varying royalty on wholesale or retail price. Submit both cassette tape and ms. Reports in 3-4 months. Ms guidelines free with SASE.

LINDSEY PUBLISHING, INC., 117 W. Harrison, #L220, Chicago IL 60605. (312)226-1458. Fax: (312)226-1248. Contact: Donna Beasley. Book publisher. Estab. 1992.
Stories: Publishes 1-2 books/year. 50% of stories are fiction. For fiction will consider African-American focus in history, adventure, sports, mystery (ages 3-13). For nonfiction will consider self-help, biography (ages 3-18). Pays authors 5-10% royalty based on wholesale price. Query. Reports in 6-8 weeks. Recently published "Peanut Butter & Bologna Sandwiches," by Pamm Jenkins, illustrated by Cortrell Harris Sr., and Cortrell Harris Jr. (Story a grandmother and grandmother who have an afternoon tea party. Guess what's on the menue!); and "Music In The Family," by Donna Renee Carter, narrated by Isaiah Robinson (ages 3-7, story of boy growing up in musical family).
Tips: "Submit query for upbeat stories that feature African-Americans in positive roles and relationships."

‡LISTENING LIBRARY, INC., One Park Ave., Old Greenwich CT 06870. (203)637-3616. Fax: (203)698-1998. Contact: Editorial Review Committee. Audiobook recording company.
Stories: Buys material outright. "Submit published books only!" SASE/IRC for return of submission. Reports in 2 months. Recorded books: *A Wrinkle in Time*, by Madeleine L'Engle (ages 9-12); and *Superfudge*, by Judy Blume (ages 5-12).
Tips: "We primarily produce works that are already published. However, we occasionally find that an audio project will arise out of original material submitted to us."

LOLLIPOP FARM ENTERTAINMENT, P.O. Box 460086, Garland TX 75046-0086. (972)497-1616. Fax: (972)437-9400. E-mail: lonnyj@aol.com. President: Lonny J. Schonfeld. Record company, live performance videotape producer. Record labels include Lollipop Farm.
Music: Releases 4-6 singles/year; 2-3 LPs/year; 2-3 CDs/year. Member of BMI. Publishes and records 10-12 songs/year. Works with composers and/or lyricists and teams collaborators. For music published, pays standard royalty of 50%; for songs recorded, pays musicians on salary for inhouse studio work, and songwriters on royalty contract (50%). Submit demo tape by mail; unsolicited submissions OK. Submit demo cassette, VHS videocassette if available with 3-5 songs and lyric sheet. "Be original and have material with a positive attitude or message. No violent material accepted." Submissions returned with SASE. Reports in 4-6 weeks. Recently published and recorded songs: "The Little Bitty Chicken," by The Warmer Brothers, recorded by Scudler and Friends on the Lollipop Farm label (pop for ages 4-10); and "Elizabeth's Lullaby," by N. Peacock and Eric Johnson, recorded by Mary Massey on the Lollipop Farm label (for ages 1-6).
Music Tips: "Keep in mind that our philosophy is that even though society has changed since the 1950s, we still believe that values such as family, education, decency, respect, and manners should be a large part of children's entertainment."
Stories: Publishes 2-4 book/cassette packages/year. 50% of stories are fiction; 50% nonfiction. For fiction and nonfiction, will consider animal, fantasy, history, sports, spy/mystery/adventure, education, human relationships (ages 4-12). Pays negotiable royalty based on wholesale price. Submit both cassette tape and ms. Reports on queries/mss in 4-6 weeks. Catalog not available. Submission guidelines free with SASE. Recently published and recorded *"Did You Know?"*, by various writers, narrated by Larry Stones (ages 4-12, educational facts, amusing stories, fun songs); *"Did You Know II?"*, by various writers, narrated by Robert Styx (ages 4-12, educational facts, amusing stories, fun songs).

OMNI 2000 INC., 413 Cooper St., Camden NJ 08102. (609)963-6400. Fax: (609)964-3291. President: Michael Nise. Music publisher, book publisher (audio books), record company. Record labels include Power Up Records. Estab. 1995.
Music: Member of BMI. Works with composers, lyricists and team collaborators. For music published, pays standard royalty of 50%; for songs recorded, pays musicians/artists on record contract, musicians on salary for inhouse studio work. "Include SASE for artist's release form. Completion is required prior to (or with) submis-

sion." Submit demo cassette with 3 songs. "Make sure product is protected and you have our release signed and returned. Don't send original masters." Reports within 3 months.

• Omni 2000 is currently setting up distribution for a children's cassette series under Century 2000 publishing, a division of Omni 2000.

Stories: For fiction and nonfiction submissions, will consider all formats (ages 2-11 and 12-17). Pays authors negotiable royalty; or outright purchase to be negotiated. Submit cassette tape of story. Reports on queries in approximately 3 months.

‡PEERMUSIC, 8159 Hollywood Blvd., Los Angeles CA 90069. (213)656-0364. Fax: (213)656-3298. E-mail: 104044.1361@compuserve.com. Website: http://www.peermusic.com. Contact: Christine Redlin. Music publisher. Estab. 1929.

Music: Member of ASCAP/BMI and others across the world. Doesn't hire staff writers for children's music. Works with composers, lyricists and team collaborators. Write for permission to submit material. Submit demo cassette with 1-4 songs and lyric sheet. Submissions returned with SASE. Reports in 1-3 months. Recently published songs: "There Was An Old Lady Who Swallowed a Fly," by Rose Bonne/Alan Mills, recorded by various artists (children's for ages 7 and up); "You Are My Sunshine," by Garner Jimmie Davis and Charles Mitchell, recorded by various artists (family, love, sing-a-long for all ages).

Tips: "Write from the heart and, because we have a TV film licensing division, think of how your song could be suited for children's films, animated films and/or cartoons."

Stories: Royalty varies. Offers $1,000 advance. Reports on queries in 4-6 weeks.

Tips: "Submit your strongest material on DAT or cassette and include lyric sheets. We do not take 'unsolicited' material. Please be sure submissions come in with legal representative, i.e.; manager, agent or attorney."

‡PELICAN PUBLISHING COMPANY, P.O. Box 3110, Gretna LA 70054. (504)368-1175. Fax: (504)368-1195. E-mail: kathleenelican.com. Website: http://www.pelicanpub.com. Promotion Director: Kathleen Calhoun Nettleton. Book publisher. Estab. 1926.

Stories: Published 12 cassettes/CDs/year. 100% of stories are fiction. For fiction, will consider animal, humor, regional holiday (ages 5-8). Pays authors royalties. Submit outline/synopsis and 2 sample chapters. Reports on queries in 1 month; on mss in 3 months. Catalog free for 9x12 SAE with 7 first-class stamps. Ms guidelines are free for SASE. Recently published and recorded story tapes: *An Irish Night Before Christmas/A Leprechaun's St. Patrick's Day*, written and narrated by Sarah Kirwan Blazek (ages 5-8, regional holiday/ethnic); and *Jenny Giraffe Discovers Papa Noel/Jenny Giraffe and the Streetcar Party*, written and narrated by Cecilia Casrill Dartez (ages 5-8, animal stories set in New Orleans).

Tips: "Be sure there is a book involved and that the topic is specific enough to fit our list (examine our catalog). Be able to provide music (either original or public domain) and possibly musicians."

PEOPLE RECORDS, 8929 Apache Dr., Beulah CO 81023. (719)485-3191. Fax: (719)485-3500. E-mail: dvanman@fone.net. Contact: Helene Van Manen. Music publisher, record company. Estab. 1986.

Music: Releases 1 LP/year; 1 CD/year. Member of BMI. Publishes and records 10 children's songs/year. For music published, pays standard royalty of 50%. Submit demo tape by mail—unsolicited submissions OK. Submit demo cassette with 3 songs and lyric sheet. Submission returned with SASE. Reports in 3 months. Recently published and recorded "Don't Whine," by Dave and Helene Van Manen, recorded by The Van Manens on People Records (folk music for ages 3-12); "Trees," by Dave and Helene Van Manen, recorded by The Van Manens on People Records (swing music for ages 3-12).

Music Tips: "Songs for children should be singable, fun and catchy. Do not be afraid of simplicity—some of the best songs for kids (and even adults) are very simple songs."

PERIDOT RECORDS, P.O. Box 8846, Cranston RI 02920. (401)785-2677. Owner/President: Amy Parravano. Music publisher, record company. Record labels include Peridot. Estab. 1992.

Music: Releases 2 singles/year; 2 LPs/year; 1 CD/year. Member of ASCAP, BMI. Publishes 1-4 and records 2-6 children's songs/year. Works with composers and/or lyricists and team collaborators. For music published, pays standard royalty of 50%; for songs recorded, pays songwriters on royalty contract. Submit demo tape by mail; unsolicited submissions OK. Submit demo cassette with 1-10 songs and lyric sheet. Reports in 2-3 months. Recently recorded songs: "Fingerprints" and "If I Were A Tree," written by Amy Parranino, recorded by Amy Beth on Peridot Records (folk/children, ages 1-10). .

Music Tips: "Send something with 'commercial-novelty' flair. 'Kid-test' songs when developing musical story ideas."

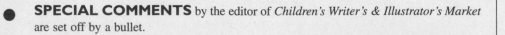

● SPECIAL COMMENTS by the editor of *Children's Writer's & Illustrator's Market* are set off by a bullet.

Stories: For nonfiction, will consider biography, education, history.

PRAKKEN PUBLICATIONS, INC., P.O. Box 8623, 3970 Varsity Dr., Ann Arbor MI 48107. (313)975-2800. Fax: (313)975-2787. E-mail: prakken@cyberzone_inc.com. Publisher: George Kennedy. Magazine publisher. Estab. 1934.
Stories: Publishes 3-4 books/videos/year. 100% nonfiction. Will consider any genre of nonfiction (ages 3-8). Authors are paid 10% royalty based on net sales. Other payment negotiable. Advance not standard practice but possibly negotiable. Submit outline/synopsis and sample chapters. Reports on queries in 2 weeks; mss in 6 weeks if return requested and SASE enclosed. Catalog free on request. Submission free with SASE.
Tips: "Nonfiction material write an educational slant would be preferred. Career explorations for younger children is a newer area of present interest."

RADIO AAHS, 5501 Excelsior Blvd., Minneapolis MN 55416. (612)926-1280. Fax: (612)926-8014. Music Director: Don Michaels. Radio network. Estab. 1990.
Stories: Submit cassette tape of story.

RHYTHMS PRODUCTIONS/TOM THUMB MUSIC, P.O. Box 34485, Los Angeles CA 90034-0485. President: R.S. White. Multimedia production cassette and book packagers. Record label, Tom Thumb—Rhythms Productions. Estab. 1955.
Music: Member of ASCAP. Works with composers and lyricists. For songs recorded pays musicians/artists on record contract, songwriters on royalty contract. Submit a cassette demo tape or VHS videotape by mail—unsolicited submissions OK. Requirements: "We accept musical stories. Must be produced in demo form, and must have educational content or be educationally oriented." Reports in 2 months. Recorded songs: "Adventures of Professor Whatzit & Carmine Cat," by Dan Brown and Bruce Crook (6 book and cassette packages); "First Reader's Kit" (multimedia learning program); and "Learn About" cassettes; all on Tom Thumb label.

SATURN, A division of Rock Dog Records, P.O. Box 3687, Hollywood CA 90028. (213)661-0259. Fax: (310)641-5074. VP A&R: Gerry North. Record company. Estab. 1987.
Stories: Publishes 2 book/cassettes and 2 cassette/CDs/year. 99% of stories are fiction; 1% nonfiction. For fiction, will consider fantasy, adventure, mystery, animal (ages 3-5). Payment negotiable. Query. "No phone calls please." Reports on queries in 1 month. Published songs: "Four Eyed Freddie" and "The Green Grickled Monster," both recorded at Saturn Studio (children's stories).
Tips: "Send typed script. If you want a reply or your materials returned, be sure to include SASE."

SMARTY PANTS AUDIO/VIDEO, 15104 Detroit, Suite #2, Lakewood OH 44107-3916. (216)221-5300. Fax: (216)221-5348. President: S. Tirk. Music publisher, book publisher, record company. Record labels include Smarty Pants, Smarty Time, High Note, S.P.I. Estab. 1988.
Music: Releases 25 LPs/year; 25 CDs/year. Member of BMI. Publishes 5-10 songs/year; records 10-20 songs and stories/year. Hires staff writers for children's music. Works with composers, lyricists, team collaborators. Buys all rights to material. Call first and obtain permission to submit material. Submit demo cassette and videocassette if available; 3 or 4 songs and lyric sheet. Material must be copyrighted. SASE/IRC for return of submission. Reports in 2 weeks. Recorded songs: "Songs of Paddington Bear" and "Sing with Paddington Bear," both written by Paul Parnes and recorded by Stewart Lewis on the Smarty Pants label (children's music for ages 3-8).
Music Tips: "Keep it upbeat, topical and clear." Sees big name artists trying to crack children's market.
Stories: Publishes 8 book/cassette packages/year; 2 cassettes/CDs/year. 100% of stories are fiction. Considers animal, fantasy aimed at ages 3-8. Work purchased outright. Submit both cassette tape and manuscript. Reports on queries/mss in 2 weeks. Catalog free on request. Call for guidelines. Published and recorded story tapes: *The Tale of Squirrel Nutkin* and *The Tale of Jemima Puddleduck*, both written by Beatrix Potter, narrated by Kathy Garver (ages 3-8).
Story Tips: "We look for stories that are similar to or follow-ups to the classics."

STEMMER HOUSE PUBLISHERS, 2627 Caves Rd., Owings Mills MD 21117. (410)363-3690. Fax: (410)363-8459. President: Barbara Holdridge. Book publisher.
Stories: Catalog for 9×12 SAE and $1.01 postage. Ms guidelines for SASE. "We only record selected books previously published by Stemmer House. Therefore it's necessary to submit a manuscript rather than a tape." Recorded story tapes: *The Wily Witch*, by Godfried Bomans, narrated by Tammy Grimes, John Houseman (ages 5-10, fairy tales).

TOOTER SCOOTER MUSIC, 195 S. 26th St., San Jose CA 95116. (408)286-9840. Fax: (408)286-9845. A&R: Gradie O'Neal. Music publisher, record company. Record labels include Rowena Records. Estab. 1969.
Music: Releases 6 CDs/year. Member of BMI, ASCAP. Works with composers, lyricists. For music published, pays standard royalty of 50%; for songs recorded, pays musicians/artists on record contract. Submit demo tape by mail; unsolicited submissions OK. Submit demo cassette with 1-4 songs, lyric sheet and SASE. Submissions returned with SASE. Reports in 2 weeks. Recently recorded songs: "It's Good to Read," by Johnny Gitar, recorded by Johnny Gitar on Rowena label (English and Spanish for ages 6-12).

TVN-THE VIDEO NETWORK, 31 Cutler Dr., Ashland MA 01721. (508)881-1800. Fax: (508)881-1800. Producer: Gregg C. McAllister. Video publisher. Estab. 1986.
Music: Publishes and records 8 children's songs/year for video and multimedia projects. Member of ASCAP and BMI. Hires staff writers for children's music. Pays on a work-for-hire basis. Pays musicians on salary for inhouse studio work. Submit demo cassette, VHS videocassette if available. "Reports on an as needed basis only." Recorded "Tugboat" and "My Dad and Me."

TWIN SISTERS PRODUCTIONS, INC., Suite D, 1340 Home Ave., Akron OH 44310. (330)633-8900. Fax: (330)633-8988. President: Kim Thompson. CEO: Karen Hilderbrand. Music publisher, record company. Estab. 1987.
Music: Releases 12 singles/year; 12-18 LPs-cassettes/year. Publishes and records 120 children's songs/year. Works with composers and teams collaborators. Pays musicians on salary for inhouse studio work. Call first and obtain permission to submit material. Submit demo cassette with lyric sheet and VHS videocassette. Not necessary to include lyric or lead sheets. List past history of successes. SASE/IRC for return of submission. Reports in 1 month. Recorded songs: "Did You Know That Monkeys Like to Swing?," by Kim Thompson and Karen Hilderbrand, recorded by Greg Fortson on the Twin Sisters Productions label (children's music for ages 2-7); "The Tiger's Loose" by Kim Thompson and Karen Hilderbrand, recorded by Greg Fortson on the Twin Sisters Productions label (children's, music for ages 2-7).
Tips: "Send a professional-sounding recording, labelled with all information—name, phone number, etc. Children's music is starting to be widely recognized in mainstream music. Independent labels are major contributors."

WATCHESGRO MUSIC PUBLISHING CO., Watch Us Climb, 9208 Spruce Mountain Way, Las Vegas NV 89134-6024. (702)363-8506. President: Eddie Lee Carr. Music publisher, record company. Record labels include Interstate 40 Records, Tracker Records. Estab. 1970.
Music: Releases 10 singles/year; 5 12-inch singles/year; 1 LP/year; 1 CD/year. Member of BMI. Publishes 15 and records 4 children's songs/year. Works with composers, lyricists. For music published, pays standard royalty of 50%; for songs recorded, pays musicians/artists on record contract, musicians on salary for inhouse studio work. Write or call first and obtain permission to submit a cassette tape. Does not return unsolicited material. Reports in 1 week.

WE LIKE KIDS!, produced by KTOO-FM, 360 Egan Dr., Juneau AK 99801. (907)586-1670. Fax: (907)586-3612. Producer: Jeff Brown. Producer of children's radio show.
Music: Releases 50 programs/year. Member of Children's Music Network; National Storytelling Association. Submit demo tape by mail; unsolicited submissions OK. Submit demo cassette, vinyl, CD.
Music Tips: "The best advice we could give to anyone submitting songs for possible airplay is to make certain that you give your best performance and record it in the best way possible. A mix of well-honed songwriting skills, an awareness of a variety of international musical styles, and the advent of home studios have all added up to a delightful abundance of quality songs and stories for children."

WORLD LIBRARY PUBLICATIONS A division of J.S. Paluch Co., 3815 N. Willow Rd., Schiller Park IL 60176. (708)678-0621. General Editor: Laura Dankler. Music publisher. Estab. 1945.
Music: Publishes 75-100 children's songs/year. Works with composers. For music published pays 10% of sales. Making contact: Submit demo cassette tape and lead sheet by mail; unsolicited submissions OK. "Please submit no more than five works at one time. If it is not a full score, we do require a cassette. Should be liturgical. We are primarily a Roman Catholic publisher." Reports in 3 months. Published children's songs and collections by Jim Marchionda, Julie Howard and the Crayons, Joe Mattingly and the Newman Singers, Steve Warner and the Notre Dame Folk Choir, Ed Bolduc, Paul Tate, Dolores Hruby, Mary Kay Beall, Carl Schalk, Jeffrey Honore and many others.

Greeting Cards, Puzzles & Games

In this section you'll find companies that produce puzzles, games, greeting cards and other items (like coloring books, stickers and giftwrap) especially for kids. These are items you'll find in children's sections of bookstores, toy stores, departments stores and card shops.

Because these markets create an array of products, their needs vary greatly. Some may need the service of freelance writers for greeting card copy or slogans for buttons and stickers. Others are in need of illustrators for coloring books or photographers for puzzles. Artists should send in copies of their work that art directors can keep on file—never originals. Carefully read through the listings to find a company's needs, and send for guidelines if they're offered, and catalogs if they're available, just as you would for a book or magazine publisher.

If you'd like to find out more about the greeting card industry beyond the market for children, there are a number of resources to help you. *Greetings Today* is the official publication of the Greeting Card Association. For information call (800)627-0932. Illustrators should check out *The Complete Guide to Greeting Card Design & Illustration*, by Eva Szela (North Light Books) and *Greeting Card Designs*, by Joanne Fink (PBC Intl. Inc.). For a complete list of companies, consult the latest edition of *Artist's & Graphic Designer's Market*. Writers should see *How to Write & Sell Greeting Cards, Bumper Stickers, T-shirts and Other Fun Stuff*, by Molly Wigand (Writer's Digest Books).

LICENSING YOUR ARTWORK

If you're not quite sure what it means to license your work, it's pretty easy to explain. An artist sells certain pieces to certain companies to be reproduced on certain products. The companies manufacture the products and market them to stores. Just as in book publishing, artists usually receive an advance and a percentage of the sales. Designs could appear on greeting cards, mugs, posters, ceramics, picture frames, or paper products, such as plates, cups and tablecloths for a child's birthday party.

Licensing is a great way to get a lot of mileage out of a single design. If you create a piece for a magazine article, you get paid once. If you create a piece for a licensed product, you make money each time the items sell. If you have time (to find the right company for your work), money (for postage, reference material, maybe even trade shows), and the right idea, you could end up in lucrative deal with a licensing company.

Finding the right company for you takes research. There are several sources of information and advice on the industry available. *Accessories Resources* offers international listings of trade shows throughout the year—attending a show is a great way to get a feel for the industry. It's published by Business Journals, Inc., 50 Day St., Norwalk CT 06856, (203)853-6015. *EMP Licensing Letter Sourcebook* lists hundreds of companies that use licensed art on their products, as well as the kinds of items they produce. It's published by EMP Communications, Inc., 160 Mercer St., Third Floor, New York NY 10012, (212)941-0099.

Be sure to read the Insider Report with licensing queen Mary Engelbreit on page 276. Engelbreit talks about starting her licensing empire and gives advice to other artists "with unique talents and big dreams."

Information on companies listed in the previous edition but not included in this edition of Children's Writer's & Illustrator's Market *may be found in the General Index.*

*S.S. ADAMS COMPANY, P.O. Box 850, Neptune NJ 07754. E-mail: ssadams@monmouth.com Contact: C.S. Adams. Estab. 1906. Novelty company. Manufactures practical joke and magic items. 100% of products are made for kids or have kids' themes.
Illustration: Needs comic illustrations for practical jokes and magic tricks. Looking for 1930s-'50s style comic illustrations that reproduce well in $1 \times 1''$ area. To contact, send cover letter, b&w photocopies. Reports in 1 month. Materials not returned. Pays on acceptance. Buys all rights.

AMCAL, 2500 Bisso Lane, #500, Concord CA 94520. (415)689-9930. Fax: (415)689-0108. Editor/Art Director: Judy Robertson. Estab. 1975. Cards, calendars, desk diaries, boxed Christmas cards, limited edition prints and more.
Illustration: Receives over 150 submissions/year. "AMCAL publishes high quality full color, narrative and decorative art for a wide market from traditional to contemporary. "Currently we are very interested in country folk art styles. Know the trends and the market. Juvenile illustration should have some adult appeal. We don't publish cartoon, humorous or gag art, or bold graphics. We sell to mostly small, exclusive gift retailers. Submissions are always accepted for future lines." To contact, send samples, photocopies, slides and SASE for return of submission. Reports in approx. 1 month. Pays on publication. Pay negotiable/usually advance on royalty. Rights purchased negotiable. Guideline sheets for #10 SASE and 1 first-class stamp.

ARISTOPLAY, LTD., P.O. Box 7028, Ann Arbor MI 48107. (313)995-4353. Fax: (313)995-4611. Website: http://www.aristoplay.com. Product Development Director: Lorraine Hopping Egan. Art Director: Jack Thompson. Estab. 1979. Produces educational board games and card decks, activity kits—all educational subjects. 100% of products are made for kids or have kids' themes.
Illustration: Needs freelance illustration and graphic designers (including art directors) for games and card decks. Makes 2-4 illustration assignments/year. To contact, send cover letter, résumé, published samples or color photocopies. Reports back in 1 month if interested. For artwork, pays by the project, $500-5,000. Pays on acceptance (½-sketch, ½-final). Buys all rights. Credit line given.
Photography: Buys photography from freelancers. Wants realistic, factual photos.
Tips: "Creating board games requires a lot of back and forth in terms of design, illustration, editorial and child testing; the more flexible you are, the better. Also, factual accuracy is important." Target age group 4-14. "We are an educational game company. Writers and illustrators working for us must be willing to research the subject and period of focus."

A/V CONCEPTS CORP., 30 Montauk Blvd., Oakdale NY 11769. (516)567-7227. Fax: (516)567-8745. Editor: Laura Solimene. President: Philip Solimene. Estab. 1969. "We are an educational publisher. We publish books for the K-12 market—primarily language arts and math and reading." 20% of products are made for kids or have kids' themes.
Writing: Needs freelance writing for classic workbooks only: adaptations from fine literature. Makes 5-10 assignments/year. To contact, send cover letter and writing samples and 9×12 SASE. Reports in 3 weeks. For writing assignments, pays by the project ($700-1,000). Pays on publication. Buys all rights.
Illustration: Needs freelance illustration for classic literature adaptations, fine art, some cartoons, super heroes. Makes 15-20 illustration assignments/year. Needs "super hero-like characters in four-color and b&w." To contact, send cover letter and photocopies. Reports back in 3 weeks. For artwork, pays by the project (range: $200-1,000). Pays on publication. Buys all rights.
Tips: Submit seasonal material 4 months in advance. "We're getting into CD-ROM development."

THE AVALON HILL GAME CO., 4517 Harford Rd., Baltimore MD 21214. (410)254-9200. Fax: (410)254-0991. President: Jackson V. Dott. Editor: A. Eric Dott. Art Director: June Kim. Jean Baer. Estab. 1958. Produces *Girl's Life* magazine for girls ages 7-14. *Girl's Life* is promoted through the Girl Scouts of America. 50% of material written and illustrated by freelancers. Buys 50 freelance projects/year; receives 500 submissions annually.
Writing: Makes 6 writing assignments/month; 36/year. To contact send cover letter, résumé, client list, writing samples. Reports back only if interested. Pays on publication. Buys all rights. Credit line given.
Illustration: Makes 12 illustration assignments/month. Prefers styles pertaining to general interest topics for girls. To contact send cover letter, résumé, published samples, portfolio. Reports in 1 month. Pays on acceptance. Buys all rights. Credit line given.

‡AVANTI PRESS, INC., 2500 Penobscot Bldg., Detroit MI 48226. (313)961-0022. Submit images to this address: Avanti, Suite 602, 84 Wooster, New York NY 10012. (212)941-9000. Art Researcher: Claire O'Dea. Estab. 1979. Greeting card company. Publishes photographic greeting cards—nonseasonal and seasonal.
Photography: Purchases photography from freelancers. Buys stock and assigns work. Buys approximately 50-75 stock images/year. Makes approximately 20-30 assignments/year. Wants "narrative, storytelling images, graphically strong and colorful!" Uses b&w/color prints; 35mm, $2\frac{1}{4} \times 2\frac{1}{4}$ and 4×5 transparencies. To contact,

"Call for submission guidelines—no originals!!" Reports in 2 weeks. Returns materials with SASE. "We pay either a flat fee or a royalty which is discussed at time of purchase." Pays on acceptance. Buys exclusive product rights (world-wide card rights). Credit line given. Photographer's guidelines for SASE.
Tips: At least 50% of products have kids' themes. Submit seasonal material 9 months-1 year in advance. "All images submitted should express some kind of sentiment which either fits an occasion or can be versed and sent to the recipient to convey some feeling."

THE BEISTLE COMPANY, P.O. Box 10, Shippensburg PA 17257. (717)532-2131. Fax: (717)532-7789. Product Manager: C. Michelle Luhrs-Wiest. Art Director: Brad Clever. Estab. 1900. Paper products company. Produces decorations and party goods, bulletin board aides, posters—baby, baptism, birthday, holidays, educational. 50% of products are made for kids' or have kids themes.
Illustration: Needs freelance illustration for decorations, party goods, school supplies, point-of-purchase display materials and educational aides. Makes 20 illustration assignments/year. Prefers fanciful style, cute 4- to 5-color illustration in gouache. To contact, send cover letter, résumé, client list, promo piece. To query with specific ideas, phone or write. Reports only if interested. Materials returned with SASE; materials filed. Pays by the project or by contractual agreement; price varies according to type of project. Pays on acceptance. Buys all rights. Artist's guidelines available for SASE.
Photography: Buys photography from freelancers. Buys stock and assigns work. Makes 30-50 assignments/year. Uses 35mm, 2¼×2¼, 4×5 transparencies. To contact, send cover letter, résumé, slides, client list, promo piece. Reports only if interested. Materials returned if accompanied with SASE; materials filed. Pays on acceptance. Buys first rights. Credit line sometimes given—depends on project. Guidelines available for SASE.
Tips: Submit seasonal material 6-8 months in advance.

BEPUZZLED/LOMBARD MARKETING, INC., 22 E. Newberry Rd., Bloomfield CT 06002. (860)769-5723. Fax: (860)769-5799. Creative Services Manager: Sue Tyska. Estab. 1987. Publishes mystery jigsaw puzzles, mystery dinner games. 30% of products are for kids or have kids' themes.
Writing: Needs freelance writing for short mystery stories. Makes 15-20 writing assignments/year. To contact, send cover letter and writing samples. Reports back in 3 weeks. Pays by the project ($1,800). Pays on publication. Buys all rights. No credit line given.
Photography: Needs freelance photographers for mystery jigsaw puzzles. Makes 20-30 photography assignments/year. Preferences announced when needed. To contact, send cover letter, résumé, client list and color promo pieces. Reports back in 2 months. Pays by the project. Pays on publication. Buys all rights.
Tips: "Send seasonal material six months in advance. Send SASE for guidelines. Submissions should be short and include idea of writing style, and an outline of ideas for visual and literal clues (six each, some with red herrings)."

‡**BURGOYNE INC.**, 2030 E. Byberry Rd., Philadelphia PA 19116. (215)677-8000. Art Studio Manager: Mary Beth Burgoyne. Contact: Christine Cathers Donohue. Estab. 1907. Greeting card company. Publisher of Christmas and everyday cards.
Illustration: Interested in illustrations for greeting cards. To contact, send cover letter. To query with specific ideas, send slides, published samples. Be sure to include a SASE. Reports in 2 months. Materials filed. Pays on acceptance. Buys greeting card US and worldwide rights. Credit line sometimes given. Artist's guidelines for SASE.
Tips: "We are looking for new traditional Christmas artwork with a detailed children's book look. We are also looking for juvenile birthday and all-occasion artwork year round."

CREATE-A-CRAFT, P.O. Box 941293, Plano TX 75094-1293. Contact: Editor. Estab. 1967. Produces greeting cards, giftwrap, games, calendars, posters, stationery and paper tableware products for all ages.
Illustration: Works with 3 freelance artists/year. Buys 3-5 designs/illustrations/year. Prefers artists with experience in cartooning. Works on assignment only. Buys freelance designs/illustrations mainly for greetings cards and T-shirts. Also uses freelance artists for calligraphy, P-O-P displays, paste-up and mechanicals. Considers pen & ink, watercolor, acrylics and colored pencil. Prefers humorous and "cartoons that will appeal to families. Must be cute, appealing, etc. No religious, sexual implications or off-beat humor." Produces material for all holidays and seasons. Contact only through artist's agent. Some samples are filed; samples not filed are not returned. Reports only if interested. Write for appointment to show portfolio of original/final art, final reproduction/product, slides, tearsheets, color and b&w. Original artwork is not returned. "Payment depends upon the assignment, amount of work involved, production costs, etc. involved in the project." Buys all rights. For guidelines and sample cards, send $2.50 and #10 SASE.

 LISTINGS NEW TO THIS EDITION are marked with a double dagger.

INSIDER REPORT

'If your ship doesn't come in, swim out to it'

Many aspiring illustrators seek out children's picture books as a place to call home—where their talent will become known as a distinct and innovative commodity, where they can bring to life the stories of a variety of authors, and where they can count on steady work.

Mary Engelbreit was no exception. In 1977, as a young illustrator from St. Louis, Engelbreit carted her portfolio to New York, hoping to find her niche. Instead—in what she took as an insult—she was advised to try her hand at greeting cards.

Try her hand she did, and the result is a one-woman cottage industry with greeting card sales of $14 million annually, some 350 product licenses, five retail outlets in malls across the Midwest, a magazine bearing her name (*Mary*

Mary Engelbreit

Engelbreit's Home Companion) and, finally, a picture book (Hans Christian Andersen's *The Snow Queen*, published in 1993). She has also published a series of decorating books, and has begun a decorating column syndicated in newspapers throughout the United States.

Pointedly, one of the taglines that accompanies her illustrations reads "We Don't Care How They Do It In New York." Others might be more familiar with "Life Is Just a Chair of Bowlies," or "Home Is Where One Starts From." She counts among her artistic influences Johnny Gruelle (who illustrated Raggedy Ann and Andy) and Joan Walsh Anglund, which is evident in her homespun patterns of cherries and checkers, her cherubic children, and in particular her ongoing character of Ann Estelle (whom she has called a self-portrait), a bespectacled girl of indefinable age with bobbed hair and an impossibly broad-brimmed hat.

Engelbreit started at the bottom of the pack. A self-trained illustrator, her first deal was the sale of three greeting card designs for $150. She then decided to produce and sell her own cards, a move which created the need for an office and studio in the basement of her St. Louis home. By 1985, she was ready to take a display to the National Stationery Show in New York. She exhibited 12 cards, at a trade convention where typically hundreds of designs are included in each display. But her work attracted attention, and she contracted with a publisher for a calendar and a licensing deal. In 1986, her card sales topped $1 million, and she expanded the business to concentrate on licensing as an outlet for her designs.

Trends typically begin on the coasts, but Engelbreit's appeal is rooted firmly in the Midwest, reflecting its values, customs and sense of family life. And while her artwork is not strictly for children, its simplicity and heartfelt sincerity appeal to the child in the many fans of her work. Here, Engelbreit discusses the road less travelled she took to success, and offers advice for illustrators considering the same path.

INSIDER REPORT, *Engelbreit*

St. Louis-based illustrator and one-woman cottage industry Mary Engelbreit turned rejection into spectacular success. Sent packing by a New York publisher of children's picture books, Engelbreit continued creating and selling her own images, first for other greeting card companies and later her own. "I knew my stuff would really sell well if I could just get it out there," she says. It has: Engelbreit's designs such as this one can be found on some 350 products, from greeting cards to gifts, stationery and home furnishings. Diversity has been key to her success—in addition to the product licensing, Engelbreit has launched a magazine, *Mary Engelbreit's Home Companion*, and several books featuring her inimitable illustrations.

Your path to success is unusual in that you were not formally educated in art. Do you recommend this route to other aspiring illustrators?

By the time I had reached my senior year in high school, I was ready to get to work. Besides, as a result of being on my own, no one was ever telling me that this was or wasn't the way to do it, so I just drew the way I wanted, and it happened to be different than anything else that was out there.

If I had been in school, I think I probably would have been toeing the party line. Honestly, I don't think I would be doing this right now. I'd be working in an agency or an art gallery somewhere. This route was better for me because I don't do very well in that kind of structured setting. I do much better on my own. For others it may be different.

Why did you choose to start your own business when you did?

I started my own business because the first company I worked with just wasn't doing what I wanted to do—and I knew my stuff would sell really well if I could just get it out there. Plus, I'm a control freak, and I just wanted to do it myself. I didn't want to wait. Now I don't recommend that route to everybody. It took a lot of time and a lot of money. You really have to be dedicated.

When I started, we just walled off part of the basement and it was really tiny. On one side of the room, we stacked up all of the cards and on the other side of the room, we had a desk. We were only there for about six months. When you consider that 12 years later we have 40 employees in a converted Greek Orthodox church, the growth is amazing.

The key to any successful business is a trustworthy business partner. Phil Delano is just that—he's also my husband. Together, we built this business by trusting our instincts. A caption in one of my illustrations says it best—"if your ship doesn't come in, swim out to it."

INSIDER REPORT, *continued*

In 1985, you took 12 cards to the National Stationery Show, and your modest exhibit attracted a lot of attention, not to mention a licensing deal. Was that show a turning point for you?

Oh, definitely. And the reason it attracted attention was that we had already been out there, so the reps and the stores knew who we were. I don't think we would have gotten so much attention had we gone out there cold. People recognized the artwork and us, and they knew my artwork would sell.

We got a licensing agent at that show—I don't think we could have gotten our foot in the door otherwise. Sure, agents take a percentage of what you make. But they know the business. Licensing might go even more slowly without one.

What's essential to success in licensing your artwork?

I would say to always try to keep your copyright—which you might not be able to do right at the beginning. Ask a really good attorney to look over your contracts. Sign a contract for the shortest amount of time possible; that way, you can make sure there's a way to take control later on if you need to. Get specific about what the licensee is buying your drawing for, which products they plan to put it on, and how long they plan to do it.

Research the potential licensee and don't jump into anything. You have to spend a little time with these people before you go into business with them. Make sure that the licensee understands why you do the art that you do, how much it means to you, and how important it is that it looks good on a product. It's worth taking the time to get to know the people you're doing business with a little bit before you sign the contract. Life's too short to deal with jerks.

You've terminated contracts with more than 20 licensees over quality issues. Is it difficult to maintain quality standards in licensing arrangements?

Quality standards are established in the licensing agreement right from the start. That protects my artwork while preserving the integrity of the product line. We approve every product through every phase of production to help maintain our quality standards.

How do you manage to solely produce all the artwork that bears your name?

I have an excellent art staff. A lot of times, one of my core designs needs to be adapted to fit a product. The staff artists help do that by adding borders or changing the shape of the design to fit the product. We work with each company to re-format the designs to better suit their products.

How have the greeting card and licensing markets changed since you entered them?

Nowadays, those companies are always looking for new artists. Even though they may do just a few cards, I think it's a great way to get your art out there to show people.

Do you get a special sense of satisfaction with publication of *The Snow Queen*? Did that project bring closure to that dream, or are you planning future book illustration projects?

It was very exciting to do that book—especially when it reached the *Publishers Weekly* Children's Bestseller List. But there were things about the book that the publishing company changed without talking to me. The company put borders on it that I was not expecting to see. I did learn a lesson about designing the whole book. I just finished 18

INSIDER REPORT, *continued*

illustrations for a 19th-century poem entitled *My Symphony*, by William Henry Channing. The poem lists ways to lead a virtuous life.

What advice would you share with aspiring artists who have unique talents and big dreams?

The most important thing I could tell anybody is to have an attorney. Don't think you're saving money by having your dad or your husband or friend look at the contract. It's important to have an attorney and you have to operate as a business from the word go.

You have to remember that you're the one with the talent who's offering the licensees the gift to be cashed in on. You're certainly bringing something to the table, too, which you're entitled to be paid for.

Also, proper timing is overrated. There's always a reason not to do things—it's too expensive, or it's not the best time, or this or that—but I believe there are wonderful opportunities sailing by, and you have to be ready to grab them.

—*Anne Bowling*

Ann Estelle is a recurring character of Mary Engelbreit, who has called the bespectacled girl a self-portrait. Ann Estelle's sweetness and pluck seem to capture the Midwestern spirit and homespun flavor of Engelbreit's art. When she was young, people told her that being an artist was not a realistic way to make a living, but Engelbreit was not discouraged. "I believed in myself," she says, "and now I'm living my dream."

Tips: Submit 6 months in advance. "Demonstrate an ability to follow directions exactly. Too many submit artwork that has no relationship to what we produce. No phone calls accepted."

CREATIF LICENSING CORP., 31 Old Town Crossing, Mt. Kisco NY 10549. (914)241-6211. E-mail: creatifli c@aol.com. President: Paul Cohen. Estab. 1975. Gift industry licensing agency. Publishes greeting cards, puzzles, posters, calendars, fabrics, home furnishings, all gifts. 75% of products are made for kids or have kids' themes.
Illustration: Needs freelance illustration for children's greeting cards, all gift and home furnishings. Makes many illustration assignments/month. Uses both color and b&w artwork. To contact, send cover letter, résumé, client list, published samples, photocopies, portfolio, promo piece and SASE. Reports in 1 month. Materials returned with SASE; materials filed. For greeting cards, pays royalty and advance. For other artwork, pays royalty and advance. Pays on acceptance or publication. Artist's guidelines available for SASE.
Tips: Submit seasonal material 8-12 months in advance.

DESIGN DESIGN INC., P.O. Box 2266, Grand Rapids MI 49501. (616)774-2448. President: Don Kallil. Creative Director: Tom Vituj. Estab. 1986. Greeting card company.
Writing: Needs freelance writing for children's greeting cards. For greeting cards, prefers both rhymed and unrhymed verse ideas. To contact, send cover letter and writing samples. Materials returned with SASE; materials not filed. For greeting cards, pays flat fee. Buys all rights or exclusive product rights; negotiable. No credit line given. Writer's guidelines for SASE.
Illustration: Needs freelance illustration for children's greeting cards and related products. To contact, send cover letter, published samples, color or b&w photocopies, color or b&w promo pieces or portfolio. Returns materials with SASE. Pays by royalty. Buys all rights or exclusive product rights; negotiable. Artist's guidelines available for SASE.
Photography: Buys stock and assigns work. Uses 4×5 transparencies or high quality 35mm slides. To contact, send cover letter with slides, stock photo list, published samples and promo piece. Materials returned with SASE; materials not filed. Pays royalties. Buys all rights or exclusive product rights; negotiable. Photographer's guidelines for SASE.

EPI GROUP LIMITED, 131 S. Rodeo Dr., Beverly Hills CA 90212. (310)887-4300. Fax: (310)887-4400. Vice President: Merryl Lambert. Estab. 1989. Paper products company. Publishes puzzles, activity kits, nature kits, games, books and plush toys, posters for nature and educational markets. 80% of products are made for kids or have kids' themes.
Writing: Needs freelance writing for children's books. Makes "hundreds of" freelance writing assignments/ year. To contact, send cover letter and writing samples. To query with specific ideas, submit overview with sample. Reports back only if interested. Materials returned with SASE; materials filed. Pays on acceptance. Buys all rights; negotiable. Credit line given.
Illustration: Needs freelance illustration for books/activity kits. Makes "hundreds of" illustration assignments/ year. Prefers animal/nature illustrations for packaging, posters, activity books, games, etc. Uses both b&w and color artwork. To contact, send photocopies and promo pieces. To query with specific ideas, submit samples with overview. Reports only if interested. Materials returned with SASE; materials filed. Pays on acceptance. Buys all rights; negotiable. Credit line given.
Photography: Buys stock and assigns work. Buys stock infrequently. Makes "hundreds of" assignments/year. Uses 4×5 prints. To contact, send promo piece. Reports only if interested. Returns material with SASE; materials filed. Pays on acceptance. Buys all rights; negotiable. Credit line given.
Tips: Submit seasonal material six months in advance.

EVERYTHING GONZO!, P.O. Box 1322, Roslyn Heights NY 11577. (516)488-8825. Fax: (516)358-7463. Owner: H.J. Fleischer. Toy designer and manufacturer. Designs, licenses, manufactures toys, gifts and related products. Manufactures novelties (educational, impulse, creative), puzzles, games; publishes booklets. 100% of products are made for kids or have kids' themes.
Illustration: Needs freelance illustration for toy concepts. Makes 100 illustration assignments/year. Uses both color and b&w artwork. To contact, send cover letter, résumé, published samples, portfolio, photocopies, promo pieces. To query with specific ideas, write to request disclosure form first. Reports only if interested. Materials returned with SASE; materials filed. For other artwork, pays by the hour($10); negotiable royalty. Pays on acceptance. Credit line sometimes given.
Photography: Buys photography from freelancers. Works on assignment only. Uses transparencies. To contact, send cover letter, published samples, portfolio, promo piece. Reports only if interested. Materials returned; materials filed. Pays on acceptance. Credit line sometimes given.
Tips: Submit seasonal material 6 months in advance. "Interested in unique toy/game/product concepts."

FAX-PAX USA, INC., 37 Jerome Ave., Bloomfield CT 06002. (203)242-3333. Fax: (203)242-7102. Editor: Stacey L. Savin. Estab. 1990. Buys 1 freelance project/year. Publishes art and history flash cards. Needs include US history, natural history.
Writing/Illustration: Buys all rights. Pays on publication. Cannot return material.
Tips: "We need concise, interesting, well-written 'mini-lessons' on various subjects including U.S. and natural

history."

FOTOFOLIO/ARTPOST, 536 Broadway, New York NY 10012. (212)226-0923. Editorial Director: Ron Schick. Estab. 1976. Greeting card company. Also publishes fine art and photographic postcards, notecards, posters, calendars. New children's line.
Illustration: Needs freelance illustration for children's greeting cards, calendars and coloring books. To contact, send cover letter, published samples, photocopies, slides, promo piece. Reports back only if interested. Returns materials with SASE. Buys materials not filed. Rights negotiable. Credit line given. Artist's guidelines not available.
Photography: Buys photography from freelancers. Buys stock. To contact, send cover letter, slides, stock photo list, published samples and promo piece. Reports back only if interested. Returns material with SASE. Pays on usage. Rights negotiable. Credit line given.

GALISON BOOKS, 28 W. 44th St., New York NY 10036. (212)354-8840. Fax: (212)391-4037. Website: http://www.galison.com. Editor: Ellen Hogan. Estab. 1978. Paper products company. Publishes museum-quality gift products, including notecards, journals, address books and jigsaw puzzles. Publishes children's jigsaw puzzles with images licensed from popular children's books. 10% of products are made for kids or have kids' themes.
Writing: Makes 5 writing assignments/year.
Illustration: Needs freelance illustration for greeting cards, jigsaw puzzles, journals, address books and recipe notecards. Makes 24 illustration assignments/year. Uses color artwork only. To contact, send cover letter, published samples and color promo piece. Reports back only if interested. Returns materials with SASE; materials filed. Pays flat fee. Credit line given. Artist's guidelines not available.
Photography: Buys photography from freelancers. Buys stock. Wants b&w fine art photography, some color themes—cats, dogs, dance, cities, nature. Uses 4×5 or larger transparencies. To contact, send cover letter, stock photo list, published samples or duplicate slides. Reports back only if interested. Returns materials with SASE; materials filed. Pays flat fee. Pays on publication. Credit line given. Photographer's guidelines available for SASE.
Tips: Christmas images should be submitted 1½ years in advance.

GREAT AMERICAN PUZZLE FACTORY, INC., 16 S. Main St., S. Norwalk CT 06854. (203)838-4240. Fax: (203)838-2065. E-mail: gapfctad@aol.com. Art Director: Anne Mulligan. Estab. 1976. Produces puzzles. 30% of products are made for kids or have kids' themes.
Illustration: Needs freelance illustration for puzzles. Makes over 20 freelance assignments/year. To contact, send cover letter, color photocopies and color promo pieces (no slides or original art) with SASE. Reports in 2 months. Artists guidelines available for SASE. Rights purchased vary. Buys all rights to puzzles. Pays on publication. Pay varies.
Photography: Needs local cityscapes for regional puzzles. "Photos that we have used have been of wildlife. We do occasionally use city skylines. These are only for custom jobs, though, and must be 4×5 or larger format."
Tips: Targets ages 4-12 and adult. "Go to a toy store and look at puzzles. See what is appropriate. No slides. Send color copies (3-4) for style. Looking for whimsical, fantasy and animal themes with a bright, contemporary style. Not too washy or cute. We often buy reprint rights to existing work. Graphic, children's-book style work is ideal for puzzles."

GREAT SEVEN, INC., Unit 503, 3870 Del Amo Blvd., Torrance CA 90503. (310)371-4555. Vice President: Ronald Chen. Estab. 1984. Paper products company. Publishes educational and fun stickers for children and teenage markets. 100% of products are made for kids or have kids' themes.
Illustration: Needs freelance illustration for children's fun stickers. Makes 120 illustration assignments/year. Wants "kid themes." To contact, send published samples and b&w photocopies. To query with specific ideas, write to request disclosure form first. Reports back only if interested. Returns material with SASE; materials filed. Pays on acceptance. Buys all rights. No credit line given. Artist's guidelines not available.
Tips: Seasonal material should be submitted 10 months in advance.

*INNOVA, P.O. Box 36, Redmond WA 98073. (206)746-7774. Fax: (206)451-3959. E-mail: kenesa@aol.com. Owner: Ken Jacobson. Estab. 1981. Paper products company and producer of educational and strategic games. Publishes coloring books, games, books. 10% of products are made for kids or have kids' themes.
Writing: To contact, send cover letter and writing samples. Reports in 3 months only if interested. Materials

returned with SASE; materials filed. Payment is negotiated. Buys all rights. Credit line given.

Illustration: Makes 1-2 illustration assignments/year. To contact, send cover letter and published samples. Reports in 3 months. Materials returned with SASE. Payment is negotiated. Pays on publication. Buys all rights. Credit line given.

Photography: Buys stock and assigns work. To contact, send cover letter and published samples. Reports in 3 months. Material returned if accompanied with SASE; materials filed. Payment is negotiated. Buys all rights. Credit line given.

INTERCONTINENTAL GREETINGS LTD., 176 Madison Ave., New York NY 10016. (212)683-5830. Fax: (212)779-8564. Art Director: Robin Lipner. Estab. 1964. 100% of material freelance written and illustrated. Produces greeting cards, scholastic products (notebooks, pencil cases), novelties (gift bags, mugs), tin gift boxes, shower and bedding curtains. 30-40% of products are made for kids or have kids' themes.

Writing: "We use very little writing except for humor." Makes 4 writing assignments/year. To contact, send cover letter, résumé, client list and writing samples with SASE. Reports in 4-6 weeks. Pays advance of $20-100 and royalty of 20% for life. Pays on publication. Contracts exclusive product rights. Credit line sometimes given.

Illustration: Needs children's greeting cards, notebook cover, photo albums, gift products. Makes 3 illustration assignments/month. Prefers primarily greeting card subjects, suitable for gift industry. To contact, send cover letter, résumé, client list, published samples, photocopies, slides and promo piece with SASE. Reports in 4-6 weeks. For greeting cards pays 20% royalty for life. For other artwork pays 20% royalty for life. Pays on publication. Buys exclusive product rights for contract period of 2 years. Credit line sometimes given.

Photography: Needs stylized and interesting still lifes, studio florals, all themed toward the paper and gift industry. Guidelines available for SASE.

Tips: Target group for juvenile cards: ages 1-10. Illustrators: "Use clean colors, not muddy or dark. Send a neat, concise sampling of your work. Include some color examples, a SASE to issue return of your samples if wanted."

INTERNATIONAL PLAYTHINGS, INC., 120 Riverdale Rd., Riverdale NJ 07457. (973)831-1400. Fax: (973)616-7775. Product Manager: Kim McCue. Estab. 1968. Toy/game company. Distributes and markets children's toys, games and puzzles in specialty toy markets. 100% of products are made for kids or have kids' themes.

Illustration: Needs freelance illustration for children's puzzles and games. Makes 20-30 illustration assignments/year. Prefers fine-quality, original illustration for children's puzzles. Uses color artwork only. To contact, send published samples, slides, portfolio, or color photocopies or promo pieces. Reports in 1 month only if interested. Materials filed. For artwork, pays by the project (range: $500-2,000). Pays on publication. Buys one-time rights, negotiable.

Tips: "Mail correspondence only, please. No phone calls."

JILLSON & ROBERTS GIFT WRAP, 5 Watson Ave., Irvine CA 92618. (714)859-8781. Art Director: Josh Neufeld. Estab. 1973. Paper products company. Makes gift wrap/gift bags. 20% of products are made for kids or have kids' themes.

Illustration: Needs freelance illustration for children's gift wrap. Makes 6-12 illustration assignments/year. Wants children/baby/juvenile themes. To contact, send cover letter. Reports in 1 month. Returns material with SASE; materials filed. For wrap and bag designs, pays flat fee of $250. Pays on publication. Rights negotiable. Artist's guidelines for SASE.

Tips: Seasonal material should be submitted up to 3½ months in advance. "We produce two lines of gift wrap per year: one everyday line and one Christmas line. The closing date for everyday is June 30th and Christmas is September 15."

LOVE GREETING CARD CO. INC., 1717 Opa-Locka Blvd., Opa-Locka FL 33054. (305)685-5683. Editor: Norman Drittel. Estab. 1980. Greeting card, paper products and children's book company. Publishes greeting cards (Muffy 'N' Pebbles), posters, small books. 20% of products are made for kids or have kids' themes.

Writing: Needs freelance writing for children's greeting cards. Makes 2 writing assignments/month; 12/year. Prefers rhymed verse ideas. To contact, send writing samples. To query with specific ideas, contact Norman Drittel. Reports in 2 months. Materials returned with SASE; materials filed. For greeting cards, pays flat fee of $50-100. Pays on acceptance. Buys one-time rights, reprint rights; negotiable. Credit line given. Writer's guidelines available for SASE.

Illustration: Needs freelance illustration for children's greeting cards, book material. Makes 2 illustration assignments/month; 12/year. Prefers 8-10 page books. Uses color artwork only. To contact, send published samples, portfolio. Reports in months. Materials returned with SASE; materials filed. For greeting cards, pays flat fee of $100-250. For other artwork, pays by the project (range: $500-2,500). Pays on acceptance. Rights negotiable. Credit line given. Artist's guidelines available for SASE.

Photography: Buys photography from freelancers. Buys stock and assigns work. Buys 20 stock images/year. Makes 5 assignments/year. Wants children, any subject. Uses color prints; 8×10 transparencies. To contact, send slides, portfolio. Reports in 2 months. Materials returned with SASE; materials filed. Pays per photo (range for $100-150) for b&w/color. Pays on acceptance. Rights negotiable. Credit line given. Guidelines available for SASE.

Tips: Submit seasonal material 6 months in advance.

MARCEL SCHURMAN COMPANY, Schurman Design, 101 New Montgomery St., 6th Floor, San Francisco CA 94105. Creative Director: Diana Ruhl. Greeting card company. Publishes greeting cards, gift wrap, stationery, bags, journals and note cards. 20% of products are made for kids or have kids' themes.

Writing: Needs freelance writing for children's greeting cards. Makes 2-3 writing assignments/month; 50/year. For greeting cards, prefers unrhymed verse ideas. To query with specific ideas, write to request disclosure form first. Reports in 6 weeks. Materials returned with SASE; sometimes files material. For greeting cards, pays flat fee of $75-125 on acceptance. Writer's guidelines available for SASE.

Illustration: Needs freelance illustration for children's greeting cards. Makes 60 illustration assignments/month; 800/year. Uses color artwork only. To contact, send color photocopies. To query with specific ideas, send letter with or without samples. Reports in 1 month. Materials returned if accompanied by SASE; materials filed. For greeting cards pays advance of $300 against 5% royalty for 3 years. Pays "when final art is approved." Credit line given. Artist's guidelines available for SASE.

Photography: Buys photography from freelancers. Buys stock and assigns work. Uses 4×5 transparencies. To contact, send slides. Reports in 1 month. Materials returned with SASE. Materials returned or filed. Pays advance of $300 and 5% royalties. Pays "when final art is approved." Buys exclusive product rights, worldwide, 3-year period. Credit line given. Guidelines for SASE.

Tips: Submit seasonal ideas 6-8 months in advance.

*NOVO CARD PUBLISHERS, INC., 4513 N. Lincoln, Chicago IL 60625. (773)769-6000. Fax: (773)769-6769. Contact: Thomas Benjamin, art production. Estab. 1926. Greeting card company. Company publishes greeting cards, note/invitation packs and gift envelopes for middle market. Publishes greeting cards (Novo Card/Cloud-9). 20% of products are made for kids or have kids' themes.

Writing: Needs freelance writing for children's greeting cards. Makes 400 writing assignments/year. Other needs for freelance writing include invitation notes. To contact send writing samples. To query with specific ideas, write to request disclosure form first. Reports back in 1 month only if interested. Materials returned only with SASE; materials filed. For greeting cards, pays flat fee of $2/line. Pays on acceptance. Buys all rights. Credit line sometimes given. Writer's guidelines available for SASE.

Illustration: Needs freelance illustration for children's greeting cards. Makes 1,000 illustration assignments/year. Prefers just about all types: traditional, humor, contemporary, etc. To contact, send published samples, slides and color photocopies. To query with specific ideas write to request disclosure form first. Reports in 1 month. Materials returned with SASE; materials filed. For greeting cards, pay negotiable. Pays on acceptance. Rights negotiable. Credit line sometimes given. Artist's guidelines available for SASE.

Photography: Buys stock and assigns work. Buys 30-40 stock images/year. Wants all types: prefers contemporary images for the time being. Uses color and b&w prints; 35mm transparencies. To contact, send slides, stock photo list, published samples, paper copies acceptable. Reports in 1 month. Materials returned with SASE; materials filed. Pays negotiable rate. Pays on acceptance. Rights negotiable. Credit line sometimes given. Guidelines for SASE.

Tips: Submit seasonal material 10-12 months in advance. "Novo has extensive lines of greeting cards: everyday, seasonal (all) and alternative lives (over 24 separate lines of note card packs and gift enclosures). Our lines encompass all types of styles and images."

P.S. GREETINGS/FANTUS PAPER PRODUCTS, 5060 N. Kimberly Ave., Chicago IL 60630. (773)725-9308. Art Director: Jennifer Dodson. Greeting card company. Publishes boxed and individual counter cards. Publishes greeting cards.

Writing: Needs freelance writing for children's greeting cards. Makes 1-10 writing assignments/year. Looks for writing which is "appropriate for kids to give to relatives." To contact, send writing samples. Reports in 6 weeks. Material returned only if accompanied with SASE; materials filed. For greeting cards, pays flat fee. Pays on acceptance. Buys all rights. Credit line given. Writer's guidelines for SASE.

Illustration: Needs freelance illustration for children's greeting cards. Makes about 100 illustration assignments/year. "Open to all mediums, all themes—use your creativity!" To contact, send published samples (up to 20 samples of any nature) and photocopies. Reports in 6 months. Returns materials with SASE; materials filed. For greeting cards, pays flat fee. Pays on acceptance. Buys all rights. Credit line given. Artist's guidelines for SASE.

Photography: Buys photography from freelancers. Buys stock. Buys 25-50 stock images/year. Wants florals, animals, seasonal (Christmas, Easter, valentines, etc.). Uses transparencies (any size). To contact, send slides. Reports in 6 weeks. Materials returned with SASE; materials filed. Pays on acceptance. Buys all rights. Credit line given. Photographer's guidelines for SASE.

Tips: Seasonal material should be submitted 6 months in advance.

*PAINTED HEARTS & FRIENDS, 1222 N. Fair Oaks Ave., Los Angeles CA 91103. (818)798-3633. Fax: (818)793-7385. Chairman of the Board: David Mekelburg. Co-owner: Susan Kinney. Estab. 1988. Material produced includes greeting cards.

 ● Painted Hearts & Friends is placing special emphasis on the children's market.

Illustration: Buys 5 freelance projects/year. Material returned with SASE. Reports in 1 week. Pays on publication.

Tips: Submit seasonal material 1 year in advance.

*PANDA INK, P.O. Box 5129, West Hills CA 91308-5129. (818)340-8061. Fax: (818)883-6193. Owner: Art/Creative Director: Ruth Ann Epstein. Estab. 1981. Greeting card company and producer of clocks, magnets, bookmarks. Produces Judaica—whimsical, metaphysical, general, everyday. Publishes greeting cards. 10% of products are made for kids or have kids' themes.
Writing: Needs freelance writing for children's greeting cards. Makes 10 writing assignments/month. For greeting cards, accepts both rhymed and unrhymed verse ideas. Looks for greeting card writing which is Judaica or metaphysical. To contact, send cover letter, ask for guidelines, send SASE. To query with specific ideas, write to request disclosure form first. Reports in 1 month. Materials returned with SASE; materials filed. For greeting cards, pays flat fee of $3-20. Pays on acceptance. Rights negotiable. Credit line sometimes given. Writer's guidelines available for SASE.
Illustration: Needs freelance illustration for children's greeting cards, magnets, bookmarks. Makes 2-3 illustration assignments/year. Needs Judaica (Hebrew wording), metaphysical themes. Uses color artwork only. To contact, send cover letter. To query with specific ideas, write to request disclosure form first. Reports in 1 month. Materials returned with SASE; materials filed. Payment is negotiable. Pays on acceptance. Rights negotiable. Credit line sometimes given. Artist's guidelines available for SASE.
Tips: Submit seasonal material 1 year in advance. "Follow our guidelines. No 'shoe box' art."

PEACEABLE KINGDOM PRESS, 707B Heinz Ave., Berkeley CA 94710. (510)644-9801. Fax: (510)644-9805. E-mail: artdog@microweb.com. Website: http://www.pkpress.com. Editor, Creative Development: Gail Peterson. Art Director: Olivia Hurd. Estab. 1983. Produces posters, greeting cards, gift wrap and related products. Uses images from classic children's books. 80-90% of products are made for kids or have kids' themes.
Illustration: Needs freelance illustration for children's greeting cards and posters. Makes 40 illustration assignments/year. To contact, send cover letter and color photocopies. Contact Molly Gauld or Gail Peterson, creative directors. Reports in 4 weeks. Pays on publication with advance. Pays 5-10% of wholesale for greeting cards. Buys rights to distribution worldwide. Artist's guidelines available for SASE.
Tips: "We only choose from illustrations that are from published children's book illustrators, or commissioned art by established children's book illustrators. Submit seasonal and everyday greeting cards one year in advance."

‡PICTURA INC., P.O. Box 2058, Four Andrews Dr., West Paterson NJ 07424. (201)890-1070. Fax: (201)890-1292. Graphic Artist: Nando Caldarone. Estab. 1980. Greeting card company. Publishes novelties ("Lisi" X-mas puzzle), puzzles, books ("The Velveteen Rabbit," illustrated by Donna Green). 25% of products are made for kids or have kids' themes.
Writing: Needs freelance writing for children's greeting cards. For greeting cards, prefers both rhymed and unrhymed verse ideas. To contact, send résumé and writing samples. To query with specific ideas, write to request disclosure form first. Reports in 2 months. Materials returned with SASE; materials filed. Pay varies according to artist and project. Writer's guidelines available for SASE.
Illustration: To contact, send résumé and photocopies. To query with specific ideas, write to request disclosure form first. Reports in 2 months. Materials returned with SASE; materials filed. Pay varies according to artist and project. Artist's guidelines available for SASE.
Photography: Buys stock and assigns work. Uses transparencies. To contact, send résumé and color promo piece. Reports in 2 months. Returns material with SASE; materials filed. Pay varies according to artist and project. Guidelines available for SASE.
Tips: Submit seasonal material 1 year in advance.

*PLUM GRAPHICS INC., P.O. Box 136, Prince St. Station, New York NY 10012. Phone/fax: (212)337-0999. Owner: Yvette Cohen. Estab. 1983. Greeting card company. Produces die-cut greeting cards for ages 5-105. Publishes greeting cards and message boards.
Writing: Needs freelance writing for greeting cards. Makes 4 writing assignments/year. Looks for "greeting card writing which is fun. Tired of writing which is boring." To contact, send SASE for guidelines. Contact: Michelle Ingram. Reports in 2 months. Materials returned with SASE; materials filed. For greeting cards, pays flat fee of $40. Pays on publication. Buys all rights. Writer's guidelines available for SASE.
Illustration: Needs freelance illustration for greeting cards. Makes 10-15 freelance illustration assignments/year. Prefers very tight artwork, mostly realism. Uses color artwork only. To contact, send b&w photocopies. Contact: Yvette Cohen. Reports only if interested. Materials returned with SASE; materials filed. For greeting cards, pays flat fee of $350-450 "plus $50 each time we reprint." Pays on publication. Buys exclusive product rights. Credit line given.
Tips: Submit seasonal material 1 year in advance. "Go to a store and look at our cards and style before submitting work."

POCKETS OF LEARNING LTD., 31-G Union Ave., Sudbury MA 01776. (800)635-2994. Fax: (800)370-1580. Product Manager: Kathy Calderini. Estab. 1989. Educational soft toy company. Specializes in design, manufacture and distribution of high-quality educational cloth books, soft sculptures, wallhangings, travel bags and gifts. 100% of products are made for children ranging from birth to 6 years old.
Illustration: Needs freelance illustration for educational cloth toys. Makes 5 illustration assignments/year. "We introduce 20-30 new products per year, including cloth books, travel bags, soft sculpture and wallhangings."

Uses both color and b&w artwork. To contact, send cover letter, slides, photocopies. To query with specific ideas, write to request disclosure form first. Pays on acceptance. Buys all rights.

‡**RECO INTERNATIONAL CORP.**, 138-150 Haven Ave., Pt. Washington NY 11050. (516)767-2400. President: Heio W. Reich. Estab. 1967. Collector's plate producer.
Illustration: Needs freelance illustration for collector's plates—children's subjects mainly, but also western, Indian, flowers, animals, fantasy and mystical. Makes 60-100 assignments/year. Uses color artwork only. To contact, send portfolio. Submit specific ideas. Reports in 6 weeks. Materials returned with SASE; materials filed. For greeting cards, pays flat fee and royalty. For other artwork, pays royalty and advance. Pays on acceptance. Buys exclusive product rights. Artist's guidelines available for SASE after review of portfolio.
Tips: 60% of products are made for kids or have kids' themes. Submit seasonal material 6-10 months in advance (although rarely uses seasonal work).

SCANDECOR INC., 430 Pike Rd., Southampton PA 18966. (215)355-2410. Product Manager: Lauren H. Karp. Poster publisher. Publishes posters for the children's market. 75% of products are made for kids or have kids' themes.
Writing: Needs freelance writing for posters. Makes 20 writing assignments/year. For posters, prefers rhymed verse ideas. To contact, send writing samples. To query with specific ideas, send SASE. Reports in 2 months. Materials returned with SASE. Pays on publication. Rights negotiable. Credit line given. Writer's guidelines available for SASE.
Illustration: Needs freelance illustration for children's posters. Makes 20 illustration assignments/year. Prefers poster art in children's themes. Uses color artwork only. To contact, send color photocopies, color promo piece. To query with specific ideas, send SASE. Reports in 2 months. Materials returned with SASE; materials filed. Pays on publication. Rights negotiable. Credit line given. Artist's guidelines available for SASE.
Photography: Buys photography from freelancers. Buys stock and assigns work. Buys 100 stock images/year. Makes 10 assignments/year. Wants animals (in studio), children (model-released), cars, motorcycles, action sports. Uses color and b&w prints; 35mm, 2¼×2¼, 4×5, 8×10 transparencies. To contact, send stock photo list, promo piece. Reports in 2 months. Materials returned with SASE; materials filed. Pays on usage. Rights negotiable. Credit line given. Guidelines available for SASE.
Tips: "We don't use seasonal material. Please look at the types/quality of photography/illustration being used for published products. We are working with more freelancers now than ever."

SMART ART, INC., P.O. Box 661, Chatham NJ 07928-0661. (973)635-1690. Fax: (973)635-2011. E-mail: smartartnj@aol.com. President: Barb Hauck-Mah. Estab. 1992. Greeting card company. Publishes photo-insert cards for card, gift and photo shops. About 10% of products are made for kids or have kids' themes.
Illustration: Needs freelance illustration for photo-insert cards. Makes 12-14 illustration assignments/year. Uses color artwork only. To contact, send color photocopies. To query with specific ideas, write to request confidentiality form. Reports in 2-3 months. Materials returned with SASE; materials not filed. For greeting cards, pays annual royalties for life of card or 5 years. Pays on publication. Credit line given. Artist's guidelines available for SASE.
Tips: Submit seasonal material 6-8 months in advance. "Smart Art specializes in a unique, premium quality line of photo-insert cards for the holidays, baby announcements, weddings and all-season occasions. Our cards feature watercolor or collage borders on textured, recycled paper. Designs should complement horizontal and vertical photos. Generally, our freelance designers are new to the greeting card/paper goods industry. Artists come from varied backgrounds, including an art teacher, a textile designer and several children's book illustrators. We are looking for 'border design' artwork rendered in pen & ink with watercolors or in cut/torn paper. We are interested in artists who can create interesting abstract textures as well as representational designs."

‡**STANDARD PUBLISHING**, 8121 Hamilton Ave., Cincinnati OH 45231. (513)931-4050. Fax: (513)931-0950. Director: Diane Stortz. Christian Education Editor: Ruth Frederick. Creative Director: Colleen Davis. Estab. 1866. Publishes children's books and teacher helps for the religious market. 75% of products are made for kids or have kids' themes.
● Standard also has a listing in Book Publishers.
Writing: Considers puzzle books, activity books and games. Reports in 3 months. Pays on acceptance. Buys all rights. Credit line given.
Illustration: Needs freelance illustration for puzzle, activity books, teacher helps. Makes 6-10 illustration assign-

ments/year. To contact, send cover letter and photocopies. Reports back in 3 months if interested. Pays on acceptance. Buys all rights. Credit line given.

Photography: Buys a limited amount of photos from freelancers. Wants mature, scenic and Christian themes.

Tips "Many of our projects are developed inhouse and assigned. Study our catalog and products; visit Christian bookstores."

TALICOR, INC., 4741 Murrieta St., Chino CA 91710. (909)517-0076. President: Lew Herndon. Estab. 1971. Game manufacturer. Publishes games (adults' and children's). 80% of products are made for kids or have kids' themes.

Illustration: Needs freelance illustration for games. Makes 14 illustration assignments/year. To contact, send promo piece. Reports only if interested. Materials returned with SASE; materials filed. For artwork, pays by the hour, by the project or negotiable royalty. Pays on acceptance. Buys negotiable rights.

Photography: Buys stock and assigns work. Buys 6 stock images/year. Makes 6 assignments/year. Uses 4×5 transparencies. To contact, send color promo piece. Reports only if interested. Materials returned with SASE; materials filed. Pays per photo, by the hour, by the day or by the project (negotiable rates). Pays on acceptance. Buys negotiable rights.

Tips: Submit seasonal material 6 months in advance.

TEDCO, INC., 498 S. Washington St., Hagerstown IN 47346. (317)489-4527. Fax: (317)489-5752. Sales Director: Jane Shadle. Estab. 1982. Toy manufacturer. Produces educational toys: The Original Gyroscope, Gyros Gyroscope, prisms, magnet kits and science kits. Manufactures novelties, games, gyroscopes, prisms. 100% of products are made for kids or have kids' themes.

Writing: To contact, send cover letter, résumé, writing samples. Materials returned with SASE; materials filed. "We have never hired a freelance writer. We would be interested in learning more about available talent."

‡ZOLAN FINE ARTS, LTD., P.O. Box 656, Hershey PA 17033. (717)534-2446. Fax: (717)534-1095. E-mail: donaldz798@aol.com. Website: http://www.catalogs4collectors.com. President: Jennifer Zolan. Estab. 1993. Commercial and fine art studio creating and marketing original oil paintings of early childhood. 100% of products are made for kids or have kids' themes.

Writing: Needs freelance writing for stories and poems about the art, and ad copy. Makes 7-8 writing assignments/month. To contact, send cover letter, client list and writing samples. Reports in 2-4 weeks only if interested. Materials returned with SASE; materials filed if interested. Pays $40-80/hour, or $50-150/project. Pays on acceptance. Rights: negotiable.

Photography: Buys stock and assigns work. Makes 8-12 assignments/year. Wants "candid, heart-warming and endearing photos of children with high emotional appeal between the ages of 2-4. Looking for human interest type of photographs evoking pleasant and happy memories at early childhood. Photos are used for artist reference only." Uses color and b&w prints; 35mm, $2\frac{1}{4} \times 2\frac{1}{4}$, 4×5 or 8×10 transparencies. To contact, send cover letter, client list. Reports only if interested. Materials returned if accompanied with SASE; materials not filed. Pays per photo (range: $200-1,000 for b&w and color). Pays on acceptance. Buys "exclusive artist reference rights." Guidelines available for SASE.

Tips: Submit seasonal material 6 months in advance. "Writers should have the love of early childhood capturing the essence and feelings of the artwork and have ability to write in various ranges from ad copy to stories. Photos should have high emotional appeal and tell a story. We are happy to work with amateur and professional photographers. Photos are used for artist reference only. Please write or e-mail for guidelines before submitting work."

Play Publishers & Producers

Writing plays for children and family audiences is a special challenge. Whether creating an original work or adapting a classic, plays for children must hold the attention of audiences that often include children and adults. Using rhythm, repetition and dramatic action are effective ways of holding the attention of kids. Pick subjects children can relate to, and never talk down to them.

Theater companies often have limited budgets so plays with elaborate staging and costumes often can't be produced. Touring companies want simple sets that can be moved easily. Writers should keep in mind that they may have as few as three actors, so roles may have to be doubled up.

Many of the companies listed in this section produce plays with roles for adults and children, so check the percentage of plays written for adult and children's roles. Most importantly, study the types of plays a theater wants and doesn't want. Many name plays they've recently published or produced, and some may have additional guidelines or information available.

Information on play publishers listed in the previous edition but not included in this edition of *Children's Writer's & Illustrator's Market* **may be found in the General Index.**

A.D. PLAYERS, 2710 W. Alabama, Houston TX 77098. (713)526-2721. Estab. 1967. Produces 4-5 children's plays/year in new Children's Theatre Series; 1-2 musical/year. Produces children's plays for professional productions.
- A.D. Players has received the Dove family approval stamp; an award from the Columbia International Film & Video Festival; and a Silver Angel Award.

Needs: 99-100% of plays/musicals written for adult roles; 0-1% for juvenile roles. "Cast must utilize no more than four actors. Need minimal, portable sets for proscenium or arena stage with no fly space and no wing space." Recently produced plays: *The Selfish Giant*, by Dr. Gillette Elvgren Jr. (a story of a child's sacrificial love, for ages 5-12); and *The Lion, the Witch and the Wardrobe*, dramatized by le Clanche du Rand, story by C.S. Lewis (Lewis's classic story of love, faith, courage and giving, for ages 5-14). Does not want to see large cast or set requirements or New Age themes.

How to Contact: Query with synopsis, character breakdown and set description; no tapes until requested. Will consider simultaneous submissions and previously performed work. Reports in 6-12 months.

Terms: Buys some residual rights. Pay negotiated. Submissions returned with SASE.

Tips: "Children's musicals tend to be large in casting requirements. For those theaters with smaller production capabilities, this can be a liability for a script. Try to keep it small and simple, especially if writing for theaters where adults are performing for children. We are interested in material that reflects family values, emphasizes the importance of responsibility in making choices, encourages faith in God and projects the joy and fun of telling a story."

AMERICAN STAGE, P.O. Box 1560, St. Petersburg FL 33731. (813)823-1600. Managing Director: Jody Kielbasa. Estab. 1977. Produces 3 children's plays/year. Produces children's plays for professional children's theater program, mainstage, school tour, performing arts halls.

Needs: Limited by budget and performance venue. Subject matter: classics and original work for children (ages K-12) and families. Recently produced plays: *The Little Prince*, by Antoine De Saint-Exupery; adapted by Julia Flood (grades K-12). Does not want to see plays that look down on children. Approach must be that of the child or fictional beings or animals.

How to Contact: Query with synopsis, character breakdown and set description. Will consider simultaneous submissions and previously performed work. Reports in 6 months.

Terms: Purchases "professional rights." Pays writers in royalties (6-8%); $25-35/performance. SASE for return of submission.

Tips: Sees a move in plays toward basic human values, relationships and multicultural communities.

*AMERICAN STAGE FESTIVAL, 14 Court St., Nashua NH 03060. (603)889-2330. Fax: (603)889-2336. Artistic Director: Matthew Parent. Estab. 1972. Produces 5 children's plays and 4 children's musical plays/year.

Needs: American Stage Festival is a non-equity, educational aim of professional LORT theater—summer season. 75% of plays/musicals written for adult roles; 25% for juvenile roles. Requirements include limited cast size (under 10) and a minimal, tourable set. Musical needs: Piano orchestration. Recently produced plays: *Aladdin & the Wonderful Lamp*, by Jack Neary (traditional play for ages 5-12); and *Rapunzel*, by Jacque Lamanc (traditional play for ages 5-12).
How to Contact: Query with synopsis, character breakdown and set description. Include sample cassette if possible. Will consider simultaneous submissions and previously performed work. Reports back only if interested.
Terms: Buys subsidiary rights. Pays negotiable royalty/performance. Submissions returned with SASE.

‡ANCHORAGE PRESS, INC., P.O. Box 8067, New Orleans LA 70182. (504)283-8868. Fax: (504)866-0502. Editor: Orlin Corey. Estab. 1935. Publishes 6-8 children's plays/year; 2-3 children's musicals/year.
Needs: "There is no genre, subject of preferred interest. We want plays of high literary/theatrical quality. Like music, such material—by nature of the stage—will appeal to any age capable of following a story. Obviously some appeal more to primary ages, some secondary." Does not want send-ups—cutesies—jargon-laden—pendantic/subject specific. "Plays—like ice cream—work only if they are superb. Teaching is not the purpose of theatre—entertainment is, and that may include serious subjects fascinatingly explored." Recently produced plays: *The Orphan Train*, by Aurand Harris (play about lives of 10 children who rode "orphan" trains of 1914 for ages 7-18); *Tokoloshe*, by Pieter Scholtz (Zulu tale of a waiter-sprite and a modern little Zulu girl seeking her father for ages 5-9).
How to Contact: Query for guidelines first. Will consider simultaneous submissions and previously performed work "essential to be proven." Reports 3 months.
Terms: Buys all stage rights. Pays royalty (varies extensively from 50% minimum to 80%). Submissions returned with SASE.
Tips: "Obtain guidelines and get a catalog first."

APPLE TREE THEATRE, 595 Elm Place, Suite 210, Highland Park IL 60035. (847)432-8223. Fax: (847)432-5214. Produces 3 children's plays/year.
Needs: Produces professional, daytime and educational outreach programs for grades 4-9. 98% of plays written for adult roles; 2% for juvenile roles. Uses a unit set and limited to 9 actors. No musicals. Straight plays only. Does not want to see: "children's theater," i.e. . . . Peter Rabbit, Snow White. Material *must* be based in social issues. Recently produced plays: *Number the Stars* (based on Lois Lowry's Newbery Medal-winning novel about the Holocaust experience in Denmark for grades 4-9); and *The Pearl*, by John Steinbeck (grades 4-9).
How to Contact: Query first. Query with synopsis, character breakdown and set description. Will consider simultaneous submissions and previously performed work. Reports in 2 months.
Terms: Pay negotiated per contract. Submissions returned with SASE.
Tips: "Never send an unsolicited manuscript. Include reply postcard for queries."

BAKER'S PLAYS, 100 Chauncy St., Boston MA 02111. (617)482-1280. Fax: (617)482-7613. Associate Editor: Raymond Pape. Estab. 1845. Publishes 10-20 children's plays/year; 2 musicals/year.
Needs: 80% of plays/musicals written for adult roles; 20% for juvenile roles. Subject matter: full lengths for family audience and full lengths and one act plays for teens."
How to Contact: Submit complete ms, score and tape of songs. Reports in 3-8 months.
Terms: Obtains worldwide rights. Pays writers in royalties (amount varies).
Tips: "Know the audience you're writing for before you submit your play anywhere. 90% of the plays we reject are not written for our market."

‡BILINGUAL FOUNDATION OF THE ARTS, 421 N. Avenue 19th, Los Angeles CA 90031. (213)225-4044. Fax: (213)225-1250. Artistic Director: Margarita Galban. Estab. 1973. Produces 6 children's plays/year; 4 children's musicals/year.
Needs: Produces children's plays for professional productions. 60% of plays/musicals written for adult roles; 40% for juvenile roles. No larger than 8 member cast. Recently produced plays: *Second Chance*, by A. Cardona and A. Weinstein (play about hopes and fears in every teenager for teenagers); *The Circle*, by Liane Schirmer (play about violence for teenagers).
How to Contact: Plays: Query with synopsis, character breakdown and set description and submit complete ms. Musicals: Query with synopsis, character breakdown and set description and submit complete ms with score. Will consider simultaneous submissions and previously performed work. Reports in 4 months.
Terms: Pays royalty; per performance; buys material outright; "different with each play."

---

‡ **LISTINGS NEW TO THIS EDITION** are marked with a double dagger.

BIRMINGHAM CHILDREN'S THEATRE, P.O. Box 1362, Birmingham AL 35201-1362. (205)458-8181. Fax: (205)458-8895. E-mail: bctamin@aol.com. Website: http://www.bham.net/bct. Executive Director: Charlotte Lane Dominick. Estab. 1947. Produces 8-10 children's plays/year; 1-2 children's musicals/year.

Needs: "BCT is an adult professional theater performing for youth and family audiences September-May." 99% of plays/musicals written for adult roles; 1% for juvenile roles. "Our 'Wee Folks' Series is limited to four cast members and should be written with preschool-grade 1 in mind. We prefer interactive plays for this age group. We commission plays for our 'Wee Folks' Series (preschool-grade 1), our Children's Series (K-6) and our Young Adult Series (6-12)." Recently produced plays: *Teddy Roosevelt & the Star-Spangled Christmas Tree*, by Elliott Street (historical, holiday musical for ages 5-12); *Three Billy Goats Gruff*, by Jean Pierce (classic fable for ages 3-6). Does not want plays which have references to witches, spells, incantations, evil magic or devils. No adult language. Will consider musicals, interactive theater for Wee Folks Series. Prefer mainstage limited to 4-7 cast members.

How to Contact: Query first, query with synopsis, character breakdown and set description. Reports in 4 months.

Terms: Buys negotiable rights. Submissions returned with SASE.

Tips: "We would like our commissioned scripts to teach as well as entertain. Keep in mind the age groups (defined by each series) that our audience is composed of. Send submissions to the attention of Charlotte Dominick, executive director."

BOARSHEAD: PROFESSIONAL THEATER, (formerly Boarshead: Michigan Public Theater), 425 S. Grand Ave., Lansing MI 48933. (517)484-7800. Fax: (517)484-2564. Artistic Director: John Peakes. Director of P.R., Marketing and Outreach: Cathy Hansel. Estab. 1966. Produces 3 children's plays/year.

Needs: Produces children's plays for professional production. Majority of plays written for young adult roles. Prefers 5 characters or less for touring productions, 5 characters for mainstage productions; one unit set, simple costumes. Recently produced plays: *The Lion, the Witch & the Wardrobe*, by Joseph Robinette (fantasy for ages 6-12); *1,000 Cranes*, by Katharine Schultz Miller; *Step on a Crack*, by Susan Zeder (family play for ages 6-12). Does not want to see musicals.

How to Contact: Query with synopsis, character breakdown and set description. Send "Director of P.R., Marketing and Outreach." Include 10 pages of representative dialogue. Will consider previously performed work. Reports in 2 weeks on queries; 4 months "if we ask for submissions."

Terms: Pays writers $15-25/performance. Submissions returned with SASE. If no SASE, send self-addressed stamped post card for reply.

CALIFORNIA THEATRE CENTER, P.O. Box 2007, Sunnyvale CA 94087. (408)245-2979. Artistic Director: Gayle Cornelison. Estab. 1975. Produces 15 children's plays and 3 musicals for professional productions.

Needs: 75% of plays/musicals written for adult roles; 20% for juvenile roles. Prefers material suitable for professional tours and repertory performance; one-hour time limit, limited technical facilities. Recently produced *Jungle Book*, adapted by Will Huddleston (Kipling's classic for ages 4th grade-up); *Heidi*, by Gayle Cornelison (classic for ages K-up). Does not want to see arcane, artsy, cute material.

How to Contact: Query with synopsis, character breakdown and set description. Send to: Will Huddleston. Will consider previously performed work. Reports in 4 months.

Terms: Rights negotiable. Pays writers royalties; pays $35-50/performance. Submissions returned with SASE.

Tips: "We sell to schools, so the title and material must appeal to teachers who look for things familiar to them. We look for good themes, universality. Avoid the cute."

CHILDREN'S STORY SCRIPTS, Baymax Productions, Suite 130, 2219 W. Olive Ave., Burbank CA 91506-2648. (818)563-6105. Fax: (818)563-2968. E-mail: baymax@earthlink.net. Website: http://home.earthlink.net/~baymax. Editor: Deedra Bebout. Estab. 1990. Produces 1-10 children's scripts/year.

Needs: "Except for small movements and occasionally standing up, children remain seated in Readers Theatre fashion." Publishes scripts sold primarily to schools or wherever there's a program to teach or entertain children. "All roles read by children except K-2 scripts, where kids have easy lines, leader helps read the narration. Prefer multiple cast members, no props or sets." Subject matter: scripts on all subjects that dovetail with classroom subjects. Targeted age range—K-8th grade, 5-13 years old. Recently published stories: *Booga the Caveman Discovers Oil*, by Helen Ksypka (about Neanderthals and petroleum, grades 4, 5, 6); *Celebrate*, by M. Donnaleen Howett (10 holiday poems for grades 3-6). No stories that preach a point, no stories about catastrophic disease or other terribly heavy topics, no theatrical scripts without narrative prose to move the story along, no monologues or 1-character stories.

How to Contact: Submit complete ms. Will consider simultaneous submissions and previously performed work (if rights are available). Reports in 2 weeks.

Terms: Purchases all rights; authors retain copyrights. "We add support material and copyright the whole package." Pays writers in royalties (10-15% on sliding scale, based on number of copies sold). SASE for reply and return of submission.

Tips: "We're only looking for stories related to classsroom studies—educational topics with a freshness to them. Our scripts mix prose narration with character dialogue—we do not publish traditional, all-dialogue plays." Writer's guidelines packet available for business-sized SASE with 2 first-class stamps. Guidelines explain what

Children's Story Scripts are, give 4-page examples from 2 different scripts, give list of suggested topics for scripts.

CIRCA '21 DINNER THEATRE, P.O. Box 3784, Rock Island IL 61204-3784. (309)786-2667. Producer: Dennis Hitchcock. Estab. 1977. Produces 3 children's plays or musicals/year.
Needs: Produces children's plays for professional productions. 95% of plays/musicals written for adult roles; 5% written for juvenile roles. "Prefer a cast of four to eight—no larger than ten. Plays are produced on mainstage sets." Recently produced plays: *Hunchback of Notre Dame*, by Brad Haskins and Linda Brinkerhoff (ages 6-10) and *Alice In Wonderland*, by Prince Street Players (ages 4-10).
How to Contact: Send complete script with audiotape of music. Reports in 3 months.
Terms: Payment negotiable.

I.E. CLARK PUBLICATIONS, P.O. Box 246, Schulenburg TX 78956. (409)743-3232. Fax: (409)743-4765. General Manager: Donna Cozzaglio. Estab. 1956. Publishes 3 children's plays/year; 1 or 2 children's musicals/year.
Needs: Medium to large casts preferred. Publishes plays for all ages. Published plays: *Little Women*, by Thomas Hischak (dramatization of the Alcott novel for family audiences); *Heidi*, by Ann Pugh, music by Betty Utter (revision of our popular musical dramatization of the Johanna Spyri novel). Does not want to see plays that have not been produced.
How to Contact: Submit complete ms and audio or video tape. Will consider simultaneous submissions and previously performed work. Reports in 2-4 months.
Terms: Pays writers in negotiable royalties. SASE for return of submission.
Tips: "We publish only high-quality literary works. Please send only one manuscript at a time."

CONTEMPORARY DRAMA SERVICE, Division of Meriwether Publishing Ltd., 885 Elkton Dr., Colorado Springs CO 80907-3557. (719)594-4422. Fax: (719)594-9916. Executive Editor: Arthur L. Zapel. Estab. 1979. Publishes 50 children's plays/year; 6-8 children's musicals/year.
Needs: 15% of plays/musicals written for adult roles; 85% for juvenile roles. Recently published plays: *Treasure Island*, by James DeVita (an adaptation of the book, for ages 10-16); *Alice's Adventures* (an adaptation of two Lewis Carrol classics for ages 10 to adult). "We publish church plays for elementary level for Christmas and Easter. Most of our secular plays are for teens or college level." Does not want to see "full-length, three-act plays unless they are adaptations of classic works or have unique comedy appeal."
How to Contact: Query with synopsis, character breakdown and set description; "query first if a musical." Will consider simultaneous submissions or previously performed work. Reports in 4-6 weeks.
Terms: Purchases first rights. Pays writers royalty (10%) or buys material outright for $200-1,000. SASE for return of submission.
Tips: "If the writer is submitting a musical play an audiocassette of the music should be sent. We prefer plays with humorous action. A writer should provide credentials of plays published and produced."

THE COTERIE, 2450 Grand, Kansas City MO 64108. Phone/fax: (816)474-6785. Artistic Director: Jeff Church. Estab. 1979. Produces 7 children's plays/year; 1 children's musical/year.
Needs: "Prefer casts of between 5-7 no larger than 15." Produces children's plays for professional productions. 80% of plays/musicals written for adult roles; 20% for juvenile roles. "We produce original plays, musicals and literary adaptations for ages five through adult." Produced plays: *Amelia Lives*, by Laura Annawyn Shamas (one-woman show on Amelia Earhart, for 6th grade through adult); *Dinosaurus*, by Ed Mast and Lenore Bensinger (Mobil Oil workers discover cavern of dinosaurs, for ages 5 through adult). "We do *not* want to see 'camp' adaptations of fairytales."
How to Contact: Query with synopsis, sample scene, character breakdown and set description. Reports in 8-10 months.
Terms: Rights purchased "negotiable." Pays writers in royalties per play of approximately $1,000-1,500. SASE for return of submission.
Tips: "We're interested in adaptations of classic literature with small casts, simple staging requirements; also multicultural topics and biography plays of Latin and African-American figures. There is a need for non-condescending material for younger age groups (5-8) and for middle school (ages 9-13)."

A SELF-ADDRESSED, STAMPED ENVELOPE (SASE) should always be included with submissions within your own country. When sending material to other countries, include a self-addressed envelope (SAE) and International Reply Coupons (IRCs).

CREEDE REPERTORY THEATRE, P.O. Box 269, Creede CO 81130. (719)658-2541. Fax: (719)658-2343. Artistic Director: Richard Baxter. Estab. 1966. Produces 1 children's play/year; 1 musical/year.
Needs: Limited to 4-6 cast members and must be able to tour. Produces children's plays for summer theater, school or professional productions. 100% of plays/musicals written for adult roles. Publishes plays for ages K-12. Recently produced plays: *Coyote Tales*, by Daniel Kramer and Company (Native American Coyote legend, for grades K-6); and *The Two of Us*, by Michael Frayn (contemporary relationship story, for ages 12-adult).
How to Contact: Query first, submit complete ms and score, or query with synopsis, character breakdown and set description. Will consider simultaneous submissions and previously performed work. Reports in 1 year.
Terms: Pays writers in royalties (5%); pays $15-30 per performance.
Tips: Sees trends in "non-sexist, non-traditional casting and Native American/Hispanic American interest. No fairy tales unless non-traditional."

EL CENTRO SU TEATRO, 4725 High, Denver CO 80216. (303)296-0219. Fax: (303)296-4614. Artistic Director: Anthony J. Garcia. Estab. 1971. Produces 6 children's plays/year.
Needs: "We are interested in plays by Chicanos or Latinos that speak to that experience. We do not produce standard musicals. We are a culturally specific company." Recently produced *Joaquim's Christmas*, by Anthony J. Garcia (children's Christmas play for ages 7-15); and *The Dragonslayer*, by Silviana Woods (young boy's relationship with grandfather for ages 7-15). Does not want to see "cutesy stuff."
How to Contact: Query with synopsis, character breakdown and set description. Will consider simultaneous submissions and previously performed work. Reports in 6 months. Buys regional rights.
Terms: Pays writers per performance: $35 1st night, $25 subsequent. Submissions returned with SASE.
Tips: "People should write within their realm of experience but yet push their own boundaries. Writers should approach social issues within the human experience of their character."

ELDRIDGE PUBLISHING CO. INC., P.O. Box 1595, Venice FL 34284. (941)496-4679. Fax: (941)493-9680. E-mail: info@histage.com. Website: http://www.histage.com or http://www.95church.com. Editor: Nancy Vorhis. Estab. 1906. Publishes approximately 25 children's plays/year; 2-3 children's musicals/year.
Needs: Prefers simple staging; flexible cast size. "We publish for junior and high school, community theater and children's theater (adults performing for children), all genres, also religious plays." Recently published plays: *Mother Goose Inc.*, by Steve Murray (fairytale characters go MTV, ages 12-14); *Agatha Christie Never Took Trig*, by Jeffrey Smart (comedy/mystery at a high school party, ages 12-18). Prefers work which has been performed or at least had a staged reading.
How to Contact: Submit complete ms, score and tape of songs (if a musical). Will consider simultaneous submissions ("please let us know, however"). Reports in 2 months.
Terms: Purchases all dramatic rights. Pays writers royalties of 50%; 10% copy sales; buys material outright for $200-500.
Tips: "Try to have your work performed, if at all possible, before submitting. We're always on the lookout for comedies which provide a lot of fun for our customers. But other more serious topics which concern teens, as well as intriguing mysteries, and children's theater programs are of interest to us as well. We know there are many new talented playwrights out there and we look forward to reading their fresh scripts."

ENCORE PERFORMANCE PUBLISHING, P.O. Box 692, Orem UT 84059. (801)225-0605. Fax: (807)765-0489. E-mail: encoreplay@aol.com. Website: http://www.Encoreplay.com. Contact: Mike Perry. Estab. 1978. Publishes 20-30 children's plays/year; 10-20 children's musicals/year.
Needs: Prefers close to equal male/female ratio if possible. Adaptations for K-12 and older. 60% of plays written for adult roles; 40% for juvenile roles. Recently published plays: *Boy Who Knew No Fear*, by G. Riley Mills/Mark Levenson (adaptation of fairy tale, ages 8-16); *Two Chains*, by Paul Burton (about drug abuse, ages 11-18).
How to Contact: Query first with synopsis, character breakdown, set description and production history. Will only consider previously performed work. Reports in 2 months.
Terms: Purchases all publication and production rights. Author retains copyright. Pays writers in royalties (50%). SASE for return of submission.
Tips: "Give us issue and substance, be controversial without offense. Use a laser printer! Don't send an old manuscript. Make yours look the most professional."

FLORIDA STUDIO THEATRE, 1241 N. Palm Ave., Sarasota FL 34236. (941)366-9017. Artistic Director: Richard Hopkins. Estab. 1980. Produces 3 children's plays/year; 1-3 children's musicals/year.
Needs: Produces children's plays for professional productions. 50% of plays/musicals written for adult roles; 50% for juvenile roles. "Prefer small cast plays that use imagination more than heavy scenery." Will consider simultaneous submissions and previously performed work.
How to Contact: Query with synopsis, character breakdown and set description. Reports in 3 months. Rights negotiable. Pay negotiable. Submissions returned with SASE.
Tips: "Children are a tremendously sophisticated audience. The material should respect this."

THE FREELANCE PRESS, P.O. Box 548, Dover MA 02030. (508)785-8250. Managing Editor: Narcissa Campion. Estab. 1979. Produces 3 musicals and/or plays/year.

Needs: Casts are comprised of young people, ages 8-15, and number 25-30. "We publish original musicals on contemporary topics for children and adaptations of children's classics (e.g., Rip Van Winkle)." Published plays: *The Tortoise and the Hare* (based on story of same name, for ages 8-12); *Monopoly*, 3 (young people walk through board game, for ages 11-15).

● The Freelance Press does not accept plays for adult performers.

How to Contact: Submit complete ms and score with SASE. Will consider simultaneous submissions and previously performed work. Reports in 3 months.

Terms: Pays writers 10% royalties on book sales, plus performance royalties. SASE for return of submission.

SAMUEL FRENCH, INC., 45 W. 25th St., New York NY 10010. (212)206-8990. Fax: (212)206-1429. Editor: Lawrence Harbison. Estab. 1830. Publishes 2 or 3 children's plays/year; "variable number of musicals."

Needs: Subject matter: "all genres, all ages. No puppet plays. No adaptations of any of those old 'fairy tales.' No 'Once upon a time, long ago and far away.' No kings, princesses, fairies, trolls, etc."

How to Contact: Submit complete ms and demo tape (if a musical). Reports in 2-8 months.

Terms: Purchases "publication rights, amateur and professional production rights, option to publish next 3 plays." Pays writers "book royalty of 10%; variable royalty for professional and amateur productions. SASE for return of submissions.

Tips: "Children's theater is a very tiny market, as most groups perform plays they have created themselves or have commissioned."

THE GROWING STAGE THEATRE, In Residence at the Palace, Rt. 183, Netcong NJ 07857. (973)347-4946. Executive Director: Stephen L. Fredericks. Estab. 1982. Produces 5 mainstage children's shows, a summer production for the whole family. Equity touring production to schools and other organizations. Professional actors work with community actors.

Needs: 60% of plays/musicals written for adult roles; 40% for juvenile roles. Produced: *Aladdin*, by Perry Arthur Kroeger, (adaptation from classic tale, for K-8th grade); and *The Pied Piper of Hamelin, AZ*, by Stephen L. Fredericks and Perry Arthur Kroeger (adaptation of classic poem, K-6th grades). Plays for young audiences only.

How to Contact: Query with synopsis, character breakdown and set description. Will consider previously performed work. Reports in 1 month.

Terms: "Contracts are developed individually." Pays $25-75/performance. Submissions returned with SASE.

Tips: "There's an overabundance on issue-oriented plays. Creativity, quality, the standards we place on theater aimed at adults should not be reduced in preparing a script for young people. We, together, are forming the audience of tomorrow. Don't repel young people by making the theater another resource for the infomercial—nurture, challenge and inspire them."

HAYES SCHOOL PUBLISHING CO. INC., 321 Pennwood Ave., Wilkinsburg PA 15221. (412)371-2373. Fax: (412)371-6408. Estab. 1940.

Needs: Wants to see supplementary teaching aids for grades K-12. Interested in all subject areas, especially music, foreign language (French, Spanish, Latin), early childhood education.

How to Contact: Query first with table of contents, sample page or activities. Will consider simultaneous and electronic submissions. Reports in 4-6 weeks.

Terms: Purchases all rights. Work purchased outright. SASE for return of submissions.

INDIANA REPERTORY THEATRE, 140 W. Washington, Indianapolis IN 46204. (317)635-5277. Artistic Director: Janet Allen. Estab. 1971. Produces 3 children's plays/year. Produces children's plays for professional productions.

Needs: 100% of plays written for adult roles. Limit 8 in cast, 75 minute running time. Recently produced plays: *Tales from the Arabian Nights*, by Michael Dixon; *Red Badge of Courage*, adaptation by Thomas Olson. Does not want to see preschool and K-4 mate

How to Contact: Query with synopsis, character breakdown and set description to Richard Roberts, literary manager. Will consider previously performed work. Reports in 6 months.

Terms: Pays writers negotiable royalty (6%) or commission fee. Submissions returned with SASE.

JEWISH ENSEMBLE THEATRE, 6600 W. Maple Rd., West Bloomfield MI 48322. (810)788-2900. Fax: (248)788-5160. Artistic Director: Evelyn Orbach. Estab. 1989. Produces children's plays for professional productions.

Needs: Is producing one children's play and is looking for additional scripts to create a repertoire. Prefers small casts and unit set. Recently produced play: *Shades of Grey*, by Eden Cooper Sage and Marshall Zweig (about inter-generational conflicts for middle and high school audience).

How to Contact: Send submission to Evelyn Orbach, artistic director. Reports on submissions in 6 months.

Tips: "Plays are toured to various schools and youth organizations. Our needs require a play as a teaching tool—usually values. No longer than 40-45 min. to be done by a small adult professional cast."

THE MUNY FIRST STAGE, (formerly The Muny Student Theatre), 634 N. Grand, 12th Floor, St. Louis MO 63103. (314)652-5213. Fax: (314)533-3345. Executive Artistic Director: Christopher Limber. Estab. 1979. Produces 5 children's plays/year; 1 or 2 children's musicals/year.

Needs: "We produce a touring and mainstage season September-May and offer extensive theater classes throughout the entire year." 100% of plays/musicals written for adult roles; 40% for juvenile roles. Prefers cast of 4 or 5 equity actors, for touring productions; no limit for mainstage productions. "Tour sets are limited in size." Produced plays: *Meet Willie*, adapted by Chris Limber (introduction to Shakespeare for 4th grade-adult); *On The Rays of The Sun* by Patton Hasegawa (about African heros and heroines for 1st grade-adult).
How to Contact: Query with synopsis, character breakdown and set description. Will consider simultaneous submissions and previously performed work. Reports in 3 months.
Terms: Rights negotiable.
Tips: "We emphasize diverse ethnic casting and multicultural material. Tour shows should fit into the school curriculum. The Muny First Stage's mission is to introduce theater to young people, to encourage creative learning and to develop future theater audiences. The company is now one of the most comprehensive theater education programs in Missouri. Each year the company reaches more than 100,000 students through its resident touring company, professional storytellers, mainstage productions and theater classes. As film and television become more sophisticated, we're seeing a focus on theatricality, imaginative use of the live theater medium; use of young actors in major roles; opera for young performers; strong adaptations of classics which highlight contemporary issues."

THE NEW CONSERVATORY THEATRE CENTER, 25 Van Ness Ave., San Francisco CA 94102-6033. (415)861-4914. Fax: (415)861-6988. Executive Director: Ed Decker. Estab. 1981. Produces 3 children's plays/year.
Needs: Limited budget and small casts only. Produces children's plays as part of "a professional theater arts training program for youths ages 4-19 during the school year and 2 summer sessions. The New Conservatory also produces educational plays for its touring company. We do not want to see any preachy or didactic material." Recently produced plays: *The Little Prince*, by Antoine de Saint-Exupery (self awareness, for ages 5-13); *Dinosauraus*, by Elenore Bensinger (environmental issues, for ages 7-10).
How to Contact: Query with synopsis, character breakdown and set description, or submit complete ms and score. Reports in 3 months.
Terms: Rights purchased negotiable. Pays writers in royalties. SASE for return of submission.
Tips: Sees trend in: "addressing socially relevant issues for young people and their families."

NEW PLAYS INCORPORATED, P.O. Box 5074, Charlottesville VA 22905-0074. (804)979-2777. E-mail: patwhitton@aol.com. Publisher: Patricia Whitton. Estab. 1964. Publishes 2 or 3 plays/year; 1 or 2 children's musicals/year.
Needs: Publishes "generally material for kindergarten through junior high." Recently published: *Ms. Courageous*, by Joanna Kraus (lives of famous women scientists, for ages 10-12); *Now You See It, Now You Don't*, by Patrica Sternberg (musical story theatre fables, for ages 5-10). Does not want to see "adaptations of titles I already have. No unproduced plays; no junior high improvisations."
How to Contact: Submit complete ms and score. Will consider simultaneous submissions and previously performed work. Reports in 2 months (usually).
Terms: Purchases exclusive rights to sell acting scripts. Pays writers in royalties (50% of production royalties; 10% of script sales). SASE for return of submission.
Tips: "Write the play you really want to write (not what you think will be saleable) and find a director to put it on."

NEW YORK STATE THEATRE INSTITUTE, 155 River St., Troy NY 12180. (518)274-3200. Fax: (518)274-3815. E-mail: nysti@crisny.org. Website: http://www.crisny.org/not-for-profit/nysti. Artistic Director: Patricia B. Snyder. Estab. 1976. Produces 5 children's plays/year; 1-2 children's musicals/year.
Needs: Produces family plays for professional theater. 90% of plays/musicals are written for adult roles; 10% for juvenile roles. Does not want to see plays for children only. Produced plays: *The Snow Queen*, by Adrian Mitchell and Richard Penslee (ages 10-100).
How to Contact: Query with synopsis, character breakdown and set description; submit tape of songs (if a musical). Will consider simultaneous submissions and previously performed work. Reports in 1 month for queries. SASE for return of submission.
Tips: Writers should be mindful of "audience *sophistication*. We do not wish to see material that is childish. Writers should submit work that is respectful of young people's intelligence and perception—work that is appropriate for families, but that is also challenging and provocative."

‡OMAHA THEATER COMPANY FOR YOUNG PEOPLE, (formerly Emmy Gifford Children's Theater), 201 Farnam St., Omaha NE 68102. (402)345-4852. Artistic Director: James Larson. Estab. 1949. Produces 9 children's plays/year; 1 children's musical/year.
Needs: Produces children's plays for professional productions. 100% of plays/musicals written for adult roles. Need plays with small casts, no fly space necessary. Does not want to see adult plays. Recently produced plays: *Frog and Toad*, by Karen Abbott (about friendship for ages 5-9); and *Lyle the Crocodile*, by Kevin Kling (about family identity for ages 5-9).
How to Contact: Will consider simultaneous submissions, electronic submissions via disk or modem, or

previously performed work. Submission method: Query first. Reports in 6 months. Pays writers in royalties (6%). Submissions returned with SASE.

THE OPEN EYE THEATER, (formerly The Open Eye: New Stagings), P.O. Box 959, Margaretville NY 12455. Phone/fax: (914)586-1660. Producing Artistic Director: Amie Brockway. Estab. 1972 (theater). Produces 3 plays/year for a family audience. Most productions are with music, but are not musicals.
Needs: "Casts are usually limited to six performers. Technical requirements are kept to a minimum for touring purposes." Produces professional productions combining professional artists and artists-in-training (actors of all ages). Recently produced plays: *The Nightingale*, by William E. Black and Amie Brockway (adaptation of Hans Christian Andersen story for ages 6-adult); and *Selkie*, by Laurie Brooks Gollobin (based on Selkie legend for ages 8-adult).
How to Contact: "No videos or cassettes. Letter of inquiry only." Will consider previously performed work. Reports in 6 months.
Terms: Rights agreement negotiated with author. Pays writers 1-time fee or royalty negotiated with publisher. SASE for return of submission.
Tips: "Send letter of inquiry only. We are interested in plays for a multigenerational audience (eight-adult)."

‡PHOENIX THEATRE'S COOKIE COMPANY, 100E. McDowell, Phoenix AZ 85004. (602)258-1974. Fax: (602)253-3626. Artistic Director: Alan J. Prewitt. Estab. 1980. Produces 4 children's plays/year.
Needs: Produces theater with professional adult actors performing for family audiences. 95% of plays/musicals written for adult roles; 5% for juvenile roles. Requires small casts (4-7), small stage, mostly 1 set, flexible set or ingenious sets for a small space. "We're just starting to do plays with music—no musicals per se." Does not want to see larger casts, multiple sets, 2 hour epics. Recently produced *Alice In Wonderland*, by Alan J. Prewitt (based on classic, bilingual—Spanish for grades K-6); and *The Magic Flute*, by Alan J. Prewitt (based on opera— intro to opera for grades K-6).
How to Contact: Plays/musicals: Query with synopsis, character breakdown and set description. Will consider simultaneous submissions. Reports back only if interested.
Terms: Submissions returned with SASE.
Tips: "Only submit innovative, imaginative work that stimulates imagination and empowers the child. We specialize in producing original scripts based on classic children's literature."

PIONEER DRAMA SERVICE, P.O. Box 4267, Englewood CO 80155. (303)779-4035. Fax: (303)779-4315. E-mail: piodrama@aol.com. Website: http://www.pioneerdrama.com. Publisher: Steven Fendrich. Estab. 1960. Publishes 20 plays and musicals/year.
Needs: Subject matter: Publishes plays for ages preschool-high school. Recently published plays/musicals: *Coney Island of Dr. Moreau*, by Tim Kelly (musical comedy spoof for junior and senior high school on up); and *Fighting For My Self*, by Renee Clark (a series of scenes depicting young women's struggle for self-esteem in today's society for ages junior high on up). Wants to see "script, scores, tapes, pics and reviews."
How to Contact: Query with synopsis, character breakdown and set description. Submit complete ms and score (if a musical). Will consider simultaneous submissions, CAD electronic submissions via disk or modem, previously performed work. Contact: Lynne Zborowski, submissions editor. Reports in 3 months.
Terms: Purchases all rights. Pays writers in royalties (10% on sales, 50% royalties on productions).

PLAYERS PRESS, INC., P.O. Box 1132, Studio City CA 91614-0132. (818)789-4980. Vice President: R. W. Gordon. Estab. 1965. Publishes 10-20 children's plays/year; 3-10 children's musicals/year.
Needs: Subject matter: "We publish for all age groups." Published plays: *Silly Soup*, by Carol Kirty (comic children's play for ages 5-15); *Indian Tales*, by William-Alan Landes (American Indian musical).
How to Contact: Query with synopsis, character breakdown and set description; include #10 SASE with query. Considers previously performed work only. Reports on query in 2-4 weeks; submissions in 1-12 months.
Terms: Purchases stage, screen, TV rights. Payment varies; work purchased possibly outright upon written request. Submissions returned with SASE.
Tips: "Submit as requested—query first and send only previously produced material. Entertainment quality is on the upswing and needs to be directed at the world, no longer just the U.S. Please submit with two #10 SASEs plus ms-size SASE. Please do not call."

PLAYS, The Drama Magazine for Young People, 120 Boylston St., Boston MA 02116-4615. (617)423-3157. Managing Editor: Elizabeth Preston. Estab. 1941. Publishes 70-75 children's plays/year.
Needs: "Props and staging should not be overly elaborate or costly. There is little call among our subscribers for plays with only a few characters; ten or more (to allow all students in a class to participate, for instance) is preferred. Our plays are performed by children in school from lower elementary grades through junior-senior high." 100% of plays written for juvenile roles. Subject matter: Audience is lower grades through junior/senior high. Recently published plays: *The Fastest Thimble in the West*, by Claire Boiko (about succeeding as sheriff in the Old West without using a gun for junior and senior high); and *Mother Saves Her Day*, by Mildred Hark and Noel McQeen (about finding the perfect Mother's Day gift, for middle and lower grades). "Send nothing downbeat—no plays about drugs, sex or other 'heavy' topics."

How to Contact: Query first on adaptations of folk tales and classics; otherwise submit complete ms. Reports in 2-3 weeks.

Terms: Purchases all rights. Pay rates vary. Guidelines available; send SASE. Sample copy $3.50.

Tips: "Get your play underway quickly. Above all, plays must be entertaining for young people with plenty of action, fast-paced dialogue and a satisfying conclusion. Any message imparted should be secondary to the entertainment value. No sex, drugs, violence, alcohol."

PLAYS FOR YOUNG AUDIENCES, P.O. Box 4267, Englewood CO 80155-4267. (303)779-4035. Fax: (303)779-4315. E-mail: piodrama@aol.com. Website: http://www.pioneerdrama.com. Submissions Editor: Lynne Zbrowski. Publisher: Steven Fendrich. Estab. 1989. Publishes 12 plays and 8 musicals/year.

Needs: "We are looking for plays with simple sets up to 90 minutes long." Publishes plays for preschool-12th grade audience. Recently produced plays: *Nifty Fifties*, by Tim Kelly and Bill Francoeur (musical comedy for junior high/high school); and *Thumbelina*, by Vera Morris (classic for children's family theater). Wants to see "script, score, tape, pictures and reviews."

How to Contact: Query with synopsis, character breakdown and set description; submit complete ms and score (if a musical). Will consider simultaneous submissions, electronic submissions via disk or modem, previously performed work. Contact: Lynne Zborowski, submissions editor. Reports in 3-4 months.

Terms: Purchases all rights. Pays writers in royalties (10% in sales, 50% on productions).

Tips: "Send query letter. Learn about our market by obtaining catalog and guidelines. Look at our website."

SEATTLE CHILDREN'S THEATRE, P.O. Box 9640, Seattle WA 98109. Literary Manager and Dramaturg: Deborah Frockt. Estab. 1975. Produces 6 full-length children's plays/year; 1 full-length children's musical/year. Produces children's plays for professional productions (September-June).

Needs: 95% of plays/musicals written for adult roles; 5% for juvenile roles. "We generally use adult actors even for juvenile roles." Prefers no turntable, no traps. Produced plays: *The Rememberer*, adapted by Steven Dietz (Native American girl struggles to maintain her cultural legacy when she is forced to attend boarding school in 1912 for ages 8 and up); *Afternoon of the Elves*, adapted by Y. York, book by Janet Taylor Lisle (friendship, imagination, getting to know those you think are different for ages 8 and up). Does not want to see anything that condescends to young people—anything overly broad in style.

How to Contact: Accepts agented scripts or those accompanied by a professional letter of recommendation (director or dramaturg). Reports in 6-12 months.

Terms: Rights vary. Payment method varies. Submissions returned with SASE.

Tips: "Please *do not* send unsolicited manuscripts. We welcome queries by all populations and encourage queries by women and minorities. We prefer sophisticated material (our weekend performances have an audience that is half adults). All shows SCT produces are multiracially cast."

STAGE ONE: THE LOUISVILLE CHILDREN'S THEATRE, 5 Riverfront Plaza, Louisville KY 40202-3300. (502)589-5946. Fax: (502)588-5910. E-mail: kystageone@aol.com. Website: http://www.stageone.org. Producing Director: Moses Goldberg. Estab. 1946. Produces 6-8 children's plays/year; 1-4 children's musicals/year.

Needs: Stage One is an Equity company producing children's plays for professional productions. 100% of plays/ musicals written for adult roles. "Sometimes we do use students in selected productions." Produced plays: *Young Black Beauty*, by Aurand Harris (about a colt growing up for ages 6-12); and *John Lennon & Me*, by Cherie Bennett (about cystic fibrosis; peer acceptance for ages 11-17). Does not want to see "camp or condescension."

How to Contact: Submit complete ms, score and tape of songs (if a musical); include the author's résumé if desired. Will consider simultaneous submissions, electronic submissions via disk or modem and previously performed work. Reports in 3-4 months.

Terms: Pays writers in royalties (5-6%) or $25-75/performance.

Tips: Looking for "stageworthy and respectful dramatizations of the classic tales of childhood, both ancient and modern; plays relevant to the lives of young people and their families; and plays directly related to the school curriculum."

STUDIO ARENA THEATRE SCHOOL, 710 Main St., Buffalo NY 14202. (716)856-8025, ext. 1770. Fax: (716)856-3415. Education Director: Robert Rutland. Artistic Director: Gavin Cameron Well. Estab. 1927. Produces 2-6 children's plays/year.

Needs: Studio Arena Theatre School is both a professional company and a school. 70% of plays/musicals written for adult roles; 30% for juvenile roles. "We like our touring productions to feature four to five actors and transport easily. Our student productions must feature a large cast (20) with many quality roles for young women. We are interested in musical adaptations of literature classics for student audiences ten years old. We also produce musicals on our main stage during the summer, but we've tended to stick to known works with a wide audience appeal." Recently produced plays: *Mother Earth*, by Wendy Peters ("reduce, reuse, recycle" for elementary audience); and *Super Science*, by Lisa Lewis (about magic and science for elementary audience).

How to Contact: Plays: Query with synopsis, character breakdown and set description; submit complete ms. Musicals: Query with synopsis, character breakdown and set description; submit complete ms and score; tape with songs acceptable also. Will consider simultaneous submissions, electronic submissions via disk/modem and previously performed work. Reports in 6 months.

Terms: Pays $25-50/performance. Submissions returned with SASE.

Tips: "Because we are both a school and a professional company, the material we seek cuts across a wide spectrum. We lean toward educational material that would be recognized by our audience with the occasional use of other work. We also have an Equity main stage that produces other work (non-children's theater)."

TADA!, 120 W. 28th St., New York NY 10001-6109. (212)627-1732. Fax: (212)243-6736. E-mail: tada@ziplink. net. Website: http://www.tadatheater.com. Artistic Director: Janine Nina Trevens. Estab. 1984. Produces 5 staged readings of children's plays and musicals/year; 0-1 children's plays/year; 2-3 children's musicals/year.

Needs: "All actors are children, ages 8-17." Produces children's plays for professional, year-round theater. 100% of plays/musicals written for juvenile roles. Recently produced musicals: *The Little Moon Theater*, book by Michael Slade, music/lyrics by Joel Gelpe (traveling performance troupe travels around the country fulfilling wishes for ages 3 and up); *Maggie and the Pirate*, book/lyrics by Winnie Holzman, music by David Evans (Maggie and her friends search for her kidnapped cricket; when they find the kidnapper, disguised as a pirate, they also find a new friend for ages 3 and up). Does not want to see fairy tales or material that talks down to children.

How to Contact: Query with synopsis, character breakdown and set description; submit complete ms, score and tape of songs (if a musical). Reports in 6 months "or in October following the August deadline for our Annual Playwriting Competition. (Send two copies of manuscript if for competition)."

Terms: Rights purchased "depend on the piece." Pays writers in royalties of 1-6% and/or pays commissioning fee. SASE a must for return of submissions.

Tips: "For plays for our Annual Playwriting Competition, submit between January and August 15. We're looking for plays with current topics that specific age ranges can identify with, with a small cast of children and one or two adults. Our company is multi-racial and city-oriented. We are not interested in fairy tales. We like to produce material that kids relate to and that touches their lives today."

‡MARK TAPER FORUM, P.L.A.Y.—Performing for Los Angeles Youth, 135 N. Grand Ave., Los Angeles CA 90012. (213)972-7574. Fax: (213)972-0746. Artistic Director: Gordon Davidson. Estab. 1967. Produces 1 play/year; varying number of musicals/year. "Sometimes our children's play is a musical."

Needs: P.L.A.Y. (Performing for Los Angeles Youth), the Mark Taper Forum's theater for young audiences program, tours Southern California schools with one 50-minute play a year. 100% of plays/musicals written for adult roles. Maximum 6 actors. Does not want to see: Plays that have no relevance to the lives of young mostly urban people. Recently produced plays: *The Square Root of Terrible*, by Kelly Stuart (about girls and math anxiety for grades K-6); and *Bocòn*, by Lisa Loomer (about a boy fleeing political repression in South America for grades K-6).

How to Contact: Plays/musicals: Query with short description of play and 5-10 sample pages of dialogue. Will consider simultaneous submissions. Reports in 2 months.

Terms: Pays $20-30/performance. Submissions returned with SASE.

THEATRE FOR YOUNG AMERICA, 4881 Johnson Dr., Mission KS 66205. (913)831-2131. Artistic Director: Gene Mackey. Estab. 1974. Produces 9 children's plays/year; 3-5 children's musicals/year.

Needs: "We use a small cast (4-7), open thrust stage." Theatre for Young America is a professional equity company. 90% of plays/musicals written for adult roles; 10% for juvenile roles. Produced plays: *The Wizard of Oz*, by Jim Eiler and Jeanne Bargy (for ages 6 and up); *A Partridge in a Pear Tree*, by Lowell Swortzell (deals with the 12 days of Christmas, for ages 6 and up); *Three Billy Goats Gruff*, by Gene Mackey and Molly Jessup (Norwegian folk tales, for ages 6 and up).

How to Contact: Query with synopsis, character breakdown and set description. Will consider simultaneous submissions and previously performed work. Reports in 2 months.

Terms: Purchases production rights, tour rights in local area. Pays writers in royalties or $10-50/performance.

Tips: Looking for "cross-cultural material that respects the intelligence, sensitivity and taste of the child audience."

‡THE THEATRE STUDIO INC., 750 Eighth Ave., #200, New York NY 10036. (212)719-0500. Artistic Director: A.M. Raychel. Estab. 1980. Produces 6 children's plays/year. "We would like to produce more." Produces no children's musicals. "We would like to start producing."

Needs: Produces children's plays for professional productions. 80% of plays written for adult roles; 20% for juvenile roles. Minimal sets; minimal casts; minimal musicians. Recently produced plays: *Time is Money*, by Matt (runaway kid, for teenagers); *White Meat*, by Melissa Galvez (family Thanksgiving for teenagers).

How to Contact: Plays: Submit complete ms. Prefers one act plays (up to 45 min.). Musicals: Query first. Prefers one act musicals (up to 45 min.). Will consider simultaneous submissions and previously performed work. Reports in several months.

Terms: No pay. Submissions returned with SASE.

THEATREWORKS/USA, 890 Broadway, New York NY 10003. (212)677-5959. Fax: (212)353-1632. Associate Artistic Director: Barbara Pasternack. Estab. 1960. Produces 3-4 children's plays and musicals/year.

Needs: Cast of 5 or 6 actors. Play should be 1 hour long, tourable. Professional children's theatre comprised of adult equity actors. 100% of shows are written for adult roles. Produced plays: *Curious George*, book and lyrics by Thomas Toce, music by Tim Brown (adaptation, for grades K-3); *Little Women*, by Allan Knee, incidental music by Kim Oler and Alison Hubbard (adaptation, for grades 4-8). No fractured, typical "kiddy theater" fairy tales or shows written strictly to teach or illustrate.

How to Contact: Query first with synopsis, character breakdown and sample songs. Will consider previously performed work. Reports in 6 months.

Terms: Pays writers royalties of 6%. SASE for return of submission.

Tips: "Plays should be not only entertaining, but 'about something.' They should touch the heart and the mind. They should not condescend to children."

THIS MONTH ON STAGE, P.O. Box 62, Hewlett NY 11557-0062. (800)536-0099. E-mail: dlonstage@aol.com. Publisher: David Lefkowitz. Estab. 1991. Publishes 1-2 children's plays/year.

Needs: Prefers material for older audiences, or universally relevant material. Does not want to see: Patronizing, moralistic, Sunday School, etc.

How to Contact: Submit complete ms. Will consider simultaneous submissions and electronic submissions via disk/modem. Reports in 4-6 months.

Terms: Buys one-time rights. Work purchased outright ($1-2); copies. Submissions returned with SASE (separate SASE for each ms please).

Tips: "Ask yourself: will adults enjoy it too?"

THE YOUNG COMPANY, 14 Court St., Nashua NH 03060. (603)889-2330. Fax: (603)889-2336. Producing Director: Troy Siebels. Estab. 1984. Produces 3-4 children's plays/year; 2-3 children's musicals/year.

Needs: "Scripts should not be longer than an hour, small cast preferred; very small production budgets, so use imagination." The Young Company is a professional training program associated with American Stage Festival, a professional theater. Produced plays/musicals: *How To Eat Like A Child* (on being a kid and enjoying it a lot for ages 4-12); and *The Phantom Tollbooth* (for ages 7-14). Prefers adaptations with name recognition to young audiences. Does not want to see condescending material.

How to Contact: Query with synopsis, character breakdown and sample score.

Terms: Purchases first production credit rights on all future materials. Pays small fee and housing for rehearsals.

Tips: Looks for "concise and legible presentation, songs that further dramatic action. Develop material with strong marketing possibilities. See your work in front of an audience and be prepared to change it if your audience doesn't 'get it.' Don't condescend to your audience. Tell them a *story*."

Young Writer's & Illustrator's Markets

The listings in this section are special because they publish work of young writers and artists (under age 18). Some of the magazines listed exclusively feature the work of young people. Others are adult magazines with special sections for the work of young writers. There are also a few book publishers listed that exclusively publish the work of young writers and artists. Many of the magazines and publishers listed here pay only in copies, meaning authors and illustrators receive one or more free copies of the magazine or book to which they contributed.

As with adult markets, markets for children expect writers to be familiar with their editorial needs before submitting. Many of the markets listed will send guidelines to writers stating exactly what they need and how to submit it. You can often get these by sending a request with a self-addressed, stamped envelope (SASE) to the magazine or publisher, or by checking a publication's website (some have added web addresses to their listings). In addition to obtaining guidelines, read through a few copies of any magazines you'd like to submit to—this is the best way to determine if your work is right for them.

A number of kids' magazines are available on newsstands or in libraries. Others are distributed only through schools, churches or home subscriptions. If you can't find a magazine you'd like to see, most editors will send sample copies for a small fee.

Before you submit your material to editors, take a few minutes to read Before Your First Sale on page 6 for more information on proper submission procedures. You may also want to check out two other sections—Contest & Awards and Conferences & Workshops. Listings in these sections marked with an asterisk (*) are open to students (some exclusively). Additional opportunities for writers can be found in *Market Guide for Young Writers* (Writer's Digest Books) and *A Teen's Guide to Getting Published: the only writer's guide written by teens for teens*, by Danielle and Jessica Dunn (Prufrock Press). More information on these books are given in the Helpful Resources section in the back of this book.

Information on companies listed in the previous edition but not included in this edition of *Children's Writer's & Illustrator's Market* may be found in the General Index.

THE ACORN, 1530 Seventh St., Rock Island IL 61201. (309)788-3980. Newsletter. Estab. 1989. Audience consists of "kindergarten-12th grade students, parents, teachers and other adults. Purpose in publishing works for children: to expose children's manuscripts to others and provide a format for those who might not have one. We want to present wholesome writing, material that will entertain and educate—audience grades K-12." Children must be K-12 (put grade on manuscripts). Guidelines available for SASE.
Magazines: 100% of magazine written by children. Uses 6 fiction pieces (500 words); 20 pieces of poetry (32 lines). No payment; purchase of a copy isn't necessary to be printed. Sample copy $2. Subscription $10 for 4 issues. Submit mss to Betty Mowery, editor. Send complete ms. Will accept typewritten, legibly handwritten and/or computer printout. Include SASE. Reports in 1 week.
Artwork: Publishes artwork by children. Looks for "all types; size 4×5. Use black ink in artwork." No payment. Submit artwork either with ms or separately to Betty Mowery. Include SASE. Reports in 1 week.
Tips: "My biggest problem is not having names on the manuscripts. If the manuscript gets separated from the cover letter, there is no way to know whom to respond to. Always put name, age or grade and address on manuscripts, and if you want your material returned enclose a SASE. Don't send material with killing of humans or animals, or lost love poems or stories."

AMELIA MAGAZINE, 329 "E" St., Bakersfield CA 93304-2031. (805)323-4064. Magazine. Published quarterly. Strives to offer the best of all genres. Purpose in publishing works for children: wants to offer first opportunities to budding writers. Also offers the annual Amelia Student Award for high school students. Submissions from young writers must be signed by parent, teacher or guardian verifying originality. Guidelines are not specifically for young writers; they cover the entire gamut of publication needs.

Magazines: 3% of magazine written by children. Uses primarily poetry, often generated by teachers in creative writing classes. Uses 1 story in any fiction genre (1,500 words); 4 pieces of poetry, usually haiku (3 lines). Would like to receive more general poetry from young writers. Pays in copies for haiku; $2-10 for general poetry. Regular $35 rate for fiction or nonfiction. Submit mss to Frederick A. Raborg, editor. Submit complete ms (teachers frequently submit student's work). Will accept typewritten ms. Include SASE. Reports in 3 weeks.

Artwork: Publishes artwork and photography by children; "have not yet, however." Looks for photos no smaller than 5×7; artwork in any method; also cartoons. Pays $5-20 on publication. Submit well-protected artwork with SASE. Submit artwork/photos to Frederick A. Raborg, Jr., editor. Include SASE. Reports in 3 weeks.

Tips: "Be neat and thorough. Photos should have captions. Cartoon gaglines ought to be funny; try them out on someone before submitting. We want to encourage young writers, because the seeds of literary creativity are sown quite young with strong desires to read and admiration for the authors of those early readings."

AMERICAN GIRL, 8400 Fairway Place, Middleton WI 53562. (608)836-4848. Fax: (608)831-7089. Website: http://www.pleasantco.com. Bimonthly magazine. Audience consists of girls ages 8-12 who are joyful about being girls. Purpose in publishing works by young people: self-esteem boost and entertainment for readers. Young writers should be 8-12 years old. "We don't have writer's guidelines for children's submissions. Instruction for specific solicitations appears in the magazine."

Magazines: 5% of magazine written by young people. "A few pages of each issue feature articles that include children's answers to questions or requests that have appeared in a previous issue of *American Girl*." Pays in copies. Submit to address listed in magazine. Will accept legibly handwritten ms. Include SASE. Reports in 8-12 weeks.

Tips: "Please, no stories, poems, etc. about American Girls Collection Characters (Felicity, Samantha, Molly, Kirsten, Addy or Josefina)."

THE APPRENTICE WRITER, % Gary Fincke, Susquehanna University, Selinsgrove PA 17870-1001. (717)372-4164. Fax: (717)372-4310. E-mail: gfincke@susqu.edu. Magazine. Published annually. "Writing by high school students and for high school students." Purpose in publishing works by young people: to provide quality writing by students which can be read for pleasure and serve as a text for high school classrooms. Work is primarily from eastern and northeastern states, but will consider work from other areas of US. Students must be in grades 9-12. Writer's guidelines available for SASE.

Magazines: Uses 15 short stories (prefers under 5,000 words); 15 nonfiction personal essays (prefers under 5,000 words); 60 poems (no word limit) per issue. Pays in copies to writers and their schools. Submit mss to Gary Fincke, editor. Submit complete ms. Will accept typewritten mss. Include SASE. Submit ms by March 15. Responds by May of each year.

Artwork/Photography: Publishes artwork and photography by children. Looks for b&w. Pays in copies to artists and their schools. Submit originals or high quality copies. Submit art and photographs to Gary Fincke, editor. Include SASE. Submit artwork by March 15. Responds by May of each year.

BLUE JEAN MAGAZINE, P.O. Box 90856, Rochester NY 14609. (716)654-5070. E-mail: editors@bluejeanmag.com. Bimonthly national magazine. "*Blue Jean Magazine* portrays real teen girls on the verge of changing the world. Our cover stories profile interesting and exciting teen girls in action. You will find no supermodels, tips on dieting or fashion spreads on our pages. We publish teen-produced poetry, artwork, photography, fiction and much more!" Audience is girls ages 12-19. Purpose in showcasing work by young people: "to stay true to what really matters, which is publishing what young women are thinking, saying and doing." Writer's guidelines available on request for SASE.

Magazine: 90% of magazine written by young people. Uses 1 fiction story; 8-14 nonfiction stories (250-3,000 words); 1-3 poems. Pays adult freelancers $75 per Real Health issue, After High School article. Payment will be sent with 2 complimentary issues within 30 days of publication. Submit ms to Victoria E. Nam, executive editor. Submit complete mss per submission guidelines. Will accept typewritten mss. Include SASE. Reports in 3-4 months at most. "Many times within two months."

Artwork: Publishes artwork and photography by teens. Will consider a variety of styles! Artwork must be submitted by a teen artist (ages 12-19). Submit art between 2 pieces of paperboard or cardboard. Submit artwork/photos to Victoria E. Nam, executive editor. Include SASE with enough postage for return. Reports in 3-4 months.

A SELF-ADDRESSED, STAMPED ENVELOPE (SASE) should always be included with submissions within your own country. When sending material to other countries, include a self-addressed envelope (SAE) and International Reply Coupons (IRCs).

Tips: "Submissions may be sent via mail or e-mail. Do not inquire about your work by calling. Replies guaranteed when material sent through mail with SASE."

BOODLE, P.O. Box 1049, Portland IN 47371. (219)726-8141. Magazine published quarterly. "Each quarterly issue offers children a special invitation to read stories and poems written by others. Children can learn from the ideas in these stories and the techniques of sharing ideas in pictures and written form. Audience is ages 6-12. We hope that publishing children's writing will enhance the self-esteem of the authors and motivate other children to try expressing themselves in this form." Submission requirements: "We ask that authors include grade when written, current grade, name of school, and a statement from parent or teacher that the work is original."
Magazines: 100% of magazine written by children. Uses 12 short stories (100-500 words), 1 nonfiction piece, usually animal (100-500 words), 30 poems (50-500 words), 2 puzzles and mazes (50-500 words) per issue. Pays 2 copies of issue. Submit mss to Mavis Catalfio, editor. Submit complete ms. Will accept typewritten and legibly handwritten mss. Include SASE.
Artwork: Wants "mazes, cartoons, drawings of animals or seasons or sports which will likely match a story or poem we publish." Pays 2 copies of issue. "Drawings should be done in black ink or marker." Submit artwork to Mavis Catalfio, editor. Reports in 2 months.
Tips: Submit seasonal materials at least a year in advance. "We love humor and offbeat stories. We seldom publish sad or depressing stories about death or serious illness."

BOYS' LIFE, 1325 W. Walnut Hill Lane, P.O. Box 152079, Irving TX 75015-2079. (972)580-2366. Magazine published monthly. Audience consists of boys ages 7-18. *Boys' Life* is published by the Boy Scouts of America to make available to children the highest caliber of fiction and nonfiction, to stimulate an interest in good reading and to promote the principles of Scouting. Writer's and illustrators guidelines available for SASE. Send 9 × 12 SASE plus a check or money order for a sample issue as well as guidelines.
Magazines: Submissions from children: Small percentage of magazine written by young people under 18. Uses hobby and collecting tips for "Hobby Hows" and "Collecting" columns. Pays $10/tip. Uses jokes for "Think & Grin" column. Pays choice of $2 or copy of *Scout Handbook* or *Scout Fieldbook*/joke accepted. Several times/year uses personal stories (500 words maximum) for "Readers' Page." Pays $25. Submit mss to column. Submit complete ms. Will accept typewritten and legibly handwritten mss for consideration. Reports in 6-8 weeks. Submissions from adults: For nonfiction mss, *query first* to Mike Goldman, articles editor. All fiction mss should be double-spaced and typed copy, 1,000-1,500 words. Pays $750 and up for accepted stories. Story categories: humor, mystery, science fiction, adventure. Include SASE for return of materials. For fiction mss, send one copy of story plus cover letter. Submit to Shannon Lowry, associate editor. Include SASE.
Tips: "Study one year's worth of recent magazines before submitting."

CHILD LIFE, Children's Better Health Institute, 1100 Waterway Blvd., P.O. Box 567, Indianapolis IN 46206. (317)636-8881. Magazine. Published 8 times/year. Targeted toward kids ages 9-11. It's now a nostalgic publication reminiscent of *Child Life's* younger days in the 1920s and 1930s. It focuses on health, sports, fitness, nutrition, safety and general interest.
Magazines: "We publish jokes, riddles and poems by children." Kids should include name, address, phone number (for office use) and school photo. "No mass duplicated, multiple submissions." They no longer accept mss for fiction or nonfiction.
Tips: "We use kids' submissions from our age range—9 to 11. Those older or younger should try one of our sister publications: *Children's Digest, Children's Playmate, Humpty Dumpty's Magazine, Jack And Jill, Turtle Magazine, U*S*Kids.*"

CHILDREN'S DIGEST, Children's Better Health Institute, 1100 Waterway Blvd., P.O. Box 567, Indianapolis IN 46206. (317)636-8881. Fax: (317)684-8094. Magazine. Published 8 times/year. Audience consists of preteens. Submissions must focus on health-related theme. Writer's guidelines available on request.
Magazines: 10% of magazine written by children. Uses 1 fiction story (under 500 words), 10-15 jokes/riddles per issue. Submit mss to *Children's Digest*. Submit complete ms.

CHILDREN'S PLAYMATE, Children's Better Health Institute, P.O. Box 567, Indianapolis IN 46206. (317)636-8881. Magazine. Estab. 1929. Audience consists of children between 6 and 8 years of age. Emphasizes health, fitness, safety, good nutrition, and *good* humorous fiction for beginning readers. Writer's guidelines available on request with SASE.
Artwork: Publishes artwork by children, kids' poems, jokes/riddles, recipes, fun activities and crafts. "Prefers black line drawings on white paper. No payment for children's artwork published." No material can be returned. Submit artwork to *Children's Playmate*, Chuck Horsman, art director. Submit original poems and jokes/riddles to *Children's Playmate*.

❦**THE CLAREMONT REVIEW**, 4980 Wesley Rd., Victoria, British Columbia Canada V8Y 1Y9. (604)658-5221. Fax: (250)658-5387. E-mail: review@claremont.victoria.bc.ca. Magazine. Publishes 2 books/year by young adults. Publishes poetry and fiction with literary value by students aged 13-19 anywhere in North America. Purpose in publishing work by young people: to provide a literary venue.

Magazines: Uses 8-10 fiction stories (200-2,500 words); 25-35 poems. Pays in copies. Submit mss to editors. Submit complete ms. Will accept typewritten mss. SASE. Reports in 6 weeks (except during the summer).

Artwork: Publishes artwork by young adults. Looks for b&w copies of imaginative art. Pays in copies. Send picture for review. Negative may be requested. Submit art and photographs to editors. SASE. Reports in 6 weeks.

Tips: "Read us first—it saves disappointment. Know who we are and what we publish. We're closed July and August."

CLUBHOUSE, P.O. Box 15, Berrien Springs MI 49103. (616)471-9009. Editor: Krista Hainey. Magazine. Estab. 1949. Published monthly. Occasionally publishes items by kids. "Audience consists of kids ages 9-14; philosophy is God loves kids, kids are neat people." Purpose in publishing works by young people: to give encouragement and demonstration of talent. Children must be ages 9-14; must include parent's note verifying originality.

● Clubhouse is not accepting adult submissions through 1998.

Magazines: Uses adventure, historical, everyday life experience (fiction/nonfiction-1,200 words); health-related short articles; poetry (4-24 lines of "mostly mood pieces and humor"). Pays in prizes for children, money for adult authors. Query. Will accept typewritten, legibly handwritten and computer printout mss. "Will not be returned without SASE." Reports in 6 weeks.

Artwork: Publishes artwork by children. Looks for all types of artwork—white paper, black pen. Pays in prizes for kids. Send b&w art to Christa Hainey, editor. "Won't be returned without SASE."

Tips: "All items submitted by kids are held in a file and used when possible. We normally suggest they do not ask for return of the item."

CREATIVE KIDS, P.O. Box 8813, Waco TX 76714-8813. (800)998-2208. Fax: (254)756-3339. E-mail: creative _kids@prufrock.com. Website: http://www.prufrock.com. Editor: Libby Lindsey. Magazine published 4 times/ year. Estab. 1979. "All material is by children, for children." Purpose in publishing works by children: "to create a product that provides children with an authentic experience and to offer an opportunity for children to see their work in print. *Creative Kids* contains the best stories, poetry, opinion, artwork, games and photography by kids ages 8-14." Writers ages 8-14 must have statement by teacher or parent verifying originality. Writer's guidelines available on request with SASE.

Magazines: Uses "about 6" fiction and nonfiction stories (800-900 words); poetry, plays, ideas to share (200-750 words) per issue. Pays "free magazine." Submit mss to submissions editor. Will accept typewritten mss. Include SASE. Reports in 1 month.

Artwork/Photography: Publishes artwork and photos by children. Looks for "any kind of drawing, cartoon, or painting." Pays "free magazine." Send original or a photo of the work to submissions editor. No photocopies. Include SASE. Reports in 1 month.

Tips: "*Creative Kids* is a magazine by kids, for kids. The work represents children's ideas, questions, fears, concerns and pleasures. The material never contains racist, sexist or violent expression. The purpose is to provide children with an authentic experience. A person may submit one piece of work per envelope. Each piece must be labeled with the student's name, birth date, grade, school, home address and school address. Include a photograph, if possible. Recent school pictures are best. Material submitted to *Creative Kids* must not be under consideration by any other publication. Items should be carefully prepared, proofread and double checked (perhaps also by a parent or teacher). All activities requiring solutions must be accompanied by the correct answers. Young writers and artists should always write for guidelines and then follow them. It is very frustrating to receive submissions that are not complete."

CREATIVE WITH WORDS, Thematic anthologies, Creative with Words Publications, P.O. Box 223226, Carmel CA 93922. Fax: (408)655-8627. Editor: Brigitta Geltrich. Nature Editor: Bert Hower. Publishes 12 anthologies/year. Estab. 1975. "We publish the creative writing of children (two anthologies written by children; ten anthologies written by all ages)." Audience consists of children, schools, libraries, adults, reading programs. Purpose in publishing works by children: to offer them an opportunity to get started in publishing. "Work must be of quality, original, unedited, and not published before; age must be given (up to 19 years old)." SASE must be enclosed with all correspondence and mss. Writer's guidelines and theme list available on request with SASE.

Books: Considers all categories except those dealing with death, violence, pornography and overly religious. Uses fairy tales, folklore items (up to 1,200 words) and poetry (not to exceed 20 lines, 46 characters across). Published *Nature Series: Skies, Land, Forests, Seas*; *Dinosaurs & Dragons*; and *Relationships* (all children and adults). Pays 20% discount on each copy of publication in which fiction or poetry by children appears. Submit mss to Brigitta Geltrich, editor. Query; child, teacher or parent can submit; teacher and/or parents must verify

---

🍁 **CANADIAN LISTINGS** are marked with a maple leaf.

originality of writing. Will accept typewritten and/or legibly handwritten mss. SASE. "Will not go through agents." Reports in 1-2 months after deadline of any theme.

Artwork/Photography: Publishes artwork, photos and computer artwork by children (language art work). Pays 20% discount on every copy of publication in which work by children appears. If artwork is commissioned, payment is in subscription. Submit artwork to Brigitta Geltrich, editor.

Tips: "Enjoy the English language, life and the world around you. Look at everything from a different perspective. Be less descriptive and use words wisely. Let the reader experience a story through a viewpoint character, don't be overly dramatic."

ECLECTIC RAINBOWS, 1538 Tennessee Walker Dr., Roswell GA 30075-3152. (770)587-5711. E-mail: ltdennison@aol.com. Magazine. Published annually. Purpose in publishing works by young adults: the satisfaction of giving a "born" writer a start and encouragement.

Magazines: 1 article/issue written by young people. Pays on publication $10-25; $10 reprints. Poetry pays in copies only. Submit mss to Linda T. Dennison, editor/publisher. If you query, be detailed in your outline. Submit complete ms if unpublished and don't have clips. Will accept "laser printed quality" mss only. "No handwritten or dot matrix submissions will be read." Include SASE. Reports in 2-3 months.

Artwork/Photography: "No solo photos. With ms only." Submit photos only—no slides, no original art. "No payment for photos—they are used only to accompany your story—but they do mean I'll pay a bit more for the story."

Tips: "Keep trying—each nonsuccess teaches you more about what you need to do to succeed. Seek out *ruthless* criticism for maximum growth at fastest speed. Older teens have only realistic chance. Writing and subject must be adult in nature and suitable for *E.R.* Nostalgia and what I did on summer break—no. Under age 16: save your money. This is *not* your market. We're partial to the environment, world affairs, politics, celebrities, humor, astrology and other 'New Age' topics, and anything else that piques your interest. You should always express a strong and well-articulated point of view, preferably your own."

FREE SPIRIT PUBLISHING INC., 400 First Ave. North, Suite 616, Minneapolis MN 55401-1730. (612)338-2068. Fax: (612)337-5050. E-mail: help4kids@freespirit.com. Publishes 15-20 books/year. "We specialize in SELF-HELP FOR KIDS®. We aim to help kids help themselves. We were the *first* publisher of self-help materials for children, and today we are the *only* publisher of SELF-HELP FOR KIDS® materials. Our main audience is children and teens, but we also publish for parents, teachers, therapists, youth workers and other involved in caring for kids. Our main interests include the development of self-esteem, self-awareness, creative thinking and problem-solving abilities, assertiveness and making a difference in the world. We do not publish fiction or poetry. We feel that children have important things to say. They have critical things to share and can reach and teach others the same age in a way that adults cannot. Most of our authors have degrees in education, psychology, social work, and/or counseling. We also accept submissions from young people ages 14 and older. Please send a letter from a parent/guardian/leader verifying originality." Request catalog, author guidelines, and "student guidelines" before submitting work.

Books: Publishes self-help for kids, how-to, classroom activities. Pays advance and royalties. Submit mss to Elizabeth Verdick, acquisitions editor. Send query and sample table of contents. Will accept typewritten mss. SASE required. Reports in 3-4 months.

Artwork/Photography: Free Spirit accepts artwork and photography by children. Submit to Elizabeth Verdick, acquisitions editor.

Tips: "Free Spirit publishes very specific material, and it helps when writers request and study our catalog before submitting work to us. We also will send information on how to become a Free Spirit author. We do not accept general self-help books, autobiographies or children's books that feature made-up stories. Our preference is books that help kids to gain self-esteem, succeed in school, stand up for themselves, resolve conflicts and make a difference in the world. We do not publish books that have animals as the main characters."

THE FUDGE CAKE, P.O. Box 197, Citrus Heights CA 95611-0197. Magazine. Published bimonthly. Audience consists of children and young adults, grandparents, teachers, parents, etc. Purpose in publishing works by young people: to provide a showcase for young writers age 6-17. "We value the work of today's children. They have a lot to say and we feel they need an outlet to express themselves." To qualify for publication, children must be age 6-17; submit copies of original work; and include SASE. Writer's guidelines available on request. Sample copy for $3.

Magazines: Uses 2-3 pieces of fiction (all types—no erotica, 250-500 words); 15-20 poems (30 lines or less). Pays 1 copy of issue work appears in. Submit mss to Jancarl Campi, editor. Submit complete ms. Will accept typewritten form and legible handwritten mss. Include SASE. Reports in 1 month.

Tips: "Don't be afraid to use the pen—write and rewrite, then send it in. We often critique or comment on rejected ms."

FUTURIFIC, INC., Foundation for Optimism, Futurific, 305 Madison Ave., Suite 10B, New York NY 10165. Publisher: B. Szent-Miklosy. (212)297-0502. Magazine published monthly. Audience consists of people interested in an accurate report of what is ahead. "We do not discriminate by age. We look for the visionary in all people. They must write what will be. No advice or 'maybe.' We've had 21 years of accurate forecasting." Sample copy for $5 postage and handling. Writer's guidelines available on request with SASE.

Magazines: Submit mss to B. Szent-Miklosy, publisher. Will accept typewritten, legibly handwritten, computer printout, 5.25 or 3.5 inch WordPerfect diskette mss.

Artwork: Publishes artwork by children. Looks for "what the future will look like." Pay is negotiable. Send b&w drawings or photos. Submit artwork to B. Szent-Miklosy, publisher.

THE GOLDFINCH, Iowa History for Young People, 402 Iowa Ave., Iowa City IA 52240. (319)335-3916. Fax: (319)335-3935. Magazine published quarterly. Audience is 4th-8th graders. "Magazine supports creative work by children: research, art, writing. *The Goldfinch* puts the fun back into history. We publish young Iowans' work to show them that they and their creative efforts are an important part of Iowa history." Submitted work must go with the historical theme of each issue.

Magazines: 10-20% written by children. Uses at least 1 nonfiction essay, poem, story/issue (500 words). Pays complimentary copies. Submit mss with SASE to Amy Ruth, editor. Submit complete ms. Will accept typewritten, legibly handwritten, computer disk (Apple) mss. Reports in 1 month.

Artwork/Photography: Publishes artwork/photographs by children. Art and photos must be b&w. Pays complimentary copies. Query first with SASE to Amy Ruth.

Tips: "We make the subject of Iowa history come alive through short features, games/puzzles/activities, fiction and cool historical photographs."

HIGH SCHOOL WRITER, P.O. Box 718, Grand Rapids MN 55744. (218)326-8025. Editor: Heather Lutterman. Magazine published monthly during the school year. "The *High School Writer* is a magazine written *by* students *for* students. All submissions must exceed contemporary standards of decency." Purpose in publishing works by young people: to provide a real audience for student writers—and text for study. Submissions by junior high and middle school students accepted for our junior edition. Senior high students' works are accepted for our senior high edition. Students attending schools that subscribe to our publication are eligible to submit their work." Writer's guidelines available on request.

Magazines: Uses fiction, nonfiction (2,000 words maximum) and poetry. Submit mss to Robert Lemen, editor. Submit complete ms (teacher must submit). Will accept typewritten, computer-generated (good quality) mss.

Tips: "Submissions should not be sent without first obtaining a copy of our guidelines. Also, submissions will not be considered unless student's school subscribes."

HIGHLIGHTS FOR CHILDREN, 803 Church St., Honesdale PA 18431. (717)253-1080. Magazine. Published monthly. "We strive to provide wholesome, stimulating, entertaining material that will encourage children to read. Our audience is children ages 2-12." Purpose in publishing works by young people: to encourage children's creative expression. Age limit to submit is 15.

Magazines: 15-20% of magazine written by children. Uses stories and poems. Also uses jokes, riddles, tongue twisters. Features which occur occasionally: "What Are Your Favorite Books?" (8-10/year), Recipes (8-10/year), "Science Letters" (15-20/year). Special features which invite children's submissions on a specific topic: "Tell the Story" (15-20/year), "You're the Reporter" (8-10/year), "Your Ideas, Please" (8-10/year), "Endings to Unfinished Stories" (8-10/year). Pays in copies. Submit complete ms to the editor. Will accept typewritten, legibly handwritten and computer printout mss. Reports in 3-6 weeks.

Artwork: Publishes artwork by children. Pays in copies. No cartoon or comic book characters. No commercial products. Submit b&w or color artwork for "Our Own Pages." Features include "Creatures Nobody Has Ever Seen" (5-8/year) and "Illustration Job" (18-20/year). Reports in 3-6 weeks.

‡INK BLOT, 901 Day Rd., Saginaw MI 48609. Newsletter. Published monthly. "I want young writers to do their best work, learn proper form and have their work shared with others. We put our newsletter in libraries, hospitals, waiting rooms and copies to contributors." Purpose in publishing works by young people: to give children an outlet for publishing their talents; to have them write using their imagination and creativity and to share them with others. Accepts manuscripts from all ages. If student, please include age, grade and school name. Only print original works from contributors. Material is accepted from across the United States and Canada. Typewritten preferred—handwritten *neatly* OK.

Magazines: Submit mss to Margaret Larkin. Responds in 3 months. Sample copy and guidelines available for $1 (check made out to M. Larkin, editor) and include SASE. Maximum length 500 words (stories). "Must fit on one side of typewritten page."

Artwork: Publishes artwork by children. Wants small 3×3 b&w ink drawings only; especially drawings that accompany poetry and short stories. No derogatory or obscene pictures accepted. Pays in copies. Submit art to Margaret Larkin, editor, or Vicki Larkin, assistant editor. Include SASE. Reports in 3 months.

KIDSART, P.O. Box 274, Mt. Shasta CA 96067. (916)926-5076. E-mail: kidsart@macshasta.com. Art education booklets published quarterly. Publishes "hands-on art projects, open-ended art lessons, art history, lots of child-made art to illustrate." Purpose in publishing works by children: "to provide achievable models for kids—give young artists a forum for their work. We always phone before publishing works to be sure it's OK with their folks, name is spelled correctly, etc."

Artwork/Photography: Publishes artwork/photographs by children. Any submissions by children welcomed.

Pays free copies of published work. Submit artwork/photos to Kim Solga, editor. "Your originals will be returned to you in 4-6 weeks." SASE desired, but not required. Free catalog available describing KidsArt newsletter. Sample copy $3.

THE LOUISVILLE REVIEW—Children's Corner, Dept. of English, University of Louisville, 315 Bingham Humanities, Louisville KY 40292. (502)852-6801. Semiannual magazine. "We are a contemporary literary journal." Purpose in publishing works by young people: to encourage children to write with fresh images and striking metaphors. Not interested in the "cute" moral lesson on highly rhymed and metered verse. "We believe there are children writers who are as good as adult writers and therefore deserve to be published along with adult writers." Must supply SASE and permission slip from parent stating that work is original and giving permission to publish if accepted. Only accepts typewritten mss.
Magazines: 10-20% of magazine written by children. Uses poetry, any length. Pays in copies. Submit mss to Children's Corner. Submit complete ms. Will accept typewritten mss. Include SASE. Deadline December 31. Reads only January through March. Will reply by April.

MERLYN'S PEN: The National Magazine of Student Writing, P.O. Box 1058, East Greenwich RI 02818. (800)247-2027. Fax: (401)885-5222. Magazine. Published annually. "By publishing student writing, *Merlyn's Pen* seeks to broaden and reward the young author's interest in writing, strengthen the self-confidence of beginning writers and promote among all students a positive attitude toward literature. We publish 100 manuscripts annually by students in grades 6-12. The entire magazine is dedicated to young adults' writing. Our audience is classrooms, libraries and students from grades 6-12." Writers must be in grades 6-12 and must send a completed *Merlyn's Pen* cover sheet with each submission. When a student is accepted, he/she, a parent and a teacher must sign a statement of originality.
Magazines: Uses 20 short stories (no word limit); plays; 8 nonfiction essays (no word limit); 25 pieces of poetry; letters to the editor; editorials; reviews of previously published works; and reviews of books, music, movies per issue. Published authors receive 1 contributor's copy and payment of $10-125. Also, a discount is offered for additional copies of the issue. Submit up to 3 titles at one time. Will only accept typewritten mss. Reports in 10 weeks.
Tips: "All manuscripts and artwork must be accompanied by a completed copy of *Merlyn's Pen* official cover sheet for submissions. Call to request cover sheet."

NATIONAL GEOGRAPHIC WORLD, 17th and M St. NW, Washington DC 20036-4688. (202)857-7000. Magazine published monthly. Picture magazine for ages 8 and older. Purpose in publishing work by young people: to encourage in young readers a curiosity about the world around them.
● *National Geographic World* was not accepting unsolicited manuscripts at the time of publication.
Tips: Publishes art, letters, poems, games, riddles, jokes and craft ideas by children in mailbag section only. No payment given. Send by mail to: Submissions Committee. "Sorry, but *World* cannot acknowledge or return your contributions."

NEW MOON: The Magazine For Girls & Their Dreams, New Moon Publishing, Inc., P.O. Box 3620, Duluth MN 55803-3620. (218)728-5507. Fax: (218)728-0314. E-mail: newmoon@newmoon.duluth.mn.us. Website: http://newmoon.duluth.mn.us/~newmoon. Magazine. Published bimonthly. *New Moon*'s primary audience is girls ages 8-14. "We publish a magazine that listens to girls." More than 70% of *New Moon* is written by girls. Purpose in publishing work by children/teens: "We want girls' voices to be heard. *New Moon* wants girls to see that their opinions, dreams, thoughts and ideas counts." Writer's guidelines available for SASE. Reports in 2-4 months.
● To learn more about *New Moon*, see the Insider Report with Joe Kelly in the 1996 edition of *Children's Writer's & Illustrator's Market*.
Magazine: 75% of magazine written by young people. Uses 4 fiction mss (300-900 words); 12 nonfiction mss (300-900 words) per year. Submit to Tya Ward and Barbara Stretchberry, managing editors. Submit query, complete mss for fiction and nonfiction. Will accept typewritten, legibly handwritten mss and disk (IBM compatible). "We do not return unsolicited material." Please include SASE. Reports in 2-4 months.
Artwork/Photography: Publishes artwork and photography by children. Looks for cover and inside illustrations. Pay negotiated. Submit art and photographs to Tya Ward or Barbara Stretchberry, managing editors. "We do not return unsolicited material."
Tips: "Read *New Moon* to completely understand our needs."

 SPECIAL COMMENTS by the editor of *Children's Writer's & Illustrator's Market* are set off by a bullet.

RASPBERRY PUBLICATIONS INC., P.O. Box 925. Westerville OH 43086-6925. (800)759-7171. Fax: (614)899-6147. Book publisher. Publishes 6-10 books/year by children. "We believe what children write has value and children like to read what other children write." Purpose in publishing books by children: to provide opportunities for young authors to be published and motivate all children to write. Books must be written and illustrated by children from grades K-12. Writer's guidelines available for SASE. Pays royalties, but no advances.

Books: Publishes all genres of fiction; nonfiction should have educational value. Pays royalties, but no advances. Contact: Curt Jenkins, publisher; Susan Schmidt, publisher. Submit complete ms for fiction and nonfiction. Will accept typewritten, legibly handwritten and computer-printed mss. Include SASE. Reports in 3-6 months.

Artwork/Photography: Publishes artwork and photography by children. Submit to Curt Jenkins, publisher.

Tips: "Be original and creative. Make sure you have solid beginning, middle and end. The 'conflict' should have a child as the main character, and should be resolved by the child without help from adults in the story. It is best to submit photocopies of mss and color photocopies of all artwork. No originals, please. Revise, revise, revise!"

SHADOW MAGAZINE, P.O. Box 5464, Santa Rosa CA 95402-5464. Phone/fax: (707)542-7114. E-mail: brianwts@aol.com. Website: http://www.metro.net/shadow/. Quarterly magazine. "We publish exciting, quality fiction that will appeal to teens. Our work is usually both interesting to read and educationally valuable in some way. While we publish work by adults, we also feel that young adults have the ability to write stories that will be the most interesting to their peers." Material must be presented in a professional manner.

Magazines: 10-20% of magazine written by young people. Uses 4-6 short fiction stories and various nonfiction articles/essays (1,000 words). Pays 2-3 sample copies. Submit mss to Brian P. Murphy, editor-in-chief. Submit complete ms. Will accept typewritten or disk mss and via e-mail. Include SASE. Reports in 1-2 months.

Tips: "Make sure the work you submit is polished and the best you can possibly do. We comment often and make a point to respond to work by students."

SHOFAR MAGAZINE, 43 Northcote Dr., Melville NY 11747. (516)643-4598. Fax: (516)643-4598. E-mail: graysonpsc@aol.com. Managing Editor: Gerald H. Grayson. Magazine published 6 times/school year. Audience consists of American Jewish children age 9-13. Purpose in publishing works by young people: to give them an opportunity to get their work printed.

Magazines: 10% of magazine written by young people. Uses fiction/nonfiction (750-1,000 words), Kids Page items (50-150 words). Submit mss to Gerald Grayson, publisher. Submit complete ms. Will accept typewritten, legibly handwritten mss and computer disk (Mac only). SASE. Reports in 2 months.

Artwork/Photography: Publishes artwork and photography by children. Pays "by the piece, depending on size and quantity." Submit original with SASE. Reports in 1-2 months.

SKIPPING STONES, Multicultural Children's Magazine, P.O. Box 3939, Eugene OR 97403. (541)342-4956. Website: http://www.nonviolence.org/~nvweb/skipping/. Articles/Poems/Fiction Editor: Arun N. Toké. 5 issues a year. Estab. 1988. Circulation 3,000. "*Skipping Stones* is a multicultural, nonprofit, children's magazine to encourage cooperation, creativity and celebration of cultural and environmental richness. It offers itself as a creative forum for communication among children from different lands and backgrounds. We prefer work by children under 18 years old. International, minorities and under represented populations receive priority, multilingual submissions are encouraged."

● *Skipping Stones*' theme for their Youth Honor Awards 1998 is multicultural and nature awareness. Send for guidelines for move information on the awards.

Magazines: 50% written by children. Uses 5-10 fiction short stories and plays (500-750 words); 5-10 nonfiction articles, interviews, letters, history, descriptions of celebrations (500-750 words); 15-20 poems, jokes, riddles, proverbs (250 words or less) per issue. Pays in contributor's copies. Submit mss to Arun Toké, editor. Submit complete ms for fiction or nonfiction work; teacher may submit; parents can also submit their contributions. Submissions should include "cover letter with name, age, address, school, cultural background, inspiration for piece, dreams for future . . ." Will accept typewritten, legibly handwritten and computer/word processor mss. Include SASE. Responds in 3 months. Accepts simultaneous submissions.

Artwork/Photography: Publishes artwork and photography for children. Will review all varieties of ms/ illustration packages. Wants comics, cartoons, b&w photos, paintings, drawings (preferably ink & pen or pencil), 8×10, color photos OK. Subjects include children, people, celebrations, nature, ecology, multicultural. Pays in contributor's copies.

Terms: "*Skipping Stones* is a labor of love. You'll receive complimentary contributor's (up to four) copies depending on the length of your contribution and illustrations." Reports back to artists in 3 months. Sample copy for $5 and 8½×11 SAE with 4 first-class stamps.

Tips: "Let the 'inner child' within you speak out—naturally, uninhibited." Wants "material that gives insight on cultural celebrations, lifestyle, custom and tradition, glimpse of daily life in other countries and cultures. Please, no mystery for the sake of mystery! Photos, songs, artwork are most welcome if they illustrate/highlight the points. Upcoming features: How I am making a difference in the world, cooperative games and sports, religions and cultures from around the world, cycles of change: life and death, Native American cultures, street children, songs and recipes from around the world, resource conservation and sustainable lifestyles, indigenous architecture, living in the inner-city, grandparents and elders in your life, creative problem-solving approaches and substance abuse.''

SKYLARK, Purdue University Calumet, 2200 169th St., Hammond IN 46323. (219)989-2262. Editor: Pamela Hunter. Young Writers' Editor: Shirley Jo Moritz. Annual magazine. Circ. 650-1,000. 15% of material written by juvenile authors. Presently accepting material by children. "*Skylark* wishes to provide a vehicle for creative writing of all kinds (with emphasis on an attractive synthesis of text and layout), especially by writers ages 5-18, who live in the Illinois/Indiana area and who have not ordinarily been provided with such an outlet. Children need a place to see their work published alongside that of adults.'' Proof of originality is required from parents or teachers for all authors. Writer's guidelines available upon request.

Magazines: 15% of magazine written by young people. In previous issues, *Skylark* has published mysteries, fantasy, humor, good narrative fiction stories (400-1,000 words), personal essays, brief character sketches, nonfiction stories (400-650 words), poetry (no more than 16 lines). Does not want to see material that is obviously religious or sexual. Pays in contributor's copies. Submit ms to Shirley Jo Moritz, young writers' editor. Submit complete ms. Prefers typewritten ms. Must include SASE for response or return of material. Reports in 4 months. Byline given.

Artwork/Photography: Publishes artwork and photographs by children. Looks for "photos of animals, landscapes and sports, and for artwork to go along with text." Pays in contributor's copies. All artwork and photos must be b&w, 8½×11, unlined paper. Do not use pencil and no copyrighted characters. Markers are advised for best reproduction. Include name and address on the back of each piece. Package properly to avoid damage. Submit artwork/photos to Pamela Hunter, editor-in-chief. Include SASE. Reports in 5 months.

Tips: "We're looking for literary work. Follow your feelings, be as original as you can and don't be afraid to be different. Some of our children or perhaps their teachers and parents don't understand that a SASE must accompany the submission in order to get a response or reply.''

SNAKE RIVER REFLECTIONS, 1863 Bitterroot Dr., Twin Falls ID 83301. (208)734-0746. E-mail: william@ micron.net. Website: http://www.webpage.net/~william. Newsletter. Publishes 10 times/year (not published in October or December). Proof of originality required with submissions. Guidelines available on request with #10 SASE.

Magazines: 5% of magazine's poems written by children. Uses poetry (30 lines maximum). Pays in copies only. Submit mss to William White, editor. Submit complete ms. Will accept typewritten and legibly handwritten mss. #10 SASE. Reports in 1 month.

‡SPRING TIDES, 824 Stillwood Dr., Savannah GA 31419. (912)925-8800. Annual magazine. Audience consists of children 5-12 years old. Purpose in publishing works by young people: To encourage writing. Requirements to be met before work is published: must be 5-12 years old. Writers guidelines available on request.

Magazines: 100% of magazine written by young people. Uses 5-6 fiction stories (1,200 words maximum); autobiographical experiences (1,200 words maximum); 15-20 poems (20 lines maximum) per issue. Writers are not paid. Submit complete ms or teacher may submit. Will accept typewritten mss. SASE.

Artwork: Publishes artwork by children. "We have so far used only local children's artwork because of the complications of keeping and returning pieces.''

STONE SOUP, The Magazine by Young Writers and Artists, Children's Art Foundation, P.O. Box 83, Santa Cruz CA 95063. (408)426-5557. Fax: (408)426-1161. E-mail: editor@stonesoup.com. Website: http://www.stonesoup.com. Articles/Fiction Editor, Art Director: Ms. Gerry Mandel. Magazine published 6 times/year. Circ. 20,000. "We publish fiction, poetry and artwork by children through age 13. Our preference is for work based on personal experiences and close observation of the world. Our audience is young people through age 13, as well as parents, teachers, librarians.'' Purpose in publishing works by young people: to encourage children to read and to express themselves through writing and art. Writer's guidelines available upon request.

Magazines: Uses animal, contemporary, fantasy, history, problem-solving, science fiction, sports, spy/mystery/adventure fiction stories. Uses 5-10 fiction stories (100-2,500 words); 5-10 nonfiction stories (100-2,500 words); 2-4 poems per issue. Does not want to see classroom assignments and formula writing. Buys 65 mss/year. Byline given. Pays on publication. Buys all rights. Pays $10 each for stories and poems, $15 for book reviews. Contributors also receive 2 copies. Sample copy $2. Free writer's guidelines. "We don't publish straight nonfiction, but we do publish stories based on real events and experiences.'' Send complete ms to Ms. Gerry Mandel, editor. Will accept typewritten and legibly handwritten mss. Include SASE. Reports in 1 month.

Artwork/Photography: Publishes any type, size or color artwork/photos by children. Pays $10 for b&w illustrations. Contributors receive 2 copies. Sample copy $2. Free illustrator's guidelines. Send originals if possible. Send submissions to Ms. Gerry Mandel, editor. Include SASE. Reports in 1 month. Original artwork returned at job's completion. All artwork must be by children through age 13.

Tips: "Be sure to enclose a SASE. Only work by young people through age 13 is considered. Whether your work is about imaginary situations or real ones, use your own experiences and observations to give your work depth and a sense of reality.''

STONEFLOWER LITERARY JOURNAL, 1824 Nacogdoches, Suite 191, San Antonio TX 78209-2216. Magazine. Published annually. "We publish quality fiction and poetry with a section for children to age 16, which includes pen & ink drawings and b&w photography. Ours is a general reading audience with literary taste for good writing." Purpose in publishing works by young people: to encourage good writing and art among youth and to provide an outlet for their creative efforts. Submissions will be reviewed according to age group (i.e., work submitted by a child of 10 will only be compared to works by other children in his/her general age group and not to works by 16-year-olds). If possible, manuscripts should be typewritten. However, handwritten or printed submissions will be considered if legibly written. We consider: poems to 25 lines; stories to 1,000 words; and pen & ink drawings. To teachers: if you organize a school project of submissions and want the mss or artwork returned, one SASE large enough to hold all mss or artwork is acceptable. All submissions should have the name, address, age, school attending and grade clearly written on the top of all mss and on the back of artwork. Submit a separate biographical page. The student's name should appear in the upper left corner of the "bio." Hobbies, participation in other school programs and activities, prior publications or honors, favorite pastimes, plans for the future, etc., should be included in the bio. Writer's guidelines available for SASE.

Magazine: 10% of magazine written by young people. Averages 2 fiction stories/issue (1,000 words); 5-10 poems/issue (25 lines). "Best of Issue" award given. Pays small publication fee. Does not pay in copies. Submit mss to Brenda Davidson-Shaddox, editor. Submit complete fiction mss, poetry and art/photos, may submit as class project, fiction, poetry and art/photo. Will accept typewritten and legibly handwritten mss. Include SASE. Reports in up to 3 months.

Artwork/Photography: Publishes pen & ink artwork and b&w photography. No color, please. Do not fold artwork. Looks for any subject except pornography. Pen & ink drawings (or top quality copies); 8½×11, no larger. Black & white photos. Pays $5/item. Does not pay in copies. Submit to Brenda Davidson-Shaddox, editor. Include SASE. Reports in up to 3 months.

Tips: Submit quality work, clean and neat, shorter writing gets preference but only if of high standard. Keep copies of all submissions. We cannot be responsible for losses. Pay attention to guidelines and always include SASE. Submissions without SASE will be discarded. Send bio according to guidelines."

STRAIGHT MAGAZINE, Standard Publishing, 8121 Hamilton Ave., Cincinnati OH 45231. (513)931-4050. Fax: (513)931-0950. Magazine published weekly. Estab. 1951. Magazine includes fiction pieces and articles for Christian teens 13-19 years old to inform, encourage and uplift them. "*Straight* is a magazine for today's Christian teenagers. We use fiction and nonfiction to address modern-day problems from a Christian perspective." Purpose in publishing works by young people: to provide them with an opportunity to express themselves and communicate with their peers through poetry, fiction and nonfiction. Children must submit their birth dates and Social Security numbers. Writer's guidelines available on request, "included in regular guidelines."

Magazines: Uses fiction (900-1,500 words), personal experience pieces (500-900 words), poetry. Pays flat fee for poetry; 5-7¢/word for stories/articles. Submit complete mss to Heather E. Wallace, editor. Will accept typewritten and computer printout mss. Reports in 1-2 months.

Artwork/Photography: Publishes artwork and photography by children. Send samples for review for consideration for assignment. Send samples for file to Heather Wallace, editor.

Tips: "Remember that we are a religious publication. Any submissions, including poetry should have a religious slant."

‡TEXAS HISTORIAN, Texas State Historical Association, 2/306 Sid Richardson Hall, University Station, Austin TX 78712. (512)471-1525. Articles Editor: David De Boe. Magazine published 4 times a year in February, May, September and November. "The *Texas Historian* is the official publication of the Junior Historians of Texas. Articles accepted for publication must be written by members of the Junior Historians of Texas."

Magazines: Uses history articles aimed at young adults (about 2,500 words). Does not accept unsolicited mss.

TURTLE MAGAZINE, Children's Better Health Institute, 1100 Waterway Blvd., P.O. Box 567, Indianapolis IN 46206. (317)636-8881. Magazine. "*Turtle* is a health-related magazine geared toward children from ages 2-5. *Turtle* seeks to entertain, educate and encourage children in healthy eating habits and fitness. Many of the features are interactive, providing a variety of resources for learning skills development." Purpose in publishing work by children/teens: "We want children to express their creativity and have an opportunity to share it with our audience."

Magazines: Submit ms to Terry Harshman, editor. Reports in 2-3 months.

Artwork: Publishes artwork by children in the "Our Own Pictures" regular features. Does not accept art with ms submissions. There is no payment for children's artwork. All artwork must have the child's name, age and complete address on it. Submit artwork to Bart Rivers, art director. "No artwork can be returned."

VIRGINIA WRITING, Longwood College, 201 High St., Farmville VA 23909. (804)395-2160. Magazine published twice yearly. "*Virginia Writing* publishes prose, poetry, fiction, nonfiction, art, photography, music and drama from Virginia high school students and teachers. The purpose of the journal is to publish 'promise,' giving the talented young people of Virginia an opportunity to have their works published. Our audience is mainly Virginia high schools, Virginia public libraries, Department of Education offices, and private citizens. It is also used as a supplementary text in many of Virginia's high school classrooms. The children must be attending a Virginia high school, preferably in no less than 9th grade (though some work has been accepted from 8th graders).

Originality is strongly encouraged. The guidelines are in the front of our magazine or available with SASE." No profanity or racism accepted.

• *Virginia Writing* is the recipient of 12 national awards, including eight Distinguished Achievement Awards for Excellence in Educational Journalism and the Golden Lamp Honor Award as one of the top four educational magazines in the U.S. and Canada.

Magazines: 85% of magazine written by children. Uses approximately 5 fiction and nonfiction short stories, 56 poems and prose pieces per issue. Submit mss to Billy C. Clark, founder and editor. Submit complete ms. Will accept typewritten mss. Reports as soon as possible, "but must include SASE to receive a reply in the event manuscript is not accepted."

Artwork/Photography: Publishes artwork by children. Considers all types of artwork, including that done on computer. Color slides of artwork are acceptable. All original work is returned upon publication in a non-bendable, well protected package. Submit artwork to Billy C. Clark. Reports as soon as possible.

Tips: "All works should be submitted with a cover letter describing student's age, grade and high school currently attending. Submit as often as you like and in any quantity. We cannot accept a work if it features profanity or racism."

WHOLE NOTES, P.O. Box 1374, Las Cruces NM 88004-1374. (505)541-5744. Magazine published twice yearly. "We look for original, fresh perceptions in poems that demonstrate skill in using language effectively, with carefully chosen images, clear ideas and fresh perceptions. Our audience (general) loves poetry. We try to recognize excellence in creative writing by children as a way to encourage and promote imaginative thinking." Writer's guidelines available for SASE.

Magazines: Every fourth issue is 100% by children. Writers should be 21 years old or younger. Uses 30 poems/issue (length open). Pays complimentary copy. Submit mss to Nancy Peters Hastings, editor. Submit complete ms. "No multiple submissions, please." Will accept typewritten and legibly handwritten mss. SASE. Reports in 3 weeks.

Artwork/Photography: Publishes artwork and photographs by children. Looks for b&w line drawings which can easily be reproduced; b&w photos. Pays complimentary copy. Send clear photocopies. Submit artwork to Nancy Peters Hastings, editor. SASE. Reports in 3 weeks.

Tips: Sample issue is $3. "We welcome translations. Don't send your only copy of your poem. Keep a photocopy."

WORD DANCE, Playful Productions, Inc., P.O. Box 10804, Wilmington DE 19850. (302)322-6699. Magazine. Published quarterly. "We're a magazine of creative writing and art that is for *and* by children in kindergarten through grade eight."

Magazines: Uses adventure, fantasy, humorous, etc. (fiction); travel stories, poems and stories based on real life experiences (nonfiction). Publishes 250 total pieces of writing/year; maximum length: 3 pages. Submit mss to Stuart Ungar, articles editor. Sample copy $3. Free writer's guidelines and submissions form. SASE. Reports in 6-8 months.

Artwork: Illustrations accepted from young people in kindergarten through grade 8. Accepts illustrations of specific stories or poems and other general artwork. Must be high contrast. Query. Submit complete package with final art to Melissa Shapiro, art director. SASE. Reports in 6-8 months.

WRITERS' INTERNATIONAL FORUM FOR YOUNG AUTHORS, (formerly Writers' International Forum), P.O. Box 516, Tracyton WA 98393-0516. Newsletter published monthly (except December and August). Purpose in publishing works by young people: to promote strong communications skills, both in essays and in traditional fiction formats. Guidelines available for SASE.

Magazines: Publication contains a "Featured Manuscript" section in which both a young author's manuscript and our professional critique of that manuscript are published. Seeks short stories and essays (1,000 word maximum). Any genre or subject (except no horror or violence). We want well-crafted stories with traditional plots which are written in clear language, have fully developed characters and an interesting storyline. Essays must have a tight focus, make a distinct point, and back up that point with specific facts and/or experiences (preferably experiences of the young author). Pays $30 upon receipt of completed acceptance form, 2 complimentary copies and provides a written professional critique. Author's biographical information printed for every accepted manuscript. Submit mss to Sandra E. Haven, editor. Submit complete ms with cover letter stating author's age. Will accept only typewritten mss. Please send SASE for full guidelines *before* submitting. Reports in 2 months.

THE WRITERS' SLATE, (The Writing Conference, Inc.), P.O. Box 664, Ottawa KS 66067-0664. (913)242-0407. Fax: (913)242-0407. E-mail: witeconf@computer-services.com. Website: http://www.scrtec.rtec.org/writi ng. Magazine. Publishes 3 issues/year. *The Writers' Slate* accepts original poetry and prose from students enrolled in kindergarten-12th grade. The audience is students, teachers and librarians. Purpose in publishing works by young people: to give students the opportunity to publish and to give students the opportunity *to read* quality literature written by other students. Writer's guidelines available on request.

Magazines: 90% of magazine written by young people. Uses 10-15 fiction, 1-2 nonfiction, 10-15 other mss per issue. Submit mss to Dr. F. Todd Goodson, editor, Dept. of English, East Carolina University, Greenville NC

27858-4353. Submit complete ms. Will accept typewritten mss. Reports in 1 month. Include SASE with ms if reply is desired.

Artwork: Publishes artwork by young people. Bold, b&w, student artwork may accompany a piece of writing. Submit to Dr. F. Todd Goodson, editor. Reports in 1 month.

Tips: "Always accompany submission with a letter indicating name, home address, school, grade level and teacher's name. If you want a reply, submit a SASE."

WRITES OF PASSAGE, 817 Broadway, 6th Floor, New York NY 10003. Phone/fax: (212)473-7564. E-mail: wpusa@aol.com. Website: http://www.writes.org. Journal. Publishes 2 issues/year by children (spring/summer and fall/winter). "Our philosophy: 'It may make your parents cringe, your teacher blush, but your best friend will understand.' " Purpose in publishing works by young people: to give teenagers across the country a chance to express themselves through creative writing. "We publish poems and short stories written by teens across the U.S. providing an outlet for their thoughts and feelings. We provide a forum in which teenagers can share their words. It gives teens an opportunity to see that they are not alone with their fears and confusion and rewards them for creative writing. It sends a message that their thoughts are important." Writers must be 12-18 years old, work must be original, short biography should be included. "We are also accepting columns of tips and advice for our young readers to be posted on the website."

Magazines: Uses short stories (up to 4 double-spaced pages) and poetry. Pays in 2 copies. Submit to Laura Hoffman, president. Will accept typewritten and legibly handwritten mss. SASE. Reports in 2 months. Sample copies available for $6. Writer's guidelines for SASE.

Tips: "We began *Writes of Passage* to encourage teenage reading and writing as fun and desirable forms of expression and to establish an open dialogue between teenagers in every state. Our selection process does not censor topics and presents submissions according to the authors' intentions. It gives teens an opportunity to expand on what they have learned in reading and writing classes in school by opening up a world of writing in which they can be free. As a result, submissions often reveal a surprising candidness on the part of the authors, including topics such as love, fear, struggle and death and they expose the diverse backgrounds of contributors."

YOUNG VOICES MAGAZINE, P.O. Box 2321, Olympia WA 98507. (360)357-4683. E-mail: patcha@olya.n et. Magazine published quarterly. "*Young Voices* is by elementary and high school students for people interested in their work." Purpose in publishing work by young people: to provide a forum for their creative work. "Home schooled writers *definitely* welcome, too." Writer's guidelines available on request with SASE.

Magazines: Uses 15 fiction stories, 5 reviews, 10 essays and 15 poems per issue (lengths vary). Pays $5-10 on acceptance (more depending on the length and quality of the writing). Submit mss to Steve Charak. Query first. Will accept typewritten and legibly handwritten mss. SASE. Reports in 2 months.

Artwork/Photography: Publishes artwork and photography by children. "Prefer work that will show up in black and white." Pays $5 on acceptance. Submit artwork to Steve Charak. SASE. Reports in 2 months.

Tips: "Please read one or more issues before submitting work."

Resources
Clubs & Organizations

Contacts made through organizations such as the ones listed in this section can be quite beneficial for children's writers and illustrators. Professional organizations provide numerous educational, business and legal services in the form of newsletters, workshops or seminars. Organizations can provide tips about how to be better writers or artists, as well as what types of business records to keep, health and life insurance coverage to carry and competitions to consider.

An added benefit of belonging to an organization is the opportunity to network with those who have similar interests, creating a support system. As in any business, knowing the right people can often help your career, and important contacts can be made through your peers. Membership in a writer's or artist's group also shows publishers you're serious about your craft. This provides no guarantee your work will be published, but it gives you an added dimension of credibility and professionalism.

Some of the organizations listed here welcome anyone with an interest, while others are only open to published writers and professional artists. A few, those marked with an asterisk (*), are open to student membership. Others, such as the Society of Children's Book Writers and Illustrators (SCBWI), have varying levels of membership. SCBWI offers associate membership to those with no publishing credits, and full membership to those who have had work for children published. Many national organizations such as SCBWI also have regional chapters throughout the country. Write or call for more information regarding any group that sounds interesting, or check the websites of the many organizations that list them. Be sure to get information about local chapters, membership qualifications, and services offered.

Information on organizations listed in the previous edition but not included in this edition of *Children's Writer's & Illustrator's Market* may be found in the General Index.

*AMERICAN ALLIANCE FOR THEATRE & EDUCATION, Theatre Department, Arizona State University, Box 872002, Tempe AZ 85287-2002. (602)965-6064. E-mail: aateinfo@asuvm.inre.asu.edu. Website: http://www.polyglot.lss.wisc.edu/chicano/aate/. Administrative Director: Christy M. Taylor. Purpose of organization: to promote standards of excellence in theater and drama education by providing the artist and educator with a network of resources and support, a base for advocacy, and access to programs and projects that focus on the importance of drama in the human experience. Membership cost: $75 annually for individual in US and Canada, $100 annually for organization, $45 annually for students, $55 annually for retired people; add $20 outside Canada and US. Annual conference held jointly with the Educational Theatre Association in Denver CO, August 1998. Newsletter published quarterly; must be member to subscribe. Contests held for unpublished play reading project and annual awards for best play for K-8 and 1 for secondary audience. Awards plaque and stickers for published playbooks. Publishes list of unpublished plays deemed worthy of performance in newsletter and press release, and staged readings at conference.

AMERICAN SOCIETY OF JOURNALISTS AND AUTHORS, 1501 Broadway, New York NY 10036. (212)997-0947. Fax: (212)768-7414. E-mail: asja@compuserve.com. Executive Director: Alexandra Owens. Qualifications for membership: "Need to be a professional nonfiction writer published 8-10 times in general circulation publications." Membership cost: Initiation fee—$100; annual dues—$165. Group sponsors national conferences; monthly workshops in New York City. Workshops/conferences open to nonmembers. Publishes a newsletter for members that provides confidential information for nonfiction writers.

ARIZONA AUTHORS ASSOCIATION, 3509 E. Shea Blvd., #117, Phoenix AZ 85028-3339. (602)867-9001. E-mail: ggbenn@juno.com. President: Gerry Benninger. Purpose of organization: to offer professional, educational and social opportunities to writers and authors and serve as a network. Qualifications for membership: 1) must be a writer or 2) an agent, publisher, publicist, printer, etc. Membership cost: $40/year professional and associate; $50/year affiliate; $25/year student. Different levels of membership include: Professional—published writers; Associate—writers working toward publication; Affiliate—professionals in publishing industry; Student—full-time students. Holds monthly educational workshops; contact office for current calendar. Publishes newsletter providing information useful to writers (markets, book reviews, calendar of meetings and events) and news about members. Non-member subscription $25/year. Sponsors Annual Literary Contest. Awards include total of $1,000 in prizes in several categories. Contest open to non-members.

ASSITEJ/USA, % Dana Childs, P.O. Box 22365, Seattle WA 98122-0365. (206)392-2147. Fax: (206)443-0442. E-mail: assitej@aol.com. Website: http://www.exposurel.com/clients/assitej/toc.html/. Editor, *TYA Today*: Cyndi Pock. Purpose of organization: to promote theater for children and young people by linking professional theaters and artists together; sponsoring national, international and regional conferences and providing publications and information. Also serves as US Center for International Association of Theatre for Children and Young People. Membership cost: $100 for organizations with budgets below $250,000; $200 for organizations with budgets of $250,000-$999,000; $300 for organizatons with budgets over $1 million; $50 annually/individual; $30 libraries; $25 students and retirees; $65 for foreign organizations or individuals outside the US; $30 for library rate. Different levels of membership include: organizations, individuals, students, retirees, corresponding, libraries. *TYA Today* includes original articles, reviews and works of criticism and theory, all of interest to theater practitioners (included with membership). Sponsors workshops or conferences. Publishes journal that focuses on information on field in US and abroad.

‡THE AUTHORS GUILD, 29th Floor, 330 W. 42nd St., New York NY 10036-6902. (212)563-5904. Executive Director: Paul Aiken. Purpose of organization: To offer services and information materials intended to help authors with the business and legal aspects of their work, including contract problems, copyright matters, freedom of expression and taxation. Guild has 7,000 members. Qualifications for membership: Must be book author published by an established American publisher within 7 years or any author who has had 3 works, fiction or nonfiction, published by a magazine or magazines of general circulation in the last 18 months. Associate membership also available. Annual dues: $90. Different levels of membership include: associate membership with all rights except voting available to an author who has a firm contract offer from an American publisher. "The Guild offers free contract reviews to its members. The Guild conducts several symposia each year at which experts provide information, offer advice, and answer questions on subjects of interest and concern to authors. Typical subjects have been the rights of privacy and publicity, libel, wills and estates, taxation, copyright, editors and editing, the art of interviewing, standards of criticism and book reviewing. Transcripts of these symposia are published and circulated to members. The *Authors Guild Bulletin*, a quarterly journal, contains articles on matters of interest to writers, reports of Guild activities, contract surveys, advice on problem clauses in contracts, transcripts of Guild and League symposia, and information on a variety of professional topics. Subscription included in the cost of the annual dues."

❧CANADIAN SOCIETY OF CHILDREN'S AUTHORS, ILLUSTRATORS AND PERFORMERS, (CANSCAIP), 35 Spadina Rd., Toronto, Ontario M5R 2S9 Canada. (416)515-1559. Fax: (416)515-7022. Website: http://www.interlog.com/~canscaip. Office Manager: Nancy Prasad. Purpose of organization: development of Canadian children's culture and support for authors, illustrators and performers working in this field. Qualifications for membership: Members—professionals who have been published (not self-published) or have paid public performances/records/tapes to their credit. Friends—share interest in field of children's culture. Membership cost: $60 (members dues), $25 (friends dues), $30 (institution dues). Sponsors workshops/conferences. Publishes newsletter: includes profiles of members; news round-up of members' activities countrywide; market news; news on awards, grants, etc; columns related to professional concerns.

LEWIS CARROLL SOCIETY OF NORTH AMERICA, 18 Fitz Harding Place, Owingsmills MD 21117. (410)356-5110. E-mail: eluchin@erols.com. Secretary: Ellie Luchinsky. "We are an organization of Carroll admirers of all ages and interests and a center for Carroll studies." Qualifications for membership: "An interest in Lewis Carroll and a simple love for Alice (or even the Snark)." Membership cost: $20/year. There is also a contributing membership of $50. Publishes a quarterly newsletter.

THE CHILDREN'S BOOK COUNCIL, INC., 568 Broadway, New York NY 10012. (212)966-1990. Website: http://www.cbcbooks.org. Purpose of organization: "A nonprofit trade association of children's and young adult publishers, CBC promotes the enjoyment of books for children and young adults, and works with national and international organizations to that end. The CBC has sponsored National Children's Book Week since 1945." Qualifications for membership: US trade publishers and packagers of children's and young adult books and related literary materials are eligible for membership. Membership cost: "Individuals wishing to receive mailings from the CBC (our semi-annual newsletter—*CBC Features*—and our materials brochures) may be placed on our mailing list for a one-time-only fee of $60. Publishers wishing to join should contact the CBC for dues information." Sponsors workshops and seminars. Publishes a newsletter with articles about children's books and publishing, and listings of free or inexpensive materials available from member publishers. Sells reading encouragement graphics and informational materials suitable for libraries, teachers, booksellers, parents, and others working with children.

FLORIDA FREELANCE WRITERS ASSOCIATION, Cassell Network of Writers, P.O. Box A, North Stratford NH 03590. (603)922-8338. Fax: (603)922-8339. E-mail: danakcnw@moose.ncia.net. Executive Director: Dana K. Cassell. Purpose of organization: To act as a link between Florida writers and buyers of the written word; to help writers run more effective communications businesses. Qualifications for membership: "None— we provide a variety of services and information, some for beginners and some for established pros." Membership cost: $90/year. Publishes a newsletter focusing on market news, business news, how-to tips for the serious writer. Non-member subscription: $39—does not include Florida section—includes national edition only. Annual *Directory of Florida Markets* included in FFWA newsletter section. Publishes annual *Guide to CNW/Florida Writers*. Sponsors contest: annual deadline March 15. Guidelines available fall of each year. Categories: juvenile, adult nonfiction, adult fiction. Awards include cash for top prizes, certificate for others. Contest open to non-members.

*GRAPHIC ARTISTS GUILD, 90 John St., Suite 403, New York NY 10038. (212)791-3400. Fax: (212)791-0333. E-mail: paulatgag@aol.com. Website: http://www.gag.org/. Executive Director: Paul Basista, CAE. Purpose of organization: "to promote and protect the economic interests of member artists. It is committed to improving conditions for all creators of graphic arts and raising standards for the entire industry." Qualification for full membership: 50% of income derived from artwork. Associate members include those in allied fields, students and retirees. Initiation fee: $25. Full memberships $120, $165, $215, $270; student membership $55/year. Associate membership $115/year. Publishes *Graphic Artists Guild Handbook, Pricing and Ethical Guidelines* and quarterly *Guild News* (free to members, $15 to non-members). "The Guild is an egalitarian union that embraces all creators of graphics arts intended for presentation as originals or reproductions at all levels of skill and expertise. The long-range goals of the Guild are: to educate graphic artists and their clients about ethical and fair business practices; to educate graphic artists about emerging trends and technologies impacting the industry; to offer programs and services that anticipate and respond to the needs of our members, helping them prosper and enhancing their health and security, to advocate for the interests of our members in the legislative, judicial and regulatory arenas; to assure that our members are recognized financially and professionally for the value they provide; to be responsible stewards for our members by building an organization that works efficiently on their behalf."

THE INTERNATIONAL WOMEN'S WRITING GUILD, P.O. Box 810, Gracie Station, New York NY 10028. (212)737-7536. Executive Director and Founder: Hannelore Hahn. IWWG is "a network for the personal and professional empowerment of women through writing." Qualifications: open to any woman connected to the written word regardless of professional portfolio. Membership cost: $35 annually; $45 annually for foreign members. "IWWG sponsors 13 annual conferences a year in all areas of the US. The major conference is held in August of each year at Skidmore College in Saratoga Springs NY. It is a week-long conference attracting more than 400 women internationally." Also publishes a 32-page newsletter, *Network*, 6 times/year; offers health insurance at group rates, referrals to literary agents.

JEWISH PUBLICATION SOCIETY, 1930 Chestnut St., Philadelphia PA 19103-4599. (215)564-5925. Editor-in-Chief: Dr. Ellen Frankel. Children's Editor: Bruce Black. Purpose of organization: "To publish quality Jewish books and to promote Jewish culture and education. We are a non-denominational, nonprofit religious publisher. Our children's list specializes in fiction and nonfiction with substantial Jewish content for pre-school through young adult readers." Qualifications for membership: "One must purchase a membership of at least $25, which entitles the member to purchase a certain unit number of our books. Our membership is nondiscriminatory on the basis of religion, ethnic affiliation, race or any other criteria." Levels of membership include: JPS member, $25; Associate, $50; Friend, $100; Fellow, $125; Senior member, $200; Sustaining member, $500. "*The JPS Bookmark* reports on JPS Publications; activities of members, authors and trustees; JPS projects and goals; JPS history; children's books and activities." All members receive *The Bookmark* with their membership.

‡❋LEAGUE OF CANADIAN POETS, 54 Wolseley St., 3rd Floor, Toronto, Ontario M5T 1A5 Canada. (416)504-1657. Fax: (416)703-0059. Executive Director: Edita Petrauskaite. President: Linda Rogers. Inquiries to Program Manager: Sandra Drzewiecki. The L.C.P. is a national organization of published Canadian poets. Our constitutional objectives are to advance poetry in Canada and to promote the professional interests of the members. Qualifications for membership: full—publication of at least 1 book of poetry by a professional publisher; associate membership—an active interest in poetry, demonstrated by several magazine/periodical publication credits, student—an active interest in poetry, 12 sample poems required; supporting—any friend of poetry. Membership fees: full—$175/year, associate—$60, student—$30, supporting—$100. Holds an Annual General Meeting every spring; some events open to nonmembers. "We also organize reading programs in schools and public venues. We publish a newsletter which includes information on poetry/poetics in Canada and beyond. Also publish the books *Poetry Markets for Canadians*; *Who's Who in the League of Canadian Poets*; *Poets in the Classroom* (teaching guide) and its accompanying anthology of Canadian poetry *Vintage*; plus a series of cassettes. We sponsor a National Poetry Contest, open to Canadians living here and abroad." Rules: Unpublished poems of any style/subject, under 75 lines, typed, with name/address on separate sheet. $6 entry fee (includes GST) per poem. $1,000-1st prize, $750-2nd, $500-3rd; plus best 50 published in an anthology. Inquire with SASE. Contest open to Canadian nonmembers. Sponsors an annual chapbook ms contest. Organizes 2 annual awards: The Gerald Lampert Memorial Award for the best first book of poetry published in Canada in the preceding year and The Pat Lowther Memorial Award for the best book of poetry by a Canadian woman published in the preceding year. Deadline for poetry contest is January 31 each year, for awards December 31. Send SASE for more details.

*LITERARY MANAGERS AND DRAMATURGS OF THE AMERICAS, Box 355, CASTA, CUNY Grad Center, 33 W. 42nd St., New York NY 10036. (212)642-2657. Fax: (212)642-1977. E-mail: ltimmel@email.gc.cu ny.edu. LMDA is a not-for-profit service organization for the professions of literary management and dramaturgy. Student Membership: $20/year. Open to students in dramaturgy, performing arts and literature programs, or related disciplines. Proof of student status required. Includes national conference, New Dramaturg activities, local symposia, job phone and select membership meetings. Active Membership: $45/year. Open to full-time and part-time professionals working in the fields of literary management and dramaturgy. All privileges and services including voting rights and eligibility for office. Associate Membership: $35/year. Open to all performing arts professionals and academics, as well as others interested in the field. Includes national conference, local symposia and select membership meetings. Institutional Membership: $100/year. Open to theaters, universities, and other organizations. Includes all privileges and services except voting rights and eligibility for office. Publishes a newsletter featuring articles on literary management, dramaturgy, LMDA program updates and other articles of interest.

‡MOVEABLE BOOK SOCIETY, P.O. Box 11654, New Brunswick NJ 08906. Contact: Ann Montanaro. Organization of lovers of moveable (a.k.a. pop-up) books. Membership includes book artists and paper engineers, collectors, book dealers, and anyone else with an interest in moveable books. The society holds conferences and publishes a newsletter.

NATIONAL WRITERS UNION, 113 University Place, 6th Floor, New York NY 10003. (212)254-0279. Office Manager: Ron Johnson. Purpose of organization: Advocacy for freelance writers. Qualifications for membership: "Membership in the NWU is open to all qualified writers, and no one shall be barred or in any manner prejudiced within the Union on account of race, age, sex, sexual preference, disability, national origin, religion or ideology. You are eligible for membership if you have published a book, a play, three articles, five poems, one short story or an equivalent amount of newsletter, publicity, technical, commercial, government or institutional copy. You are also eligible for membership if you have written an equal amount of unpublished material and you are actively writing and attempting to publish your work." Membership cost: annual writing income under $5,000—$80/year; annual writing income $5,000-25,000—$132/year; annual writing income over $25,000—$180/year. National union newsletter quarterly, issues related to freelance writing and to union organization. Non-member subscription: $15.

PEN AMERICAN CENTER, 568 Broadway, New York NY 10012. (212)334-1660. Fax: (212)334-2181. Purpose of organization: "To foster understanding among men and women of letters in all countries. International PEN is the only worldwide organization of writers and the chief voice of the literary community. Members of PEN work for freedom of expression wherever it has been endangered." Qualifications for membership: "The standard qualification for a writer to join PEN is that he or she must have published, in the United States, two or more books of a literary character, or one book generally acclaimed to be of exceptional distinction. Editors who have demonstrated commitment to excellence in their profession (generally construed as five years' service in book editing), translators who have published at least two book-length literary translations, and playwrights whose works have been professionally produced, are eligible for membership." An application form is available upon request from PEN Headquarters in New York. Candidates for membership should be nominated by 2 current members of PEN. Inquiries about membership should be directed to the PEN Membership Committee. Friends of PEN is also open to writers who may not yet meet the general PEN membership requirements. PEN sponsors public events at PEN Headquarters in New York, and at the branch offices in Boston, Chicago, New Orleans,

---

🍁 **CANADIAN LISTINGS** are marked with a maple leaf.

San Francisco and Portland, Oregon. They include tributes by contemporary writers to classic American writers, dialogues with visiting foreign writers, symposia that bring public attention to problems of censorship and that address current issues of writing in the United States, and readings that introduce beginning writers to the public. PEN's wide variety of literary programming reflects current literary interests and provides informal occasions for writers to meet each other and to welcome those with an interest in literature. Events are all open to the public and are usually free of charge. The Children's Book Authors' Committee sponsors biannual public events focusing on the art of writing for children and young adults and on the diversity of literature for juvenile readers. The PEN/Norma Klein Award was established in 1991 to honor an emerging children's book author. The bimonthly *PEN Newsletter* covers PEN activities, features interviews with international literary figures, transcripts of PEN literary symposia, reports on issues vital to the literary community. All PEN publications are available by mail order directly from PEN American Center. Individuals must enclose check or money order with their order. Subscription: $8 for 6 issues; sample issue $2. Pamphlets and brochures all free upon request. Sponsors several competitions per year. Monetary awards range from $700-7,500.

*PUPPETEERS OF AMERICA, INC., #5 Cricklewood Path, Pasadena CA 91107. (818)797-5748. Membership Officer: Gayle Schluter. Purpose of organization: to promote the art of puppetry. Qualifications for membership: interest in the art form. Membership cost: single adult, $35; junior member, $20; retiree, $25 (65 years of age and 5 years prior membership); group or family, $55; couple, $45. Membership includes a bimonthly newsletter. Sponsors workshops/conferences. Publishes newsletter. *The Puppetry Journal* provides news about puppeteers, puppet theaters, exhibitions, touring companies, technical tips, new products, new books, films, television, and events sponsored by the Chartered Guilds in each of the 8 P of A regions. Subscription: $30.

*SCIENCE-FICTION AND FANTASY WRITERS OF AMERICA, INC., 532 La Guardia Place #632, New York NY 10012-1428. Website: http://www.sfwa.org. Executive Secretary: Peter Dennis Pautz. Purpose of organization: to encourage public interest in science fiction literature and provide organization format for writers/editors/artists within the genre. Qualifications for membership: at least 1 professional sale or other professional involvement within the field. Membership cost: annual active dues—$50; affiliate—$35; one-time installation fee of $10; dues year begins July 1. Different levels of membership include: active—requires 3 professional short stories or 1 novel published; affiliate—requires 1 professional sale or professional involvement. Workshops/conferences: annual awards banquet, usually in April or May. Open to nonmembers. Publishes newsletter. Nonmember subscription: $15 in US. Sponsors SFWA Nebula® Awards for best published science fiction in the categories of novel, novella, novelette and short story. Awards trophy.

SOCIETY OF CHILDREN'S BOOK WRITERS AND ILLUSTRATORS, 345 N. Maple Dr., Suite 296, Beverly Hills CA 90210. (310)859-9887. Website: http://www.scbwi.org. Chairperson, Board of Directors: Sue Alexander. Purpose of organization: to assist writers and illustrators working or interested in the field. Qualifications for membership: an interest in children's literature and illustration. Membership cost: $50/year. Different levels of membership include: full membership—published authors/illustrators; associate membership—unpublished writers/illustrators. Holds 100 events (workshops/conferences) around the country each year. Open to nonmembers. Publishes a newsletter focusing on writing and illustrating children's books. Sponsors grants for writers and illustrators who are members.

SOCIETY OF ILLUSTRATORS, 128 E. 63rd St., New York NY 10021-7392. (212)838-2560. Fax: (212)838-2561. Director: Terrence Brown. Purpose of organization: to promote interest in the art of illustration for working professional illustrators and those in associated fields. Membership cost: Initiation fee—$250. Annual dues for non-resident members (those living more than 125 air miles from SI's headquarters) are $248. Dues for Resident Artist Members are $428 per year; Resident Associate Members $496. Different levels of membership: *Artist Members* "shall include those who make illustration their profession" and through which they earn at least 60% of their income. *Associate Members* are "those who earn their living in the arts or who have made a substantial contribution to the art of illustration." This includes art directors, art buyers, creative supervisors, instructors, publishers and like categories. "All candidates for membership are admitted by the proposal of one active member and sponsorship of four additional members. The candidate must complete and sign the application form which requires a brief biography, a listing of schools attended, other training and a résumé of his or her professional career." Candidates for *Artist* membership, in addition to the above requirements, must submit examples of their work. Sponsors "The Annual of American Illustration." Awards include gold and silver medals. Open to nonmembers. Deadline: October 1. Sponsors "The Original Art: The Best of Children's Book Illustration." Deadline: mid-September. Call for details.

❋ **ORGANIZATIONS OPEN TO STUDENTS** are marked with an asterisk.

SOCIETY OF MIDLAND AUTHORS, % SMA, P.O. 10419, Chicago IL 60610-0419. Purpose of organization: create closer association among writers of the Middle West; stimulate creative literary effort; maintain collection of members' works; encourage interest in reading and literature by cooperating with other educational and cultural agencies. Qualifications for membership: author or co-author of a book demonstrating literary style and published by a recognized publisher, and be identified through residence with Illinois, Indiana, Iowa, Kansas, Michigan, Minnesota, Missouri, Nebraska, North Dakota, Ohio, South Dakota or Wisconsin. Membership cost: $25/year dues. Different levels of membership include: regular—published book authors; associate, nonvoting— not published as above but having some connection with literature, such as librarians, teachers, publishers and editors. Program meetings at Cliff Dwellers, 200 S. Michigan Ave., Borg-Warner Bldg. Chicago, held 5 times a year, featuring authors, publishers, editors or the like individually or on panels. Usually second Tuesday of October, November, February, March and April. Also holds annual awards dinner at Cliff Dwellers, 200 S. Michigan Ave., Chicago, in May. Publishes a newsletter focusing on news of members and general items of interest to writers. Non-member subscription: $5. Sponsors contests. "Annual awards in six categories, given at annual dinner in May. Monetary awards for books published which premiered professionally in previous calendar year. Send SASE to contact person for details." Categories include adult fiction, adult nonfiction, biography, juvenile fiction, juvenile nonfiction, poetry, biography. No picture books. Contest open to non-members. Deadline for contest: January 30.

‡**TEXT AND ACADEMIC AUTHORS ASSOCIATION**, University of South Florida, St. Petersburg FL 33701. (813)553-1195. Executive Director: Ronald Pynn. Purpose of organization: to address the professional concerns of text and academic authors, to protect the interests of creators of intellectual property at all levels, and support efforts to enforce copyright protection. Qualifications for membership: all authors and prospective authors are welcome. Membership cost: $30 first year; $60 per year following years. Workshops/conferences: June each year. Newsletter focuses on all areas of interest to text authors.

VOLUNTEER LAWYERS FOR THE ARTS, 1 E. 53rd St., 6th Floor, New York NY 10022-4201. (212)319-2787 (administration); (212)319-2910 (Art Law Line) Fax: (212)752-6575. Executive Director: Amy Schwartzman. Purpose of organization: Volunteer Lawyers for the Arts is dedicated to providing free arts-related legal assistance to low-income artists and not-for-profit arts organizations in all creative fields. Over 800 attorneys in the New York area donate their time through VLA to artists and arts organizations unable to afford legal counsel. There is no membership required for our services. Everyone is welcome to use VLA's Art Law Line, a legal hotline for any artist or arts organization needing quick answers to arts-related questions. VLA also provides clinics, seminars and publications designed to educate artists on legal issues which affect their careers. Membership is through donations and is not required to use our services. Members receive discounts on publications and seminars as well as other benefits.

*****WESTERN WRITERS OF AMERICA, INC.**, 1012 Fair St., Franklin TN 37064. (615)791-1444. Fax: (615)791-1444. Secretary/Treasurer: James A. Crutchfield. Purpose of organization: to further all types of literature that pertains to the American West. Membership requirements: must be a *published* author of Western material. Membership cost: $75/year ($90 foreign). Different levels of membership include: Active and Associate—the 2 vary upon number of books published. Holds annual convention. Publishes bimonthly magazine focusing on market trends, book reviews, news of members, etc. Non-members may subscribe for $30 ($40 foreign). Sponsors contests. Spur awards given annually for a variety of types of writing. Awards include plaque, certificate, publicity. Contest open to nonmembers.

WRITERS CONNECTION, P.O. Box 24770, San Jose CA 95154-4770. (408)445-3600. Fax: (408)445-3609. Editor: Jan Stiles. Vice President/Program Director: Meera Lester. Purpose of organization: to provide services and resources for writers. Qualifications for membership: interest in writing or publishing. Membership cost: $45/year. Conferences: Selling to Hollywood and various genre conferences, including writing for children. Publishes a newsletter focusing on writing and publishing (all fields except poetry), how-to, markets, contests, tips, etc., included with membership. Subscription $25.

*❦**WRITERS' FEDERATION OF NEW BRUNSWICK**, Box 37, Station A, 404 Queen St., Fredericton, New Brunswick E3B 4Y2 Canada. (506)459-7228. Website: http://www.sjfn.nb.ca/community_hall/W/Writers_F EDERATION_NB/index.htm. Project Coordinator: Anna Mae Snider. Purpose of organization: "to promote the work of New Brunswick writers and to help them at all stages of their development." Qualifications for membership: interest in writing. Membership cost: $30, basic annual membership; $20, student/unemployed; $40, family membership; $50, institutional membership; $100, sustaining member; $250, patron; and $1,000, lifetime member. Holds workshops/conferences. Publishes a newsletter with articles concerning the craft of writing, member news, contests, markets, workshops and conference listings. Sponsors annual literary competition (for New Brunswick residents). Categories: fiction, nonfiction, poetry, children's literature—3 prizes per category of $200, $100, $30; Alfred Bailey Prize of $400 for poetry ms; The Richards Prize of $400 for short novel, collection of short stories or section of long novel; The Sheree Fitch Prize for writing by young people (14-18 years of age). Contest open to nonmembers (residents of New Brunswick only).

❀**WRITERS GUILD OF ALBERTA**, 11759 Groat Rd., 3rd Floor, Percy Page Centre, Edmonton, Alberta T5M 3K6 Canada. (403)422-8174. Fax: (403)422-2663. E-mail: writers@compusmart.ab.ca. Website: http://www.writersguildofalberta.ca. Executive Director: Mr. Miki Andrejevic. Purpose of organization: to provide meeting ground and collective voice for the writers in Alberta. Membership cost: $60/year; $20 for seniors/students. Holds workshops/conferences. Publishes a newsletter focusing on markets, competitions, contemporary issues related to the literary arts (writing, publishing, censorship, royalties etc.). Nonmembers may subscribe to newsletter. Subscription cost: $60/year. Sponsors annual literary awards program in 7 categories (novel, nonfiction, short fiction, children's literature, poetry, drama, best first book). Awards include $500, leather-bound book, promotion and publicity. Open to nonmembers.

WRITERS OF KERN, P.O. Box 6694, Bakersfield CA 93386-6694. (805)871-5834. Open to published writers and any person interested in writing. Dues: $35/year, $20 for students. Types of memberships: professional, writers with published work; associate—writers working toward publication, affiliate—beginners and students. Monthly meetings held on the fourth Saturday of every month, except September which is conference month, with speakers who are authors, agents, etc., on topics pertaining to writing; critique groups for several fiction genres, nonfiction, journalism and screenwriting which meet weekly or biweekly. Members receive a monthly newsletter with marketing tips, conferences and contests; access to club library; discount to annual conference. Annual conference held the third Saturday in September; annual writing contest with winners announced at the conference. Send SASE for information.

Conferences & Workshops

Writers and illustrators eager to expand their knowledge of the children's industry should consider attending one of the many conferences and workshops held each year. Whether you're a novice or seasoned professional, conferences and workshops are great places to pick up information on a variety of topics and network with experts in the publishing industry, as well as your peers.

Many conferences and workshops included here focus on children's writing or illustrating and related business issues. Others appeal to a broader base of writers or artists, but still provide information that can be useful in creating material for children. Illustrators may be interested in painting and drawing workshops, for example, while writers can learn about techniques and meet editors and agents at general writing conferences. Workshops in this section that are open to student participants are marked with an asterisk (*).

Listings in this section provide details about what conference and workshop courses are offered, where and when they are held, and the costs. Some of the national writing and art organizations also offer regional workshops throughout the year. Write or call them for information.

Artists can find a detailed directory of annual art workshops offered around the globe in the March, June, September and December issues of *The Artist's Magazine*. Writers should consult the May issue of *Writer's Digest*.

Members of the Society of Children's Book Writers and Illustrators can find information on conferences in national and local SCBWI newsletters. Nonmembers may attend SCBWI events as well. A number of local SCBWI conferences are listed in this section. For information on SCBWI's annual national conference, contact them at (818)888-8760 or check their website for a complete calendar of events (http://www.scbwi.org).

Information on conferences listed in the previous edition but not this edition of *Children's Writer's & Illustrator's Market* may be found in the General Index.

AMERICAN CHRISTIAN WRITERS CONFERENCE, P.O. Box 110390, Nashville TN 37222. 1(800)21-WRITE or (615)834-0450. Website: http://www.ecpa.org/acw. Director: Reg Forder. Writer and illustrator workshops geared toward beginner, intermediate and advanced levels. Classes offered include: fiction, nonfiction, poetry, photography, music, etc. Workshops held in two dozen US cities. Call or write for a complete schedule of conferences. 75 minutes. Maximum class size: 30 (approximate). Cost of conference: $99, 1-day session; $169, 2-day session; $229, 3-day session (discount given if paid 30 days in advance).

BE THE WRITER YOU WANT TO BE—MANUSCRIPT CLINIC, Villa 30, 23350 Sereno Court, Cupertino CA 95014. (415)691-0300. Contact: Louise Purwin Zobel. Writer workshops geared toward beginner, intermediate and advanced levels. "Participants may turn in manuscripts at any stage of development to receive help with structure and style, as well as marketing advice. Manuscripts receive some written criticism and an oral critique from the instructor, as well as class discussion." Annual workshop. Usually held in the spring. Registration limited to 20-25. Cost of workshop: $45-65/day, depending on the campus; includes an extensive handout. SASE for more information.

‡BUTLER UNIVERSITY CHILDREN'S LITERATURE CONFERENCE, 4600 Sunset Drive, Indianapolis IN 46208. (317)940-9861. Fax: (317)940-9930. E-mail: sdaniell@butler.edu. Contact: Shirley Daniell. Writer and illustrator conference geared toward intermediate level. Annual conference held in late January. Registration limited to 300. Cost of conference: $80; includes meals and registration. Write for more information. "The conference is geared toward three groups: teachers, librarians and writers/illustrators."

‡CAPE COD WRITERS CONFERENCE, Cape Cod Writers' Center, % The Conservatory, W. Barustable MA 02668. (508)375-0516. Contact: Executive Director. Writer conference and workshops geared toward beginner, intermediate and professional levels. Annual conference. Conference held third week in August. Cost of conference includes $60 to register; $85 per course (we offer 9); manuscript evaluation, $60; personal conference, $30. Write for more information. "We also offer four state-of-the-genre seminars—one on each Sunday in October. Both conference and seminar schedules include children's writing. The summer conference includes young adult fiction.

*CELEBRATION OF CHILDREN'S LITERATURE, 51 Mannakee St., Office of Continuing Education, Room 220, Rockville MD 20850. (301)251-7914. Fax: (301)251-7937. E-mail: ssonner@cc.mc.md.us. Senior Program Director: Sandra Sonner. Writer and illustrator workshops geared toward all levels. Topics include Creating a Series; Style and Techniques of Illustrating; What is Literature?; Sorting out Good Books; Knowledge of Reviewing Books; How are Books Recommended; Researching and Writing; Recordings for Children's Books. Annual workshop. Registration limited to 200. Writing/art facilities, continuing education classrooms and large auditorium. Cost of workshop: $60/Montgomery County residents; $80/out-of-county; includes workshops, box lunch and coffee. Write for more information.

CHARLESTON WRITERS' CONFERENCE, English Dept., College of Charleston, Charleston SC 29424. (803)953-5659. Fax: (803)953-3180. E-mail: allenp@cofc.edu. Contact: Director. Writer workshops geared toward beginner and intermediate levels. Features sessions on craft and marketing. Annual conference. Conference held March 19-22, 1998. Cost of workshop: $150; includes tuition and all functions. For individual manuscript critiques, a separate fee is charged ($40). Write for more information.

CHILDREN'S LITERATURE CONFERENCE, Hofstra University, U.C.C.E., Hempstead NY 11549. (516)463-5016. Fax: (516)463-4833. E-mail: dcelcs@hofstra.edu. Writers/Illustrators Contact: Lewis Shena, associate dean, Liberal Arts Studies. Writer and illustrator workshops geared toward all levels. Emphasizes: fiction, nonfiction, poetry, submission procedures, picture books. Workshops held May 16. Length of each session: 1 hour. Registration limited to 35/class. Cost of workshop: approximately $60; includes 2 workshops, reception, lunch, 2 general sessions, and panel discussion with guest speakers and/or critiquing. Write for more information. Co-sponsored by Society of Children's Book Writers & Illustrators.

‡*CHILDREN'S WRITER'S CONFERENCE, St. Charles County Community College, P.O. Box 76975, 103 CEAC, St. Peters MO 63376-0975. (314)213-8000 ext. 4108. Fax: (314)209-0772. E-mail: cccohn22@aol.com. SCBWI MO Regional Advisor: Carolyn Cohn. Writer and illustrator conference geared toward beginner, intermediate, advanced and professional levels. Conference speakers and topics include: "The Structure of Mystery," by Connie Hiser; "How to Make a Dummy for your Picture Book" by Sandra Griffin; "What Happens When Your Manuscript is Accepted" by Dawn Weinstock, editor; "Multicultural Aspects of Picture Books" by V. Rahaman; "Nonfiction that Sells" by Bev Letchworth; "Writing—Hobby or Vocation?" by Chris Kelleher. Annual conference held in late October/early November. Registration limited to 50-70. Cost of conference: $50-60; includes one day workshop (8:00 a.m. to 5:00 p.m.) plus lunch. Write for more information.

THE COLLEGE OF NEW JERSEY WRITERS' CONFERENCE, (formerly Trenton State College Writer's Conference), English Dept,, The College of New Jersey, Hillwood Lakes CN 4700, Trenton NJ 08650-4700. (609)771-3254. Director: Jean Hollander. Writer workshops geared toward all levels. Offers workshop in children's literature. Workshops held in April of every year. Length of each session: 2 hours. Registration limited to 50. Cost of workshop: $50 (reduced rates for students); includes conference, workshop and ms critique. Write for more information.

*THE COLUMBUS WRITERS CONFERENCE, P.O. Box 20548, Columbus OH 43220-0176. (614)451-3075. Fax: (614)451-0174. E-mail: angelapl28@aol.com. Director: Angela Palazzolo. Writer workshops geared toward all levels. "Since its inception in 1993, the conference has offered a wide variety of topics including writing in the following markets: children's, young adult, movie/television, humor, suspense, science fiction/fantasy, travel, educational and greeting card. Other topics' have included writing the novel, the short story, the nonfiction book; playwriting; finding and working with an agent; independent publishing; book reviewing; technical writing; and time management for writers. Specific sessions that have pertained to children: children's writing, children's markets, writing and publishing children's poetry and stories. Annual conference. Conference held in September. Cost of conference: $89 for early registration; $105 regular registration. Includes attendance at conference, continental breakfast, lunch and a networking/refreshments session. $28 for pre-conference dinner/program. Write for more information.

✳ WORKSHOPS OPEN TO STUDENTS are marked with an asterisk.

*PETER DAVIDSON'S WRITER'S SEMINAR; HOW TO WRITE A CHILDREN'S PICTURE BOOK SEMINAR, 982 S. Emerald Hills Dr., P.O. Box 497, Arnolds Park IA 51331-0497. Seminar Presenter: Peter Davidson. "This seminar is for anyone interested in writing and/or illustrating children's picture books. Beginners and experienced writers alike are welcome. If participants have a manuscript in progress, or have an idea, they are welcome to bring it along to discuss with the seminar presenter." *How to Write a Children's Picture Book* is a one-day seminar devoted to principles and techniques of writing and illustrating children's picture books. Topics include Definition of a Picture Book, Picture Book Sizes, Developing an Idea, Plotting the Book, Writing the Book, Illustrating the Book, Typing the Manuscript, Copyrighting Your Work, Marketing Your Manuscript and Contract Terms. Seminars are presented year-round at community colleges. Even-numbered years, presents seminars in Minnesota, Iowa, Nebraska, Kansas, Colorado and Wyoming. Odd-numbered years, presents seminars in Illinois, Minnesota, Iowa, South Dakota, Missouri, Arkansas and Tennessee (write for a schedule). One day, 9 a.m.-4 p.m. Cost of workshop: varies from $42-59, depending on location; includes approximately 35 pages of handouts. Write for more information.

DEEP SOUTH WRITERS CONFERENCE, % English Dept. USL Box 44691, Lafayette LA 70504. (318)482-6910. E-mail: jlm8047@usl.edu. Professor, English: Sylvia Iskander. Writer workshops geared toward beginner and intermediate levels. Illustrator workshops geared toward beginner level. Topics offered include age-appropriateness, development of character and plot, and submission of mss (including query letter). Annual workshop. Workshop held third or fourth weekend in September. Registration limited to 10 people. Writing/art facilities available: special equipment can be made available if enough advanced notice is given. Cost of workshop: $40 and conference registration of $25-50, depending on status. Payment entitles workshop participants to workshop and all conference craft lectures and readings. Submit ms at least 3 weeks in advance (by end of August). Ms (not art) will be duplicated for all members of the workshop to critique. Write for more information.

‡DUKE CREATIVE WRITER'S WORKSHOP, Box 90702, Room 203, The Bishop's House, Durham NC 27708. (919)684-2827. Fax: (919)681-8235. E-mail: kprice@mail.duke.edu. Website: http://www.learnmore.duke .edu. Program Coordinator: Kim Price. Writer workshops geared toward intermediate to advanced levels. The Creative Writer's Workshop allows each participant to explore creative writing in-depth with the instructor of their choice. Each instructor focuses on a particular style or area of creative writing; for example, Short Fiction, Personal Narrative, Playwriting, Poetry and others. Annual workshop. Every summer there are 2 1-week sessions in July. Registration limited to 40. All participants have access to University facilities including computer clusters, libraries and classrooms. Costs for 1997 were $750 for this 1-week residential session. This cost includes room, board, activity and course expenses, special events and meals, and 1 camper T-shirt. Interested participants are requested to send a sample of their writing and a letter of introduction prior to registration. Write or call for more information.

‡*DUKE YOUNG WRITER'S CAMP, P.O. Box 90702, Room 203, The Bishop's House, Durham NC 27708. (919)684-2827. Fax: (919)681-8235. E-mail: kprice@mail.duke.edu. Website: http://www.learnmore.duke.edu. Program Coordinator: Kim Price. Writer workshops geared toward beginner and intermediate levels. The Young Writer's Camp offers courses that help participants to increase their skills in Creative Writing, Expository Writing and Journalism. The courses are divided into lower and upper age groups. Specific examples of courses offered this summer for the older age group are: Writing the Short Story, Essays Made Fun and Film Review. Some examples of the lower age group classes are: Humor Writing, Children's Literature and Journal Writing. Annual workshop. Every summer there are 3 2-week sessions in June and July. Registration limited to 140. All participants have access to University facilities including computer clusters, libraries and classrooms. Costs for 1997 were $1,175 for residential campers and $610 for day campers. The cost for residential campers includes room, board, activity and course expenses, and 1 camp T-shirt. The cost for day campers includes all course expenses, and 1 camp T-shirt. Write or call for more information.

FISHTRAP, INC., P.O. Box 38, Enterprise OR 97828. (541)426-3623. Fax: (541)426-3324. Director: Rich Wandschneider. Writer workshops geared toward beginner, intermediate, advanced and professional levels. Not specifically writing for children, although we have offered occasional workshops such as "The Children's Picture Book." A series of eight writing workshops (enrollment 12/workshop) and a writers' gathering is held each July; a winter gathering concerning writing and issues of public policy (e.g. "Violence," "Fire") is held in February. During the school year Fishtrap brings writers into local schools and offers occasional workshops for teachers and writers of children's and young adult books. Also brings in "Writers in Residency" (10 weeks). Cost of workshop: $40-210 for 1-4 days; includes workshop only. Food and lodging can be arranged. College credit is available for $39/hour. Please contact for more information.

---

‡   **LISTINGS NEW TO THIS EDITION** are markets with a double dagger.

*FLORIDA CHRISTIAN WRITERS CONFERENCE, 2600 Park Ave., Titusville FL 32780. (407)269-6702, ext. 202. Fax: (407)383-1741. E-mail: writer@digital.net. Website: http://www.Kipertek.com/writer. Conference Director: Billie Wilson. Writer workshops geared toward all levels. "We offer 48 one-hour workshops and 7 five-hour classes. Approximately 24 of these are for the children's genre: Seeing Through the Eyes of an Artist; Characters . . . Inside and Out; Seeing Through the Eyes of a Child; Picture Book Toolbox; and CD-ROM & Interactive Books for Children. Annual workshop held January 29 through February 2, 1998; February 18-22, 1999; and February 24-28, 2000. We have 30 publishers and publications represented by editors teaching workshops and reading manuscripts from the conferees. The conference is limited to 200 people. Usually workshops are limited to 25-30. Advanced or professional workshops are by invitation only via submitted application." Cost of workshop: $400; includes food, lodging, tuition and manuscript critiques and editor review of your manuscript. Write for more information.

*FLORIDA SUNCOAST WRITERS' CONFERENCE, Department of English, University of South Florida, Tampa FL 33620-6600. (813)974-1711. Fax: (813)974-2270. Directors: Ed Hirshberg and Steve Rubin. Writer workshops geared toward beginner through advanced levels. Emphasizes writing for children and young adults (including craft, marketing, etc.). Workshops held first weekend in February. Class sizes range from 30-100. Cost of workshop: $125; $110 for students/teachers; includes all sessions, receptions, panels. Conference is held on St. Petersburg campus of USF. Call for information.

GREAT LAKES WRITER'S WORKSHOP, Alverno College, 3401 S. 39th St., P.O. Box 343922, Milwaukee WI 53234-3922. (414)382-6176. Fax: (414)382-6332. Assistant Director: Cindy Jackson. Writing workshops geared toward beginner and intermediate levels; subjects include writing techniques/focuses such as character development, scene development, etc.; techniques for getting over writer's block; marketing strategies; and publishing strategies. Annual workshop. Workshop held on a weekend in July. Average length of each session: 2 hours. Workshop is currently being redeveloped into a weekend format. Write for more information.

‡GREEN RIVERS WRITERS NOVELS-IN-PROGRESS WORKSHOP, 11906 Locust Rd., Middletown KY 40243-1413. (502)245-4902. President: Mary O'Dell. Writer workshops geared toward intermediate and advanced levels. Workshops emphasize novel writing. Format is 6 novelist instructors working with small groups (5-7 people); one of these novelists may be young adult novelist. Workshop held March 17-23, 1998. Registration limited to 49. Participants will need to bring own computers, typewriters, etc. Private rooms are available for sleeping, working. No art facilities. Cost of workshop: $350; includes organization membership, buffet banquet with agents and editors, registration, manuscript reading fee (60 pages approximately with outline/synopsis). Writers must supply 40-60 pages of manuscript with outline, synopsis or treatment. Write for more information. Conference held on Shelby Campus at University of Louisville; private rooms with bath between each 2 rooms. Linens furnished. $20 per night.

*THE HEIGHTS WRITER'S CONFERENCE, Sponsored by Writer's World Press, P.O. Box 24684, Cleveland OH 44124-0684. (216)481-1974. Fax: (216)481-2057. E-mail: writersworld@juno.com. Conference Director: Lavern Hall. Writer workshops geared toward beginner, intermediate, advanced and professional levels. Program includes 1-hour seminars and 2 2½-hour workshops. "Our workshop topics vary yearly. We *always* have children's literature." Annual workshop held first Saturday in May. Registration is open for seminars. The 2 teaching workshops are limited to 25 and pre-registration is a must. Cost of conference: $75; includes continental breakfast, registration packet, lunch, seminars and/or workshops, general session and networking reception at the end of the day. SASE for brochure.

"HELP! I'M A WRITER" SEMINAR, (formerly "Writing for the Local Church . . . and Beyond"), P.O. Box 12624, Roanoke VA 24027. Phone/fax: (540)342-7511. E-mail: ccmbbr@juno.com. Director: Betty Robertson. Writer and illustrator workshops geared toward beginner and intermediate levels. Includes sessions on stories for children, puppet scripts, puzzles, curriculum. Workshops held on invitation; various locations. Cost of workshop: $24.95-34.95; includes comprehensive handbook, refreshments, free magazine samples. Write for more information.

HIGHLAND SUMMER CONFERENCE, Box 7014 Radford University, Radford VA 24142. (540)831-5366. Fax: (540)831-5004. E-mail: gedwards@runet.edu. or jasbury@runet.edu. Website: http://www.runet.edu/~arsc. Director: Grace Toney Edwards. Assistant to the Director: Jo Ann Asbury. Writer workshops geared toward beginner, intermediate and advanced levels. Emphasizes Appalachian literature. Annual workshop. Workshop held June 15-26, 1998 (last 2 weeks in June annually). Registration limited to 20. Writing facilities available: computer center. Cost of workshop: Regular tuition plus $25 conference fee (housing/meals extra). Must be registered student or special status student. Write for more information. Past visiting authors include: Wilma Dykeman, Sue Ellen Bridgers, George Ella Lyon, Lou Kassem, Jim Wayne Miller.

HIGHLIGHTS FOUNDATION WRITERS WORKSHOP AT CHAUTAUQUA, Dept. CWL, 814 Court St., Honesdale PA 18431. (717)253-1192. Fax: (717)253-0179. Conference Director: Jan Keen. Writer workshops geared toward those interested in writing for children; beginner, intermediate and advanced levels. Classes offered include: Children's Interests; Writing Dialogue; Beginnings and Endings; Rights; Contracts; Copyrights; Science Writing. Annual workshop. Workshops held July 18-25, 1998, at Chautauqua Institution, Chautauqua, NY. Registration limited to 100/class. Cost of workshop: $1,485; includes tuition, meals, conference supplies. Cost does not include housing. Call for availability and pricing. Scholarships are available for first-time attendees. Write for more information.

*HOFSTRA UNIVERSITY SUMMER WRITERS' CONFERENCE, Hofstra University, UCCE, Hempstead NY 11549. (516)463-5016. Fax: (516)463-4833. E-mail: dcelcs@hofstra.edu. Assistant Dean of Liberal Arts Studies: Lewis Shena. Writer workshops geared toward all levels. Classes offered include fiction, nonfiction, poetry, children's literature, stage/screenwriting and other genres. Children's writing faculty has included Pam Conrad, Johanna Hurwitz, Tor Seidler and Jane Zalben, with Maurice Sendak once appearing as guest speaker. Annual workshop. Workshops held for 2 weeks in July commencing the first Monday after July 4. Each workshop meets for 2½ hours daily for a total of 25 hours. Students can register for 2 workshops, schedule an individual conference with the writer/instructor and submit a short ms (less than 10 pages) for critique. Enrollees may register as certificate students or credit students. Cost of workshop: certificate students enrollment fee is approximately $350 plus $26 registration fee; 2-credit student enrollment fee is approximately $900 undergraduate and $1,682 graduate; 4-credit student enrollment fee is approximately $1,682 undergraduate and $1,762 graduate. On-campus accommodations for the sessions are available for approximately $350/person. Students may attend any of the ancillary activities, a private conference, special programs and social events.

‡*INSPIRATIONAL WRITERS ALIVE, Rt. 4, Box 81-H, Rusk TX 75785. Director: Maxine E, Holder. Guest speaker for 1998: Pam Zollman. Topics: Focus and Writing for Children. Bi-Annual conference held 1st Saturday in August (August 1st for 1998). Registration usually 60-75 conferees. Writing/art facilities available: First Baptist Church, Christian Life Center, Houston TX. Cost of conference: approximately $100. Write for more information. "Annual IWA Contest presented. Manuscripts critiqued along with one-on-one 15 minute sessions with speaker(s). (Extra ms. if there is room.)"

INTERNATIONAL WOMEN'S WRITING GUILD "REMEMBER THE MAGIC" ANNUAL SUMMER CONFERENCE, P.O. Box 810, Gracie Station, New York NY 10028. (212)737-7536. Executive Director: Hannelore Hahn. Writer and illustrator workshops geared toward all levels. Offers 60 different workshops—some are for children's book writers and illustrators. Also sponsors 13 other events throughout the US. Annual workshops. Workshops held the 3rd week in August. Length of each session: 1 hour-15 minutes; sessions take place for an entire week. Registration limited to 400. Cost of workshop: $350 (plus $350 room and board). Write for more information. "This workshop always takes place at Skidmore College in Saratoga Springs NY."

*THE IUPUI NATIONAL YOUTH THEATRE PLAYWRITING DEVELOPMENT WORKSHOP AND SYMPOSIUM, 425 N. University Blvd., Suite 309, Indianapolis IN 46202-5140. (317)274-0566. Fax: (317)278-1025. E-mail: wmccrear@iupui.edu. Literary Manager: W. Mark McCreary. "The purpose of the Symposium is to provide a forum in which we can examine and discuss those principles which characterize good dramatic literature for young people and to explore ways to help playwrights and the promotion of quality drama. Publishers, playwrights, directors, producers, librarians and educators join together to examine issues central to playwriting." Biennial workshop. Workshop held spring 1999. Cost of workshop varies, "usually less than $100." Holds playwriting competition. Send SASE for guidelines and entry form. Deadline: September 1, 1998.

I'VE ALWAYS WANTED TO WRITE BUT—BEGINNERS' CLASS, Villa 30, 23350 Sereno Ct., Cupertino CA 95014. (415)691-0300. Contact: Louise Purwin Zobel. Writer workshops geared toward beginner and intermediate levels. "This seminar/workshop starts at the beginning, although the intermediate writer will benefit, too. There is discussion of children's magazine and book literature today, how to write it and how to market it. Also, there is discussion of other types of writing and the basics of writing for publication." Annual workshops. "Usually held several times a year; fall, winter and spring." Sessions last 1-2 days. Cost of workshop: $45-65/day, depending on the campus; includes extensive handout. Write with SASE for more information.

LET'S WRITE, WRITERS' GUILD OF ACADIANA, (formerly Do Write, Writer's Guild of Acadiana), P.O. Box 51532, Lafayette LA 70505-1532. Contact: Marilyn Conting (318)981-5153 or Ro Foley (318)234-8694. Writer conference geared toward beginner and intermediate levels. "We invite children's writers and agents, among other genres. The conference is not geared only to children's writings." Annual conference. Conference held April 3-4, 1998. Registration limited to 125. Cost of workshop: $90 member/$115 nonmember; includes 2 days of about 20 various sessions, some geared to children's writers; Friday night dinner, Saturday continental breakfast and luncheon; Friday and Saturday autograph teas; a chance to have your ms looked at by agents. Also includes a year membership to Writer's Guild of Acadiana. Write for more information.

LIGONIER VALLEY WRITERS CONFERENCE, P.O. Box B, Ligonier PA 15658-1602. (412)238-5749. Fax: (412)593-2113. Director: Tina Thoburn. Writer and illustrator workshops geared toward intermediate level. Workshops are geared toward developing stories and characters that lend themselves to clear illustration. Annual workshop. Minimal facilities available. Cost of workshop: $250; includes tuition and a luncheon. Write for more information.

*JACK LONDON WRITERS' CONFERENCE, 135 Clark Dr., San Mateo CA 94402-1002. (415)615-8331. Fax: (415)342-9155. Coordinator: Marlo Faulkner. Writer workshops geared toward beginner, intermediate, advanced and professional levels. Sample workshop subjects include agents/editors, editing and poetry. Annual workshop. Workshop held the first or second weekend in March. The conference is a program of speakers, panels and workshops—writing depends on the workshop leader. Cost of workshop: $95; includes continental breakfast, lunch, all programs and Ask a Pro sessions. Write for more information.

MANHATTANVILLE WRITERS' WEEK, Manhattanville College, 2900 Purchase St., Purchase NY 10577. (914)694-3425. Fax: (914)694-3488. Dean, Adult and Special Programs: Ruth Dowd. Writer workshops geared toward beginner, intermediate and advanced levels. Writers' week offers a special workshop for writers interested in children's/young adult writing. We have featured such workshop leaders as: Patricia Gauch, Patricia Horner, Elizabeth Winthrop and Lore Segal. Annual workshop held last week in June. Length of each session: one week. Cost of workshop: $600 (non-credit); includes a full week of writing activities, 5-day workshop on children's literature, lectures, readings, sessions with editors and agents, etc. Workshop may be taken for 2 graduate credits. Write for more information.

MAPLE WOODS COMMUNITY COLLEGE WRITERS' CONFERENCE, 2601 NE Barry Rd., Kansas City MO 64156. (816)437-3011. Director Community Education: Paula Schumacher. Writer workshops geared toward beginner, intermediate levels. Various writing topics and genres covered. Conference held September 26, 1998. Length of each session: 1 hour. Registration limited to 250. Cost of workshop: $68; includes continental breakfast, refreshments and two networking sessions.

♣MARITIME WRITERS' WORKSHOP, Department Extension & Summer Session, P.O. Box 4400, University of New Brunswick, Fredericton, New Brunswick E3B 5A3 Canada. (506)453-4646. Fax: (506)453-3572. E-mail: extensin.unb.ca. Coordinator: Glenda Turner. Week-long workshop on writing for children, general approach, dealing with submitted material, geared to all levels and held July 5-11, 1998. Annual workshop. 3 hours/day. Group workshop plus individual conferences, public readings, etc. Registration limited to 10/class. Cost of workshop: $325 tuition; includes tuition only. Meals and accommodations extra. 10-20 ms pages due before conference (deadline announced). Scholarships available.

*MIDLAND WRITERS CONFERENCE, Grace A. Dow Memorial Library, 1710 W. St. Andrews, Midland MI 48640-2968. (517)835-7151. Fax: (517)835-9791. E-mail: kred@vlc.lib.mi.us. Conference Chair: Katherine Redwine. Writer and illustrator workshops geared toward all levels. "Each year, we offer a topic of interest to writers of children's literature. Last year, Gloria Whelan spoke on writing historical fiction for children." Classes offered include: how to write poetry, writing for youth, your literary agent/what to expect. Annual workshop. Workshops held usually second Saturday in June. Length of each session: concurrently, 4 1-hour and 2 2-hour sessions. Maximum class size: 40. "We are a public library." Cost of workshop: $60; $50 seniors and students; includes choice of workshops and the keynote speech given by a prominent author (last year Roger Ebert). Write for more information.

*MIDWEST WRITERS' CONFERENCE, 6000 Frank Ave. NW, Canton OH 44720-7599. (330)499-9600. Fax: (330)494-6121. E-mail: druhe@stork.kent.edu. Assistant Director: Debbie Ruhe. Writer workshops geared toward beginner, intermediate and advanced levels. Topics include: Fiction, Nonfiction, Juvenile Literature, Poetry and a rotating category. Titles for Juvenile Literature have included Writing as Power, Writing for Children, and Lifting Them Up to Our Windows: Writing for Kids. Annual conference. Conference held early October. Length of each session: 1 hour. Registration limited to 400 total people. Cost of workshop: $65; includes Friday afternoon workshops, keynote address, Saturday workshops, box lunch, up to 2-ms entries in contest. Write for more information.

‡MIDWEST WRITERS WORKSHOP, College of Communication, Ball State University, Muncie IN 47306. (765)285-6000. Fax: (765)285-6002. Director: Earl L. Conn. Writer workshops geared toward intermediate level. Topics include fiction and nonfiction writing. Annual workshop. Workshop held July 29-August 1, 1998. Registration tentatively limited to 135. Cost of workshop: $175; includes everything but room and meals. Write for more information.

MISSISSIPPI VALLEY WRITERS CONFERENCE, 3403 45th St., Moline IL 61265. Conference Director: David R. Collins. Writer workshops geared toward all levels. Classes offered include Juvenile Writing—1 of 9 workshops offered. Annual workshop. Workshops held June 7-12, 1998; usually it is the second week in June each year. Length of each session: Monday-Friday, 1 hour each day. Registration limited to 20 participants/workshop. Writing facilities available: college library. Cost of workshop: $25 registration; $50 to participate in 1 workshop, $90 in 2, $30 for each additional; $25 to audit a workshop. Write for more information.

*MONTROSE CHRISTIAN WRITER'S CONFERENCE, 5 Locust St., Montrose PA 18801-1112. (717)278-1001. Fax: (717)278-3061. E-mail: mbc@epix.net. Executive Director: Jim Fahringer. Writer workshops geared toward beginner, intermediate and advanced levels. Annual workshop. Workshop held in July. Cost of workshop: $90-100; includes tuition. Write for more information.

MOUNT HERMON CHRISTIAN WRITERS CONFERENCE, Mount Hermon Christian Conference Center, P.O. Box 413, Mount Hermon CA 95041-0413. (408)335-4466. Fax: (408)335-9218. E-mail: mhtalbott@aol.com. Director of Specialized Programs: David R. Talbott. Writer workshops geared toward all levels. Emphasizes religious writing for children via books, articles; Sunday school curriculum; marketing. Classes offered include: Suitable Style for Children; Everything You Need to Know to Write and Market Your Children's Book; Take-Home Papers for Children. Workshops held annually over Palm Sunday weekend: April 3-7, 1998. Length of each session: 5-day residential conferences held annually. Registration limited 45/class, but most are 10-15. Conference center with hotel-style accommodations. Cost of workshop: $450-675 variable; includes tuition, resource notebook, refreshment breaks, full room and board for 13 meals and 4 nights. Write for more information.

THE NATIONAL WRITERS ASSOCIATION CONFERENCE, Suite 424, 1450 S. Havana, Aurora CO 80012. (303)751-7844. Executive Director: Sandy Whelchel. Writer workshops geared toward all levels. Classes offered include marketing, agenting, "What's Hot in the Market." Annual workshop. "In 1997 the workshop will be held in Denver, Colorado, June 13-15. Write for more information.

‡NEW ENGLAND WRITERS' WORKSHOP AT SIMMONS COLLEGE, 300 The Fenway, Boston MA 02115. (617)521-2220. Fax: (617)521-3199. Conference Administrator: Cynthia Grady. Writers' workshops geared toward intermediate and advanced levels. Writing workshops focusing on novels and short stories. We may be adding a children's literature section for 1998. Annual workshop. Workshop held mid-June, Monday-Friday. Registration limited to 45. Writing facilities available: computer labs and equipment in library. Cost of workshop: $550; includes workshop, individual ms consultation. Write for more information.

NORTH CAROLINA WRITERS' NETWORK FALL CONFERENCE, P.O. Box 954, Carrboro NC 27510. (919)967-9540. Fax: (919)929-0535. E-mail: ncwn@sunsite.unc.edu. Website: http://sunsite.unc.edu/ncwriters. Writer workshops geared toward beginner, intermediate, advanced and professional levels. "We offer workshops and critique sessions in a variety of genres: fiction, poetry, children's. Past young adult and children's writing classes include: 'Everybody's Got a Story to Tell—or Write!' with Eleanora Tate; 'Writing Young Adult Fiction' with Sarah Dessen." Annual conference. Conference held November 20-22, 1998 (Winston-Salem, NC). Cost of workshop: approximately $130-145, includes workshops, panel discussions, 3 meals.

*NORTHWEST OKLAHOMA WRITERS WORKSHOP, P.O. Box 5994, Enid OK 73702-5994. (405)237-2744. E-mail: scrybr8@prodigy.net. Website: http://www.geocities.com/Athens/Acropolis/8817/. Workshop Chairman: Bev Walton-Porter. Writer workshops geared toward beginner, intermediate, advanced and professional levels. Annual workshop. Workshop held in spring (usually March). Cost of workshop: $40; includes registration, handouts. Write or call for more information. "Our workshops are not geared, per se, to children's writers. We generally have one speaker for the day. Past speakers were Norma Jean Lutz, Mary Elizabeth Lynn, Deborah Bouziden, Anna Meyers (the only time we've had a children's writer), Sandra Soli and Marcia Preston. The speaker for the 1998 workshop has not yet been determined. "Look for details around February in *Writer's Digest* or *Byline Magazine*."

*OHIO KENTUCKY INDIANA CHILDREN'S LITERATURE CONFERENCE, % Greater Cincinnati Library Consortium, 3333 Vine St., Suite 605, Cincinnati OH 45220. (513)751-4422. Fax: (513)751-0463. E-mail: gclc@uc.edu. Website: http://www.libraries.uc.edu/gclc/. Staff Development Coordinator: Ronald Frommeyer. Writer and illustrator conference geared toward all levels. 1997 conference keynote speakers: Isaac Olaleye, Chris Soentpiet, Louise Borden. Tristate Authors & Illustrators Showcase; workshops by children's literature specialists/authors/illustrators including: Marie Bradby, Omope Carter Daboiku, Sue Eades, Mary Kay Kroeger, Katherine Roundtree and Anita Haller (storytelling). Annual conference. Conference held November 7, 1998. Registration limited to 250. Cost of conference: $25; includes registration/attendance at all workshop sessions, coffee break, lunch, author/illustrator signings. Write for more information.

OKLAHOMA FALL ARTS INSTITUTES, P.O. Box 18154, Oklahoma City OK 73154. (405)842-0890. Fax: (405)848-4538. Website: okarts@telepath.com. Assistant Program Director: Linda DeBerry. Writer and illustrator workshops geared toward intermediate, advanced and professional levels. Writing topics include children's writing, fiction, nonfiction, poetry, art of teaching writing, painting, drawing, printmaking. Annual workshop. Visual arts workshop held in early October; writing workshops in late October. Registration is limited to 20 participants per workshop; 5 workshops each weekend. Cost of workshop: $450; includes tuition, double-occupancy room and board. Write for more information. "Catalogues are available. Each workshop is taught by a professional artist of national reputation."

OUTDOOR WRITERS ASSOCIATION OF AMERICA ANNUAL CONFERENCE, 2155 E. College Ave., State College PA 16801-7204. (814)234-1011. Fax: (814)234-9692. E-mail: 76711.1725@compuserve.com.

Meeting Planner: Eileen King. Writer workshops geared toward all levels. Annual workshop. Workshop held in June. Cost of workshop: $130; includes attendance at all workshops and most meals. Attendees must have prior approval from Executive Director before attendance is permitted. Write for more information.

OZARK CREATIVE WRITERS, INC. CONFERENCE, 6817 Gingerbread Lane, Little Rock AR 72204. (501)565-8889. Fax: (510)565-7220. Counselor: Peggy Vining. Writer's workshops geared to all levels. "All forms of the creative process dealing with the literary arts. We have expanded to songwriting. We invite excellent speakers who are selling authors. We also promote writing by providing competitions in all genres." Always the second full weekend in October at Inn of the Ozarks in Eureka Springs AR (a resort town). Held October 5-7, 1998. Morning sessions are given to main attraction author . . . 6 1-hour satellite speakers during each of the 2 afternoons. Two banquets. "Approximately 200 attend the conference yearly . . . many others enter the creative writing competition." Cost of registration/contest entry fee approximately $40-50. Includes entrance to all sessions, contest entry fees. "This does not include meals or lodging. We block off 70 rooms prior to August 15 for OCW guests." Send #10 SASE for brochure by May 1st. "Reserve early. Camping is available."

PENNWRITERS ANNUAL CONFERENCE, 103 N. Elmer Ave., Suite 4, Sayre PA 18840. (717)888-1365. Fax: (717)888-4402. E-mail: pptc@cyberquest.com. Conference Coordinator: Candy Zulkosky. Writer workshops geared to all levels. Annual workshop. Workshop usually held third weekend in May. Cost of workshop: $90; includes Saturday workshops, lunch, book signing tea. Additional fee for networking dinner Friday and Saturday nights and breakfast Sunday. Write for more information. Other workshops and 1-day seminars on writing for children as well as other category genre are held by Pennwriters throughout the year. For more information contact Candy Zulkosky. "Pennwriters is dedicated to helping beginners—getting valuable information into their hands, helping them with the basics. We also do a lot for our members who have become published by sponsoring book signings, sending out newsletters and providing other help."

‡*PERSPECTIVES IN CHILDREN'S LITERATURE CONFERENCE, School of Education, 226 Furcolo Hall, University of Massachusetts, Amherst MA 01003-3035. (413)545-4325 or (413)545-1116. Fax: (413)545-2879. E-mail: rudman@educ.umass.edu. Director of Conference: Dr. Masha K. Rudman. Writer and illustrator workshops geared to all levels. Emphasis varies from year to year. "We always have an editor who brings us up to date on the status of children's literature and we always have at least two illustrators. Next year one of them will be Ashley Bryan. Presentors talk about how they broke into publishing and what guides them now." Next conference held April 4, 1998, 8 am-4 pm, 4 sessions approximately 1 hour each. Registration limited to 500. Cost of workshop: $55, $50 for SCBWI members; includes lunch, snacks and drinks, 10% discount on books purchased. $178 package for 1 academic credit also available; a 1-page response to either 2 workshops or 1 workshop and 1 keynote speaker required.

*PHOTOGRAPHY: A DIVERSE FOCUS, 895 W. Oak St., Zionsville IN 46077-1208. Phone/fax: (317)873-0738. Director: Charlene Faris. Writer and illustrator workshops geared to beginners. "Conferences focus primarily on children's photography; also literature and illustration. Annual conferences are held very often throughout year." Registration is not limited, but "sessions are generally small." Cost of conference: $150 (2 days), $80 (1 day). "Inquiries with an SASE only will receive information on seminars."

PORT TOWNSEND WRITER'S CONFERENCE, Centrum, P.O. Box 1158, Port Townsend WA 98368. (310)385-3102. Director: Sam Hammil. Writer workshops geared toward intermediate, advanced and professional levels. Emphasizes writing for children and young adults. Classes offered include: poetry, fiction, nonfiction and writing for children. Workshops held 10 days in mid-July. Registration limited to 16/class. Writing facilities available: classrooms. Cost of workshop: $425 tuition, open enrollment $300. Publication list for master class. Write for more information. $100 deposit necessary. Applications accepted after December 1 for following July; workshops fill by February.

GARY PROVOST'S WRITERS RETREAT WORKSHOP, (formerly Writers Retreat Workshop), % Write It/Sell It, South Lancaster MA 01561. (800)642-2494 (for brochure). Writer workshops geared toward beginner, intermediate and advanced levels. Workshops are appropriate for writers of full length novels for children/YA. Also, for writers of all novels or narrative nonfiction. Annual workshop. Workshops held in May. Registration limited to small groups: beginners and advanced. Writing facilities available: private 9 with desks. Cost of workshop: $1,595; includes tuition, food and lodging for 9 nights, daily classes, writing space, time and assignments, consultation and instruction. Requirements: short synopsis required to determine appropriateness of novel for our nuts and bolts approach to getting the work in shape for publication. Write for more information. For complete details, call 800 number.

ROBERT QUACKENBUSH'S CHILDREN'S BOOK WRITING AND ILLUSTRATING WORK-SHOP, 460 E. 79th St., New York NY 10021-1443. Phone/fax: (212)744-3822. E-mail: naap95@aol.com. (E-mail inquirers please include mailing address). Contact: Robert Quackenbush. Writer and illustrator workshops geared toward all levels. Emphasizes picture books from start to finish. Also covered is writing fiction and nonfiction for middle grades and young adults, if that is the attendees' interest. Current trends in illustration are also covered. Workshops held fall, winter and summer. Courses offered fall and winter include 10 weeks each—1½ hour/week; July workshop is a full 5-day (9 a.m.-4 p.m) extensive course. Registration limited to 10/class. Writing and/or art facilities available; work on the premises; art supply store nearby. Cost of workshop: $650 for instruction. Cost of workshop includes instruction in preparation of a ms and/or book dummy ready to submit to publishers. Attendees are responsible for arranging their own hotel and meals, although suggestions are given on request for places to stay and eat. "This unique five-day workshop, held annually since 1982, provides the opportunity to work with Robert Quackenbush, a prolific author and illustrator of children's books with more than 160 fiction and nonfiction books for young readers to his credit, including mysteries, biographies and songbooks."

SAN DIEGO STATE UNIVERSITY WRITERS' CONFERENCE, The College of Extended Studies, San Diego CA 92182-1920. (619)594-2517. Fax: (619)594-8566. E-mail: ealcaraz@mail.sdsu.edu. Website: http://rohan.sdsu.edu/dept/extstd/writers.html. Conference Facilitator: Erin Grady Alcaraz. Writer workshops geared toward beginner, intermediate and advanced levels. Emphasizes nonfiction, fiction, screenwriting, advanced novel writing; includes sessions specific to writing and illustrating for children. Workshops held third weekend in January each year. Registration limited. Cost of workshop: $215 if preregistered before January 10; includes Saturday reception, 2 lunches and all sessions and 1 read and critique appointment with an editor or agent. Write for more information or see our home page at the above Website.

‡SANDY COVE CHRISTIAN WRITERS CONFERENCE, 251 Water Works Rd., Coatesville PA 19320. (610)384-8125. Fax: (610)384-8125. Director: Gayle Roper. Writers conference geared to beginner and advanced writers. Offers 2-hour session for children's writers and 2-3 editors of children's publications are guest speakers. Annual conference beginning 1st Sunday in October. Cost of conference is $250; includes 5 continuing workshops, 45 one-time classes, keynote, editorial evaluations. Write for more information. "Sandy Cove is a general writing conference with children's writing as one aspect among many."

SEATTLE CHRISTIAN WRITERS CONFERENCE, P.O. Box 11337, Bainbridge Island WA 98110. (206)842-9103. Fax: (206)842-0536. Director: Elaine Colvin. Writer workshops geared toward all levels. Past conferences have featured subjects such as 'Making It to the Top as a Children's Book Author,' featuring Debbie Trafton O'Neal. Quarterly workshop (4 times/year). Workshop held September, January, March, June. Cost of workshop: $25. Write for more information.

SNAKE RIVER INSTITUTE, P.O. Box 128, Wilson WY 83014. (307)733-2214. Fax: (307)739-1710. E-mail: snakeriverinst@wyoming.com. Website: http://www.wyoming.com/jacksonhole/sri/. Writer and illustrator workshops geared toward all levels. "Our workshops are not geared specifically to children's writing and illustrating. However, we do offer a variety of writing and painting classes. They change every year." Workshop held summers—May-September; 3-5 day seminars. Registration limited to 15. Cost of workshop: $195-950; depends on the class—may include food, lodging. "We are a nonprofit organization. We offer arts and humanities classes based on the history and culture of the West. Classes are a variety of painting, photography, writing and history." Write for more information.

‡SOCIETY OF CHILDREN'S BOOK WRITERS AND ILLUSTRATORS—CAROLINAS ANNUAL FALL CONFERENCE, 104 Barnhill Place, Chapel Hill NC 27514-9224. (919)967-2452 or (910)288-6606. Fax: (919)929-6643. E-mail: 73522.1456@compuserve.com. Coordinator: Ellen Bryant Lloyd. Writer and illustrator conference geared toward beginner, intermediate, advanced and professional levels. Sessions include "How to Write a Children's Book and Get It Published" by Keynote speaker Barbara Seuling. Other speakers include Marilee Robinson, *Highlights for Children*; Virginaia Writght Frierson, author/illustrator; Jackie Ogburn, former editor Lothrop, Lee & Shepherd; Ludli Grey; Cathy Dubrowski (early readers); Fran Davis (nonfiction). Annual conference held late October or early November. Cost of conference is $60 for SCBWI members before October 1st, $65 after October 1st. $65 for NCWN members before October 1st, $75 after October 1st. $70 for nonmembers before October 1st, $75 after October 1st. Critiques for writing. Portfolios will be displayed, not critiqued. Write for more information.

SOCIETY OF CHILDREN'S BOOK WRITERS AND ILLUSTRATORS—FLORIDA REGION, 2158 Portland Ave., Wellington FL 33414. (561)798-4824. E-mail: barcafer@aol.com. Florida Regional Advisor: Barbara Casey. Writer and illustrator workshops geared toward beginner, intermediate, advanced and professional levels. Subjects to be announced. Annual workshop. Workshop held second Saturday of September in the meeting rooms of the Palm Springs Public Library, 217 Cypress Lane, Palm Springs FL. Registration limited to 100/class. Cost of workshop: $50 for members, $55 for non-members. Special rates are offered through the West Palm Beach Airport Hilton Hotel for those attending the conference who wish to spend the night. Write for more information.

SOCIETY OF CHILDREN'S BOOK WRITERS AND ILLUSTRATORS—HAWAII, 2355 Ala Wai Blvd. #502, Honolulu HI 96815-3404. (808)926-0115. E-mail: dmasters@sprynet.com. Regional Advisor: Elaine Masters. Writer and illustrator conferences geared toward all levels. Conferences feature general topics—writing, illustrating, publishing and marketing; also specific skills workshops teach plotting, characterization, etc. Quarterly workshops. Workshops held February 15 and April, 1998. Cost varies, includes instruction and light refreshments. Reduced rate for SCBWI members. Open to nonmembers. SASE for more information.

‡SOCIETY OF CHILDREN'S BOOK WRITERS AND ILLUSTRATORS—ILLINOIS SPRING RETREAT—THE WRITE CONNECTION: 3 ACQUIRING EDITORS, 2408 Elmwood, Wilmette IL 60091. (847)256-4494. Fax: (847)256-9462. E-mail: esthersh@aol.com. Regional Advisor, SCBWI-Illinois: Esther Hershenhorn.
● The workshop is held in Woodstock, Illinois.
Writer workshops geared toward intermediate, advanced and professional levels. Offers teaching sessions; open mike; ms critiques; panel discussions; editor presentations. Biannual workshop. Workshop held Friday, May 15-Sunday, May 17, 1998. Registration limited to 55. Writing facilities available: shared and individual rooms. Cost of workshop: $235 SCBWI members; $260 non-members; includes room, board, meals, snacks. "Manuscript critiques available for $30—must be mailed in by March 1, 1998."

SOCIETY OF CHILDREN'S BOOK WRITERS AND ILLUSTRATORS—INDIANA SPRING WRITERS' CONFERENCE, P.O Box 36, Garrett IN 46738. E-mail: 70334.1145@compuserve.com. Conference Directors: Lola M. Schaefer and Sarah Murray-Palmer. Writer and illustrator workshops geared toward all levels. All are geared toward children's writers and illustrators. Conference held annually in June. 1998 conference: June 13. Length of each session: 45 minutes to 1½ hours. Cost of workshop: approximately $55; includes meal and workshops. Write for more information.

*SOCIETY OF CHILDREN'S BOOK WRITERS AND ILLUSTRATORS—MICHIGAN WORKING WRITERS AND ILLUSTRATORS RETREAT, 5859 124th Ave., Fennville MI 49408. (616)561-2850. Retreat Chair: Joan Donaldson. Writer and illustrator workshops geared toward intermediate and advanced levels. Topics include critique groups for both writers or illustrators of children's literature. This year will feature a hands-on writing workshop; ms/dummy workshopping group sessions (peer critique facilitated by an experienced writer and/or illustrator); and editors' workshops on writing adventure stories and marketing (workshop subjects vary from year to year). Annual workshop. Workshop held October 23-25. Registration limited to approximately 40. Cost of workshop $170 (to members); includes meals, lodging, registration. Those wishing an individual ms critique by a member of the faculty should send a copy of their ms, neatly typed and double-spaced, with a check for $35 to Joan Donaldson before September 6. (Limit: complete picture book text, or 1 chapter of a novel or nonfiction work, or a complete magazine story.) Write for more information.

SOCIETY OF CHILDREN'S BOOK WRITERS AND ILLUSTRATORS—MIDSOUTH SPRING CONFERENCE, (formerly Society of Children's Book Writers and Illustrators—Tennessee/Kentucky Spring Conference), Box 3342, Clarksville TN 37043-3342. (615)358-9849. E-mail: czauthor@aol.com. Regional Advisor: Cheryl Zach. Writer workshop geared toward all levels. Illustrator workshops geared toward beginner and intermediate levels. Previous workshop topics have included Editor's Perspective, Writing Query Letters, Writing Picture Books, Marketing Your Artwork, Mining History for Ideas, What Books Do Children's Librarians Want To See?, Whodunit: Writing Juvenile Mysteries, Writing About Koalas and Quantum Physics, Writing a Series, Successful School Visits, Book Contracts, Writing for Magazines. Workshop held in the spring (April 5, 1998). 1 day. Cost of workshop: $60 SCBWI members, $65 nonmembers; includes all day of workshops and lunch. Registration limited to 100. "SCBWI-Midsouth 1998 is scheduled for April 25 in Nashville." Send SASE for flier.

SOCIETY OF CHILDREN'S BOOK WRITERS AND ILLUSTRATORS—MINNESOTA, 7060 Valley Creek Rd., Suite 115215, Woodbury MN 55125. (612)739-0119. E-mail: kidlit@juno.com. Minnesota Regional Advisor: Peg Helminski. Writer and illustrator workshops geared toward beginner, intermediate, advanced and professional levels. All of our workshops and conferences focus on the needs of children's writers and illustrators. Critique sessions and portfolio reviews are often available. "We try to have at least one full day conference and one evening event per year." Conferences are held in April and October. Cost of conference: varies $20-85. Full day conferences usually include luncheon, coffee breaks and snack. Evening workshops usually include snack. SASE for more information 6 weeks prior to each event.

‡SOCIETY OF CHILDREN'S BOOK WRITERS AND ILLUSTRATORS—NEW YORK—CONFERENCE IN CHILDREN'S LITERATURE, P.O. Box 20233, Park West Finance Station New York NY 10025-1511. Conference Chairman: Kimberly Colen. Writer and illustrator conference geared toward all levels. Annual conference. Workshop held usually the first or second Saturday in November. Length of each session: 1 hour, 15 minutes. Registration limited to 400. Cost of conference: $75, nonmembers; $70, members; includes continental breakfast, lunch and a day of meeting authors, illustrators, publishers, editors and agents. Write for more information.

SOCIETY OF CHILDREN'S BOOK WRITERS AND ILLUSTRATORS—NORCAL RETREAT AT ASILOMAR, 1316 Rebecca Dr., Suisun CA 94585-3603. (707)426-6776. Fax: (707)427-2885. Regional Advisor: Bobi Martin. Writer and illustrator workshops geared toward beginner, intermediate, advanced and professional levels. Emphasizes various topics from writing or illustrating picture books to young adult novels. Past speakers include agents, publishers, editors, published authors and illustrators. Annual workshop. Workshop generally held last weekend in February; Friday evening through Sunday lunch. Registration limited to 65. Rooms are shared with 1 other person. Desks available in most rooms. All rooms have private baths. Cost of workshop: $225 SCBWI members; $250 nonmembers; includes shared room, 6 meals, ice breaker party and conference. A full scholarship is available to SCBWI members. Call Bobi Martin for application procedure. Registration opens October 1st and usually is full by October 31st. A waiting list is formed. SASE for more information. "This is a small retreat with a relaxed pace."

‡*SOCIETY OF CHILDREN'S WRITERS AND ILLUSTRATORS—NORTH CENTRAL TEXAS, c/o Conference co-Director Diane Roberts (writers' contact), 6840 Fortnue Road, Fort Worth TX 76116. (817)738-5390. E-mail: DRaccoon@aol.com or Conference co-Director Peggy Freeman, (illustrators' contact) 734 Walnut Ridge Court, Cedar Hill TX 75104. (972)299-9739. E-mail: freeman@webwide.com. Annual conference geared toward professional writers and illustrators. "We usually have an editor from major NY publisher, agent, authors, illustrators and art directors. Jane Yolen is a confirmed speaker for 1998." Conference held October 10, 1998. Conference includes arts roundtable for showing portfolios, manuscript consultations. Cost of conference: $55 for SCBWI members, $60 for non-members, includes lunch and all-day conference. For an extra $25 fee art and manuscript consultations by speakers are available. Must submit by a deadline about 3 months before conference. Write to Diane Roberts (writers) or Peggy Freeman (illustrators) for more information. Conference is held in the Dallas/Ft. Worth Metroplex.

SOCIETY OF CHILDREN'S BOOK WRITERS AND ILLUSTRATORS—SOUTHERN BREEZE (ALABAMA/GEORGIA/MISSISSIPPI REGION), P.O. Box 26282, Birmingham AL 35260. Fax: (205)979-0274. E-mail: joanbroer@aol.com. Regional Advisor: Joan Broerman. "The fall conference offers more than 20 workshops on craft, from entry level to professional track, picture books to young adult. This year also includes a panel discussion titled 'Tracking the Trends.' Annual workshop. Workshop held October 17, 1998. Cost of workshop: $50-60 for SCBWI members; $60-80 for nonmembers; ms critiques and portfolio review available for additional cost. Write for more information (include SASE). "Our spring conference, Springmingle!, is in different parts of the three-state region. Springmingle '98! will be held in Hattiesburg, MS in mid-March 1998." Preregistration important for both conferences.

‡SOCIETY OF CHILDREN'S BOOKS WRITERS AND ILLUSTRATORS—SOUTHERN CALIFORNIA; ILLUSTRATOR'S DAY, 5632 Van Nuys Blvd., #292, Van Nuys CA 91401. (818)785-7282. Co-regional Advisor: Julie Williams. Illustrators sessions geared toward all levels. Emphasizes illustration and illustration markets. Conference includes presentations by art director, children's book editor, and artist/author-illustrators. This conference has been held annually in the fall, but will be in February beginning with February 1999. "Editors and art directors will view portfolios. We want to know whether or not each conferee is bringing a portfolio." Cost of conference: $70-85; included entire day of speakers and open marketplace ($10 extra for private portfolio review.)

‡SOCIETY OF CHILDREN'S BOOKS WRITERS AND ILLUSTRATORS—SOUTHERN CALIFORNIA; WRITER'S DAY, 5632 Van Nuys Blvd., #292, Van Nuys CA 91401. (818)785-7282. Co-regional Advisor: Julie Williams. A one-day conference for children's books writers geared toward all levels. Emphasizes fiction and nonfiction writing for children from picture books through young adult. Conference includes presentations by a children's book editor and children's book authors. Annual conference held in spring. Cost of conference: $70-85; includes entire day of speakers and a Writer's Day Contest.

SOCIETY OF CHILDREN'S BOOK WRITERS AND ILLUSTRATORS—VENTURA/SANTA BARBARA FALL CONFERENCE, 1001 Hillview Lane, Simi Valley CA 93065. (805)581-1906. Regional Advisor: Alexis O'Neill. Writers conference geared toward all levels. "We invite editors, authors and author/illustrators and agents. We have had speakers on the picture book, middle grade, YA, magazine and photo essay books. Both fiction and nonfiction are covered." Conference held in November from 9:00 a.m.-4 p.m. on Saturdays. Cost of conference $55; includes all sessions and lunch. Write for more information.

SOCIETY OF CHILDREN'S BOOK WRITERS & ILLUSTRATORS—WISCONSIN ANNUAL FALL RETREAT, Rt. 1, Box 137, Gays Mills WI 54631. (608)735-4707. Fax: (608)735-4700. E-mail: pfitsch@mwt.net. Regional Advisor: Patricia Pfitsch. Writer workshops geared toward working writers. Some years we offer group critique sessions with faculty and participant participation—each full time participant receives critique from well-known editors, writers and or agents as well as other participants. Also talks by faculty on various aspects of writing and selling your work. "We try to have major New York editors, agents and well-known writers on the faculty. The entire retreat is geared *only* to children's book writing." Annual workshop. Retreat held in October or November, from Friday evening to Sunday afternoon. Registration limited to approximately 60. Cost of workshop: about 15-25; includes room, board and program. Critique may be extra. "We strive to offer an informal weekend with an award-winning children's writer, an agent or illustrator and an editor from a trade house in New York in attendance." There's usually a waiting list by mid-July. Send SASE for flier.

‡*SOFER, THE JEWISH WRITERS WORKSHOP, 555 Skokie Blvd., Suite 225, Northbrook IL 50062. (847)509-0990 ext. 12. Fax: (847)509-0970. E-mail: dunnfried@aol.com. Assistant Director: Deanne Dunn Friedman. Writers conference geared toward the intermediate, advanced and professional levels. Session cover creative nonfiction, fiction and playwriting. Speakers have included Roger Kamenetz and Howard Schwartz. Annual workshop held in August. Registiration limited to 100. Cost of workshop is $235-350, depending on chosen lodging and includes programming, lodging and meals. "We do ask for a writing sample, but acceptance is not based on it. Though most workshop leaders are not children's writers, they can advise on writing for children. We usually have several attendees who are children's writers." Write for more information.

‡SOUTH CAROLINA CHRISTIAN WRITERS CONFERENCE, P.O. Box 12624, Roanoke VA 24027. Phone/fax: (540)342-7511. E-mail: ccmbbr@juno.com. Director: Betty Robinson. Writer conference geared toward all levels. Annual conference. Conference held September 16, 1998. Cost of conference: $29.95 (early); $39.95 (regular tuition); includes free magazine samples, refreshments, choice of workshops. Write for more information.

*SOUTHEASTERN WRITER'S CONFERENCE, 5952 Alma Hwy., Waycross GA 31503. Phone/fax: (912)285-9159. Secretary: Nelle McFather. Writer workshops geared toward beginner and intermediate levels. Offers a 5-session juvenile writing class. Annual conference held on St. Simon's Island, GA. Conference held June 21-26, 1998. Registration limited to 100. Cost of workshops: $245; includes tuition only. "Attendees may submit one chapter of three different manuscripts for free professional critiques."

SOUTHWEST WRITERS WORKSHOP, Suite B, 1338 Wyoming Blvd. NE, Albuquerque NM 87112. (505)293-0303. Fax: (505)237-2665. Website: http://www.US1.net/sww/. Contact: Carol Bruce-Fritz, executive director. Writer workshops geared toward all genres at all levels of writing. Various aspects of writing covered. Examples from conferences: Preconference workshops on the juvenile/young adult/novel taught by Penny Durant; on picture books by April Halprin Wayland; on Writing a Juvenile Novel in 6 weeks by Shirley Raye Redmond; on writing for children's magazines by C. Walskel (of Cricket). Annual conference. Conference held September 18-20, 1998 at Albuquerque Convention Center. Length of each session: Friday-Sunday. Cost of workshop: $250 (approximately); includes all workshops and meals. Also offers ongoing writers' groups (for $35/year, offers 2 monthly meetings and occasional workshops). Write for more information.

SPACE COAST WRITERS GUILD, Box 804, Melbourne FL 32902. (407)727-0051. President: Dr. Edwin J. Kirschner. Guild geared toward beginner through professional writer levels. "Fact and Fiction" Speaker Series held annually; 5th-grade teacher and student writing contests conducted in the fall on the Space Coast of Florida. Call for more information.

‡*SPLIT ROCK ARTS PROGRAM, University of Minnesota, 306 Wesbrook Hall, 77 Pleasant St. SE, Minneapolis MN 55455-0216. (612)624-6800. Fax: (612)625-2568. E-mail: srap@mail.cee.umn.edu. Registrar: Danielle Porter. Writer and illustrator workshops geared toward intermediate, advanced and professional levels. Workshops offered in writing and illustrating books for children and young people. Workshops begin in July for 5 weeks. Two college credits available. Registration limited to 16 per class. Workshops held on the University of Minnesota-Duluth campus. Cost of workshop: $390; includes tuition and fees. Amounts vary depending on course fee, determined by supply needs, etc. "Moderately priced on-campus housing available." Complete catalogs available March 15. Call or write anytime to be put on mailing list. Some courses fill very early.

*STATE OF MAINE WRITERS' CONFERENCE, 47 Winona Ave., P.O. Box 7146, Ocean Park ME 04063-7146. (207)934-9806 (summer). (413)596-6734 (winter). Fax: (413)796-2121. E-mail: rburns0@kraken.mvnet.w nec.edu. Chairman: Richard F. Burns. Writers' workshops geared toward beginner, intermediate, advanced levels. Emphasizes poetry, prose, mysteries, editors, publishers, etc. Annual conference held August 25-28, 1998. Cost of workshop: $85 ($40 for students 22 and under); includes all sessions and banquet, snacks, poetry booklet. Send SASE for more information.

‡*SUMMER WRITING PROGRAM AT THE UNIVERSITY OF VERMONT, 322 S. Prospect St., Burlington VT 05401. (802)656-5796. Fax: (802) 656-0306. Website: http://uvmce.uvm.edu:443/sumwrite.htm. Coordinator: Heather Laszlo. Writer/Illustrator workshop geared toward beginner, intermediate, advanced and professional levels. Sessions include "Writing Picture Books for Children." Annual workshop held in July. Registration limited to 12 per workshop. Writing and art facilities available: computer labs. Cost of workshop: $790 for credit in-state (VT) or 0 credits out-of-state. $1682 for 3 credits out-of-state (subject to change for 1998). Writing sample required (up to 5 pages), brief bio sketch and $25 fee. Write for more information. "We offer room and board for participants, 2 week residency is $675 and 3 weeks is $950 (subject to change for 1998). We offer a host of student and faculty readings, picnics, one-and half-day seminars—plenty of opportunities to talk to and mingle with participants and faculty. Free and easy environment—supportive and friendly."

‡*UMKC/WRITERS PLACE WRITERS WORKSHOPS**, University of Missouri—Kansas City, 5100 Rockhill Rd., 215 55B, Kansas City MO 64110-2499. (816)235-2736. Fax: (816)235-5279. E-mail: mckinlem@s mtpgate.umkc.edu. Continuing Education Manager: Mary Ann McKinley. Writer workshops geared toward intermediate, advanced and professional levels. Semi-annual workshops. Workshop held in fall and spring. Registration limited to 25. Cost of workshop: $65. "Credit fees vary depending on level. Write for more information.

♣*VANCOUVER INTERNATIONAL WRITERS FESTIVAL**, 1243 Cartwright St., Vancouver, British Columbia V6H 4B7 Canada. (604)681-6330. Fax: (604)681-8400. E-mail: vifw@axionet.com. Website: http:// www.axionet.com/writerfest. Producer: Alma Lee. "The mission of the Vancouver International Writers Festival is to encourage an appreciation of literature and to promote literacy by providing a forum where writers and readers can interact. This is accomplished by the production of special events and an annual Festival which feature writers from a variety of countries, whose work is compelling and diverse. The Festival attracts over 11,000 people and presents approximately 40 events in four venues during five days on Granville Island, located in the heart of Vancouver. The first 3 days of the festival are programmed for elementary and secondary school students." Annual festival. Held third week in October (5-day festival). All writers who participate are invited by the producer. The events are open to anyone who wishes to purchase tickets. Cost of events ranges from $10-15.

*VASSAR INSTITUTE OF PUBLISHING AND WRITING: CHILDREN'S BOOKS IN THE MARKETPLACE**, Box 300, Vassar College, Poughkeepsie NY 12604-0540. (914)437-5903. Fax: (914)437-7209. E-mail: mabruno@vassar.edu. Website: http://www.vassar.edu. Program Coordinator: Maryann Bruno. Director: Barbara Lucas. Writer and illustrator conference geared toward all levels. Emphasizes "the editorial, production, marketing and reviewing processes, on writing fiction and nonfiction for all ages, creating the picture book, understanding the markets and selling your work." Workshop usually held in mid-June. Length of each session: 3½-hour morning critique sessions, afternoon and evening lectures. Registration limited to 25/class (with 2 instructors). Cost of conference: approximately $800, includes room, board and tuition for all critique sessions, lectures and social activities. "Proposals are pre-prepared and discussed at morning critique sessions. Art portfolio review given on pre-prepared works." Write for more information. "This conference gives a comprehensive look at the publishing industry as well as offering critiques of creative writing and portfolio review."

♣THE VICTORIA SCHOOL OF WRITING**, 607 Linden Ave., Victoria, British Columbia V8V 4G6 Canada. (250)385-8982. Fax: (250)995-9391. E-mail: writeawy@islandnet.com. Website: http://www.islandnet.com/ ~writeawy. Director: Margaret Dyment. Writer conference geared toward intermediate level. In the 1997 conference there will be 1 workshop on writing for children and young adults. Annual conference. Workshop held July 15-18, 1997. Registration limited to 100. Conference includes close mentoring from established writers. Cost of conference: $395 (Canada); $290 (U.S.); includes tuition and 1 brunch. To attend, submit 3-10 pages of writing samples. Write for more information.

VIRGINIA CHRISTIAN WRITERS CONFERENCE**, P.O. Box 12624, Roanoke VA 24027. Phone/fax: (540)342-7511. E-mail: ccmbbr@juno.com. Director: Betty Robertson. Writer conference geared toward all levels. Annual conference. Conference held April 4, 1998. Cost of conference: $29.95 (early); $39.95 (regular tuition); includes free magazine samples, refreshments, choice of workshops. Write for more information.

WELLS WRITERS' WORKSHOP**, 69 Broadway, Concord NH 03301. (603)225-3774. Fax: (603)225-9162. E-mail: forbine@forbine.mv.com. Coordinator: Vic Levine. Writer workshops geared toward beginner and intermediate levels. "Sessions focus on careful plot preparation, economical text and artwork relationship, as well as on effective writing (characterization, dialogue and exposition), with lots of time for writing." Workshops, which meet on Maine seacoast, are offered twice a year in May and September. Registration limited to 6/class. Writing facilities available: space, electrical outlets, resident Mac computer. Cost of workshop: $750. Write for more information. "I invite interested writers to call or write. I'd be happy to meet with them if they're reasonably close by. Workshop stresses the importance of getting the structure right when writing stories for children."

WESLEYAN WRITERS CONFERENCE**, Wesleyan University, Middletown CT 06459. (860)685-3604. Fax: (860)685-2441. E-mail: agreene@wesleyan.edu. Director: Anne Greene. Writer workshops geared toward all levels. "This conference is useful for writers interested in how to structure a story, poem or nonfiction piece. Although we don't always offer classes in writing for children, the advice about structuring a piece is useful for writers of any sort, no matter who their audience is." Classes in the novel, short story, fiction techniques, poetry, journalism and literary nonfiction. Guest speakers and panels offer discussion of fiction, poetry, reviewing, editing

♣ **CANADIAN LISTINGS** are marked with a maple leaf.

and publishing. Individual ms consultations available. Conference held annually the last week in June. Length of each session: 6 days. "Usually, there are 100 participants at the Conference." Classrooms, meals, lodging and word processing facilities available on campus. Cost of workshop: tuition—$450, room—$105, meals (required of all participants)—$185. "Anyone may register; people who want financial aid must submit their work and be selected by scholarship judges." Call for a brochure.

‡**WESTERN RESERVE WRITERS AND FREELANCE CONFERENCE**, Lakeland Community College, 7700 Clocktower Dr., Mentor OH 44060. (440)943-3047 or (800)OLDHAMI. E-mail: fa837@cleveland.freenet.edu. Coordinator: Lea Leever Oldham. Writer workshops geared toward all levels. Emphasizes fiction, photography, greeting card writing, science fiction, fantasy, children's writing, poetry. Classes offered include: All-day conference. Cost of workshop: $49 plus lunch. Write for more information to #110, 34200 Ridge Rd., Willoughby OH 44094. (440)943-3047.

‡**WESTERN RESERVE WRITERS MINI CONFERENCE**, 34200 Ridge Rd. #110, Willoughby OH 44094-2954. (440)943-3047 or (800)OLDHAMI. E-mail: fa837@cleveland.freenet.edu. Coordinator: Lea Leever Oldham. Writer workshops geared toward beginner, intermediate and advanced levels. Topics include query letters, marketing, editing, grammar and other specifics about selling what you write. Annual workshop. Workshop held in October at Lakeland Community College, Mentor OH. Cost of workshop: $29. Write for more information.

***WRITE FOR SUCCESS WORKSHOP: CHILDREN'S BOOKS**, 3748 Harbor Heights Dr., Largo FL 33774. (813)581-2484. Workshop Leader: Theo Carroll. Writer and illustrator workshops geared toward intermediate levels. Program covers: writing and defining the picture book, middle-grade novel, mystery and biography; finding and developing ideas; creating characters; plotting; writing dialogue; trends in publishing; developing conflict; revising. Annual workshop. Workshop held in March. Registration limited to 50-110. Cost of workshop: $85; includes hand outs and writers magazines. Write for more information.

***WILLAMETTE WRITERS ANNUAL WRITERS CONFERENCE**, 9045 SW Barbur Blvd., Suite 5A, Portland OR 97219. (503)452-1592. Fax: (503)452-0372. E-mail: wilwrite@teleport.com. Office Manager: Bill Johnson. Writer workshops geared toward all levels. Emphasizes all areas of writing, including children's and young adult. Opportunities to meet one-on-one with leading literary agents and editors. Workshops held in August. Cost of conference: $231; includes membership.

‡***WRITE PEOPLE LITERACY CONFERENCE**, P.O. Box 188, Scottville, MI 49454. Conference held at West Shore Community College, 3000 Stiles Rd, Scottville, MI 49454. (616)757-9432. Fax: (616)757-3801. Co-chair: Jacky Jeter (writers' contact) and Jean Stickney (illustrators' contact). Writer and illustrator conference geared toward: beginner, intermediate, advanced and professional levels. Conference held every other year on the first or second weekend in October. Registration to conference is not limited; however, individual sessions may be limited. Cost of conference is under $75 and includes continental breakfast Saturday, luncheon, coffee/tea/cookie breaks morning and afternoon. Friday evening is free to public. Write for more information.

‡**WRITE TO SELL WRITER'S CONFERENCE**, 8465 Jane St., San Diego CA 92129. (619)484-8575. Conference Director: Diane Dunaway. Writer and illustrator workshops geared toward beginner, intermediate, advanced and professional levels. Emphasizes How-to, Trends, Read and Critique; Workshops led by writers, editors and agents. Classes offered include: Writing the Picture Book, Middle Grade, YA, General Fiction, Nonfiction and Screen Writing; Illustrating for Children's Books. Workshops held third weekend in January. Length of each session: 50 minutes. Maximum class size: 100. Conference is held at San Diego State University; workshops are held in individual classrooms. Cost of conference: $210. Cost includes Friday evening through Sunday and 2 lunches. "Just bring chapters and/or artwork." Write for more information.

‡***THE WRITERS' CENTER AT CHAUTAUQUA**, Box 408, Chautauqua NY 14722-0408. (716)483-0381. Fax: (716)487-1281. E-mail: blsaid@mao.com. Director: Janette Martin. Writer workshops geared toward beginner and intermediate levels. Emphasizes poetry, fiction, nonfiction, at least 1 week of which is devoted to writing for children; for example, the elements of writing, slanted for children's writers: setting, characters, plot, conflict, etc. In general, workshops are a combination of teaching and editing students' work. Workshop held sometime between last week in June and last week in August. Registration limited to 25. Cost of workshop: $60. "Often a leader will invite students to submit their work for class discussion or for comments by the leader, but this is never a requirement." Write for more information. Mail should be addressed to 953 Forest Ave. Ext., RD3, Jamestown NY 14701. "A $10 membership in The Writers' Center at Chautauqua includes full information on each season, mailed out in March, with registration blank."

‡**WRITERS' FORUM**, 1570 E. Colorado Blvd., Pasadena CA 91106-2003. (818)585-7608. Coordinator of Forum: Meredith Brucker. Writer workshops geared toward all levels. Workshop held March 8, 1997. Length of session: 1 hour and 15 minutes including Q & A time. Cost of workshop: $100; includes lunch. Write for more information to Community Education, Pasadena City College, 1570 E. Colorado Blvd., Pasadena CA 91106-2003.

Contests & Awards

Publication is not the only way to get your work recognized. Contests can also be viable vehicles to gain recognition in the industry. Placing in a contest or winning an award validates the time spent writing and illustrating. Even for those who don't place, many competitions offer the chance to obtain valuable feedback from judges and other established writers or artists.

Not all of the contests here are strictly for professionals. Many are designed for those who have not yet been published. Several of the contests in this section are open to students (some exclusively). These are marked with an asterisk (*). Young writers can find additional contests in *Market Guide for Young Writers*, by Kathy Henderson (Writer's Digest Books).

When considering contests, be sure to study guidelines and requirements. Regard entry deadlines as gospel and note whether manuscripts and artwork should be previously published or unpublished. Also, be aware that awards vary. While one contest may award a significant amount of money, another may award a certificate or medal instead.

Note that some contests require nominations. For published authors and illustrators, competitions provide an excellent way to promote your work. Your publisher may not be aware of local competitions such as state-sponsored awards—if your book is eligible for a contest or award, have the appropriate person at your publishing company nominate or enter your work for consideration.

To select potential contests for your work, read through the listings that interest you, then send for more information about the types of written or illustrated material considered and other important details, such as who retains the rights to prize-winning material. A number of contests offer such information through websites given in their listings. If you are interested in knowing who has received certain awards in the past, check your local library or bookstores or consult *Children's Books: Awards & Prizes*, compiled and edited by the Children's Book Council. Many bookstores have special sections for books that are Caldecott and Newbery Medal winners.

Information on contests listed in the previous edition but not included in this edition of *Children's Writer's & Illustrator's Market* may be found in the General Index.

*AIM Magazine Short Story Contest, P.O. Box 20554, Chicago IL 60620. (773)874-6184. Contest Directors: Ruth Apilado, Mark Boone. Annual contest. Estab. 1983. Purpose of contest: "We solicit stories with social significance. Youngsters can be made aware of social problems through the written word and hopefully they will try solving them." Unpublished submissions only. Deadline for entries: August 15. SASE for contest rules and entry forms. SASE for return of work. No entry fee. Awards $100. Judging by editors. Contest open to everyone. Winning entry published in fall issue of *AIM*. Subscription rate $12/year. Single copy $4.50.

❧ALCUIN CITATION AWARD, The Alcuin Society, P.O. Box 3216, Vancouver, British Columbia V6B 3X8 Canada. (604)888-9049. Fax: (604)888-9052. Secretary: Doreen E. Eddy. Annual award. Estab. 1983. Purpose of contest: Alcuin Citations are awarded annually for excellence in Canadian book design. Previously published submissions only, "in the year prior to the Awards Invitation to enter; i.e., 1996 awards went to books published in 1995." Submissions made by the author, publishers and designers. Deadline for entries: March 15. SASE. Entry fee is $10. Awards certificate. Judging by professionals and those experienced in the field of book design. Requirements for entrants: Winners are selected from books designed and published in Canada. Awards are presented annually at the Annual General Meeting of the Alcuin Society held in late May or early June each year.

*AMERICA & ME ESSAY CONTEST, Farm Bureau Insurance, Box 30400, 7373 W. Saginaw, Lansing MI 48909-7900. (517)323-7000. Fax: (517)323-6615. Contest Coordinator: Lisa Fedewa. Annual contest. Estab. 1968. Purpose of the contest: to give Michigan 8th graders the opportunity to express their thoughts/feelings on America and their roles in America. Unpublished submissions only. Deadline for entries: mid-November. SASE for contest rules and entry forms. "We have a school mailing list. Any school located in Michigan is eligible to participate." Entries not returned. No entry fee. Awards savings bonds and plaques for state top ten ($500-1,000), certificates and plaques for top 3 winners from each school. Each school may submit up to 10 essays for judging. Judging by home office employee volunteers. Requirements for entrants: "Participants must work through their schools or our agents' sponsoring schools. No individual submissions will be accepted. Top ten essays and excerpts from other essays are published in booklet form following the contest. State capitol/schools receive copies."

‡AMERICAN ASSOCIATION OF UNIVERSITY WOMEN, NORTH CAROLINA DIVISION, AWARD IN JUVENILE LITERATURE, North Carolina Literary and Historical Association, 109 E. Jones St., Raleigh NC 27601-2807. (919)733-9375. Fax: (919)733-8807. Award Director: Dr. Jerry C. Cashion. Annual award. Purpose of award: To reward the creative activity involved in writing juvenile literature and to stimulate in North Carolina an interest in worthwhile literature written on the juvenile level. Must be published during the year ending June 30 of the year of publication. Submissions made by author, author's agent or publisher. Deadline for entries: 15 July. SASE. for contest rules. Awards a cup to the winner and winner's name inscribed on a plaque displayed within the North Carolina Division of Archives and History. Judging by Board of Award selected by sponsoring organization. Requirements for entrants: Author must have maintained either legal residence or actual physical residence, or a combination of both, in the State of North Carolina for three years immediately preceding the close of the contest period.

AMERICAS AWARD, Consortium of Latin American Studies Programs (CLASP), CLASP Committee on Teaching and Outreach, % Center for Latin America, University of Wisconsin-Milwaukee, P.O. Box 413, Milwaukee WI 53201. (414)229-5986. Fax: (414)229-2879. E-mail address: cla@csd.uwm.edu. Website: http://www.uwm.edu/Dept/CLA. Coordinator: Julie Kline. Annual award. Estab. 1993. Purpose of contest: "Two awards are given each spring in recognition of a U.S. published work (from the previous year) of fiction, poetry, folklore or selected nonfiction (from picture books to works for young adults) in English or Spanish which authentically and engagingly related to the Caribbean, or Latinos in the United States. By combining both and linking the "Americas," the intent is to reach beyond geographic borders, as well as multicultural-international boundaries, focusing instead upon cultural heritages within the hemisphere." Previously published submissions only. Submissions open to anyone with an interest in the theme of the award. Deadline for entries: January 15. SASE for contest rules and any committee changes. Awards $200 cash prize, plaque and a formal presentation at the Library of Congress, Washington DC. Judging by a review committee consisting of individuals in teaching, library work, outreach and children's literature specialists.

AMHA LITERARY CONTEST, American Morgan Horse Association Youth, P.O. Box 960, Shelburne VT 05482. (802)985-4944. Contest Director: Erica Richard. Annual contest. The contest includes categories for both poetry and essays. The 1996 theme was "If My Morgan Could Talk." Entrants should write to receive the 1998 entry form and theme. Unpublished submissions only. Submissions made by author. Deadline for entries: October 1. SASE for contest rules and entry forms. No entry fee. Awards $50 cash and ribbons to up to 5th place. "Winning entry will be published in *AMHA News and Morgan Sales Network*, a monthly publication."

AMHA MORGAN ART CONTEST, American Morgan Horse Association, Box 960, Shelburne VT 05482. (802)985-4944. Fax: (802)985-8897. E-mail: amha@together.net. Promotional Recognition Coordinator: Susan Bell. Annual contest. The art contest consists of two categories: Morgan art (pencil sketches, oils, water colors, paintbrush), Morgan specialty pieces (sculptures, carvings). Unpublished submissions only. Deadline for entries: October 1. Contest rules and entry forms available for SASE. Entries not returned. Entry fee is $2. Awards $50 first prize in 2 divisions (for adults) and AMHA gift certificates to top 5 places (for children). Judging by *The Morgan Horse* magazine staff. "All work submitted becomes property of The American Morgan Horse Association. Selected works may be used for promotional purposes by the AMHA." Requirements for entrants: "We consider all work submitted." Works displayed at the annual convention and the AMHA headquarters; published in *AMAHA News* and *Morgan Sales Network* and in color in *The Morgan Horse Magazine* (TMHA). The contest divisions consist of Junior (to age 17), Senior (18 and over) and Professional (commercial artists). Each art piece must have its own application form and its own entry fee. Matting is optional.

HANS CHRISTIAN ANDERSEN AWARD, IBBY International Board on Books for Young People, Nonnenweg 12, Postfach, CH-4003 Basel Switzerland. (004161)272 29 17. Fax: (004161)272 27 57. Award offered every two years. Purpose of award: A Hans Christian Andersen Medal shall be awarded every two years by the

---

✱ CONTESTS OPEN TO STUDENTS are marked with an asterisk.

International Board on Books for Young People (IBBY) to an author and to an illustrator, living at the time of the nomination, who by the outstanding value of their work are judged to have made a lasting contribution to literature for children and young people. The complete works of the author and of the illustrator will be taken into consideration in awarding the medal, which will be accompanied by a diploma. Previously published submissions only. Submissions are nominated by National Sections of IBBY in good standing. The National Sections select the candidates. The Hans Christian Andersen Award, named after Denmark's famous storyteller, is the highest international recognition given to an author and an illustrator of children's books. The Author's Award has been given since 1956, the Illustrator's Award since 1966. The Andersen Award is often called the "Little Nobel Prize." Her Majesty Queen Margrethe of Denmark is the Patron of the Hans Christian Andersen Awards. At the discretion of the jury the distinction "Highly Commended" may also be awarded. The Hans Christian Andersen Jury judges the books submitted for medals according to literary and artistic criteria.

*ARTS RECOGNITION AND TALENT SEARCH (ARTS), National Foundation for Advancement in the Arts, 800 Brickell Ave., Suite 500, Miami FL 33131. (305)377-1147. Fax: (305)377-1149. E-mail: nfaa@nffa.org. Website: http://www.nfaa.org. Contact: Laura Padrón. Open to students/high school seniors or 17 and 18-year-olds. Annual award. Estab. 1981. "Created to recognize and reward outstanding accomplishment in dance, music, jazz, theater, photography, visual arts and/or writing. Arts Recognition and Talent Search (ARTS) is an innovative national program of the National Foundation for Advancement in the Arts (NFAA). Established in 1981, ARTS touches the lives of gifted young people across the country, providing financial support, scholarships and goal-oriented artistic, educational and career opportunities. Each year, from a pool of nearly 8,000 applicants, an average of 400 ARTS awardees are chosen for NFAA support by panels of distinguished artists and educators. Deadline for entries: June 1 and October 1. SASE for award rules and entry forms. Entry fee is $25/35. Fee waivers available based on need. Awards $100-3,000—unrestricted cash grants. Judging by a panel of authors and educators recognized in the field. Rights to submitted/winning material: NFAA/ARTS retains the right to duplicate work in an anthology or in Foundation literature unless otherwise specified by the artist. Requirements for entrants: Artists must be high school seniors or, if not enrolled in high school, must be 17 or 18 years old. Applicants must be US citizens or residents, unless applying in jazz. Works will be published in an anthology distributed during ARTS Week, the final adjudication phase which takes place in Miami.

*BAKER'S PLAYS HIGH SCHOOL PLAYWRITING CONTEST, Baker's Plays, 100 Chauncy St., Boston MA 02111. (617)482-1280. Contest Director: Raymond Pape. Annual contest. Estab. 1990. Purpose of the contest: to acknowledge playwrights at the high school level and to insure the future of American theater. Unpublished submissions only. Deadline for entries: January 31 each year. Notification: May. SASE for contest rules and entry forms. No entry fee. Awards $500 to the first place playwright and Baker's Plays will publish the play; $250 to the second place playwright with an honorable mention; and $100 to the third place playwright with an honorable mention in the series. Judged anonymously. Open to any high school student. Teachers must not submit student's work. The first place playwright will have his/her play published in an acting edition the September following the contest. The work will be described in the Baker's Plays Catalogue, which is distributed to 50,000 prospective producing organizations. Plays must be accompanied by the signature of a sponsoring high school drama or English teacher, and it is recommended that the play receive a production or a public reading prior to the submission. "Please include a SASE."

BAY AREA BOOK REVIEWER'S ASSOCIATION (BABRA), % Chandler & Sharp, 11A Commercial Blvd., Novato CA 94949. (415)883-2353. Fax: (415)883-4280. Contact: Jonathan Sharp. Annual award for outstanding book in children's literature, open to Bay Area authors, northern California from Fresno north. Annual award. Estab. 1981. "BABRA presents annual awards to Bay Area (northern California) authors annually in fiction, nonfiction, poetry and children's literature. Purpose is to encourage Bay Area writers and stimulate interest in books and reading." Previously published submissions only. Must be published the calendar year prior to spring awards ceremony. Submissions nominated by publishers; author or agent could also nominate published work. Deadline for entries: December. No entry forms. Send 3 copies of the book to Jonathan Sharp. No entry fee. Awards $100 honorarium and award certificate. Judging by voting members of the Bay Area Book Reviewer's Association. Books that reach the "finals" (usually 3-5 per category) displayed at annual award ceremonies (spring). Nominated books are displayed and sold at BABRA's annual awards ceremonies, in the spring of each year.

JOHN AND PATRICIA BEATTY AWARD, California Library Association, 717 K. Street Suite 300, Sacramento CA 95814. (916)447-8541. Executive Director: Mary Sue Ferrell. Annual award. Estab. 1987. Purpose of award: "The purpose of the John and Patricia Beatty Award is to encourage the writing of quality children's books highlighting California, its culture, heritage and/or future." Previously published submissions only. Submissions made by the author, author's agent or review copies sent by publisher. The award is given to the author of a children's book published the preceding year. Deadline for entries: Submissions may be made January-December. Contact CLA Executive Director who will liaison with Beatty Award Committee. Awards cash prize of $500 and an engraved plaque. Judging by a 5-member selection committee appointed by the president of the California Library Association. Requirements for entrants: "Any children's or young adult book set in California and published in the U.S. during the calendar year preceding the presentation of the award is eligible for consideration."

This includes works of fiction as well as nonfiction for children and young people of all ages. Reprints and compilations are not eligible. The California setting must be depicted authentically and must serve as an integral focus for the book." Winning selection is announced through press release during National Library Week in April. Author is presented with award at annual California Library Association Conference in November.

✤**THE GEOFFREY BILSON AWARD FOR HISTORICAL FICTION**, The Canadian Children's Book Centre, 35 Spadina Rd., Toronto, Ontario M5R 2S9 Canada. (416)975-0010. Fax: (416)975-1839. E-mail: ccbc@l global.com. Website: http://www.lglobal.com/~ccbc. Program Coordinator: Jeffrey Canton. Annual award. Estab. 1988. Purpose of contest: To reward excellence in the writing of an outstanding work of historical fiction. Previously published submissions only. Submissions picked by the Children's Book Centre "based on our *Our Choice* catalogue." Must be published the previous calendar year. Writers should *not* contact the centre. No entry fee. Awards $1,000 (Canadian). Judging by a jury made up of a writer, bookseller, children's book specialist, historian, librarian. Requirements for entrants: "All books written by Canadians and selected for inclusion in *Our Choice*, will be eligible for consideration. A Canadian shall, for the purposes of the Committee, be deemed a citizen of Canada or a permanent resident who has lived in Canada for at least two years. Historical fiction is fiction in which history informs the work in a significant way and is historically authentic. An historical setting alone does not constitute a work of historical fiction."

THE IRMA S. AND JAMES H. BLACK BOOK AWARD, Bank Street College of Education, 610 W. 112th St., New York NY 10025-1898. (212)875-4452. Fax: (212)875-4558. E-mail: lindag@bnk1.bnkst.edu. Website: http://www.bnkst.edu/library/clib/isb.html. Contact: Linda Greengrass. Annual award. Estab. 1972. Purpose of award: "The award is given each spring for a book for young children, published in the previous year, for excellence of both text and illustrations." Entries must have been published during the previous calendar year (between January '97 and December '97 for 1997 award). Deadline for entries: January 1. "Publishers submit books to us by sending them here to me at the Bank Street library. Authors may ask their publishers to submit their books. Out of these, three to five books are chosen by a committee of older children and children's literature professionals. These books are then presented to children in selected second, third and fourth grade classes here and at a few other cooperating schools on the East Coast. These children are the final judges who pick the actual award. A scroll (one each for the author and illustrator, if they're different) with the recipient's name and a gold seal designed by Maurice Sendak are awarded in May."

‡***WALDO M. AND GRACE C. BONDERMAN/IUPUI YOUTH THEATRE PLAYWRITING DEVEL-OPMENT WORKSHOP AND SYMPOSIUM**, Indiana University-Purdue University at Indianapolis, 425 University Blvd. #309, Indianapolis IN 46202. (317)274-2095. Fax: (317)278-1025. E-mail: wmccrear@.iupui.e du. Director: Dorothy Webb. Entries should be submitted to W. Mark McCreary, Literary Manager. Contest every two years; next competition will be 1998. Estab. 1983. Purpose of the contest: "to encourage writers to create artistic scripts for young audiences. It provides a forum through which each playwright receives constructive criticism of his/her work and, where selected, writers participate in script development with the help of professional dramaturgs, directors and actors." Unpublished submissions only. Submissions made by author. Deadline for entries: September 1, 1998. SASE for contest rules and entry forms. No entry fee. "Awards will be presented to the top ten finalists. Four cash awards of $1,000 each will be received by the top four playwrights whose scripts will be given developmental work culminating in polished readings showcased at the symposium held on the IUPUI campus. This symposium is always held opposite years of the competition. Major publishers of scripts for young audiences, directors, producers, critics and teachers attend this symposium and provide useful reactions to the plays. If a winner is unable to be involved in preparation of the reading and to attend the showcase of his/her work, the prize will not be awarded. Remaining finalists will receive certificates." Judging by professional directors, dramaturgs, publishers, university professors. Write for guidelines and entry form.

✤**BOOK OF THE YEAR FOR CHILDREN**, Canadian Library Association, 200 Elgin St., Suite 206, Ottawa, Ontario K2P 1L5 Canada. (613)232-9625. Fax: (613)563-9895. Contact: Chairperson, Canadian Association of Children's Librarians. Annual award. Estab. 1947. "The main purpose of the award is to encourage writing and publishing in Canada of good books for children up to and including age 14. If, in any year, no book is deemed to be of award calibre, the award shall not be made that year. To merit consideration, the book must have been published in Canada and its author must be a Canadian citizen or a permanent resident of Canada." Previously published submissions only; must be published between January 1 and December 1 of the previous year. Deadline for entries: January 1. SASE for award rules. Entries not returned. No entry fee. Awards a medal. Judging by committee of members of the Canadian Association of Children's Librarians. Requirements for entrants: Contest open only to Canadian authors or residents of Canada. Winning books are on display at CLA headquarters.

✤ **CANADIAN LISTINGS** are marked with a maple leaf.

BOOK PUBLISHERS OF TEXAS, Children's/Young People's Award, The Texas Institute of Letters, % TCU Press, P.O. Box 298300, Ft. Worth TX 76129. (817)921-7822. Fax: (817)921-7333. E-mail: jalter@gamma.is .tcu.edu. Contact: Judy Alter. Send to above address for list of judges to whom entries should be submitted. Annual award. Purpose of the award: "to recognize notable achievement by a Texas writer of books for children or young people or by a writer whose work deals with a Texas subject. The award goes to the author of the winning book, a work published during the calendar year before the award is given. Judges list available each October. Submissions go directly to judges, so current list of judges is necessary. Write to above address. Deadline is first postally operative day of January." Previously published submissions only. SASE for award rules and entry forms. No entry fee. Awards $250. Judging by a panel of 3 judges selected by the TIL Council. Requirements for entrants: The writer must have lived in Texas for 2 consecutive years at some time, or the work must have a Texas theme.

THE BOSTON GLOBE-HORN BOOK AWARDS, The Boston Globe & The Horn Book, Inc., The Horn Book, 11 Beacon St., Suite 1000, Boston MA 02108. (617)227-1555. Fax: (617)523-0299. Award Directors: Stephanie Loer and Roger Sutton. Writing Contact: Stephanie Loer, children's book editor for *The Boston Globe*, 298 North St., Medfield MA 02052. Annual award. Estab. 1967. "Awards are for picture books, nonfiction and fiction. Up to two honor books may be chosen for each category." Books must be published between June 1, 1997 and May 31, 1998. Deadline for entries: May 15. "Publishers usually submit books. Award winners receive $500 and silver engraved bowl, honor book winners receive a silver plate." Judging by 3 judges involved in children's book field who are chosen by Roger Sutton, editor-in-chief for The Horn Book, Inc. (*The Horn Book Magazine* and the *Horn Book Guide*) and Stephanie Loer, children's book editor for *The Boston Globe*. "*The Horn Book Magazine* publishes speeches given at awards ceremonies. The book must have been published in the U.S. The awards are given at the fall conference of the New England Library Association."

ANN ARLYS BOWLER POETRY CONTEST, *Read* Magazine, 200 First Stamford Place, P.O. Box 120023, Stamford CT 06912-0023. (203)705-3406. Fax: (203)705-1661. E-mail: kdavis@weeklyreader.com. Website: http://www.weeklyreader.com/read.html. Contest Director: Kate Davis. Annual contest. Estab. 1988. Purpose of the contest: to reward young-adult poets (grades 6-12). Unpublished submissions only. Submissions made by the author or nominated by a person or group of people. Entry form must include signature of teacher, parent or guardian, and student verifying originality. Deadline for entries: December 12. SASE for contest rules and entry forms. No entry fee. Awards 6 winners $100 each, medal of honor and publication in *Read*. Semifinalists receive $50 each. Judging by *Read* and *Weekly Reader* editors and teachers. "Entrant understands that prize will include publication, but sometimes pieces are published in other issues." Requirements for entrants: the material must be original. Winning entries will be published in the May 1 issue of *Read* (all-student issue).

✦ANN CONNOR BRIMER AWARD, Nova Scotia Library Association, P.O. Box 36036, Halifax, Nova Scotia B3J 3S9 Canada. (902)490-5822. Fax: (902)490-5743. Award Director: Heather MacKenzie. Annual award. Estab. 1991. Purpose of the contest: to recognize excellence in writing. Given to an author of a children's book who resides in Atlantic Canada. Previously published submissions only. Submissions made by the author's agent or nominated by a person or group of people. Must be published May 1-April 30. Deadline for entries: April 30. SASE for contest rules and entry forms. No entry fee. Awards $1,000. Judging by a selection committee. Requirements for entrants: Book must be intended for children up to age 15; in print and readily available; fiction or nonfiction except textbooks.

BUCKEYE CHILDREN'S BOOK AWARD, State Library of Ohio, 65 S. Front St., Columbus OH 43215-4163. (614)644-7061. Fax: (614)728-2788. E-mail: rmetcalf@winslo.state.oh.us. Website: http://www.wp/.lib.oh .us:80/buckeyebook/. Nancy Smith, Chairperson. Correspondence should be sent to Floyd C. Dickman at the above address. Award every two years. Estab. 1981. Purpose of the award: "The Buckeye Children's Book Award Program was designed to encourage children to read literature critically, to promote teacher and librarian involvement in children's literature programs, and to commend authors of such literature, as well as to promote the use of libraries. Awards are presented in the following three categories: grades K-2, grades 3-5 and grades 6-8." Previously published submissions only. Deadline for entries: February 1. "The nominees are submitted by this date during the even year and the votes are submitted by this date during the odd year. This award is nominated and voted upon by children in Ohio. It is based upon criteria established in our bylaws. The winning authors are awarded a special plaque honoring them at a banquet given by one of the sponsoring organizations. The BCBA Board oversees the tallying of the votes and announces the winners in March of the voting year in a special news release and in a number of national journals. The book must have been written by an author, a citizen of the United States and originally copyrighted in the U.S. within the last three years preceding the nomination year. The award-winning books are displayed in a historical display housed at the Columbus Metropolitan Library in Columbus, Ohio."

BYLINE MAGAZINE CONTESTS, P.O. Box 130596, Edmond OK 73013. E-mail: bylinemp@aol.com. Website: http://www.bylinemag.com. Contest Director: Marcia Preston. Purpose of contest: *ByLine* runs 4 contests a month on many topics to encourage and motivate writers. Past topics include first chapter of a novel, children's fiction, children's poem, nonfiction for children, personal essay, general short stories, valentine or love poem, etc. Send SASE for contest flier with topic list. Unpublished submissions only. Submissions made by the author. "We do not publish the contests' winning entries, just the names of the winners." SASE for contest rules and entry forms. Entry fee is $3-4. Awards cash prizes for first, second and third place. Amounts vary. Judging by qualified writers or editors. List of winners will appear in magazine.

*BYLINE MAGAZINE STUDENT PAGE, P.O. Box 130596, Edmond OK 73013. (405)348-5591. E-mail: bylinemp@aol.com. Website: http://www.bylinemag.com. Contest Director: Marcia Preston, publisher. Estab. 1981. "We offer student writing contests on a monthly basis, September through May, with cash prizes and publication of top entries." Previously unpublished submissions only. "This is not a market for illustration." Deadline for entries varies. "Entry fee usually $1." Awards cash and publication. Judging by qualified editors and writers. "We publish top entries in student contests. Winners' list published in magazine dated 2 months past deadline." Send SASE for details.

RANDOLPH CALDECOTT MEDAL, Association for Library Service to Children, Division of the American Library Association, 50 E. Huron, Chicago IL 60611. (312)280-2163. Executive Director ALSC: Susan Roman. Annual award. Estab. 1938. Purpose of the award: to honor the artist of the most distinguished picture book for children published in the US (Illustrator must be US citizen or resident.) Must be published year preceding award. Deadline for entries: December. SASE for award rules. Entries not returned. No entry fee. "Medal given at ALA Annual Conference during the Newbery/Caldecott Banquet."

CALIFORNIA WRITERS' CLUB 1998 WRITING CONTEST, California Writers' Club, 3975 Kim Ct., Sebastopol CA 95472. (707)823-8128. "Ask for award rules before submitting entries." Award offered every year. Next conference, June 26-28, 1998. Purpose of the award: "To celebrate good writing." Categories: adult short stories, adult novels, adult nonfiction, juvenile fiction or nonfiction, picture books, poetry and scripts. Unpublished submissions only. Deadline for entries: May 1, 1998. SASE for award rules and entry forms. Entrires are not returned. Entry fee is $10 for each submission. Awards are full conference registration for 7 first prize winners ($435 value) or $200 cash (top prize winners read their pieces at CWC Conference at Asilomar); $100, second; $50, third. "Open to all."

*CALIFORNIA YOUNG PLAYWRIGHTS CONTEST, Playwrights Project, Suite 215, 1450 Frazee Rd., San Diego CA 92108. (619)298-9242. E-mail: playwrightsproject@juno.com. Director: Deborah Salzer. Open to Californians under age 19. Annual contest. Estab. 1985. "Our organization, and the contest, is designed to nurture promising young writers. We hope to develop playwrights and audiences for live theater. We also teach playwriting." Submissions required to be unpublished and not produced professionally. Submissions made by the author. Deadline for entries: April 1. SASE for contest rules and entry form. No entry fee. Award is professional productions of 3-5 short plays each year, participation of the writers in the entire production process, with a royalty award of $100 per play. Judging by professionals in the theater community, a committee of 5-7; changes somewhat each year. Works performed "in San Diego at the Cassius Carter Centre Stage of the Old Globe Theatre. Writers submitting scripts of 10 or more pages receive a detailed script evaluation letter."

*❧CANADIAN AUTHORS ASSOCIATION STUDENTS' CREATIVE WRITING CONTEST, Box 32219, 250 Harding Blvd. W., Richmond Hill, Ontario L4C 9R0 Canada. (705)653-0323. Fax: (705)653-0593. E-mail: bfarrar@learn.senecac.on.ca. Contact: Bernice Lever-Farrar. Entrants must be enrolled in secondary schools, colleges or universities and must be Canadian residents or Canadian citizens living abroad. Students must be 12-21 years of age. Students may have multiple entres, but the entry fee applies for each entry. Entries to be typed on one side of letter-sized white paper, and not published previously except in a student class anthology, student newspaper or student yearbook. Entries will not be returned. Entry fees: $5 per short story of 2,000 words or less; $5 for 3 poems of not more than 30 lines each. Awards: $500 for best story; $500 for best poem. Four Honourable Mentions in each category. All 10 winners will receive *Canadian Author* magazine for 1 year. Entry forms will be in the Winter and Spring issues of *Canadian Author*; deadline March 31, 1998.

REBECCA CAUDILL YOUNG READERS' BOOK AWARD, Illinois Reading Council, Illinois School Library Media Association, Illinois Association of Teachers of English, P.O. Box 871, Arlington Heights IL 60006-0871. (708)420-6406. Fax: (708)420-3242. Award Director Jackie Plourde. Annual award. Estab. 1988. Purpose of contest: to award the Children's Choice Award for grades 4-8 in Illinois. Submissions nominated by students. Must be published within the last 5 years. Awards honorarium, plaque. Judging by children, grades 4-8.

*❧CHICKADEE COVER CONTEST, Chickadee Magazine, Owl Communications, 179 John St., Suite 500, Toronto, Ontario M5T 3G5 Canada. (416)340-2700. Contest Director: Mitch Butler, All Your Own Editor. Annual contest. There is a different theme published each year. Announcement published each October issue. No entry fee. Winning drawing published on cover of February issue. Judging by staff of *Chickadee*. Requirements for entrants: Must be 6- to 9-year-old readers.

*❧CHICKADEE'S GARDEN EVENT, Chickadee Magazine, Owl Communications, 179 John St., Suite 500, Toronto, Ontario M5T 3G5 Canada. (416)340-2700. Contest Director: Mitch Butler, All Your Own Editor.

Annual. *Chickadee* readers are asked "to grow a favorite fruit or vegetable (anything as long as you can eat it) and submit a photo or drawing of you and your plant, and tell us why you chose the plant you did, and who helped you to care for it. Include experiences and humorous adventures along the way." Unpublished submissions only. Contest is announced in May issue. Deadline for entries: September. Results published in January issue. Judging by staff of *Chickadee*. Requirements for entrants: Must be 6-9 year-old readers.

CHILDREN'S BOOK AWARD, Federation of Children's Book Groups. The Old Malt House, Aldbourne Marlborough, Wiltshire SN8 2DW England. 01672 540629. Fax: 01672 541280. E-mail: 106311.1205@compuse rve.com. Coordinator: Marianne Adey. Purpose of the award: "The C.B.A. is an annual prize for the best children's book of the year judged by the children themselves." Categories: (I) picture books, (II) short novels, (III) longer novels. Estab. 1980. Previously unpublished submissions only. Deadline for entries: December 31. SASE for rules and entry forms. Entries not returned. Awards "a magnificent silver and oak trophy worth over $6,000 and a portfolio of children's work." Silver dishes to each category winner. Judging by children. Requirements for entrants: Work must be fiction and published during the current year (poetry is ineligible). Work will be published in current "Pick of the Year" publication.

CHILDREN'S WRITER WRITING CONTESTS, 95 Long Ridge Rd., West Redding CT 06896-1124. (203)792-8600. Contest offered every 4 months by *Children's Writer*, the monthly newsletter of writing and publishing trends. Purpose of the award: To promote higher quality children's literature. "Each contest has its own theme. Our last three were: (1) A science article for ages 6 to 8; to 850 words. (2) Folk or fairytale for ages 8 to 12; to 850 words. (3) A humorous story for ages 4 to 8; to 750 words. Any original unpublished piece, not accepted by any publisher at the time of submission, is eligible." Submissions made by the author. Deadline for entries: Last Friday in February, June and October. "We charge a $10 entry fee for nonsubscribers only, which is applicable against a subscription to *Children's Writer*." Awards 1st place—$100 or $1,000, a certificate and publication in *Children's Writer*; 2nd place—$50 or $500, and certificate; 3rd-5th places—$25 or $250 and certificates. One or two contests each year with the higher cash prizes also include $100 prizes plus certificates for 6th-12th places. To obtain the rules and theme for the current contest send a SASE to *Children's Writer* at the above address. Put "Contest Request" in the lower left of your envelope. Judging by a panel of 5 selected from the staff of the Institute of Children's Literature. "We acquire First North American Serial Rights (to print the winner in *Children's Writer*), after which all rights revert to author." Open to any writer. Entries are judged on age targeting, originality, quality of writing and, for nonfiction, how well the information is conveyed and accuracy. "Submit clear photocopies only, not originals; submission will *not* be returned. Manuscripts should be typed double-spaced. No pieces containing violence or derogatory, racist or sexist language or situations will be accepted, at the sole discretion of the judges."

CHILDREN'S WRITERS FICTION CONTEST, Goodin Williams Goodwin Literary Associates, P.O. Box 8863, Springfield MO 65801. (417)863-7670 or (417)833-5724. Coordinator: V.R. Williams. Annual contest. Estab. 1994. Purpose of contest: To promote writing for children, by giving children's writers an opportunity to submit work in competition. Unpublished submissions only. Submissions made by the author. Deadline for entries: July 31st. SASE for contest rules and entry forms. Entry fee is $5. Awards cash prize and publication in newsletter; certificates for Honorable Mention. Judging by Goodin, Williams and Goodwin. First rights to winning material acquired or purchased. Requirements for entrants: Work must be suitable for children and no longer than 800 words. "Send SASE for list of winners."

MR. CHRISTIE'S BOOK AWARD® PROGRAM, Christie Brown & Co., Division of Nabisco Ltd., 2150 Lakeshore Blvd., Toronto, Ontario M8V 1A3 Canada. (416)503-6050. Fax: (416)503-6034. Coordinator: Marlene Yustin. Competition is open to Canadian citizens, landed imigrants or books published in Canada in 1997. Annual award. Estab. 1990. Purpose of award: to honor Canadian authors and illustrators of good English/French Canadian published children's books. Contest includes three categories: Best Book for 7 and under; 8-11; and 12 and up. Submissions are made by the author, made by the author's agent, publishers. Deadline for entries: January 31. SASE for contest rules and entry forms. No entry fee. Awards a total of $45,000. Judging by a panel consisting of people in the literary/teaching community across Canada. Requirements for entrants: must be published children's literature in English or French.

COLORADO BOOK AWARDS, Colorado Center for the Book, 2123 Downing St., Denver CO 80205. (303)839-8321. Fax: (303)839-8319. E-mail: 103332.1376@compuserve.com. Website: http://www.aclin.org/code/ccftb. Award Director: Suzan Moore. Award open to adults. Annual award. Estab. 1993. Previously published submissions only. Submissions are made by the author, author's agent, nominated by a person or group of people. Deadline for entries: December 1. SASE for contest rules and entry forms. Entry fee is $30. Awards $500 and plaque. Judging by a panel of literary agents, booksellers and librarians.

CHRISTOPHER COLUMBUS SCREENPLAY DISCOVERY AWARDS, Christopher Columbus Society of the Creative Arts, #600, 433 N. Camden Dr., Beverly Hills CA 90210. (310)288-1988. Fax: (310)288-0257. E-mail: awards@screenwriters.com. Website: http://screenwriters.com. Award Director: Mr. Carlos Abreu. Annual and monthly awards. Estab. 1990. Purpose of award: to discover new screenplay writers. Unpublished submissions only. Submissions are made by the author or author's agent. Deadline for entries: August 1st and monthly (last day of month). Entry fee is $45. Awards: (1) Feedback—development process with industry experts. (2) Financial rewards—option moneys up to $10,000. (3) Access to key decision makers. Judging by entertainment industry experts, producers and executives.

‡THE COMMONWEALTH CLUB'S BOOK AWARDS CONTEST, The Commonwealth Club of California, 595 Market St., San Francisco CA 94105. (415)597-6700. E-mail: cwc@sirius.com. Website: http://www.sfgate.com/~common. Attn: James Coplan. Chief Executive Officer: Gloria Duffy. Annual contest. Estab. 1932. Purpose of contest: the encouragement and production of literature in California. Juvenile category included. Previously published submission; must be published from January 1 to December 31, previous to contest year. Deadline for entries: January 31. SASE for contest rules and entry forms. No entry fee. Awards gold and silver medals. Judging by the Book Awards Jury. The contest is only open to California writers/illustrators (must have been resident of California when ms was accepted for publication). "The award winners will be honored at the Annual Book Awards Program." Winning entries are displayed at awards program and advertised in newsletter.

*CRICKET LEAGUE, *Cricket Magazine*, P.O. Box 300, 315 Fifth St., Peru IL 61354. (815)224-6643. Address entries to: Cricket League. Monthly. Estab. 1973. "The purpose of Cricket League contests is to encourage creativity and give young people an opportunity to express themselves in writing, drawing, painting or photography. There is a contest each month. Possible categories include story, poetry, art or photography. Each contest relates to a *specific theme* described on each *Cricket* issue's Cricket League page. Signature verifying originality, age and address of entrant required. Entries which do not relate to the current month's theme cannot be considered." Unpublished submissions only. Deadline for entries: the 25th of each month. Cricket League rules, contest theme, and submission deadline information can be found in the current issue of *Cricket*. "We prefer that children who enter the contests subscribe to the magazine, or that they read *Cricket* in their school or library." No entry fee. Awards certificate suitable for framing and children's books or art/writing supplies. Judging by *Cricket* editors. Obtains right to print prize-winning entries in magazine. Refer to contest rules in current *Cricket* issue. Winning entries are published on the Cricket League pages in the *Cricket* magazine 3 months subsequent to the issue in which the contest was announced.

MARGUERITE DE ANGELI PRIZE, Bantam Doubleday Dell Books for Young Readers, 1540 Broadway, New York NY 10036. Estab. 1992. Fax: (212)782-9452 (note re: Marguerite De Angeli Prize). Annual award. Purpose of the award: to encourage the writing of fiction for children aged 7-10, either contemporary or historical; to encourage unpublished writers in the field of middle grade fiction. Unpublished submissions only. Length: between 40-144 pages. Submissions made by author or author's agent. Entries should be postmarked between April 1st and June 30th. SASE for award rules. No entry fee. Awards a $1,500 cash prize plus a hardcover and paperback book contract with a $3,500 advance against a royalty to be negotiated. Judging by Bantam Doubleday Dell Books for Young Readers editorial staff. Open to US and Canadian writers who have not previously published a novel for middle-grade readers (ages 7-10). Works published in an upcoming Bantam Doubleday Dell Books for Young Readers list.

DELACORTE PRESS PRIZE FOR A FIRST YOUNG ADULT NOVEL, Delacorte Press, Books for Young Readers Department, 1540 Broadway, New York NY 10036. (212)354-6500. Fax: (212)782-9452. Annual award. Estab. 1982. Purpose of award: to encourage the writing of contemporary young adult fiction. Previously unpublished submissions only. Mss sent to Delacorte Press may not be submitted to other publishers while under consideration for the prize. "Entries must be submitted between October 1 and New Year's Day. The real deadline is a December 31 postmark. Early entries are appreciated." SASE for award rules. No entry fee. Awards a $1,500 cash prize and a $6,000 advance against royalties on a hardcover and paperback book contract. Works published in an upcoming Bantam Doubleday Dell Books for Young Readers list. Judged by the editors of the Books for Young Readers Department of Bantam Doubleday Dell. Requirements for entrants: The writer must be American or Canadian and must *not* have previously published a young adult novel but may have published anything else. Guidelines are changing for 1998. Send SASE for new guidelines.

MARGARET A. EDWARDS AWARDS, American Library Association, 50 East Huron St., Chicago IL 60611-2795. (312)944-6780 or (800)545-2433. Fax: (312)664-7459. Annual award administered by the Young Adult Library Services Association (YALSA) of the American Library Association (ALA) and sponsored by *School Library Journal* magazine. Purpose of award: "ALA's Young Adult Library Services Association (YALSA), on behalf of librarians who work with young adults in all types of libraries, will give recognition to those authors whose book or books have provided young adults with a window through which they can view

---

‡ LISTINGS NEW TO THIS EDITION are marked with a double dagger.

their world and which will help them to grow and to understand themselves and their role in relationships, society and the world." Previously published submissions only. Submissions are nominated by young adult librarians and teenagers. Must be published five years before date of award. SASE for award rules and entry forms. No entry fee. Judging by members of the Young Adult Library Services Association. "The award will be given annually to an author whose book or books, over a period of time, have been accepted by young adults as an authentic voice that continues to illuminate their experiences and emotions, giving insight into their lives. The book or books should enable them to understand themselves, the world in which they live, and their relationship with others and with society. The book or books must be in print at the time of the nomination."

JOAN FASSLER MEMORIAL BOOK AWARD, Association for the Care of Children's Health, 7910 Woodmont Ave., Suite 300, Bethesda MD 20814. (301)654-6549. Fax: (301)986-4553. E-mail: acch@clark.net. Website: http://www.acch.org. Membership Manager: Jennifer Fincken. Competition open to adults and children. Annual award. Estab. 1989. "Award is given to the author(s) of the trade book that makes the most distinguished contribution to a child's or young person's understanding of hospitalization, illness, disabling conditions, dying and death and preventive care." Previously published submissions only. Submissions made by the author, author's agent. Must be published between 1996 and 1997. Deadline for entries: December 1. SASE for award rules and entry forms. No entry fee. Award $1,000 honorarium, plaque. Judging by multidisciplinary committee of ACCH members. Requirements for entrants: open to any writer. Display and book signing opportunities at annual conference.

DOROTHY CANFIELD FISHER CHILDREN'S BOOK AWARD, Vermont Department of Libraries, Vermont State PTA and Vermont Congress of Parents and Teachers, % Southwest Regional Library, Pierpoint Ave., Rutland VT 05701. (802)828-3261. Chairman: Sandra S. Roy. Annual award. Estab. 1957. Purpose of the award: to encourage Vermont children to become enthusiastic and discriminating readers by providing them with books of good quality by living American authors published in the current year. Deadline for entries: "January of the following year." SASE for award rules and entry forms. No entry fee. Awards a scroll presented to the winning author at an award ceremony. Judging is by the children grades 4-8. They vote for their favorite book. Requirements for entrants: "Titles must be original work, published in the United States, and be appropriate to children in grades 4 through 8. The book must be copyrighted in the current year. It must be written by an American author living in the U.S."

FLICKER TALE CHILDREN'S BOOK AWARD, North Dakota Library Association, 515 N. Fifth St., Bismarck ND 58501. (701)222-6410. Fax: (701)221-6854. Award Director: Konnie Wightman. P.O. Box 145, Kindred ND 58051. Estab. 1979. Purpose of award: to give children across the state of North Dakota a chance to vote for their book of choice from a nominated list of 10: 5 in the picture book category; 5 in the juvenile category. Also, to promote awareness of quality literature for children. Previously published submissions only. Submissions nominated by a person or group of people. Awards a plaque from North Dakota Library Association and banquet dinner. Judging by children in North Dakota.

FLORIDA STATE WRITING COMPETITION, Florida Freelance Writers Assocociation, P.O. Box A, North Stratford NH 03590. (603)922-8338. Fax: (603)922-8339. E-mail: danakinw@moose.mcia.net. Executive Director: Dana K. Cassell. Annual contest. Estab. 1984. Categories include children's short story and children's nonfiction article or book chapter (length appropriate to age category). Entry fee is $5 (members), $10 (nonmembers). Awards $75 first prize, membership second prize, book third prize, certificates for honorable mentions. Judging by teachers, editors and published authors. Judging criteria: interest and readability within age group, writing style and mechanics, originality, salability. Deadline: March 15. For copy of official entry form, send #10 SASE.

FOSTER CITY INTERNATIONAL WRITER'S CONTEST, Foster City Arts & Culture Committee, 650 Shell Blvd., Foster City CA 94404. (415)345-5731. Contest Director: Ted Lance. Open to all ages. Annual contest. Estab. 1975. Unpublished submissions only. Submissions made by the author. Deadline for entries: November 30, 1998. SASE for contest rules and entry forms. Entry fee is $10. Awards $250 cash award for first place; plus $125 for honorable mention. Judging by Peninsula Press Club. Categories include: best nonfiction (not more than 3,000 words), best humor (prose not more than 3,000 words), best story for children (not more than 2,000 words) and best poem. Entries must be typed, double-spaced on white 8½×11 paper, pages with numbers at the top right corner. Your name should not appear on any page. Attach 3×5 typed card with your name, address, phone number, manuscript title and category. Enter in one or multiple categories. No illustrated manuscripts. For each entry include a non-refundable entry fee check for $10 (payable to City of Foster City).

4-H ESSAY CONTEST, American Beekeeping Federation, Inc., P.O. Box 1038, Jesup GA 31598. (912)427-4233. Fax: (912)427-8447. E-mail: info@abfnet.org. Website: http://www.abfnet.org. Contest Director: Troy H. Fore. Annual contest. Purpose of contest: to educate youth about the beekeeping industry. 1998 essay topic: a "news event" in the bee colony—report on beekeeping activities in your community and/or state. For complete rules and details on topic, see website. Some examples are "Queen and Loyalists Flee Anarchists" (swarm leaves to set up new colony); "New Queen Takes the Throne" (bees replace failing or dead queen bee). Unpublished submissions only. Deadline for entries: before March 1. No entry fee. Awards 1st place: $250; 2nd place: $100;

3rd place: $50. Judging by American Beekeeping Federation's Essay Committee. "All national entries become the property of the American Beekeeping Federation, Inc., and may be published or used as it sees fit. No essay will be returned. Essayists *should not* forward essays directly to the American Beekeeping Federation office. Each state 4-H office is responsible for selecting the state's winner and should set its deadline so state judging can be completed at the state level in time for the winning state essay to be mailed to the ABF office before March 1, 1998. Each state winner receives a book on honey bees, beekeeping or honey. The National Winner will announced by May 1, 1998." Requirements for entrants: Contest is open to active 4-H Club members only.

DON FREEMAN MEMORIAL GRANT-IN-AID, Society of Children's Book Writers and Illustrators, 345 N. Maple Dr. #296, Beverly Hills CA 90210. (310)859-9887. Website: http://www.scbwi.org. Estab. 1974. Purpose of award: to "enable picture book artists to further their understanding, training and work in the picture book genre." Applications and prepared materials will be accepted between January 15 and February 15. Grant awarded and announced on June 15. SASE for award rules and entry forms. SASE for return of entries. No entry fee. Annually awards one grant of $1,000 and one runner-up grant of $500. "The grant-in-aid is available to both full and associate members of the SCBWI who, as artists, seriously intend to make picture books their chief contribution to the field of children's literature."

✦AMELIA FRANCES HOWARD GIBBON AWARD FOR ILLUSTRATION, Canadian Library Association, Suite 602, 200 Elgin St., Ottawa, Ontario K2P 1L5 Canada. (613)232-9625. Contact: Chairperson, Canadian Association of Children's Librarians. Annual award. Estab. 1971. Purpose of the award: "to honor excellence in the illustration of children's book(s) in Canada. To merit consideration the book must have been published in Canada and its illustrator must be a Canadian citizen or a permanent resident of Canada." Previously published submissions only; must be published between January 1 and December 31 of the previous year. Deadline for entries: January 1. SASE for award rules. Entries not returned. No entry fee. Awards a medal. Judging by selection committee of members of Canadian Association of Children's Librarians. Requirements for entrants: illustrator must be Canadian or Canadian resident. Winning books are on display at CLA Headquarters.

GOLD MEDALLION BOOK AWARDS, Evangelical Christian Publishers Association, 1969 East Broadway Rd., Suite Two, Tempe AZ 85282. (602)966-3998. Fax: (602)966-1944. E-mail: jmeegan@ecpa.org. Website: http://www.ecpa.org. President: Doug Ross. Annual award. Estab. 1978. Categories include Preschool Children's Books, Elementary Children's Books, Youth Books. "All entries must be evangelical in nature and cannot be contrary to ECPA's Statement of Faith (stated in official rules)." Deadlines for entries: December 1. SASE for award rules and entry form. "The work must be submitted by the publisher." Entry fee is $250 for nonmembers. Awards a Gold Medallion plaque.

GOLDEN KITE AWARDS, Society of Children's Book Writers and Illustrators, 22736 Vanowen St., Suite 106, West Hills CA 91307. (818)888-8760. Website: http://www.scbwi.org. Coordinator: Sue Alexander. Annual award. Estab. 1973. "The works chosen will be those that the judges feel exhibit excellence in writing, and in the case of the picture-illustrated books—in illustration, and genuinely appeal to the interests and concerns of children. For the fiction and nonfiction awards, original works and single-author collections of stories or poems of which at least half are new and never before published in book form are eligible—anthologies and translations are not. For the picture-illustration awards, the art or photographs must be original works (the texts—which may be fiction or nonfiction—may be original, public domain or previously published). Deadline for entries: December 15. SASE for award rules. Self-addressed mailing label for return of entries. No entry fee. Awards statuettes and plaques. The panel of judges will consist of two children's book authors, a children's book artist or photographer (who may or may not be an author), a children's book editor and a librarian." Requirements for entrants: "must be a member of SCBWI." Winning books will be displayed at national conference in August. Books to be entered, as well as further inquiries, should be submitted to: The Society of Children's Book Writers and Illustrators, above address.

HIGHLIGHTS FOR CHILDREN FICTION CONTEST, 803 Church St., Honesdale PA 18431. (717)253-1080. Mss should be addressed to Fiction Contest. Editor: Kent L. Brown Jr. Annual contest. Estab. 1980. Purpose of the contest: to stimulate interest in writing for children and reward and recognize excellence. Unpublished submissions only. Deadline for entries: February 28; entries accepted after January 1 only. SASE for contest rules and return of entries. No entry fee. Awards 3 prizes of $1,000 each in cash and a pewter bowl (or, at the winner's election, attendance at the Highlights Foundation Writers Workshop at Chautauqua). Judging by *Highlights* editors. Winning pieces are purchased for the cash prize of $1,000 and published in *Highlights*; semifinalists go to out-of-house judges (educators, editors, writers, etc.). Requirements for entrants: open to any writer. Winners announced in June. "The 1998 theme is 'stories that break the mold.' Length up to 900 words. Stories for beginning readers should not exceed 500 words. Stories should be consistent with *Highlights* editorial requirements. No violence, crime or derogatory humor. Send SASE for further rules and guidelines."

*HRC'S ANNUAL PLAYWRITING CONTEST, Hudson River Classics, Inc., P.O. Box 940, Hudson NY 12534. (518)828-1329. President: W. Keith Hedrick. Annual contest. Estab. 1992. Hudson River Classics is a not-for-profit professional theater company dedicated to the advancement of performing in the Hudson River

Valley area through reading of plays and providing opportunities for new playwrights. Unpublished submissions only. Submissions made by author and by the author's agent. Deadlines for entries: June 1st. SASE for contest rules and entry forms. Entry fee is $5. Awards $500 cash plus concert reading by professional actors. Judging by panel selected by Board of Directors. Requirements for entrants: Entrants must live in the northeastern US.

INDIAN PAINTBRUSH BOOK AWARD, Wyoming Library Association, P.O. Box 1387, Cheyenne WY 82003. (307)632-7622. Award Director: Laura Grott. Annual award. Estab. 1986. Purpose of award: to encourage the children of Wyoming to read good books. Previously published submissions only. Deadline for entries: April 1. Books can only be submitted for the nominations list by the children of Wyoming. No entry fee. Awards a watercolor painting. Judging by the children of Wyoming (grades 4-6) voting from a nominations list of 20. Requirements for entrants: only Wyoming children may nominate; books must be published in last 5 years, be fiction, have good reviews; final list chosen by a committee of librarians.

*INSPIRATIONAL WRITERS ALIVE! OPEN WRITERS COMPETITION, IWA, Rt. 4 Box 81-H, Rusk TX 75785-9410. (903)795-3986. Contest Director: Maxine E. Holder. Annual contest. Estab. 1990. Purpose of contest: to help aspiring writers to inspire through the inspirational/religion markets. Unpublished submissions only. Submissions made by author. Deadline for entries: April 1st. SASE for contest rules. Entry fee is $5 (devotional, short story or article); $5 (3 poems). Awards certificate of merit and cash for 1st, 2nd and 3rd place. Anthology of winning entry entitled *Timbrels of God* published every other year. Judging by well-known, published authors. Requirements for entrants: Cannot enter published material. "We want to aid especially new and aspiring writers." Contest has 5 categories—to include short story (adult), short story (for children and teens) article, daily devotions, and poetry. "*Must* include a cover sheet with every category."

IOWA TEEN AWARD, Iowa Educational Media Association, 306 E. H Ave., Grundy Center IA 50638. (319)824-6788. Contest Director: Don Osterhaus. Annual award. Estab. 1983. Previously published submissions only. Purpose of award: to allow students to read high quality literature and to have the opportunity to select their favorite from this list. Must have been published "in last 3-4 years." Deadline for entries: April 1998 for '99-2000 competition. SASE for award rules/entry forms. No entry fee. "Media specialists, teachers and students nominate possible entries." Awards an inscribed brass apple. Judging by Iowa students in grades 6-9. Requirements: Work must be of recent publication, so copies can be ordered for media center collections. Reviews of submitted books must be available for the nominating committee. Works displayed "at participating classrooms, media centers, public libraries and local bookstores in Iowa."

EZRA JACK KEATS/KERLAN COLLECTION MEMORIAL FELLOWSHIP, University of Minnesota, 109 Walter Library, 117 Pleasant St. SE, Minneapolis MN 55455. (612)624-4576. Competition open to adults. Offered annually. Deadline for entries: first Monday in May. Send request with SASE, including 52¢ postage. The Ezra Jack Keats/Kerlan Collection Memorial Fellowship from the Ezra Jack Keats Foundation will provide $1,500 to a "talented writer and/or illustrator of children's books who wishes to use the Kerlan Collection for the furtherance of his or her artistic development. Special consideration will be given to someone who would find it difficult to finance the visit to the Kerlan Collection." The fellowship winner will receive transnportation and per diem. Judging by the Kerlan Award Committee—3 representatives from the University of Minnesota faculty, one from the Kerlan Friends, and one from the Minnesota Library Association.

KENTUCKY STATE POETRY SOCIETY ANNUAL CONTEST, Kentucky State Poetry Society, % *Pegasus* editor Miriam L. Woolfolk, 3289 Hunting Hills Dr., Lexington KY 40515. (606)271-4662. Annual contest. Estab. 1966. Purpose of award: To encourage the creative mind and the continuing appreciation of poetry. Unpublished poems only. Deadline for entries: June 30. SASE for contest rules and entry forms. Student categories are free; Grand Prix, $5; all others $1. Offers more than 30 categories and awards certificates of merit and cash prizes from $3 to $200. Sponsors pick judges. Contest open to all. "One-time printing rights acquired for publication of first prize winner in the Prize Poems Issue of *Pegasus*, our annual journal (late fall/early winter issue). All other winners will be displayed at our October annual awards banquet."

KERLAN AWARD, University of Minnesota, 109 Walter Library, 117 Pleasant St. SE, Minneapolis MN 55455. (612)624-4576. Curator: Karen Nelson Hoyle. Annual award. Estab. 1975. "Given in recognition of singular attainments in the creation of children's literature and in appreciation for generous donation of unique resources to the Kerlan Collection." Previously published submissions only. Deadline for entries: November 1. Anyone can send nominations for the award, directed to the Kerlan Collection. No materials are submitted other than the person's name. Requirements for entrants: open to all who are nominated. "For serious consideration, entrant must be a published author and/or illustrator of children's books (including young adult fiction) and have donated original materials to the Kerlan Collection."

CORETTA SCOTT KING AWARD, Coretta Scott King Task Force, Social Responsibility Round Table, American Library Association, 50 E. Huron St., Chicago IL 60611. "The Coretta Scott King Award is an annual award for a book (1 for text and 1 for illustration) that conveys the spirit of brotherhood espoused by M.L. King, Jr.—and also speaks to the Black experience—for young people. There is an award jury that judges the books—

reviewing over the year—and making a decision in January. A copy of an entry must be sent to each juror. Acquire jury list from SRRT office in Chicago.''

JANUSZ KORCZAK AWARDS, Braun Center for Holocaust Studies, Anti-Defamation League, 823 United Nations Plaza, New York NY 10017. (212)885-7884. Fax: (212)949-6930. Website: http://www.adl.org. Award Director: Carol Lister. Award usually offered every 2 years. Estab. 1980. Purpose of award: "The award honors books about children which best exemplify Janusz Korczak's principles of selflessness and human dignity." Previously published submissions only; for 1998, books must have been published in 1996 or 1997. SASE for award rules and entry forms. No entry fee. Awards $1,000 cash and plaque (first prize); plaque (honorable mention). Judging by an interdisciplinary committee of leading scholars, editors, literary critics and educators. Requirements for entrants: Books must meet entry requirements and must be published in English. No entries are returned. They become the property of the Braun Center. Press release will announce winners.

‡ANNE SPENCER LINDBERGH PRIZE IN CHILDREN'S LITERATURE, The Charles A. and Anne Morrow Lindbergh Foundation, 708 S. Third St., Suite 110, Minneapolis MN 55415. (612)338-1703. Fax: (612)338-6826. E-mail: lindfdtn@mtn.org. Website: http://www.mtn.org/lindfdtn. Contest Director: Gene Bratsch. Competition open to adults. Contest is offered: annually. Estab. 1996. Purpose of contest: To recognize the children's fantasy novel judged to be the best published in the English language during the year. Prize program honors Anne Spencer Lindbergh, author of a number of acclaimed juvenile fantasies, who died in late 1993 at the age of 53. Previously published submissions only. Submissions made by author, author's agent or publishers. Must be published between January1 and December 31. Deadline for entries: November 1. Entry fee is $25. Awards $5,000 to author of winning book. Judging by panel drawn from writers, editors, librarians and teachers prominent in the field of children's literature. Requirements for entrants: Open to all authors of children's fantasy novels published during the year. Entries must include 4 copies of books submitted. Winner announced in January.

*LONGMEADOW JOURNAL LITERARY COMPETITION, % Rita and Robert Morton, 6750 N. Longmeadow, Lincolnwood IL 60646. (312)726-9789. Fax: (312)726-9772. Contest Director: Rita and Robert Morton. Competition open to students (anyone age 10-19). Held annually and published every year. Estab. 1986. Purpose of contest: to encourage the young to write. Submissions are made by the author, made by the author's agent, nominated by a person or group of people, by teachers, librarians or parents. Deadline for entries: June 30. SASE. No entry fee. Awards first place, $175; second place, $100; and five prizes of $50. Judging by Rita Morton, Robert Morton and Laurie Levy. Works are published every year and are distributed to teachers and librarians and interested parties at no charge.

*LOUISE LOUIS/EMILY F. BOURNE STUDENT POETRY AWARD, Poetry Society of America, 15 Gramercy Park, New York NY 10003-1705. (212)254-9628. Fax: (212)673-2352. E-mail: poetrysocy@aol.com. Website: http://www.poetrysociety.com. Award Director: Timothy Donnelly. Annual award. Purpose of the award: Award is for the best unpublished poem by a high or preparatory school student (grades 9-12) from the US and its territories. Unpublished submissions only. Deadline for entries: Oct. 1 to Dec. 21. SASE for award rules and entry forms. Entries not returned. "High schools can send an unlimited number of submissions with one entry per individual student for a flat fee of $10." Award: $100. Judging by a professional poet. Requirements for entrants: Award open to all high school and preparatory students from the US and its territories. School attended, as well as name and address, should be noted. PSA submission guidelines must be followed. These are printed in our fall calendar, and are readily available if those interested send us a SASE. Line limit: none. "The award-winning poem will be included in a sheaf of poems that will be part of the program at the award ceremony and sent to all PSA members."

MAGAZINE MERIT AWARDS, Society of Children's Book Writers and Illustrators, 345 N. Maple Dr. #296, Beverly Hills CA 90210. (310)859-9887. Website: http://www.scbwi.org. Award Coordinator: Dorothy Leon. Annual award. Estab. 1988. Purpose of the award: "to recognize outstanding original magazine work for young people published during that year and having been written or illustrated by members of SCBWI." Previously published submissions only. Entries must be submitted between January 31 and December 15 of the year of publication. For brochure (rules) write Award Coordinator. No entry fee. Must be a SCBWI member. Awards plaques and honor certificates for each of the 3 categories (fiction, nonfiction, illustration). Judging by a magazine editor and two "full" SCBWI members. "All magazine work for young people by an SCBWI member—writer, artist or photographer—is eligible during the year of original publication. In the case of co-authored work, both authors must be SCBWI members. Members must submit their own work." Requirements for entrants: 4 copies

✳ CONTESTS OPEN TO STUDENTS are marked with an asterisk.

each of the published work and proof of publication (may be contents page) showing the name of the magazine and the date of issue. The SCBWI is a professional organization of writers and illustrators and others interested in children's literature. Membership is open to the general public at large.

*MAJESTIC BOOKS WRITING CONTEST, Majestic Books, P.O. Box 19097, Johnston RI 02919-0097. Contest Director: Cindy MacDonald. Open to Rhode Island students only. Annual contest. Estab. 1992. Purpose of contest: to encourage students to write to the best of their ability and to be proud of their work. Unpublished submissions only. Submissions made by the author or teacher. Deadline for entries: second Friday in October. No entry fee, however, we do ask for a large self-addressed envelope (9 × 12) for our reply and certificate. Winners are published in an anthology. All entrants receive a certificate acknowledging their efforts. Judging by a panel of published writers and an English teacher. One-time publishing rights to submitted material required or purchased. Our contest is open to all students, age 6-17 in Rhode Island. *Anthology* comes off the press in December and a presentation ceremony is held for all winning students. Students must include their age, grade, school and statement of authenticity signed by the writer and a parent or teacher. Entries must be neat and will not be returned. In order to encourage all children, every entrant receives a personalized award acknowledging their efforts.

MILKWEED PRIZE FOR CHILDREN'S LITERATURE, Milkweed Editions, 430 First Ave. N., Suite 400, Minneapolis MN 55401-1473. (612)332-3192. Award Director: Emilie Buchwald, publisher/editor. Annual award. Estab. 1993. Purpose of the award: to encourage writers to turn their attention to readers in the 8-12 age group. Unpublished submissions only "in book form." Must send SASE for award guidelines. The prize is awarded to the best work for children ages 8-12 that Milkweed agrees to publish in a calendar year by a writer not published by Milkweed before. The Prize consists of $2,000 cash over and above any advance or royalties agreed to at the time of acceptance. Submissions must follow our usual children's guidelines. Must send SASE with submission form.

❧ELIZABETH MRAZIK-CLEAVER CANADIAN PICTURE BOOK AWARD, IBBY-Canada, 35 Spadina Rd., Toronto, Ontario M5R 2S9 Canada. (416)975-0010. Fax: (416)975-1839. Award Committee Chair: Mariella Berkelli. Annual contest. Estab. 1986. Award is given for outstanding illustrations in a Canadian children's book in either French or English and all genres. Previously published submissions only. Submissions made by author or publisher. Must be published the previous calendar year. Deadline for entries: end of year. Awards $1,000 Canadian and a certificate. Judging by a committee of professionals of children's literature. Requirements for entrants: Canadian citizenship.

*N.C. WRITERS' NETWORK INTERNATIONAL LITERARY PRIZES, N.C. Writers' Network, P.O. Box 954, Carrboro NC 27510. (919)967-9540. Fax: (919)929-0535. E-mail: ncwn@sunsite.unc.edu. Website: http://sunsite.unc.edu/ncwriters. Program Coordinator: Frances Dowell. Annual contest. *Thomas Wolfe Fiction Prize* (TWFP), est. 1994, awards $500 prize for best piece of fiction (short story or novel excerpt not to exceed 12 pp.), winning entry will be considered for publication in Carolina quarterly; *Paul Green Playwrights Prize* (PGPP), est. 1995, awards $500 prize for best play, any length, no musicals, winning entry will be considered for production by a consortium of North Carolina theaters. *Randall Jarrell Poetry Prize* (RJPP), est. 1990, awards $500 prize, publication and reading/reception for best poem, winning poem published in *Parnassus: Poetry in Review*. Unpublished submissions only. Submissions made by the author. Deadline for entries: TWFP—Aug. 31; PGPP—Sept. 30; RJPP—Nov. 1. SASE for award rules and entry forms. Entry fee is $7-TWFP; $7-RJPP; $10-PGPP ($7.50 for NCWN members). Judging by published writers or editors. Previous judges have included: Anne Tyler, Barbara Kingsolver, Donald Hall, Lucille Clifton, Romulus Linney.

❧THE NATIONAL CHAPTER OF CANADA IODE VIOLET DOWNEY BOOK AWARD, Suite 254, 40 Orchard View Blvd., Toronto, Ontario M5R 1B9 Canada. (416)487-4416. Award Director: Marty Dalton. Annual award. Estab. 1985. Purpose of the award: to honor the best children's English language book, by a Canadian, published in Canada for ages 5-13, over 500 words. Fairy tales, anthologies and books adapted from another source are not eligible. Previously published submissions only. Books must have been published in Canada between February 1 and January 31. Submissions made by author, author's agent; anyone may submit. Three copies of each entry are required. Must have been published during previous calendar year. Deadline for entries: January 31, 1997. SASE for award rules and entry forms. No entry fee. Awards $3,000 for the year 1998 for books published in 1997. Judging by a panel of 6, 4 IODE members and 2 professionals.

NATIONAL JEWISH BOOK AWARD FOR CHILDREN'S LITERATURE, Jewish Book Council Inc., 15 E. 26th St., New York NY 10010. (212)532-4949. Awards Coordinator: Carolyn Starman Hessel. Annual award. Estab. 1950. Previously published submissions only; must be published in 1997 for 1998 award. Deadline for entries: September 15, 1998. SASE for award rules and entry forms. Entries not returned. Entry fee is $36/ title; $72 if listed in 2 categories. Monetary awards. Judging by 3 authorities in the field. Requirements for entrants: Jewish children's books, published only for ages 2-16. Books will be displayed at the awards ceremony in NYC during Jewish Book Month, November 14—December 14, 1998.

NATIONAL WRITERS ASSOCIATION NONFICTION CONTEST, 1450 S. Havana, Suite 424, Aurora CO 80012. (303)751-7844. Executive Director: Sandy Whelchel. Annual contest. Estab. 1971. Purpose of contest: "to encourage writers in this creative form and to recognize those who excel in nonfiction writing." Submissions made by author. Deadline for entries: December 31. SASE for contest rules and entry forms. Entry fee is $15. Awards three cash prizes; choice of books; Honorable Mention Certificate. "Two people read each entry; third party picks three top winners from top five." Top 3 winners are published in an anthology published by National Writers Association, if winners agree to this. Judging sheets sent if entry accompanied by SASE.

NATIONAL WRITERS ASSOCIATION NOVEL WRITING CONTEST, 1450 S. Havana, Suite 424, Aurora CO 80012. (303)751-7844. Executive Director: Sandy Whelchel. Annual contest. Estab. 1971. Purpose of contest: "to encourage writers in this creative form and to recognize those who excel in novel writing." Submissions made by the author. Deadline for entries: April 1. SASE for contest rules and entry forms. Entry fee is $35. Awards top 3, cash prizes; 4 to 10, choice of books; 10 to 20, Honorable Mention Certificates. Judging: "two people read the manuscripts; a third party picks the three top winners from the top 5. We display our members' published books in our offices." Judging sheets available for SASE.

NATIONAL WRITERS ASSOCIATION SHORT STORY CONTEST, 1450 Havana St., Suite 424, Aurora CO 80012. (303)751-7844. Executive Director: Sandy Whelchel. Annual contest. Estab. 1971. Purpose of contest: "To encourage writers in this creative form and to recognize those who excel in fiction writing." Submissions made by the author. Deadline for entries: July 1. SASE for contest rules and entry forms. Entry fee is $15. Awards 3 cash prizes, choice of books and certificates for Honorable Mentions. Judging by "two people read each entry; third person picks top three winners." Judging sheet copies available for SASE. Top three winners are published in an anthology published by National Writers Association, if winners agree to this.

*THE NATIONAL WRITTEN & ILLUSTRATED BY . . . AWARDS CONTEST FOR STUDENTS, Landmark Editions, Inc., P.O. Box 270169, Kansas City MO 64127-0169. (816)241-4919. Fax: (816)483-3755. Contest Director: Teresa Melton. Annual awards contest with 3 published winners. Estab. 1986. Purpose of the contest: to encourage and celebrate the creative efforts of students. There are 3 age categories (ages 6-9, 10-13 and 14-19). Unpublished submissions only. Deadline for entries: May 1. For a free copy of the contest rules, send a self-addressed, business-sized envelope, stamped with 64¢ postage. "Need to send a self-addressed, sufficiently stamped (at least $3 postage) book mailer with book entry for its return. All entries which do not win are mailed back in November or December of each contest year." Entry fee is $1. Awards publication of book. Judging by national panel of educators, editors, illustrators, authors and school librarians. "Each student winner receives a publishing contract allowing Landmark to publish the book. Copyright is in student's name and student receives royalties on sale of book. Books must be in proper contest format and submitted with entry form signed by a teacher or librarian. Students may develop their illustrations in any medium of their choice, as long as the illustrations remain two-dimensional and flat to the surface of the paper." Winners are notified by phone by October 15 of each contest year. During November/December all other book entries are returned, accompanied by a list of winners and finalists. By September of the following year, all winners' books are published—after several months of pre-production work on the books by the students and the editorial and artistic staff of Landmark editions. Works are published in Kansas City, Missouri for distribution nationally and internationally.

THE NENE AWARD, Hawaii State Library, 478 S. King St., Honolulu HI 96813. (808)586-3510. Estab. 1964. "The Nene Award was designed to help the children of Hawaii become acquainted with the best contemporary writers of fiction, become aware of the qualities that make a good book and choose the best rather than the mediocre." Previously published submissions only. Books must have been copyrighted not more than 6 years prior to presentation of award. Work is nominated. Awards Koa plaque. Judging by the children of Hawaii in grades 4-6. Requirements for entrants: books must be fiction, written by a living author, copyrighted not more than 6 years ago and suitable for children in grades 4, 5 and 6. Current and past winners are displayed in all participating school and public libraries. The award winner is announced in April.

NEW ENGLAND BOOK AWARDS, New England Booksellers Association, 847 Massachusetts Ave., Cambridge MA 02139. (617)576-3070. Fax: (617)576-3091. E-mail: neba@neba.org. Award Director: Nan Sorensen. Annual award. Estab. 1990. Previously published submissions only. Submissions made by New England booksellers; publishers. Entries must be still in print and available. Deadline for entries: October 31. SASE for contest rules and entry forms. No entry fee. Judging by NEBA membership. Requirements for entrants: Author/illustrator must live in New England or write about New England. Submit written nominations only; actual books should not be sent. Member bookstores receive materials to display winners' books.

NEW ERA WRITING, ART, PHOTOGRAPHY & MUSIC CONTEST, The Church of Jesus Christ of Latter-day Saints, 50 E. North Temple, Salt Lake City UT 84150. (801)240-2951. Fax: (801)240-5997. Managing Editor: Richard M. Romney. Annual contest. Estab. 1971. Purpose of the contest: to feature the creative abilities of young Latter-day Saints. Unpublished submissions only. Submissions made by the author. Deadline for entries: January 6. SASE for contest rules and entry forms. No entry fee. Awards partial scholarships to LDS colleges,

"WE WANT TO PUBLISH YOUR WORK."

You would give anything to hear an editor speak those 6 magic words. So you work hard for weeks, months, even years to make that happen. You create a brilliant piece of work and a knock-out presentation, but there's still one vital step to ensure publication. You still need to submit your work to the right buyers. With rapid changes in the publishing industry it's not always easy to know who those buyers are. That's why each year thousands of writers and illustrators turn to the most current edition of this indispensable market guide.

Keep ahead of the changes by ordering *1999 Children's Writer's & Illustrator's Market* today! You'll save the frustration of getting your work returned in the mail stamped MOVED: ADDRESS UNKNOWN. And of NOT submitting your work to new listings because you don't know they exist. All you have to do to order the upcoming 1999 edition is complete the attached order card and return it with your payment. Order now and you'll get the 1999 edition at the 1998 price—just $19.99—no matter how much the regular price may increase! *1999 Children's Writer's & Illustrator's Market* will be published and ready for shipment in January 1999.

Keep on top of the ever-changing industry and get a jump on selling your work with help from the *1999 Children's Writer's & Illustrator's Market*. Order today—you deserve it!

Turn Over for More Great Books to Help Get Your Children's Works Published! ➡

Get Your Children's Stories Published with help from these Writer's Digest Books!

Children's Writer's Word Book

Even the most original children's story won't get published if its language usage or sentence structure doesn't speak to young readers. You'll avoid these pitfalls with this quick-reference guide full of word lists, reading levels for synonyms and more! #10316/$19.99/352 pages

The Very Best of Children's Book Illustration

Feast your eyes on this wonderful collection of the best in contemporary children's book illustration. You'll see nearly 200 full-color illustrations sure to spark your creativity. #30513/$29.95/144 pages/198 illus.

Writing and Illustrating Children's Books for Publication

Create a good, publishable manuscript in eight weeks using this self-taught writing course. Easy-to-follow lessons and exercises cover everything from getting ideas to writing, polishing and publishing. #10448/$24.95/128 pages/200 illus.

How To Write and Illustrate Children's Books and Get Them Published

Find everything you need to break into the lucrative children's market. You'll discover how to write a sure-fire seller, create captivating illustrations, get your manuscript into the right buyer's hands and more! #30082/$24.99/144 pages/115 illus.

How To Write and Sell Children's Picture Books

If you yearn to put smiles on little faces, you need this charming guide. You'll discover how to put your picture book on paper and get it published—whether you're retelling a wonderful old tale, or spinning a splendid new yarn. #10410/$7.99/192 pages

NEW!
Ten Steps to Publishing Children's Books

Discover vital information on children's publishing as you polish your writing skills. You'll find advice from professionals, case histories, checklists, exercises and more. #10534/$24.95/128 pages/150 illus.

1818 Ways to Write Better & Get Published

If you need to know it, use it, act on it, it's here—in easy-to-search, fast-reference form. These checklists detail how to name characters, overcome writer's block, how to make business contacts, 23 misconceptions about editors and editing, and much more. #10508/$12.99/224 pages/paperback

REVISED EDITION!
How to Write & Sell Your First Novel

22 accomplished authors reveal the keys to writing and publishing a successful novel in today's complicated market. #10530/$16.99/256 pages/pb

Fill out order card on reverse side and mail today!

cash prizes. Judging by *New Era* magazine editorial and design staffs. All rights acquired; reassigned to author upon written request. Requirements for entrants: must be an active member of the LDS Church, ages 12-23. Winning entries published in each August's issue.

JOHN NEWBERY MEDAL AWARD, Association for Library Service to Children, Division of the American Library Association, 50 E. Huron, Chicago IL 60611. (312)280-2163. Executive Director, ALSC: Susan Roman. Annual award. Estab. 1922. Purpose of award: to recognize the most distinguished contribution to American children's literature published in the US. Previously published submissions only; must be published prior to year award is given. Deadline for entries: December. SASE for award rules. Entries not returned. No entry fee. Medal awarded at Caldecott/Newbery banquet during annual conference. Judging by Newbery Committee.

‡THE NOMA AWARD FOR PUBLISHING IN AFRICA, Kodansha Ltd., P.O. Box 128, Witney, Oxol 0X8 5XU England. 44-1993-775235. Fax:`44-1993-709265. E-mail: maryljay@aol.com. Secretary of the Managing Committee: Mary Jay. Annual award. Estab. 1979. Purpose of award: to encourage publications of works by African writers and scholars in Africa, instead of abroad, as is still too often the case at present. Books in the following categories are eligible: scholarly or academic, books for children, literature and creative writing, including fiction, drama and poetry. Previously published submissions only. 1998 award given for book published in 1997. Deadline for entries: end of February 1998. Submissions must be made through publishers. Conditions of entry and submission forms are available from the secretariat. Entries not returned. No entry fee. Awards $10,000. Judging by the Managing Committee (jury): African scholars and book experts and representatives of the international book community. Chairman: Walter Bgoya. Requirements for entrants: Author must be African, and book must be published in Africa. "Winning titles are displayed at appropriate international book events."

NORTH AMERICAN INTERNATIONAL AUTO SHOW SHORT STORY HIGH SCHOOL POSTER CONTEST, Detroit Auto Dealers Association, 1800 W. Big Beaver Rd., Troy MI 48084-3531. (248)643-0250. Public Relations/Writing: Mary Kay McGovern. Public Relations/Art: Lynnette Steensen. Annual contest. Submissions made by the author and illustrator. Deadline to be determined for 1997. Contact DADA. SASE for contest rules and entry forms. No entry fee. five winners of the short story contest will each receive $500. Entries will be judged by an independent panel comprised of knowledgeable persons engaged in the literary field in some capacity. Entrants must be Michigan residents, including high school students enrolled in grades 9-12. Junior high school students in 9th grade are also eligible. Awards in the High School Poster Contest are as follows: Best Theme, Best Use of Color, Best Use of Graphics & Most Creative. A winner will be chosen in each category from grades 9, 10, 11 and 12. Each winner in each grade from each category will win $250. The winner of the Chairman's Award will receive $1,000. Entries will be judged by an independent panel of recognized representatives of the art community. Entrants must be Michigan high school students enrolled in grades 9-12. Junior high students in 9th grade are also eligible. Winners will be announced during the North American International Auto Show in January and may be published in the *Auto Show Program* at the sole discretion of the D.A.D.A.

THE SCOTT O'DELL AWARD FOR HISTORICAL FICTION, 1700 E. 56th St., Suite 3907, Chicago IL 60637-1936. Award Director: Mrs. Zena Sutherland. Annual award. Estab. 1981. Purpose of the award: "To promote the writing of historical fiction of good quality for children and young adults." Previously published submissions only; must be published between January 1 and December 31 previous to deadline. Deadline for entries: December 31. "Publishers send books, although occasionally a writer sends a note or a book." SASE for award rules. No entry fee. Awards $5,000. Judging by a committee of 3. Requirements for entrants: "Must be published by a U.S. publisher in the preceding year; must be by an American citizen; must be set in North or South America; must be historical fiction."

OHIOANA BOOK AWARDS, Ohioana Library Association, 65 S. Front St., Suite 1105, Columbus OH 43215. (614)466-3831. Fax: (614)728-6974. Director: Linda R. Hengst. Annual award. "The Ohioana Book Awards are given to books of outstanding literary quality. Purpose of contest: to provide recognition and encouragement to Ohio writers and to promote the work of Ohio writers. Up to six are given each year. Awards may be given in the following categories: fiction, nonfiction, children's literature, poetry and books about Ohio or an Ohioan. Books must be received by the Ohioana Library during the calendar year prior to the year the award is given and must have a copyright date within the last two calendar years." Deadline for entries: December 31. SASE for award rules and entry forms. No entry fee. Winners receive citation and glass sculpture. "Any book that has been written or edited by a person born in Ohio or who has lived in Ohio for at least five years" is eligible. The Ohioana Library Association also awards the "Ohioana Book Award in the category of juvenile books." Send SASE for more information.

OKLAHOMA BOOK AWARDS, Oklahoma Center for the Book, 200 NE 18th, Oklahoma City OK 73105. (405)521-2502. Fax: (405)525-7804. E-mail: gcarlile@oltn.odl.state.ok.us. Website: http://www.state.ok.us.~odl. oc. Annual award. Estab. 1989. Purpose of award: "to honor Oklahoma writers and books about our state." Previously published submissions only. Submissions made by the author, author's agent, or entered by a person or group of people, including the publisher. Must be published during the calendar year preceding the award.

Deadline for entries: January. SASE for award rules and entry forms. No entry fee. Awards a medal—no cash prize. Judging by a panel of 5 people for each category—a librarian, a working writer in the genre, editors, etc. Requirements for entrants: author must be an Oklahoma native, resident, former resident or have written a book with Oklahoma theme. Book will be displayed at banquet at the Cowboy Hall of Fame in Oklahoma City.

ORBIS PICTUS AWARD FOR OUTSTANDING NONFICTION FOR CHILDREN, National Council of Teachers of English, 1111 W. Kenyon Rd., Urbana IL 61801-1096. (217)328-3870, ext. 268. Chair, NCTE Committee on the Orbis Pictus Award for Outstanding Nonfiction for Children: Myra Zarnowski, Queens College, New York. Annual award. Estab. 1989. Purpose of award: to honor outstanding nonfiction works for children. Previously published submissions only. Submissions made by author, author's agent, by a person or group of people. Must be published January 1-December 31 of contest year. Deadline for entries: December 31. Call for award information. No entry fee. Awards a plaque given at the NCTE Elementary Section Luncheon at the NCTE Annual Convention in November. Judging by a committee.

THE ORIGINAL ART, Society of Illustrators, 128 E. 63rd St., New York NY 10021-7392. (212)838-2560. Fax: (212)838-2561. Annual contest. Estab. 1981. Purpose of contest: to celebrate the fine art of children's book illustration. Previously published submissions only. Deadline for entries: August 20. SASE for contest rules and entry forms. Entry fee is $20/book. Judging by seven professional artists and editors. Works will be displayed at the Society of Illustrators Museum of American Illustration in New York City October-November annually. Medals awarded.

HELEN KEATING OTT AWARD FOR OUTSTANDING CONTRIBUTION TO CHILDREN'S LITERATURE, Church and Synagogue Library Association, P.O. Box 19357, Portland OR 97280-0357. (503)244-6919. Fax: (503)977-3734. E-mail: csla@worldaccessnet.com. Website: http://www.worldaccessnet.com/~csla. Chair of Committee: Alrene Hall. Annual award. Estab. 1980. "This award is given to a person or organization that has made a significant contribution to promoting high moral and ethical values through children's literature." Deadline for entries: April 1. "Recipient is honored in July during the conference." Awards certificate of recognition and a conference package consisting of registration, all meals day of awards banquet, two nights' housing and a complementary 1 year membership. "A nomination for an award may be made by anyone. It should include the name, address and telephone number of the nominee plus the church or synagogue relationship where appropriate. Nominations of an organization should include the name of a contact person. A detailed description of the reasons for the nomination should be given, accompanied by documentary evidence of accomplishment. The person(s) making the nomination should give his/her name, address and telephone number and a brief explanation of his/her knowledge of the nominee's accomplishments. Elements of creativity and innovation will be given high priority by the judges."

*✿OWL MAGAZINE CONTESTS, Writing Contest, Photo Contest, Poetry Contest, Cover Contest, *OWL Magazine*, 370 King St. W., Suite 300, Toronto, Ontario M5V 1J9 Canada. (416)971-5275. Contact: Children's Page editor. Annual contest. Purpose of contest: "to encourage children to contribute and participate in the magazine. *Owl* also recognizes excellence in an individual or group effort to help the environment. Unpublished submissions only. Deadlines change yearly. Prizes/awards "change every year. Often we give books as prizes." Winning entries published in the magazine. Judging by art and editorial staff. Entries become the property of Owl Communications. "The contests and awards are open to children up to 14 years of age."

PEN/NORMA KLEIN AWARD FOR CHILDREN'S FICTION, PEN American Center, 568 Broadway, New York NY 10012. (212)334-1660. Awarded in odd-numbered years. Estab. 1990. "In memory of the late PEN member and distinguished children's book author Norma Klein, the award honors new authors whose books demonstrate the adventuresome and innovative spirit that characterizes the best children's literature and Norma Klein's own work." Previously published submissions only. "Candidates may not nominate themselves. We welcome all nominations from authors and editors of children's books." Deadline for entries: December. Awards $3,000 which will be given in May. Judging by a panel of 3 distinguished children's book authors. Nominations open to authors of books for elementary school to young adult readers. "It is strongly recommended that the nominator describe in some detail the literary character of the candidate's work and how it promises to enrich American literature for children."

PLEASE TOUCH MUSEUM BOOK AWARD, Please Touch Museum, 210 N. 21st St., Philadelphia PA 19103. (215)963-0667. Fax: (215)963-0424. E-mail: pleastch@libertynet.org. Website: http://www.libertynet.org/~pleastch. Public Relations and Marketing Coordinator: Katie Gorman. Annual award. Estab. 1985. Purpose of

---

✿ CANADIAN LISTINGS are marked with a maple leaf.

the award: "to recognize and encourage the publication of books for young children by American authors that are of the highest quality and will aid them in enjoying the process of learning through books. Awarded to two picture books that are particularly imaginative and effective in exploring a concept or concepts, one for children age three and younger, and one for children ages four-seven." Previously published submissions only. "To be eligible for consideration a book must: (1) Explore and clarify an idea for young children. This could include the concept of numbers, colors, shapes, sizes, senses, feelings, etc. There is no limitation as to format. (2) Be distinguished in both text and illustration. (3) Be published within the last year by an American publisher. (4) Be by an American author and/or illustrator." Deadline for entries: April 30 (submissions may be made throughout the year). SASE for award rules and entry forms. No entry fee. Judging by selected jury of children's literature experts, librarians and early childhood educators. Education store purchases books for selling at Book Award Celebration Day and throughout the year. Receptions and autographing sessions held in bookstores, Please Touch Museum, and throughout the city.

POCKETS MAGAZINE FICTION CONTEST, The Upper Room, P.O. Box 189, Nashville TN 37202-0189. (615)340-7333. Fax: (615)340-7006. E-mail: pockets@upperroom.org. Website: http://www.upperroom.org. Associate Editor: Lynn Gilliam. Annual contest. Estab. 1990. Purpose of contest: "to discover new freelance writers for our magazine and to encourage freelance writers to become familiar with the needs of our magazine." Unpublished submissions only. Submissions made by the author. Deadline for entries: August 15. SASE for contest rules and entry forms. No entry fee. Awards $1,000 and publication. Judging by *Pockets*' editors and 3 other editors of other Upper Room publications. Winner published in the magazine.

EDGAR ALLAN POE AWARD, Mystery Writers of America, Inc., 6th Floor, 17 E. 47th St., New York NY 10017. (212)888-8171. Fax: (212)888-8107. Executive Director: Priscilla Ridgway. Annual award. Estab. 1945. Purpose of the award: to honor authors of distinguished works in the mystery field. Previously published submissions only. Submissions made by the author, author's agent; "normally by the publisher." Work must be published/produced the year of the contest. Deadline for entries: November 30 "except for works only available in the month of December." SASE for award rules and entry forms. No entry fee. Awards ceramic bust of "Edgar" for winner; scrolls for all nominees. Judging by professional members of Mystery Writers of America (writers). Nominee press release sent after first Wednesday in February. Winner announced at the Edgar Banquet, held in late April.

‡✦PRIX ALVINE-BELISLE, Associations pour l'avancement des sciences et des techniques de la documentation (ASTED) Inc., 3414 Avenue Du Parc, Bureau 202, Montreal, Quèbec H2X 2H5 Canada. (514)281-5012. Fax: (514)281-8219. E-mail: info@asted.org. Award President: Josée Valiquette. Award open to adults. Annual award. Estab. 1974. Purpose of contest: To recognize the best children's book published in French in Canada. Previously published submissions only. Submissions made by publishing house. Must be published the year before award. Deadline for entrie: June 1. Awards $500. Judging by librarian jury.

*QUILL AND SCROLL INTERNATIONAL WRITING/PHOTO CONTEST, *Quill and Scroll*, School of Journalism, University of Iowa, Iowa City IA 52242. (319)335-5795. Contest Director: Richard Johns. Annual contest. Previously published submissions only. Submissions made by the author or school newspaper adviser. Must be published February 6, 1995 to February 4, 1996. Deadline for entries: February 5. SASE for contest rules and entry forms. Entry fee is $2/entry. Awards engraved plaque to junior high level sweepstakes winners. Each high school sweepstakes winner receives electric typewriter. Judging by various judges. *Quill and Scroll* acquires the right to publish submitted material in the magazine if it is chosen as a winning entry. Requirements for entrants: must be students in grades 9-12 for high school division.

READ WRITING & ART AWARDS, *Read* Magazine, 200 First Stamford Place, P.O. Box 120023, Stamford CT 06912-0023. (203)705-3406. Fax: (203)705-1661. E-mail: kdavis@weeklyreader.com. Website: http://www.weeklyreader.com/read.html. Contest Director: Kate Davis. Annual award. Estab. 1978. Purpose of the award: to reward excellence in writing and art in the categories of fiction, essay and art. Unpublished submissions only. Submissions made by the author or nominated by a person or group of people. Students in grades 6-12 are eligible to enter. Must include entry coupon and signature of teacher, parent or guardian and student. Deadline for entries: December 5. SASE for contest/award rules and entry forms. No entry fee. Awards first prize ($100), second prize ($75), third prize ($50). Prizes are given in each category, plus publication of first place winners. Judging by *Read* editorial staff. "Entrant understands that prize will include publication, but sometimes pieces are published in other issues. A story may be bought later." Work must be original. Prefer art entries in color, but b&w may be submitted. Artwork should be original in composition and execution, not *copied* from another artist's work. Prefers original artwork, although color photocopies are accepted. Art will be returned only if proper SASE is included. No tubes, boxes, loose stamps, or money—prefers artwork to be submitted flat, with chipboard or bubblewrap packaging. Published in April 1998 issue of *Read* (all-student issue).

‡TOMÁS RIVERA MEXICAN AMERICAN CHILDREN'S BOOK AWARD, Southwest Texas State University, EDU, 601 University Dr., San Marcos TX 78666-4613. (512)245-8539. Fax: (512)245-8345. E-mail: vm04@academia.swt.edu. Award Director: Dr. Velma Menchara. Competition open to adults. Annual contest.

Estab. 1995. Purpose of award: "To encourage authors, illustrators and publishers to produce books that authentically reflect the lives of Mexican American children and young adults in the American Southwest." Previously published submissions only. Submissions made by "any interested individual." Must be published during the year of consideration. Deadline for entries: February 1 post publication year. Contact Dr. Menchara for nomination forms. No entry fee. Awards $30 per book. Judging of nominations by a regional committee, national committee judges finalists. Annual ceremony honoring the book and author/illustrator is held during Hispanic Heritage Month at Southwest Texas State University.

ANNA DAVIDSON ROSENBERG AWARD FOR POEMS ON THE JEWISH EXPERIENCE, Judah L. Magnes Museum, 2911 Russell St., Berkeley CA 94705. (510)849-2710. Poetry Award Director: Paula Friedman. Annual award. Estab. 1986-87. Purpose of the award: to encourage poetry in English on the Jewish experience (writer does not need to be Jewish). Previously unpublished submissions only. Deadline for entries: August 31. SASE for award rules and entry forms by July 31. Entry forms must be included with submissions. SASE for list of winners. Awards $100-first prize, $50-second prize; $25-third prize; honorable mention certificates; *$25* Youth Commendation (poets under 19); Emerging Poet Award. Judging by committee of 3 well-published poets with editing/teaching experience. There will be a reading of top award winners in December at Magnes Museum. Prospective anthology of selected winning entries. "We request permission to use in potential anthologies." Write for entry form and guidelines *first*; entries must follow guidelines and be accompanied by entry form. *Please do not phone.*

‡PLEASANT T. ROWLAND PRIZE FOR FICTION FOR GIRLS, Pleasant Company Publications, 8400 Fairway Place, Middleton, WI 53562. Contact: Submissions Editor. Purpose of contest: "The mission of the competition is to encourage writers to turn their talents to the creation of high-quality fiction for girls, to reward talented authors of novles that successfully capture the spirit of contemporary American girls and illuminate the ways in which their lives may be personally touched by events and concerns shaping the United States today. Stories should feature a female protagonist between the ages of 8 and 12. Characters of varying cultural backgronds and family situations are welcome." Unpublished submissions only. Submissions made by author or author's agent. Deadline for entires: September 1, 1998. No entry fee. Awards $10,000 in cash and a standard contract with advance and royalty for publication of the winning book. Judging by the editors of Pleasant Company Publications, publisher of The American Girls Collection, American Girl Library, and *American Girl* magazine. Requirement for entrants: Must be U.S. resident. "Authors whose work is now being publsihed by Pleasant Company are not eligible. Manuscripts sent to Pleasant Company Publications my not be submitted to other publishers while under consideration for the Pleasant T. Rowland Prize."

‡❀SASKATCHEWAN BOOK AWARDS: CHILDREN'S LITERATURE, Saskatchewan Book Awards, Box 1921, Regina, Saskatchewan S4P 3E1 Canada. (306)569-1585. Fax: (306)569-4187. Award Director: Joyce Wells. Annual award. Estab. 1995. Previously published submissions only. Submissions made by author, author's agent or publisher. SASE for contest rules and entry forms. Entry fee is $15 (Canadian). Awards $1,000 (Canadian). Judging by two children's literature authors outside of Saskatchewan. Requirements for entrants: Must be Saskatchewan resident; book must have ISBN number; must meet above dates. Award winning book will appear on TV talk shows and be pictured on book marks distributed to libraries, schools and bookstores in Saskatchewan.

***SEVENTEEN FICTION CONTEST**, 850 Third Ave., 9th Floor, New York NY 10022. Fiction Editor: Ben Schrank. Annual contest. Estab. 1945. Fax: (212)407-9899. E-mail: seventeenm@aol.com. Unpublished submissions only. Deadline for entries: April 30. SASE for contest rules and entry forms; contest rules also published in November issue of *Seventeen*. Entries not returned. No entry fee. Awards cash prize and possible publication in *Seventeen*. Judging by "inhouse panel of editors, external readers." If first prize, acquires first North American rights for piece to be published. Requirements for entrants: "Our annual fiction contest is open to anyone between the ages of 13 and 21 who submit on or before April 30 (check November issue of *Seventeen* for details). Submit only original fiction that has not been published in any form other than in school publications. Stories should be between 1,500 and 3,000 words in length (6-12 pages). All manuscripts must be typed double-spaced on a single side of paper. Submit as many original stories as you like, but each story must include your full name, address, birth date and signature in the top right-hand corner of the first page. Your signature on submission will constitute your acceptance of the contest rules."

‡*THE SHAMROCK AWARD, Shamrock Publishing Inc. of St. Paul, 1490 Sherburne Ave., St. Paul MN 55104. (612)646-0276. Fax: (612)645-9859. E-mail: shmrckpub@aol.com. Award Director: Stefany Cruze. Competition open to adults and students. Annual contest. Estab. 1997. Purpose of award: "To help unpublished, children's autos to break into the publishing industry. Also, to descry quality, innovative and marketable stories in the picture book and middle reader, chapter book categories." Unpublished submissions only. Submissions are made by author. Deadline for entries: December 31. SASE for award rules and entry forms. Entry fee is $15. Awards $250 per category, brass shamrock, consideration of story for publication. Judging by the Shamrock Publishing editors. Requirements for entrants: unpublished fiction or nonfiction chapter book or picture book mss appropriate for middle readers; unique, educational, entertaining and marketable stories; hard-copy, typed, double spaced (approximately 100 pgs. for chapter books, 32 pgs. for picture books). Include cover letter which gives brief biography. Winner will be notified by mail on or before September 30 of the following year. Submissions will only be accepted when sent via U.S. Mail.

SHUBERT FENDRICH MEMORIAL PLAYWRIGHTING CONTEST, Pioneer Drama Service, Inc., P.O. Box 4267, Englewood CO 80155-4267. Fax: (303)779-4315. E-mail: piodrama@aol.com. Website: http://www.pioneerdrama.com. Director: Steven Fendrich. Annual contest. Estab. 1990. Purpose of the contest: "to encourage the development of quality theatrical material for educational and family theater." Previously unpublished submissions only. Deadline for entries: March 1. SASE for contest rules and entry forms. No entry fee. Application must accompany all submissions. Awards $1,000 royalty advance and publication. Upon receipt of signed contracts, plays will be published and made available in our next catalog. Judging by editors. All rights acquired with acceptance of contract for publication. Restrictions for entrants: Any writers currently published by Pioneer Drama Service are not eligible.

CHARLIE MAY SIMON BOOK AWARD, Arkansas Elementary School Council, Arkansas Department of Education, Room 302B, #4 Capitol Mall, Little Rock AR 72201. (501)682-4371. Fax: (501)682-4618. E-mail: hesterj@arkedu.k12.ar.us. Award Director: James A. Hester. Annual contest. Estab. 1970. Purpose of award: to promote reading—to encourage reading of quality literature and book discussion among children in grades 4-6. Previously published submissions only; must be published between January 1 and December 31 of calendar year preceding award; all books must have recommendations from 3 published sources. "Books are selected based on being published in previous calendar year from time of committee work; *Horn Book* is used as selection guide." Students in grades 4-6 vote on their favorite book on a reading list; the book with the most votes receives the Charlie May Simon Medallion and runner-up receives a plaque as honor book winner; reading list prepared by committee of 25 people representing cooperating organizations. No entry fee. Contest open to any book for children in grades 4-6 provided book is printed in year being considered.

*SKIPPING STONES YOUTH HONOR AWARDS, *Skipping Stones*, P.O. Box 3939, Eugene OR 97403-0939. (541)342-4956. Website: http://www.nonviolence.org/~nvweb/skipping/. Annual award. Purpose of contest: "to recognize youth, 7 to 17, for their contributions to multicultural awareness, nature and ecology, social issues, peace and nonviolence. Also to promote creativity, self-esteem and writing skills, and to recognize important work being done by youth organizations." Submissions made by the author. For 1998, the theme is "Multicultural and Nature Awareness." Deadline for entries: June 20, 1998. SASE for contest rules. Entries must include certificate of originality by parents and/or teachers, and background information on the author written by the author. Entry fee is $3. Judging by *Skipping Stones*' staff. "Up to ten awards are given in three categories: (1) Compositions—(essays, poems, short stories, travelogues, etc.) should be typed (double-spaced) or neatly handwritten. Fiction or nonfiction should be limited to 750 words; poems to 30 lines. Non-English writings are also welcome. (2) Artwork—(drawings, cartoons, paintings or photo essays with captions) should have the artist's name, age and address on the back of each page. Send the originals with SASE. Black & white photos are especially welcome. Limit: 8 pieces. (3) Youth Organizations—Tell us how your club or group works to: (a) preserve the nature and ecology in your area, (b) enhance the quality of life for low-income, minority or disabled, or (c) improve racial or cultural harmony in your school or community. Use the same format as for compositions." The 1998 winners will be published in Vol. 10, #4 (September-October 1998) issue of *Skipping Stones*.

*KAY SNOW WRITERS' CONTEST, Williamette Writers, 9045 SW Barbur Blvd. #5A, Portland OR 97219-4027. (503)452-1592. Fax: (503)452-0372. E-mail: wilwrite@teleport.com. Website: http://www.teleport.com/~wilwrite/. Contest Director: Martha Miller. Annual contest. Purpose of contest: "to encourage beginning and established writers to continue the craft." Unpublished, original submissions only. Submissions made by the author or author's agent. Deadline for entries: May 15. SASE for contest rules and entry forms. Entry fee is $10, Williamette Writers' members;, $15, nonmembers; $5, student writer. Awards cash prize of $200 per category (fiction, nonfiction, juvenile, poetry, script writing). "Judges are anonymous."

GEORGE G. STONE CENTER FOR CHILDREN'S BOOKS RECOGNITION OF MERIT AWARD, George G. Stone Center for Children's Books, The Claremont Graduate University, 131 E. 10th St., Claremont CA 91711-6188. (909)607-3670. Fax: (909)621-8390. Award Director: Doty Hale. Annual award. Estab. 1965. Purpose of the award: to recognize an author or illustrator of a children's book or a body of work exhibiting the "power to please and expand the awareness of children and teachers as they have shared the book in their classrooms." Previously published submissions only. SASE for award rules and entry forms. Entries not returned. No entry fee. Awards a scroll. Judging by a committee of teachers, professors of children's literature and librarians. Requirements for entrants: "Nominations are made by students, teachers, professors and librarians. Award made at annual Claremont Reading Conference in spring (March)."

JOAN G. SUGARMAN CHILDREN'S BOOK AWARD, Washington Independent Writers Legal and Educational Fund, Inc., #220, 733 15th St. NW, Washington DC 20005. (202)347-4973. Director: Isolde Chapin. Open to residents of D.C., Maryland, Virginia. Award offered every 2 years. Next awards presented in 1998 for publications done in 1996-1997. Estab. 1987. Purpose of award: to recognize excellence in children's literature, ages 1-15. Previously published submissions only. Submissions made by the author or author's agent or by publishers. Must be published in the 2 years preceeding award year. Deadline for entries: January 31, 1998. SASE for award rules and entry forms. No entry fee. Awards $1,000. Judging by selected experts in children's books. Requirements for entrants: publication of material; residence in DC, Maryland or Virginia. No picture-only books. Works displayed at reception for award winners and become part of the Sugarman Collection at The George Washington University.

SUGARMAN FAMILY AWARD FOR JEWISH CHILDREN'S LITERATURE, District of Columbia Jewish Community Center, 1529 16th St. N.W., Washington DC 20036. (202)518-9400. Fax: (202)518-9420. Award director: Nancy Drapin. Open to adults. Biannual award. Estab. 1994. Purpose of contest: to enrich all children's appreciation of Jewish culture and to inspire writers and illustrators for children. Newly published submissions only. Submissions are made by the author, made by the author's agent. Must be published January-December of year previous to award year. SASE for entry deadlines, award rules and entry forms. Entry fee is $25. Award at least $750. Judging by a panel of three judges—a librarian, a children's bookstore owner and a reviewer of books. Requirements for entrants: must live in the United States. Work displayed at the D.C. Jewish Community Center Library after March.

SYDNEY TAYLOR MANUSCRIPT COMPETITION, Association of Jewish Libraries, 1327 Wyntercreek Lane, Dunwoody GA 30338-3816. Fax: (770)671-8380. E-mail: m-psand@mindspring.com. Coordinator: Paula Sandfelder. Annual contest. Estab. 1985. Purpose of the contest: "This competition is for unpublished writers of fiction. Material should be for readers ages 8-11, with universal appeal that will serve to deepen the understanding of Judaism for all children, revealing positive aspects of Jewish life." Unpublished submissions only. Deadline for entries: January 15. SASE for contest rules and entry forms. No entry fee. Awards $1,000. Award will be given at the Association of Jewish Libraries annual convention. Judging by qualified judges from within the Association of Jewish Libraries. Requirements for entrants: must be an unpublished fiction writer; also, books must range from 64 to 200 pages in length. "AJL assumes no responsibility for publication, but hopes this cash incentive will serve to encourage new writers of children's stories with Jewish themes for all children."

*TREASURE STATE AWARD, Missoula Public Library, Missoula County Schools, Montana Library Assoc., 301 E. Main, Missoula MT 59802. (406)721-2005. Fax: (406)728-5900. E-mail: bammon@mtlib.org. Website: http://www.marsweb.com/~mslaplib. Award Directors: Bette Ammon and Carole Monlux. Annual award. Estab. 1990. Purpose of the award: Children in grades K-3 read or listen to a ballot of 5 picture books and vote on their favorite. Previously published submissions only. Submissions made by author, nominated by a person or group of people—children, librarians, teachers. Must be published in previous 5 years to voting year. Deadline for entries: March 20. SASE for contest rules and entry forms. No entry fee. Awards a plaque or sculpture. Judging by popular vote by Montana children grades K-3.

*VEGETARIAN ESSAY CONTEST, The Vegetarian Resource Group, P.O. Box 1463, Baltimore MD 21203. (410)366-VEGE. Fax: (410)366-8804. E-mail: vrg@vrg.org. Website: http://www.vrg.org. Address to Vegetarian Essay Contest. Annual contest. Estab. 1985. Purpose of contest: to promote vegetarianism in young people. Unpublished submissions only. Deadline for entries: May 1 of each year. SASE for contest rules and entry forms. No entry fee. Awards $50 savings bond. Judging by awards committee. Acquires right for The Vegetarian Resource Group to reprint essays. Requirements for entrants: age 18 and under. Winning works may be published in *Vegetarian Journal*, instructional materials for students. "Submit 2-3 page essay on any aspect of vegetarianism, which is the abstinence of meat, fish and fowl. Entrants can base paper on interviewing, research or personal opinion. Need not be vegetarian to enter."

*VERY SPECIAL ARTS PLAYWRIGHT DISCOVERY, (formerly Very Special Arts Young Playwrights Program), Very Special Arts, Education Office, The John F. Kennedy Center for the Performing Arts, Washington DC 20566. (202)628-2800 or 1-800-933-8721. Fax: (202)737-0725. E-mail: saraq@vsarts.org. Website: http://www.vsorg.com. Program Manager: Elena Widder. Annual contest. Estab. 1984. "All scripts must address or incorporate some aspect of disability." Unpublished submissions only. Deadline for entries: Mid April, TBA. Write to Playwright Discovery Program Manager for contest rules and entry forms. No entries returned. No entry fee. Judging by Artists Selection Committee. Entrants must be students age 25 and under, with a disability. "Script will be selected for production at The John F. Kennedy Center for the Performing Arts, Washington DC. The winning play(s) is presented each October."

*VFW VOICE OF DEMOCRACY, Veterans of Foreign Wars of the U.S., 406 W. 34th St., Kansas City MO 64111. (816)968-1117. Fax: (816)968-1157. Website: http://www.vfw.org. Annual contest. Estab. 1960. Purpose of contest: to give high school students the opportunity to voice their opinions about their responsibility to our country and to convey those opinions via the broadcast media to all of America. Deadline for entries: November 1st. No entry fee. Winners receive awards ranging from $1,000-20,000. Requirements for entrants: "Tenth-twelfth grade students in public, parochial and private schools in the United States and overseas are eligible to compete. Former national and/or first place state winners are not eligible to compete again. Contact your high school counselor or your local VFW Post to enter."

VOLUNTEER STATE BOOK AWARD, Tennessee Library Association, P.O. Box 158417, Nashville TN 37215-8417. (615)297-8316. Award Co-Chairs: Dr. Beverly N. Youree, Sue Thetford. Competition open to adults only. Annual award. Estab. 1978. Purpose of award: to promote awareness, interest, and enjoyment of good new children's and young adult literature and to promote literacy and life-long reading habits by encouraging students to read quality contemporary literature which broadens understanding of the human experience and provides accurate, factual information. Previously published submissions only. Submissions made by author, by the author's agent and nominated by a person or group of people. Must be published in 5 years prior to year of voting. SASE for contest rules and entry forms. No entry fee. Awards plaque. Judging by children. Any public or private school in Tennessee is eligible to participate. It is not required that the entire school be involved. Each participating school must have a minimum of twelve of the twenty titles per division available.

*THE STELLA WADE CHILDREN'S STORY AWARD, *Amelia* Magazine, 329 E St., Bakersfield CA 93304. (805)323-4064. Editor: Frederick A. Raborg, Jr. Annual award. Estab. 1988. Purpose of award: "With decrease in the number of religious and secular magazines for young people, the juvenile story and poetry must be preserved and enhanced." Unpublished submissions only. Deadline for entries: August 15. SASE for award rules. Entry fee is $5 per adult entry; there is no fee for entries submitted by young people under the age of 17, but such entry must be signed by parent, guardian or teacher to verify originality. Awards $125 plus publication. Judging by editorial staff. Previous winners include Maxine Kumin and Sharon E. Martin. "We use First North American serial rights only for the winning manuscript." Contest is open to all interested. If illustrator wishes to enter only an illustration without a story, the entry fee remains the same. Illustrations will also be considered for cover publication. Restrictions of mediums for illustrators: Submitted photos should be no smaller than 5×7; illustrations (drawn) may be in any medium. "Winning entry will be published in the most appropriate issue of either *Amelia*, *Cicada* or *SPSM&H*—subject matter would determine such. Submit clean, accurate copy."

‡WASHINGTON POST/CHILDREN'S BOOK GUILD AWARD FOR NONFICTION, % Patricia Markun, 4405 "W" St. NW, Washington DC 20007-1152. (202)965-0403. Annual contest. Estab. 1977. Purpose of contest: "to encourage nonfiction writing for children of literary quality. Awarded for the body of work of a leading American nonfiction author." No entry fee. Awards $1,000 and an engraved crystal paperweight. Judging by a jury of Children's Book Guild librarians and authors and a *Washington Post* book critic. "One doesn't enter. One is selected."

*WE ARE WRITERS, TOO!, Creative With Words Publications, P.O. Box 223226, Carmel CA 93922. Fax: (408)655-8627. Contest Director: Brigitta Geltrich. Semi-annual contest. Estab. 1975. Purpose of award: to further creative writing in children. Unpublished submissions only. Deadline for entries: June 1 and December 1. SASE for contest rules and entry forms. SASE for return of entries "if not winning poem." No entry fee. Awards publication in an anthology and a free copy for "Best of the Month." Judging by selected guest editors and educators. Contest open to children only (up to and including 19 years old). Writer should request contest rules. SASE with all correspondence. Age of child must be stated and manuscript must be verified of its authenticity. Each story or poem must have a title. Creative with Words Publications publishes the top 100 manuscripts submitted to the contest, and also publishes anthologies on various themes throughout the year to which young writers may also submit. Request theme list, include SASE.

WESTERN HERITAGE AWARDS, National Cowboy Hall of Fame, 1700 NE 63rd St., Oklahoma City OK 73111-7997. (405)478-2250. Fax: (405)478-4714. E-mail: nchf@aol.com. Website: http://www.nationalcowboyh alloffame.com. Director of Public Relations: Lynda Haller. Annual award. Estab. 1961. Purpose of award: The WHA are presented annually to encourage the accurate and artistic telling of great stories of the West through 15 categories of western literature, television and film, including fiction, nonfiction, children's books and poetry. Previously published submissions only; must be published the calendar year before the awards are presented. Deadline for literary entries: November 30. Deadline for film, music and television entries: December 31. SASE for award rules and entry forms. Entries not returned. Entry fee is $35. Awards a Wrangler bronze sculpture designed by famed western artist, John Free. Judging by a panel of judges selected each year with distinction in various fields of western art and heritage. Requirements for entrants: The material must pertain to the development or preservation of the West, either from a historical or contemporary viewpoint. Historical accuracy is vital. Literary entries must have been published December 1 and November 30 of calendar year. Film, music or television entries must have been released or aired between January 1 and December 31 of calendar year of entry. Works recognized during special awards ceremonies held annually at the museum. There is an autograph party preceding the awards. Film clips of award winner are shown during the awards presentation. Awards ceremonies are sometimes broadcast.

---

‡ **LISTINGS NEW TO THIS EDITION** are marked with a double dagger.

JACKIE WHITE MEMORIAL NATIONAL CHILDREN'S PLAY WRITING CONTEST, Columbia Entertainment Company, 309 Parkade Blvd., Columbia MO 65202-1447. (573)874-5628. Contest Director: Betsy Phillips. Annual contest. Estab. 1988. Purpose of contest: to find good plays for 30-45 theater school students, 6-9 grade, to perform in CEC's theater school. Previously unpublished submissions only. Submissions made by author. Deadline for entries: June 1. SASE for contest rules and entry forms. Entry fee is $10. Awards $250, production of play, travel expenses to come see production. Judging by board members of CEC and at least one theater school parent. Play is performed during the following season, i.e. 1997 winner to be presented during CEC's 1997-98 season.

‡LAURA INGALLS WILDER AWARD, Association for Library Service to Children, Division of the American Library Association, 50 E. Huron, Chicago IL 60611. (312)280-2163. Executive Director, ALSC: Susan Roman. Award offered every 3 years. Purpose of the award: to recognize an author or illustrator whose books, published in the US, have over a period of years made a substantial and lasting contribution to children's literature. Awards a medal presented at banquet during annual conference. Judging by Wilder Committee.

*PAUL A. WITTY OUTSTANDING LITERATURE AWARD, International Reading Association, Special Interest Group, Reading for Gifted and Creative Learning, School of Education, P.O. Box 32925, Fort Worth TX 76129. (817)921-7660. Award Director: Dr. Cathy Collins Block. Annual award. Estab. 1979. Categories of entries: poetry/prose at elementary, junior high and senior high levels. Unpublished submissions only. Deadline for entries: February 1. SASE for award rules and entry forms. SASE for return of entries. No entry fee. Awards $25 and plaque, also certificates of merit. Judging by 2 committees for screening and awarding. Works will be published in International Reading Association publications. "The elementary students' entries must be legible and may not exceed 1,000 words. Secondary students' prose entries should be typed and may exceed 1,000 words if necessary. At both elementary and secondary levels, if poetry is entered, a set of five poems must be submitted. All entries and requests for applications must include a self-addressed, stamped envelope."

PAUL A. WITTY SHORT STORY AWARD, International Reading Association, P.O. Box 8139, 800 Barksdale Rd., Newark DE 19714-8139. (302)731-1600. The entry must be an original short story appearing in a young children's periodical for the first time during 1997. The short story should serve as a literary standard that encourages young readers to read periodicals. Deadline for entries: The entry must have been published for the first time in the eligibility year; the short story must be submitted during the calendar year of publication. Anyone wishing to nominate a short story should send it to the designated Paul A. Witty Short Award Subcommittee Chair by December 1. Send SASE for guidelines. Award is $1,000 and recognition at the annual IRA Convention.

ALICE LOUISE WOOD OHIOANA AWARD FOR CHILDREN'S LITERATURE, Ohioana Library Association, 65 S. Front St., Suite 1105, Columbus OH 43215. (614)466-3831. Fax: (614)728-6974. E-mail: ohioana@winslo.ohio.gov. Website: http://www.oplin.lib.oh.us/OHIOANA/. Director: Linda R. Hengst. Annual award. Estab. 1991. Purpose of award: "to recognize an Ohio author whose body of work has made, and continues to make, a significant contribution to literature for children or young adults." SASE for award rules and entry forms. Award: $1,000. Requirements for entrants: "must have been born in Ohio, or lived in Ohio for a minimum of five years; established a distinguished publishing record of books for children and young people; body of work has made, and continues to make, a significant contribution to the literature for young people; through whose work as a writer, teacher, administrator, or through community service, interest in children's literature has been encouraged and children have become involved with reading."

CARTER G. WOODSON BOOK AWARD, National Council for the Social Studies, 3501 Newark St. NW, Washington DC 20016-3167. (202)966-7840. Fax: (202)966-2061. E-mail: excellence@ncss.org. Website: http://www.ncss.org. Staff Competition Coordinator: Rose-Kathryn Young Chaisson. Annual award. Purpose of contest: to recognize books relating to ethnic minorities and authors of such books. NCSS established the Carter G. Woodson Book Awards for the most distinguished social science books appropriate for young readers which depict ethnicity in the United States. This award is intended to "encourage the writing, publishing, and dissemination of outstanding social studies books for young readers which treat topics related to ethnic minorities and race relations sensitively and accurately." Submissions must be previously published. Submissions generally made by publishers "because copies of the book must be supplied to each member of the committee and copies of winning books must be provided to NCSS headquarters." Eligible books must be published in the year preceding the year in which award is given, i.e., 1997 for 1998 award. Books must be received by members of the committee by February 1. Rules, criteria and requirements are available for SASE. No entry fee. Award consists of: an announcement published in NCSS periodicals and forwarded to national and Council affiliated media. The publisher and author receive written notification of the committee decision. Reviews of award recipients and outstanding merit book are published in the NCSS official journal, *Social Education*. The award is presented at the NCSS Annual Conference in November. Judging by committee of social studies educators (teachers, curriculum supervisors and specialists, college/university professors, teacher educators—with a specific interest in multicultural education and the use of literature in social studies instruction) appointed from the NCSS membership at large.

WORK-IN-PROGRESS GRANTS, Society of Children's Book Writers and Illustrators, 345 N. Maple Dr. #296, Beverly Hills CA 90210. Fax: (310)859-4877. Website: http://www.SCBWI.org. Annual award. "The

SCBWI Work-in-Progress Grants have been established to assist children's book writers in the completion of a specific project." Five categories: (1) General Work-in-Progress Grant. (2) Grant for a Contemporary Novel for Young People. (3) Nonfiction Research Grant. (4) Grant for a work whose author has never had a book published. (5) Grant for a picture book writer. Requests for applications may be made beginning October 1. Completed applications accepted February 1-May 1 of each year. SASE for applications for grants. In any year, an applicant may apply for any of the grants except the one awarded for a work whose author has never had a book published. (The recipient of this grant will be chosen from entries in all categories.) Five grants of $1,000 will be awarded annually. Runner-up grants of $500 (one in each category) will also be awarded. "The grants are available to both full and associate members of the SCBWI. They are not available for projects on which there are already contracts." Previous recipients not eligible to apply.

*WRITER'S EXCHANGE POETRY CONTEST, R.S.V.P. Press, Box 394, Society Hill SC 29593. Contest Director: Gene Boone. Quarterly contest. Estab. 1985. Purpose of the contest: to promote friendly competition among poets of all ages and backgrounds, giving these poets a chance to be published and win an award. Submissions are made by the author. Continuous deadline; entries are placed in the contest closest to date received. SASE for contest rules and entry forms. Entry fee is $1 per poem. Awards 50% of contest proceeds, usually $35-100 varying slightly in each quarterly contest due to changes in response. Judging by Gene Boone or a guest judge such as a widely published poet or another small press editor. "From the entries received, we reserve the right to publish the winning poems in an issue of *Writer's Exchange*, a literary newsletter. The contest is open to any poet. Poems on any subject/theme, any style, to 30 lines, may be entered. Poems should be typed, single-spaced, with the poet's name in the upper left corner."

‡❤WRITERS GUILD OF ALBERTA CONTEST, 11759 Groat Rd., 3rd Floor, Edmonton, Alberta T5M 3K6 Canada. (403)422-8174. Fax: (403)422-2663. Contest Director: Darlene Diver. Competition open to adults. Annual award. Estab. 1980. Purpose: To promote excellence in children's writing. Previously published submissions only. Submissions are made by author, author's agent or publisher. Deadline for entries: December 31. Awards $500 and leather bound copy of winning book. Judging by a jury of three published children's writers. Requirements for entrants: must be resident of Alberta for 12 of the past 18 months. Winning work will be displayed at all conferences and libraries in the province.

*WRITER'S INTERNATIONAL FORUM CONTESTS, *Writer's International Forum*, P.O. Box 516, Tracyton WA 98393-0516. Contest Director: Sandra E. Haven. Estab. 1991. Purpose of contest: to inspire excellence in the traditional short story format. "We like identifiable characters, strong storylines, and crisp, fresh endings. We particularly like helping new writers, writers changing genres and young writers." Unpublished submissions only. Submissions made by the author. Deadlines, fees, and cash award prizes vary per contest. SASE for dates of each upcoming contest, contest rules and entry forms. Judging by *Writer's International Forum* staff. "We reserve the right to publish cash award winners." Please state genre of story and age of intended audience (as "ages 9-11") in cover letter. Contest winners announced in future issue. Word count restrictions vary with each contest. Some contests require following a theme or other stipulation. Please request guidelines for contest you want to enter.

*WRITING CONFERENCE WRITING CONTESTS, The Writing Conference, Inc., P.O. Box 664, Ottawa KS 66067-0664. (913)242-0407. Fax: (913)242-0407. E-mail: witeconf@computer-services.com. Contest Director: John H. Bushman. Annual contest. Estab. 1988. Purpose of contest: to further writing by students with awards for narration, exposition and poetry at the elementary, middle school and high school levels. Unpublished submissions only. Submissions made by the author or teacher. Deadline for entries: January 12. SASE for contest rules and entry form. No entry fee. Awards plaque and publication of winning entry in *The Writers' Slate*, March issue. Judging by a panel of teachers. Requirements for entrants: must be enrolled in school—K-12th grade.

*YEARBOOK EXCELLENCE CONTEST, *Quill and Scroll*, School of Journalism, University of Iowa, Iowa City IA 52242. (319)335-5795. Executive Director: Richard Johns. Annual contest. Estab. 1987. Previously published submissions only. Submissions made by the author or school yearbook adviser. Must be published between November 1, 1996 and November 1, 1997. Deadline for entries: November 1. SASE for contest rules and entry form. Entry fee is $2 per entry. Awards National Gold Key; sweepstakes winners receive plaque; seniors eligible for scholarships. Judging by various judges. Winning entries may be published in *Quill and Scroll* magazine.

❤YOUNG ADULT CANADIAN BOOK AWARD, The Canadian Library Association, Suite 602, 200 Elgin St., Ottawa, Ontario K2P 1L5 Canada. (613)232-9625. Fax: (613)563-9895. Contact: Committee Chair. Annual award. Estab. 1981. Purpose of award: "to recognize the author of an outstanding English-language Canadian book which appeals to young adults between the ages of 13 and 18 that was published the preceding calendar year. Information is available for anyone requesting. We approach publishers, also send news releases to various journals, i.e., *Quill & Quire*." Entries are not returned. No entry fee. Awards a leather-bound book. Requirement for entrants: must be a work of fiction (novel or short stories), the title must be a Canadian publication in either hardcover or paperback, and the author must be a Canadian citizen or landed immigrant. Award given at the Canadian Library Association Conference.

YOUNG READER'S CHOICE AWARD, Pacific Northwest Library Association, Box 352930, University of Washington, Graduate School of Library and Information Science, Seattle WA 98195-2930. (206)543-1897. Secretary: Carol Doll. Award Director: named annually. Annual award for published authors. Estab. 1940. Purpose of award: "to promote reading as an enjoyable activity and to provide children an opportunity to endorse a book they consider an excellent story." Previously published submissions only; must be published 3 years before award year. Deadline for entries: February 1. SASE for award rules and entry forms. No entry fee. Awards a silver medal, struck in Idaho silver. "Children vote for their favorite (books) from a list of titles nominated by librarians, teachers, students and other interested persons."

‡*THE ANNA ZORNIO MEMORIAL CHILDREN'S THEATRE PLAYWRITING AWARD, University of New Hampshire Theatre in Education Program, Department of Theatre and Dance, Paul Creative Arts Center, 30 College Rd., University of New Hampshire, Durham NH 03824-3538. (603)862-2291. Fax: (603)862-2908. Contact: Julie Brinker. Contest every 4 years; next contest is 2001. Estab. 1979. Purpose of the award: "to honor the late Anna Zornio, an alumna of The University of New Hampshire, for dedication to and inspiration of children's theater playwriting. Open to playwrights who are residents of the U.S. and Canada. Production should run about 45 minutes." Unpublished submissions only. Submissions made by the author. Deadline for entries: September 1, 2001. SASE for award rules and entry forms. No entry fee. Awards $1,000 plus guaranteed production. Judging by faculty committee. Acquires rights to campus production. Write for details.

Helpful Resources

The editor of *Children's Writer's & Illustrator's Market* suggests the following books, periodicals and websites to keep you informed on writing and illustrating techniques, trends in the field, business issues, industry news and changes, and additional markets.

BOOKS

CHILDREN'S WRITER GUIDE TO 1998, (annual), The Institute of Children's Literature, 95 Long Ridge Rd., West Redding CT 55104. (800)443-6078.

CHILDREN'S WRITER'S WORD BOOK, by Alijandra Mogilner, Writer's Digest Books, 1507 Dana Ave., Cincinnati OH 45207. (800)289-0963.

GETTING STARTED AS A FREELANCE ILLUSTRATOR OR DESIGNER, by Michael Fleischman, North Light Books, 1507 Dana Ave., Cincinnati OH 45207. (800)289-0963.

GUIDE TO LITERARY AGENTS, (annual) edited by Don Prues, Writer's Digest Books, 1507 Dana Ave., Cincinnati OH 45207. (800)289-0963.

HOW TO SELL YOUR PHOTOGRAPHS & ILLUSTRATIONS, by Elliot & Barbara Gordon, North Light Books, 1507 Dana Ave., Cincinnati OH 45207. (800)289-0963.

HOW TO WRITE A CHILDREN'S BOOK & GET IT PUBLISHED, by Barbara Seuling, Charles Scribner's Sons, 1230 Avenue of the Americas, New York NY 10020. (212)702-2000.

HOW TO WRITE AND ILLUSTRATE CHILDREN'S BOOKS AND GET THEM PUBLISHED, edited by Treld Pelkey Bicknell and Felicity Trottman, Writer's Digest Books, 1507 Dana Ave., Cincinnati OH 45207. (800)289-0963.

HOW TO WRITE AND SELL CHILDREN'S PICTURE BOOKS, by Jean E. Karl, Writer's Digest Books, 1507 Dana Ave., Cincinnati OH 45207. (800)289-0963.

HOW TO WRITE, ILLUSTRATE, AND DESIGN CHILDREN'S BOOKS, by Frieda Gates, Lloyd-Simone Publishing Company, distributed by Library Research Associates, Inc., Dunderberg Rd. RD 6, Box 41, Monroe NY 10950. (914)783-1144.

LEGAL GUIDE FOR THE VISUAL ARTIST, by Tad Crawford, North Light Books, 1507 Dana Ave., Cincinnati OH 45207. (800)289-0963.

MARKET GUIDE FOR YOUNG WRITERS, Fifth Edition, by Kathy Henderson, Writer's Digest Books, 1507 Dana Ave., Cincinnati OH 45207. (800)289-0963.

A TEEN'S GUIDE TO GETTING PUBLISHED, by Danielle Dunn & Jessica Dunn, Prufrock Press, P.O. Box 8813, Waco TX 76714-8813. (800)998-2208.

TEN STEPS TO PUBLISHING CHILDREN'S BOOKS, by Berthe Amoss & Eric Suben, Writer's Digest Books, 1507 Dana Ave., Cincinnati OH 45207. (800)289-0963.

THE ULTIMATE PORTFOLIO, by Martha Metzdorf, North Light Books, 1507 Dana Ave., Cincinnati OH 45207. (800)289-0963.

YOU CAN WRITE CHILDREN'S BOOKS, by Tracey Dils, Writer's Digest Books, 1507 Dana Ave., Cincinnati OH 45207. (800)289-0963.

THE WRITER'S DIGEST GUIDE TO MANUSCRIPT FORMATS, by Dian Dincin Buchman & Seli Groves, Writer's Digest Books, 1507 Dana Ave., Cincinnati OH 45207. (800)289-0963.

THE WRITER'S ESSENTIAL DESK REFERENCE, Second Edition, Writer's Digest Books, 1507 Dana Ave., Cincinnati OH 45207. (800)289-0963.

WRITING AND ILLUSTRATING CHILDREN'S BOOKS FOR PUBLICATION: TWO PERSPECTIVES, by Berthe Amoss and Eric Suben, Writer's Digest Books, 1507 Dana Ave., Cincinnati OH 45207. (800)289-0963.

WRITING & PUBLISHING BOOKS FOR CHILDREN IN THE 1990s: THE INSIDE STORY FROM THE EDITOR'S DESK, by Olga Litowinsky, Walker & Co., 435 Hudson St., New York NY 10014. (212)727-8300.

WRITING BOOKS FOR YOUNG PEOPLE, Second Edition, by James Cross Giblin, The Writer, Inc., 120 Boylston St., Boston MA 02116-4615. (617)423-3157.

WRITING FOR CHILDREN & TEENAGERS, Third Edition, by Lee Wyndham and Arnold Madison, Writer's Digest Books, 1507 Dana Ave., Cincinnati OH 45207. (800)289-0963.

WRITING WITH PICTURES: HOW TO WRITE AND ILLUSTRATE CHILDREN'S BOOKS, by Uri Shulevitz, Watson-Guptill Publications, 1515 Broadway, New York NY 10036. (212)764-7300.

PUBLICATIONS

BOOK LINKS, editor Judith O'Malley, American Library Association, 50 E. Huron St., Chicago IL 60611. (800)545-2433. *Magazine published 6 times a year (September-July) for the purpose of connecting books, libraries and classrooms. Features articles on specific topics followed by bibliographies recommending books for further information. Subscription: $18.95/year.*

CHILDREN'S BOOK INSIDER, editor Laura Backes, P.O. Box 1030, Fairplay CO 80440-1030. (800)807-1916. E-mail: mail@write4kids.com. Website: http://www.write4kids.com. *Monthly newsletter covering markets, techniques and trends in children's publishing. Subscription: $29.95/year. Official update source for* Children's Writer's & Illustrator's Market, *featuring quarterly lists of changes and updates to listings in CWIM.*

CHILDREN'S WRITER, editor Susan Tierney, The Institute of Children's Literature, 95 Long Ridge Rd., West Redding CT 55104. (800)443-6078. *Monthly newsletter of writing and publishing trends in the children's field. Subscription: $24/year; special introductory rate: $15.*

THE FIVE OWLS, editor Susan Stan, Hamline University Crossroads Center, MS-C1924, 1536 Hewitt Ave., St. Paul MN 55104. (612)644-7377. Fax: (612)641-2956. *Bimonthly newsletter for readers personally and professionally involved in children's literature. Subscription: $35/year.*

THE HORN BOOK MAGAZINE, editor-in-chief Robert Sutton, The Horn Book Inc., 11 Beacon St., Suite 1000, Boston MA 02108. (617)227-1555. E-mail: magazine@hbook.com. *Bimonthly guide to the children's book world including views on the industry and reviews of the latest books. Subscription: $42/year; special introductory rate: $24.95.*

THE LION AND THE UNICORN: A CRITICAL JOURNAL OF CHILDREN'S LITERATURE, editors Jack Zipes and Louisa Smith, The Johns Hopkins University Press—Journals Publishing Division, 2175 N. Charles St., Baltimore MD 21218-4319. (410)516-6987. *Magazine published 3 times a year serving as a forum for discussion of children's literature featuring interviews with authors, editors and experts in the field. Subscription: $26/year.*

ONCE UPON A TIME . . ., editor Audrey Baird, 553 Winston Court, St. Paul MN 55118. (612)457-6233. Website: http://members.aol.com/OUATMAG/. *Quarterly magazine for children's writers and illustrators and those interested in children's literature. Subscription: $19/year.*

PUBLISHERS WEEKLY, editor-in-chief Nora Rawlinson, Bowker Magazine Group, Cahners Publishing Co., 249 W. 17th St., New York NY 10011. (800)278-2991. *Weekly trade publication covering all aspects of the publishing industry; includes coverage of the children's field (books, audio and video) and spring and fall issues devoted solely to children's books. Subscription: $139/year. Available on newsstands for $4/issue. (Special issues are higher in price.)*

SOCIETY OF CHILDREN'S BOOK WRITERS AND ILLUSTRATORS BULLETIN, editors Stephen Mooser and Lin Oliver, SCBWI, 22736 Vanowen St., Suite 106, West Hills CA 91307. (818)888-8760. *Bimonthly newsletter of SCBWI covering news of interest to members. Subscription with $50/year membership.*

WEBSITES

CBCONLINE, THE WEBSITE OF THE CHILDREN'S BOOK COUNCIL: http://www.cbcbooks.org/
This site includes a complete list of CBC members with addresses, names and descriptions of what each publishes, and links to publishers' websites. Also offers previews of upcoming titles from members; articles from CBC Features, the Council's newsletter; and their catalog.

CHILDREN'S LITERATURE WEB GUIDE: http://www.ucalgary.ca/~dkbrown/index.html
This site includes stories, poetry, resource lists, lists of conferences, links to book reviews, lists of awards (international), and information on books from classic to contemporary.

CHILDREN'S MUSIC WEB GUIDE: http://www.childrensmusic.org
This site includes an index of children's music sites on the web, a database of children's music events in the U.S. and worldwide, an e-mail forum for children's music professionals and enthusiasts, a music magazine with activities for kids, and links to other sites.

CHILDREN'S WRITERS RESOURCE CENTER: http://www.write4kids.com
This site includes highlights from the newsletter Children's Book Insider*; definitions of publishing terms; answers to frequently asked questions; information on trends; information on small presses; a research center for Web information; and a catalog of material available from CBI.*

KIDS 'N STUFF WRITING FOR CHILDREN HOMEPAGE: http://pages.prodigy.com/childrens_writers/
Site coordinator Jody Blosser includes articles for writers, lists of resources, lists of clubs and organizations, and links to other sites including companion site A World of Pictures. Blosser is looking for articles from writers to include on the page.

ONCE UPON A TIME: http://members.aol.com/OUATMAG/
This companion site to Once Upon A Time *magazine offers excerpts from recent articles, notes for prospective contributors, and information about OUAT's 10 regular columnists.*

THE PURPLE CRAYON: http://www.users.interport.net/~hdu/
Editor Harold Underdown's site includes articles on trends, business, and cover letters and queries as well as interviews with editors and answers to frequently asked questions. He also includes links to a number of other sites helpful to writers.

THE SLUSH PILE: http://www.theslushpile.com/
Editor Laura Belgrave's site offers a wealth of tips for writers such as information on submissions, agents, copyright, cover and query letters, a glossary of publishing terms, online and offline resources and frequently asked questions. (See Before Your First Sale for Belgrave's "Seven Deadly Sins of Submission.")

SOCIETY OF CHILDREN'S BOOK WRITERS AND ILLUSTRATORS: http://www.scbwi.org
Site coordinator Bruce Balan includes information on awards and grants available to SCBWI members, a calendar of events listed by date and region, a list of publications available to members, and a site map for easy navigation. Balan welcomes suggestions for the site from visitors.

A WORLD OF PICTURES WEBSITE FOR CHILDREN'S ILLUSTRATORS:
http://pages.prodigy.com/picbooks/
Site coordinator Kimberly Dahl includes a wealth of articles on marketing and self-promotion; articles for beginners; a detailed list of resources; an illustrators' forum and message board; and links to a number of other sites with descriptions including companion site Kids 'n Stuff. Note: A World of Pictures was getting ready to change URLs at press time.

WRITES OF PASSAGE: http://www.writes.org
Run by Writes of Passage *(a literary magazine for teens), this site includes features from the magazine; links to a list of teen resources on the Web, including high school and college newspapers and online dictionaries; and a database of high school websites.*

Glossary

Advance. A sum of money a publisher pays a writer or illustrator prior to the publication of a book. It is usually paid in installments, such as one half on signing the contract; one half on delivery of a complete and satisfactory manuscript. The advance is paid against the royalty money that will be earned by the book.

All rights. The rights contracted to a publisher permitting the use of material anywhere and in any form, including movie and book club sales, without additional payment to the creator. (See The Business of Writing & Illustrating.)

Anthology. A collection of selected writings by various authors or gatherings of works by one author.

Anthropomorphization. The act of attributing human form and personality to things not human (such as animals).

ASAP. As soon as possible.

ASCAP. American Society of Composers, Authors and Publishers. A performing rights organization.

Assignment. An editor or art director asks a writer, illustrator or photographer to produce a specific piece for an agreed-upon fee.

B&W. Black & white.

Backlist. A publisher's list of books not published during the current season but still in print.

Biennially. Occurring once every 2 years.

Bimonthly. Occurring once every 2 months.

Biweekly. Occurring once every 2 weeks.

BMI. Broadcast Music, Inc. A performing rights organization.

Book packager. A company that draws all elements of a book together, from the initial concept to writing and marketing strategies, then sells the book package to a book publisher and/or movie producer. Also known as book producer or book developer.

Book proposal. Package submitted to a publisher for consideration usually consisting of a synopsis, outline and sample chapters. (See Before Your First Sale.)

Business-size envelope. Also known as a #10 envelope. The standard size used in sending business correspondence.

Camera-ready. Refers to art that is completely prepared for copy camera platemaking.

Caption. A description of the subject matter of an illustration or photograph; photo captions include persons' names where appropriate. Also called cutline.

CD-ROM. Compact disc read-only memory. Non-erasable electronic medium used for digitalized image and document storage capable of holding enormous amounts of information. A computer user must have a CD-ROM drive to access a CD-ROM.

Clean-copy. A manuscript free of errors and needing no editing; it is ready for typesetting.

Clips. Samples, usually from newspapers or magazines, of a writer's published work.

Concept books. Books that deal with ideas, concepts and large-scale problems, promoting an understanding of what's happening in a child's world. Most prevalent are alphabet and counting books, but also includes books dealing with specific concerns facing young people (such as divorce, birth of a sibling, friendship or moving).

Contract. A written agreement stating the rights to be purchased by an editor, art director or producer and the amount of payment the writer, illustrator or photographer will receive for that sale. (See The Business of Writing & Illustrating.)

Contributor's copies. The magazine issues sent to an author, illustrator or photographer in which her work appears.

Co-op publisher. A publisher that shares production costs with an author, but, unlike subsidy publishers, handles all marketing and distribution. An author receives a high percentage of royalties until her initial investment is recouped, then standard royalties.

Copy. The actual written material of a manuscript.

Copyediting. Editing a manuscript for grammar usage, spelling, punctuation and general style.

Copyright. A means to legally protect an author's/illustrator's/photographer's work. This can be shown by writing ©, the creator's name, and year of work's creation. (See The Business of Writing & Illustrating.)

Cover letter. A brief letter, accompanying a complete manuscript, especially useful if responding to an editor's request for a manuscript. May also accompany a book proposal. (See Before Your First Sale.)

Cutline. See caption.

Disk. A round, flat magnetic plate on which computer data may be stored.

Division. An unincorporated branch of a company.

Dummy. Handmade mock-up of a book.

Electronic submission. A submission of material by modem or on computer disk.

E-mail. Electronic mail. Messages sent from one computer to another via a modem or computer network.

Final draft. The last version of a polished manuscript ready for submission to an editor.

First North American serial rights. The right to publish material in a periodical for the first time, in the United States or Canada. (See The Business of Writing & Illustrating.)

Flat fee. A one-time payment.

Galleys. The first typeset version of a manuscript that has not yet been divided into pages.

Genre. A formulaic type of fiction, such as horror, mystery, romance, science fiction or western.

Glossy. A photograph with a shiny surface as opposed to one with a non-shiny matte finish.

Gouache. Opaque watercolor with an appreciable film thickness and an actual paint layer.

Halftone. Reproduction of a continuous tone illustration with the image formed by dots produced by a camera lens screen.

Hard copy. The printed copy of a computer's output.

Hardware. All the mechanically-integrated components of a computer that are not software—circuit boards, transistors and the machines that are the actual computer.

Hi-Lo. High interest, low reading level. Pertains mostly to books for beginning adult readers.

Home page. The first page of a World Wide Web document.

Imprint. Name applied to a publisher's specific line of books.

Interactive. A type of computer interface that takes user input, such as answers to computer-generated questions, and acts upon them.

Internet. A worldwide network of computers that offers access to a wide variety of electronic resources.

IRC. International Reply Coupon. Sold at the post office to enclose with text or artwork sent to a foreign buyer to cover postage costs when replying or returning work.

Keyline. Identification, through signs and symbols, of the positions of illustrations and copy for the printer.

Layout. Arrangement of illustrations, photographs, text and headlines for printed material.

Line drawing. Illustration done with pencil or ink using no wash or other shading.

Mechanicals. Paste-up or preparation of work for printing.

Middle reader. The general classification of books written for readers ages 9-11.

Modem. A small electrical box that plugs into the serial card of a computer, used to transmit data from one computer to another, usually via telephone lines.

Ms (mss). Manuscript(s).

One-time rights. Permission to publish a story in periodical or book form one time only. (See The Business of Writing & Illustrating.)

Outline. A summary of a book's contents in 5-15 double-spaced pages; often in the form of chapter headings with a descriptive sentence or two under each heading to show the scope of the book.

Package sale. The sale of a manuscript and illustrations/photos as a "package" paid for with one check.

Payment on acceptance. The writer, artist or photographer is paid for her work at the time the editor or art director decides to buy it.

Payment on publication. The writer, artist or photographer is paid for her work when it is published.

Photostat. Black & white copies produced by an inexpensive photographic process using paper negatives; only line values are held with accuracy. Also called stat.

Picture book. A type of book aimed at preschoolers to 8-year-olds that tells a story primarily or entirely with artwork.

Print. An impression pulled from an original plate, stone, block, screen or negative; also a positive made from a photographic negative.

Production house. A film company that creates video material including animation, special effects, graphics, filmstrips, slides, live action and documentaries.

Proofreading. Reading a typescript to correct typographical errors.

Query. A letter to an editor designed to capture her interest in an article or book you propose to write. (See Before Your First Sale.)

Reading fee. Money charged by some agents and publishers to read a submitted manuscript.

Reprint rights. Permission to print an already published work whose first rights have been sold to another magazine or book publisher. (See The Business of Writing & Illustrating.)

Response time. The average length of time it takes an editor or art director to accept or reject a query or submission and inform the creator of the decision.

Rights. The bundle of permissions offered to an editor or art director in exchange for printing a manuscript, artwork or photographs. (See The Business of Writing & Illustrating.)

Rough draft. A manuscript that has not been checked for errors in grammar, punctuation, spelling or content.

Roughs. Preliminary sketches or drawings.

Royalty. An agreed percentage paid by a publisher to a writer, illustrator or photographer for each copy of her work sold.

SAE. Self-addressed envelope.

SASE. Self-addressed, stamped envelope.

SCBWI. The Society of Children's Book Writers and Illustrators. (See listing in Clubs & Organizations section.)

Second serial rights. Permission for the reprinting of a work in another periodical after its first publication in book or magazine form. (See The Business of Writing & Illustrating.)

Semiannual. Occurring once every 6 months.

Semimonthly. Occurring twice a month.

Semiweekly. Occurring twice a week.

Serial rights. The rights given by an author to a publisher to print a piece in one or more periodicals. (See The Business of Writing & Illustrating.)

Simultaneous submissions. Queries or proposals sent to several publishers at the same time. (See Before Your First Sale.)

Slant. The approach to a story or piece of artwork that will appeal to readers of a particular publication.

Slush pile. Editors' term for their collections of unsolicited manuscripts.

SOCAN. Society of Composers, Authors and Music Publishers of Canada. A performing rights organization.

Software. Programs and related documentation for use with a computer.

Solicited manuscript. Material that an editor has asked for or agreed to consider before being sent by a writer.

Speculation (spec). Creating a piece with no assurance from an editor or art director that it will be purchased or any reimbursements for material or labor paid.

Stat. See photostat.

Subsidiary rights. All rights other than book publishing rights included in a book contract, such as paperback, book club and movie rights. (See The Business of Writing & Illustrating.)

Subsidy publisher. A book publisher that charges the author for the cost of typesetting, printing and promoting a book. Also called a vanity publisher.

Synopsis. A brief summary of a story or novel. Usually a page to a page and a half, single-spaced, if part of a book proposal.

Tabloid. Publication printed on an ordinary newspaper page turned sideways and folded in half.

Tearsheet. Page from a magazine or newspaper containing your printed art, story, article, poem or photo.

Thumbnail. A rough layout in miniature.

Transparencies. Positive color slides; not color prints.

Unsolicited manuscript. Material sent without an editor's or art director's request.

Vanity publisher. See subsidy publisher.

Word processor. A computer that produces typewritten copy via automated text-editing, storage and transmission capabilities.

World Wide Web. An Internet resource that utilizes hypertext to access information. It also supports formatted text, illustrations and sounds, depending on the user's computer capabilities.

Work-for-hire. An arrangement between a writer, illustrator or photographer and a company under which the company retains complete control of the work's copyright. (See The Business of Writing & Illustrating.)

Young adult. The general classification of books written for readers ages 12-18.

Young reader. The general classification of books written for readers ages 5-8.

Age-Level Index

This index lists book and magazine publishers by the age-groups for which they publish. Use it to locate appropriate markets for your work, then carefully read the listings and follow the guidelines of each publisher. Use this index in conjunction with the Subject Index to further narrow your list of markets. Listings new to this edition are marked with a double dagger (‡).

BOOK PUBLISHERS

Picture books (preschoolers to 8-year-olds)

ABC, All Books For Children; Abingdon Press; ‡Acropolis Books; Advocacy Press; Africa World Press; African American Images; Aladdin Paperbacks; Alyson Publications, Inc.; American Bible Society; Atheneum Books for Young Readers; A/V Concepts Corp.; Bantam Doubleday Dell; Barrons Educational Series; Behrman House Inc.; ‡Benefactory, The; Bess Press; ‡Beyond Words Publishing, Inc.; Blackbirch; ‡Blue Sky Marketing; Boingo; Boyds Mills; ‡Bright Lamb; ‡Browndeer; Callaway Editions; Candlewick; Carolrhoda; ‡Cartwheel; Chariot; Charlesbridge; Children's Book Press; ‡Children's Library; ‡China Books; Christian Publications; Chronicle; Concordia; Crossway; Crown; CSS Publishing; Dawn; Dial; ‡DK Ink; ‡DK Publishing; Down East; Dutton; E.M. Press; Eerdmans; Evan-Moor; Farrar; ‡First Story; Fitzhenry & Whiteside; Free Spirit; ‡Front Street; Geringer, Laura; Gibbs Smith; Godine, David R.; Golden; Grapevine; Greene Bark; Greenwillow; Grolier; ‡Grosset; HaChai; Harcourt; HarperCollins; Hendrick-Long; Highsmith; ‡Hinterland; Holiday House; Holt, Henry; Houghton Mifflin; Humanics; Huntington House; Hyperion Books; Hyperion Press; Ideals; Incentive; Jalmar; ‡Jewish Lights; Jewish Publication Society; Kar-Ben Copies; ‡Key Porter; Knopf; Laredo; ‡Levine, Arthur; Little, Brown; Lodestar Books; Lollipop Power; Lothrop; Lowell House Lowell House; Lucas/Evans Books Inc.; McClanahan; McElderry; Mage; Magination; Meadowbrook; Millbrook Press; Mondo; Morehouse; Morris, Joshua; Multnomah; ‡Nelson, Tommy; ‡New Canaan; ‡New Hope; ‡North-South; Open Hand; Orca; Orchard; ‡Ottenheimer; ‡Otter Creek; Our Child; Owen, Richard C.; Pages; Parenting; Pauline; Peachtree; Pelican; Perspectives; Philomel; Phoenix Learning; Press-Tige; Price Stern Sloan; ‡Prometheus; Putnam's; Random House; ‡Red Deer; ‡Sadlier, William H.; Seedling; ‡Shamrock; Silver Moon; Simon & Schuster; Soundprints; Speech Bin; Standard; Stemmer House; Stoddart; ‡Summit; ‡Sword of The Lord; Treasure; Tricycle; Troll; ‡Tundra; ‡Turtle; Tyndale; ‡UAHC; University Classics; Volcano; Walker; Whispering Coyote; ‡Woman's Missionary; World Book; Writers Press; Zino; ‡Zondervan

Young readers (5- to 8-year olds)

ABC, All Books For Children; ‡Acropolis Books; Advocacy Press; Africa World Press; African American Images; Aladdin Paperbacks; Alyson Publications, Inc.; American Bible Society; Atheneum Books for Young Readers; A/V Concepts Corp.; Bantam Doubleday Dell; Barrons Educational Series; Behrman House Inc.; ‡Benefactory, The; Bess Press; Bethany House Publishers; Blackbirch; Blue Sky Press; Boingo; Boyds Mills; ‡Bright Lamb; Bright Ring; ‡Browndeer; Callaway Editions; Candlewick; Carolrhoda; ‡Cartwheel; Chariot; Chicago Review; Christian Ed.; Christian Publications; Chronicle; Concordia; Coteau; Crossway; Crown; CSS Publishing; Davenport, May; Dial; ‡DK Ink; ‡DK Publishing; Dutton; E.M. Press; Eerdmans; Enslow; Evan-Moor; Farrar; Feminist Press; ‡First Story; Fitzhenry & Whiteside; Free Spirit; Friends United; Geringer, Laura; Godine, David R.; Golden; Grapevine; Greene Bark; Greenwillow; Grolier; ‡Grosset; HaChai; Harcourt; HarperCollins; Hendrick-Long; Highsmith; Holiday House; Houghton Mifflin; ‡Huckleberry; Humanics; Huntington House; Hyperion Books; Hyperion Press; Ideals; Incentive; Jalmar; Jewish Publication Society; Jones, Bob; Just Us Books; Kaeden; Kar-Ben Copies; ‡Key Porter; Knopf; Laredo; Little, Brown; Lodestar Books; Lollipop Power; Lothrop; Lowell House; Lucas/Evans

Books Inc.; McElderry; Magination; Meadowbrook; Messner, Julian; Millbrook Press; ‡Miracle Sound; Mitchell Lane; Morehouse; Morgan Reynolds; Morris, Joshua; Multnomah; ‡Nelson, Tommy; ‡New Canaan; ‡New Hope; Northland; Open Hand; Orca; Orchard; ‡Otter Creek; Our Child; Owen, Richard C.; Pages; Parenting; Pauline; Peachtree; Pelican; Perspectives; Philomel; Phoenix Learning; Planet Dexter; Players Press; Press-Tige; Price Stern Sloan; ‡Prometheus; Putnam's; Rainbow; Random House; ‡Red Deer; Reidmore; ‡Ronsdale; Rosen; ‡Sadlier, William H.; ‡Shamrock; Silver Moon; Simon & Schuster; Speech Bin; Standard; Stemmer House; Stoddart; Storey; ‡Summit; ‡Sword of The Lord; Treasure; Troll; Tyndale; ‡UAHC; University Classics; Volcano; Walker; Weigl Educational; Weiss, Daniel; Whitecap; Williamson; ‡Woman's Missionary; World Book; Writers Press; Zino; ‡Zondervan

Middle readers (9- to 11-year-olds)

ABC, All Books For Children; ‡Acropolis Books; Advocacy Press; Africa World Press; African American Images; Aladdin Paperbacks; Alyson Publications, Inc.; American Bible Society; Atheneum Books for Young Readers; A/V Concepts Corp.; Avon Books; B&B Publishing, Inc.; Bantam Doubleday Dell; Barrons Educational Series; ‡Beech Tree Books; Behrman House Inc.; Bess Press; Bethany House Publishers; Blackbirch; Boingo; Boyds Mills; Bright Ring; ‡Browndeer; Callaway Editions; Candlewick; Carolrhoda; Chariot; Chicago Review; Children's Book Press; ‡China Books; Christian Ed.; Christian Publications; Chronicle; Clear Light; Concordia; Coteau; Crossway; Crown; CSS Publishing; Dial; ‡DK Ink; ‡DK Publishing; Down East; Dutton; E.M. Press; Eerdmans; Enslow; Evan-Moor; Facts on File; Farrar; Fawcett; Feminist Press; Fitzhenry & Whiteside; Free Spirit; Friends United; ‡Front Street; Geringer, Laura; Gibbs Smith; Godine, David R.; Golden; Grapevine; Greenhaven; Greenwillow; Grolier; ‡Grosset; HaChai; Harcourt; HarperCollins; Hendrick-Long; Highsmith; Holiday House; Holt, Henry; Houghton Mifflin; ‡Huckleberry; Humanics; Huntington House; Hyperion Books; Hyperion Press; Incentive; Jalmar; ‡Jewish Lights; Jewish Publication Society; Jones, Bob; Kar-Ben Copies; ‡Key Porter; Knopf; Laredo; Lerner; ‡Levine, Arthur; Little, Brown; Lodestar Books; Lorimer; Lothrop; Lowell House; Lucas/Evans Books Inc.; Lucent; McElderry; Meadowbrook; Meriwether; Milkweed; Millbrook Press; Mitchell Lane; Mondo; Morehouse; Morgan Reynolds; Morris, Joshua; Multnomah; ‡Nelson, Tommy; ‡New Canaan; ‡New Hope; Oliver Press; Open Hand; Orca; Orchard; ‡Otter Creek; Our Child; Pages; PaperStar; Parenting; Pauline; Peachtree; Pelican; Philomel; Phoenix Learning; Planet Dexter; Players Press; Pleasant Co.; Press-Tige; Price Stern Sloan; ‡Prometheus; Putnam's; Rainbow; Random House; ‡Red Deer; Reidmore; ‡Ronsdale; Rosen; ‡Sadlier, William H.; St. Anthony Messenger; ‡Shamrock; Silver Moon; Simon & Schuster; Southwest Parks; Speech Bin; Standard; Stemmer House; Sterling; Storey; ‡Summit; ‡Sword of The Lord; Thistledown; Troll; Tyndale; ‡UAHC; University Classics; Volcano; Walker; ‡Ward Hill; Weigl Educational; Weiss, Daniel; Whitecap; Wiley, John; ‡Woman's Missionary; World Book; Zino; ‡Zondervan

Young adults (ages 12 and up)

‡Acropolis Books; Africa World Press; African American Images; Aladdin Paperbacks; Alyson Publications, Inc.; American Bible Society; Atheneum Books for Young Readers; A/V Concepts Corp.; Avon Books; B&B Publishing, Inc.; Bantam Doubleday Dell; Barrons Educational Series; Beach Holme Publishers; ‡Beech Tree Books; Behrman House Inc.; Bethany House Publishers; Blackbirch; Blue Sky Press; Boyds Mills; ‡Browndeer; Candlewick; Chariot; Chicago Review; Children's Book Press; ‡China Books; Christian Publications; Chronicle; Clear Light; Concordia; Crossway; CSS Publishing; Davenport, May; Dial; ‡DK Ink; ‡DK Publishing; Dutton; E.M. Press; Enslow; Facts on File; Farrar; Fawcett; Feminist Press; Fitzhenry & Whiteside; Free Spirit; ‡Freestone; Friends United; ‡Front Street; Geringer, Laura; Godine, David R.; Golden; Grapevine; Greenhaven; Greenwillow; Grolier; ‡Grosset; Harcourt; HarperCollins; Hendrick-Long; Highsmith; Holiday House; Holt, Henry; Houghton Mifflin; ‡Huckleberry; ‡Hunter House; Huntington House; Hyperion Books; Jalmar; Jewish Publication Society; Jones, Bob; Knopf; Laredo; Lerner; ‡Levine, Arthur; Lion Books; Little, Brown; Lodestar Books; Lorimer; Lothrop; Lowell House; Lucas/Evans Books Inc.; Lucent; McElderry; Meriwether; Millbrook Press; Mitchell Lane; Mondo; Morehouse; Multnomah; ‡Nelson, Tommy; ‡New Canaan; ‡New Hope; Oliver Press; Open Hand; Orca; Orchard; Our Child; Pages; Pauline; Peachtree; Pelican; Philomel; Phoenix Learning; Players Press; Press-Tige; Price Stern Sloan; ‡Prometheus; Putnam's; Rainbow; ‡Red Deer; Reidmore; ‡Ronsdale; Rosen; ‡Sadlier, William H.; St. Anthony Messenger; Silver Moon; Simon & Schuster; Speech Bin; Standard;

Stemmer House; Stoddart; ‡Summit; ‡Sword of The Lord; Thistledown; Tricycle; Troll; ‡Tundra; ‡UAHC; University Classics; Volcano; Walker; ‡Ward Hill; Weigl Educational; Weiss, Daniel; Wiley, John; ‡Woman's Missionary; World Book; ‡Zondervan

MAGAZINES

Picture-oriented material (preschoolers to 8-year-olds)

Babybug; Bread for God's Children; Chickadee; Focus on the Family Clubhouse; Focus on the Family Clubhouse Jr.; Friend; Highlights for Children; Hopscotch; Humpty Dumpty's; Ladybug; Nature Friend; Science Weekly; Scienceland; Skipping Stones; Story Friends; ‡Together Time; Totally Fox Kids; Turtle; Wonder Time; Your Big Backyard

Young readers (5- to 8-year-olds)

ASPCA Animal Watch; Bread for God's Children; Chickadee; Children's Playmate; ‡Discoveries; Dyna-Math; ‡First Opportunity; Focus on the Family Clubhouse; Focus on the Family Clubhouse Jr.; Friend; Highlights for Children; Hopscotch; Jack And Jill; My Friend; National Geographic World; Nature Friend; Pockets; Racing for Kids; Read; School Mates; Science Weekly; Scienceland; Skipping Stones; Soccer Jr.; Spider; Straight; Totally Fox Kids; U*S* Kids; Writers' International Forum; Your Big Backyard

Middle readers (9- to 11-year-olds)

Advocate; ‡American Girl; ASPCA Animal Watch; Boys' Life; Bread for God's Children; Calliope; Cat Fancy; Child Life; Children's Digest; Cobblestone; Counselor; Cricket Magazine; Crusader; ‡Crystal Ball; ‡Curiocity; Current Health 1; ‡Discoveries; Discovery; Disney Adventures; Dolphin Log; DynaMath; Faces; Focus on the Family Clubhouse; Focus on the Family Clubhouse Jr.; Friend; Goldfinch; Guide; Guideposts for Kids; High Adventure; Highlights for Children; Hopscotch; Jack And Jill ; Junior Scholastic; Kids World; My Friend; National Geographic World; Nature Friend; Odyssey; On The Line; OWL; Pockets; Power and Light; Racing for Kids; R-A-D-A-R; Ranger Rick; School Mates; Science Weekly; Shofar; Skipping Stones; Soccer Jr.; 3-2-1 Contact; Totally Fox Kids; Touch; U*S* Kids; W.O.W. (Wild Outdoor World); Writers' International Forum; Young Judaean

Young adults (ages 12 and up)

Advocate; AIM Magazine; ‡All About You; American Cheerleader; ‡blue jean; Bread for God's Children; Calliope; ‡Career World; ‡Careers & Colleges; Cat Fancy; Challenge; Cobblestone; Cricket Magazine; Crusader; ‡Crystal Ball; ‡Curiocity; Current Health II; Dolphin Log; ‡Dramatics; DynaMath; Exploring; Faces; Florida Leader; For Seniors Only; Guide; High Adventure; Hobson's Choice; I.D.; Junior Scholastic; Keynoter; ‡Kids' Wall Street News; ‡Listen; National Geographic World; Nature Friend; New Era; Odyssey; On Course; On The Line; Power and Light; Racing for Kids; react; Scholastic Math Magazine; School Mates; Science Weekly; Science World; Seventeen; Shadow; ‡Sharing the Victory; Skipping Stones; Soccer Jr.; Street Times; Student Leadership Journal; Teen Life; 'TEEN; Teenage Teenage Christian; ‡3-2-1 Contact; Touch; What! A Magazine; With; Writers' International Forum; Young Salvationist

Subject Index

This index lists book and magazine publishers by the fiction and nonfiction subject area in which they publish. Use it to locate appropriate markets for your work, then carefully read the listings and follow the guidelines of each publisher. Use this index in conjunction with the Age-Level Index to further narrow your list of markets. Listings new to this edition are marked with a (‡).

BOOK PUBLISHERS: FICTION

Adventure

ABC, All Books For Children; Advocacy Press; Africa World Press; Avon Books; Bantam Doubleday Dell; Barrons Educational Series; ‡Beech Tree Books; Bess Press; Bethany House Publishers; ‡Beyond Words Publishing, Inc.; Blue Sky Press; Boyds Mills; ‡Bright Lamb; Callaway Editions; ‡Cartwheel; ‡Children's Library; Christian Ed.; Concordia; Coteau; Crossway; Dial; Down East; Dutton; Farrar; Feminist Press; Fitzhenry & Whiteside; Friends United; Geringer, Laura; Gibbs Smith; Godine, David R.; Golden; Grapevine; Greene Bark; Grolier; ‡Grosset; HaChai; Harcourt; HarperCollins; ‡Hinterland; Holiday House; Holt, Henry; Houghton Mifflin; Hyperion Books; Ideals; Jewish Publication Society; Jones, Bob; Just Us Books; Kaeden; Kar-Ben Copies; Knopf; Laredo; Lerner; Little, Brown; Lodestar Books; Lorimer; Lothrop; Lowell House; McElderry; Milkweed; Mondo; Morris, Joshua; ‡Nelson, Tommy; ‡New Canaan; ‡New Dawn; Northland; Orca; ‡Otter Creek; Pages; PaperStar; Paws IV; Peachtree; Perfection Learning; Philomel; Piñata; Place In The Woods; Pleasant Co.; Press-Tige; Pride; Putnam's; Random House; ‡Red Deer; ‡Ronsdale; Roussan; Seedling; ‡Shamrock; Standard; Stoddart; ‡Sword of The Lord; Thistledown; Time-Life for Children; Tyndale; Whispering Coyote; Whitman, Albert; Writers Press; Zino

Animal

ABC, All Books For Children; ‡Acropolis Books; Advocacy Press; Alyson Publications, Inc.; Atheneum Books for Young Readers; Bantam Doubleday Dell; Barrons Educational Series; Bess Press; ‡Beyond Words Publishing, Inc.; Blue Sky Press; Boyds Mills; Callaway Editions; Candlewick; ‡Cartwheel; ‡Children's Library; Chronicle; Compass Prod.; Crown; Dawn; Dial; ‡DK Publishing; Dutton; Eerdmans; Farrar; Geringer, Laura; Godine, David R.; Golden; Grapevine; Grolier; ‡Grosset; Harcourt; HarperCollins; Holiday House; Houghton Mifflin; Humanics; Hyperion Books; Ideals; Jones, Bob; Kaeden; ‡Key Porter; Knopf; Little, Brown; Lodestar Books; Lothrop; McClanahan; Milkweed; Minstrel; Mondo; Morris, Joshua; Northland; Orchard; ‡Otter Creek; OWL Books; Pages; Paws IV; Peachtree; Perfection Learning; Philomel; Place In The Woods; ‡Playskool; Pleasant Co.; Press-Tige; Pride; Putnam's; Random House; ‡Red Deer; ‡Ronsdale; Seedling; ‡Shamrock; Simon & Schuster; Soundprints; Speech Bin; Standard; Stemmer House; Stoddart; ‡Sword of The Lord; Time-Life for Children; Troll; University Classics; Walker; Whispering Coyote; Whitman, Albert; Zino

Anthology

Bess Press; Blue Sky Press; Candlewick; ‡Cartwheel; ‡Children's Library; ‡DK Publishing; Farrar; Harcourt; HarperCollins; Houghton Mifflin; Hyperion Books; ‡Key Porter; Knopf; Lee & Low; Lodestar Books; Lothrop; Lowell House; Meriwether; ‡New Dawn; Orchard; Owen, Richard C.; Pages; Piñata; Press-Tige; Simon & Schuster; Thistledown; Troll

Concept

ABC, All Books For Children; Advocacy Press; Africa World Press; Barrons Educational Series; Bess Press; Bethany House Publishers; Blue Sky Press; ‡Bright Lamb; Callaway Editions; Candlewick; ‡Cartwheel; ‡Children's Library; Dial; Farrar; Feminist Press; Geringer, Laura; Grapevine; Grolier; ‡Grosset;

Dial; ‡DK Publishing; Down East; Dutton; Farrar; Feminist Press; Fitzhenry & Whiteside; Friends United; Geringer, Laura; Godine, David R.; Golden; Grapevine; ‡Grosset; HaChai; Harcourt; HarperCollins; Hendrick-Long; Holt, Henry; Houghton Mifflin; ‡Huckleberry; Humanics; Hyperion Books; Ideals; Jewish Publication Society; Jones, Bob; Just Us Books; Kaeden; Kar-Ben Copies; Knopf; Lee & Low; Little, Brown; Lodestar Books; Lothrop; Mondo; Morehouse; Morgan Reynolds; ‡New Canaan; Northland; Open Hand; Orca; Orchard; Pacific View; Pages; Peachtree; Pelican; Perfection Learning; Philomel; Pleasant Co.; Pride; Putnam's; Random House; ‡Red Deer; ‡Ronsdale; Roussan; Simon & Schuster; Soundprints; Stoddart; Time-Life for Children; Troll; Walker; Whispering Coyote; Whitman, Albert; Writers Press

Humor

Alyson Publications, Inc.; Avon Books; Bantam Doubleday Dell; Bess Press; Bethany House Publishers; Blue Sky Press; Boyds Mills; Candlewick; ‡Cartwheel; Children's Book Press; ‡Children's Library; Concordia; Coteau; Crossway; Crown; Davenport, May; ‡DK Publishing; Farrar; Fitzhenry & Whiteside; Geringer, Laura; Gibbs Smith; Golden; Grapevine; Grolier; ‡Grosset; Harcourt; Holt, Henry; Houghton Mifflin; Hyperion Books; Ideals; Kaeden; Kar-Ben Copies; Knopf; Little, Brown; Lodestar Books; Lothrop; Lowell House; Meriwether; Milkweed; Minstrel; Mondo; ‡Nelson, Tommy; ‡New Dawn; Northland; Orca; ‡Otter Creek; Owen, Richard C.; OWL Books; Pages; PaperStar; Peachtree; Perfection Learning; Place In The Woods; ‡Playskool; Press-Tige; Pride; Putnam's; ‡Red Deer; ‡Shamrock; Simon & Schuster; Stoddart; Thistledown; Time-Life for Children; Whispering Coyote; Whitman, Albert

Multicultural

ABC, All Books For Children; Advocacy Press; Africa World Press; African American Images; A/V Concepts Corp.; Barrons Educational Series; Beach Holme Publishers; Bess Press; Bethany House Publishers; ‡Beyond Words Publishing, Inc.; Blue Sky Press; ‡Bright Lamb; Candlewick; Carolrhoda; ‡Cartwheel; Children's Book Press; ‡Children's Library; ‡China Books; Chronicle; Coteau; Dutton; Farrar; Feminist Press; Fitzhenry & Whiteside; Geringer, Laura; Gibbs Smith; Golden; Grolier; Harcourt; HarperCollins; ‡Hinterland; Holt, Henry; Houghton Mifflin; ‡Huckleberry; Hyperion Books; Ideals; Jones, Bob; Just Us Books; Kaeden; Kar-Ben Copies; Knopf; Laredo; Lee & Low; Lerner; Little, Brown; Lodestar Books; Lollipop Power; Lorimer; Lothrop; Mage; Magination; Milkweed; Mondo; ‡New Dawn; ‡New Hope; Northland; Open Hand; Orca; Orchard; Our Child; Owen, Richard C.; Pages; PaperStar; Paulist; Perfection Learning; Philomel; Piñata; Place In The Woods; Press-Tige; Pride; Putnam's; ‡Red Deer; ‡Ronsdale; ‡Sadlier, William H.; Seedling; ‡Shamrock; Stemmer House; Stoddart; Tricycle; Walker; ‡Ward Hill; Whitman, Albert; Williamson; Woman's Missionary; Zino

Nature/Environment

ABC, All Books For Children; Advocacy Press; Alyson Publications, Inc.; Barrons Educational Series; Beach Holme Publishers; Bess Press; ‡Beyond Words Publishing, Inc.; Blue Sky Press; Callaway Editions; Candlewick; Carolrhoda; ‡Cartwheel; ‡Children's Library; Chronicle; Coteau; Crown; Dawn; Dial; Down East; Dutton; E.M. Press; Farrar; Fitzhenry & Whiteside; Gibbs Smith; Godine, David R.; Golden; Grapevine; ‡Grosset; Harcourt; HarperCollins; Houghton Mifflin; Humanics; Ideals; Jones, Bob; Kaeden; ‡Key Porter; Knopf; Lerner; Little, Brown; Lothrop; Lowell House; Milkweed; Mondo; Morris, Joshua; ‡New Dawn; Northland; Orca; Orchard; ‡Otter Creek; Owen, Richard C.; OWL Books; Pages; Peachtree; Perfection Learning; Philomel; Press-Tige; Pride; ‡Red Deer; ‡Ronsdale; Seedling; ‡Shamrock; ‡Sierra Club; Soundprints; Stemmer House; Time-Life for Children; Tricycle; Troll; University Classics; Whitman, Albert

Poetry

‡Acropolis Books; Advocacy Press; Beach Holme Publishers; Blue Sky Press; Boyds Mills; Candlewick; ‡Cartwheel; Chronicle; Dial; Dutton; Eerdmans; Farrar; Geringer, Laura; Godine, David R.; Grapevine; Harcourt; HarperCollins; Hyperion Books; Knopf; Lee & Low; Lothrop; McElderry; Meadowbrook; Orchard; Owen, Richard C.; Pages; Peachtree; Perfection Learning; Philomel; Piñata; Press-Tige; ‡Red Deer; ‡Ronsdale; Simon & Schuster; Thistledown; Troll; Whispering Coyote

Problem Novels

Avon Books; Barrons Educational Series; Bethany House Publishers; Boyds Mills; Chronicle; Dial; DK Publishing; E.M. Press; Farrar; Feminist Press; HaChai; Harcourt; Houghton Mifflin; Hyperion Books; Jewish Publication Society; Knopf; Lerner; Lorimer; Lothrop; Magination; ‡Nelson, Tommy; ‡New Dawn; Orca; Pages; Philomel; Piñata; Place In The Woods; Press-Tige; Pride; Putnam's; ‡Red Deer; Roussan; Troll; University Classics; Whitman, Albert

Religious

‡Acropolis Books; Bethany House Publishers; Christian Publications; Compass Prod.; Concordia; Crossway; CSS Publishing; Dial; E.M. Press; Eerdmans; Farrar; Forward Movement; Friends United; Golden; HaChai; Harcourt; HarperCollins; Holt, Henry; Huntington House; ‡Jewish Lights; Jewish Publication Society; Kar-Ben Copies; Knopf; Lothrop; Meriwether; Morehouse; Morgan Reynolds; Morris, Joshua; Multnomah; ‡Nelson, Tommy; ‡New Canaan; ‡New Hope; Our Sunday Visitor; Pauline; Paulist; Pelican; Press-Tige; ‡Sadlier, William H.; Standard; ‡Sword of The Lord; Time-Life for Children; Tyndale; ‡UAHC; ‡Zondervan

Romance

Avon Books; Bethany House Publishers; Farrar; Fawcett; Houghton Mifflin; Hyperion Books; Jewish Publication Society; Just Us Books; Knopf; Pages; Thistledown; Troll

Science Fiction

Alyson Publications, Inc.; Callaway Editions; Candlewick; ‡Cartwheel; ‡Children's Library; Compass Prod.; Coteau; Dial; Dutton; Farrar; Fawcett; Harcourt; HarperCollins; Houghton Mifflin; Hyperion Books; Ideals; Kaeden; ‡Key Porter; Knopf; Little, Brown; Lodestar Books; Lothrop; Lowell House; ‡New Dawn; Orchard; Owen, Richard C.; Perfection Learning; Press-Tige; Roussan; ‡Shamrock; Simon & Schuster; Thistledown; Walker

Special Needs

Alyson Publications, Inc.; A/V Concepts Corp.; Carolrhoda; Fairview; Farrar; Houghton Mifflin; Humanics; Jalmar; Kar-Ben Copies; Knopf; Lothrop; Magination; ‡New Dawn; Orca; Our Child; Perfection Learning; Philomel; Press-Tige; Putnam's; Seedling; Speech Bin; University Classics; Whitman, Albert

Sports

Avon Books; Bantam Doubleday Dell; Bess Press; Bethany House Publishers; Candlewick; ‡Cartwheel; Dial; ‡DK Publishing; Farrar; Feminist Press; Fitzhenry & Whiteside; Geringer, Laura; ‡Grosset; Harcourt; Holt, Henry; Houghton Mifflin; Hyperion Books; Ideals; Jewish Publication Society; Jones, Bob; Kaeden; ‡Key Porter; Knopf; Lerner; Lorimer; Lothrop; Lowell House; Mondo; Morgan Reynolds; ‡Nelson, Tommy; Orchard; Owen, Richard C.; Pages; PaperStar; Peachtree; Perfection Learning; Place In The Woods; Press-Tige; Putnam's; Random House; Roussan; Seedling; ‡Shamrock; Standard; Time-Life for Children; Troll

Suspense/Mystery

Alyson Publications, Inc.; Avon Books; Bantam Doubleday Dell; Barrons Educational Series; Bethany House Publishers; Callaway Editions; Candlewick; ‡Cartwheel; ‡Children's Library; Christian Ed.; Compass Prod.; Concordia; Coteau; Crossway; Dial; DK Publishing; Dutton; Farrar; Feminist Press; Fitzhenry & Whiteside; Geringer, Laura; Gibbs Smith; Godine, David R.; Golden; Grapevine; Harcourt; HarperCollins; Holt, Henry; Houghton Mifflin; Hyperion Books; Jewish Publication Society; Jones, Bob; Just Us Books; Kaeden; Kar-Ben Copies; ‡Key Porter; Knopf; Laredo; Lerner; Little, Brown; Lodestar Books; Lorimer; Lothrop; Lowell House; McElderry; Mega-Books; Milkweed; Minstrel; ‡Nelson, Tommy; ‡New Canaan; Northland; Orca; Orchard; ‡Otter Creek; Pages; PaperStar; Perfection Learning; Place In The Woods; Pleasant Co.; Press-Tige; Pride; Putnam's; Random House; Roussan; ‡Shamrock; Simon & Schuster; Standard; Stoddart; ‡Sword of The Lord; Thistledown; Time-Life for Children; Troll; Tyndale; Whitman, Albert

BOOK PUBLISHERS: NONFICTION

Activity Books

American Bible Society; A/V Concepts Corp.; Bess Press; Bright Ring; Candlewick; Chicago Review; Concordia; Crown; Davenport, May; DK Publishing; Evan-Moor; Fairview; Farrar; Gibbs Smith; Godine, David R.; ‡Grosset; Gryphon House; Harcourt; HarperCollins; Highsmith; Houghton Mifflin; ‡Huckleberry; Humanics; ‡Hunter House; Ideals; Incentive; Jalmar; ‡Jewish Lights; Kaeden; Kar-Ben Copies; Lion Books; Little, Brown; Lodestar Books; Lowell House; McClanahan; Meadowbrook; Meriwether; Millbrook Press; Morris, Joshua; ‡Nelson, Tommy; ‡Ottenheimer; ‡Otter Creek; Pages; Paws IV; ‡Peel; Perfection Learning; Place In The Woods; Players Press; ‡Playskool; Pleasant Co.; Press-Tige; Pride; Rainbow; Rhache; Speech Bin; Sterling; ‡Summit; ‡Sword of The Lord; Tricycle; Troll; Tyndale; University Classics; Wiley, John; Williamson; World Book

Animal

‡Acropolis Books; Atheneum Books for Young Readers; ‡Benefactory, The; Bess Press; Blackbirch; Blue Sky Press; Boyds Mills; Candlewick; Carolrhoda; ‡Cartwheel; ‡Children's Library; Chronicle; Compass Prod.; Copper Beech; Crown; Dawn; Dial; ‡DK Publishing; Down East; Dutton; Enslow; Evan-Moor; Facts on File; Farrar; Godine, David R.; Golden; Grolier; ‡Grosset; Harcourt; HarperCollins; Holiday House; Houghton Mifflin; Humanics; Ideals; Jones, Bob; Kaeden; ‡Key Porter; Knopf; Lerner; Little, Brown; Lodestar Books; Lothrop; McClanahan; Millbrook Press; Mondo; Morris, Joshua; Northland; Orchard; ‡Ottenheimer; ‡Otter Creek; Owen, Richard C.; OWL Books; Pages; Peachtree; Perfection Learning; Place In The Woods; ‡Playskool; Press-Tige; Putnam's; Random House; Rhache; ‡Ronsdale; Rosen; Seedling; Soundprints; Southwest Parks; Stemmer House; Sterling; Storey; ‡Sword of The Lord; Time-Life for Children; Troll; University Classics; Walker; Whitecap; Whitman, Albert; Wiley, John; Williamson; World Book

Arts/Crafts

Abbeville Kids; ‡Benefactory, The; Bright Ring; Chicago Review; Chronicle; Concordia; Copper Beech; Farrar; Fitzhenry & Whiteside; Gibbs Smith; Golden; Grolier; ‡Grosset; Harcourt; Houghton Mifflin; ‡Huckleberry; Humanics; Ideals; Incentive; Kar-Ben Copies; Knopf; Lerner; Lion Books; Little, Brown; Lowell House; Millbrook Press; OWL Books; Pages; Paws IV; Philomel; Pleasant Co.; Press-Tige; Rainbow; Rhache; Sterling; Storey; ‡Summit; Tricycle; University Classics; Wiley, John; Williamson; World Book

Biography

Atheneum Books for Young Readers; B&B Publishing, Inc.; ‡Beech Tree Books; ‡Beyond Words Publishing, Inc.; Blackbirch; Blue Sky Press; Boyds Mills; Candlewick; Carolrhoda; ‡Cartwheel; Chronicle; Copper Beech; Coteau; Crown; Dial; ‡DK Publishing; Dutton; Eerdmans; Enslow; Evan-Moor; Facts on File; Farrar; Feminist Press; Fitzhenry & Whiteside; Godine, David R.; Greenhaven; Grolier; ‡Grosset; Harcourt; HarperCollins; Hendrick-Long; Holiday House; Houghton Mifflin; ‡Huckleberry; Humanics; Incentive; Jewish Publication Society; Jones, Bob; Just Us Books; Kaeden; Kar-Ben Copies; Knopf; Lee & Low; Lerner; Lion Books; Little, Brown; Lodestar Books; Lothrop; McElderry; Millbrook Press; Minstrel; Mitchell Lane; Mondo; Morgan Reynolds; Oliver Press; Pages; Pauline; Paulist; Paws IV; Peachtree; Pelican; Perfection Learning; Philomel; Piñata; Press-Tige; Putnam's; Random House; ‡Ronsdale; Rosen; Simon & Schuster; Stemmer House; ‡Sword of The Lord; Troll; Walker; ‡Ward Hill; Whitman, Albert; Wiley, John

Careers

Advocacy Press; B&B Publishing, Inc.; Crown; ‡DK Publishing; Enslow; Facts on File; Farrar; Fitzhenry & Whiteside; Grolier; Harcourt; Houghton Mifflin; Humanics; Kaeden; Kar-Ben Copies; ‡Key Porter; Laredo; Lerner; Millbrook Press; Owen, Richard C.; Perfection Learning; Players Press; Press-Tige; Rhache; Rosen; ‡Summit; Troll; Walker; Weigl Educational; Whitman, Albert; Williamson; World Book

Concept

ABC, All Books For Children; Africa World Press; Alyson Publications, Inc.; B&B Publishing, Inc.; Barrons Educational Series; Bess Press; Blackbirch; Blue Sky Press; Candlewick; ‡Cartwheel; Compass Prod.; Copper Beech; ‡DK Publishing; Farrar; Golden; Grolier; ‡Grosset; Harcourt; Holiday House; Houghton Mifflin; Humanics; Ideals; Ideals; Jones, Bob; Kar-Ben Copies; Lerner; Little, Brown; Lodestar Books; Lothrop; Lowell House; McClanahan; Magination; Millbrook Press; ‡Ottenheimer; OWL Books; Pages; Paulist; ‡Playskool; Press-Tige; Putnam's; Rhache; Rosen; Seedling; Simon & Schuster; Standard; Time-Life for Children; Tricycle; University Classics; Whitman, Albert; Wiley, John; World Book

Cooking

Bright Ring; ‡Children's Library; Chronicle; Copper Beech; Farrar; Golden; Houghton Mifflin; Humanics; Ideals; Kar-Ben Copies; Lerner; Little, Brown; Lowell House; Pelican; Pleasant Co.; Press-Tige; Rhache; Rosen; Williamson

Geography

B&B Publishing, Inc.; ‡Beyond Words Publishing, Inc.; Blackbirch; Boyds Mills; Candlewick; Charlesbridge; ‡Children's Library; Chronicle; Copper Beech; ‡DK Publishing; Evan-Moor; Facts on File; Farrar; Fitzhenry & Whiteside; Golden; Grolier; HarperCollins; Holiday House; Houghton Mifflin; Humanics; Incentive; Jones, Bob; Kaeden; Lerner; Little, Brown; Lowell House; Millbrook Press; Mondo; ‡New Canaan; Oliver Press; ‡Ottenheimer; Owen, Richard C.; Pages; Perfection Learning; Press-Tige; Reidmore; Southwest Parks; Sterling; Time-Life for Children; Tricycle; Whitman, Albert; Wiley, John; World Book

Health

‡Beyond Words Publishing, Inc.; Copper Beech; Crown; Enslow; Facts on File; Fairview; Farrar; Fitzhenry & Whiteside; Grolier; Harcourt; Houghton Mifflin; Humanics; ‡Hunter House; Ideals; Incentive; Kaeden; Laredo; Lerner; Lowell House; Lucent; Magination; Millbrook Press; Parenting; Pelican; Perfection Learning; Press-Tige; Rhache; Speech Bin; ‡Summit; Time-Life for Children; Tricycle; Troll; University Classics; Walker; Whitman, Albert; Wiley, John; Williamson; World Book

Hi-Lo

A/V Concepts Corp.; Barrons Educational Series; Bess Press; Facts on File; Farrar; Fitzhenry & Whiteside; Grolier; Harcourt; Houghton Mifflin; Humanics; ‡Key Porter; Lerner; Lodestar Books; Perfection Learning; Place In The Woods; Press-Tige; Rosen; Seedling

History

Africa World Press; Atheneum Books for Young Readers; B&B Publishing, Inc.; Bess Press; ‡Beyond Words Publishing, Inc.; Blackbirch; Blue Sky Press; Boyds Mills; Candlewick; Carolrhoda; ‡Cartwheel; ‡Children's Library; Chronicle; Copper Beech; Coteau; Crown; Dial; Down East; Dutton; Eerdmans; Enslow; Evan-Moor; Farrar; Feminist Press; Fitzhenry & Whiteside; Friends United; Godine, David R.; Greenhaven; Grolier; ‡Grosset; Harcourt; Hendrick-Long; Houghton Mifflin; ‡Huckleberry; Humanics; Ideals; Incentive; Jewish Publication Society; Jones, Bob; Kaeden; Kar-Ben Copies; Knopf; Lee & Low; Lerner; Lion Books; Little, Brown; Lodestar Books; Lowell House; Lucent; McElderry; Millbrook Press; Morgan Reynolds; ‡New Canaan; Northland; Oliver Press; Open Hand; Orchard; Pages; Peachtree; Pelican; Perfection Learning; Philomel; Place In The Woods; Players Press; Pleasant Co.; Press-Tige; Pride; Putnam's; Random House; Reidmore; Rhache; ‡Ronsdale; Soundprints; Southwest Parks; ‡Sword of The Lord; Time-Life for Children; Troll; Walker; ‡Ward Hill; Whitman, Albert; Williamson; World Book; Writers Press; Zino

Hobbies

Avon Books; Bright Ring; Carolrhoda; Chicago Review; ‡Children's Library; Crown; Enslow; Farrar; Fitzhenry & Whiteside; Grolier; Harcourt; Houghton Mifflin; Humanics; Ideals; Kaeden; Lerner; Lion Books; Lowell House; Millbrook Press; OWL Books; Pages; Perfection Learning; Place In The Woods; Pleasant Co.; Press-Tige; Random House; Rhache; Sterling; Storey; ‡Summit; Troll; Walker; Whitman, Albert; Wiley, John; World Book

How-to

Barrons Educational Series; Copper Beech; Farrar; Gibbs Smith; Grapevine; Grolier; Harcourt; HarperCollins; Houghton Mifflin; ‡Huckleberry; Humanics; Kaeden; Knopf; Lerner; Lion Books; Magination; Meriwether; Mondo; ‡New Canaan; OWL Books; Pages; Place In The Woods; Planet Dexter; Players Press; Pleasant Co.; Press-Tige; Rhache; Rosen; Sterling; Storey; ‡Summit; Tricycle; Wiley, John; Williamson; World Book

Multicultural

Advocacy Press; Africa World Press; African American Images; American Bible Society; A/V Concepts Corp.; B&B Publishing, Inc.; Bess Press; ‡Beyond Words Publishing, Inc.; Blackbirch; Blue Sky Press; Boyds Mills; Carolrhoda; ‡Cartwheel; ‡China Books; Chronicle; Clear Light; Coteau; Dutton; Facts on File; Fairview; Farrar; Feminist Press; Fitzhenry & Whiteside; Godine, David R.; Grolier; Harcourt; HarperCollins; Hendrick-Long; Houghton Mifflin; ‡Hunter House; Incentive; Jones, Bob; Kaeden; Kar-Ben Copies; Knopf; Lee & Low; Lerner; Lion Books; Little, Brown; Lodestar Books; Lothrop; Lucent; Mage; Magination; Millbrook Press; Mitchell Lane; Mondo; Morehouse; Morgan Reynolds; ‡New Hope; Northland; Oliver Press; Open Hand; Orchard; Our Child; Owen, Richard C.; Pacific View; Pages; Paulist; Pelican; Perfection Learning; Philomel; Piñata; Place In The Woods; Players Press; Press-Tige; Pride; Putnam's; Reidmore; ‡Ronsdale; Rosen; Seedling; Stemmer House; Sterling; Tilbury House; Walker; ‡Ward Hill; Weigl Educational; Whitman, Albert; Williamson; Woman's Missionary; Zino

Music/Dance

Avon Books; Bright Ring; Copper Beech; Crown; Farrar; Fitzhenry & Whiteside; Harcourt; Houghton Mifflin; Humanics; ‡Hunter House; Kaeden; Knopf; Lerner; Millbrook Press; Pelican; Philomel; Players Press; Press-Tige; Rhache; Seedling; Sterling; Troll; Walker; Whitman, Albert; Williamson

Nature/Environment

ABC, All Books For Children; American Bible Society; B&B Publishing, Inc.; ‡Benefactory, The; ‡Beyond Words Publishing, Inc.; Blue Sky Press; Boyds Mills; Bright Ring; Candlewick; Carolrhoda; ‡Children's Library; Chronicle; Copper Beech; Coteau; Crown; Dawn; Dial; Down East; Dutton; Eerdmans; Enslow; Evan-Moor; Facts on File; Farrar; Fitzhenry & Whiteside; Gibbs Smith; Godine, David R.; Golden; Greenhaven; Grolier; ‡Grosset; Harcourt; HarperCollins; Holiday House; Houghton Mifflin; Humanics; Ideals; Incentive; Jones, Bob; Kaeden; ‡Key Porter; Knopf; Learning Triangle; Lerner; Little, Brown; Lodestar Books; Lothrop; Lucent; Millbrook Press; Mondo; Morris, Joshua; Orchard; ‡Ottenheimer; ‡Otter Creek; Owen, Richard C.; OWL Books; Pages; Paws IV; Peachtree; Pelican; Perfection Learning; Planet Dexter; Press-Tige; ‡Prometheus; Putnam's; Reidmore; Rhache; ‡Ronsdale; Rosen; ‡Sierra Club; Simon & Schuster; Southwest Parks; Standard; Stemmer House; Sterling; Storey; Time-Life for Children; Tricycle; Troll; University Classics; Walker; Whitecap; Whitman, Albert; Wiley, John; Williamson; World Book

Reference

American Bible Society; B&B Publishing, Inc.; Barrons Educational Series; Behrman House Inc.; Bess Press; ‡Beyond Words Publishing, Inc.; Blackbirch; Copper Beech; ‡DK Publishing; Facts on File; Farrar; Fitzhenry & Whiteside; Grolier; Harcourt; Highsmith; Houghton Mifflin; Humanics; ‡Key Porter; ‡Legacy; Lowell House; McClanahan; Millbrook Press; ‡Nelson, Tommy; ‡New Canaan; ‡Ottenheimer; Pages; Players Press; Press-Tige; Rainbow; Rhache; Simon & Schuster; Sterling; ‡Sword of The Lord; Time-Life for Children; Wiley, John; World Book

Religious

Abingdon Press; ‡Acropolis Books; American Bible Society; Bethany House Publishers; Christian Ed.; Christian Publications; Compass Prod.; Concordia; Crown; CSS Publishing; Eerdmans; Facts on File; Farrar; Forward Movement; Friends United; Harcourt; Huntington House; Ideals; ‡Jewish Lights; Jewish Publication Society; Kaeden; Kar-Ben Copies; ‡Legacy; Meriwether; Morehouse; Morris, Joshua; Multnomah; ‡Nelson, Tommy; ‡New Canaan; ‡New Hope; ‡Ottenheimer; Pauline; Paulist; Pelican; Press-Tige;

Rainbow; Rosen; ‡Sadlier, William H.; St. Anthony Messenger; Standard; ‡Sword of The Lord; Time-Life for Children; Treasure; Tyndale; ‡UAHC; Walker; ‡Woman's Missionary; ‡Zondervan

Science

A/V Concepts Corp.; B&B Publishing, Inc.; ‡Beyond Words Publishing, Inc.; Blackbirch; Bright Ring; Carolrhoda; Charlesbridge; ‡Children's Library; Chronicle; Copper Beech; Crown; ‡DK Publishing; Evan-Moor; Facts on File; Farrar; Feminist Press; Gibbs Smith; Golden; Grapevine; Grolier; ‡Grosset; Harcourt; Holiday House; Houghton Mifflin; Humanics; Ideals; Incentive; Kaeden; ‡Key Porter; Knopf; Learning Triangle; Lerner; Lodestar Books; Lothrop; Lowell House; Millbrook Press; Mondo; OWL Books; Pages; Perfection Learning; Planet Dexter; Press-Tige; Pride; ‡Prometheus; Reidmore; Rhache; Rosen; Seedling; Sterling; Time-Life for Children; Tricycle; Walker; Whitman, Albert; Wiley, John; Williamson; World Book

Self Help

‡Acropolis Books; Advocacy Press; American Bible Society; A/V Concepts Corp.; Avon Books; Barrons Educational Series; Bethany House Publishers; Fairview; Farrar; Free Spirit; Grapevine; Humanics; ‡Hunter House; Jalmar; Knopf; Lerner; Little, Brown; Lowell House; Morehouse; ‡Nelson, Tommy; Parenting; Paulist; Perfection Learning; Place In The Woods; Pleasant Co.; Press-Tige; ‡Prometheus; Rhache; Rosen; ‡Summit; University Classics; Volcano; Wiley, John; Williamson

Social Issues

Advocacy Press; Alyson Publications, Inc.; American Bible Society; B&B Publishing, Inc.; Barrons Educational Series; Bethany House Publishers; Carolrhoda; Chronicle; Coteau; DK Publishing; Dutton; Enslow; Facts on File; Fairview; Farrar; Feminist Press; Fitzhenry & Whiteside; Greenhaven; Grolier; Harcourt; Holiday House; Houghton Mifflin; Humanics; ‡Hunter House; Jalmar; Kar-Ben Copies; Knopf; Lerner; Little, Brown; Lodestar Books; Lucent; Millbrook Press; Morehouse; Morgan Reynolds; Pages; Parenting; Paulist; Perfection Learning; Perspectives; Place In The Woods; ‡Playskool; Press-Tige; Pride; ‡Prometheus; Putnam's; ‡Ronsdale; Rosen; Tricycle; Volcano; Walker; ‡Ward Hill; Whitman, Albert

Special Needs

American Bible Society; Blackbirch; Carolrhoda; Davenport, May; Fairview; Farrar; Grolier; Houghton Mifflin; Humanics; Lerner; Magination; Our Child; Perfection Learning; Place In The Woods; Press-Tige; Putnam's; Rhache; Rosen; Speech Bin; University Classics; Volcano; Whitman, Albert; Zino

Sports

Avon Books; Bess Press; ‡Cartwheel; Compass Prod.; Copper Beech; Crown; ‡DK Publishing; Enslow; Facts on File; Farrar; Fitzhenry & Whiteside; Grolier; ‡Grosset; Harcourt; Holiday House; Houghton Mifflin; Humanics; Ideals; Jewish Publication Society; Kaeden; ‡Key Porter; Knopf; Lerner; Lowell House; Lucent; Millbrook Press; Mondo; Morgan Reynolds; Owen, Richard C.; Pages; Pelican; Perfection Learning; Place In The Woods; Pleasant Co.; Press-Tige; Random House; Rosen; Seedling; Standard; Sterling; Time-Life for Children; Troll; Walker

Textbooks

Advocacy Press; A/V Concepts Corp.; Bess Press; Farrar; Grapevine; Gryphon House; Houghton Mifflin; Humanics; Jalmar; Laredo; ‡New Canaan; Phoenix Learning; Players Press; Press-Tige; Reidmore; ‡Sadlier, William H.; Speech Bin; University Classics; Weigl Educational

MAGAZINES: FICTION

Adventure
Advocate; ASPCA Animal Watch; Boys' Life; Boys' Quest; Calliope; Challenge; Children's Digest; Counselor; Cricket Magazine; Crusader; ‡Curiocity; ‡Discoveries; Discovery; Disney Adventures; Flicker Magazine; Focus on the Family Clubhouse; Focus on the Family Clubhouse Jr.; Friend; Guideposts for Kids; Highlights for Children; Humpty Dumpty's; I.D.; Kids at Home; Kids World; Ladybug; My Friend; Odyssey; On Course; Pockets; Power and Light; R-A-D-A-R; Read; Seventeen; Shadow; Spider; Street Times; Teen Life; Teenage Christian; Touch; Turtle; U*S* Kids; Wonder Time; Writers' International Forum; Your Big Backyard

Animal
ASPCA Animal Watch; ‡blue jean; Boys' Life; Boys' Quest; Cat Fancy; Challenge; Chickadee; Children's Digest; Children's Playmate; Cricket Magazine; Crusader; Flicker Magazine; Focus on the Family Clubhouse; Focus on the Family Clubhouse Jr.; Friend; Guideposts for Kids; Highlights for Children; Humpty Dumpty's; I.D.; Jack And Jill ; Kids at Home; Ladybug; My Friend; R-A-D-A-R; Ranger Rick; Read; Scholastic Math Magazine; Seventeen; Shadow; Skipping Stones; Spider; Touch; Turtle; U*S* Kids; Your Big Backyard

Contemporary
Advocate; ‡American Girl; ‡blue jean; Boys' Life; Bread for God's Children; Challenge; Children's Digest; Children's Playmate; Cricket Magazine; Crusader; ‡Curiocity; ‡Discoveries; Discovery; Disney Adventures; Faces; Friend; Guideposts for Kids; Highlights for Children; Humpty Dumpty's; I.D.; Jack And Jill ; Kids at Home; Kids World; ‡Listen; My Friend; New Era; On Course; On The Line; Pockets; Power and Light; Read; Seventeen; Shadow; Shofar; Skipping Stones; Spider; Story Friends; Straight; Street Times; Teen Life; 'TEEN; Teenage Christian; Touch; Turtle; U*S* Kids; With; Wonder Time; Writers' International Forum; Young Salvationist

Fantasy
Advocate; Beckett; ‡blue jean; Boys' Life; Children's Digest; Children's Playmate; Cricket Magazine; ‡Crystal Ball; ‡Curiocity; Discovery; Disney Adventures; Highlights for Children; Hobson's Choice; Humpty Dumpty's; Ladybug; Ranger Rick; Read; Seventeen; Shadow; Spider; Street Times; Touch; Turtle; With; Writers' International Forum; Your Big Backyard

Folktales
Advocate; ASPCA Animal Watch; ‡blue jean; Calliope; Children's Digest; Children's Playmate; Cricket Magazine; ‡Crystal Ball; Faces; Flicker Magazine; Focus on the Family Clubhouse; Focus on the Family Clubhouse Jr.; Friend; Guideposts for Kids; Highlights for Children; Humpty Dumpty's; I.D.; Jack And Jill ; Kids at Home; Kids World; Ladybug; Odyssey; Pockets; Read; Seventeen; Shadow; Spider; Street Times; Touch; Turtle

Health
Advocate; Challenge; Children's Digest; Flicker Magazine; Focus on the Family Clubhouse; Focus on the Family Clubhouse Jr.; For Seniors Only; Guideposts for Kids; Holidays & Seasonal Celebrations; Humpty Dumpty's; Jack And Jill ; ‡Listen; Read; Seventeen; Shadow; Straight; Touch; Turtle; U*S* Kids

History
AIM Magazine; ‡American Girl; ASPCA Animal Watch; Beckett; Boys' Life; Boys' Quest; Calliope; Challenge; Children's Digest; Children's Playmate; Counselor; Cricket Magazine; Faces; Flicker Magazine; Focus on the Family Clubhouse; Focus on the Family Clubhouse Jr.; Friend; Goldfinch; Guideposts for Kids; Highlights for Children; Hopscotch; Humpty Dumpty's; I.D.; Jack And Jill ; Kids at Home; Odyssey; On Course; On The Line; Read; Seventeen; Shadow; Spider; Street Times; Teen Life; Touch; Turtle; U*S* Kids

Humorous

Advocate; Beckett; Boys' Life; Boys' Quest; Bread for God's Children; Chickadee; Children's Digest; Children's Playmate; Cricket Magazine; Crusader; ‡Curiocity; Discovery; Disney Adventures; Flicker Magazine; For Seniors Only; Friend; Guideposts for Kids; Highlights for Children; Hopscotch; Humpty Dumpty's; I.D.; Jack And Jill ; Kids World; Ladybug; ‡Listen; My Friend; New Era; On Course; On The Line; Power and Light; R-A-D-A-R; Ranger Rick; Read; School Mates; Seventeen; Shadow; Shofar; Skipping Stones; Spider; Story Friends; Straight; Street Times; Teen Life; 'TEEN; Teenage Christian; Touch; Turtle; U*S* Kids; With; Writers' International Forum; Your Big Backyard

Multicultural

AIM Magazine; ‡American Girl; ASPCA Animal Watch; ‡blue jean; Counselor; Cricket Magazine; Crusader; Faces; ‡First Opportunity; Flicker Magazine; Focus on the Family Clubhouse; Focus on the Family Clubhouse Jr.; Friend; Guideposts for Kids; Highlights for Children; Holidays & Seasonal Celebrations; Humpty Dumpty's; I.D.; Kids at Home; Kids World; Ladybug; Pockets; Power and Light; Read; Shadow; Skipping Stones; Spider; Story Friends; Street Times; Student Leadership Journal; Teen Life; Touch; Turtle; U*S* Kids; With; Wonder Time; Young Salvationist; Your Big Backyard

Nature/Environment

Advocate; ASPCA Animal Watch; ‡blue jean; Boys' Quest; Bread for God's Children; Challenge; Chickadee; Children's Digest; ‡Chirp; Counselor; Cricket Magazine; Crusader; Flicker Magazine; Focus on the Family Clubhouse; Focus on the Family Clubhouse Jr.; Guideposts for Kids; Highlights for Children; Holidays & Seasonal Celebrations; Hopscotch; Humpty Dumpty's; I.D.; Kids at Home; Kids World; Ladybug; ‡Listen; My Friend; On The Line; Pockets; Power and Light; R-A-D-A-R; Read; Shadow; Skipping Stones; Spider; Story Friends; Touch; Turtle; U*S* Kids; Wonder Time; Writers' International Forum; Your Big Backyard

Problem-Solving

Advocate; ASPCA Animal Watch; Boys' Life; Boys' Quest; Challenge; Children's Digest; Counselor; Crusader; ‡Discoveries; Flicker Magazine; Friend; Guideposts for Kids; Humpty Dumpty's; Jack And Jill ; Kids World; Ladybug; ‡Listen; On The Line; Pockets; Power and Light; Read; Shadow; Spider; Story Friends; Straight; Street Times; Teen Life; 'TEEN; Teenage Christian; Touch; Turtle; U*S* Kids; With; Writers' International Forum

Religious

Bread for God's Children; Challenge; Counselor; Crusader; ‡Discoveries; Faces; Flicker Magazine; Friend; Guideposts for Kids; I.D.; My Friend; New Era; On Course; On The Line; Pockets; Power and Light; Seventeen; Shadow; Shofar; Story Friends; Straight; Student Leadership Journal; Teen Life; Teenage Christian; ‡Together Time; Touch; With; Wonder Time; Writers' International Forum; Young Judaean; Young Salvationist

Romance

Advocate; ‡blue jean; Guideposts for Kids; New Era; Read; Seventeen; Shadow; Teen Life; 'TEEN; Touch; With; Writers' International Forum

Science/Fiction

Advocate; Boys' Life; Children's Digest; Children's Playmate; ‡Crystal Ball; ‡Curiocity; Discovery; Disney Adventures; Focus on the Family Clubhouse; Focus on the Family Clubhouse Jr.; Guideposts for Kids; Highlights for Children; Hobson's Choice; Hopscotch; I.D.; Kids World; Ladybug; My Friend; New Era; Ranger Rick; Read; Seventeen; Shadow; Spider; Teen Life; With; Writers' International Forum

Sports

Advocate; Beckett; Bread for God's Children; Children's Digest; Children's Playmate; Counselor; Cricket Magazine; Discovery; Disney Adventures; Flicker Magazine; Focus on the Family Clubhouse; Focus on the Family Clubhouse Jr.; Guideposts for Kids; Highlights for Children; Hopscotch; Humpty Dumpty's; I.D.; Jack And Jill; Kids at Home; Kids World; Ladybug; ‡Listen; New Era; On Course; On The Line; Read; R-A-D-A-R; Seventeen; Shadow; Shofar; Spider; Straight; Teen Life; Teenage Christian; Turtle; U*S* Kids; With; Young Salvationist

Suspense/Mystery

Advocate; ‡American Girl; Boys' Life; Children's Digest; Children's Playmate; Cricket Magazine; ‡Curiocity; Discovery; Disney Adventures; Friend; Guideposts for Kids; Hopscotch; Humpty Dumpty's; I.D.; Kids at Home; Kids World; Ladybug; R-A-D-A-R; Read; Seventeen; Shadow; Spider; 'TEEN; Teenage Christian; Turtle; U*S* Kids; Writers' International Forum

Travel

Guideposts for Kids

MAGAZINES: NONFICTION

Adventure

W.O.W. (Wild Outdoor World)

Animal

Advocate; ASPCA Animal Watch; Boys' Life; Boys' Quest; Cat Fancy; Challenge; Chickadee; Child Life; Children's Digest; Children's Playmate; Cricket Magazine; Crusader; ‡Curiocity; Discovery; Disney Adventures; Dolphin Log; DynaMath; Flicker Magazine; Focus on the Family Clubhouse; Focus on the Family Clubhouse Jr.; Friend; Girls' Life; Guide; Guideposts for Kids; Highlights for Children; Hopscotch; Humpty Dumpty's; I.D.; Jack And Jill ; Kids at Home; ‡Kids' Wall Street News; Kids World; Ladybug; ‡LiveWire; National Geographic World; Nature Friend; New Moon; OWL; R-A-D-A-R; Ranger Rick; react; Read; Scholastic Math Magazine; Science World; Scienceland; Seventeen; Shadow; Skipping Stones; Spider; Story Friends; Teenage Christian; ‡3-2-1 Contact; Touch; Turtle; U*S* Kids; W.O.W. (Wild Outdoor World); Your Big Backyard

Arts/Crafts

Advocate; ASPCA Animal Watch; blue jean; Boys' Quest; Calliope; Cat Fancy; Challenge; Chickadee; Child Life; Children's Digest; Children's Playmate; ‡Chirp; Counselor; Crayola Kids; Cricket Magazine; Crusader; Curiocity; ‡Dramatics; DynaMath; Faces; Flicker Magazine; Focus on the Family Clubhouse; Focus on the Family Clubhouse Jr.; Friend; Girls' Life; Goldfinch; Highlights for Children; Holidays & Seasonal Celebrations; Hopscotch; Humpty Dumpty's; I.D.; Jack And Jill ; Kids at Home; Ladybug; ‡Listen; LiveWire; My Friend; National Geographic World; New Moon; Odyssey; On The Line; OWL; R-A-D-A-R; Scholastic Math Magazine; Scienceland; Shadow; Spider; Street Times; Teenage Christian; ‡Together Time; Turtle; U*S* Kids; Your Big Backyard; ZILLIONS

Biography

Advocate; Calliope; Children's Digest; Children's Playmate; Cobblestone; Counselor; Cricket Magazine; Crusader; ‡Crystal Ball; ‡Curiocity; Discovery; Disney Adventures; Florida Leader; Friend; Girls' Life; Goldfinch; Guide; Guideposts for Kids; High Adventure; Highlights for Children; Hopscotch; I.D.; ‡Kids' Wall Street News; Kids World; National Geographic World; New Era; Odyssey; On The Line; Read; Scienceland; Shadow; Skipping Stones; Teen Life; Teenage Christian; Their Dreams; What! A Magazine

Careers

Advocate; ‡All About You; American Cheerleader; ASPCA Animal Watch; ‡blue jean; ‡Career World; ‡Careers & Colleges; Challenge; Child Life; Crusader; ‡Dramatics; ‡First Opportunity; Flicker Magazine; Florida Leader; For Seniors Only; Girls' Life; Guideposts for Kids; Highlights for Children; Hopscotch; I.D.; Keynoter; Kids at Home; ‡Kids' Wall Street News; Kids World; New Moon; On Course; Read;

Scholastic Math Magazine; Scienceland; Seventeen; Shadow; Street Times; Teen Life; 'TEEN; Teenage Christian; Touch; ‡Twist; What! A Magazine; ZILLIONS

Concept

Advocate; Flicker Magazine; Guideposts for Kids; Humpty Dumpty's; I.D.; Kids World; Ladybug; New Moon; Read; Science World; Shadow; Street Times; What! A Magazine

Cooking

Advocate; Boys' Quest; Calliope; Child Life; Children's Digest; Children's Playmate; ‡Curiocity; Dyna-Math; Flicker Magazine; Focus on the Family Clubhouse; Focus on the Family Clubhouse Jr.; Friend; Girls' Life; Guideposts for Kids; Holidays & Seasonal Celebrations; Hopscotch; Humpty Dumpty's; Jack And Jill ; Ladybug; National Geographic World; Odyssey; On The Line; Pockets; Scienceland; Shadow; Spider; 'TEEN; Turtle; U*S* Kids

Fashion

Advocate; American Cheerleader; DynaMath; Guideposts for Kids; Seventeen; Shadow; Touch

Games/Puzzles

Advocate; Boys' Quest; Calliope; Challenge; Chickadee; Child Life; Children's Digest; Children's Play-mate; Class Act; Cobblestone; Counselor; Crayola Kids; Cricket Magazine; Crusader; Discovery; Disney Adventures; Dolphin Log; DynaMath; Faces; Flicker Magazine; Focus on the Family Clubhouse; Focus on the Family Clubhouse Jr.; For Seniors Only; Friend; Goldfinch; Guide; Guideposts for Kids; Highlights for Children; Holidays & Seasonal Celebrations; Hopscotch; Humpty Dumpty's; Kids World; My Friend; National Geographic World; New Era; New Moon; Odyssey; On The Line; OWL; Pockets; Power and Light; R-A-D-A-R; react; Read; Scholastic Math Magazine; School Mates; Scienceland; Shadow; Shofar; Skipping Stones; Spider; Teen Life; Teenage Christian; Touch; Turtle; U*S* Kids; Your Big Backyard; ZILLIONS

Geography

ASPCA Animal Watch; Challenge; Children's Digest; Cricket Magazine; ‡Curiocity; Dolphin Log; Flicker Magazine; Guideposts for Kids; Highlights for Children; Holidays & Seasonal Celebrations; Hopscotch; I.D.; Junior Scholastic; Kids at Home; ‡Kids' Wall Street News; National Geographic World; Science World; Shadow; Spider; Turtle

Health

‡All About You; American Cheerleader; Black Belt for Kids; ‡blue jean; Boys' Life; ‡Careers & Colleges; Challenge; Child Life; Children's Digest; Children's Playmate; Current Health I; Current Health II; Dyna-Math; ‡First Opportunity; Flicker Magazine; Focus on the Family Clubhouse; Focus on the Family Club-house Jr.; For Seniors Only; Girls' Life; Guideposts for Kids; Highlights for Children; Holidays & Seasonal Celebrations; Hopscotch; Humpty Dumpty's; I.D.; Keynoter; ‡Kids' Wall Street News; ‡Listen; My Friend; National Geographic World; New Moon; On The Line; react; Scholastic Math Magazine; Science World; Scienceland; Seventeen; Shadow; Straight; 'TEEN; Teenage Christian; ‡3-2-1 Contact; Turtle; ‡Twist; U*S* Kids; What! A Magazine; Young Salvationist; ZILLIONS

History

Advocate; ASPCA Animal Watch; Beckett; Black Belt for Kids; Boys' Life; Boys' Quest; Bread for God's Children; Calliope; Challenge; Children's Digest; Children's Playmate; Cobblestone; Counselor; Cricket Magazine; DynaMath; Faces; Flicker Magazine; Focus on the Family Clubhouse; Focus on the Family Clubhouse Jr.; Friend; Girls' Life; Goldfinch; Guideposts for Kids; Highlights for Children; Holidays & Seasonal Celebrations; Hopscotch; I.D.; Jack And Jill ; Junior Scholastic; Keynoter; Kids at Home; ‡Kids' Wall Street News; Kids World; My Friend; National Geographic World; New Era; New Moon; On The Line; R-A-D-A-R; Read; Scholastic Math Magazine; Scienceland; Shadow; Shofar; Skipping Stones; Spi-der; Street Times; Student Leadership Journal; Teen Life; Teenage Christian; U*S* Kids; Young Judaean

Hobbies

Advocate; ASPCA Animal Watch; Beckett; Challenge; Children's Digest; Cricket Magazine; Crusader; ‡Curiocity; DynaMath; Flicker Magazine; Focus on the Family Clubhouse; Focus on the Family Clubhouse Jr.; Girls' Life; Hopscotch; Humpty Dumpty's; Kids at Home; Kids World; ‡Listen; My Friend; National Geographic World; New Moon; On Course; On The Line; R-A-D-A-R; react; Scholastic Math Magazine; Seventeen; Shadow; Straight; Teenage Christian; U*S* Kids; What! A Magazine; ZILLIONS

How-to

Advocate; American Cheerleader; Black Belt for Kids; ‡blue jean; Boys' Quest; ‡Career World; ‡Careers & Colleges; Challenge; Children's Digest; Children's Playmate; Class Act; Crayola Kids; Cricket Magazine; ‡Crystal Ball; ‡Dramatics; DynaMath; ‡First Opportunity; Flicker Magazine; Florida Leader; For Seniors Only; Friend; Guideposts for Kids; Hobson's Choice; Hopscotch; Humpty Dumpty's; Jack And Jill ; Keynoter; Kids World; My Friend; On The Line; Power and Light; R-A-D-A-R; Scholastic Math Magazine; Scienceland; Seventeen; Shadow; Teenage Christian; ‡3-2-1 Contact; Touch; U*S* Kids; With; ZILLIONS

Humorous

Advocate; ‡All About You; Beckett; Boys' Quest; ‡Careers & Colleges; Challenge; Chickadee; Child Life; Children's Digest; Children's Playmate; Cricket Magazine; Crusader; DynaMath; Flicker Magazine; Florida Leader; Focus on the Family Clubhouse; Focus on the Family Clubhouse Jr.; For Seniors Only; Friend; Girls' Life; Guide; Guideposts for Kids; Highlights for Children; Hopscotch; Humpty Dumpty's; I.D.; Jack And Jill ; Keynoter; Kids World; Ladybug; ‡LiveWire; My Friend; New Moon; On Course; On The Line; OWL; R-A-D-A-R; Ranger Rick; Read; Scholastic Math Magazine; Seventeen; Shadow; Shofar; Skipping Stones; Story Friends; Straight; Teen Life; Teenage Christian; Touch; ‡Twist; U*S* Kids; What! A Magazine; With; ZILLIONS

Interview/Profile

Advocate; AIM Magazine; ‡All About You; ASPCA Animal Watch; Black Belt for Kids; ‡Career World; ‡Careers & Colleges; Challenge; Child Life; Children's Digest; Cobblestone; Counselor; Cricket Magazine; Crusader; ‡Crystal Ball; ‡Curiocity; Discovery; Disney Adventures; Dolphin Log; ‡Dramatics; Exploring; Faces; ‡First Opportunity; Flicker Magazine; Florida Leader; Focus on the Family Clubhouse; Focus on the Family Clubhouse Jr.; For Seniors Only; Girls' Life; Goldfinch; Guideposts for Kids; Highlights for Children; Hobson's Choice; I.D.; Jack And Jill ; Junior Scholastic; ‡Kids' Wall Street News; Kids World; LiveWire; My Friend; National Geographic World; New Moon; On Course; OWL; Pockets; Power and Light; R-A-D-A-R; react; Read; Scholastic Math Magazine; School Mates; Seventeen; Shadow; ‡Sharing the Victory; Shofar; Skipping Stones; Story Friends; Straight; Street Times; Student Leadership Journal; Teen Life; Teenage Christian; ‡3-2-1 Contact; Touch; ‡Twist; U*S* Kids; What! A Magazine; Young Salvationist

Math

Boys' Quest; DynaMath; ‡First Opportunity; Guideposts for Kids; Holidays & Seasonal Celebrations; Hopscotch; Ladybug; New Moon; Scholastic Math Magazine; Shadow; Spider

Multicultural

AIM Magazine; ASPCA Animal Watch; ‡blue jean; Challenge; Crayola Kids; Cricket Magazine; Dolphin Log; ‡Dramatics; DynaMath; ‡First Opportunity; Flicker Magazine; Girls' Life; Guide; Guideposts for Kids; Highlights for Children; Holidays & Seasonal Celebrations; I.D.; Junior Scholastic; Kids at Home; LiveWire; National Geographic World; New Moon; Scholastic Math Magazine; Shadow; Skipping Stones; Spider; Story Friends; Street Times; Student Leadership Journal; Teen Life; 'TEEN; ‡3-2-1 Contact; Touch; Turtle; U*S* Kids; With; Young Salvationist

Nature/Environment

Advocate; ASPCA Animal Watch; Boys' Life; Challenge; Chickadee; Children's Digest; Counselor; Cricket Magazine; Crusader; ‡Curiocity; Current Health I; Discovery; Disney Adventures; Dolphin Log;

DynaMath; Flicker Magazine; Focus on the Family Clubhouse; Focus on the Family Clubhouse Jr.; Girls' Life; Guideposts for Kids; Holidays & Seasonal Celebrations; Humpty Dumpty's; I.D.; Junior Scholastic; Keynoter; Kids at Home; ‡Kids' Wall Street News; Kids World; Ladybug; ‡Listen; My Friend; National Geographic World; Nature Friend; New Moon; OWL; R-A-D-A-R; Ranger Rick; react; Read; Scholastic Math Magazine; Science World; Scienceland; Shadow; Skipping Stones; Spider; Story Friends; Student Leadership Journal; ‡3-2-1 Contact; Turtle; U*S* Kids; W.O.W. (Wild Outdoor World); What! A Magazine; Your Big Backyard; ZILLIONS

Problem-Solving

Advocate; American Cheerleader; Boys' Quest; ‡Careers & Colleges; Challenge; Counselor; Crusader; Current Health II; DynaMath; Exploring; ‡First Opportunity; Flicker Magazine; Florida Leader; Friend; Guide; Guideposts for Kids; Highlights for Children; I.D.; Jack And Jill ; Keynoter; Kids World; Ladybug; ‡Listen; My Friend; New Moon; Power and Light; R-A-D-A-R; Scholastic Math Magazine; Scienceland; Shadow; Skipping Stones; Spider; Straight; Street Times; Teen Life; 'TEEN; Teenage Christian; Touch; With; Wonder Time; Young Salvationist; ZILLIONS

Religious

Bread for God's Children; Challenge; Counselor; Crusader; Faces; Flicker Magazine; Friend; Guide; Guideposts for Kids; High Adventure; Highlights for Children; I.D.; My Friend; New Era; On Course; Pockets; Power and Light; Seventeen; Shadow; Shofar; Skipping Stones; Straight; Student Leadership Journal; Teenage Christian; Touch; With; Wonder Time; Young Judaean; Young Salvationist

Science

Advocate; ASPCA Animal Watch; Boys' Life; Boys' Quest; Challenge; Chickadee; Children's Digest; Counselor; Crayola Kids; Cricket Magazine; Crusader; ‡Crystal Ball; ‡Curiocity; Dolphin Log; DynaMath; ‡First Opportunity; Flicker Magazine; Focus on the Family Clubhouse; Focus on the Family Clubhouse Jr.; Girls' Life; Guideposts for Kids; Highlights for Children; Hobson's Choice; Holidays & Seasonal Celebrations; Humpty Dumpty's; I.D.; Jack And Jill ; Kids at Home; ‡Kids' Wall Street News; Kids World; Ladybug; ‡LiveWire; My Friend; National Geographic World; New Moon; Odyssey; OWL; R-A-D-A-R; react; Read; Scholastic Math Magazine; Science Weekly; Science World; Shadow; Spider; ‡3-2-1 Contact; Turtle; U*S* Kids; What! A Magazine

Social Issues

Advocate; ASPCA Animal Watch; ‡blue jean; ‡Careers & Colleges; Challenge; Counselor; Crusader; ‡Curiocity; DynaMath; Flicker Magazine; Florida Leader; Focus on the Family Clubhouse; Focus on the Family Clubhouse Jr.; For Seniors Only; Guideposts for Kids; Highlights for Children; I.D.; Junior Scholastic; Keynoter; Kids' Wall Street News; Kids World; National Geographic World; New Era; New Moon; On Course; OWL; Power and Light; R-A-D-A-R; react; Read; Seventeen; Shadow; Straight; Street Times; Student Leadership Journal; Teen Life; 'TEEN; Teenage Christian; Touch; ‡Twist; U*S* Kids; What! A Magazine; With; Wonder Time; Young Judaean; Young Salvationist; ZILLIONS

Sports

Advocate; ‡All About You; American Cheerleader; Beckett; Black Belt for Kids; Boys' Life; ‡Careers & Colleges; Challenge; Child Life; Children's Digest; Children's Playmate; Counselor; Cricket Magazine; Crusader; ‡Curiocity; Discovery; Disney Adventures; DynaMath; Flicker Magazine; Florida Leader; Focus on the Family Clubhouse; Focus on the Family Clubhouse Jr.; For Seniors Only; Friend; Girls' Life; Guideposts for Kids; Highlights for Children; Humpty Dumpty's; I.D.; Jack And Jill ; Kids at Home; ‡Kids' Wall Street News; Kids World; ‡Listen; ‡LiveWire; My Friend; National Geographic World; New Era; New Moon; On Course; On The Line; OWL; Racing for Kids; react; Read; Scholastic Math Magazine; Seventeen; Shadow; ‡Sharing the Victory; Skipping Stones; Soccer Jr.; Straight; Teen Life; Teenage Christian; Touch; Turtle; U*S* Kids; W.O.W. (Wild Outdoor World); What! A Magazine; ZILLIONS

Travel

Advocate; Black Belt for Kids; ‡Careers & Colleges; Challenge; Chickadee; Children's Digest; Children's Playmate; Cobblestone; Crayola Kids; Cricket Magazine; ‡Curiocity; Exploring; Faces; Flicker Magazine; Florida Leader; For Seniors Only; Girls' Life; Guideposts for Kids; Highlights for Children; Kids at Home; ‡Kids' Wall Street News; National Geographic World; New Era; New Moon; OWL; Power and Light; R-A-D-A-R; Ranger Rick; Read; Shadow; Skipping Stones; 'TEEN; Teenage Christian; Touch; U*S* Kids

Photography Index

This index lists markets that buy photos from freelancers. It's divided into book publishers, magazines and greeting cards. It's important to carefully read the listings and follow the guidelines of each publisher to which you submit. Listings new to this edition are marked with a double dagger (‡).

BOOKS

Abbeville Kids; Abingdon Press; Absey; ‡Acropolis Books; American Bible Society; A/V Concepts Corp.; B&B Publishing, Inc.; Beach Holme Publishers; Behrman House Inc.; Bethany House Publishers; Blackbirch; Blue Sky Press; Boingo; Boyds Mills; Carolrhoda; ‡Cartwheel; Chicago Review; ‡China Books; Chronicle; Coteau; Dial; DK Publishing; Dutton; Fitzhenry & Whiteside; Focus; Free Spirit; Grolier; ‡Grosset; Gryphon House; Harcourt; ‡Huckleberry; ‡Hunter House; Huntington House; Incentive; Jalmar; ‡Jewish Lights; Just Us Books; Lerner; Little, Brown; Lodestar Books; Lorimer; Lowell House Lowell House; Mariposa; Millbrook Press; ‡Miracle Sound; Mondo; Morehouse; Multnomah; ‡New Hope; Oliver Press; ‡Ottenheimer; Our Sunday Visitor; Owen, Richard C.; OWL Books; Pages; Pauline; Phoenix Learning; Place In The Woods; ‡Playskool; Pleasant Co.; Press-Tige Press-Tige; Price Stern Sloan; Pride; Rainbow; ‡Red Deer; Reidmore; Rhache; Rosen; St. Anthony Messenger; Seedling; Silver Burdett; Silver Moon; Southwest Parks; Speech Bin; Storey; ‡Sword of The Lord; Time-Life for Children; Troll; Tyndale; UAHC; Weigl Educational; Whitecap; Whitman, Albert; Williamson; Woman's Missionary; World Book

MAGAZINES

Advocate; AIM Magazine; American Cheerleader; ASPCA Animal Watch; Beckett; Boys' Quest; Calliope; Careers & Colleges; Cat Fancy; Challenge; Chickadee; Child Life; Children's Digest; Children's Playmate; Cobblestone; Discovery; Disney Adventures; Dolphin Log; ‡Dramatics; Faces; ‡First Opportunity; Flicker Magazine; Florida Leader; Focus on the Family Clubhouse; Focus on the Family Clubhouse Jr.; For Seniors Only; Girls' Life; Goldfinch; Guideposts for Kids; Hobson's Choice; Holidays & Seasonal Celebrations; Hopscotch; Junior Scholastic; LiveWire; My Friend; National Geographic World; New Moon: The Magazine for Girls & Their Dreams; Odyssey; On Course; OWL; Pockets; Power and Light; react; School Mates; Scienceland; ‡Sharing the Victory; Skipping Stones; Spider; Story Friends; Straight; Student Leadership Journal; Teen Life; ‡3-2-1 Contact; ‡Together Time; Totally Fox Kids; Turtle; U*S* Kids; With; Young Salvationist; Your Big Backyard

GREETING CARDS

Aristoplay, Ltd.; ‡Avanti Press, Inc.; Beistle Company, The; Design Design Inc.; EPI Group Limited; Everything Gonzo!; Fotofolio/Artpost; Galison Books; Innova; Love Greeting Card Co. Inc.; Marcel Schurman Company; P.S. Greetings/Fantus Paper Products; Scandecor Inc.; ‡Standard Publishing; Talicor, Inc.

General Index

A double dagger (‡) appears before listings that are new to this edition. Companies that appeared in the 1997 edition of *Children's Writer's & Illustrator's Market* but do not appear in this edition are identified witih a two-letter code explaining why the market was omitted: **(ED)**—Editorial Decision; **(NS)**—Not Accepting Submissions; **(NR)**—No (or late) Response to Listing Request; **(OB)**—Out of Business; **(RR)**—Removed by Market's Request.

More Great Books for Writers!

Ten Steps to Publishing Children's Books—Get published in the popular genre of children's books! You'll discover vital tips from successful writers and illustrators to help you polish the skills necessary to make your dream come true. Plus, the input of editors offers a unique perspective from the publishing side of the industry. *#10534/$24.95/128 pages/150 illus.*

The Children's Writer's Word Book—Even the most original children's story won't get published if its language usage or sentence structure doesn't speak to young readers. You'll avoid these pitfalls with this fast-reference guide full of word lists, reading levels for synonyms and much more. *#10316/$19.99/352 pages*

Writing and Illustrating Children's Books for Publication: Two Perspectives—Discover how to create a good, publishable manuscript in only eight weeks! You'll cover the writing process in its entirety—from generating ideas and getting started, to submitting a manuscript. Imaginative writing and illustrating exercises build on these lessons and provide fuel for your creative fires! *#10448/$24.95/128 pages/200 b&w illus., 16 page color insert*

How to Write and Illustrate Children's Books and Get Them Published—Find everything you need to know about breaking into the lucrative children's market. You'll discover how to write a sure-fire seller, how to create fresh and captivating illustrations, how to get your manuscript into the right buyer's hands and more! *#30082/$24.99/144 pages/70 color, 45 b&w illus.*

The Very Best of Children's Book Illustration—Feast your eyes on this wonderful collection of the best in contemporary children's book illustration. You'll see nearly 200 full-color illustrations sure to spark your creativity. *#30513/$29.95/144 pages/198 color illus.*

How to Write and Sell Children's Picture Books—Learn how to put your picture book on paper and get it published—whether you're retelling a wonderful old tale or spinning a splendid new yarn. *#10410/$17.99/192 pages*

Grammatically Correct: The Writer's Guide to Punctuation, Spelling, Style, Usage and Grammar—Write prose that's clear, concise and graceful! This comprehensive desk reference covers the nuts-and-bolts basics of punctuation, spelling and grammar, as well as essential tips and techniques for developing a smooth, inviting writing style. *#10529/$19.99/352 pages*

The Writer's Essential Desk Reference—Get quick, complete, accurate answers to your important writing questions with this companion volume to *Writer's Market*. You'll cover all aspects of the business side of writing—from information on the World Wide Web and other research sites, to opportunities with writers' workshops and the basics on taxes and health insurance. *#10485/$24.99/384 pages*

The Writer's Digest Dictionary of Concise Writing—Make your work leaner, crisper and clearer! Under the guidance of professional editor Robert Hartwell Fiske, you'll learn how to rid your work of common say-nothing phrases while making it tighter and easier to read and understand. *#10482/$19.99/352 pages*

How to Write Attention-Grabbing Query & Cover Letters—Use the secrets John Wood reveals to write queries perfectly tailored, too good to turn down! In this guidebook, you will discover why boldness beats blandness in queries every time, ten basics you *must* have in your article queries, ten query blunders that can destroy publication chances and much more. *#10462/$17.99/208 pages*

The Writer's Digest Guide to Manuscript Formats—No matter how good your ideas, an unprofessional format will land your manuscript on the slush pile! You need this easy-to-follow guide on manuscript preparation and presentation—for everything from books and articles, to poems and plays. *#10025/$19.99/200 pages*

The Complete Guide to Writing & Selling the Christian Novel—One of the most respected figures in Christian publishing shares her extensive knowledge on how to write and publish spiritual fiction successfully. *#10544/$14.99/265 pages/pb.*

Roget's Super Thesaurus, 2nd Edition—This complete, easy-to-use guide is organized to help you find exactly what you need—and find it *fast*. It also contains the only reverse dictionary in any thesaurus. *#10541/$19.99/672 pages/pb.*